SEVENTH EDITION

Argumentation and Debate

CRITICAL THINKING FOR
REASONED DECISION MAKING

SEVENTH EDITION

Argumentation and Debate

CRITICAL THINKING FOR REASONED DECISION MAKING

AUSTIN J. FREELEY
John Carroll University

Wadsworth Publishing Company
Belmont, California
A Division of Wadsworth, Inc.

Communications Editor: Kris Clerkin
Editorial Assistant: Tamiko Verkler
Production: Mary Douglas
Print Buyer: Randy Hurst
Designer: Janet Bollow
Copy Editor: Elizabeth Judd
Technical Illustrator: Evanell Towne
Compositor: Beacon Graphics
Cover: Charles Fuhrman

Printed in the United States of America
1 2 3 4 5 6 7 8 9 10 — 94 93 92 91 90

Library of Congress Cataloging-in-Publication Data
Freeley, Austin J.
    Argumentation and debate : critical thinking for reasoned decision making / Austin J. Freeley. — 7th ed.
        p.   cm.
    Includes bibliographical references.
    ISBN 0-534-12006-7
    1. Debates and debating.   2. Decision-making.   I. Title.
PN4181.F68   1990
808.53 — dc20
                                                    89-22439
                                                        CIP

To Trudie

Preface

Today's students will spend most of their lives in the twenty-first century. Will they be better prepared for the twenty-first century than their forebears were for the twentieth?

As the 20th century approached, a Boston newspaper asserted that the telephone couldn't work and that it would be of no practical value if it could. A British scientist remarked that the electric light was a novelty that would soon "fade away." A physicist declared that radio had no practical value. Charles H. Duell, the commissioner of the U.S. Office of Patents advised President McKinley to abolish the patent office, arguing that "everything that can be invented has been invented."

The one thing we can confidently predict about the 21st century is that it will be unlike anything we expect.

This prediction will come as no surprise to today's students, for they have grown up in the greatest era of change in human history. The world's store of knowledge doubled from 1750 to 1950 and again from 1950 to 1960. Since 1960 the sum total of knowledge has doubled every five years. By the year 2000 there will be more than one thousand times more knowledge than there was in 1900. Today's students will occupy the major decision-making positions in the early decades of the twenty-first century. They will be called upon to face problems we cannot even imagine and to reach decisions based on evidence that does not now exist. Ninety-seven percent of everything known at the start of the twenty-first century will have been discovered since today's students were born. We live in an information society. Peter Drucker noted, "Knowledge has already become the primary industry, the industry that supplies the economy the essential and central resources of production." New knowledge and its application comes unevenly. Had the automobile industry developed and applied knowledge as the computer industry has done in the last forty years, a Rolls-Royce would cost $2.50

and get two million miles to the gallon. Uneven though change may be, no phase of our lives is untouched by what some see as the rise of a new civilization, The Third Wave, which will profoundly challenge our old assumptions, ways of thinking, formulas, dogmas, and ideologies. To deal with this fast-emerging clash of new values, technologies, geopolitical relationships, life styles, and modes of communication, we will need a means of critical thinking to arrive at reasoned decisions on the complex, urgent, and unprecedented issues that will confront us.

Futurists predict that in the years beyond 2000 we will see whole new industries develop and revolutionize our lives. Chemical fuel cells will enable us to build electric cars that can travel over a thousand miles without recharging. Superconductors will transform the transmission and production of electricity. Synthetic-fuel technology will create a permanent oil glut. We will solve the problems of the fusion nuclear reactor and develop an inexhaustible form of clean energy. Advances in medical technology will mean that life spans of 100 years will no longer be unusual.

We will be able to solve the problems of world hunger and poverty. Herman Kahn predicted that the per-capita income of the world, which was about $200 when our country was founded and which is about $2,000 today, will grow to $20,000 in the twenty-first century.

We will see a continuing revolution in computers. We will develop voice operated computers. The speed of computers will increase by whole orders of magnitude at a time. We will create artificial intelligence. In the very early twenty-first century a computer the size of a cigar box will be able to store the equivalent of ten Libraries of Congress.

Are these predictions for the twenty-first century more accurate than the predictions made for the twentieth century? Only time will tell. But of this much we can be certain: We *will* need a means of critical thinking to arrive at reasoned decisions on the complex, urgent, and unprecedented issues that will confront us.

Knowledgeable teachers of argumentation recognize that the accelerated rate of change has had a marked impact on the field of argumentation and debate. In many important ways we no longer analyze arguments, conduct research, build cases, or conduct debates in the way we did ten or even five years ago. Not only is more knowledge available today than ever before, it is also more accessible. In the field of argumentation and debate each new academic year brings change as newly emerging theory and practice come to the fore. While the change in any one year is small, the incremental growth of change over a few years mandates a new edition.

This seventh edition of *Argumentation and Debate*, it is hoped, retains and reinforces the features that have led to its wide use for over a quarter of a century by seven "generations" of students, and at the same time, brings before today's student the significant changes of our constantly developing field of study. This edition draws on the various Summer Conferences on Argumentation and the National Developmental Conferences on Forensics. It also draws on the proceedings of major professional conventions, research from the related fields of behavioral science and communication theory, and the "shop talk" of tournaments. These sources have provided new material on the recent developments in argumentation theory and the changes in debate practices that are added to the foundation of classical and modern principles. For example, this edition, in keeping with contemporary practice, focuses on *critical thinking* and *reasoned* decision making. This edition provides new treatment on value and quasi-policy debating, designed to give the students insight to the vastly expanded field of CEDA debate. The section on cross-examination debating has again been expanded to help both CEDA and NDT debaters. Throughout the text new examples have been provided on many topics.

Additional changes in this edition include new material on the burden of proof considered from both the judicial perspective and the policy perspective. A chapter (restored from earlier editions) deals with the structure of reasoning so important to both critical thinking and debating. The treatment of statistical evidence has been expanded to help the student with this often difficult concept. New material has been provided on stock issues for both CEDA and NDT debaters together with new material on stock issue questions and stock issue statements. The chapters on case include new information on debate cases (illustrated with examples from the actual debates presented in the appendixes) and on speaker responsibilities that will meet the needs of both CEDA and NDT debaters. The treatment of the flow sheet has been expanded to make this critical yet often difficult concept more readily understandable for the student. New material on the slippery slope and utopian counterplans will aid the student's understanding of these strategies. The new material on mock trial debating will be welcomed by many.

The appendixes include a new presidential debate and for the first time both CEDA and NDT national final debates. They provide a wealth of contemporary examples for the instructor and student. The lists of CEDA and NDT propositions have been updated. The glossary is entirely new and should prove to be a useful and convenient reference.

This book is designed for all who are interested in using critical thinking to reach reasoned decisions. It is designed specifically for the undergraduate course in argumentation and debate, but it may be used in any broadly liberal course for students who seek self-realization and who desire to prepare themselves for effective participation in a democratic society.

The instructor may assign the chapters in any order adapted to the needs of the students. The instructor may take a broad overview of the field of argumentation and debate; focus on CEDA or NDT debate; or focus on critical thinking.

I wish to record my thanks to Robert Kully of California State University, Los Angeles; Ronald J. Matlon of Towson State University; Steven R. Brydon of California State University, Chico; and Charles Kneupper of the University of Texas who offered thoughtful, insightful, and practical advice for the seventh edition. Thanks are also due to Kristine Clerkin of Wadsworth Publishing Company, whose editorial work on this edition is sincerely appreciated, and to Mary Douglas who facilitated the production of this book. Over the years many of the students I have taught and judged have contributed to this edition as well as earlier editions. They have helped me refine my thinking and develop more cogent statements on many matters, and they have provided many of the examples which may be found throughout this text.

Austin J. Freeley

Contents

10 Obstacles to Clear Thinking 159

11 Requirements of the Case 172

12 Building the Affirmative Case 187

13 Building the Negative Case 214

14 Refutation 243

SEVENTH EDITION

Argumentation and Debate

CRITICAL THINKING FOR
REASONED DECISION MAKING

1

Critical Thinking

A growing number of colleges and universities are establishing the requirement that their students study critical thinking. The executive order establishing California's requirement states:

> Instruction in *critical thinking* is designed to achieve an understanding of the relationship of language to logic, which would lead to the ability to analyze, criticize, and advocate ideas, to reason inductively and deductively, and to reach factual or judgmental conclusions based on sound inferences drawn from unambiguous statements of knowledge or belief. The minimal competence to be expected at the successful conclusion of instruction in critical thinking should be the ability to distinguish fact from judgment, belief from knowledge, and skills in elementary inductive and deductive processes, including an understanding of the formal and informal fallacies of language and thought.

Competency in critical thinking is rightly viewed as a requisite intellectual skill for self-realization as an effective participant in human affairs, for the pursuit of higher education, and for successful participation in the highly competitive world of business and the professions. Debate is today, as it has been since classical times, one of the best methods of learning and applying the principles of critical thinking.

Many of the most significant and critical communications of our lives are conducted in the form of debates. These may be intrapersonal communications, where we weigh the pros and cons of an important decision in our own minds; or they may be interpersonal communications, where we listen to a debate conducted to secure our decision or participate in a debate to secure the decision of others.

Success or failure in life is largely determined by our ability to make wise decisions for ourselves and to secure the decisions we want from others. Much of our significant, purposeful activity is concerned with making required decisions. Whether to join a campus organization, go to graduate school, accept a certain job offer, buy a car or house, move to another city, invest in a certain stock, or vote for Smith—these are just a few of the thousands of decisions we may have to make. Often, intelligent self-interest or a sense of responsibility will require us to secure certain decisions from others. We may want a scholarship, a particular job, a customer for our product, or a vote for a certain candidate.

Some people make decisions by flipping a coin. Others act on the whim of the moment or respond unthinkingly to the pressures of the "hidden persuaders." If the problem is trivial—the movies tonight?—the use of these methods is of no consequence. For important matters, however, mature adults require a reasoned means of decision making. They seek the greatest possible assurance that their decisions are justified by good reasons based on true evidence and valid reasoning.

Argumentation is reason giving in communicative situations by people whose purpose is the justification of acts, beliefs, attitudes, and values. This definition is based on a definition adopted at the National Developmental Conference on Forensics.[1] Toulmin makes a similar point when he asks, "What kind of *justificatory activities* must we engage in to convince our fellows that these beliefs are based on 'good reasons'?"[2] *Good reasons* may be defined as "reasons which are psychologically compelling for a given audience, which make further inquiry both unnecessary and redundant—hence justifying a decision to affirm or reject a proposition."[3] Note that what constitutes good reasons for one audience may not be good reasons for another. When Ayatollah Ruhollah Khomeini ordered his followers to murder novelist Salmon Rushdie for writing the "blasphemous" *The Satanic Verses*, Khomeini's command and his "good reason," "blasphemy" of the Prophet, were considered to be so compelling to Khomeini's followers that Rushdie, a British subject living in Britain, went into hiding under British police protection and publishers and booksellers around the world feared for the safety of their employees and customers. In most of the world "blasphemy" is not perceived as a good reason for murder, and in America freedom of the press, enshrined in the First Amendment to the Constitution, is perceived as a good reason for allowing an author to express just about any opinion. The debater's task is to discover the justificatory activities that the decision renderers will accept and to develop the good reasons that will lead them to agree with the desired conclusion—or, of course, to reject those reasons advanced by an opponent.

First we will consider debate as a method of critical thinking. Then we will consider some other methods of decision making and see how they relate to argumentation and debate.

---

[1] James H. McBath, ed., *Forensics as Communication* (Skokie, Ill.: National Textbook Co., 1975), p. 11.
[2] Stephen Toulmin, *Knowing and Acting* (New York: Macmillan, 1976), p. 138.
[3] David Zarefsky, "Criteria for Evaluating Non-Policy Argument," *Perspectives on Non-Policy Argument*, ed. Don Brownlee, sponsored by CEDA (privately published, 1980), p. 10.

I. Debate

Debate is the process of inquiry and advocacy, the seeking of reasoned judgment on a proposition. Debate may be used by the individual to reach a decision in his or her own mind, or it may be used by an individual or a group seeking to secure a decision from others.

As debate specifically provides reasoned arguments for and against a given proposition, it also provides opportunities for critical thinking. Society, as well as the individual, must have an effective method of reaching reasoned decisions. A free society is so structured that many of its decisions are reached through debate. Our law courts and our legislative bodies are specifically designed to create and perpetuate debate as the method of reaching decisions. In fact, any organization that conducts its business according to parliamentary procedure has selected debate as its method. Debate pervades our society at decision-making levels.

From the earliest times to the present, thoughtful people have recognized the importance of debate for the individual and society. Plato, whose dialogues were an early form of cross-examination debate, defines rhetoric as "a universal art of winning the mind by arguments, which means not merely arguments in the courts of justice, and all other sorts of public councils, but in private conference as well."[4]

Aristotle lists four values for *rhetoric*.[5] First, it prevents the triumph of fraud and injustice. Aristotle argues that truth and justice are by nature more powerful than their opposites. When decisions are not made as they should be, speakers with right on their side have only themselves to blame for the outcome. Thus, it is not enough to know the right decision ourselves; we must be able to argue for that decision before others.

Second, rhetoric is a method of instruction for the public. Aristotle points out that situations exist wherein scientific arguments are of no avail; the speaker must then instruct the audience by framing arguments with the help of common knowledge and commonly accepted opinions. Congressional debates on arms limitations or tax policies are examples of this. The general public, and indeed the majority of the Congress, lacks the specialized knowledge to follow highly sophisticated technical arguments. Skilled partisans who have the expertise to understand the technical data must reformulate their reasons in ways that can be comprehended by both Congress and the public.

Third, rhetoric makes us see both sides of a case. By arguing both sides, no aspect of the case will escape us, and we will be prepared to refute our opponents' arguments.

Fourth, rhetoric is a means of defense. Often a knowledge of argumentation and debate will be necessary to protect ourselves or our interests. Aristotle states: "If it is a disgrace to a man when he cannot defend himself in a bodily way, it would be odd not to think him disgraced when he cannot defend himself with reason. Reason is more distinctive of man than is bodily effort."

[4]Plato, *Phaedrus*, 261. Cooper and Jowett use slightly different terms in translating this passage. This statement draws from both translations.

[5]See: Aristotle, *Rhetoric*, I, 1.

Similarly, in the nineteenth century, John Stuart Mill placed great emphasis on the value of debate:

> If even the Newtonian philosophy were not permitted to be questioned, mankind could not feel as complete assurance of its truth as they now [1858] do. The beliefs which we have the most warrant for, have no safeguard to rest on, but a standing invitation to the whole world to prove them unfounded. If the challenge is not accepted, or is accepted and the attempt fails, we are far enough from certainty still; but we have done the best that the existing state of human reason admits of; we have neglected nothing that could give the truth the chance of reaching us; if the lists are kept open, we may hope that if there be a better truth, it will be found when the human mind is capable of receiving it; and in the meantime we may rely on having attained such approach to truth as is possible in our day. This is the amount of certainty attainable by a fallible being, and this is the sole way of attaining it.[6]

The United States Senate designated, as Senate Immortals, five senators who had shaped the history of our nation by their ability as debaters: Henry Clay, Daniel Webster, John C. Calhoun, Robert M. La Follette, Sr., and Robert A. Taft. The triumvirate of Webster, Clay, and Calhoun towered over all others and were the near unanimous choice of senators and scholars alike. These commanding figures might well be included in a list of the world's great debaters. As John F. Kennedy, then a freshman senator, pointed out, "For over thirty years they dominated the Congress and the country, providing leadership and articulation on all the great issues of the growing nation."[7] La Follette and Taft were selected as the outstanding representatives of the progressive and conservative movements in the twentieth century. In honoring these "immortals," the Senate recognized the importance of debate in determining the course of American history. John Quincy Adams considered Webster's reply in his debate with Hayne to be "the most significant act since the founding of the Constitution."[8] Indeed, it would be impossible to understand the history of the United States without a knowledge of the great debaters and their debates.

Our laws not only are made through the process of debate but are applied through debate as well. The famous attorney Joseph N. Welch has stated:

> America believes in what lawyers call "the adversary system" in our courtrooms, including our criminal courts. It is our tradition that the District Attorney prosecutes hard. Against him is the lawyer hired by the defendant, or supplied by the court if the defendant is indigent. And the defendant's lawyer defends hard. We believe that truth is apt to emerge from this crucible. It usually does.[9]

We need debate not only in the legislative assembly and the courtroom but in all areas of human activity, since most of our liberties are directly or indirectly depen-

---

[6]John Stuart Mill, *On Liberty* (New York: Burt, n.d.), pp. 38–39.

[7]John F. Kennedy, Speech in the Senate, May 1, 1957, from a press release.

[8]Ibid.

[9]Joseph N. Welch, "Should a Lawyer Defend a Guilty Man?" *This Week* magazine, December 6, 1959, p. 11. Copyright 1959 by the United Newspapers Magazine Corporation. Reprinted by permission of *This Week* magazine and Joseph N. Welch.

dent on debate. As Walter Lippmann has pointed out, one of our most cherished liberties, freedom of speech, can be maintained only by creating and perpetuating debate:

> Yet when genuine debate is lacking, freedom of speech does not work as it is meant to work. It has lost the principle which regulates and justifies it — that is to say, dialectic conducted according to logic and the rules of evidence. If there is no effective debate, the unrestricted right to speak will unloose so many propagandists, procurers, and panderers upon the public that sooner or later in self-defense the people will turn to the censors to protect them. It will be curtailed for all manner of reasons and pretexts, and serve all kinds of good, foolish, or sinister ends.
>
> For in the absence of debate unrestricted utterance leads to the degradation of opinion. By a kind of Gresham's law the more rational is overcome by the less rational, and the opinions that will prevail will be those which are held most ardently by those with the most passionate will. For that reason the freedom to speak can never be maintained by objecting to interference with the liberty of the press, of printing, of broadcasting, of the screen. It can be maintained only by promoting debate.[10]

Not only do we need debate to maintain freedom of speech but also to provide a methodology for innovation and judgment about matters related to contemporary problems. As Chaim Perelman, the Belgian philosopher-rhetorician whose works in rhetoric and argumentation have become increasingly influential among the forensic community, has pointed out:

> If we assume it to be possible without recourse to violence to reach agreement on all the problems implied in the employment of the idea of justice we are granting the possibility of formulating an ideal of man and society, valid for all beings endowed with reason and accepted by what we have called elsewhere the universal audience.[11]
>
> I think that the only discursive methods available to us stem from techniques that are not demonstrative — that is, conclusive and *rational* in the narrow sense of the term — but from argumentative techniques which are not conclusive but which may tend to demonstrate the *reasonable* character of the conceptions put forward. It is this recourse to the rational and reasonable for the realization of the ideal of universal communion that characterizes the age-long endeavor of all philosophies in their aspiration for a city of man in which violence may progressively give way to wisdom.[12]

Thus we see the age-long concern of philosophers and statesmen with debate as an instrument for dealing with the problems of society. It is easy, then, to understand why debate is pervasive in our society. It is in the interest of the individual to know the principles of argumentation and debate and to be able to apply them in reaching and in securing decisions. It is in the interest of society to encourage debate both to

[10]Walter Lippmann, *Essays in the Public Philosophy* (Boston: Little, Brown, 1955), pp. 129–130. Reprinted by permission.

[11]Chaim Perelman and L. Olbrechts-Tyteca, *Traité de l'argumentation, La nouvelle rhétorique* (Paris: Presses Universitaires de France, 1958), Sec. 7.

[12]Chaim Perelman, *The Idea of Justice and the Problem of Argument*, trans. John Petrie (New York: Humanities Press, 1963), pp. 86–87.

protect the individual and to provide a means whereby society may reach reasoned decisions.

II. Individual Decisions

Whenever the conditions necessary to the solution of a problem are within the control of the individual, the problem may be solved by personal decision. If the problem is "Shall I go to the basketball game tonight?" and if the price of admission and a means of transportation are at hand, the decision can be made individually. If, however, a friend's car is needed to get to the game, then his or her decision to furnish the transportation must be secured.

Complex problems, too, are subject to individual decision. American business offers many examples of small companies that grew into major corporations while still under the individual control of the founder. Some computer companies that began in the 1970s as one-person operations burgeoned into multi–million dollar corporations with the original inventor still making all the major decisions. Some of the multi–billion dollar leveraged buyouts of the 1980s were put together by daring—some would say greedy—financiers, who made the day-to-day and even hour-to-hour decisions individually. When Carter called for the curtailment of the sale of wheat to the Soviet Union following its invasion of Afghanistan, when Reagan sent troops into Grenada, and when Bush chose Quayle as his Vice President they used different methods of decision making, but the ultimate decision was an individual one.

Whenever we have to make an individual decision of any importance, we may find it advantageous to debate the matter. This debate may take place in our minds as we weigh the pros and cons of the problem, or we may arrange for others to debate the problem for us. For instance, many governmental decisions can be made only by the President. Walter Lippmann points out that debate is the only satisfactory way by which the great issues of our times can be decided:

> A president, whoever he is, has to find a way of understanding the novel and changing issues which he must, under the Constitution, decide. Broadly speaking . . . the president has two ways of making up his mind. The one is to turn to his subordinates—to his chiefs of staff and his cabinet officers and undersecretaries and the like, and to direct them to argue out the issues and to bring him an agreed decision. . . .
>
> The other way is to sit like a judge at a hearing where the issues to be decided are debated. After he has heard the debate, after he has examined the evidence, after he has heard the debaters cross-examine one another, after he has questioned them himself, he makes his decision. This is the method intended by the authors of the National Security Act. . . .
>
> It is a much harder method in that it subjects the president to the stress of feeling the full impact of conflicting views, and then to the strain of making his decision, fully aware of how momentous it is. But there is no other satisfactory way by which momentous and complex issues can be decided.[13]

[13]Walter Lippmann, "How to Make Decisions," *New York Herald Tribune*, March 3, 1960. Reprinted by permission.

As Senator Henry M. Jackson has stressed, the most important role of the National Security Council is to provide just this sort of debate for the President.[14]

Kennedy used Cabinet sessions and National Security Council meetings to provide debate to illuminate diverse points of view, expose errors, and challenge assumptions before he reached decisions.[15] As he gained experience in office, he placed greater emphasis on debate. One historian points out: "One reason for the difference between the Bay of Pigs and the missile crisis was that fiasco instructed Kennedy in the importance of uninhibited debate in advance of major decision."[16] Kennedy, Johnson, Nixon, Ford, and Carter all had special assistants, often from the academic world, who had access to the White House Situation Room and to most of the secrets of government. Their job was to make sure that the President had all the information and insights he needed and to clarify and define the options open to the President and the consequences likely to flow from them.[17] When this wise policy was apparently not adhered to during the Reagan administration, the Iran-Contra affair followed.

We may never be called on to render the final decision on great issues of national policy — but we are constantly concerned with decisions important to ourselves where debate can be applied in similar ways. Youth is increasingly involved in the decisions of the campus, community, and society in general; it is in intelligent self-interest that these decisions be reached after reasoned debate.

When we reach an individual decision, we can put it into effect if we control the necessary conditions. If we need the consent or cooperation of others to carry out our decision, we must find a means of securing the appropriate response from them by debate — or by group discussion, persuasion, propaganda, coercion, or a combination of methods.

III. Group Discussion

Decisions may be reached by group discussion when the members of the group (1) agree that a problem exists, (2) have compatible standards of value, (3) have compatible purposes, (4) are willing to accept the consensus of the group, and (5) are relatively few in number. When these conditions are met and when all relevant evidence and arguments are carefully weighed, group discussion is a reasoned means of decision making.

Despite considerable differences — Reagan took office calling Russia "the evil empire" — Reagan and Gorbachev were able to make important decisions on arms control. Overriding the differences there was agreement on the conditions necessary to reach a decision on this specific problem. In contrast, other international problems have remained unresolved as the conditions necessary to reach a decision were missing.

---

[14]See Henry M. Jackson, "Organizing for Survival," *Foreign Affairs*, Vol. 38 (March 1956), pp. 446–456.
[15]See Theodore C. Sorensen, *Decision-Making in the White House* (New York: Columbia University Press, 1963), p. 59.
[16]Arthur M. Schlesinger, Jr., *Imperial Presidency* (Boston: Houghton Mifflin, 1973), p. 215.
[17]See Henry A. Kissinger, *The White House Years* (Boston: Little, Brown, 1979).

If the group is much larger than fifteen or twenty, profitable discussion becomes difficult or impossible. A group of senators can discuss a problem in committee, but not on the floor of the Senate. The Senate is too large for discussion; here debate must be used. Of course, informal debate may take place within the discussion process. Discussion may be a precursor of debate.[18] If the differences cannot be solved by discussion, debate is the logical recourse. Or if the group, such as a Senate committee, reaches a decision by discussion, it may then be necessary to debate it on the floor to carry the Senate as a whole.

Like an individual, a group may act on its decision only insofar as it has the power to do so. If the performance of its plan requires the consent or cooperation of others, the group must use other means to secure their decision to cooperate.

IV. Persuasion

Purposeful persuasion is defined as communication intended to influence the acts, beliefs, attitudes, and values *of others*. Clearly, one method of persuasion is debate. Persuasion is not, however, limited to seeking reasoned judgments, as is debate, nor does persuasion require reasoned arguments both for and against a given proposition. The "Marlboro Man" advertising campaign must have been judged as highly effective persuasion by the company that ran it for many years; but it did not seek the kind of reasoned judgment that one associates with debate.

Frequently the persuader hopes to have the field alone and avoids situations where another side of the argument might be presented. The cigarette companies accepted the ban on TV advertising without the prolonged court battle that many expected. The reason for this may have been that the television stations were required to give equal time to public service announcements against cigarettes. The tobacco companies apparently found it more advantageous to direct their advertising dollars to media that did not have an equal-time requirement.

Persuaders select the type of persuasive appeals they believe to be best adapted to their audience. These may include such diverse communications as the act of marching on a picket line, such clever ploys as Senator Ted Kennedy's "Where was George?" reference to the Iran-Contra affair at the 1988 Democratic Convention, or the stately formality of a debate before the Supreme Court. (Audience Analysis is considered in Chapter 14.)

Persuaders reach a decision on the problem before they begin the process of persuasion. They continue the process of persuasion until they solve the problem by persuading others to accept the decision or until they are convinced that further efforts at persuasion are pointless. In their efforts to influence others, they may find it necessary or advantageous to join with other persuaders and become propagandists or to face the opposition and become debaters. Thus they must know the principles of argumentation and debate in order to secure the desired judgment. This knowledge is also a defense against the persuasion of others. If we subject their appeals to critical

---

[18]See James H. McBurney, James M. O'Neill, and Glen E. Mills, *Argumentation and Debate* (New York: Macmillan, 1951), p. 67.

analysis, we increase our opportunity of making reasoned decisions. If persuaders advocate a decision we believe unsound, we may find it necessary to become debaters and advocate the conclusion we believe to be wise.

Unintended persuasion occurs when one receives a message not intended for that particular receiver — one might overhear a private conversation between two strangers in an elevator and be influenced by it — or when a person unknowingly communicates to and influences others in an unintended way.

V. **Propaganda**

Propaganda is the use of persuasion by a group (often a closely knit organization) in a sustained, organized campaign using multiple media for the purpose of influencing a mass audience. Historically propaganda is associated with religious, social, or political movements. Today the term has been expanded to include commercial advertising campaigns. The term first came into common usage in 1622 when Pope Gregory XV established the Sacred Congregation for Propagating the Faith. What in the view of the faithful could be more commendable than spreading the faith? In 1933 when Hitler appointed Dr. Joseph Goebbels as his Minister of Propaganda, the word took on a different connotation. What in the view of non-Nazis could be more evil than spreading Nazism? Thus even to the present day, propaganda is often perceived as a pejorative term. An official of a women's liberation group recently said: "We've been conducting an extensive educational campaign to inform the public of the necessity of making abortion on demand available to women on welfare. It was going very well until the churches unleashed a bunch of propagandists to work against us." Thus, in everyday language, *we* educate or give information, while *they* propagandize.

Of course, the end does not justify the means. Propaganda, like persuasion, may be viewed as good or bad only in relation to the degree that it is based on true evidence and valid reasoning. Examples of questionable methods may be found in the Allied propaganda in the United States prior to America's entry into the First World War. At that time extensive use was made of distorted or false atrocity stories. Other examples may be found in communist propaganda, which makes extensive use of the technique of the "big lie." During any Middle East crisis both Israel and the Arab countries conducted propaganda compaigns in the United States designed to sway public opinion in their favor. Each side obviously thought of theirs as good and the other's as bad.

Examples of propaganda used for good purposes may be found in the various campaigns designed to get the public to drive safely or to recognize the symptoms of cancer; these examples are usually based on sound evidence and reasonable inference. Other examples may be found in churches that conduct campaigns to persuade people to act in accordance with the Ten Commandments or in colleges that conduct campaigns to raise funds.

Propagandists reach a decision on a problem before they begin the process of propaganda. They continue their campaign until they solve the problem by persuading others to accept their decision or they are convinced that further efforts are pointless. In their efforts to influence others, propagandists may find it necessary or advantageous to face their opponents and become debaters. In such cases, they need a knowledge of argumentation and debate. If their evidence is true and their reasoning valid and if their appeals are carefully selected, the campaign will have the greatest opportunity for success. If any of the conditions is lacking, the opportunity for success is diminished.

On the other hand, a knowledge of argumentation and debate is an important defense against the propaganda campaigns constantly seeking to influence our decisions. Unless we subject propaganda to critical analysis, we will be unable to distinguish the good from the bad. We will lose our ability to make reasoned decisions and become hapless puppets manipulated by the "hidden persuaders."

VI. Coercion

Coercion is defined as the threat or use of force. Parents use coercion when they take a box of matches from a baby; society uses coercion to confine criminals to a prison; the nation uses coercion when it goes to war. A free society places sharp restrictions on the use of coercion. The amount of coercion parents may use on a child is limited; criminals may be sentenced to prison only after they have an opportunity for debate on the charges against them; the United States may declare war only after the advocates of war win a debate in Congress. Even undeclared wars, such as the Vietnam conflict, require Congressional sanction in the form of joint resolutions and military appropriations. In a free society the use of coercion as a method of solving problems — by private individuals or the state — is generally prohibited except in those special cases where its use has been found necessary after debate. A totalitarian society, on the other hand, is characterized by sharply limited debate and by almost omnipresent coercion.[19]

Coercion may be used to influence a decision. The existence of the coercive powers of the state is a strong logical appeal against a decision to commit a crime; and for some it may be the only effective appeal. In debating policy propositions, affirmative debaters almost always provide for coercion in their plan; they include an "enforcement plank" providing fines, imprisonment, or some other penalty for those who do not obey or who seek to circumvent the requirements of the plan.

A decision to use coercion is likely to be socially acceptable and effective when that decision is made after full and fair debate. Baron Karl von Clausewitz's classic definition of war as the "continuation of diplomacy by other means" indicates that war, the ultimate form of coercion, is a method of problem solving to be selected after a careful debate on the possible risks and possible advantages.

Brainwashing, a term that became familiar during the Korean War, is a specialized use of coercion as a method of securing a decision. It is defined as the use of coercion in combination with a blend of sound and specious argument, persuasion, propaganda, and rigidly controlled group discussion in a situation where intensive and unremitting pressure is applied by a controlling group — an army, secret police organization, or a band of terrorists — to controlled individuals — prisoners — for the purpose of securing from the prisoners a decision to profess publicly the ideas dictated by their captors. As an essential ingredient of brainwashing the captors punish any

[19]See Aleksandr I. Solzhenitsyn, *The Gulag Archipelago* (New York: Harper & Row, 1974).

"wrong" statement or attitude by physical or mental torture, or conditioning, and reward a "right" statement or attitude by granting some desirable privilege. The first objective is to produce prisoners free from visible signs of torture and so conditioned that they will profess the ideas of their captors in a convincing manner and in an apparently uncontrolled situation. The ultimate objective is to condition the prisoners so thoroughly that they come to believe the ideas dictated to them and to act in accordance with the dictated ideas even after their release. Brainwashing is a form of coercion, because it is dependent upon the complete physical control of the subjects for an indefinite period of time.

A knowledge of argumentation is a basic factor in the administration of brainwashing, for those who administer it seek to convince prisoners by logical and pseudological argument. Endless pressures are designed to condition the prisoners to believe that their side is "logically" wrong and that the captors' side is "logically" right.

The same kind of knowledge may be a defense against brainwashing, in that prisoners can detect the false evidence and invalid reasoning of their captors and thus may prove to be unprofitable subjects. In the cases of prominent persons, however, when a totalitarian state has found it profitable to make extraordinary efforts, even well-educated persons have succumbed to brainwashing.

Totalitarian states are not the only practitioners of brainwashing. Some religious sects or cults have brainwashed or "programmed" their followers, with tragic results. In response to this, some anguished parents have hired "deprogrammers" to counter-brainwash their children in an effort to offset the cults' influence.

VII. Combination of Methods

It is often necessary to use a combination of methods in reaching a decision to a problem. The social context will determine the methods most suitable for reaching decisions on a given problem.

The solution to a problem requiring the consent or cooperation of others may extend over a considerable period of time and may require use of all the methods of decision making. For example, through *individual decision* a person might determine that "nonrefundable beverage containers cause unacceptable litter and should be prohibited."

Because that person is powerless to put such a decision into effect alone, he or she must use *persuasion* to influence friends to join in the decision. They may use the process of *group discussion* to decide how to proceed toward their objective. They might find it necessary to organize a group for raising funds and work together for a period of months or years to conduct a *propaganda* campaign directed toward the voters of the state. During this campaign many individuals might serve to *persuade* or *debate*. Eventually, a bill might be introduced into the state legislature.

After *discussion* in committee hearings and a number of *debates* on the floor of the legislature, there would be a final *debate* to determine the disposition of the bill. If enacted into law, *coercion* would be provided to ensure compliance. The validity of the law would probably be tested by *debates* in the law courts to determine its constitutionality. In cases of violation of the law, *coercion* could be applied only as the result of *debates* in the law courts. The extent to which brainwashing, a specialized form of *coercion*, may be used by cults or individuals raises complex Constitutional issues that have not been resolved by the courts.

How do we reach a decision on this problem or on any other matter of importance? We are all under constant pressure to make unreasoned decisions. Unquestionably many people often use unreasoned means to make decisions. What is the method most likely to lead to a wise decision? Our only assurance of wise judgments is in the use of critical thinking. In many situations argumentation's emphasis on reasoned considerations and debate's confrontation of opposing sides give us our best or only opportunity to reach reasoned conclusions. The point of view here is that it is in the public interest to promote debate and that it is in the intelligent self-interest of the individual to know the principles of argumentation and to be able to apply critical thinking in debate.

Exercises

1. List ten types of business or professional activities in which a knowledge of argumentation and debate would be an important asset. Explain why.

2. Can you find any significant business or professional activities in which a knowledge of argumentation and debate would not be an important asset? Explain why.

3. Prepare a brief paper in which you list recent examples of the following:
   a. A debate in a campus organization to which you belong.
   b. A group discussion in a campus organization to which you belong.
   c. A persuasive speech that you have heard on campus.
   d. Evidence of a propaganda campaign you have seen on campus.
   e. Evidence of the use of coercion you have heard of on a campus.

4. Prepare a brief paper in which you list recent examples of the following:
   a. An individual decision, apparently made after debate, on an important public matter.
   b. A group discussion in which a decision of public importance was made.
   c. A persuasive speech by a national figure on a matter of public importance.
   d. A current propaganda campaign on a matter of national importance.
   e. The use of coercion to enforce a decision on a matter of public importance.

5. Prepare for a class discussion on the question "How important was their debating ability to the careers of the 'Senate Immortals'?"

6. Prepare to participate in a class discussion in which you explain why you agree or disagree with one or more of the following statements:
   a. Mill, as quoted on page 4   b. Welch, as quoted on page 4
   c. Lippmann, as quoted on page 5   d. Perelman, as quoted on page 5

7. Prepare to participate in a class discussion on the following statements. What do you think prompted the speaker to make the statement? Do you agree with his or her view?
   a. "If all my possessions and powers were to be taken from me with one exception, I would choose to keep the power of speech, for by it I could soon recover all the rest." — Daniel Webster

b. "The most valuable form of public speaking is debate."—William Jennings Bryan

c. "It seems to me that stronger than any other group, tougher in intellectual fiber, keener in intellectual interest, better equipped to battle with coming problems, are the college debaters."—Alexander Meiklejohn, late President of Amherst College

d. "The training I received in speech and debate has been more valuable to me than all the rest of my training put together."—William O'Neill, former Chief Justice, Ohio Supreme Court

e. "I believe that training in debate should be a most valuable preparation for a career in business. Forty years in the business world certainly indicates to me that the ability to present a position clearly and forcefully, to detect the flaws or weaknesses in the presentation of an opposite position and rapidly decide how to bring these flaws or weaknesses to light and then counter them convincingly is of the utmost value to most businessmen. It is an ability which is essential in almost every form of negotiations, whether it be contract negotiations, labor negotiations, negotiations with Government agencies or representatives, or in fact any sort of negotiations. This ability is inherent in every successful salesman. It is essential in dealing with organizational matters in a person's own business. It is not too much to say that such ability—objectively applied to one's own personal problems—can spell the difference between personal success and failure."—M. J. Rathbone, former President, Standard Oil Company of New Jersey

f. "Among the marks of an educated person are the abilities to think intelligently, to hold convictions, and to speak clearly and persuasively on public issues. We at Harvard are committed to the high standard of education represented by these marks, and one measure of these indicators is the formal debate. We are happy, therefore, to have so many representatives of other academic institutions join us in this activity."—Derek C. Bok, President, Harvard University

g. "No college freshman can project twenty-five years to decide what he needs to learn—subject matter is easily forgotten and in today's world, the knowledge explosion makes constant learning an inevitability. But all adults today need to be able to communicate with clarity, to articulate ideas, to reason, to separate key facts from the barrage of ideas we all are exposed to every day.

"No single activity can prepare one better than debating—the ability to think on one's feet, to form conclusions rapidly, to answer questions logically and with clarity, to summarize ideas are all processes which forensic activities develop and develop well."—Helen M. Wise, Past President, National Education Association

h. "Debate trained me to analyze and articulate the complex national problems that confront our country. Too, it was tremendous help in campaign debates for my House and Senate seats . . . I derived benefits from it far beyond the normal extracurricular and curricular activity that it encompassed."—Richard S. Schweiker, Secretary of Health and Human Services.

2

Applied and Academic Debate

Debate may be classified into two broad categories: applied and educational. *Applied debate* is conducted on propositions in which the advocates have a special interest and the debate is presented before a judge or audience with power to render a binding decision on the proposition. *Academic debate* is conducted on propositions in which the advocates usually have an academic interest; it is presented before a judge or audience usually without direct power to render a decision on the proposition—indeed, in academic debate the judge is instructed to disregard the merits of the proposition and to render the decision on the merits of the debate; and the purpose of the debate is to provide educational opportunities for the participants.

I.   Applied Debate

Applied debate may be classified as special debate, judicial debate, parliamentary debate, and nonformal debate. This chapter will consider each of these classifications of debate briefly; academic debate will then be considered in more detail.

A. Special Debate

Special debate is conducted under special rules drafted for a specific occasion. Perhaps the best-known examples are the Lincoln-Douglas debates of 1858, the Kennedy-Nixon debates of 1960, the Ford-Carter debates of 1976, the Carter-Reagan debate of 1980, the Reagan-Mondale debates of 1984, and the Bush-Dukakis debates of 1988. These were formal debates, yet they were neither judicial nor parliamentary; they were conducted under special rules agreed on by the debaters. Debates between Presidential candidates now seem to be a firmly established part of the American political scene. In the 1988 primary campaigns, which included a multiplicity of candidates, series of debates were held by both parties. While the formats of these debates left much to be desired, they did at least bring the candidates together face to face and provided the voters with a better opportunity to compare the candidates than was usually available in primary campaigns. Although this type of debate is most frequently associated with political figures and campaign issues, it may be used by anyone on any proposition; it merely requires the agreement of opposing advocates to come together under the provisions of a special set of rules drafted for the occasion.

B. Judicial Debate

Judicial debate is conducted in the law courts or before quasi-judicial bodies. It is conducted under the rules of a court of law and has as its purpose the prosecution or defense of individuals charged with violation of the law or the determination of issues of law alleged to be applicable to specific cases before the court.

Judicial debate may be observed in any law court from the Supreme Court of the United States to a local court. In its academic form, judicial debate (known as moot-court debate) is used by law schools as a method of preparing students for their later debates in court.

The principles of argumentation and debate apply to judicial debate. Since judicial debate is also very much concerned with sometimes highly technical rules of procedure — which may vary considerably from federal to state courts, from one state to another, and from one type of court to another within a given state — the specific methods of judicial debate are not considered here. Mock trial debate, which emulates the form of courtroom debate without the emphasis on rules of procedure and admissibility, is considered later (see Chapter 18, Section I-D).

C. Parliamentary Debate

Parliamentary debate is conducted under the rules of parliamentary procedure. It has as its purpose the passage, amendment, or defeat of motions and resolutions that come before a parliamentary assembly.

The practice of parliamentary debate may be observed in the Senate or House of Representatives of the Congress, the legislatures of the several states, city councils, town governing bodies, and at the business meetings of various organizations, such as the national convention of a major political party or a meeting of a local fraternity chapter. In its educational form, parliamentary debate may be known as a model Congress, a model state legislature, a model United Nations Assembly, a mock political convention, or other similar designations.

The principles of argumentation and debate apply to parliamentary debate. The special provisions of parliamentary procedure that also apply to this type of debate are considered in Chapter 19.

D. Nonformal Debate

Nonformal debate is conducted without the formal rules found in special, judicial, parliamentary, and academic debate. This is the type of debate that newspapers or television commentators usually refer to when they speak of the "abortion debate," the "tax policy debate," and other controversies that engage public interest. The term "nonformal" has no reference to the formality or informality of the occasion in which the debate may take place. A President's State of the Union Address — a very formal speech — may be a part of a nonformal debate; or a rap session in a college fraternity — a very informal situation — may also be part of a nonformal debate.

Examples may be found in national political campaigns, in community debates about pollution of water or a new school bond issue, in business debates about the policies of a corporation, in colleges on matters of educational policy or the allocation of the college budget, or in the contests for the various offices in student politics. On the family level, nonformal debates may revolve around such matters as who will have the car tonight or the choice of a college.

II. Academic Debate

Academic debate is conducted under the direction of an educational institution for the purpose of providing educational opportunities for its students. Most schools and colleges today conduct programs of academic debate; it is almost inevitable that every educated person at some time will be a participant in some form of debate. Clearly the question before us is not whether or not we will participate in debate — our participation as decision renderers or advocates is inevitable. The only question is whether our participation will be effective. The purpose of academic debate is to enable us to become effective in this essential art.

A. Backgrounds of Academic Debate

A history of academic debate would fill many volumes. There are, however, a few salient facts we may consider here. The beginnings of debate are lost in the remote reaches of the earliest recorded history. Civilized people began debating at least 3,000 years ago: Chinese scholars conducted important philosophical debates during the Chou Dynasty (1122–255 B.C.). Homer's (about 900 B.C.) epic poems, the *Iliad* and the *Odyssey*, contain speeches, which Quintilian cites as examples of the arts of legal pleading and deliberation, that may be regarded as embryonic debates. The *Rhetoric* of Aristotle (384–322 B.C.) laid the foundation of argumentation and debate and is influential even to the present day.

Academic debate began at least 2,400 years ago when the scholar Protagoras of Abdera (481–411 B.C.), known as the father of debate, conducted debates among his students in Athens. Corax and Tisias founded one of the earliest schools of rhetoric, specializing in teaching debate so that students might plead their own cases in the law courts of ancient Sicily.

Debate flourished in the academies of the ancient world and in the medieval universities where rhetoric was installed as one of the seven liberal arts. Perhaps the first intercollegiate debate in the English-speaking world took place in the early 1400s at Cambridge University between students of Oxford and Cambridge. The debating programs at British universities have long been a principal training ground for future members of Parliament.

Debating has been an important part of the American educational scene from the earliest times. Debating flourished in the colonial colleges; disputations were a required part of the curriculum, and debates were frequently a featured part of the commencement ceremonies. Almost all of the leaders of the Revolution and the early national period were able debaters who had studied argumentation in the colonial colleges or in the innumerable community debating "societies," "lyceums," and "bees" that flourished throughout the land.

Intercollegiate debating began in the later part of the 1800s, and interscholastic debating followed soon after. In the early part of this century, however, intercollegiate debates were relatively rare events. Normally a college would schedule only a few intercollegiate debates during an academic year, and large audiences would assemble to watch the few students who were privileged to participate in these unusual events. Recognition of the value and importance of academic debate has increased steadily during this century, however. Tournament debating was introduced in the 1920s but was a little-used phenomenon until twenty years later. During the 1920s to 1940s, contract debating prevailed. A college team would send out contracts to other college teams specifying such details as which team had which side of the proposition, how judges would be selected, provisions for housing, meals, and so on, and indicating a willingness to reciprocate as host on some future occasion. When a sufficient number of signed contracts were returned, a tour was arranged and the team departed by car, bus, or train for a few days or a week or two of debating. Usually the schedule called for one debate a day, although in such major cities as Boston, New York, Washington, or Chicago, two debates a day might be scheduled. On rare occasions teams traveled coast to coast on private railroad cars.

In the post–World War II era, tournament debating came to be *the* mode of debating. In 1947 the U.S. Military Academy began the National Debate Tournament (NDT) at West Point. Tournament debating proliferated and teams soon had their choice of many different tournaments at nearby or distant colleges on almost any weekend between October and April. Swing tournaments evolved; two relatively nearby colleges would schedule tournaments back-to-back during the winter break so that, instead of one or two debates a day, teams could now schedule two tournaments in a week.

In 1967 the American Forensic Association assumed responsibility for the National Debate Tournament, and the NDT has been hosted by a different college each year since then. By 1967 the NDT had become *the* dominant force in intercollegiate debating, and virtually all teams geared their programs to winning a place in the NDT or emulated the practices of teams that were successful in the NDT. In 1971 CEDA (the Cross Examination Debate Association) was established to provide an alternative to NDT debating, one which would meet a perceived need by placing greater emphasis on communication. (The use of cross-examination debating is not a distinguishing factor between the two approaches; since 1974–1975 the NDT has used the cross examination format.) CEDA — which began using off-topic (non-NDT) policy propositions — has used value propositions since 1975. After a modest start as the South West Debate Association, CEDA has burgeoned nationally and is now the most widely used mode of intercollegiate debating. The American Debate Association was established in 1983 to foster the growth of what it perceived as "reasonable" policy debate. In NDT and ADA debates there is an explicit consideration of policy; in CEDA debates there is an implicit consideration of policy. In academic debate the student must know and adapt to the preferences and expectations of the judges identified with these organizations (see Chapter 15, Analysis of the Audience, and Chapter 17, Judging Philosophies.) NDT and ADA debaters often find it necessary to consider and debate values, whereas CEDA debaters often find it necessary to consider and debate the policy implications of values. In applied debate the interrelationship of value and policy is so entwined that one often must debate both.

B. Organization of Academic Debate

Academic debate is by no means limited to the classroom and the argumentation course. Most colleges and schools conduct a program of academic debate through the organization of a debating team, which provides a means for students to obtain additional opportunities beyond the traditional course offerings. Academic credit is often given for participation in the debate program — a program usually open to any qualified undergraduate. The director of forensics conducts the program so as to provide training opportunities for students new to debate and maximum challenge for the more experienced students.

As the designation "director of forensics" suggests, most debating teams today have been broadened to include other forensic activities in addition to debate. "*Forensics* is defined as an educational activity primarily concerned with using an argumentative perspective in examining problems and communicating with people."[1] Recognizing that many forensic programs have been expanded to include a wide variety of public address and individual events in addition to debate, the 1984 definition continues:

> Forensics is viewed as a form of rhetorical scholarship which takes various forms, including debate, public address, and the interpretation of literature. Forensics serves as a curricular and co-curricular laboratory for improving students' abilities in research, analysis, and oral communication. Typically, forensic activities are conducted in a competitive environment so as to motivate students and accelerate the learning process. Forensics remains an ongoing, scholarly experience, uniting students and teachers, in its basic educational purpose.[2]

---

[1]This definition, adopted at the Second National Developmental Conference on Forensics at meetings in Evanston, Illinois, in 1984, reaffirmed the definition adopted at the First National Developmental Conference on Forensics held in Sedalia, Colorado, in 1974.
[2]Ibid.

American Forensic Association: Statement of Principles

Recognizing that the free interchange and objective evaluation of ideas through such forensic activities as public speaking, discussion, and debate are essential to the maintenance of a democratic society, the American Forensic Association herewith records this statement of principles, which it believes should govern academic training in these disciplines.

- We believe that forensic activity should create opportunities for intensive investigation of significant contemporary problems.
- We believe that forensic activity should promote the use of logical reasoning and the use of the best available evidence in dealing with these problems.
- We believe that forensic activity should develop the ability to select, arrange, and compose material clearly and effectively.
- We believe that forensic activity should train students in the sincere and persuasive presentation of this material to the appropriate audience.
- We believe that forensic activity should stimulate students to honest and original effort.
- We believe that interscholastic and intercollegiate competition should be used to motivate students to their best efforts in attaining these objectives.
- We further believe that forensic activities should be under the responsible direction of a qualified faculty member, whose duty it should be to maintain and support the above principles.

C. Values of Academic Debate

Because debating is an ancient discipline that is thriving in modern educational institutions, it may be well to consider briefly some of the values of academic debate that are responsible for its increasing prominence on the educational scene. Although not all these values are unique to debate, the well-conducted academic debate program is an important means of attaining these values. Indeed, for many students it is the best or sometimes the only means of attaining full realization of these values.

1. Debate provides preparation for effective participation in a free society. Debate is an inherent condition of a free society. Our Constitution provides for freedom of speech. Our legislatures, our courts, and most of our private organizations conduct their business through the medium of debate. Because debate is so widespread at decision-making levels, the citizen's ability to vote intelligently or to use his or her right of free speech effectively is limited without a knowledge of debate. As we know from history, freedoms unused or used ineffectively are soon lost. Citizens educated in debate can have hopes of attaining truly effective participation in a free society (*see inset*).

2. Debate offers preparation for leadership. The ultimate position of leadership is the Presidency of the United States. Schlesinger cites two indispensable requirements an effective President must meet. The first is "to point the republic in one or another direction."

> The second requirement is to explain to the electorate why the direction the President proposes is right for the nation. Reagan understood, as Carter never did, that politics is ultimately an educational process. Where Carter gave the impression of regarding presidential speeches as disagreeable duties, to be rushed through as perfunctorily as possible, Reagan knew that the speech is a vital weapon of presidential leadership. His best speeches had a structure and an argument. They were well written and superbly delivered. They were potent vehicles for the President's charm, histrionic skill and genius for simplification.[3]

It is interesting to note that Schlesinger's second requirement echoes the definition of argumentation given on page 2. While few, if any, of the readers of this text will become President, many will aspire to positions of leadership. And an indispensable requirement of leadership—not only in politics, but in almost all areas of human endeavor—is that the leader explain why the direction proposed is right.

3. Debate offers training in argumentation. From classical times to the present, argumentation professors have found that debate is the best method of providing training in this discipline. Debate provides an unexcelled opportunity for students to apply the theories of argumentation under conditions designed to increase their knowledge and understanding of these theories and proficiency in their use. As an educational method, debate provides excellent motivation for learning, since the student has both the short-term goal of winning a decision or an award in a tournament and the long-term goal of increasing knowledge and ability. This combination of short-term and long-term motivations provides for an optimum learning situation. The constant evaluation of student achievement, in the form of decisions rendered on debates, provides frequent opportunities to encourage growth and progress and to detect and remedy misunderstandings or misapplications.

4. Debate provides for investigation and intensive analysis of significant contemporary problems. Thoughtful educators have long been concerned that students and the general public often have only a superficial knowledge of significant contemporary problems. In addition to acquiring a knowledge of the principles of argumentation, debaters also have the opportunity to investigate in depth and to analyze intensively the various significant contemporary problems that form the basis of the propositions under debate. In the course of a debating career, students will acquire a better-than-average knowledge of current problems, as well as skill in applying methods that will enable them to analyze critically the problems they will encounter in the future. As Baldwin points out, the true aim of rhetoric—the energizing of knowledge—is necessarily correlated with inquiry and with policy.[4] In debate, students learn both to acquire knowledge and to energize that knowledge.

---

[3]Arthur M. Schlesinger, Jr., *The Cycles of American History* (Boston: Houghton Mifflin, 1986), p. 293.
[4]See Charles Sears Baldwin, *Medieval Rhetoric and Poetic* (New York: Macmillan, 1928), p. 3.

5. Debate develops proficiency in critical thinking. Through study of argumentation and practice in debate, students participate in an educational process specifically designed to develop their proficiency in critical thinking. Winston Brembeck investigated whether a college course in argumentation and debate, as taught at eleven different colleges, improved critical-thinking scores on a standardized test and found that the argumentation students outgained the control students by a statistically significant amount. Ted R. Jackson found that the critical-thinking ability of 100 college debaters (in comparison with 147 nondebaters) improved by a statistically significant amount after one season of intercollegiate debating.[5] The debater learns to apply the principles of critical thinking not only to problems that emerge in the relative leisure and comfort of research or the briefing session but also to problems that arise in the stress of debate.

6. Debate is an integrator of knowledge. Educators are constantly searching for methods of synthesizing knowledge. Debate has long served as a means of achieving this goal. Baird comments: "Again the exponents of a synthesis of knowledge and the broader view of a problem can well take a leaf from the practical experience and method of the arguer and discussant. Almost any problem at which the debater works cuts across these fields of knowledge."[6] For example, in debating the proposition dealing with the problem of guaranteed annual wages, debaters must have at least a minimal acquaintance with the principles of argumentation, economics, political science, sociology, psychology, finance, business management, labor relations, government, history, and philosophy. They will, of course, learn the principles and details of these disciplines through the appropriate departments of the college or through independent study; however, through debate they can integrate their knowledge of these various problems and bring them to bear upon a significant contemporary problem. For many students debate is their first and often their most intensive and valuable experience in interdisciplinary studies.

7. Debate develops proficiency in purposeful inquiry. Debate is preceded by inquiry. Of necessity the debater must be well informed of all the relevant aspects of the problem to be debated. The extent to which debate motivates the student to undertake purposeful inquiry in the form of the study of significant contemporary problems, to apply the principles of critical thinking to those problems, and to integrate the knowledge acquired from various disciplines is suggested by a former college debater:

> [In just six years] high school and college debaters were introduced to such vital and contemporary issues as compulsory arbitration of labor disputes, world government, electoral college reforms, price and wage controls, FEPC, and tariff revision. Each of these big topics raised subsidiary, but equally important public questions.

[5]Both the Brembeck and the Jackson studies are reported in Richard Huseman, Glen Ware, and Charles Gruner, "Critical Thinking, Reflective Thinking, and the Ability to Organize Ideas: A Multi-Variate Approach," *Journal of the American Forensic Association*, Vol. 9 (Summer 1972), pp. 261–262.

[6]A. Craig Baird, "General Education and the Course in Argumentation," *The Gavel*, Vol. 38 (March 1956), p. 59. Reprinted by permission of Delta Sigma Rho.

Study and debate of such topics serves as an introduction to the social sciences for many undergraduates whose major studies are in the humanities or the sciences. My first reading in *Foreign Affairs, American Economic Review, American Political Science Review, The Annals,* law reviews, regional quarterlies, and other social science journals was in search of materials relevant to debate topics. I suspect that many an undergraduate relies on debating for his important contact with social science. . . .

While I do not mean to say that thoroughness can be measured by length, I think it interesting and significant that the volume of my and my colleague's research on FEPC and free trade was about equal to that which went into my master's thesis of two hundred thirty pages on a question of public law.[7]

Indeed the debater is frequently working on the cutting edge of contemporary problems, studying matters well in advance of the time they emerge as subjects of general public concern. As Robinson pointed out in the preceding quotation, the debater seeks out the scholarly journals where significant problems are often first reported and studied. The general public draws its information from television and the popular press, which may not report these matters until months or years later. For example, the "greenhouse" (p. 200) and the "beef" (p. 233) disadvantages were considered "exotic" by nondebaters who heard them in 1978 and 1979; by 1989 stories on these subjects were common fare in general circulation publications.

An examination of the lists of national debate propositions (see Appendixes D and E) will reveal that debaters were in fact working on the cutting edge, considering major contemporary problems in advance of the general public. Perhaps the most striking example of foresight in discerning future public policy issues may be found in the then highly controversial 1954–1955 NDT proposition on the diplomatic recognition of communist China. It was not until Nixon's historic visit to China seventeen years later that the United States extended diplomatic recognition to China.

The recognition of the necessity to conduct inquiry in sometimes unfamiliar fields, and the knowledge of principles that will make that inquiry purposeful and effective, will serve students well in many of their later undertakings.

8. Debate emphasizes quality instruction. Debate is based on a close tutorial relationship between faculty and students. Concerned educators are worried about the implications of mass classes and impersonal teaching. The debate class provides an effective solution to this problem by providing a tutorial relationship between the faculty and the student. Such classes are usually relatively small and there are many opportunities for interaction between the students and the professor as they prepare for class debates or other class projects. This valuable process is enhanced by the feedback that usually follows such projects. Most of the educational activity of the debate program as well is carried out in a tutorial situation where the Director of Forensics or one of the assistants works with the two members of the debate team as they plan their research, develop their affirmative case, and plan their negative strategies or with a group of four students after a practice debate as they critique the debate in-depth and plan for further improvement. As this tutorial relationship is rarely lim-

---

[7]James Robinson, "A Recent Graduate Examines His Forensic Experience," *The Gavel,* Vol. 38 (March 1956), p. 62. Reprinted by permission of Delta Sigma Rho.

ited to one quarter or semester, and often extends over four years, it provides a valuable opportunity for a personal education in the all-too-often impersonal world of higher education.

9. Debate encourages student scholarship. Debate establishes high standards of research and scholarly achievement that are rarely equaled in undergraduate courses. Some students fear that the time spent on debate may have an adverse effect on their grades. Experience proves the contrary to be true. Intercollegiate debaters report that their work in debate is a significant factor in helping them write better exams, prepare better term papers, and obtain better results in graduate school admission examinations. This, of course, is the predictable result of the values considered in this section. The scholarly skills the debater develops through research, organization, and presentation and defense of a debate case are directly transferable to many areas of scholarly endeavor. Added to this is the challenge to do one's best that debate provides. In the classroom the professor typically makes "reasonable" assignments that the "average" student can fulfill. In intercollegiate debate the student's opponent is rarely "reasonable" or "average." As we recognize in point 7 earlier, good debaters will do far more research than a reasonable professor would ever assign for a term paper and will present it with far more skill and defend it far more ably than would be required in a classroom report. Preparing for and participating in major tournaments can truly be a mind-expanding experience that gives students the incentive to work at the very maximum of their capabilities and enables them to discover their real potential.

Argumentation courses and participation in intercollegiate debate are traditional training grounds for prelaw students. In a study of 98 law school deans, Swanson found that 69.9 percent would advise prelaw students to take a course in argumentation, and 70.3 percent recommended participation in intercollegiate debate. The deans also indicated that prelaw students "needed training in the skills of public speaking" (81.9 percent), "practical experience in the use of research techniques" (84.2 percent), "training in the application of the principles of logical reasoning" (89.6 percent), and "training in the techniques of refutation and rebuttal" (75.8 percent).[8]

While such training and experience are of obvious value to the prelaw student, it is easy to see that they would be important assets in many areas of graduate study and business and professional endeavor.

10. Debate develops the ability to make prompt, analytical responses. In the 1988 Presidential campaign, Dukakis—who had an 18-point lead in the early polls—shrugged off Bush's attacks and let them go unanswered. One of Bush's more effective attacks was to criticize Dukakis for vetoing a bill requiring teachers to lead the Pledge of Allegiance each day. "'Dukakis' strategy of shrugging off attacks suddenly stopped looking presidential and started looking weak,' said a top aide. . . . Months after Bush first raised the issue, Dukakis finally responded."[9] This failure to make a prompt, analytical response to this and other attacks that Dukakis apparently judged

[8]From a paper by Don R. Swanson, "Debate as Preparation for Law: Law Deans' Reactions," presented at the Western Speech Communication Association convention, 1970.
[9]*Time*, November 21, 1988, p. 47.

to be frivolous was considered by many observers to be important factors in Dukakis' defeat. In today's world of instant communication, a candidate lets an attack go unanswered at his peril. (See Chapter 3, Section III, "Presumption and Burden of Proof.") In the same way a senator, business executive, or private citizen may be in a position that requires a prompt, analytical response. The student learns to do this in debate; cross-examination requires an instant response, and response to an argument made in an opponent's speech must be prepared during the speech or in the fleeting time allowed between speeches.

11. Debate develops critical listening. In their pioneer work on listening, Nichols and Stevens's research found that "on the average we listen at approximately a 25 percent level of efficiency."[10] If we allow our attention to wander while an opponent speaks, our reply will be ineffective and "off the mark." And if we miss 75 percent of our opponents' arguments, we will be destroyed. Debaters soon learn to listen to their opponents with sharply focused critical attention, recording their arguments precisely on the flow sheet so that their own responses may be precisely to the point as they adapt the very words of their opponents, turning the subtleties and limitations heard to their own advantage. The ability to listen critically is widely recognized as an important attribute of the educated person. Nichols and Stevens found that a top executive of a large industrial plant reported "perhaps 80 percent of my work depends on my listening to someone, or upon someone else listening to me."[11] The debater begins to develop this important skill of critical listening from the very first debate.

12. Debate develops proficiency in writing. Many debates are conducted in writing. The daily "debates" on the editorial page of USA Today are only one example. However, as a practical matter, we most often think of debate as oral argument. Given this fact, how then does debate develop proficiency in writing? Don't we just "talk on our feet" when we debate? As we have seen, debate does, indeed, develop the ability to make prompt, analytical responses (see point 10). However, as we will discover, much of the debate is written in advance of delivery. The first affirmative constructive speech is almost invariably a manuscript speech, which means that it is written and rewritten, revised and edited as the advocates seek to develop the most effective statement of their position. In the same way, many portions of other speeches, negative briefs, generic blocks, and other arguments are the product of careful writing and extensive rewriting, as well as skillful adaptation to previous speeches.

The writing proficiency that the student develops in debate pays dividends in the first instance by enabling the debater to present arguments more cogently and effectively and thus to win the vote of the judge. The skills learned in writing for debate, however, carry over to many other fields. The student will find that the writing skills learned in debate can be profitably applied in all courses in writing term papers and in writing better answers to essay exams. After graduation the demand for writing proficiency is great in almost any responsible business or professional career.

---

[10]Ralph G. Nichols and Leonard A. Stevens, *Are You Listening?* (New York: McGraw-Hill, 1957), p. ix.
[11]Ibid., p. 141.

13. Debate encourages mature judgment. Scholars in the field of general semantics tell us that many problems in human affairs result from the misevaluation and misunderstanding that come from considering complex problems in the context of a one- or two-valued orientation. Educational debate provides an opportunity for students to consider significant problems in the context of a multivalued orientation. They learn to look at a problem from many points of view. As debaters analyze the potential affirmative cases and the potential negative cases, including the possibility of negative counter plans, they begin to realize the complexity of most contemporary problems and to appreciate the worth of a multivalued orientation; as they debate both sides of a proposition under consideration, they learn not only that most problems of contemporary affairs have more than one side but also that even one side of a proposition embodies a considerable range of values.

Sometimes at the start of an academic year some debaters may, on the basis of a hastily formulated opinion, feel that only one side of a proposition is "right." After a few debates, however, such students usually request an assignment on the other side of the proposition. By the end of a year, in which they have debated on both sides of the proposition, they learn the value of suspending judgment until they have investigated and analyzed a reasonable amount of evidence and reasoning. The necessity of advocating one side of the proposition in a debate has also taught them that decisions may not be postponed indefinitely. When, at the end of the year, they finally formulate their personal position on the proposition, it may or may not be the same as it was at the start of the season; but this time it will be a position that they have reached after due consideration and that they can defend logically.

14. Debate develops courage. Debate helps students to develop courage by requiring them to formulate a case and defend it against strong opposition. In debate, students' cases will come under attack. It would be easy to push the panic button, beat a disorderly retreat, and avoid the problems. They can't do this, however. The situation requires that they defend their position. They must have the courage of their convictions. They must discipline themselves, concentrate on the problem, organize thoughts, and present refutation. Well-prepared debaters find that they *can* defend their position, that their opponents are only human; they thus gain new confidence in themselves and in their ability to function in a competitive situation.

15. Debate encourages effective speech composition and delivery. Since composition and delivery of the debate speech are among the factors that determine the effectiveness of arguments, debaters are encouraged to select, arrange, and present their materials in accordance with the best principles of public speaking. Debating places a premium on extemporaneous delivery, requiring speakers to think on their feet. Typically, debaters will speak before many different audiences: a single judge in the preliminary round of a tournament, a group of businesspeople at a service club, or a radio or TV audience. Each of these situations provides new challenges for students. Constant adaptation to the audience and to the speech situation develops flexibility and facility in thinking and speaking.

16. Debate develops social maturity. Debate provides an opportunity for the student to travel to different colleges and meet students and faculty members from various parts of the country. With the dawning of the jet age, many colleges developed continental debate programs, and it is by no means unusual for a team to participate in tournaments on the East Coast, the West Coast, the Deep South, the New England States, and many points in between in the course of a year. Previously there were Eastern, Midwestern, Southern, and Western cases and styles of debating. Now that debating is a continental activity, these regional differences have largely disappeared. Association in both the businesslike atmosphere of the debate and the pleasantly informal social situations that accompany most debates and tournaments helps students to acquire social amenities, poise, and assurance. Amid the competition of a tournament, they learn that they must accept victory or defeat gracefully and that they must respond courteously to the criticism of a judge regardless of the decision. The incidental educational benefit that comes from the opportunity of meeting professors from a number of different colleges in an informal social situation has significant value.

17. Debate develops essential proficiencies. At its essence, debate is an educational activity that provides students with the opportunity to develop a high level of proficiency in writing, thinking, reading, speaking, and listening. These are essential competencies that leading educators and educational groups have termed vital to intellectual advancement. There has been remarkable consensus on this question in every major study of education in the United States in recent years: proficiency in oral communication is essential to academic competency. The following studies are representative of this pressing need (emphasis added):

1. The National Commission on Higher Education Issues, in a recent study, identified the "fundamental competencies in reading, *writing*, *speaking*, mathematical techniques, and *reasoning*" as the requisite intellectual skills for the pursuit of higher education (*Summary Recommendations of the National Commission on Higher Education Issues*).

2. The National Commission on Excellence in Education, chaired by David Gardner, echoed the same views and specified the same competencies, including both *oral* and *written* communication in its enumeration of necessary skills (*A Nation at Risk*, U.S. Department of Education, National Commission on Excellence in Education).

3. The Education Commission for the States' Task Force on Education for Economic Growth, whose members included governors, business leaders and educators, assessed the critical needs of the education–commerce nexus and concluded that educational preparation for the "very competitive world of international commerce and trade" must include the essential language competencies of "reading," "*writing*," "*speaking* and *listening*" (*Action for Excellence*, Report of the Task Force on Education for Economic Growth, Education Commission for the States).

4. In its 1983 report, the College Entrance Examination Board also listed "speaking and listening" among what it termed the "Basic Academic Competencies." "The Basic Academic Competencies are the broad intellectual skills essential to effective work in all fields of college study. They provide a link across disciplines of knowledge although they are not specific to any particular discipline. The Basic Aca-

demic Competencies are reading, *writing, speaking* and *listening*, mathematics, *reasoning* and studying" (*Academic Preparation for College*, The College Board).

5. A proposal for strengthening public education issued by the Paideia Group, whose membership includes Mortimer Adler, Jacques Barzun, and Ernest Boyer, among others, specified the requisite intellectual skills for the educational process: "The skills to be acquired are the skills of reading, *writing, speaking, listening*, observing, measuring, estimating and calculating. They are linguistic, mathematical and scientific skills. They are the skills that everyone needs in order to learn anything, in school or elsewhere" (*Paideia Proposal*, The Paideia Group).

6. The American Association for the Advancement of Science in a report prepared by the National Council on Science and Technology Education stated that students should be able to "distinguish good arguments from bad ones" (*Project 2061 Phase 1 Reports*, The American Association for the Advancement of Science).

Debate is distinctive because of its unique dialectical form, providing the opportunity for intellectual clash in the testing of ideas. The creation of an argument is one of the most complex cognitive acts a student can engage in. To create an argument, a student is required to research issues (which requires knowledge of how to use libraries and data banks), organize data, analyze the data, synthesize different kinds of data, and evaluate information with respect to the quality of conclusions it may point to. To form an argument after this process, a student must understand how to reason, must be able to recognize and critique different methods of reasoning, and must have an understanding of the logic of decision making. The successful communication of arguments to audiences reflects another cognitive skill: the ability to communicate complex ideas clearly with words. Finally, the argumentative interaction of students in a debate reflects an even more complex cognitive ability — the ability to process the arguments of others quickly and to reformulate or adapt or defend previous positions.[12]

III. Ethical Standards for Debate

Because we use debate as a means of influencing human behavior, the mature, responsible advocate will be concerned with ethical standards for debate. The Second National Developmental Conference on Forensics adopted "Ethical Guidelines for Students" and "Ethical Guidelines for Educators." These guidelines are recorded here and are earnestly recommended for your thoughtful consideration. They represent the most extensive statement on ethical standards for debate to have been developed by the forensic community.

A. Ethical Guidelines for the Student

Students participating in forensics are obligated to adhere to high ethical standards. Here we are concerned with the ethical choices students make for themselves, not with the standards to be applied by critics or judges. An ethical commitment by stu-

---

[12]Adapted from "A Rationale for Forensics as Education," adopted at the Second National Developmental Conference on Forensics, Evanston, Illinois.

dents is essential because the value of forensics is directly dependent on the integrity of those involved. For that reason, it is the duty of each student to participate honestly, fairly, and in such a way as to avoid communicational behaviors that are deceptive, misleading, or dishonest. Students should strive to place forensic competitions in a proper perspective as ethical decisions are pondered. The goal of winning must be evaluated within a framework that considers strategic choices in light of the educational value of such choices. Forensic contests are not ends in themselves but means to an end.

Furthermore, student participants must remember that forensics is an oral, interactive process. It is the student's duty to aspire to the objective of effective oral expression of ideas. When ideas are expressed in an unintelligible fashion, the forensic process is abused. The interactive dimension of forensics suggests that behaviors that belittle, degrade, demean, or otherwise dehumanize others are not in the best interests of forensics because they interfere with the goals of education and personal growth. The ethical forensic competitor recognizes the rights of others and communicates with respect for opponents, colleagues, and critics.

Student advocates should compete with respect for the principles and objectives of reasoned discourse. Students who invent definitions involving unwarranted shifts in the meanings of words fail to maintain a respect for the integrity of language. Students who deliberately employ specious reasoning as a strategem fail to maintain a respect for the integrity of the forensic decision-making process. . . .

Evidence plays an important role in forensic advocacy. Arguments can be no stronger than the evidence supporting them. If the evidence is misrepresented, distorted, or fabricated, the conclusions drawn are meaningless and ethically suspect. In order to understand these implications, the advocate should be familiar with the role of evidence in critical decision making, as well as with the methods of scholarship in discovering and recording evidence. The content of, and citations for, evidence used by advocates should be open to inspection by their opponents. Advocates should use only evidence that is in the public domain and, hence, open to critical evaluation by others.

Advocates should clearly identify, during their speeches, the source of all the evidence they use. Such identification should include available information relevant to the credibility of the author, the source of publication, and the date. Omitting the source of evidence denies the audience the opportunity to evaluate the quality of the information. Since the strength of evidence depends on the qualifications of the individual being quoted, this information is critical to any evaluator of the argument.

Advocates are responsible for the integrity of all the evidence they utilize, even when the evidence is not researched by the individual advocate. An advocate should not introduce evidence that is distorted or fabricated. In determining whether evidence has been distorted, the advocate should ask if the evidence deviates from the quality, quantity, probability, or degree of force of the author's position on the point in question. Any such deviation should be avoided, because such alteration can give undue rhetorical force to an advocate's argument. . . .

Students competing in forensic contests share a unique opportunity to learn and to experience personal growth. This environment serves the goals of forensics best when student participants recognize their responsibility to preserve and promote opportunities for such a forensic education. Students should remember that forensic contests are often subject to public scrutiny and that reaction to forensic practices may aid or inhibit the future course taken by the forensic activity. Thus, students should carefully consider the values inherent in the claims they advance and in the behaviors they display. Communication that engenders ill will and disrespect for forensics ultimately reduces the utility of forensics for all who participate in it and should, therefore, be avoided.

As indicated at the outset, this document is intended to outline an ethic for the entire forensic community. Although it explicitly identifies certain direct participants in the activity, there are other, less centrally involved but nonetheless vitally important members of the community upon whom ethical responsibilities fall. Because forensics is an invaluable educational experience that can benefit all students, academic institutions may be ethically obligated to offer this experience and to commit the resources that will ensure its availability and quality. Similarly, alumni of forensic programs, having benefited themselves from this experience, may be ethically obligated to work for the continued availability of the experience for others. The future of forensics is in the hands of *all* members of the community.

Honest differences of opinion exist within the forensic community as to whether certain practices should be considered ethical or unethical. The surest guide to the debater and the director may be found in answering this question: "Am I more concerned with enduring ethical standards and educational objectives than with the short-term goal of winning a debate?" If the answer is an honest "yes," the decision about a particular practice will probably be an ethically sound one.

B. Ethical Guidelines for Educators

In any forensic program, the decisions made by participants as they carry out the diverse facets of the program have ethical implications. It is the responsibility of the forensic educator to maximize the opportunity for ethical development and behavior among all participants. Because the educator normally assumes a variety of roles, including those of coach, judge, and tournament administrator, it is important to consider separately the ethical responsibilities that each of these roles implies.

Because forensics is primarily an educational activity, educators in their capacity as coaches should emphasize learning before competitive success and teach this view to their students. Because students differ in talent, experience, motivation, and purpose, pedagogical methods should be adapted to student needs; at the same time, however, coaching efforts should supplement, not substitute for, student efforts. Because many forensic events are laboratories in argumentation, the educator should strive to teach students the principles and objectives of sound reasoning. Regardless of event, forensics is sponsored by academic institutions that maintain high standards of learning; therefore, the educator should strive to teach students the rigors of scholarship. Forensics is inherently characterized by a diversity of approaches and activities that, nonetheless, possess a common interest in the advancement of forensic excellence. Thus, recalling that tolerance is a virtue, educators should avoid prejudicially denigrating other educators, students, programs, or activities. Because all students can benefit from forensic experience at some level and because all students — at whatever level — require and deserve educators' attention and efforts, educators should strive to treat all students fairly and to promote equality of opportunity for appropriate and challenging learning experiences.

Judges and critics are an integral part of the educational process in forensics; they are contributing participants in a process that seeks the full, free testing of ideas and, at the same time, are the primary reinforcers of student behavior, both good and bad. As such, judges must delicately balance two considerations; the need for rigorous examination of any and all views, however unpopular, unrealistic, or repugnant, and the guidance and direction of student behavior, attitudes, and beliefs in socially responsible ways. By nature, all judging is interventionary to some degree; hence, all judges are ethically obligated to balance these considerations, applying their expertise as judges in good faith. The following guidelines are intended to assist judges in their determinations.

Judges should act always to promote and protect the process of intellectual exchange. Student creativity in the selection and construction of discourse is to be affirmed for the purpose of promoting the sound testing of ideas, and intervention by judges on the basis of prejudice or personal preference is to be discouraged. Judges should strive at all times to render impartial decisions and fully to disclose their reasons according to tournament rules of procedure; they should, therefore, attempt to remove themselves from situations in which conflicts of interest or prejudices are likely to jeopardize such decisions. Recognizing that determination of authorial intent is problematic, judges of interpretive events should respect diverse student interpretations. Judges are ethically obligated to enforce the rules of the tournaments or events in which they participate. Moreover, judges have a positive obligation to discourage actions inimical to the forensic process. Recognizing the crucial importance of the veracity and quality of evidence and other materials, we believe student intention to be irrelevant to the evaluation of violations of evidence standards; judges should discount the probative force of material not conforming to the standards discussed below and should apply appropriate sanctions. In other areas, where considerations of intent or circumstance do bear on the evaluation of actions, judges should act according to their consciences, recognizing that it is not always a judge's task to enforce every student or coach responsibility. It is the primary responsibility of the educator as coach, rather than as judge, to regulate the content of student speeches.

In determining whether and to what extent to intervene, critics of debate should consider, in addition, that the adversarial nature of debate offers a good but imperfect means of revealing the weaknesses or undesirability of substantive positions and *may* lessen the need for intervention.

Finally, because the critic's role is an inherently educative one, all judges should strive for competence and conscientiousness in deliberation, including familiarity with accepted standards of forensic excellence. Coaches who employ non- or paraprofessional critics to fulfill their tournament judging obligations are responsible for ensuring that such critics will be able to provide a high-quality learning experience for students.

In administering tournaments, educators should strive to ensure that all students have an equal opportunity to excel. Educators should be particularly cognizant of the issues involved in scheduling and the assignment of judges and should seek to promote high-quality and fair learning experiences for all contestants. Furthermore, tournaments should not be designed to operate at a profit, and relevant professional codes should be followed.

In recruiting students, the educator should be cautious, open, and forthright. Students are free to attend the schools of their choice and free to transfer; educators nonetheless should be sensitive to the problem of tampering with other programs, should not recruit students under conditions that would compromise the learning experiences of existing students, and should be honest in evaluating the relative strengths and weaknesses of the programs and institutions in question. At all times, the best interests of the student (including other academic nonforensic interests) should take precedence over the competitive interests of the recruiting program.

The forensic educator assumes additional ethical responsibilities regardless of specific role. In all capacities, educators function as role models to other educators, to graduate students or other assistant educators, and to students; therefore, they should aspire to the highest ethical standards in their own conduct. They should act professionally at all times and with respect for the dignity and civil rights of students; in particular, harassment of, or discrimination against, students on the basis of race, gender, age, religion, national origin, or similarly irrelevant traits is condemned. Educator should not overburden students so that the latter's nonforensic educational aims and activities are jeopardized. Educators also should inform participants of the ethical choices inherent in forensic competition and the nature and desirability of ethical conduct. They should assist students in developing the capacity for critical self-observation of motives and actions, in exploring alternative ethical decisions, and in making wise choices. In order to emphasize the importance of ethical conduct, educators should devise positive reinforcements for exemplary conduct and apply appropriate sanctions for unethical behavior when needed. Additionally, educators should scrutinize the ways in which tournament rules and formats foster or hinder ethical conduct and should develop innovations consonant with ethical ideals. In short, the forensic educator should foster ethical attitudes and behaviors among all members of the forensic community.

Exercises

1. Find an example of a special debate in a recent political campaign. Prepare a brief report in which you describe the procedures used by the debaters.

2. Attend a court trial. Prepare a brief report in which you describe the judicial debate. How was it similar to academic debate? How different?

3. Analyze a nonformal debate currently in the news. Prepare a brief report in which you identify the leading debaters on each side and the principal issues of the debate.

4. Prepare a brief report on the history of academic debate at your college. By special arrangement with your instructor, you may present a longer report on this subject as a term paper.

5. Find a recent article on the values of debate in the publications of the speech associations or forensic honoraries. (Your instructor will give you the names of the publications available in your library.) Prepare a brief report on the article.

6. Prepare a five-minute speech, suitable for presentation at a freshman orientation program at your college, in which you set forth the values of academic debate.

7. Participate in a class discussion in which you consider the relative importance of the essential proficiencies developed by debate.

8. Participate in a class discussion in which you develop a statement of ethical guidelines to govern class debates.

3

Stating the Controversy

Debate is a means of settling differences. Therefore, there must be a difference of opinion or a conflict of interest before there can be a debate. If everyone is in agreement on a fact, or value, or policy, there is no need for debate; the matter can be settled by unanimous consent. Thus it is pointless to attempt to debate "Resolved: That two plus two equals four" — there is simply no controversy about this statement. Controversy is an essential prerequisite of debate. Controversies, to be considered intelligently, must be clearly stated. Vague understanding results in vague decisions. Someone disturbed by the problem of inflation might say, "Mortgage rates are too high — everything is too expensive," and arrive at an unprofitable decision, such as "We ought to do something about this." But if a precise question is posed — such as "What can be done to curb inflation?" — then a profitable area of discussion is opened up. One or more judgments can be phrased in the form of debate propositions, motions for parliamentary debate, or bills for legislative assemblies.

The statement "Resolved: That the federal government should adopt a program of compulsory wage and price controls" clearly identifies one of the possible ways of dealing with inflation in a form suitable for debate.

I.   Defining the Controversy

In order to have a profitable debate, the basis for argument must be clearly defined. If we merely talk about "inflation," "abortion," or "crime," we are likely to have a rap session, providing a pleasant way to spend a few hours but not affording the most profitable basis for argument. For example, the statement "Resolved: That the pen is mightier than the sword" fails to provide a basis for argument. If this statement means that the written word is for some purposes more effective than physical force, we can identify a problem area: the comparative effectiveness of writing or physical force for a specific purpose.

Although we now have a general subject, we have not yet stated a problem. It is still too broad, too loosely stated to promote well-organized argument. What sort of writing are we concerned with — poems, novels, government documents, or what? What does "effectiveness" mean in this context? What kind of physical force — fists, dueling swords, military occupation, nuclear weapons, or what? A more specific question might be "Would a mutual defense treaty or a visit by our fleet be more effective in assuring Laurania of our support in a certain crisis?" The basis for argument could be phrased in a debate proposition such as "Resolved: That the United States should enter into a mutual defense treaty with Laurania." Negative advocates might oppose this proposition by arguing that fleet maneuvers would be a better solution.

II.   Phrasing the Debate Proposition

In argumentation and debate the term *proposition* means a *statement of judgment that identifies the central issue in controversy.* The advocate desires to have others accept or reject the proposition. Debate provides for organized argument *for* and *against* the proposition: those arguing in favor of the proposition present the affirmative side; those arguing against it, the negative side. To promote intelligent and effective argumentation, a debate proposition must have certain characteristics.

A. Controversy

As we saw at the opening of this chapter, "controversy is an essential prerequisite of debate." Thus the debate proposition must clearly state the controversy.

B. One Central Idea

If a proposition has more than one central idea, it may lead to needless confusion. Consider the proposition "Resolved: That the Philosophy Club deplores abortions and lotteries as immoral." While there are some who would agree with this proposition, there are really two subjects for argument here. Some might deplore abortions and laud lotteries; others might take the opposite view. Two such central ideas should be placed in separate propositions and debated separately. If this resolution were introduced into parliamentary debate, any member of the House could move to amend the original motion into two separate motions. If the amendment were passed (only a simple majority is required), then the two motions could be debated separately.

C. Unemotional Terms

The proposition should be stated in unemotional terms. It should not include loaded language giving special advantage to the affirmative or the negative. Consider the proposition "Resolved: That cruel, sadistic experimenters should be forbidden to torture defenseless animals pointlessly." The heavily loaded, emotional language gives the affirmative an unreasonable advantage. "Resolved: That vivisection should be illegal" states the proposition in dispassionate terms. Although emotionally loaded terms have persuasive value, they have no place in a debate proposition.

"Resolved: That everyone should have the right to work" places an almost impossible burden on the negative—who can oppose the right to work? "Resolved: That the requirement of membership in a labor organization as a condition of employment should be illegal" states the problem in reasonably objective terms. Although probably no word is completely neutral to everyone, one can and must try to minimize the evaluative aspects of a proposition. The wording of the proposition must be such that reasonable participants on either side will accept it as accurately describing the controversy to be debated.

D. Precise Statement of the Affirmative's Desired Decision

The proposition should represent a statement of the decision the affirmative desires. It should set forth the decision clearly and precisely so that, if adopted, the affirmative advocates will have achieved their purpose. The proposition "Resolved: That the power of the federal government should be increased" is vague and indefinite. If the affirmative should win a debate on such a proposition, what would they have won? Actually nothing. Once it was agreed that the powers of the federal government should be increased, it would be necessary to proceed to another debate on the specific power in question. People who might favor increasing the power of the federal government by allowing it to make military appropriations for three, rather than two, years might well oppose an increase in the power of the federal government that would allow it to abolish the states.

A proposition such as "Resolved: That the President of the United States should be permitted to veto individual items in appropriation bills" states a specific decision clearly. The phrasing of the proposition must be clear, specific, devoid of ambiguous terms, and precise in the statement of the desired decision.

Although the decision desired by the affirmative must be stated with precision, the proposition sometimes allows the affirmative considerable latitude in its analysis of the status quo and permits the option of several plans in implementing that decision. For example, the proposition "Resolved: That the federal government should grant annually a specific percentage of its income tax revenue to the state governments" indicated the plan to be used but allowed the affirmative considerable latitude in analyzing the status quo and in developing the details within the plan. Thus some affirmatives called for the plan to improve the financing of general state and local services, whereas others focused on such specific problems as improved financing of the administration of criminal justice, mental health, or health care generally, and still others developed a quite different analysis and called for adopting the proposition as a means of checking the power of the military-industrial complex.

Such "open-ended" propositions realistically reflect the fact that different persons may support one policy for a variety of reasons. As the saying goes, "Politics makes strange bedfellows," and in applied debate we often find unlikely combinations of legislators supporting a bill for widely different reasons.

Phrasing the Proposition for Academic Debate

The additional requirements for propositions used in academic debate are as follows.

Significant Contemporary Problem

In choosing a problem for educational debate, directors of forensics seek not only a well-phrased proposition but also one that will provide an opportunity for exploring a significant problem of current interest to students, judges, and audiences. Since the topic should be one on which information is readily available, national debate propositions deal with matters of current national or international concern. Educators also seek a problem that will remain in the news during the academic year so that the topic will remain challenging and the debaters can continue to find new evidence and argument.

When "right-to-work" laws were the subject of a national debate proposition, the educators who chose that problem expected that neither Congress nor the majority of the states would enact "right-to-work" legislation during the time the proposition was being debated. Had such laws been enacted, the status quo in the field of labor legislation would have changed and the debate proposition would have required rephrasing. Even on such a rephrased proposition, debates would have been anticlimactic.

Sometimes the status quo may change dramatically and require substantial changes in affirmative cases without necessitating a change in the proposition. During the academic year in which the proposition concerning "federal control of the supply and utilization of energy" was debated, a number of such changes occurred. Early in the season some affirmative teams argued that "the Arab nations might embargo oil." Negative teams confidently denied this possibility, but the Arabs did in fact embargo oil early in the season. Some affirmative teams then argued for gas rationing as the only means of dealing with the oil embargo. As the academic year went on, however, it became apparent that, although some states imposed limitations on gas sales, no real-world support existed for federal rationing. During that year many teams found it necessary to redraft their affirmative cases for almost every tournament, for the status quo changed repeatedly as new policies became operative or as new evidence became available.

The statement of the proposition must be affirmative in both form and intent. The proposition "Resolved: That the United States should not give direct economic aid to foreign countries" is in negative form. The use of negative phrasing would violate sound debate practice, since it would confuse the audience and needlessly complicate the advocates' problem in presenting their cases.

The proposition "Resolved: That the jury system should be abolished" is negative in its intent. The flaw here is that the proposition represents an interim goal and does not provide a clear and precise statement of the decision desired by the affirmative. If the jury system were abolished and nothing provided in its place, all accused criminals would go free as there would be no means of trying them. The proposition "Resolved: That juries should be replaced by a panel of three judges" represents a statement of a decision some affirmatives might advocate.

Equal Conflicting Evidence and Reasoning

In applied debates the evidence and reasoning may strongly favor one side. In the law courts, attorneys may defend clients when the evidence against them is almost overwhelming. In the legislative assembly, the minority leader may fight for an almost hopeless cause. In academic debate, however, the objective is not to secure, or prevent, the adoption of a proposition. Rather, it is to use the proposition to provide opportunities to learn about argumentation and debate, as well as about the subject itself. For educational purposes, preference is given to propositions that give both sides an approximately equal opportunity to build a strong case.

Single Declarative Sentence

In the interests of clarity, and because of the limited amount of time available, academic debate propositions are limited to a single declarative sentence. In applied debates, the proposition may be as long as necessary; for instance, a bill in Congress is a specialized form of debate proposition and may extend for many printed pages.

Avoidance of Ambiguity

Of course, one should seek to avoid ambiguity to the greatest extent possible in all debate propositions. The Second National Developmental Conference on Forensics made the following recommendations specifically for academic debate:

Take care when using any encompassing term such as "all," "every," or "any";

Take care when using vague or compounding words or phrases such as "greater" or "any and all";

Seek consultation with linguistics experts on the phrasing and interpretation of debate propositions;

Specify clearly the nature and direction of the change or decision;

Seek wording that will balance the need for maintaining interest over a period of time with the need to limit the topic in order to create a meaningful level of research and discussion.

In addition to the criteria for any debate proposition considered here, there are certain additional requirements for a proposition to be used in academic debate. (*See inset on pp.* 36–37.)

III. Presumption and Burden of Proof

The concepts of "presumption" and "burden of proof" are more easily understood through another term often used in connection with them — *status quo.*

Choosing the Proposition for Academic Debate

Each year the Committee on Intercollegiate Debate and Discussion (CIDD) publishes the national debate proposition for use by colleges and universities having NDT (National Debate Tournament) programs. The Cross Examination Debate Association (CEDA) announces a proposition for use by colleges and universities having CEDA programs. A second CEDA proposition is announced in the winter for use in the second half of the academic year. The Second National Developmental Conference on Forensics has recommended narrower, more specific versions of the national resolution for novice debaters. The CIDD also announces an "off-topic" proposition for those colleges desiring another alternative. Tournament debating makes the use of national debate propositions indispensable. If the students attempted to debate a different proposition for each tournament, or even if they attempted to debate a number of different propositions during the year, they would acquire considerable experience in research methods but very limited experience in sound debating. The first few academic debates on a new proposition are often tentative and experimental. After a number of debates on a proposition, the learning situation is far more profitable.

Since most academic debating is on a national intercollegiate debate proposition, it is well to know how such propositions are chosen. The care devoted to the selection of these propositions suggests something of the care that the individual should exercise in phrasing propositions for his or her own use.

The CIDD consists of representatives of Delta Sigma Rho–Tau Kappa Alpha, Phi Rho Pi, and Pi Kappa Delta (the national forensic honorary organizations), the American Forensic Association, and the Speech Communication Association. After careful study and research, the committee submits several propositions having the greatest potential as *national* propositions to a preferential ballot by the nation's directors of forensics. The proposition receiving the greatest preferential vote is announced as the national proposition. The national discussion question and the "off-topic" proposition are chosen at the same time and in the same manner. The CEDA propositions are selected in a similar manner by that organization. NDT national propositions are always propositions of policy; CEDA uses propositions of value or quasi-policy; the ADA uses the NDT national proposition; the NDT "off-topic" proposition may be either value or policy.

Status quo means the existing state of things. At one time capital punishment was legal in the United States. It was the status quo. Then the Supreme Court ruled the existing capital punishment statutes unconstitutional. The status quo then became one of no capital punishment. Subsequently, some states enacted new capital punishment laws that met the Supreme Court's criteria, and some executions took place in those states. Thus the status quo is that some states permit capital punishment under specific circumstances. Partisans on both sides are seeking to change this status quo. Some want to expand capital punishment to all states whereas others want to abolish it altogether.

Presumption may be viewed from two perspectives — the judicial perspective and the policy perspective.

The *judicial perspective* is used when the option exists of continuing the structure of the status quo. With this option, there may, of course, be minor repairs and other modifications, but the essential features of the status quo will continue until good and sufficient reason is given to justify a change. This perspective is mandated in the courts, for example, where the accused must be presumed innocent (the status quo) until proved guilty.

From the judicial perspective the *presumption* favors the status quo. The existing state of affairs will continue until good and sufficient reason is given for changing it. In debates using the judicial perspective, the presumption favors the status quo and the affirmative has the burden of proof.

The burden of proof is defined as the risk of the proposition. It is the obligation of the advocates who affirm the proposition to prove their case. They must provide good and sufficient reason for adopting the proposition and must convince those who render the decision. If they do not carry the burden of proof, they will lose all that they hoped to gain were the proposition adopted.

These concepts are aptly summed up in the maxim, *"If it ain't broke, don't fix it."*[1]

The *policy perspective* is used when change is inherent in the status quo. Recent history provides an excellent example of this. In 1984 President Reagan, the incumbent President, ran for reelection. That year the voters had the option of voting for President Reagan (the status quo) or for his opponent, Walter Mondale. In 1988 Reagan was barred by the Constitution from running for a third term. Thus change was inevitable; the voters did not have the option of supporting the status quo (voting for Reagan) but had to choose between two departures from the status quo — George Bush or Michael Dukakis. As is typical in such cases, one choice represented a greater change in the status quo than the other.

From the policy perspective the *presumption* favors the position that provides the greatest advantages while incurring the least disadvantages. In debates on *value propositions* the presumption favors the position of the greater over the lesser value; for example, in debates on the "testing for controlled substances" proposition the issue in many debates was does "privacy" outweigh "safety"?

How does one determine *the burden of proof* in such cases? The classic rule of burden of proof applies: *One who asserts must prove.*

Let us now look at a few examples to see how these concepts work. We will consider first some examples from the judicial perspective.

Do you favor the Equal Rights Amendment to the Constitution? Do you favor a Right to Life Amendment to the Constitution? The status quo is the Constitution as it now exists. If you want to change the Constitution, you have the burden of proof. In this case you must convince both houses of Congress to pass your amendment, you must convince the President to sign it, and then you must convince 38 states to ratify it. This is the burden of proof we place on those who would change our Constitution.

Is the present immigration policy of the United States good or bad? Good or bad, it is the status quo. It will continue in effect until those who believe it bad can, by showing good and sufficient reason for changing it, convince a majority of the House

---

[1]The same idea was expressed earlier by Viscount Falkland in more stately prose, "When it is not necessary to change, it is necessary not to change."

and the Senate to agree to pass a new bill and convince the President to sign the bill creating a new policy.

The concept of presumption is a vital part of our legal system. Did Richard Roe rob the Cook County National Bank? Our laws explicitly require that a person be presumed innocent until proved guilty. The status quo is that Richard Roe is innocent, and the police department and the district attorney must convince a jury that he is guilty before he can be sentenced. (Unfortunately, this principle of law is sometimes distorted. The accused in a well-publicized case may have a "trial by news media" and be "proved guilty" in the minds of the prospective jurors before the courtroom trial begins. British law is much stricter than American law in prohibiting pretrial publicity of the accused.)

The lobbyist who would change our immigration law has the burden of proof of convincing the House, the Senate, and the President. The district attorney who would convict Richard Roe has the burden of proof of convincing the jury.

In our law courts, different standards prevail for the burden of proof in different circumstances. Before a grand jury, only "probable cause" need be proved to secure an indictment; in a criminal trial, the prosecutor must establish proof "beyond a reasonable doubt" to secure a guilty verdict; in a civil case the verdict commonly is based on a "preponderance of evidence." Outside the courtroom, reasonable persons usually apply this standard and base their decisions on important matters on a "preponderance of evidence." The judge in legal proceedings will instruct the jury as to what constitutes "probable cause" or "reasonable doubt." The concepts of burden of proof and presumption made the front page of *The New York Times* and other newspapers across the country when the Supreme Court ruled that in sex discrimination cases "an employer has the legal burden of proving that its refusal to hire or promote someone is based on legitimate and not discriminatory reasons." In the same decision the Court ruled that the employer has to show only by "a preponderence of evidence" that its reasons were legitimate and not by the more rigorous standard of "clear and convincing proof" as required by a lower court.[2] Outside the courtroom, we do not have predetermined definitions of what constitutes a "preponderance of evidence," and a definition of that concept may become a critical issue of the debate as the debaters seek to convince the decision renderers that theirs is a satisfactory definition within the context of the debate. (See Chapter 4, Section II-B.)

In certain situations in parliamentary debate, the affirmative must obtain a two-thirds or a three-quarters majority to carry its burden of proof. In order to convict Richard Roe of robbing the Cook County National Bank the prosecutor must convince 100 percent of the jury. If one juror is not convinced of Roe's guilt, he cannot be convicted.

If we want to obtain a new federal law, we must convince a majority of the House, a majority of the Senate, and the President. If the President vetoes the law, we must convince two-thirds of the House and two-thirds of the Senate. If the law is challenged in the courts, we may have to convince a majority of the Supreme Court Justices of its constitutionality. This is the burden we place on those who seek new federal legislation.

Let us now consider a few examples from the policy perspective.

[2]*The New York Times*, May 2, 1989, p. 1.

In some cases change may be inherent in the status quo. In such cases, there is a presumption in favor of *a* change, but *not* in favor of any *particular* change. A typical example may be found in the automobile industry. Most companies have a policy of making annual model changes. But while new models come out each year, the designers advocating model X have the burden of proof to convince their company that model X is better than model Y or model Z or any other model under consideration. In some situations there is no status quo — when it comes time to elect freshman class officers there are no incumbents.

Thus, when the status quo provides for a change or when a change is inherent in the status quo, the advocates of a new policy or of possible change have the burden of proof. In similar circumstances, the advocates of a specific value (as in a CEDA debate where the affirmative advocates the specific value called for in the resolution) have the burden of proof. The classic rule of burden of proof applies to all of these situations: One who asserts must prove.

The affirmative — the one advancing an assertion — has the burden of proof. The question then arises: What amounts to satisfactory proof? The answer depends on the rules governing the debate and the judgment of the person or group empowered to decide. As a minimum the affirmative must go more than halfway in convincing those who render the decision. If 49 percent of the members of your club vote *for* a motion and 51 percent vote against it, the motion fails. If 50 percent vote for the motion and 50 percent against it, the motion fails.

Note that there is a distinction between *the* burden of proof and *a* burden of proof, and that this distinction applies to *both the judicial and the policy perspective. The* burden of proof always rests on the affirmative; it must prove that the proposition should be adopted. However, *a* burden may rest on either the affirmative or the negative. Whoever introduces an issue or contention into the debate has *a* burden of proof. The advocate must support the argument he or she introduces. During a trial, for example, the prosecution may allege that Richard Roe committed a robbery in Chicago. Richard Roe may claim that he was in New York at the time of the robbery. Richard Roe now has assumed a burden of proof; he must prove his alibi. In a debate on the "testing for controlled substances" proposition, if the negative introduces the argument that "privacy" outweighs "safety," they have assumed a burden of proof.

Either side may have *a burden of refutation.* A burden rests on the advocate whose case is weakened by an argument advanced by their opponent. They must refute that argument or suffer damage to their case. In Richard Roe's case, if Roe introduces evidence to establish that he was in New York at the time of the robbery, the prosecution has a burden of refutation. The Chicago district attorney must refute that evidence or Roe will go free. In the "controlled substances" case, the affirmative must refute the negative's "safety" argument or face a serious loss.

A tie is thus impossible in debate. The affirmative either carries its burden of proof or it does not. Even in a debate with one judge, a common situation in academic debate, a tie is impossible. If the judge discerns that both teams have done an equal job, he or she must render a decision for the negative because the affirmative has failed to carry its burden of proof. Reasonable people follow this principle in making individual decisions. If the arguments pro and con are equal — if they just cannot make up their minds — they decline to support the affirmative's proposal.

IV. Types of Debate Propositions

Debate propositions may deal with controversies of *fact*, *value*, or *policy*. We will first consider propositions of fact, then value, and finally policy.

A. Propositions of Fact

In a debate on a proposition of fact, the affirmative maintains that a certain thing is true, while the negative maintains that it is false. Our law courts are almost entirely concerned with propositions of fact. Typical propositions of legal debates are, in effect, "Resolved: That John Doe is guilty of murder," or "Resolved: That this is the last will and testament of Richard Roe," or "Resolved: That the plaintiff's constitutional rights were violated in this trial." Typical debates on propositions of fact outside the courtroom would include "Resolved: That inflation will decline next year," or "Resolved: That others conspired with Lee Harvey Oswald to kill President Kennedy." This latter proposition of fact was the subject of extensive public debate when the twenty-fifth anniversary of Kennedy's death triggered an outpouring of articles, books, and television shows on this controversy.

Propositions of fact are also often debated as a part of debates on propositions of value or propositions of policy, since it is frequently essential to establish relevant facts before we can reach decisions about values or policies.

B. Propositions of Value

In a debate on a proposition of value, the affirmative maintains that a certain belief, value, or fact is justified, that it conforms to the definition or criteria appropriate to evaluate the matter at issue. The negative maintains that the definition or criteria is inappropriate or that the matter at issue does not conform to the definition or criteria. Typical propositions of value are, in effect, "Resolved: That abortion is immoral," or "Resolved: That television is a vast wasteland."

One of the most readily recognizable differences between a proposition of value and a proposition of policy is that the policy proposition requires the affirmative to propose a plan to implement its policy. The proposition of value does not provide for a plan; rather the affirmative seeks our support for a claim that (1) endorses a value, for example, "Resolved: That compulsory national service for all qualified U.S. citizens is desirable," or (2) chooses one value over another, for example, "Resolved: That inflation is a greater threat to American society than unemployment," or (3) rejects a value, for example, "Resolved: That the emphasis on competitive athletics is deleterious to American society."

Quasi-policy propositions are propositions that express a value judgment about a policy. Typical quasi-policy propositions include the "compulsory national service" proposition just cited and many CEDA propositions, such as "Resolved: That a unilateral freeze by the United States on the production and development of nuclear weapons would be desirable." While a plan is not explicit in quasi-policy propositions, it is implicit and the debaters may find it necessary to debate the policy implications of the proposition.

An example of fact and value judgments leading to policy considerations occurred in the first Bush-Dukakis debate in 1988. Bush, who was known to favor the "sanctity of life" (a value position) and to regard abortions as "killings" (a fact position), was asked, ". . . if abortions were to become illegal, do you think women who have them should go to jail?" (a policy position).

Bush replied, "I haven't sorted out the penalties. . . I'm for the sanctity of life, and once that illegality is established, then we can come to grips with the penalty side, and of course, there's got to be some penalties to enforce the law." This response was judged to be weak and ineffective by some observers.

Dukakis promptly focused on the policy implications of Bush's values by saying, "Well, I think that the Vice President is saying that he's prepared to brand a woman a criminal for making this decision."[3]

While we may sometimes debate facts, values, or policies by themselves, we will find that on many occasions it is necessary to consider all of them together.

C. Propositions of Policy

In a debate on a proposition of policy, the affirmative maintains that a policy or course of action should be adopted, while the negative maintains that this policy should be rejected. Most debates in legislative assemblies are on propositions of policy. Typical debates in Congress, state legislatures, and city councils are, in effect, "Resolved: That the proposed tax bill should be enacted" or "Resolved: That the Senate should advise and consent to the nomination of Joseph Doakes as Ambassador to France." In private organizations as well, most debates are on propositions of policy: "Resolved: That the Speech Communication Association should hold its annual convention in Chicago" or "Resolved: That Compact Motors, Inc., should pay a quarterly dividend of fifty cents per share of common stock" or "Resolved: That more dormitories should be established on this campus." Recall, as we have noted in Section B, that a plan to implement the policy is an essential part of the affirmative's case. In debates on policy propositions, propositions of value often arise as important issues. In debates on the proposition of policy "Resolved: That the federal government should significantly strengthen the regulation of mass media communication in the United States," it was sometimes necessary to debate as essential issues "Resolved: That First Amendment rights are the most important of all our rights" and "Resolved: That pretrial publicity denies a fair trial to defendants in criminal trials" (both propositions of value).

Exercises

1. Examine the following "propositions." Which are well phrased? Which violate the criteria of a well-phrased proposition? What criteria do they violate? Rephrase the incorrect propositions so that they meet the requirements for academic debate.
   a. Inadequate parking facilities on campus.
   b. The threat posed by the Soviet Union's policy of hegemony.

[3]See the *New York Times*, September 26, 1988, p. 11, for the full text of this exchange.

   c. Should our college abandon intercollegiate athletics?

   d. The present method of electing the President of the United States should be improved.

   e. The United States should reject a system of national health care.

   f. The federal income tax rate should be limited to a maximum of 25 percent, and labor unions should be subject to the antitrust laws.

   g. College entrance requirements should be stricter.

   h. The present agricultural price support program is beneficial to the American people.

2. Phrase one proposition of fact, one of value, and one of policy for each of the following areas:

   a. current social problems

   b. labor-management relations

   c. federal fiscal policies

   d. U.S. foreign policy

   e. a current campus problem

3. From the newspapers, newsmagazines, and radio and television broadcasts of the past week, discover what problems are currently being debated in Congress or in the nation. Phrase propositions of fact, value, and policy on five problems currently being debated nationally. Phrase these fifteen propositions in a manner suitable for academic debate.

4. From the newspapers, newsmagazines, and radio and television broadcasts of the past week, find five examples of quasi-policy propositions that are currently being debated in Congress or in the nation.

5. Prepare a five-minute speech for delivery in class in which you state a proposition of policy and demonstrate how it meets the criteria of a well-phrased proposition for academic debate.

4

Analyzing the Controversy

The proposition for debate may be formulated by one of the advocates in the debate, by agreement between the opposing advocates, or by someone other than the actual advocates. If a student at a business meeting of a college organization introduces a motion "Resolved: That the dues of this organization should be increased five dollars a semester," he or she is formulating a proposition for debate. Before Lincoln and Douglas held their famous debates, they agreed on the propositions they would use when they met. Frequently, an attorney first learns of the proposition to be debated in a court case when retained by a client.

Regardless of how the proposition is chosen, our first task as advocates is to analyze the proposition and the total controversy area from which it is derived. We must define the terms of the proposition and discover the issues involved. Words or terms in the proposition must be defined *within the context of the proposition*. For example, we cannot define or even pronounce the word *polish* until we know the context in which it is used. Analysis of the proposition's relationship to the problem area — the political, legal, social, or other relevant contexts from which it arises — may reveal further terms that require definition and new concepts that will aid in the development of issues.

I. The Importance of Defining Terms

The definition of terms is often an essential part of debate. In some instances, the opposing advocates will come to quick agreement on the definition of terms, and the debate will move on to other issues. In other cases, the locus of the debate may be the definition of a key term or terms, and definitions become the "voting issue" that decides the debate.

Many intercollegiate debate propositions call for the "federal government" to adopt a certain policy. Often the term is self-evident in the context of the proposition, and no definition is necessary. In debates on the "mass media" proposition, the affirmative merely designates the appropriate federal agency (for example, the Federal Communications Commission or the Federal Trade Commission) to carry out its policy, and the debate moves on to other issues. However, sometimes other terms in the proposition (for instance, "mass media") become critical issues of the debate. Not infrequently the negative will raise the issue of topicality and argue that the affirmative's plan is not the best definition of the proposition. In debates on propositions of value, the clash on definition or criteria may be crucial to the outcome of the debate.

In debates outside the educational setting, the same situation prevails. In some debates, the definition of terms is easy and obvious — they need only be stated "for the record," and the debate proceeds to other issues. In other debates, however, the definition may be all-important. Physicians, clergy, and ethicists conduct long, hard-fought debates on the critical issue of the definition of life. When does life begin? At conception, when the fetus becomes capable of survival outside the womb, when brain life begins, or at the moment of birth?

Exactly the opposite problem arose and continues in debates over the use of organ transplants. When does death occur — when breathing stops, when the heart stops, or when the brain ceases to function? Some states have debated this issue and adopted new definitions of death; in other states, the debate continues.

What does "affirmative action" mean? Americans have debated that term for decades. The Civil Rights Act of 1964 empowers courts to order affirmative action in certain circumstances but doesn't define the term. Dictionaries generally define "affirmative" but not "affirmative action." *Black's Law Dictionary* (1968) defines "affirmative action" but in the context of the 1935 National Labor Relations Act. In 1978 the affirmative action Bakke case reached the Supreme Court. The brethren firmly ducked the issue. Brennan's minority opinion used the term more than ten times but did not define it. Powell's majority opinion never used the term.[1] Some able law professors have offered their notions of what the term means, but they remain only notions. Given the context of the debate (that is, law), the only definition that will matter is the definition decreed by a majority of the Supreme Court.

Terms that do not actually occur in the proposition itself, but which an advocate expects to occur in the course of the debate, should also be defined. The words "cyclical," "frictional," and "hidden" did not appear in the proposition "Resolved: That the federal government should establish a national program of public work for the unemployed." Yet since references to these types of unemployment recurred in debates on the proposition, it was necessary for the debaters to define them.

In debates on this same proposition, dictionary definitions of the individual words "public" and "work" did little to provide a profitable explanation of the meaning of

---

[1]See Gertrude Block, "New Wine in an Old Bottle: The Etymology of Affirmative Action," *Academe*, Vol. 66 (Feb. 1980), pp. 54–56.

the proposition or to furnish a basis for argument. Advocates found it necessary to define the term "public work" rather than the individual words; and, by referring to the use of this phrase in legislation, they were able to provide a useful definition.

In analyzing the problem, advocates must carefully consider all possible definitions of all the terms. In presenting their cases, however, they will define only those terms that might be unfamiliar to their audience or about which they and their opponents might differ. In debating the proposition "Resolved: That Congress should be given the power to reverse decisions of the Supreme Court," it would probably be unnecessary to define "Congress" and "Supreme Court." It would be necessary, however, to define "reverse" and "decisions," since the legal usage of these terms is different from the popular usage, and opposing advocates sometimes differ in their interpretations of these words within the context of this proposition.

Consider the old brainteaser—when a tree falls in a forest but nobody hears it, does it make a sound? The answer, of course, is totally dependent on your definition of sound. If sound is defined as waves in the air, the answer is yes. If sound is defined as the subjective experience of hearing, the answer is no.

The terms of a debate proposition may be defined in a variety of ways. In order to make the basis of the argument explicit, advocates should choose the method or combination of methods best suited to the requirements of the proposition and to the interests of the audience. It is important to define terms carefully to ensure a profitable debate.

II. Methods of Defining Terms

A. Basic Methods

1. Example. Giving an example is often an effective method of defining terms. In debates on the national program of public work proposition, affirmative teams sometimes defined terms by saying "By a national program of public work we mean a program similar to the WPA of the 1930s," thus giving their audience a specific example of the type of program they proposed.

2. Common Usage. In the interest of accuracy and precision, debate propositions must sometimes contain technical terms. Often these terms can be defined effectively by referring to common usage. In debates on the proposition "Resolved: That the requirement of membership in a labor organization as a condition of employment should be illegal," some affirmative teams defined an important term by saying "By 'labor organizations' we mean the type of organization popularly referred to as unions." This reference to common usage usually served to establish a definition acceptable to both teams and clear to the audience. Although the word "unions" served well as a definition, it would not have been an acceptable term for use in the proposition. Many important "unions" operate under the legal title of "brotherhoods," "associations," "federations," or other names; and most important legislation regulating unions speaks of "labor organizations." Had the word "unions" been used in the proposition, it might have led to some pointless quibbles on whether or not such legislation would apply to organizations such as the railroad brotherhoods.

Sometimes terms in common usage are widely misunderstood. The *New York Times* called 12 A.M. and 12 P.M. "the trickiest times on the clock." Does 12 A.M. designate midday or midnight? Is 12 P.M. lunchtime or bedtime? Railroads avoid the problem by using schedule times like 12:01 A.M. or 11:59 P.M. The military, too, avoids the problem by using twenty-four-hour time; noon is 1200 and midnight is 2400. According to the nation's highest authority on time, the Naval Observatory, "there is no 12 A.M. or 12 P.M., only noon and midnight."[2] When time is critical, as it may be in contracts, on birth or death certificates, and in interpreting many other documents, it is advisable to use terms that are defined by a recognized authority.

3. Authority. Some terms may be defined most effectively by referring to an authority qualified to state the meaning and usage of the term. Dictionaries, encyclopedias, and books or articles by recognized scholars are often used as authority for a particular definition. In debates on nationalization of the basic nonagricultural industries, some debaters defined "nationalization" by quoting *Webster's Dictionary*, *Black's Law Dictionary*, or various encyclopedia articles. In debates on "tax sharing," advocates often defined "a specific percentage of federal income tax revenue" by quoting Walter Heller, who had done much of the basic writing on this subject, or other economists who had written about this problem or who had testified before Congressional committees.

Time magazine chided the Nebraska legislature for failure to consult a recognized authority:

> ... Burling was acquitted on largely lexicological grounds. The state legislature misspelled the drug's chemical name when it passed the bill that outlawed it in 1986. Thus Burling could not be convicted of possessing the substance specified by the lawmakers. The correct spelling is methylenedioxymethamphetamine, not methylenedioxyethamphetamine [note the omission of a letter *m*] as the law had it. Next time they ban a drug in Nebraska, they'd better consult a pharmacological dictionary.[3]

In legal matters the only definition that counts is the one upheld by the Supreme Court. What does "request" mean? Section 1915 (d) of Title 28 of the United States Code says that federal district judges may "request" lawyers who practice before the federal courts to undertake uncompensated representation of the poor. Justice John Paul Stevens, in a dissenting opinion, held that "request" should be understood to mean "respectfully command." Justice William J. Brennan, Jr. held in the 5 to 4 majority opinion that "in everyday speech request means to ask, petition or entreat, not to require or command."[4]

4. Operation. Some terms are best defined if the advocate provides an operational definition and explains the function or special purpose represented by the terms in a specific context. Debates on the proposition "Resolved: That the nonagricultural industries should guarantee their employees an annual wage" required careful defini-

---

[2] *New York Times*, November 29, 1987, p. 19.
[3] *Time*, December 12, 1988, p. 33.
[4] *The New York Times*, May 2, 1989, p. 8.

tion of the phrase "guarantee . . . an annual wage." Some affirmative advocates chose to provide an operational definition, defining these terms by presenting their plan. One debater said:

> We propose a plan whereby the employer places the sum of five cents per employee hour worked in a trust fund until that fund equals 50 percent of the average annual payroll of that company for the past five years. When an employee is laid off, he may then draw from his fund a sum equal to 75 percent of his average weekly pay for the previous year less such state unemployment compensation as he may receive for 52 weeks or until he is rehired.

The use of operation as a method of definition is often linked with the presentation of a plan and is a helpful way of explaining a complex matter.

5. Negation. Sometimes a term may be defined effectively by indicating what it does not mean. In debates on nationalization of basic industries, some teams defined "basic industries" by combining negation with example, saying "We do not mean the corner drugstore, we do not mean retail businesses, we do not mean service businesses; we mean steel, autos, transportation, mining, oil, and gas."

6. Comparison and Contrast. Some terms may be best understood if they are compared to something familiar to the audience or contrasted with something within the common experience of the audience. In debates on the "mass media" proposition, some negative teams offered a counterplan and proposed the creation of an agency "similar to the National Association of Broadcasters" to regulate newspapers and claimed an advantage from the fact that their plan called for voluntary regulation in contrast with the affirmative's proposal of federal regulation.

7. Derivation. One of the standard methods of defining words is to trace their development from their original or radical elements. Thus, in a debate on fair employment practices, it would be possible to define the word "prejudice" by pointing out that the word derived from the Latin words "prae" and "judicium" meaning "before judgment." Definition by derivation has limited use in argumentation and debate, because the advocate is usually concerned with the contemporary usage of the word within a specific context.

8. Combination of Methods. Since most propositions of debate contain several terms that must be defined, no one of the methods mentioned is likely to be satisfactory for the definition of all of the terms. If any term is particularly difficult to define, or if it is of critical importance in the debate, the advocate may find it desirable to use more than one method of definition in order to make the meaning clear.

B. Provide a Satisfactory Definition

A satisfactory definition is one that *meets the expectations of those who render the decision*.

In CEDA debate the judges usually expect a *reasonable definition*. In NDT debate the judges usually expect the *best definition in the debate*. This difference should not surprise the student. In applied debate the decision renderers often have different expectations about decisions in different situations. As we saw earlier (in Chapter 3,

Criteria to Prove a Satisfactory Definition

1. **Prove your definition is officially stipulated as the correct one for this resolution.** This criterion is of great value in the law courts, where many definitions are stipulated by statute and have been upheld by the highest courts so often that appeal is pointless. A kilogram is defined by an international agreement; a watt is a standard unit of measure in the United States; drugs are defined by official pharmacopoeias. Such exotic terms as black hole, gigaflop, pulsar, and quasar, although not officially defined, have universally accepted definitions in the scientific community. Of course, any definition *could* be changed, but changes in official or universally accepted definitions come only after exhaustive debate.

2. **Prove that your definition is grammatically correct.** The presumptions are that the framers of the proposition are knowledgeable in the conventions of English grammar and syntax, that each word in the proposition is there for a good reason, and that each word further refines the meaning of the sentence. Thus you must prove that your definition considers all the terms of the proposition and that none of the terms is redundant or contradictory.

3. **Prove that your definition is derived from the appropriate field.** Many propositions contain specialized terms. If the subject is nuclear weapons, you must prove that your definition is the one used by nuclear physicists. If the subject is economics, you must prove that your definition is the one used by economists.

4. **Prove that your definition is based on common usage.** Many of the terms in debate propositions are words in common usage. Since debate is a public activity,

---

Section III), the law courts have different standards for defining the burden of proof in different situations. In our personal lives, too, we frequently apply differing standards. Our definition of satisfactory medical care would no doubt vary if we had a sprained ankle or if we were confronted with a life-threatening illness.

Sometimes advocates offer unusual definitions — definitions that are not consistent with the expectations of the opposing advocates. The use of "trick" or "squirrel" definitions to catch an opponent off guard, or to gain some other advantage, is specifically *not recommended*. A *squirrel* definition or the resultant case is one that the affirmative hopes in the first instance will find the negative unprepared and in the second instance that it can convince the judge to accept. One example of a squirrel case was found in debates on the proposition "Resolved: That greater controls should be imposed on the gathering and utilization of information about United States citizens by government agencies." Early in the season most negatives expected that the affirmative cases would deal with abuses of computerized credit information. One squirrel case called for legislation to prohibit the gathering and utilization of information about citizens who used marijuana. (The affirmative argued that if the police and prosecutors were prohibited from gathering and utilizing such information, they would devote their time and energies to more important crimes.) Of course, once this case became well known it lost an essential characteristic of a squirrel case — it no longer found negative teams unprepared. The advocate who depends on trick or

you must be able to prove that your definition is consistent with the common usage of the general public.

5. Prove that your definition is consistent with policy or value makers' usage. Debaters are arguing that we, the public, should adopt or reject a certain policy or value. You must prove that your definition is consistent with the usage of the makers of policy and value in the public forums; for example, prove your definition is consistent with the definition used in Congressional debates on the subject.

6. Prove your definition meets the intent of the framers. Cautions were given against this method earlier. As noted in Section II-B, while this criterion may be compelling in applied debate in the courtroom, the intent of the framers is often elusive and indeed may be impossible to discover in academic debate or in applied debate outside the courtroom.

Note that the debater will rarely use all these criteria to prove that the definition used is satisfactory. Initially, the definition is stated succinctly with only the minimum evidence essential to establish the claim. Only if the definition comes under attack does the debater move to a full-scale justification of the definition.

To attack an opponent's definition, one opens with a full-scale attack to prove that the definition does not meet one or more of the criteria just discussed.

Note too that the criteria listed here, although widely used, are not all-inclusive. Depending on the nature of the proposition, other criteria may well be discovered and applied to prove or disprove the claim that the definition is satisfactory.

---

squirrel cases will find that they are usually quickly exposed and defeated by competent opposition. Not every unusual definition, however, should be regarded as a trick or squirrel definition. The apparently unusual definition might take the opposing team by surprise only because they had failed to do a thorough job of analyzing the proposition.

Debaters are sometimes advised to look for the "intent of the framers" of the proposition. Such advice draws on an august precedent: Often what attorneys do when arguing a case before the Supreme Court is to consult the legislative debate that surrounded the enactment of the law at issue in an effort to discover the intent of Congress. Most debate propositions, however, do not stem from Congressional debate. There is often little or no record to provide evidence of the "intent of the framers," so this well-intentioned advice is often of little value in academic debate.

How then, can one prove that a definition is satisfactory? By giving those who render the decision good reasons to accept that definition.

What are some of the good reasons one might advance to prove that a specific definition is satisfactory? The reasons will be different with different propositions and different decision renderers, but some of the most frequently used criteria are shown in the inset on pp. 50–51.

To prove that a definition is *reasonable* one must establish that the definition meets the relevant criteria.

To prove that a definition is the *best in the debate* one must establish that the definition meets the relevant criteria in ways that are *superior* to opposing definitions.

C. The Meaning of "Should" — Fiat Power

Most propositions on matters of policy contain the word "should" — for example, "Resolved: That such and such *should* be done." In a debate on a policy proposition, "should" means that intelligent self-interest, social welfare, or the national interest prompts this action, and that it is both desirable and workable. When the affirmative claims a policy "should" be adopted, it must show that the policy is practical — but it is under no obligation to show it *will* be adopted. The affirmative must give enough detail to show it would work. It may be impossible, within the time limitations of the debate, for the affirmative to give all the details, but it must at least show the outline of its policy and indicate how the details could be worked out. For example, in a debate on federal aid to education, the affirmative could not reasonably be expected to indicate how much money each state would receive under its plan, but it would be obliged to indicate the method by which the amount of the grants would be determined. It is pointless for the negative to seek to show that the affirmative's plan could not be adopted by demonstrating that public opinion is against it or that the supporters of the plan lack sufficient voting strength in Congress.

Public opinion and a majority of congresspeople were opposed to the income tax at one time; yet, when the advocates of the income tax demonstrated that it *should* be adopted, the Sixteenth Amendment was enacted. In the same way it could be demonstrated that at a given time the Eighteenth, Nineteenth, Twenty-first, or Twenty-sixth Amendments of the Constitution could not possibly have been passed — too many people were opposed to prohibition, opposed to woman's suffrage, opposed to the repeal of the Eighteenth Amendment, opposed to lowering the voting age to eighteen — yet all these amendments were passed after the advocates of these measures won debates showing they *should* be adopted. Thus, in an academic debate on a policy proposition, *constitutionality is never an issue*. If the affirmative proves that a certain policy *should* be adopted, it has also proved that, if necessary, the Constitution should be amended. In the same way, if the affirmative's proposal is presently illegal or outside the scope of existing law, it has, by showing that its proposal should be adopted, demonstrated that the necessary enabling legislation should be enacted.

Thus the negative, in academic debate, cannot argue "Congress will never pass the affirmative's plan" and proceed to prove that because of attitudinal barriers, political interest, or for some other reason the affirmative plan can never get enough votes to enact their proposal. The affirmative may simply "fiat" their proposal and reply that Congress *should* enact the plan. The affirmative need only demonstrate that its proposal ought to be adopted and need not consider the political or attitudinal barriers that thus far have prevented its enactment.

The negative must avoid the "should–would" argument, which is pointless in academic debate.[4] The point is not *would* — but *should* — the affirmative's proposal be

---

[4]"Should–would" arguments may be of considerable importance in applied debate. A political leader might feel that a certain policy *should* be adopted but, recognizing that it would be impossible to marshal sufficient support, decide not to make the fight for it, feeling it is better to conserve energy and credibility for the possible. For example, some of President Reagan's advisors urged that the Constitution *should* be amended to ban abortions and to permit school prayer. Reagan sympathized with their proposals, but declined to lead an all-out legislative battle for them, apparently feeling Congress *would* not enact them.

adopted. The negative may, of course, focus on the workability of the policy and seek to demonstrate that a given policy, if adopted, would not work or would produce significant disadvantages.

For example, in debating the "government control of the supply and utilization of energy" proposition, the negative could not argue that Congress would not pass gasoline rationing because it was so unpopular with members of Congress and their constituents. The affirmative could simply "fiat" rationing — that is, argue that it *should* be passed. The negative could, however, argue that because rationing was so unpopular it would not work; that there would be widespread violations and black markets; that the system would break down; and thus that the affirmative could not achieve any advantage.

Fiat power is the power of the affirmative to focus the debate on whether a given policy *should* be adopted and to dismiss as irrelevant any arguments about whether that policy *will* be adopted. The purpose of fiat power is to require the debaters to debate the merits of the proposition and not the political machinations of how one might garner the votes necessary for enactment. Note too the limitations of fiat power: The affirmative may use fiat power to focus on *should*, but fiat power goes no further. The affirmative may *not* fiat that advantages will flow from its plan; the advantages must be proved. The affirmative may *not* fiat attitudes; for example, the affirmative may not fiat that all citizens will love gas rationing and will eagerly comply with their plan. Some additional uses and limitations of fiat power will be considered in Chapter 12, Section III-A (see pp. 196–197).

III. Issues

Issues are those critical claims *inherent* in the proposition that the affirmative must establish. The negative must defeat at least one stock issue in order to win. Issues may be readily recognized since they are claims with answers that *directly* prove or disprove the proposition. If the issues are established, then the proposition must prevail. As debaters begin analysis of the proposition, they phrase the issues as questions — "Did John Doe kill Richard Roe with malice?" Issues, in the analysis stage, are phrased in the form of questions to which the affirmative must answer *yes*; and the negative must answer *no* to at least one issue or there is no debate. When the issues are presented in a debate, the advocate phrases them as declarative sentences — "John Doe killed Richard Roe with malice."

Stock issues are standard claims that are applicable to many propositions. They will be considered in detail in the following sections.

Potential issues are all of the possible answers to the stock issues questions. In any given debate, however, it is unlikely that all of the potential issues will be used. (See Section III-C, "The Number of Issues.")

Admitted issues are those issues that one side concedes. For example, in debates on the proposition "Resolved: That the federal government should implement a program that guarantees employment opportunities for all U.S. citizens in the labor force," some affirmatives introduced the issue "millions of U.S. citizens are unemployed." In view of the evidence the affirmative could produce to support this issue, many negative advocates readily admitted this issue. Some negatives introduced the issue "millions of unemployed do not suffer economic hardship." In view of the evidence the negative could produce to support this issue, many affirmatives quickly admitted this issue. It is usually a wise policy for debaters to admit those issues they cannot win and concentrate their efforts on those issues they have a chance of winning.

The *issues of the debate* (the "actual issues") are those issues that actually are introduced into the debate and on which the opposing advocates clash. For example, the potential issues on a certain proposition might be: A, B, C, D, E, F, G, H, I, and J. The affirmative might introduce issues A, B, C, D, E, and F. The negative might admit issues B and C, introduce issue G, and seek to refute issues A, D, E, and F. The potential issues H, I, and J were not introduced by either side and thus did not enter into this debate. The issues of this debate were A, D, E, F, and G.

The *ultimate issue* arises when there is only one issue remaining in dispute. In *some* debates the clash may narrow down to one contended issue, known as the ultimate issue. In the preceding example the affirmative might have won issues A, D, E, and F early in the debate, leaving only issue G in dispute. G thus became the ultimate issue of this debate.

Contentions are statements offered in support of an issue. Pertinent evidence is organized into cogent arguments to support each issue. Usually several contentions are offered in support of an issue. The affirmative may fail to establish some of the remaining contentions and still win its case, provided that the remaining contentions have enough probative force to establish the issue.

A. Discovering the Issues

One of the first problems confronting the advocate in preparing to debate on a proposition is discovering the issues. In a courtroom debate, the issues are often stated explicitly in the law applicable to the case before the court. For example, if the proposition before the court is, in effect, "Resolved: That John Doe murdered Richard Roe," in most jurisdictions the issues would be:

1. Richard Roe is dead.
2. John Doe killed Richard Roe.
3. John Doe killed Richard Roe unlawfully.
4. John Doe killed Richard Roe following premeditation.
5. John Doe killed Richard Roe with malice.

If the prosecution fails to prove any one of these issues, John Doe cannot be convicted of murder; however, he might be convicted of manslaughter or some other lesser charge if some of the issues were proved.

In debates outside the courtroom, the issues are seldom so explicitly stated. It is up to the advocates to discover them by one of several possible methods. First of all, a careful definition of the terms of the proposition will aid the advocate in discovering some of the issues of the debate. As the terms are defined, important aspects of the proposition will become apparent and reveal at least some of the issues. In debates on "a national program of public work for the unemployed," the definition of the word "unemployed" was important. If "unemployed" was defined as including housewives who were seeking part-time work, this definition suggested the issue question, "Do the unemployed have the skills necessary for a public work program?"

In addition, stock issues — the standard questions applicable to many propositions — may be used profitably in the early analysis of the problem. As standard questions, they are not sufficiently specific to the issues of a particular proposition; but they often aid the advocate in the formulation of the actual issues.

1. Stock Issues on Propositions of Value. The stock issues in a debate on a proposition of *fact or value* are drawn from the two basic elements of the affirmative case: definition and designation. Since academic debate is more often concerned with propositions of value than with propositions of fact, we will refer to propositions of fact only briefly and consider propositions of value in much more detail.

In their briefest form, the stock issues may be phrased as:

1. Definitive issues
   a. What are the *definitions* of the key terms?
   b. What are the *criteria* for the values?
2. Designative issues
   a. Do the facts *correspond* to the definitions?
   b. What are the *applications* of the values?

With this brief statement in mind, we can proceed to a more detailed consideration of the stock issues.

Let us turn first to the murder trial of John Doe that we just considered. This trial, of course, is a debate on a proposition of *fact*. The definitive issue in this trial is the legal definition of murder. The designative issues in this trial are the five issues — (1) Richard Roe is dead, and so on — that the prosecuting attorney must prove in order to establish that the facts correspond to the definition of murder, thus proving that John Doe is guilty of murdering Richard Roe.

In a law court debate on a proposition of fact the issues are often neatly spelled out in the applicable law. In most debates outside the courtroom, however, the issues must be discovered by a careful analysis of the proposition.

Consider the value proposition "Resolved: That commercial television is more detrimental than beneficial to American society." What are the *definitions* of the key terms? We will certainly have to define "commercial television" and "American society." (See Section II-B.)

What are the *criteria* to define the value terms — "detrimental" and "beneficial"? (Again see Section II-B.)

As we consider the *application* of the values, additional issues may be discovered. The affirmative might argue that "detrimental" applies to programming that emphasized sports, soap operas, and escapist entertainment, whereas "beneficial" applied to programming that emphasized classical drama, classical music, and scholarly lectures. The negative might reply that the application of such values would drive viewers away, which in turn would drive sponsors away. With little or no advertising revenue, the television stations would have to turn to the government for revenue; thus the government would become the arbiter of television programming. Such government control, the negative might argue, would be far more detrimental than the programming the affirmative indicted. The affirmative might respond by arguing that the application of its values would raise the intellectual level of American society—that in time the public would come to appreciate its "beneficial" programming and that the quality of American society would be improved.

Note that as the debaters began to consider the policy applications of the values they have moved into a quasi-policy debate. In such debates the negative may well offer "value objections" that are very similar to the policy issue of "disadvantages." Additional issues long associated with policy debate become essential in quasi-policy debate. Since quasi-policy debate involves the consideration of policy issues, we will consider them next.

2. Stock Issues for Propositions of Policy. The stock issues for the proposition of policy are drawn from the three basic elements of the affirmative case: justification, plan, and advantages. In their briefest form, the stock issues may be phrased as:

1. Justification
   a. Is the problem *inherent* in the status quo?
   b. Is the problem *significant?*
2. Plan
   a. Is the plan *workable?*
   b. Does the plan *solve* the problem?
3. Advantages
   a. Does the plan produce *advantages?*
   b. Do the advantages outweigh the *disadvantages?*

With this brief statement in mind, we can then proceed to a more detailed consideration of the stock issues.

Is there a *justification* for a change in the status quo (that is, are there specific *needs*, evils, undesirable factors, shortcomings, unmet *goals* or *criteria*, unattained *advantages* or *alternative justifications* that constitute good reasons for changing the status quo)? Are these conditions *significant* enough to warrant a change in the status quo? (Significance may be demonstrated either quantitatively or qualitatively—or, best of all, *both* quantitatively and qualitatively.) Are these conditions *inherent* in the status quo? Are they *caused* by the status quo? (Inherency may be demonstrated as being either structural, attitudinal, or, again best of all, *both* structural and attitudinal.) Is it impossible to eliminate these conditions by repairs, adjustments, or improvements within the framework of the status quo? Is any negative proposal to repair or adjust the problems of the status quo unsatisfactory?

Is there a *plan* to solve the problems cited as justification for adopting the proposition? Is the plan *topical* (that is, is it directly related to the proposition)? Is the plan *workable?* Does the plan have *solvency* (that is, will it solve the problems)? Is any possible negative counterplan topical and thus capable of being absorbed into the affirmative's plan? Is the counterplan unworkable or lacking in solvency?

Will the plan achieve the claimed *advantages* (that is, will it satisfy the justification offered by the affirmative, meet the needs cited by the affirmative, attain the goals or criteria cited by the affirmative)? Will the plan produce no disadvantages as great as or greater than those existing in the status quo? Will any possible negative counterplan produce greater disadvantages than the status quo or the plan? Are the advantages *inherent* in the plan (that is, will they necessarily flow from the adoption of the plan)? Are the advantages *unique* to the plan (that is, can they be obtained without adopting the plan)? Are the advantages *significant?* Do they outweigh the disadvantages?

3. Using Stock Issues. After carefully defining the terms of the proposition and the related terms from the area of controversy, and applying the appropriate stock issues, the advocate will formulate a preliminary statement of the potential issues of the debate.

Both the affirmative and the negative use stock issues in their analysis. The affirmative uses stock issues as they seek to discover the issues they will advance. The negative uses stock issues as they seek to anticipate the issues they must refute and the issues, such as disadvantages, that they will advance.

A practical method for the advocate to follow in beginning analysis is:

First: Ask the stock issue as a *question:* Is there a justification for a change in the status quo of the type called for in the resolution? Is the problem inherent in the status quo? And so on.

Second: Answer each of these questions with the statement of a *potential* issue of the debate.

The following example shows how the stock issues may be used: Some debaters started their analysis of the proposition "Resolved: That law enforcement agencies in the United States should be given greater freedom in the investigation and prosecution of crime" by asking the stock issue question "Is there a *justification* for a change in the status quo?" In their preliminary reading, some of them came across a number of articles arguing that law enforcement agencies needed more money to upgrade the quality of police personnel and to purchase more equipment. They tentatively phrased the potential issue "Law enforcement agencies *need* more money to fight crime." As they continued their analysis, defined the term "greater freedom," and considered the stock issue "Is this *inherent* in the status quo?" they decided that "more money" was not consistent with their definition of "greater freedom" and that a shortage of funds was not inherent in the status quo. Thus they rejected the potential issue they had tentatively selected and continued their analysis.

As these debaters continued their preliminary research, they decided that the major evil in the status quo was organized crime and that it was a serious enough problem to warrant a change. Further study led to the conclusion that the use of the telephone was essential to the operation of organized crime. They also concluded that status quo legislation inherently prevented law enforcement agencies from using wiretap evidence in court and that if the police were given "greater freedom"—by the legalization of wiretaps and making evidence thus obtained admissible in court—they would be able to combat crime more successfully. These conclusions led to formulation of the following potential *need* issue as *justification* for a change in the status quo:

Organized crime is a major national problem.

Next the debaters asked, "Is the need quantitatively significant?" After considering various alternatives, they formulated the following potential issues:

Organized crime loots billions from legitimate businesses.

Organized crime evades billions in taxes.

The debaters continued their preliminary exploration by asking, "Is the need qualitatively significant?" This question led to the development of the potential issue:

Organized crime murders and maims thousands.

Next the debaters asked, "Are these conditions inherent in the status quo?" After reviewing the evidence they had at hand the debaters developed the following potential issues:

The use of the telephone is essential to the operation of organized crime.

Present restrictions on the use of wiretaps reduce the effectiveness of law enforcement agencies in combating organized crime.

Next the debaters asked the stock issue questions, "Is there a plan to meet this problem? Is the plan workable? Will the plan solve the problem? After considering a number of possible alternatives, they developed a plan providing potential statements of agency, mandates, enforcement, funding and staffing, and addendum (see Chapter 12, Section III-A) as their answers to these stock issue questions.

The debaters continued their analysis by asking the stock issue question, "Will this plan produce advantages?" Their analysis led them to claim the following potential advantage contentions:

The plan will provide an effective weapon against organized crime.

The plan will have the additional advantage of reducing all crime.

The plan will extend the right of privacy of law-abiding citizens by providing effective regulation against unauthorized wiretapping.

These potential issues represent the debaters' preliminary analysis of the problem. At this point they have moved from general stock questions to potential issues specifically adapted to the proposition. These potential issues must now be tested by further research to determine whether the evidence will in fact support the claimed issues. The debaters must discover whether there are effective objections to their plan — whether their plan will produce disadvantages greater than the claimed advantages. On the basis of further study, they will no doubt modify their potential issues. They may try them out in a few practice debates. Experience may lead them to rethink some or all of the potential issues. They have, however, taken the essential first step: they have moved from the general to the specific and have begun a meaningful analysis of the proposition.

In similar fashion, the advocate who is debating propositions of value must analyze the subject area and move from the general stock issues to the specific issues inherent in the proposition.

Using the "commercial television" proposition, consider a real-world example of value, and later policy, debate that took place a few years ago and continues, although in a somewhat different form, to the present. Opponents of cigarette commercials on television argued that such commercials were "detrimental," and they established the *criterion* that "encouraging sales of products that caused illness and death was detrimental."

Turning to the next issue, the affirmative sought to demonstrate that the subject *met* the criterion by drawing on the Surgeon General's Report, which argued that there was a link between cigarette smoking and illness and death among the general public.

Significance was established by the same report, which claimed a link between cigarette smoking and many thousands of deaths.

The *inherency* issue gave the affirmative the most difficulty. People had been smoking cigarettes for years before commercial television came into existence, and cigarette manufacturers were also advertising lavishly in other media. The debate came to an inconclusive end when the negative withdrew from the field. The law required that equal time be given to anticigarette commercials, and the cigarette companies decided to direct their advertising to media that did not have the equal-time requirement.

B. Introduction of Issues

1. Introduction by Either Side. In both value and policy debate the affirmative must introduce the issues necessary to establish a *prima facie case*—one that provides good and sufficient reason for adopting the proposition. As a starting point, a prima facie case must provide effective issue statements to answer each of the stock issue questions. (See Chapter 11, Section I.) If the negative detects flaws in the affirmative case, it has the responsibility of introducing the appropriate issues to refute the affirmative. For example, the affirmative case *should* be so clearly topical that it is unnecessary for the affirmative to prove that it is. In such a case, it is clearly pointless for the negative to attack it, and this issue will not be argued. If it is not topical, however, the negative must "attack topicality." (See Chapter 13, Sections II and III, for a consideration of the issues the negative may introduce.) If the affirmative is using a "needs analysis" case, it will certainly introduce one or more "need" issues. In proving these issues, the affirmative might argue that the status quo cannot be repaired, or it might wait to see if the negative seeks to provide repairs and then argue the specific negative repairs. "Workability," for example, might or might not become a critical issue, and it might or might not be introduced by either side. In debates on the Twenty-Sixth Amendment, "workability" was never argued—it was self-evident that the voting age *could* be lowered to eighteen—the affirmative did not have to prove it, and it would have been pointless for the negative to attempt to disprove it. In debates on the "further development of nuclear weapons" proposition, workability was almost invariably a critical issue. The negative was almost certain to introduce the issue. Recognizing this possibility, some affirmatives sought to preempt the argument by introducing the issue first. The affirmative will claim "advantages" for their plan and be prepared for a negative attack on this issue. The issue of "disadvantages," however, will be argued only if the negative introduces it.

It is readily apparent that advocates must discover and prepare to deal with *all* potential issues of the proposition — not just those issues they find it most convenient to deal with. Any potential issue may become an issue of the debate.

Note that, although the affirmative must carry all of the stock issues, it is not necessarily required to carry all of the contentions. In the example just considered, the affirmative must carry the stock issue of advantage. Simply carrying the first advantage contention (the plan will provide an effective weapon against organized crime) might be sufficient to do so, even if the affirmative lost the second and third advantage contentions.

2. The Counterplan. One of the potential issues of any policy debate is "Is the plan proposed by the affirmative the best possible way to solve the problems of the status quo?" If the negative denies that there are any serious problems in the status quo, this potential issue does not become an issue of the debate. The negative, however, may find it desirable to admit that there are certain problems in the status quo and may introduce a counterplan to meet these problems, as is shown in Chapter 13. In such a case the negative introduces this issue, and the affirmative may then argue: (1) the counterplan is topical (not competitive with the proposition), and thus the affirmative may absorb it into its plan; or (2) the counterplan is not workable; or (3) the counterplan lacks solvency; or (4) the counterplan produces disadvantages greater than the status quo or the affirmative's plan; or any combination of these attacks as can be applied to the counterplan.

C. The Number of Issues

The number of issues varies from one proposition to another and can be discovered only by careful analysis of the problem. In general, the number of issues is rather small. There are usually four to six issues in dispute in the typical intercollegiate debate. If advocates claim a large number of "issues," they may be confusing supporting contentions with issues. It is usually to the advantage of the affirmative to try to narrow the number of issues of the debate. If the affirmative can secure the admission of the negative, or if it can quickly establish three out of four issues, for example, then it can concentrate its efforts on proving the remaining issue.

It is usually to the advantage of the negative to seek to establish as many issues of debate as possible. By keeping the maximum possible number of issues in dispute, the negative hopes to force the affirmative to prove every issue and to deny the affirmative the opportunity of concentrating on a few issues of its own choosing. Either team, however, may find it advisable to drop a nonessential issue it is losing and concentrate on the critical issues it feels that it can and must win.

In debates on the "guarantee employment opportunities" proposition, as mentioned previously, the affirmative had excellent evidence to establish the issue "millions are unemployed." Many negatives chose to admit the issue and concentrated on other issues. Some, however, adopted the strategy of clashing with this issue (they argued that the figures were flawed as they included millions of short-term unemployed who were only mildly inconvenienced and sustained no real harm from brief unemployment). This contention, of course, forced the affirmative to spend time reestablishing the issue at the cost of devoting less time to extending or defending other issues. Neither side can manufacture issues just to waste its opponent's time — capable advocates would quickly expose such a trick. Both teams have an obligation to develop the issues essential to their position. It is wise strategy, however, to drop a noncritical, lost issue and concentrate on the issues that can be won. If an affirmative "turned around" the negative's first disadvantage (that is, proved that, instead of being a disadvantage, it was actually an advantage that helped the affirmative), the negative might choose to drop that issue and concentrate on the second disadvantage that it felt it was winning and argue that this disadvantage alone outweighed all of the affirmative's advantages. Thus it is not uncommon to find fewer issues in contention at the close of the debate than there were at the beginning.

D. Phrasing the Issues

The issues must be so phrased as to provide maximum logical and persuasive impact on those who render the decision. First, the well-phrased issue will preview and then bring into focus the line of argument to be developed. Second, the issue must be phrased persuasively. Third, the issue must be phrased concisely. Fourth, taken as a whole, the issues must be so phrased as to provide a coherent organization for the case and admit of smooth transition from one issue to another. Students will find it worthwhile to review Chapter 15 (Presenting the Case: Composition) and Chapter 16 (Presenting the Case: Delivery) as they begin to put their phrasing of the issues into final form.

Some students debating "Resolved: That executive control of U.S. foreign policy should be significantly curtailed" wanted to curtail executive control by prohibiting the executive from carrying out covert operations in foreign countries. They *might* have phrased the first need issue as "American foreign policy objectives of combating communism, protecting the innocent, and preserving peace are seriously impeded when it becomes a matter of public knowledge that the United States has in fact engaged in covert operations to overthrow hostile regimes." They *might* have phrased the second issue as "Neither reducing the number of covert operations nor limiting covert operations to those most likely to succeed will effectively avoid the adverse publicity that will follow when the operations become public knowledge." *Instead*, they wisely phrased the issues as "Discovery of covert operations undermines American objectives" and "The only way to prevent discovery is to end all operations."

The phrasing actually used is clearly superior and meets the criteria considered earlier in this section. Most often, however, the issue will first occur to an advocate in a rambling, disjointed form. The experienced advocate knows that well-phrased issues are the result of careful rewriting and skillful editing.

Well-phrased issues give advocates in academic debate one of the best opportunities to "take control of the flow sheet" and lodge their arguments, *exactly as they want them stated*, in the mind of the judge. The importance of phrasing issues with precision is by no means limited to students in academic debate. In almost any circumstances, advocates are more likely to achieve their objective if the issues are crisply and coherently stated rather than buried in a discursive presentation. The importance of well-phrased issues becomes more critical if advocates attain enough prominence to be quoted on even a local radio or television news program. The advocates quickly learn that their entire speech is almost never presented; rather, they feel lucky if as much as a sixty-second "clip" of their speech is used. In such circumstances, wise speakers quickly learn to phrase their issues effectively. The same considerations, although to a somewhat lesser degree, apply to newspapers, which often quote portions of a speech but only infrequently publish full texts.

E. The Substructure of the Issues

The same considerations that apply to the phrasing of the issues also apply to the substructure of the issue. The contentions — that is, the supporting arguments used to establish an issue — must be phrased with care so that they too will provide the maximum logical and persuasive impact on those who render the decision.

Consider the substructure of the issues cited in the previous section:

I. Discovery of covert operations undermines American objectives.
  A. Discovery strengthens communism.
  B. Discovery injures the innocent.
  C. Discovery threatens peace.
II. The only way to prevent discovery is to end all operations.
  A. Discovery of some operations is inevitable.
  B. Discovery is unpredictable.

The reiteration of the concept of "discovery" on which the advocate wished to focus and the concise phrasing of the contentions helped the advocate to establish the case more effectively.

F. The Issues and the Decision Makers

Advocates must consider the attitudes and values of those who render the decision as they decide what issues they will introduce and how they will handle them. In debating the "comprehensive medical care for all citizens" proposition, some debaters quickly discovered the issue "comprehensive medical care for all citizens will inflate taxes by prolonging lives." The argument was irrefutable. If the plan worked as well as the affirmative claimed it would, the negative could prove that vast numbers of elderly indigents would linger on for years in an unproductive state consuming more and more tax dollars in medical and welfare costs. Despite the overwhelming logical force of the argument, the debaters decided against introducing the issue. They felt the values of most American audiences are such that they would reject the idea of denying poor people medical care so that they might die earlier and thus save taxes.

Before a group of business managers, the "cost issue," if the plan requires the expenditure of tax monies, is one that the negative will almost certainly argue. The negative will maximize the tax burden, while the affirmative will seek to minimize it. Many business people are well aware of the enormous taxes they are already paying and are predisposed to resist any new or additional taxes. Cost may well become the critical issue of the debate and provide the negative with its best opportunity of winning. California's tax-cutting Proposition 13 proved very popular with the voters of that state and triggered a series of tax-cutting proposals across the nation. Before student groups, negatives often find that the "cost issue" is less critical. Many students are beneficiaries of tax-spending programs and have not yet felt the personal burden of paying heavy taxes. Before such audiences the negative may decide to drop the cost issue or to transform its material and argue that the affirmative plan will "distort social priorities" because its cost is so great that it precludes or reduces other more desirable programs. Thus, in arguing the "medical care" proposition, some negatives maintained that, rather than spend the money on medical care, more lives would be saved and the quality of life improved if the money were spent to provide better food and housing for the poor.

Even the highly qualified professional judges ideally found in academic debate cannot totally divorce themselves from their value systems. Thus, if in a debate on the "medical care" proposition, a negative introduced as a counterplan the issue "euthanasia for anyone who is hospitalized more than once a year," it must expect that the judge will evaluate almost any affirmative objection as sufficient to defeat the counterplan.

As students begin to make final selection of issues and to plan their handling of those issues, they may find it helpful to study Chapter 15 (Presenting the Case: Composition), especially Section I ("Analysis of the Audience").

Exercises

1. Prepare a brief paper in which you define the terms of the current national NDT or CEDA debate proposition. Your instructor may call for a class discussion of your definitions.

2. From the newspapers and newsmagazines of the past month find an example of an argumentative speech on a proposition of policy by a public figure. Prepare a brief paper in which you identify the speaker and the occasion, state the proposition, and state the issues set forth. If necessary, rephrase the speaker's words to form a clear and correct statement of the proposition and issues; be careful, however, to preserve the speaker's ideas. Do you agree with the speaker's choice of issues?

3. Prepare a three-minute speech for delivery in class in which you (a) state a proposition of policy or value, as determined by your instructor, (b) define the terms, (c) state the issues. The class will be asked to evaluate your statement of the proposition, definition of terms, and statement of the issues. Prepare an outline of this speech to hand to your instructor.

4. Your instructor will divide the class into groups of two students. Each group will select a proposition of value or policy. One student, acting as an affirmative speaker, will present a three-minute speech to (a) state the proposition, (b) define the terms, and (c) state the issues. The other student, acting as a negative speaker,

will (a) accept the definitions or offer superior ones, (b) accept the statement of issues, revise the issues if advisable, or offer additional issues if advisable.

5. Attend an intercollegiate debate and prepare a brief paper in which you report the definition of terms and statement of issues presented in the debate. Evaluate the ability of the debaters in defining terms and discovering issues. Evaluate the ability of the debaters in phrasing the issues and contentions.

5

Exploring the Controversy

Once we have analyzed the controversy and formulated a statement of the potential issues, our next step is to explore the controversy. Advocates who seek to present their position intelligently and to convince others to concur with them must be thoroughly familiar with the controversy. They must undertake an organized program of research so that they may explore fully all relevant aspects of the issues. Careful research will provide a firm foundation that will give them confidence in the case that they will later build. The potential issues formulated in the analysis of the controversy will help to give direction to their exploration of it. The process of analyzing and exploring the controversy are interwoven, and advocates will continue to move from one to the other of these two processes as long as they are concerned with the proposition. They must be innovative and creative in their search for evidence and issues and then be coolly and dispassionately analytical in evaluating findings and planning further research. On the basis of their exploration, they may find it necessary to rephrase the issues they originally developed or to develop new issues or, if the proposition is subject to rephrasing, they may find it desirable to revise the proposition.

In formal debate, a restatement of the proposition cannot be done unilaterally; it requires the consent of all parties concerned. The intercollegiate debater, the attorney in the law court, and other advocates must often debate on a proposition that is not subject to revision. In informal debate in government and business, advocates—for persuasive purposes—often make serious and sometimes successful attempts to change the wording and meaning of the proposition unilaterally. For example, opponents of abortion prefer to speak of the "right to life," and supporters of euthanasia prefer to state their proposal as "death with dignity" rather than as "mercy killing." In parliamentary debate, the proposition may be amended by a simple majority vote; in many conference and discussion situations, the problem may be revised by informal action. In any event, the advocate will continue exploration, constantly revising the case on the basis of new information.

I.   Brainstorming for Ideas

Traditionally, advocates seek to develop a case by a careful, orderly, deliberate, logical process. Although the case they finally present must be logically sound, advocates sometimes find it advantageous to shorten the logical processes while gathering ideas for their case. Sometimes the solution to a problem is found by means of an "intuitive leap," a "hunch," a "lucky break," an "inspiration," or serendipity. The advocate may just happen to look into an obscure reference and make a critical inference or find exactly the piece of evidence needed to complete a chain of reasoning; or consider a seemingly improbable plan "just for the fun of it" and find that it meets the needs perfectly; or follow up an apparently irrelevant lead and uncover an important precedent; or consider an impractical proposal that will lead to a highly practical solution.

A dramatic example of how one may use inferences to make a creative leap from sketchy data occurred when an inference reader in the Central Intelligence Agency, who was assigned to read Russian newspapers, noted that a small Soviet town's soccer team, perennial born losers, suddenly began winning games and catapulted to the top of their league. At the inference reader's urging, an overflight was made of the town, revealing a hidden military installation. The Soviets had carefully camouflaged the installation but forgot that its technicians would notably improve the town's soccer team. Thus skilled inference reading revealed an important secret.

It is for the express purpose of uncovering ideas that might otherwise be ignored or delayed that the advocate uses *brainstorming*. Many situations arise in which it may be profitable to use brainstorming: in defining terms or discovering issues, in finding materials for the argument, in connection with the problems of evidence or reasoning, in building the case, or in many other areas. Although brainstorming is not a substitute for the ways of dealing with problems considered in other chapters, it is a supplement that may help in many situations.

In a typical brainstorming session, the participants sit around a table. They make a deliberate effort to create an informal atmosphere in which everyone is encouraged to contribute and no one is permitted to criticize. They are usually most successful when following certain guidelines (*see inset on p. 67*).

Brainstorming is often deceptively simple. The idea evolved may evoke the comment "Why, anyone could have thought of that." This is often true. The point is that in many cases no one had thought of the idea earlier, and perhaps no one would have thought of that particular idea if it had not been for the brainstorming session. Many of the ideas evolved in brainstorming sessions are pure "fluff." However, if only one important idea is evolved that otherwise might never have been considered, the technique is worthwhile.

Method of Brainstorming

1. **The size of the group is limited.** Brainstorming has been found to work better in small groups. Fifteen is usually considered to be a maximum workable size. Groups as small as two or three have been effective, and it is even possible for an individual to apply the method of brainstorming alone.

2. **The time devoted to a brainstorming session is limited.** Because the objective of brainstorming is to produce a large number of ideas and to avoid any critical evaluation *during the session,* it is usually desirable to limit a session to one hour or less; many profitable sessions have been limited to between 20 and 40 minutes.

3. **The problem is announced in advance.** The person calling the brainstorming session announces the problem he or she wants the group to consider, either at the start of the session or a day or two in advance.

4. **All participants are encouraged to contribute.** Since the objective is to secure the maximum possible number of ideas, everyone is urged to participate. The leader can encourage contributions by creating a friendly, informal atmosphere. Participants are urged not only to originate ideas but also to modify and extend ideas presented by others.

5. **No organized pattern is followed.** Whereas traditional discussion follows a careful pattern of reflective thinking, brainstorming deliberately follows no pattern. The objective is to provide an atmosphere for the *trigger effect* in which an idea, even a bad or irrelevant one, once expressed, may trigger a good idea.

6. **No criticism is permitted.** No criticism or evaluation of ideas should be permitted *during the session.* Since criticism, at this stage, tends to discourage contributions and decreases the possibility of the "trigger effect," the leader must suppress criticism and strive to maintain an atmosphere in which everyone feels free to contribute.

7. **All ideas are recorded.** All ideas, including those that seem worthless at first glance, must be recorded. The most widely used method is probably that of assigning two or three members of the group to write ideas on a blackboard as rapidly as they are expressed. Other methods include the use of an "idea tree"—a short pole is set in the center of the table and participants write out their ideas and attach them to the "tree" with Scotch tape—or the "cracker barrel"—a basket is placed on the table and participants write their ideas on pieces of paper and toss them into the "barrel." No matter which method is used, all ideas should be recorded and forwarded to the person or group responsible for evaluation.

8. **The ideas are subject to rigorous evaluation.** Once the brainstorming session is over and the ideas have been recorded in some usable form, they are then subjected to thorough evaluation. Sometimes the ideas are duplicated and sent to the participating individuals for their evaluation. In many cases they are forwarded to a policymaking group or to the individual responsible for making decisions for screening and testing. The ideas gathered during brainstorming may serve as springboards for concepts that will be developed more fully during evaluation.

One group of college students debating "a national program of public work for the unemployed" found that early in the season their affirmative teams were having a great deal of difficulty with their plan, which called for a massive program of urban renewal to provide jobs. Their negative opponents were defeating the plan by pointing out that few of the unemployed had the skills necessary for construction work. The debaters held a brainstorming session from which they evolved the idea that the affirmative plan did not have to call for construction work. Then they proceeded to develop a new plan that called for conservation, service, and maintenance work that unskilled persons could easily perform. This plan might have evolved by some other means, of course, but this particular group of advocates was unable to develop an effective plan until they brainstormed the problem.

II. Sources of Material

Most often the advocates turn to the library as their first source of material. Resources, physical arrangements, and loan policies of libraries vary enormously, and advocates are well advised to spend some time browsing through the library in order to acquire a general familiarity with its collections and organization so that later search for information may be purposeful and effective. Librarians are usually eager to assist a person doing serious research, and their help can be a valuable asset to the advocate.

A. General References

Exploration usually begins with an effort to acquire general information on the problem. As the advocate acquires a general knowledge of the problem, he or she is in a position to develop more specific lines of inquiry and to seek more specialized information. Among the more important general references are the *card catalog* (whether literally on cards or on a computer) and *The Library of Congress Subject Heading Index*, usually located near the card catalog, which indicates the subject headings the card catalog uses and lists related headings and the various encyclopedias, almanacs, and yearbooks located in the reference room.

Valuable references for newspapers include the *Newspaper Index*, *NewsBank*, and *Editorials on File*. Important references for periodical literature include *Readers' Guide to Periodical Literature*, *Magazine Index*, and *Business Index*.

Often the advocate will wish to learn more about specific individuals to establish the expertness of "witnesses." Useful biographical references are *Who's Who* (worldwide in scope, but primarily British), *Who's Who in America*, *Who's Who in the East* (and similar publications for other geographic regions of the United States), *Who's Who of American Women*, *Dictionary of American Biography*, and the *Biography Index*.

B. Special References

Special biographical directories list individuals prominent in certain fields. *Who's Who in American Education* and the *Directory of American Scholars* list educators and scholars, and similar directories may be found for other professions.

General references perform a valuable function by providing the advocate with important information on the proposition and by suggesting further avenues of exploration. Almost invariably, however, the general references do not provide the depth of specialized information the advocate needs; further information may be sought in special reference works. Some of the more specialized references include the *Statistical Abstract of the United States* (a very highly regarded source of such data), the United Nation's *Demographic Yearbook*, the *Congressional Record*, and the *Monthly Catalogue of Government Documents*.

Be alert for references to committee hearings on your subject. Your representative and senators have a limited supply of copies for free distribution to constituents on a first-come, first-served basis. If the hearings are recent and appear to be valuable, a quick phone call or prompt letter to your representative or senator will be worthwhile. If the supply of free copies is exhausted, a copy may be available in your library or can be obtained from a Government Printing Office Book Store; consult your phone book under "United States Government."

A special reference work on each year's NDT debate resolution is prepared by the Library of Congress Legislative Reference Service and is available free from your representative or senator. Further valuable resources include the *Congressional Information Service Index*, the *Public Affairs Information Service Bulletin*, the *Congressional Quarterly's* weekly review of news on issues before Congress (start with the most recent issue and work backward; the index is cumulative), the *Monthly Catalog of Government Documents*, *Index to Government Periodicals*, and *Editorial Research Reports*. Be sure to check *Bibliography Index* to find bibliographies on your subject. *Presidential Papers* provides the full text of the current President's speeches, press releases, and press conferences.

Be sure to consult the abstracts of your subject area, such as *Psychological Abstracts* or *Sociological Abstracts*. Important indexes are available for almost all subject areas such as: *Social Science Index, Social Sciences Citation Index, Religion Index, Essay and General Literature Index, Humanities Index,* and *Education Index*. Don't overlook such sources of scholarly information as ERIC or *Dissertation Abstracts*. For legal matters consult *Black's Law Dictionary* (an old standby), *U.S. Law Week, Index to Legal Periodicals*, and the *Supreme Court Reporter*. (When quoting a Supreme Court decision, be certain to record the name of the justice and whether the quote is from a majority, concurring, or dissenting opinion.)

Your initial research should cover the broadest possible base of potentially useful sources. If you are preparing to debate a value proposition, don't limit yourself to the *Sociological Index* and the *Humanities Index*; if you are preparing for a policy proposition, don't limit yourself to the *Public Affairs Information Service Bulletin* and the *Congressional Information Service Index*. Important evidence on both value and policy is not so discretely isolated, and the wise advocate will seek out evidence wherever it may be found.

One of the best methods for locating special references is to answer certain questions. The answers will suggest many sources of information (*see inset on p. 70*).

Information secured from sources suggested by answers to the "who is for it or against it" questions must be viewed with special care. It is often easy information to obtain, because those whose interests are affected by the proposition are usually anx-

Locating References: Questions

1. **Who is concerned with the proposition?** We may find that persons and organizations concerned with a problem include those with an academic interest in it, those interested in the potential influence of the proposition, and even those unwilling as yet to take a public stand on the problem. For example, if we are seeking information on the "higher education" proposition, our answer to the question "Who is concerned with the proposition?" would include the various associations of educators, economists, political scientists, businesspeople, labor organizations, and organizations in other related fields. The scholarly associations and their journals seldom take an official position for or against legislation, but their journals carry significant articles about contemporary problems in the area of their special interest. The education journals, in particular, yielded a number of significant articles on this proposition.

2. **Who is interested in securing the adoption of the proposition?** The answer to this question will often lead the advocate to one of the most prolific sources of information. A search for information on "higher education" would lead the advocate to the Department of Education, for example, which took the lead in presenting the administration's arguments in favor of the proposition.

3. **Who is interested in preventing the adoption of the proposition?** The answer will often lead the advocate to another prolific source of information. The advocate interested in "higher education" found, for example, that the National Association of Manufacturers published a good deal of material opposed to the proposition.

ious to give the widest possible dissemination to their arguments. At the same time, the very fact that their interests are affected by the problem may mean that the information they distribute is not completely objective or accurate.

Problems of possible bias, conflicting evidence, and conflicting interpretations of the same evidence are, of course, inherent in argumentation. If there were no controversy, there would be no debate. Information from interested parties cannot be rejected out of hand merely because of possible bias. Frequently, parties to a dispute are the best — indeed sometimes the only — sources of information about the dispute. The clash of conflicting evidence and opinion is the lifeblood of argumentation and gives advocates excellent opportunities to get to the root of the matter. In studying conflicting evidence and opinion, advocates must apply the tests of evidence and reasoning considered in later chapters. A searching and rigorous examination of the conflict will help to separate fact from wishful thinking and logical issues of the debate from emotion-laden slogans.

If labor and management *disagree* about a certain proposal to aid the unemployed and if reports issued by the Bureau of Labor Statistics, the AFL–CIO, and the NAM all *agree* that the unemployment rate is x percent, the advocate is probably safe in deciding that the unemployment rate will not be an issue of the debate. The real issue may be "Is x percent too high?" The search for the answer to this question may lead to the profitable exploration of previously overlooked economic and sociology journals. If the AFL–CIO and the NAM disagree about the cost of the proposal, the advocate may well conclude that cost will be a major issue of the debate and may decide to search the conflicting arguments to find the reasons for the differences in the cost estimates. Does the labor report speak only of the first-year cost, whereas the management report speaks of a ten-year total? A precise analysis of the conflicting figures, together with a careful checking of relevant data from impartial sources, may lead to accurate cost estimates.

Another important source of special references are the think tanks. Four of the best known are the American Enterprise Institute (conservative), the Brookings Institute (liberal), the Hudson Institute (conservative), and the Club of Rome (liberal). All publish important studies prepared by qualified scholars. These studies, which (not surprisingly) occasionally contradict one another, deal with matters of public interest and are often quoted in journal articles, news stories, and in public debate. The advocate will find it desirable to obtain the original document and consult the full text. Many, but not all, of these studies are available in your library. For insurance the debater may find it advisable to write to these think tanks and ask for their current catalog. (Their addresses are available in your library; the first two think tanks are the most prolific.)

Resources vary from one library to another, so check with your reference librarian to learn the specific resources available in your facility. If a specific publication you need is not available locally, ask the librarian to run a computer search on its availability at other libraries. Of course, many reference materials are not available for interlibrary loans, and such loans are often too slow for the debater who needs to use the evidence next week. However, if you know an important document is available in a relatively nearby library, it may be worth the trip.

C. Current Periodicals and Newspapers

Because advocates are most often concerned with a proposition of current interest, they may expect that information relating to the proposition will appear from time to time in the daily press, weekly newsmagazines, and monthly magazines. Resourceful advocates will maintain a constant program of scanning current publications for articles related to their problem. Their daily reading should include the *New York Times* and at least one other metropolitan daily. The Sunday *New York Times'* "News of the Week in Review" section is a helpful summary of current events. Weekly reading should include such newsmagazines as *Time, Newsweek,* or *U.S. News & World Report.* If the proposition is related to a particular field, advocates should add the special publications of that area to their research list. For example, if they are concerned with a business problem, they should read the *Wall Street Journal, Business Week, Fortune,* the *AFL–CIO News,* and the *Monthly Labor Review,* together with some of the trade papers and newsletters of the specific area under consideration.

Advocates should make a special point of reading publications with many different editorial policies. Much of their opponents' evidence and argument may come from publications with which they disagree. If they study this information in its original source, they will be in a better position to deal with it in the debate.

D. Databases

Databases constitute valuable research tools. Some of the most specialized databases contain crucial or classified material; and, as their annual subscriptions can cost several hundred thousand dollars, they are available only to government agencies, think tanks, or large corporations. Some of the nonclassified financial databases do not publicize their subscription rates, perhaps because "If you have to ask the price, you can't afford it."

The next level of databases are designed for general use but are so expensive that they are available only in libraries, which means, however, that they are available to the student since the user pays only for the time the search takes. "Dialog," "BRS," and "SDC Orbit" are excellent sources and have a wide variety of subsystems. The cost to use the subsystems varies from a few dollars to a few hundred dollars an hour. However, as the average search takes only three minutes, efficient database searches are within the budget of the average student and are enormously cost effective.

Databases supply information in one of four formats: (1) a bibliographic citation, (2) an abstract, (3) a full text (obviously the most expensive format. Do you really want the full text of a *New York Times* article? If a bibliographic citation would do just as well, you could view the article on microfilm and read it without charge.), or (4) numerical data (for example, today's official estimate of the unemployment rate in the United States, as contrasted with last week's or last month's), the most recent information likely to be available in printed sources.

The key to successful and cost-effective use of databases is to enter carefully structured searches. It is strongly recommended that one who is just beginning to use databases should consult with a reference librarian. One debater, beginning work on the "hazardous waste" proposition, entered a too-broad search and the computer indicated that over 15,000 items were available. Even the most dedicated debater would be daunted at the prospect of plowing through over 15,000 books and articles. Quick consultation with the reference librarian enabled the debater to fine-tune the search and come up with 187 items. When the abstracts were printed out, for less than three minutes of computer time, the debater had a far more extensive list of references than could have been compiled in many hours of manual checking. Some of the items were classified by the debater as "URGENT: for immediate reading," others were discarded as "probably useless," and the remaining articles were assigned various priorities. A further cost-saving option is available: You may elect to have the printout mailed to you rather than have the data sent by wire. This option will save you the long-distance phone charges but will involve a time lag of two or three days. You may decide which is the better option in a given situation.

The next levels of databases are much less expensive both for their one-time membership fee and for their search-time charges. They are designed for use on personal computers. If you have a personal computer, you will need a modem (to connect to a phone line) and a printer or a disk drive on which you can download (copy) the results of your database search. "Delphi" (which can gain access to library databases), "The Source," "CompuServe," "Dialog Knowledge Index," and "BRS after Dark" are excellent sources. They are designed for non–prime-time use (when the phone rates are cheapest), which is an added feature for the researcher who enjoys working after normal business hours and a real advantage for the college student who has classes during the day. Here again, learning to enter the optimum search is important; if you can "log on" and locate specific information with cobra-like quickness, you can draw on vast resources at minimum cost.

We have made no attempt to give exact costs or precise information about database capabilities in this discussion. The cost undoubtedly will have changed by the time you read these words. The history of databases, though brief, is encouraging: Each year the costs have declined and the quality has improved. Many students have personal computers in their homes or dormitories, and database searches are generally available through libraries.

E. A Specific Example

How, specifically, does one go about utilizing the resources just cited in order to undertake serious research on a subject? B. F. Magnan, of the Library Services Division of the Congressional Research Service of the Library of Congress, provided a helpful Research Guide for students debating the proposition "Resolved: That the United States federal government should significantly increase exploration and/or development of space beyond the Earth's mesosphere." Although the following excerpt is specific to this proposition, it can serve as an excellent model for anyone undertaking research on a contemporary problem involving federal legislation.

Books

Library of Congress subject headings are used in many library catalogs nationwide. This partial listing of subject headings may be used to identify books in the Library of Congress catalog and other library catalogs on space issues.

Search Terms:
Artificial satellites
Astronautics
Astronautics and civilization
Budget — United States
Manned space flight
Outer space — Exploration
Space law
Space stations
United States — Economic policy
United States — Social policy

The search terms listed above may also be used for online commercial access to Library of Congress bibliographic records.

Journal Articles

Citations to journal articles and other materials about space can be found in a number of printed indexes and online bibliographic databases. The materials covered by the printed indexes are briefly described here and the appropriate search terms are also listed.

Online bibliographic databases enable the researcher to locate citations to journal articles and other materials quickly by using a computer terminal to search a machine-readable file. Online databases allow the researcher to combine search terms in ways that are impossible in a printed index or library catalog and to simultaneously search material that would be contained in printed index volumes covering several years. The availability of various indexes online is indicated in the description of the tools.

Magazine Index. *Magazine Index* provides citations to materials in hundreds of popular magazines, focusing on coverage of current affairs, leisure time activities, arts, sports, and science and technology. The *Index* is available online commercially.

Search Terms:
Artificial satellites
Astronautical research
Astronautics
Astronautics and state
Budget — planning
Space colonies
Space flight
Space sciences
Space shuttles
Space weapons

Public Affairs Information Service Bulletin (PAIS). *PAIS* is a subject index of books, pamphlets, government publications, reports of public and private agencies, and periodical articles relating to economic and social conditions, public administration, and international relations. *PAIS* is available online commercially.

Search Terms:
Budget, Government
Satellites, Artificial
Space flight
Space, outer
Space research
Space stations
Space technology
United States — Economic policy
United States — Social policy

Readers' Guide to Periodical Literature. The *Readers' Guide* is an author/subject index to periodicals of general interest published in the United States.

Search Terms:
Artificial satellites
Budget
Space colonies
Space flight
Space research

Business Periodicals Index. *Business Periodicals Index* is a subject index to articles appearing in English language business periodicals. The *Index* is issued monthly and cumulated quarterly and annually.

Search Terms:
Astronautics
Budget
Program budgeting
Satellites, Artificial
Space flight
Space research
Space vehicles

Legislative Information

Congressional activities on space issues may be monitored by searching the following printed publications.

Congressional Record. The *Congressional Record* provides an edited transcript of the activities on the floor of the House and the Senate. It is published each day Congress is in session. Subject and name indexes are published biweekly and cumulated annually.

Search Terms:
Budget of the United States
National Aeronautics and Space Administration
Space policy
Space program
Space sciences

Congressional Record Abstract Files. The *Congressional Record Abstract Files* (CR) contain abstracts of material in the *Congressional Record* from the 94th Congress, 2d session to the present. A typical entry includes the abstract, bill numbers, indexing terms, and page number references to the full text of the *Congressional*

Record, and the date of the *Record*. These files have full-text retrieval capabilities, making it possible for researchers to formulate their own search terms in addition to using terms that are part of a controlled searching vocabulary. The CR files are commercially available to the general public.

Search Terms:
Artificial satellites
Astronautics
Space law
Space policy
Space sciences

Bills and Resolutions

Congressional Quarterly Weekly Report. *Congressional Quarterly Weekly Report* provides current information on congressional activities, the progress of major bills, and background information on major policy issues. Important recent articles are indexed on the back cover of each issue. Consult this index under the heading "Budget" and "Defense." A quarterly and an annual index are also issued. Congressional Quarterly also publishes an annual publication that cumulates material appearing in the weekly reports during a year. This publication is entitled *CQ Almanac*. *Congressional Quarterly Weekly Report* is available online through the *NEXIS* library.

Search Terms:
Appropriations
Budget
Defense
Foreign policy

Congressional Quarterly Almanac. See description above.

Search Terms:
Budget, U.S.
Missiles [for ASAT]
National Aeronautics and Space Administration
Satellites
Space and space programs
Space policy

National Journal. *National Journal* provides information on important executive branch and congressional actions. In addition to the annual index, the back cover of each issue also contains a brief index to recent articles. Consult this index under the headings "Defense" and "Budget."

Search Terms:

Economy, domestic

National Aeronautics and Space Administration

Digest of Public General Bills and Resolutions. The *Digest* summarizes the essential features of public bills and resolutions and changes made in them during the legislative process. The *Digest* is published during each session of Congress in two cumulative issues and a final issue at the conclusion of the session provides subject indexes.

Search Terms:

Economic policies and conditions

Public finance and budgets

Space
   Artificial satellites
   Communication satellites
   Space policy

Major Legislation of the Congress (MLC). The *MLC* provides summaries of selected major legislation arranged by subject. It includes background on the issues and information on the content and status of major bills affecting that issue. The publication may be examined at a government depository library or purchased from the Government Printing Office. Search under the headings "Space issues" in the table of contents.

Search Terms:

Budget and government spending

National defense and security

Science and technology

Congressional Publications

CIS Index. (Index to the Publications of the United States Congress) The *CIS Index*, produced by the Congressional Information Service, abstracts all congressional publications with the exception of the *Congressional Record*. The *Index* is published monthly and cumulated quarterly and annually. Each issue of the *Index* is divided into index and abstract portions. The *Index* is commercially available online.

Search Terms:

Astronautics

Budget of the U.S.

Communication satellites

International cooperation in astronautics

Space commercialization

Space programs

Space research

Space shuttle

Space stations

Space weapons

Copies of recently issued hearings and committee prints should be requested directly from the issuing committee. Congressional hearings and committee prints may also be found in the collections of government depository libraries.

Government Publications

Monthly Catalog of United States Government Publications. The *Monthly Catalog* lists documents issued by all branches of the federal government. The catalog has monthly, semiannual, and annual indexes arranged by author, title, subject, keywords, and series/report title. The *Monthly Catalog* is commercially available online.

Search Terms:

Headings starting with the word Astronautics

Headings starting with the words Artificial satellites

Headings starting with the word Budget

Headings starting with the word Space

Weekly Compilation of Presidential Documents. The *Weekly Compilation of Presidential Documents* contains statements, messages, and other Presidential materials released by the White House during the preceding week. The *Weekly Compilation* has weekly, quarterly, and annual indexes.

Search Terms:

Arms and munitions

Budget, Federal

Outer-space weapons

Space program

Newspaper Articles

The following indexes may be used to locate newspaper articles on space issues.

New York Times Index. The *New York Times Index* provides extensive abstracts for articles appearing in the *New York Times*.

Search Terms:

Astronautics

Budgets and budgeting

Satellites

Space

Space weapons

United States — Finances — Budgets and budgeting

Bell & Howell Newspaper Indexes. The *Bell & Howell Newspaper Indexes* list articles appearing in the *Chicago Tribune, Chicago Sun-Times, Denver Post, Detroit News, Houston Post, Los Angeles Times, New Orleans Times-Picayune, San Francisco Chronicle,* and *Washington Post.*

Search Terms:

Artificial satellites

Space (Outer)

Space exploration

Space stations

Space vehicles

United States Govt. — Budget

Official Washington Post Index. The *Index* provides access to all substantial newsworthy items in this paper.

Search Terms:

Artificial satellites

Astronautics

Budget — United States

Reusable space vehicles

Spaceships

Space stations

National Newspaper Index. *National Newspaper Index*, produced by Information Access Corporation, is available online as part of the Lockheed Dialog system, and provides front-page to back-page indexing on current affairs topics in the *Christian Science Monitor, New York Times, Wall Street Journal, Los Angeles Times,* and the *Washington Post.*

Nexis. The *NEXIS* online library provides access to wire service articles from the Associated Press, United Press International, and Reuters, articles from the *Washington Post* and journal articles. The journals indexed include *Newsweek* and *U.S. News & World Report.* In addition to providing citations and abstracts of the materials included in the data base, *NEXIS* makes the full text of the articles available on-line. *NEXIS* also provides access to the *New York Times Information Bank*, which is a current affairs database containing citations to the *New York Times* and many other newspapers and journals.

Newssearch. *Newssearch* is the daily update of *Magazine Index*, *National Newspaper Index*, and *Legal Resources Index* in the Lockheed Dialog system. It provides front-page to back-page indexing of the *Christian Science Monitor*, *Wall Street Journal*, and *New York Times*, as well as popular magazines, law journals, and legal newspapers.

F. Other Sources

Information may also be obtained through interviews and correspondence. The answers to the three questions in the inset will suggest persons with whom the advocate should seek an interview or correspondence.

Caution: Interviews and correspondence will provide both *leads* to evidence and evidence that is *admissible* in the debate. It is important to know the distinction.

1. Interviews. Interviews with subject-matter experts are often very valuable sources of information. The value of any interview depends to a considerable extent on our advance preparation; carefully planned preliminary research will enable us to ask meaningful questions. The student debater is in an excellent position to secure interviews with faculty members, and often interviews can be arranged with members of Congress, business executives, labor leaders, and others who have special knowledge of the subject of the debate proposition.

Consider a hypothetical case: In the course of an interview with Dr. Hamilton, an economics professor on your campus, you might ask about a study that your opponents often cited and that you found particularly difficult to refute. If Dr. Hamilton replies "The Back Bay Study is seriously flawed because they failed to consider...," you have a *lead*. You can't quote Dr. Hamilton's statement in a debate because, within the limitations of academic debate, you cannot prove you are quoting this professor accurately. At the first opportune moment, ask Dr. Hamilton "How can we document the flaws in this study?" If Dr. Hamilton replies by citing a scholarly article in one of the economic journals, and if your examination of the article provides a detailed statement of the flaws in the Back Bay Study, you are covered. By citing the article to which the economics professor gave you a *lead*, you now have evidence that is *admissible* in the debate.

There are many other important interviews the advocate can study. Radio and television stations often present interviews with national or world figures on problems of contemporary importance ("Meet the Press," "This Week," "Face the Nation," and "Firing Line" are examples). Magazines also often publish interviews in which prominent persons are quizzed about important problems; these can serve as important sources of information. Note that the same distinction between leads and admissible evidence applies here. An interview in a magazine is clearly admissible evidence; it is available in the public record and may be used without any question on that score.

However, your recollection of what the Secretary of the Treasury said on "Meet the Press" last Sunday is just that—your recollection. As such it constitutes a lead and nothing more. Of course, if the Monday newspapers quote the Secretary's statement, the problem is solved. Otherwise you must request a transcript of the program, and you cannot use the evidence until the transcript arrives. In intercollegiate debate, convention wisely requires that the advocate must document evidence from sources available in the public domain.

2. Correspondence. Correspondence is often a fruitful source of information. A helpful starting point in the search for information is the list of associations and societies in the United States published in the *World Almanac*. Hundreds of organizations are listed, ranging from "Abolish Capital Punishment, American League to" through "Zoologists, American Society of." Most of these organizations and other special-interest groups are willing to answer thoughtful letters asking intelligent questions in the area of their concern.

Often advocates will discover organizations that strongly support or oppose the proposition under consideration. Some of these maintain elaborate propaganda agencies. Through correspondence, advocates can often obtain press releases, special papers, data sheets, pamphlets, booklets, and other materials not ordinarily available through libraries. Here, too, it is important to note the distinction between a lead and admissible evidence. For example, let us suppose that, in response to your request for a transcript of the House Hearings on Unemployment, your representative not only sends you the Hearings but adds a personal note stating "I feel these Hearings are unnecessarily gloomy. My view is that we will see a substantial drop in unemployment beginning in the next quarter." The Hearings, of course, are admissible evidence. The letter is not because, within the limitations of academic debate, it is impossible to authenticate the letter. It is, however, a valuable lead. Phone your representative immediately and ask whether the prediction can be documented. If your representative refers you to a think-tank study that was published recently and has gone almost unnoticed in the press, you may—when you get a copy of the study—have valuable admissible evidence.

III. Reading with a Purpose

Advocates can make brainstorming work by preparing a carefully drafted outline of the ideas and sources suggested in brainstorming. From this list, they should develop a selected bibliography for use in research and a selected list of publications for monitoring. While doing research and monitoring, they can revise and refine the bibliography and list of monitored publications. This process of brainstorming, research, and revising will continue until the first debate, which will often trigger further brainstorming and research that will continue as long as the proposition is debated.

When students are asked to monitor the daily press or weekly newsmagazines, they sometimes protest: "But I don't have time to read all those newspapers and magazines." Perhaps they do not have time to read an entire newspaper every day; but when they read for the purpose of finding information on a specific problem, they are not asked to read an entire newspaper. It takes only a few minutes to scan the bulky *New York Times* to determine whether it contains an article on inflation, unemployment, population stabilization, or an international conflict.

IV. Reading Critically

More literature is probably available on any contemporary, controversial problem than advocates can possibly read in the time available. Research, then, must be planned for both breadth and discrimination, so that time is used efficiently. Advocates must seek out sources representative of the various points of view related to the problem in order to understand possible lines of argument. Since much writing on any contemporary problem is likely to be a restatement of other writings, or a highly superficial treatment, discriminating advocates will seek out original sources, articles in scholarly or professional journals, writings by qualified authorities, and reports by competent and objective persons, giving preference to sources with established reputations for accuracy.

An article on nuclear weapons appearing in the *Bulletin of the Atomic Scientists*, for example, is more likely to contain accurate and significant information than is an article on the same subject in the Sunday supplement of a local newspaper. The full text of the Secretary of State's speech on a foreign policy problem may contain some carefully phrased qualifications that are omitted in the brief summary appearing in a newsmagazine.

Advocates cannot read everything written about the problem. They must be critical in their reading to select representative, authoritative, accurate, and significant material for careful, detailed study.

V. Recording Materials

At the start of the exploration of a problem, advocates will find it desirable to adopt a systematic method of recording materials so they may readily use the information assembled from many different sources.

Candidates for the Presidency and other major political offices have developed an effective solution to this problem. They have scores of thousands of items of information from their own speeches, articles, and newspaper interviews and those of their opponents fed into a computer. These data are so organized that in seconds the computer can produce all of the candidate's, or a selected opponent's, statements on a specific subject on a printout. Such data files, once so expensive that they were a rarity, are now inexpensive and commonplace among college debaters and, indeed, among all serious advocates.

Advocates may use any method — 3 × 5 cards, 8½ × 11 sheets, material assembled in steel filing cabinets, or in computer data files, and so on — that their needs require and their resources permit. Many advocates find that they must develop a portable library they can take with them on the campaign plane or into the boardroom, the courtroom, or the classroom.

Intercollegiate debaters have evolved a successful method of recording materials by using thousands of 3 × 5 or 4 × 6 file cards, assembled in file boxes carried in sturdy sample cases. Although the advocate will use only a relatively few cards in any one debate, experienced NDT debaters find it desirable to have thousands of pieces of information immediately available to meet the possible arguments of their opponents. The file is usually supplemented by one or two attaché cases in which the debater carries bulkier material. Rather than copying lengthy material, the advocate often finds it desirable to clip a table or a statement from a newspaper or magazine article. These sheets are often carried in lightweight transparent plastic jackets to protect them from wear and tear. Sometimes it is desirable to have available the full text of key Senate committee hearings, a particularly authoritative book, or other frequently cited documents. CEDA debate places a lesser premium on bulk of evidence, and CEDA debaters typically carry less impedimentia. Nonetheless they must develop an efficient method of transporting a considerable body of evidence. How much evidence does one need in applied debating? The answer is: whatever it takes to win your argument. In a class debate a few dozen well-chosen evidence cards may be sufficient. Some lawsuits have required literally truckloads of evidence. Most advocates prefer to have too much rather than not enough evidence available to them. In academic debate, if some little-used evidence becomes critical, you must either have it with you or lose whatever issue the evidence might win for you if it were available. In applied debate you might — but it's only a slim chance — be able to persuade the court or stockholders meeting to adjourn while you send an assistant across town, or across the country, to recover little-used, but now crucial evidence that you left behind.

While reading source material, advocates should have at hand a supply of cards on which to record (1) all information that may help in supporting their stand on the proposition and (2) all information that may be of help to opponents. They should record the information shown on the annotated sample card (*see inset*).

If advocates record only one piece of information on each card, they will be able to handle the material more flexibly. Such flexibility will be an asset when they organize their material. The sample card (page 84) shows a convenient method of recording information.

If several advocates are working together — as a college debating team, members of a law firm, or a group of congressmen — the task of exploring the problem may be divided, with each member of the group being assigned the responsibility of covering thoroughly a certain segment of the source material. Under this system the information recorded by each member is pooled in a computer data file. Although executives and attorneys often delegate much of the "spadework" to secretaries or law clerks, they often find, as advocates, they must do much of the research personally. Only the person who actually presents the case can fully appreciate the implications of certain information and determine which avenues of exploration must be more fully developed. A story, which just might be true, is told of an American history professor who specialized in Lincoln and who for years had his graduate assistants enter every known fact of Lincoln's life into a computer file. When the time came for the professor to demonstrate his awesome data file to his colleagues, he invited them to ask any question about any event in Lincoln's life. One colleague asked, "When was Lincoln

Sample Evidence Card

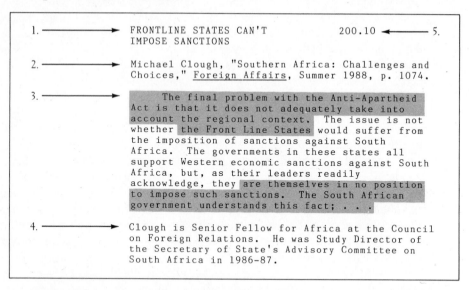

1. ──────▶ FRONTLINE STATES CAN'T   200.10 ◀──── 5.
IMPOSE SANCTIONS

2. ──────▶ Michael Clough, "Southern Africa: Challenges and Choices," <u>Foreign Affairs</u>, Summer 1988, p. 1074.

3. ──────▶   The final problem with the Anti-Apartheid Act is that it does not adequately take into account the regional context. The issue is not whether the Front Line States would suffer from the imposition of sanctions against South Africa. The governments in these states all support Western economic sanctions against South Africa, but, as their leaders readily acknowledge, they are themselves in no position to impose such sanctions. The South African government understands this fact; . . .

4. ──────▶ Clough is Senior Fellow for Africa at the Council on Foreign Relations. He was Study Director of the Secretary of State's Advisory Committee on South Africa in 1986-87.

1. **Subject Heading** (This heading will aid advocates when they later organize their material.)

2. **Statement of the Source of Information** This statement should include the title of the publication, the name of the author if known, the publisher, the page number, the date of publication, and the date of the information if it is different from the date of publication.

killed?" The professor smiled benignly as he entered this obviously "softball" query. No answer was forthcoming. The computer had hundreds of items on Lincoln's assassination but not one on Lincoln's killing; no one had programmed the computer to treat assassination as equal to killing.

The more important a message, the more intensive must exploration of the problem be. Presidential candidates must be knowledgeable on a wide variety of subjects. From the "kitchen cabinets" and "brain trusts" of earlier times, they have now developed vast staffs of researchers, speech writers, and subject-matter experts to brief them on every potential issue and to develop position papers on every potential problem. A large staff obviously enables the advocate to cover more ground. The method of exploring the problem, however, is the same for the student debater and the Presidential candidate.

It must be noted that a speaker who uses a piece of evidence must accept full responsibility for it. Thus, while much of the "nitty gritty" research may be done by a law clerk, a justice of the Supreme Court—and not the clerk—is responsible for what is said in the justice's opinion. Consequently, whenever an advocate finds an

3. Statement of Desired Information A verbatim quotation of the source material is always preferred. It is permissible to omit irrelevant material by ellipsis (. . .) or to paraphrase. The use of ellipsis or paraphrase must always be indicated when the information is recorded and must always be acknowledged when the information is presented; and the advocate must be careful to preserve the intention of the source quoted. Material to be emphasized may be highlighted by marking it with a yellow felt-tip marker.

4. Relevant Supplementary Information Sometimes the value of the material is enhanced by supplementary information. Consequently, the advocate may wish to include some information on the author's qualifications, the nature of the organization publishing the material, or other significant details. When an author is quoted only a few times it is usually most convenient to include this information on each card. When there are many citations from the same author, some debaters prefer to prepare a master bibliography section for their files and record the information once, there, rather than repeat it many times on multiple cards.

5. A Quick Retrieval Number Each card should be assigned a number so that the advocate may classify and organize the cards in a manner that permits quick retrieval. (See Section VI, "Organizing Materials.") Thus cards may be quickly located and pulled from the file for use in a debate. The retrieval number also permits the quick and accurate refiling of the cards after the debate so that they may be ready for use again in the future.

---

important piece of evidence that has come from someone else, he or she should, for both ethical and practical reasons, go back to the original source and verify the quotation.

Consider the case of a debater arguing the "comprehensive health care" proposition. He came across a card, researched by a colleague, that quoted an excellent source as saying:

> The AFL–CIO and Senator Kennedy have been outspoken in condemnation of the United States as being listed as fifteenth or sixteenth in the infant mortality tables as compared to such other nations as Sweden, Denmark, France, England, etc.

Without verifying the quotation, he used this apparently "devastating" evidence to indict American health care. Imagine his embarrassment when his better-prepared opponent turned to the original source and read the next two sentences:

> However, as the Medical Year Book of the World Health Organization points out, the figures on which these statistics are based are not truly comparable. In many European countries an infant mortality is recorded as a stillborn child if the infant did not survive for as much as five days and hence the death does not appear in the infant mortality tables.

VI. **Organizing Materials**

Advocates must not only have a wealth of information, but that information must be instantly available to them. The method used by intercollegiate debaters will be considered here; however, it may be adapted to any type of advocacy.

As a first step the advocate should classify information cards as *affirmative, first negative,* or *second negative,* indicating these classifications by an abbreviation placed on each card or by different colors of cards.

The second step is to classify the cards according to the *issues* the advocate has developed. The affirmative file will consist of the issues necessary to develop the affirmative case together with the evidence necessary to establish the case in the first affirmative speech and to defend and extend the case in the second affirmative speech. The first negative file contains the issues and evidence necessary to attack the affirmative's case. The second negative file, in a policy debate, will contain the issues and evidence necessary to attack the affirmative's plan; in a value debate the second negative file will contain the issues and evidence necessary to establish the undesirable consequences of adopting the resolution. (See "Basic CEDA Speaker Responsibilities" in Chapters 12 and 13.)

A system of indexing the file cards should be developed to enable the advocate to locate any card quickly. At the beginning of a season of debating "Resolved: That the federal government should establish a national program of public work for the unemployed," an affirmative team used the following main divisions in preparing their affirmative file:

Affirmative

A 100   Rationale
A 200   Definitions
A 300   Need
A 310   Unemployment harmful
A 320   Unemployment increasing
A 330   Unmet need for public work
A 400   Inherency
A 500   Plan
A 600   Advantages
A 700   Answers to negative attacks
A 800   Unemployment statistics
A 900   Qualifications of authorities

As the advocates built their case, they developed further refinements for their classifications of information cards. Under "Unemployment harmful," for instance, the debaters quickly established subheadings of "A 310.1 Harm to the individual," "A 310.2 Harm to families," "A 310.3 Harm to society," "A 310.4 Harm to economy." This decimal system of organizing materials makes it convenient for advocates to add new information to their file.

A negative team preparing to debate the "comprehensive medical care" proposition used the following main divisions to organize their files:

First Negative

1N 100   Rationale
1N 200   Not topical
1N 300   Other goals more important
1N 400   Quality of medical care satisfactory
1N 500   Method of delivering medical care satisfactory
1N 600   Minor repairs

Second Negative

2N 100   Plan not workable
2N 200   Plan not achieve advantages
       2N 210   Not remove economic barrier
       2N 220   Not remove fear barrier
       2N 230   Not remove ignorance barrier
       2N 240   Not remove transportation barrier
       2N 250   Not provide physicians in ghettos or rural areas
2N 300   Disadvantages

As with the affirmative file just considered, these first drafts of negative files were soon expanded by the debaters. Here too the decimal system makes it convenient for the advocates to add new information and further refine their files.

The objective is to provide as many subheadings as are necessary to make essential information instantly available. Index cards may be used to indicate subdivisions, and colored metal "flags" may be used to indicate cards with particularly important information. While the examples shown here are drawn from the files of student debaters, it is obvious that any advocate who must organize a large mass of data must develop some comparable system.

In some cases advocates will find that a given piece of information might appropriately be placed under more than one classification. Multiple cards recording the same information should be prepared and inserted in the proper places, with a cross-reference to other locations to avoid repetition.

Careful exploration of the problem is essential to intelligent advocacy. Reasonable and prudent people will give little time and less credence to the person who "doesn't know what he's talking about." Debaters who thoroughly study the appropriate sources of information, who organize their research effectively, who read purposefully and critically, who record materials accurately, and who organize them effectively are taking an important step toward responsible and effective advocacy. Only well-prepared advocates can hope to gain and hold the attention of a critical audience, contend against well-informed opposition, and secure a decision from reasonable and prudent people.

Exercises

1. Find the answers to each of the following questions and indicate the source of your information:
   a. What percentage of college students are black? Hispanic? Asian?
   b. What percentage of college and university faculty members are women?
   c. What percentage of the current federal budget is spent on defense? On welfare?
   d. Define poverty.
   e. How has the value of the dollar changed since one year ago? Since five years ago? Since ten years ago?
   f. What are the qualifications of Milton Friedman to speak on economic matters?
   g. How many nuclear power reactors are there in the United States?
   h. How much does pollution cost?
   i. How many abortions were performed in the United States last year?
   j. How much oil did the United States import last year? How much oil did the United States export?
   k. How much military aid has the United States given to Israel?

2. Select a proposition that may be used for the following exercises and for later classroom debates:
   a. Prepare a list of general references useful in exploring this specific problem.
   b. Prepare a list of special references useful in exploring this specific problem.
   c. Hold a brainstorming session in class on this proposition, and record the ideas suggested. At the next meeting of the class evaluate the ideas. Did the ideas suggested in the brainstorming session "trigger" any additional ideas? What percentage of the ideas had practical value?
   d. Prepare a number of evidence cards (the number to be specified by your instructor) on this specific problem.
   e. Organize the evidence cards according to a system that will provide for the effective use of this information in a debate.

6

Evidence

Evidence is the raw material of argumentation. It consists of facts, opinions, and objects that are used to generate proof. The advocate brings together the raw materials and, by the process of reasoning, produces new conclusions.

We cannot undertake critical thinking without a sound basis of evidence. The use of evidence is not limited to debates — although debates give us an excellent means of learning about evidence. Even in unstructured disputes in informal settings we must necessarily seek out evidence. Who won the first Heisman trophy? Just what does your warranty cover? I can't believe the campus paper said that! These and countless other matters are best settled by referring to the appropriate evidence.

The impact that the evidence will have on the decision renderers will depend on their perceptions and values. In intercollegiate debate, the judge is expected to evaluate evidence coolly and dispassionately, setting aside any preconceived notions and weighing the data critically. This is a good model for us to follow when we are called on to make important decisions. Yet we must recognize that in almost any situation the judge or the audience will be influenced by the *source* of the message (that is, the advocate or the publication the advocate quotes), the *message* itself, the *channel* (for example, face-to-face communication, radio or television, and so on), and as *receiver* (that is, the receiver's values and perceptions).

As we saw earlier, we probably could, after some debate, establish that the unemployment rate in the United States is x percent. Once that fact was established, we would proceed to the more difficult matter of establishing that x percent was an acceptable or unacceptable rate of unemployment. The college professor serving as debate judge would probably feel empathy for the scholarly opinion of a professor of economics. An unemployed person in the audience might attach most weight to a labor leader's view, while a banker in the audience might be most impressed by a statement from the chairperson of the Federal Reserve Board; and a student in the audience might evaluate the evidence on the basis of personal experience — is unemployment a remote concept considered only in economics classes, or was one of the student's parents just laid off at the auto plant?

In previous chapters we considered how advocates assemble and organize information as they analyze and explore the problem. In this chapter we will consider the evidence itself, and in the next chapter we will consider tests to be applied to evidence. Later chapters will consider the composition of the case (Chapter 15) and delivery of the case (Chapter 16), thus gaining an understanding of the interrelationship of evidence with source, message, channel, and receiver. By understanding evidence and its interrelation with communication, we will be in a better position to evaluate arguments presented for our decision or to construct good reasons to serve as justification for the decisions we desire to secure from others.

Evidence may be classified as direct or presumptive. *Direct evidence* is evidence that tends to show the existence of a fact in question without the intervention of the proof of any other fact. In a debate on "tax sharing," the claim that "forty-four states now have state income taxes" could be established or refuted by reference to the *World Almanac* or some other reliable source. In argument, direct evidence is most frequently used to establish supporting contentions rather than to prove the proposition itself. If irrefutable evidence existed in proof of the proposition, there would be no point in debating it. At one time, for example, the proposition "Resolved: That the United States can land men on the moon" was debatable. Today there is simply no point in debating the proposition.

Presumptive evidence, or indirect or circumstantial evidence, is evidence that tends to show the existence of a fact in question by proof of another fact or other facts from which the fact in question may be inferred. In debates on the "hazardous waste" proposition students had many occasions to argue presumptive evidence. When someone lived (usually unknowingly at the time) near a site where hazardous waste had been buried and contracted cancer years later, could it be presumed that the hazardous waste was the cause of the cancer? Many civil suits turned on this issue and many state legislatures enacted laws addressing this question. In many cases the courts ruled that the presumption was strong enough to justify a verdict for the plaintiff.

As a practical matter, much time and effort is spent on presumptive evidence. "But you can't convict a person on circumstantial evidence!" students sometimes protest. On the contrary — many people are convicted on circumstantial evidence. If there is strong direct evidence of the guilt of the accused, the case seldom comes to trial; under such circumstances the accused usually finds it advisable to "plea bargain" (plead guilty to a lesser charge in exchange for a lighter sentence).

I. Sources of Evidence

Evidence is introduced into an argument from various sources. By understanding the uses and limitations of the sources of evidence, we will be more discerning in reaching our own decisions or in developing arguments for the decision of others.

A. Judicial Notice

Judicial notice is the quickest, simplest, and easiest way of introducing evidence into an argument. *Judicial notice* (the term is borrowed from the law courts) is the process whereby certain evidence may be introduced without the necessity of substantiating it.

In almost any argument, it is necessary to refer to various matters of common knowledge, in order to lay the foundation for other evidence to be introduced later and to set the argument in its proper context. Certain matters, which we might reasonably expect any well-informed person to know, may be presented as evidence simply by referring to them. Certain cautions, however, must be observed in the use of judicial notice.

1. The evidence must be introduced. Advocates cannot expect those who render the decision to build a case for them; they cannot plead "But I thought everybody knew that." If it is important to know certain evidence in order to understand the case, then the advocate must introduce that evidence. The Supreme Court summed up this principle, which applies to legal pleadings as well as other types of argumentation, when it ruled: "A judge sees only with judicial eyes and knows nothing respecting any particular case of which he is not informed judicially."

2. The evidence must be well known. The instrument of judicial notice may be used only for those matters that are really common knowledge. When the "energy" proposition was debated, the existence of an oil shortage could be established by judicial notice; the extent of the shortage was another matter, however. To establish this, the debater had to produce evidence that would very likely be attacked with conflicting evidence. If advocates introduce little-known evidence merely by judicial notice, they may anticipate that there will be some doubt in the minds of those who render the decision. The Supreme Court made this sound principle of argumentation a part of our legal structure when it ruled: "Courts should take care that requisite notoriety exists concerning the matters on which they take judicial notice, and every reasonable doubt upon the subject should be resolved in the negative." A "perfect example" of judicial notice is considered in Chapter 8, Section II-E. Note that well-known evidence is often perishable. For example, the date of Pearl Harbor is burned indelibly in the minds of your grandparents; the assassination of President Kennedy is firmly implanted in the minds of your parents. They can tell you where they were, who they were with, and what they were doing at the time they learned of these events. You may, or may not, remember the dates or any details of these events from reading about them in school years after they occurred.

3. The evidence may be refuted. Evidence offered by judicial notice is usually presented in the expectation that it will be accepted without question by the opposition. Such evidence, like all evidence, is subject to possible refutation. In debates on "right-to-work" laws, some affirmative debaters sought to establish by judicial notice that "there is widespread corruption in labor unions." Negative debaters, however, usually refused to allow this claim and introduced evidence designed to refute it.

In presenting evidence through judicial notice, the advocates ask, in effect, that their opponents and those rendering the decision suspend the tests of evidence and accept their assertion as an established fact not requiring proof. The opposing advocates allow such evidence to go unchallenged at their peril. If the evidence actually is irrefutable, there is no point in raising an objection. If the evidence is refutable and the opposing advocates fail to raise an objection, then they have only themselves to blame if those who render the decision accept the evidence as an established fact.

The use of judicial notice is not uncommon in academic debate. It is most likely to be found toward the end of the academic year, when there is a certain body of evidence and argument related to the current national debate proposition that has become common knowledge to "everybody" in the forensic community. In these circumstances judicial notice will be effective if (1) the evidence is so well known to the opposing team that it will concede the point by failing to attempt to refute it and (2) the evidence is so well known to the judge, or judges, that it will weigh in the decision as if it were fully developed rather than merely asserted.

Judicial notice is not limited to the courtroom or academic debate, however. It may be used in any circumstances where the evidence is, in fact, well known to those who render the decision. Thus an executive at a board meeting might argue "We can't use this incentive plan—remember Ernst and Whinney's report on how it would affect our tax situation?" If the report is well known to the board, and all accept its conclusion that the incentive plan would hurt the company's tax position, the proposal may well be defeated by this brief use of judicial notice.

The advocate must remember that what is well known to the "in-group" may be unfamiliar to others. Thus, the use of a critical piece of evidence by judicial notice might be devastating in the final round of a major tournament and limply ineffective in an exhibition debate before a Kiwanis Club. The brief reminder that might clinch an argument before knowledgeable board members might be meaningless at a stockholders' meeting; the stockholders of a large corporation could not be expected to be familiar with the details of every report submitted to the board of directors.

B. Public Records

Public records are often used as a source of evidence. Indeed, on many matters they are the most important evidence, since private individuals or organizations lack the authority or resources to assemble much of the evidence that can be found only in public records. Public records include all documents compiled or issued by or with the approval of any governmental agency. In this category are such diverse materials as the *Congressional Record*, federal and state statute books, birth certificates, deeds, reports of Congressional hearings, and the minutes of a town meeting. Official records are usually highly regarded. The fact that they are public records, however, does not mean that they should be accepted uncritically. A public record containing the report of a Congressional committee might be the best possible source of information on the amount of money the United States spent on direct economic aid to foreign countries in a certain year, since a committee has power to compel officials to produce their records and testify under oath. The same report might contain the testimony of witnesses on the value of this economic aid. Their testimony would not necessarily be the best possible expert opinion on that subject, however. They might be great and impartial authorities, or they might be highly prejudiced lobbyists.

C. Public Writings

Public writings, another frequently used source of evidence, include all written material, other than public records, made available to the general public. In this category are such diverse materials as the *Encyclopaedia Britannica* and the sensational scandal magazine, the college textbook and the campus humor magazine, the *World Almanac* and fiction, or a Brookings Institution report and an astrologer's chart. Some public writings command high prestige and are likely to be accepted readily; others are more likely to be disbelieved than believed. Obviously, the value of public writings varies tremendously.

D. Private Writings

Caution: Private writings and testimony of witnesses, like the interviews and correspondence considered in Chapter 5, Section II-F, will provide both *leads* to evidence and evidence that is *admissible* in the debate. As noted earlier, it is important that the advocate know the distinction.

Private writings include all written material prepared for private rather than public use. Some private writings are designed to become public records at a later date. Wills, for example, become public records when they are probated; contracts become public records if they are brought into court for adjudication. Any private writing may become a public record if it is included in the records of a court or a governmental agency, or it may become a public writing if it is made available to the general public. Most private writings, however, are prepared for a limited circulation among selected individuals. In this category are such diverse materials as a privately owned company's financial statement prepared by a certified public account, a student's class notes, a diary, or a personal letter.

Private writings may be carefully prepared documents designed to report events with great precision and to reflect carefully considered judgments, or they may be incomplete and studded with offhand comments or facetious remarks. Since private writings constitute an important source of evidence, care should be taken to determine who prepared the document and under what circumstances. It should be noted here that personal letters are not customarily introduced as evidence in academic debate. The reason may be that it is usually impossible to authenticate a personal letter within the limitations of an academic debate. Thus, if private writings become public writings, they are clearly admissible in the form of public writings. If they remain private writings, they are leads that may guide one to admissible evidence.

E. Testimony of Witnesses

The testimony of witnesses is one of the most common sources of evidence. Testimony given in court or before a governmental body is usually presented under oath and is subject to the penalties of perjury or contempt. Testimony outside the courtroom is not subject to the same legal restrictions and is usually more informal: Management officials usually give testimony on the operation of their company at a stockholders' meeting; the president of a company may ask the plant superintendent for an oral report on the utility of a new machine; the freshman may ask a sophomore for advice on what courses to take. In fact, much of our day-to-day business and social activity is based on the testimony of witnesses. The value of such testimony may vary considerably. Clearly the testimony of a witness at a Congressional hearing is readily admissible by citing the hearings. The "testimony" of your political science professor in a classroom lecture is *not* admissible in academic debate; but it may constitute a valuable lead that will enable you to find admissible evidence.

F. Personal Inspection

When personal inspection is used as a source of evidence, something is presented for examination to the persons rendering the decision: The automobile salesperson may invite customers to lift the hood and inspect the motor; a stockbroker may show the financial statement of a company to a client; or a senator may bring a bag of groceries into the Senate chamber for use during a speech on inflation. The college student is frequently asked to perform personal inspection: The geology professor may offer a sample of rock for the inspection of the class; the economics professor may sketch a supply-and-demand curve on the blackboard; or the music professor may play a portion of a recording for a music appreciation class.

Personal inspection is frequently used in courtroom debates: Attorneys often show juries and judges the murder weapon, arrange for them to visit the scene of the crime, or show them the plaintiff's injuries. Evidence presented through personal inspection has been carefully selected and arranged by someone to support a particular argument; it must therefore be examined with care.

II.   Types of Evidence

A. Judicial or Extrajudicial Evidence

Evidence is usually classified as judicial or extrajudicial. *Extrajudicial evidence* is also known as "extralegal" or "incompetent" evidence. The word "incompetent" has no bad connotation when used in this sense; it merely means "not admissible in court." Extrajudicial evidence is used to satisfy persons about the facts requiring proof in any situation other than a legal proceeding and is subject only to the usual tests of evidence. *Judicial evidence*, also known as "legal" or "competent" evidence, is evidence that is admissible in court. Such evidence must satisfy not only the usual tests of evidence but also the various technical rules of legal evidence.

In legal proceedings, certain otherwise perfectly good evidence is excluded. For example, if we are trying to decide whether a certain man's testimony is trustworthy, we are interested in knowing whether or not he has a criminal record. Such evidence, however, is often excluded from courtroom debates. Thus, if someone says, "That evidence couldn't be admitted in court," the objection is irrelevant unless the debate actually is taking place in court.

B. Primary or Secondary Evidence

Evidence is often classified as primary or secondary. *Primary evidence* is the best evidence that the circumstances admit. It affords the greatest certainty of the matter in question; and it is original or firsthand evidence. *Secondary evidence* is evidence that falls short of this standard, since by its nature it suggests there is better evidence of the matter in question. Thus an examination of Chapters 6 and 7 of this book is *primary* evidence that this book contains two chapters on evidence; a friend's statement that this book contains two chapters on evidence is *secondary* evidence.

In debating the "law enforcement" proposition, students came across many newspaper and magazine stories that quoted the FBI's *Uniform Crime Reports* as reporting that the crime rate had gone up 16 percent that year. These sources were, of course, secondary evidence of the FBI's report. Thoughtful debaters checked the primary evidence, the FBI report itself. There they found the caution that the statistics should not be used for year-to-year comparisons. (One reason for this caution was that at the time this proposition was debated many police departments had just recently computerized their record keeping. The fact that they were much more efficient in counting and reporting crime was not in itself statistically valid evidence of any change in the number of crimes actually committed.) Many secondary sources omitted this caution, and debaters who depended on secondary evidence sustained embarrassing defeats at the hands of debaters who sought out the primary evidence.

Primary evidence is stronger than secondary evidence because there is less possibility of error. Secondary evidence is weaker than primary evidence because it does not derive its value solely from the credibility of the witness, but rests largely on the veracity and competence of others. In any argument the prudent advocate seeks to use primary evidence whenever possible.

C. Written or Unwritten Evidence

Written evidence is evidence supplied by writings of all kinds: books, newspapers, and magazines, as well as less frequently used types of writing such as roman numerals carved on the cornerstone of a building. *Unwritten evidence* includes both oral testimony and objects offered for personal inspection.

In arguments outside the courtroom, written evidence generally is given greater weight than oral evidence because it is easier to substantiate. In a recent intercollegiate debate, a negative speaker introduced unwritten, secondary evidence by saying:

> Last week I had the opportunity to talk with Senator _____ when he visited in my home town, and he told me that . . .

Then the negative debater quoted a statement strongly critical of the affirmative's position. An affirmative speaker replied to this by using written evidence:

> We have no way of knowing how accurately the negative quoted Senator _____ nor of knowing what the senator said in a private interview. However, we do have a record of the considered opinion of the senator on this subject as he expressed it in an article in the *New York Times Magazine* of last week when he stated . . .

The affirmative debater then quoted a carefully qualified statement that indicated only minor reservations about the affirmative's position. Which of the speakers quoted the senator correctly? Perhaps both. The senator may have changed his mind; or, more likely, the two statements represented the difference between an offhand comment and a considered opinion. In any event, the judge accepted the statement of the affirmative speaker, since he could better substantiate his evidence.

On the other hand, we often accept and act upon oral evidence even when it is hearsay. If a professor says to some students "Last night the dean told me that the president told him that the trustees have decided to raise the tuition next year," the students might well decide immediately that they will have to raise more money for next fall's tuition. As was noted earlier (in Chapter 5, Section II-F), while unwritten evidence is not used in academic debate, it may provide valuable leads to written evidence, which can be used in academic debate.

D. Real or Personal Evidence

Real evidence is furnished by objects placed on view or under inspection. In the courtroom, real evidence may consist of fingerprints, scars, or weapons. Outside the courtroom a farmer may be asked to inspect test plots in which different types of seed are used; a customer might be invited to taste a new grocery product; a student might be invited to examine a famous painting in a museum; or an executive might be asked to examine a new computer.

We are constantly offered pseudo or real evidence in the form of newspaper advertisements and television commercials. Vast sums of money are lavished on producing evidence designed to convince us to buy a product or vote for or against a candidate. Pictures of a car effortlessly speeding up a mountain road or of an opposition candidate caught at a particularly inept moment are offered as "real" evidence of the performance of the car or of the candidate's qualifications. It is important to realize that such "real" evidence is selected and prepared by someone. Consequently, if we hope to make a critical judgment about this evidence, we must apply the appropriate tests of evidence both to the evidence itself and to the persons who prepared it.

Personal evidence is evidence furnished by persons, and it may be in the form of oral or written testimony. The credibility we attach to personal evidence depends in large part on the competence and honesty we attribute to the person providing the testimony.

E. Lay or Expert Evidence

Evidence is usually classified as lay or expert. As a practical matter, however, it is often difficult to distinguish between the well-informed layperson and the expert. Representatives and senators, for example, may or may not be experts on the subjects they speak about. However, because their official position gives them unusual opportunities to acquire special knowledge on many subjects, they are often regarded as experts by popular audiences. The able intercollegiate debater who has spent an academic year in a superior forensic program studying a national intercollegiate debate proposition might be qualified as a minor expert on that proposition.

Lay evidence is provided by persons without any special training, knowledge, or experience in the matter under consideration. Such evidence is useful in areas that do not require special qualifications. In debates on "right-to-work" laws, the testimony of "rank-and-file" union members or managers of small businesses was often important. These people often had no special knowledge of law, economics, sociology, or even of unions generally. They were, however, able to give important evidence as to how certain union practices had affected them.

In general, the courts will allow laypersons to testify on matters of fact, but will not allow them to testify as to their opinion. This limitation may well be followed in argumentation outside the courtroom as well. Laypersons, assuming they meet the qualifications of a good witness, are usually competent to testify on a matter of fact they have observed; their opinion of the significance of the fact, however, is another matter. The testimony of a "rank-and-file" steelworker as to how many members of his or her local attended the meeting at which a strike vote was taken would be good evidence, assuming that the steelworker is an honest and competent person. His or her opinion about the effect of a steel strike on the national economy, however, cannot be considered as more valuable than that of any other layperson of comparable education and intelligence. Only an expert, in this case probably an economist, could give us a meaningful opinion.

Expert evidence is evidence provided by persons with special training, knowledge, or experience in the matter under consideration. In the courtroom, expert testimony is permitted only when the inference to be drawn requires something more than the equipment of everyday experience. This guideline, too, is a wise limitation to follow in argumentation outside the courtroom. Although the testimony of an expert is essential in certain matters, the expert should not be used unnecessarily.

The courts further require that the special competence of experts be established before they are allowed to offer opinion evidence. It is advisable to follow this practice in all argumentation. Remember that an expert is expert in certain areas only and that he or she is a layperson in all other areas.

The qualifications of a witness should be studied carefully before that person is accepted as an expert. The fact that persons are well known or that their views appear in print does not establish them as experts. Intercollegiate debaters are constantly required to distinguish between the expert and the pseudoexpert. Each year the national debate proposition deals with some subject of contemporary significance. A number of articles on this subject appear in the press. Some are thoughtful analyses written by experts; others are superficial treatments turned out under the pressure of a deadline by writers who may know less about the subject than the typical college debater.

"Argument from authority" Is a phrase sometimes used to indicate that expert opinion is presented to establish a contention in an argument. Expert opinion should be used only when a matter at issue cannot be established readily by other evidence. Intercollegiate debaters and others who cannot establish themselves as experts often find it advantageous to introduce the opinions of experts to sustain certain contentions. In debates on the "compulsory wage and price controls" proposition, some negative speakers contended that controls merely intensified inflationary pressures, whereas affirmative speakers maintained they were the solution to inflation. The judges in these debates had little basis for accepting the opinion of one college student in preference to that of another. Consequently, the debaters found it necessary to introduce as evidence the opinion of experts who commanded the respect of the judges.

In any matter likely to be the subject of a debate, there will probably be expert opinion on both sides. Economists will differ on the merits of a certain tax policy; physicians will differ on the merits of a certain drug; lawyers will differ in their opinion about whether or not a certain merger violates the antitrust laws; advertising people will differ on the merits of a certain advertising campaign. An important problem in both applied and academic debates is that of establishing a preponderance of expert opinion — not by simply marshaling *more* experts than the opposition but by using testimony from *better-qualified* experts whose opinions may be related directly to the matter at hand.

The scientific study is a form of expert evidence that advocates eagerly seek out in an effort to establish greater credibility for their claims. Arguments about the credibility of studies are often crucial to the outcome of a debate. Newell maintains that a *study* is unique

> in that we are provided not only with opinions (the conclusions of the study) but also the facts (observations/data) on which those opinions are based; we are provided not only facts but also with an explanation of how the observations were made; and we are provided not only statistics but also with an expert interpretation of the statistics. A study then is evidence which includes an argument for its own credibility. This unique combination gives a study the potential to "carry more weight," to be more conclusive and more credible than other types of evidence.[1]

Advocates who introduce studies into a debate must be prepared to give good reasons why the studies should be accepted; those whose case is harmed by the studies must be prepared to give good reasons why the studies should be rejected. Newell offers these recommendations:

> Reasonably, the person who introduces the study into the round needs to give some standard or warrant for the credibility of the study. Three major factors determine the extent of proof necessary: (1) the controversial nature of the study's conclusion, (2) the existence of counterstudies, and (3) the importance or controversy of the policy claim. The warrant may range anywhere from general qualification of the expertise of the researcher, to evidence from other sources proclaiming the study to be good or acceptable, to specific explanation and support for the external and internal validity.
>
> . . . The arguments indicting a study are generally of five types. In hierarchical order, according to persuasive power, they are: (1) counterstudies disprove, (2) the study is flawed — specific indictments by experts, (3) the study is flawed — general indictments by experts, (4) the study is flawed — specific indictments by the debater, and (5) general indictments by the debater. "The study is flawed" just means that something is wrong with either the internal or external validity.[2]

[1]Sara E. Newell, "The 'Study' as Evidence and Argument in Academic, Policy Debate," in *Proceedings of the Summer Conference on Argumentation*, ed. Jack Rhodes and Sara Newell (sponsored by the Speech Communication Association and the American Forensic Association) (privately published, 1980), p. 296.
[2]Ibid., p. 302.

F. Prearranged or Casual Evidence

Prearranged evidence is created for the specific purpose of recording certain information for possible future reference. Many public records and public writings are of this type. Political leaders often make an effort to get their views "on the record," so that at election time they will have evidence that they supported measures of interest to their constituents. The average person has a considerable amount of prearranged evidence: birth certificates, driver's licenses, marriage certificates, deeds to property, Social Security cards, insurance policies, receipts, canceled checks, contracts, military discharge papers, or a transcript of college records. Prearranged evidence is valuable because it is usually created near the time that the event in question took place; and, since it is intended for future reference, it is usually prepared with care. On the other hand, since this kind of evidence is *arranged*, it may be subject to the influence of those arranging it.

Casual evidence is created without any effort being made to create it and is not designed for possible future reference. When a newspaper photographer snapped a human-interest picture of a "good Samaritan" helping a motorist whose car had broken down and was blocking rush-hour traffic, he had no intention of creating evidence. It just happened to be a light news day, and the editor decided to run the picture with the names of the motorist and the good Samaritan together with a brief story about the traffic tie-up. Some months later that casual evidence became important evidence in a criminal trial. The good Samaritan was accused of bank robbery. The circumstantial evidence against the good Samaritan was strong; his car matched the description of the robber's car even to a similar dent on the left-rear fender, and his physical description matched that of the robber. The accused had no alibi; he could not remember where he had been at the time of the robbery four months earlier. These facts, together with other circumstances, made his future look very bleak until his attorney, doing research on an unrelated case, just happened to come across the newspaper story, which established that at the time of the robbery his client had been in a city a hundred miles away.

This casual evidence led to a prompt acquittal. Casual evidence is valuable because the party concerned did nothing to create the evidence. The accused did not know a photographer was coming to the scene of the traffic jam, and he did not ask him to take his picture or to publish it. As the accused did nothing to create the evidence, the jury was all the more ready to believe it was genuine and not a prepared alibi. The weakness of casual evidence is that its value is usually not known at the time it is created, often no effort is made to preserve it, and a later effort to recall events may be subject to uncertainty. In this case, it was just sheer luck that the picture appeared in the paper together with the accused's name and the fact that it was taken at the height of the morning rush hour on a particular day.

G. Negative Evidence

Negative evidence is the absence of evidence that might reasonably be expected to be found were the issue in question true. For example, if the name of a person cannot be found in an official list of graduates of your college, this absence of evidence is negative evidence that he or she did not graduate from your college. Negative evidence played an important part in at least one Presidential election. In 1884, a New York clergyman called the Democrats the party of "rum, Romanism, and rebellion" in a speech at a reception attended by Blaine, the Republican candidate. Blaine's failure to repudiate this statement was taken by many voters as negative evidence that he agreed with it. Some historians regard this as the critical turning point in the election in which Blaine was defeated and Cleveland elected.

Negative evidence was highly important in the investigations of the assassination of President Kennedy. Official investigations established that *no evidence* of a conspiracy existed. Yet rumors of conspiracies persist and have spawned many books, articles, and television programs. Is the absence of any evidence of a conspiracy proof that there was no conspiracy? Or is it proof that the investigators were not thorough enough?

Negative evidence must be introduced into the argument with care; advocates should claim negative evidence only when they are certain that there is an absence of the evidence in question.

Even if careful investigation establishes that the evidence is indeed missing, is it missing for the reason you claim? This difficulty of negative evidence can be illustrated by a case from World War II. Germany developed and stockpiled huge amounts of the deadly nerve gases Tabun, Sarin, and Soman.[3] German scientists who studied Allied scientific journals found no reference to these chemicals. Since this absence of any reference to these chemicals was exactly what one would expect to find as the result of efficient censorship, the Germans concluded that the Allies had discovered the gases and probably had large supplies on hand. The fear of retaliation apparently led the Germans to decide not to use their gases during the war. Actually the chemicals were not mentioned in the Allied journals simply because no Allied scientist had discovered the gases. Their existence was unknown until advancing Allied troops stumbled on the German supplies after VE-Day.

Fortunately, we are rarely faced with such complex tasks as confronted German wartime intelligence. A typical use of negative evidence in everyday affairs might be as follows. An executive receives an attractive opportunity to purchase some merchandise from an out-of-town firm. The price is very favorable, but he does not know the firm — will it really deliver merchandise of the quality claimed? The executive directs an assistant to look into the matter. The assistant calls the Better Business Bureau in the firm's city and inquires. The reply indicates that the firm has been doing business in that city for twenty-five years and that only six complaints have been received about the firm in the past year, with all adjusted to the satisfaction of the customers. The executive would probably take this lack of unsettled complaints as satisfactory negative evidence that the firm is reputable.

H. Evidence Aliunde

Evidence aliunde, also known as "extraneous" or "adminicular" evidence, is used to explain or clarify other evidence. Often the meaning or significance of evidence is not

---

[3]These compounds are designated GA, GB, and GD in the United States; their less volatile liquid counterparts are known as V-agents.

apparent upon the presentation of the evidence per se; therefore, that evidence must be explained by the presentation of other evidence.

In debates on free trade, some debaters introduced as expert evidence the opinion of certain economists that free trade would be beneficial because it would permit the operation of the principle of comparative advantage. Unless those who rendered the decision understood the principle of comparative advantage, this evidence was of little value until the debaters introduced additional evidence to explain the concept.

Evidence is used in extraordinarily complex combinations in argumentation. One piece of evidence may often be classified under several types. In a debate on the "increase exploration and/or development of space" proposition, one affirmative speaker offered the following evidence from *Time* magazine to establish an advantage:

> "One of the six crew members [of the aborted *Discovery* mission] is Charles Walker, 35, an engineer with McDonnell Douglas and the shuttle's first ambassador for private enterprise. Walker's in-flight task is to concoct a mystery drug for Johnson & Johnson, using a technique called electrophoresis, which in the zero gravity of space can separate biological compounds 700 times as efficiently as on earth. Judging by the many clues the principals have dropped, the substance *could be a one shot cure for diabetes.*"

The identification of the types of evidence represented by this statement will help us to analyze it. Obviously it is *written* evidence from a *public record*, that is, *Time*. Clearly, it is *secondary* evidence as *Time* isn't telling who the "principals" are. It *may* be *expert* evidence, as is suggested by the use of the word "principals"; but we don't know who made the statement or what the credentials of the principals are. It is probably *unwritten evidence*, "clues" tend to be "dropped" in off-the-record comments. Certainly, had the clues appeared in, say, *The New England Journal of Medicine*, *Time* would have cited such a prestigious source. This evidence in its current form is useless, as the affirmative debater who used it — just once — quickly found out. Clearly evidence aliunde is needed to clarify this evidence before it will have real impact in establishing the value of preparing biological compounds in space.

III. The Probative Force of Evidence

We are concerned not only with the sources and types of evidence but also with its *probative force*. Evidence may only partially substantiate a matter at issue, or it may be strong enough to justify the claim conclusively in the minds of those who render the decision. Baseball fans engaged in a pleasant disputation on the question "Who won the Most Valuable Player Award last year?" will probably settle the matter conclusively by reference to a standard almanac. If the question was "Who was the greatest baseball player of all time?" a conclusive answer is probably impossible; the game has changed too much over the years. Ty Cobb and Babe Ruth were unquestioned greats of yesteryear, but there is no practical way of comparing them with today's greats. Thus the standards necessary to establish a conclusive answer probably could not be agreed on.

The often-heard question "If we can put a person on the moon, why can't we solve the energy crisis or clean up the inner cities?" provides excellent examples of the probative force of evidence. Once the political decision was made to spend the money to put a person on the moon, the problem was limited to its scientific and engineering aspects. The scientific and engineering communities had developed agreed-on standards that allowed them to establish conclusive proof that a moon landing could be made, and the mission was accomplished.

Solving the energy crisis or cleaning up the inner cities, however, involves not just accepted scientific and engineering facts but also complex political and social problems involving conflicting values and perceptions. Thus the probative force of evidence will be determined by the decision renderers, and the task of the advocates remains that of discovering evidence that will have the desired impact in justifying their claim.

A. Partial Proof

Partial proof is used to establish a detached fact in a series of facts tending to support the issue in dispute. In debating the proposition of guaranteed annual wages, affirmative debaters sometimes sought to introduce evidence of seasonal fluctuations in employment as partial evidence in support of their need issue. In a murder trial, the prosecution would usually have to introduce evidence to prove malice on the part of the accused toward the murdered person — partial evidence in the series of facts the prosecution would seek to establish in order to prove the charge of murder. Evidence that only partially substantiates the advocate's contention is of little value in itself. However, when several pieces of partial evidence are brought together, their combined effect may be very strong. Indeed, taken together they might become conclusive.

B. Corroborative Proof

Corroborative proof, also known as "cumulative" or "additional" proof, is strengthening or confirming evidence of a different character in support of the same fact or proposition. In debates on free trade, some advocates sought to show that free trade would harm domestic industry. Evidence showing one industry that would be harmed was of some value in establishing this contention. Evidence that a number of industries would be harmed made the contention stronger. A defendant in a trial might claim he was out of town on the day the crime took place. One witness who saw him in another city on the day in question could furnish evidence of his alibi. His alibi would be stronger, however, if he could produce several witnesses to corroborate the fact that he was in another city.

C. Indispensable Proof

Indispensable proof is evidence without which a particular issue cannot be proved. In courtroom debates it is relatively easy to identify indispensable evidence. In a murder trial, for example, the prosecution must introduce evidence to establish the actual death of the person alleged to have been murdered.

In argumentation outside the courtroom, the indispensable evidence necessary to establish the proposition is usually less well defined than in legal proceedings, but careful examination of the proposition will indicate certain matters that must be proved. In a debate on "wage and price controls," the affirmative must introduce evidence showing that such controls will work to control inflation.

D. Conclusive Proof

Conclusive proof is evidence that is incontrovertible, either because the law will not permit it to be contradicted or because it is strong and convincing enough to override all evidence to the contrary and to establish the proposition beyond reasonable doubt. Evidence that may not be contradicted in legal proceedings varies from one jurisdiction to another. Outside the courtroom no evidence is arbitrarily safe from refutation and is conclusive only on its merits. The advocate always seeks to find such evidence; but on matters likely to be the subject of debate, conclusive evidence that applies directly to the proposition is seldom available. Obviously, once conclusive evidence is presented on a proposition, that proposition is no longer debatable. More often such evidence is found to support subsidiary matters related to the proposition. In debates on "right-to-work" laws, for example, some advocates were able to introduce conclusive evidence of corrupt practices in labor-management relations; they were not able, however, to introduce conclusive evidence that "right-to-work" laws would eliminate such corrupt practices.

Evidence is an essential ingredient in all argumentation. We cannot make intelligent decisions without evidence. The value of one piece of evidence, however, may vary considerably from that of another piece of evidence. Therefore, when we evaluate evidence presented to us for our decision, we must accept the good and reject the defective. In the same manner, when we seek the decision of others, we must evaluate evidence carefully so that we may use sound evidence in our case; and we must be able to evaluate the evidence of our opponents so that we may expose their defective evidence. Those seeking to reach a reasoned decision on evidence will find it desirable to apply the *tests of evidence* considered in the next chapter.

Exercises

1. Select one contention related to the current national intercollegiate debate proposition—NDT or CEDA, as your instructor specifies. Bring to class two examples of each of the following classifications of evidence:
   a. Direct evidence to prove this contention
   b. Presumptive evidence in support of this contention

2. From newspapers or newsmagazines published within the past week, find examples of the use of the following sources of evidence to support a contention:
   a. Judicial notice
   b. Public records
   c. Public writings
   d. A source that was originally a private writing
   e. Testimony of a witness

Bring to class a brief paper in which you classify the evidence, identify the contention advanced by the writer, and attach a clipping of the supporting evidence.

3. Obtain the text of a recent public speech by a well-known national figure on a matter of current importance. Prepare a brief paper in which you classify the evidence:

a. By type

b. By the probable probative force the evidence had on the audience addressed by the speaker

4. Attend an intercollegiate debate, and take careful note of the evidence presented in the debate. Prepare a brief paper in which you classify evidence:

a. By type

b. By the probable probative force it had on the judge

Compare this with the paper you prepared for Exercise 3. Who used *more* evidence, the public figure or the debaters? Why? Who did the better job of giving the audience good reason for accepting the evidence?

7

Tests of Evidence

Evidence is the raw material of argumentation. It provides the building blocks with which the advocate constructs the case. If the evidence is true, the advocate can construct a strong case. If the evidence is weak or flawed, the case can never be sound. Thus we must consider the tests of evidence.

I. Uses of Tests of Evidence

The previous chapter considered the sources and the types of evidence; this chapter considers tests that may be applied to evidence. There are three important uses for such tests.

A. To Test the Credibility of One's Own Evidence

In the construction of their cases, advocates will discover a great deal of evidence. Before they include any of it in their cases, they must apply the tests of evidence, rejecting what is weak and inconclusive and using only what stands up under examination. By applying the tests of evidence, they may also anticipate the probable refutation of their opponents and prepare to meet it.

The tests of evidence must also be applied to problems outside the debate situation. The political leader must weigh intelligence reports, the executive must evaluate reports of market trends, the college student must appraise studies of employment opportunities in various fields. Throughout life, we are all required to formulate propositions, gather evidence on those propositions, and evaluate that evidence as a part of the process of making decisions. Intelligent self-interest and our sense of responsibility to those affected by our decisions require that we apply the tests of evidence with care.

B. To Test the Credibility of Evidence Advanced by an Opponent

While preparing their own cases, advocates must also seek out evidence that will be of value to opponents, apply the appropriate tests to it, and plan refutation. As a debate develops, they will discover the evidence actually used by opponents and be prepared to test and refute it, if possible, during the debate. It should be noted that the responsibility of applying the tests of evidence and of refuting evidence rests on the party whose case is damaged by the evidence. If our case is adversely affected by certain evidence used by our opponents and we do not refute it, we may find that the decision renderers will accept even weak evidence at its face value. Indeed, the absence of refutation may enhance the value of the evidence.

C. To Test the Credibility of Evidence Advanced for a Decision

Although we may participate in debates only on rare occasions, there are innumerable occasions on which we are required to render decisions. As citizens, as consumers, and simply as social beings, we find that evidence is constantly directed to us for our evaluation. If we fail to evaluate the evidence of a candidate's qualifications, we may share the responsibility for a poor government; if we fail to evaluate the evidence of the merits of a product, we may suffer inconvenience or financial loss. In fact, any time we fail to apply the tests of evidence, we run the risks inherent in an unwise decision. The rewards of applying such tests are correspondingly great. As we apply them, we increase our opportunities for making sound decisions and gaining all the benefits that come with wise decisions.

II. Tests of Credible Evidence

Some writers are "interested in the intuitive probability judgments people make about the probity and diagnostic value of evidence."[1] It is no doubt true that people sometimes rely on their intuition in testing the credibility of evidence (and for other matters too). Aristotle, when composing his famous *Rhetoric*, observed how the statesmen of Athens argued. No doubt they drew on both their intuition and the lessons they learned at the schools of rhetoric. Intuition, however, is an uncertain guide when one seeks good reasons for sound judgments. It may result in serendipity or it may play us false. Gambling casinos grow rich on intuitive players who bet on their hunches. The occasional player who develops a winning system is promptly barred from the casinos.

The tests of credible evidence considered here are drawn from the long history of argumentation and are presented to give the advocate a system that, it is hoped, will

[1]Charles Arthur Willard, "Some Speculations about Evidence," *Proceedings of the Summer Conference on Argumentation*, ed. by Jack Rhodes and Sara Newell. Sponsored by the Speech Communication Association and the American Forensic Association (privately published, 1980), p. 271.

Questions for Testing Evidence Credibility

In general, affirmative answers to these questions imply that the evidence is credible; negative answers imply a weakness in the evidence.

- Is there enough evidence? (See II-A.)
- Is the evidence clear? (See II-B.)
- Is the evidence consistent with other known evidence? (See II-C.)
- Is the evidence consistent within itself? (See II-D.)
- Is the evidence verifiable? (See II-E.)
- Is the source of the evidence competent? (See II-F.)
- Is the source of the evidence unprejudiced? (See II-G.)
- Is the source of the evidence reliable? (See II-H.)
- Is the evidence relevant? (See II-I.)
- Is the evidence statistically sound? (See II-J.)
- Is the evidence the most recent available? (See II-K.)
- Is the evidence cumulative? (See II-L.)

serve as a surer guide than intuition in evaluating evidence. The tests of evidence can be stated in the form of questions (*see inset above*). As indicated in the previous chapter, all evidence obviously does not have the same degree of cogency, and thoughtful persons will want to test the degree of cogency they may reasonably expect will be assigned to the evidence by the decision renderers. Let us now discuss the tests in detail.

A. Sufficient Evidence

The advocate must provide enough evidence to support the matter at issue. How much is enough? Logically, advocates must provide evidence that is more convincing than the opposing evidence. Naturally, they seek conclusive evidence, but, since such evidence is often not available, they must settle for a fair preponderance of evidence. In the civil courts, the verdict is based on a "preponderance of evidence." In important matters outside the civil courtroom, reasonable men and women usually also apply this standard and base their decisions on a "preponderance of evidence." The national intercollegiate debate propositions, for example, always have some evidence — but less than conclusive evidence — on each side. Usually the ability of the advocates determines which side will establish a fair preponderance of evidence. It should be remembered that in an argumentative situation the advocates seek to convince those who render the decision rather than to convince their opponents.[2] They need to persuade only those who judge the debate that they have a fair preponderance of evidence.

---

[2]In some argumentative situations, the opponent may render the decision by conceding; for example, in a civil suit for personal injury damages, the defense attorney may seek to convince the plaintiff's attorney that his or her case is so weak that it would be better to accept a modest out-of-court settlement rather than to run the risk of the jury awarding no damages. Or, of course, vice versa.

B. Clear Evidence

The advocate must provide evidence that is clear or that, by means of evidence aliunde, can be made clear. In a classroom debate on the "mass media" proposition an affirmative team built a case to ban violence on television. These debaters were delighted when they discovered a newspaper article by a columnist who was a psychiatrist and research director of the National Coalition on Television Violence in which he said:

> The surgeon general's expert panel concluded the evidence is overwhelming. Violent entertainment has a harmful effect on viewers.[3]

At first the debaters greeted the evidence with great pleasure. An excellent source seemed to be saying exactly what they wanted. But was the evidence clear? Without evidence aliunde, it is *not* clear. (See Section II-H, "Evidence Aliunde," in Chapter 6.) What is meant by violence? (Professional football or professional hockey? Saturday morning children's cartoons? Or a televised play featuring a few murders?) Nor is it clear what "harmful" meant—something trivial or something catastrophic? The negative would be quick to point out the lack of clarity in this particular piece of evidence. The affirmative debaters wisely concluded they must find additional evidence to clarify this evidence in the minds of the judge. Their further research turned up evidence that the surgeon general's report was sixteen years old. They decided that if Congress had not acted on the report in sixteen years, they must have found the evidence unconvincing. The affirmative decided they would seek evidence that was clear, primary (see Section II-B in Chapter 6), and the most recent (see Section II-K in this chapter).

C. Evidence Consistent with Other Known Evidence

Advocates must determine whether the evidence is consistent with other known evidence. If it is, they may be able to strengthen their evidence by corroborative evidence; if it is not, they must be prepared to demonstrate that their evidence is more credible than other known evidence, or that other known evidence is not applicable in this particular case. If business executives offer evidence that the unit cost of a certain product will decrease as production increases, their evidence is consistent with the experience of many manufacturing firms. Thus this evidence will be consistent with other known evidence.

This test, however, clearly does not prohibit the advocates from using or considering evidence that is inconsistent with other known evidence. For example, in debating the "guaranteed employment opportunities" proposition, some students found evidence indicating, as might be expected, that unemployment was related to many harms: It was correlated with ill health, divorce, child abuse, crime, and suicide. This finding was consistent with other known evidence and provided the students with recent studies on the very point they wanted to make. Other students, researching the same proposition, came across other studies indicating that employment also was related to harms: The stress associated with working and the hazards of on-the-job accidents were likewise correlated with ill health, divorce, child abuse, crime, and suicide. Given the

[3]Thomas E. Radecki, "We Must Curb TV Violence," *USA Today*, October 24, 1988, p. 10A.

general acceptance of the work ethic in American society, most audiences would tend to accept the first piece of evidence — we all "know" that employment is good and unemployment is bad. Those debaters who chose to use the second piece of evidence were confronted with the task of demonstrating to the decision renderers that the credentials of their expert were superior, that their expert's evidence was more recent; and they had to supply other good reasons why evidence inconsistent with other known evidence should, in this particular case, be accepted.

Advocates should not disregard evidence merely because it is inconsistent with other known evidence but should recognize that such evidence must be studied with particular care. The advocate must be prepared to have the evidence attacked by opponents and must anticipate possible audience resistance. In most human affairs, of course, some known evidence is available on either side of a proposition. For example, will the stock market go up next month? There is probably some evidence indicating a rise, some indicating a decline.

D. Evidence Consistent Within Itself

Advocates must study the evidence carefully and determine whether it is consistent within itself. In debating the "law enforcement" proposition, some negative debaters cited evidence that rape was decreasing (going on to argue that the affirmative's plan for a change in the way that rape trials were conducted was thus unnecessary). Well-prepared affirmative debaters turned to the same source and quoted the following statement:

> The rates are for reported crimes only; they are not an accurate index of crimes actually committed. In many metropolitan areas an unknown number of crimes go unreported by victims. This is especially true of the crimes of rape, burglary, and larceny. Additionally, figures may be distorted for political reasons.

Thus, while the statistical tables did indeed show a decrease in the crime of rape, the text of the document itself contained a serious disclaimer about the accuracy of the statistics. The evidence was clearly not consistent within itself.

As another example, a group campaigning for a higher tax rate for a local school district issued a pamphlet in which they maintained that the increased revenue would go for increased teachers' salaries — an increase they argued was necessary to maintain quality education in the school district (quality education was a popular issue in this school district). An examination of the proposed budget printed in the pamphlet, however, revealed that most of the additional tax revenues would go for the purchase of additional school buses and to pay bus drivers and bus maintenance workers (busing was an unpopular issue in this school district).

E. Verifiable Evidence

Advocates must always be able to verify their evidence — that is, authenticate, confirm, and substantiate it. In gathering evidence, the advocates should be careful to check evidence against other sources to satisfy themselves about its validity before presenting it, and they should present whatever supporting evidence may be necessary to their audience. They should also be careful to identify the source of their evidence so that those who render the decision may verify it themselves if they wish. For example, in a debate on economic policy a speaker might say:

> According to *Newsweek*, December 26, 1988, p. 41, inflation fell from 13 percent to 4 percent during Reagan's administration.

The audience now has the opportunity to consult *Newsweek* and verify that *Newsweek* did indeed make that statement. This would probably be sufficient to establish the claim about the budget in most debates. If the audience were skeptical or doubted the magazine's accuracy, the speaker might find it desirable to offer further opportunity for verification by citing the appropriate fiscal-year reports of the Treasury Department's Office of Management and Budget or the appropriate *Economic Reports of the President*. Verification of a claim, of course, is more impressive if one can demonstrate that various independent sources verify the claim (see "Cumulative Evidence," Section II-L).

F. Competent Source of Evidence

Advocates must determine whether or not the source of the evidence is actually qualified to testify on the matter at issue. When the source of evidence is a *layperson*, the following tests should be applied:

1. *Did the witness have an opportunity to observe the matter in question?* Once a popular journalist spent a week in the Soviet Union and on his return wrote an article entitled "What's Going On Inside the Kremlin," in which he reported secret foreign policy decisions of the communist leaders. One might reasonably ask if the writer, who was an expert journalist but a layman on matters of foreign policy or espionage, actually had an opportunity to learn about secret decisions made inside the Kremlin.

2. *Was the witness physically capable of observing the matter in question?* In a trial a witness once claimed that he would be able to identify a robber he had seen at a distance of approximately 100 yards; yet he was unable to read a clock in the courtroom only 30 yards from the witness stand. One might reasonably ask if the witness were physically capable of seeing the person he claimed he saw.

3. *Was the witness mentally capable of reporting his or her observations?* Even a normal person may be questioned when claiming that he or she can perform unusual mental feats. For example, at a certain trial a defendant testified in great detail about the routine events of a business day five years previous, but he was unable to recall any details of other business days at approximately the same time. One might reasonably ask if the witness were mentally capable of recalling all of the details he claimed he remembered.

   A person's powers of observations may be influenced by circumstances surrounding the event. A standard psychology class experiment involves two students who rush into the classroom, fight, and then rush out. When the professor asks the class to describe the incident, he or she often receives widely differing reports. We must know too whether the witness had any interest in making a mental effort to observe and remember the event. How many people attended last year's commencement ceremonies at your college? Ask a few people who were present. Probably very few made any effort to count the audience.

If the source of evidence is an *expert*, then the following tests would be applied in addition to the tests applicable to a lay witness.

4. *Does the witness have official signs of respectability?* If claiming to be a physician, does the witness have a medical degree? If claiming to be an economist, does he or she have a doctorate in that field? In other words, does the witness have expert credentials? The fact that a physician has all the proper credentials of a surgeon does not, of course, guarantee that the operation will be a success. However, even though some persons without proper credentials have performed successful surgery, few of us would care to entrust our lives to an amateur brain surgeon.

5. *Is the witness well regarded by other authorities?* If an expert witness is highly regarded by others in the field in which he or she claims special competence, then the opinions have added weight. If a physician is an officer of the appropriate medical associations, is accredited in a specialty, has presented papers at medical conventions, is a professor of medicine at an accredited medical school — then it is reasonable to conclude that this person is well regarded by other authorities in medicine. Similar signs of professional regard should be sought in other areas.

G. Unprejudiced Source of Evidence

Advocates must be careful to determine whether the source of evidence is prejudiced. In many cases persons testify about matters in which they have an interest; in some cases those who are personally interested in the matter at hand are the only witnesses available. Are these persons free from prejudice? Do they report matters objectively or in a manner most favorable to their own interests? The advocate must determine whether the witness has an interest in the matter at issue and whether this interest is likely to influence his or her testimony. In a debate on direct foreign economic aid, a negative debater quoted the administrator of the aid program in a certain country as testifying "The program is highly efficient; waste is less than one-tenth of 1 percent." An affirmative debater replied:

> Of course he said the program was efficient. What could you expect him to do, admit that the program was inefficient and get fired? Let's see what a Congressional committee found when they investigated this program. . . .

Whenever possible, it is better to do what the affirmative debater did in this case; that is, introduce testimony from a disinterested source.

The *reluctant witness* is a witness who furnishes evidence against his or her own interests or prejudices. This, of course, is even stronger evidence than that coming from a disinterested source. Throughout his long fight against impeachment, President Nixon had counted on Republican loyalists who had ably defended him in the House Judiciary Committee proceedings. When new evidence was released after the committee hearings concluded, Nixon at first glossed over its importance. But within hours of the release of the transcripts, all Republican members of the committee indicated that the new facts "were legally sufficient to sustain at least one count against the President" and that they would vote for impeachment. Apparently, this reluctant reversal of their previous position was a major factor in convincing Nixon his case was hopeless. Three days later he resigned.

H. Reliability of Evidence

Advocates must be careful to determine whether the source of evidence is trustworthy. Does the source of evidence have a reputation for honesty and for previous accuracy in similar matters? Presidential elections afford interesting examples of the reliability of sources of evidence. Official results of Presidential elections are not known for several days following the election; yet the national news services have established such a reputation for reliability in reporting results that we invariably accept and act on their unofficial returns, which are announced the night of or the day following the election. The polls predicting the results of Presidential elections have earned a good reputation for accuracy and are generally considered to be reliable evidence. Evidence offered by the candidates themselves predicting the outcome of an election is notoriously unreliable. Typically front-runners in the polls will deprecate the polls for fear their supporters will become overconfident and fail to turn out the vote and this could cause a defeat. Candidates who are trailing in the polls also deprecate the predictions for fear their supporters will become discouraged and fail to turn out the vote, causing a defeat to become a rout.

If advocates can demonstrate that the source of their evidence is reliable, they increase the credibility of that evidence; if they can demonstrate that the source of their opponent's evidence is not reliable, then they have cast doubt on that evidence.

I. Relevance of Evidence

Advocates must be careful to determine whether or not the evidence is actually related to the matter at issue. Sometimes evidence is offered that is not relevant to the issue or has only the appearance of relevancy. The popular phone-in polls using area code 900 generate much doubtful evidence. The public is asked to call one number to register a "yes" vote, another for a "no" vote, or different numbers for different candidates; many variations are possible. The deficiency is that only those who feel strongly enough to spend the toll charged for each call are likely to phone in and, of course, those who feel *very* strongly can make multiple calls — hardly relevant evidence of how the general public would vote.

J. Statistically Sound Evidence

Occasionally advocates may find it necessary to use evidence in the form of statistics; however, such evidence should be introduced into a speech only when absolutely necessary. President Reagan, for example — who could draw on all the resources of the federal government for statistical evidence — would use statistics in a speech *only* if he could not make his point without them. When he did use statistics, he would "round off" figures and simplify and dramatize the statistics as much as possible. This is a sound practice for all speakers to follow, since most audiences find statistics dull, uninteresting, difficult to follow, and easy to forget. Statistical evidence is always prepared by someone, is almost always written evidence, and is usually expert or allegedly expert; it is therefore subject to the usual tests of evidence. Strictly speaking, there are no special tests for statistics that are not implied in the other tests of evidence. However, since the form of statistical evidence is specialized, the following tests will aid the advocate in evaluating this evidence:

1. *Have accurate statistics been collected?* Many people are reluctant to appear socially unacceptable or uninformed. Consequently, when a pollster calls they tend to give what they perceive as a socially acceptable response, they say they intend to vote when they don't, offer what they believe to be less controversial opinions, or express a view — any view — to cover up their ignorance of an issue. In one study almost a third of the respondents offered an opinion when asked about the nonexistent "Public Affairs Act."

    If the survey is conducted by telephone it should be noted that women answer the phone 70 percent of the time. A poll that doesn't take this into account by making extra calls to get enough men is likely to be skewed. The advocate must search for evidence that will establish the accuracy of the statistics collected.

2. *Have the statistics been classified accurately?* If you want the best place to go skiing, what do you look for? The folks at Rand McNally ignored Colorado's world class resort areas in their top ten list of the best cities for skiing, ranking Detroit no. 1, Los Angeles no. 2, and Akron-Canton, Ohio, no. 3. "This is insane!" protested Colorado ski resort owners. Six of their state's ski resorts are among the nation's ten busiest, with Vail the no. 1 pick of skiers.

    The author of *Sports Places Rated: Ranking America's Best Places to Enjoy Sports* said the ranking made "perfect sense." The choice was based on federally defined metropolitan statistical areas. All of Colorado's world class ski resorts are just outside such areas. The scoring was based on the total ski lift capacity within the metro area where the city was located. Detroit has five ski areas in its three-county metro area, but none of them are on mountains by any stretch of the imagination. How do you classify the best places for skiing? By chair lift capacity in metropolitan statistical areas or by the big slopes?

    Students debating the proposition on direct foreign economic aid came to realize the importance of accurate classification of statistics. Some sources listed foreign aid expenditures as amounting to billions; others listed these expenditures as 700 million, 500 million, or other amounts. The difference depended on how the person preparing the statistics classified military aid, defense support, technical assistance, and other types of aid.

3. *Has the sampling been accurate?* The ratings of television programs are based on such tiny samples that some Congressional observers wonder if they are not meaningless. Some statisticians claim they can predict a Presidential election with only a few thousand respondents — if they have just the right proportion of urban residents, farmers, Northerners, Southerners, college graduates, manual laborers, native Americans, naturalized citizens, and so on.

    Getting such a sample, however, is very difficult. Many pollsters would rather interview prosperous-looking people who live in good residential areas than go into the slums to find the requisite number of unskilled laborers. Some ghetto dwellers view pollsters as representatives of "the Establishment" and refuse to reply to questions or give misleading answers. A number of psychological studies are based on responses given by college sophomores — mainly because many sophomores are enrolled in psychology classes, and it is convenient to test them. But one may question whether college sophomores are representative of the general public.

4. *Have the units been accurately defined?* A kilowatt-hour is a reasonably well-defined unit, but what is a "work week"? Students debating the proposition on guaranteed annual wages discovered that there are many different definitions for this phrase. It is reported that the Soviet Union has more military divisions than the United States, but how does the reporter define the unit "division"? Soviet and American divisions differ in size and power; there are also differences between combat and service divisions. Similar definitions are needed for statistics on "the family": That unit is defined one way for tax purposes, another way in housing statistics, and in still other ways in other statistics.

5. *Are the data statistically significant?* Almost any set of statistics will show certain variations. Are the variations significant? Statistical differences are considered significant only if the sample is sufficiently large and representative, and if allowance has been made for the necessary margin of error, seasonal fluctuations, and other factors. If one student has a score of 120 on an IQ test and another student has a score of 121, the difference is not statistically significant. If you toss a coin ten times and it comes up heads eight times, the result is not statistically significant. Figures showing the extent of unemployment in December and June are not significant unless allowance has been made for seasonal differences.

6. *Is the base of the percentage reasonable?* Whenever statistical evidence is reported in percentages, the advocate must be careful to discover the base from which the percentage was determined. Has the value of the American dollar gone up or down? It all depends on the date used as the base. During the Summer Olympics in Los Angeles, things were so peaceful that the police insisted that crime in certain sections had somehow dropped 250 percent. *Newsweek* noted wryly, "Anything over 100 percent seems to imply that some lawbreakers had switched to performing good deeds."

7. *Do the visual materials report the data fairly?* Statistical evidence is often reported in the visual form. Visual materials are helpful in overcoming audience apathy toward statistics and, when prepared fairly, in clarifying complex data. However, visual materials can also be used to distort statistical evidence. Therefore, the advocate must be careful to determine whether the various charts, diagrams, pictograms, and other visual materials presented really interpret the data fairly. For example, assume that the following figures for the production of a certain type of machine tool are absolutely accurate:

	United States	Soviet Union
Last year	1,000,000	5,000
This year	1,010,000	10,000

Now consider the diagrams (*see inset*) and how they slant these figures. In the first two, the choice of units used on the vertical axis of the graph produces two quite

Visual Materials: Examples

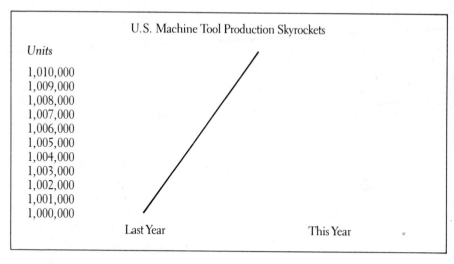

U.S. Machine Tool Production Skyrockets

Units

1,010,000
1,009,000
1,008,000
1,007,000
1,006,000
1,005,000
1,004,000
1,003,000
1,002,000
1,001,000
1,000,000

Last Year   This Year

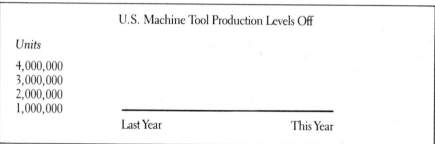

U.S. Machine Tool Production Levels Off

Units

4,000,000
3,000,000
2,000,000
1,000,000

Last Year   This Year

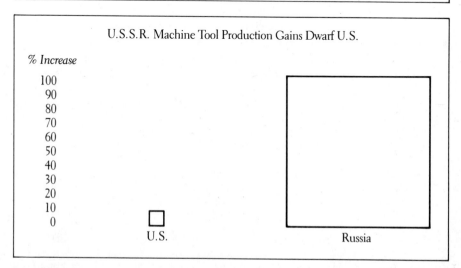

U.S.S.R. Machine Tool Production Gains Dwarf U.S.

% Increase

100
90
80
70
60
50
40
30
20
10
0

U.S.   Russia

different pictures; in the third graph, the height of each bar is reasonably accurate, but a distorted picture is created by using a much wider bar for the Soviet Union. The caption above each diagram adds to the distortion.

These few simple examples only begin to suggest the possibility of distortion in visual materials. The advocate must study carefully each visual aid presented in the argument to determine whether it is an accurate or a distorted presentation of the data.

8. *Is only reasonable precision claimed for the statistics?* If greater precision is attributed to the statistics than they deserve, we may reach unwarranted conclusions. One of the 1948 polls, which predicted Dewey's election over Truman, correctly showed Dewey to be in the lead. Dewey's lead, however, was less than the margin of error in the poll. Those who predicted that Dewey would win on the basis of this poll were attributing unreasonable precision to the poll. Sometimes claims of unreasonable precision are made for statistics, and evidence that may merit little consideration is often given undue weight when it is presented in statistical form.

In their desire to satisfy the demand for quantification, journalists, legislative reference clerks, and others often provide us with "imaginary numbers."[4] Consider the following examples of imaginary numbers as they appeared in the press:

1,750,000 Cheered Candidate as He Drove through New York

U.S. Has Coal Reserves for 400 Years

17 Million Americans Go to Bed Hungry Every Night

The thoughtful reader will immediately recognize that unreasonable precision has been claimed for all of these figures. No reporter riding in a press car behind a candidate could count 1,750,000 people as the motorcade drove along, and some of the people in the crowd certainly were not cheering—they were just waiting to cross the street. The coal reserves statement probably means "at the present rate of consumption." But no one knows what the demand for coal will be in 10, 50, or 100 years, let alone what it will be in 200, 300, or 400 years. The statement about the 17 million hungry Americans overlooks the fact that on any given day 20 million Americans are on a diet and should be going to bed hungry. Thus this figure proves that 3 million Americans cheat on their diets. (If you agree with the conclusion in the previous sentence, please reread this entire section.)

9. *Are the data interpreted reasonably?* Sometimes "the thing speaks for itself" and no interpretation is necessary.[5] Usually, however, someone reports the data and draws conclusions from them; and that someone may have an interest in supporting a

[4]The term is used here to indicate that the numbers come from the writer's imagination, with little or no warrant from the real world. In higher mathematics an imaginary number is a multiple of the square root of minus one.

[5]The legal maxim is *res ipsa loquitur*. A classic example would be that of a patient who, after undergoing surgery, is found to have a sponge in his abdomen. The patient, who was under anesthesia at the time, cannot testify that the surgeon did wrong. Usually there are no witnesses to the wrongdoing; if any of the other physicians or nurses present at the operation had noticed the error, they would have told the surgeon, who would have corrected the situation before the incision was closed. The plaintiff's lawyer would argue *res ipsa loquitur* — sponges simply are not supposed to be left in a patient's abdomen; therefore, the surgeon must have done wrong. The *res ipsa loquitur* argument, although very powerful in this case, is not necessarily conclusive. Now, however, the surgeon's lawyer would have the burden of proving that the sponge had somehow been introduced into the patient's abdomen by some other surgeon at some other time.

particular point of view. For example, assume that the following figures on the cost of widgets are absolutely accurate:

Month	Cost of Widgets	Increase from January	Increase from Previous Month
Jan.	$1.00	—	—
Feb.	1.10	10%	10 %
Mar.	1.20	20%	9.6%
Apr.	1.30	30%	9.1%
May	1.40	40%	7.8%
June	1.50	50%	7.1%
July	1.60	60%	6.7%
Aug.	1.70	70%	6.2%

With these data before them, the advocates may make a number of accurate but different statements. On one hand they might say, "The price of widgets has increased by seventy cents in eight months." Or they might say, "The price of widgets soared a staggering 70 percent in runaway inflation in just eight months." On the other hand, the advocates might take a more sanguine view and say, "Last month the price of widgets rose only 6.2 percent." Or they might report, "Inflation is ending; for the sixth consecutive month there has been a decreasing rate of increase in the cost of widgets."

Which is safer, travel by commercial aviation or travel by car? The statistical method favored by the airlines examines passenger-miles traveled. In this method, you multiply the number of passengers in a plane or car by the number of miles flown or driven by each vehicle to reach the result. Viewed this way, scheduled commercial airline travel had .06 death for each 100 million passenger-miles flown in the most recent 10-year period; cars had 2 fatalities for each 100 million passenger-miles driven in the same time period. This suggests that commercial airplanes are 33 times safer than cars.

However, if you prefer driving to flying, you might prefer the vehicle-miles method. This method completely ignores how many people are in the vehicle. Viewed this way, commercial airplanes had 6.6 fatalities per 100 million vehicle-miles while cars had only 3 fatalities for each 100 million vehicle-miles. This method suggests that cars are more than twice as safe as commercial airplanes.

Thus it is clear that the advocate should review statistical data in as much detail as possible and determine if the interpretation is reasonable or if other equally reasonable interpretations are possible.

10. *Are the questions unbiased?* Even polls taken at the same time can produce dramatically different results depending on how the question is phrased. The July 11, 1988, issue of *U.S. News & World Report* provided some striking examples on pages 44 and 45:

ABORTION

Constitutional amendment "prohibiting abortions"?
For 29%
Against 67%

Constitutional amendment "protecting the life of the unborn"?
For 50%
Against 39%

GUN CONTROL

"Waiting period and background check before guns can be sold"?
For 91%
Against 6%
"National gun-registration program costing about 20% of all dollars now spent on crime control"?
For 37%
Against 61%

WELFARE

"Are we spending too much, too little or about the right amount on welfare"?
Too little 22%
"Are we spending too much, too little or about the right amount on assistance to the poor"?
Too little 61%

The perspective or spin (see Chapter 15, Section V-C) given to a question may have a profound effect on the response elicited. We might be surprised and worried if the same person expresses radically different judgments depending on how the question is put to him or her. Yet that happens frequently. A group of doctors was asked: "Imagine that the U.S. is preparing for the outbreak of an unusual disease, which is expected to kill 600 people. Two alternative programs to combat the disease have been proposed. Assume that the exact scientific estimate of the consequences of the programs is as follows: If program A is adopted 200 lives will be saved. If program B is adopted, there is 1/3 probability that 600 people will be saved and 2/3 probability that no people will be saved. Which of the two programs do you favor?" The vast majority of doctors, 72% of them, opted for program A.

Another group of doctors was given the same "cover story" as the first, but they were asked to choose among the following alternatives: "If program C is adopted, 400 people will die. If program D is adopted, there is 1/3 probability that nobody will die, and 2/3 probability that 600 people will die. Which of the two programs do you favor?" Only 22 percent of the doctors opted for C. The odd thing is that C is just a different way of phrasing A.[6] And D, of course, is only a different way of phrasing B. The spin can indeed make a difference. The wise advocates will be aware of spin control and give careful consideration to how the question was phrased.

K. The Most Recent Evidence

Old evidence may sometimes be more valuable than recent evidence. If we want to know certain facts about the voyage of the *Mayflower*, a document dated 1620 may be more valuable than one dated 1920. A map made in 1000 A.D. was important evidence

---

[6]Leo Katz, *Bad Acts and Guilty Minds: Conundrums of the Criminal Law* (Chicago: University of Chicago Press, 1987), pp. 4–5.

supporting the claim of many scholars that Leif Ericson's Norsemen reached Labrador, the New England coast, and Martha's Vineyard long before Columbus discovered the New World. Often, however, the recency of evidence is an important factor in establishing its value. If the facts of a situation are subject to change, or if opinions about a certain matter are subject to revision, then we want the most recent information available. For example, this month's estimate by the Bureau of the Census of the population of the United States is more valuable evidence of the size of the population than a report issued by the same bureau a year ago.

In many cases more recent evidence, merely because it is more recent, is sufficient to refute older evidence. In debates on the "mass media" proposition, some affirmative teams called for a ban on the advertising of diet drinks containing saccharin. Their justification was that a several-years-old Canadian study indicated a 60 percent increased risk of bladder cancer among saccharin users. The value of this evidence sharply depreciated when, three-quarters of the way through the debate season, a series of new studies appeared that reported "There is no saccharin induced epidemic of bladder cancer in this country" and that people who use moderate amounts of saccharin "can be assured that their excess risk of cancer, if present at all, is quite small and little cause for concern." Since new evidence is constantly being developed on matters that are likely to be subjects of debate, the advocates must make a special point of assembling the most recent evidence and making proper allowance for it in their case.

L. Cumulative Evidence

Although one piece of evidence is sometimes sufficient to establish a given contention, advocates are usually in a stronger position if they can offer several pieces of evidence from different sources or of different types to substantiate their contentions. In debates on the issue of nuclear power plant safety, for example, the opinion of one eminent scientist might be offered to establish a certain contention. This contention would be more firmly established, however, if the advocate could show that the same conclusion was shared by the Nuclear Regulatory Commission, the Kemeny Commission, the Union of Concerned Scientists, the Institute of Nuclear Power Operations, and the National Academy of Sciences.

III. Tests of Audience Acceptability

In addition to tests of credible evidence, the advocate must also apply tests of audience acceptability. Some evidence that might appear credible to us may not be acceptable to the audience; therefore the advocate must consider not only how the audience views the credibility of the evidence but also the acceptability of the evidence to the audience. The audience, of course, may be a single judge in an academic debate, the whole voting population of the United States in a Presidential election, or any group of decision renderers. One method of audience analysis is considered in Chapter 15; only certain tests of audience acceptability are considered here. These tests can be stated in the form of questions (*see inset*). Let us now discuss these tests in detail.

Questions for Testing Audience Acceptability

In general, affirmative answers to these questions indicate that the evidence will probably be acceptable to audiences; negative answers indicate that it probably will not be acceptable to audiences.

- Is the evidence consistent with the beliefs of the audience? (See III-A.)
- Is the source of the evidence acceptable to the audience? (See III-B.)
- Is the evidence suited to the level of the audience? (See III-C.)
- Is the evidence consistent with the motives of the audience? (See III-D.)
- Is the evidence consistent with the norms of the audience? (See III-E.)
- Is the evidence documented for the audience? (See III-F.)

A. Consistency with Audience Beliefs

A negative answer to the tests of evidence previously considered implies some weakness in the evidence. A negative answer to the question of consistency with audience beliefs, however, does not carry such an implication; obviously, advocates occasionally must use evidence that is not consistent with audience beliefs. However, when they use such evidence, the advocates must anticipate audience resistance to this particular evidence and make special provisions to overcome this resistance. Therefore, the advocates must analyze their audiences and determine their beliefs on the various pieces of evidence they plan to use.

An excellent example of how the audience's beliefs condition their response to political candidates was found in the 1988 Presidential election. In the Democratic primaries Dukakis proudly *boasted* that he was "a card carrying member of the American Civil Liberties Union." The liberal Democrats who voted in the primaries saw this as evidence that Dukakis' views were consistent with theirs. This evidence was credited with contributing to his winning the nomination. In the general election Bush *accused* Dukakis of being "a card carrying member of the ACLU." In the general election many more conservative voters saw this as evidence that Dukakis' views were inconsistent with theirs. This evidence was credited with contributing to Bush's victory.

The importance of audience beliefs is not limited to political campaigns; there are ardent partisans for nonpolitical issues as well. The experienced advocate will recognize that in many audiences there are partisans who will interpret evidence from the point of view of their own beliefs. The task of the advocate is to find evidence that will be acceptable to as many members of the audience as possible.

B. Source Acceptable to the Audience

Again, a negative answer to this question does not imply any weakness in the evidence itself; rather, it indicates a problem the advocate must overcome. We know that audiences tend to believe some sources more readily than others. If evidence comes from a source that has high prestige in the minds of the audience, it is likely to be accepted with little or no question; if it comes from a source without special prestige for the audience, it must stand on its own merits; if it comes from a source held in low regard by the audience, it may be discredited regardless of its intrinsic merits. The advocates, then, should try to use sources of evidence that are acceptable to the audience. If they find it necessary to use sources with low prestige, they must establish the credibility of the source, at least in this special case. When they find it absolutely essential to use sources toward which the audience is hostile, then they must overcome this hostility.

An excellent example of this problem occurred when the proposition "the federal government should control the supply and utilization of energy" was debated. When the Arabs embargoed oil and raised prices, there were serious shortages in many parts of the country and prices rose sharply. How much of the shortage was due to the Arab embargo? How much of the price increase was caused by the increase in the price of imported oil? The oil companies had one answer. Government agencies had another. Consumer advocates had a third answer. Which source would the audience believe? It depended almost entirely on the audience's attitude toward the various sources. One debater solved the problem by citing figures from consumer advocate Ralph Nader and argued that, as even Nader admitted that imports were down *x* percent, the audience should accept that figure as accurate. The proconsumer members of the audience felt they had to agree with their hero; and the probusiness members of the audience, while feeling the actual figure was much higher, were pleased to see an old rival admit there was some truth on their side. As Hovland, Janis, and Kelley point out:

> The debater, the author of scientific articles, and the news columnist all bolster their contentions with quotations from figures of prestige. . . . When acceptance is sought by using arguments in support of the advocated view, the perceived expertness and trustworthiness of the communicator may determine the credence given them. . . . Sometimes a communication presents only a conclusion, without supporting argumentation, and its acceptance appears to be increased merely by attributing it to a prestigeful or respected source.[7]

If, for example, advocates wished to cite certain evidence that had appeared in the *New York Times*, *National Geographic*, *Ladies Home Journal*, and *Field and Stream*, they would be well advised to cite the source with the highest prestige for their audience. Hovland, Janis, and Kelley found that the credibility of a message seems to be related to the particular magazine in which it appears.[8] Students debating the "law enforcement" proposition found confirmation of this fact. Some excellent articles relating to the proposition, written by highly regarded, well-qualified sources, appeared in *Playboy* magazine. When the debater said "As Superintendent Parker said in last month's *Playboy* . . . ," audiences usually interrupted the quotation with chuckles. Apparently, the audiences associated the magazine more readily with the centerfold for which it is famous than with the quality articles it sometimes publishes. President Carter certainly learned that lesson when an interview he had granted appeared in *Playboy* shortly before the Presidential elections. The interview generated more nega-

---

[7]Carl L. Hovland, Irving L. Janis, and Harold H. Kelley, "Credibility of the Communicator" in *Dimensions in Communication*, 2nd ed., eds. James H. Campbell and Hal W. Hepler (Belmont, Calif.: Wadsworth, 1970), pp. 146 ff.

[8]Ibid., p. 147.

tive publicity for Carter than almost any other single incident in the campaign and led him ruefully to admit during the third television debate of the campaign, "If I should ever decide in the future to discuss my deep Christian beliefs . . . I'll use another forum besides *Playboy.*"[9]

C. Evidence Suited to Audience Level

Is the evidence too technical or too sophisticated for the audience to understand? In debates on the issue of nuclear power plant safety, some of the primary evidence was so technical in nature that it could be understood only by a physics professor. When debating before lay audiences, the advocates were forced to discard the primary evidence and turn to secondary evidence that made approximately the same point in simpler terms.

D. Consistency with Audience Motives

Advocates occasionally must use evidence not in keeping with the values and attitudes of the audience. In such cases, they must expect audience resistance. Some advocates debating the "mass media" proposition used cases calling for restraints on publication of information about the identity of CIA agents (giving as their justification that events in Iran and Afghanistan made it necessary to increase U.S. intelligence-gathering capabilities). Some judges, thinking of earlier CIA abuses, ignored the affirmative's carefully qualified plan and said, "I simply cannot vote to give the CIA unchecked powers."

E. Consistency with Audience Norms

Certain audiences have well-defined norms for evaluating evidence, and the advocate must be aware of and adapt to these norms before such audiences. If you wish to argue a point of law before a group of lawyers you will find that they have definite ideas about how legal arguments should be made. In the same way scientists, physicians, accountants, policymakers, philosophers, and others usually impose specific standards for evaluating evidence as acceptable. Thus the norms that a group of scientists will impose on evidence used to establish a scientific hypothesis will be much more rigorous than the data needed to establish a proposition before a lay audience.

F. Evidence Documented for the Audience

We saw earlier that the evidence must be verifiable. In order to give the audience the opportunity to verify the evidence, the speaker must provide documentation within his or her speech at the time of evidence presentation. In an academic debate, the judge expects such documentation, and the wise debater will fulfill the judge's expectations. Indeed, the American Forensic Association in its statement of "Standards" adjures:

> Debaters should document their evidence accurately and completely. Complete documentation should generally consist of author, credentials, publication, and year. This information in addition to page numbers should be available when requested by the judge or opponents.

[9]See Paul F. Boller, Jr., *Presidential Campaigns* (New York: Oxford University Press, 1984), p. 352.

To avoid any misunderstanding, it is emphasized that this information should be presented *in the speech*.

As the student of communication theory knows, not only the debate judge but the general public as well reacts to documentation. Rosenthal points out:

> In short, verifiability is the primary linguistic factor in enforcing a statement's credibility, not because the listener *will* verify the statement but because he or anyone else *can* verify it. . . . This opens up the possibility that measurement of the degree of verifiable content in a message may provide an index of its credibility to the receiver.[10]

An experimental study by Fleshler, Ilardo, and Demoretcky led them to conclude:

> It is evident that message documentation was the primary variable that determined evaluations of message and speaker. Concrete message documentation resulted in significantly more positive evaluations of the message and the speaker.[11]

Exercises

1. Find three advertisements in newspapers published within the past week in which advertisers use evidence to support their arguments. Prepare a brief paper in which you apply the appropriate tests of evidence to the advertisements. Attach copies of the advertisements to your paper.

2. Find three editorials in newspapers published within the past week in which the writer uses evidence to support his or her argument. Prepare a brief paper in which you apply the appropriate tests of evidence to the editorials. Attach copies of the editorials to your paper.

3. Find three examples of the use of statistical evidence in newspapers or newsmagazines published within the past week. Prepare a brief paper in which you apply the appropriate tests of evidence to the statistics. Attach copies of the statistics to your paper.

4. Find three examples of the use of visual aids to present statistical evidence in newspapers or newsmagazines published within the past week. Prepare a brief paper in which you apply the appropriate tests of evidence to the visual aids. Attach copies of the visual aids to your paper.

5. Attend an intercollegiate debate and prepare a brief paper in which you report three examples of evidence used in the debate. Apply the appropriate tests of evidence to each of these examples.

6. Attend an intercollegiate debate and prepare a brief paper in which you report three examples of evidence used in the debate and the way in which the opposing

---

[10]Paul I. Rosenthal, "Specificity, Verifiability, and Message Credibility," *Quarterly Journal of Speech*, Vol. 57 (December 1971), p. 400. Italics in original.

[11]Helen Fleshler, Joseph Ilardo, and Joan Demoretcky, "The Influence of Field Dependence, Speaker Credibility Set, and Message Documentation on Evaluations of Speaker and Message Credibility," *Southern Speech Communication Journal*, Vol. 39 (Summer 1974), p. 400.

team applied the test of evidence to refute this evidence. Evaluate the effectiveness with which the tests of evidence were applied.

7. Prepare a three-minute speech for presentation in class, in which you develop an argument supported by carefully chosen evidence. Other members of the class will be invited to apply the tests of evidence to see if your evidence is sound. Prepare an outline of your speech in which you indicate the types of evidence used and hand this outline to your instructor.

8. Prepare a three-minute speech for presentation in class, in which you develop an argument supported by evidence. In your speech deliberately include some carefully concealed unsound evidence. Other members of the class will be invited to apply the tests of evidence to see if they can discover the invalid evidence. Prepare an outline of your speech in which you indicate the types of evidence used and the invalid evidence and hand this outline to your instructor.

8

The Structure of Reasoning

For centuries philosophers, rhetoricians, debaters, and others have been concerned with the structure of reasoning. In this chapter we will consider the two structures most widely used today. First, we will turn to the structures of Aristotle, whose *syllogism* and *enthymeme* have been standard tools of reasoning for centuries and are still the basis of much reasoning today. Next we turn to a contemporary logician, Stephen Toulmin, whose concept of the elements of any argument (Section II) is now widely accepted. His tools—claims, grounds, warrants, backing, modal qualifications, and possible rebuttals—have come into common usage.

The formal structure of these methods of reasoning gives us special opportunities to make piercing and precise *analyses* of lines of reasoning and to *test* their validity. The methods and terminologies of both the classical and contemporary structures are widely used in present-day argumentation, and students are well advised to have a working knowledge of both.

I. The Classical Structures

Two special forms of deductive reasoning are the *syllogism* and the *enthymeme*. By using these structures for the purpose of analysis, we can apply the appropriate tests of formal validity to the reasoning we encounter as we explore the problem, to the reasoning we develop for our own case, and to the reasoning we meet in our opponent's case.

Tests: Categorical Syllogism

1. The categorical syllogism must have three terms—no more and no less.
These terms may be represented by the letters A, B, and C, as follows: Major Term: B; Middle Term: A; Minor Term: C. *Example:*

Major Premise: All A's are B's.   ——Middle Term
Minor Premise: C is an A.————   ——Minor Term
   Conclusion: Therefore, C is a B.——Major Term

2. Every term must be used twice in the categorical syllogism—no more and no less.

3. A term must be used only once in any premise.

4. The middle term must be used in at least one premise in an unqualified or universal sense. In the syllogism on legal insanity, the middle term was correctly *distributed,* referring to *all* legally insane persons. The middle term is incorrectly distributed in the following example, because (A) is qualified (*some*). Consequently, the conclusion of this syllogism is invalid.

Major Premise: Some politicians (A) are corrupt (B).
Minor Premise: Richard Roe (C) is a politician (A).
   Conclusion: Therefore, Richard Roe (C) is corrupt (B).

5. A term may be distributed in the conclusion only if it has been distributed in the major or minor premise. The following is an example of an *illicit major*—a major term that is distributed in the conclusion but not in the major premise.

Major Premise: All communists (A) want the United States to cut defense spending (B).
Minor Premise: Congressman Zilch (C) is not a communist (A).
   Conclusion: Therefore, Congressman Zilch (C) does not want the United States to cut defense spending (B).

A. Syllogisms

We will consider three types of syllogisms: (1) categorical, (2) disjunctive, and (3) conditional. First, however, let us consider the structure of all types of syllogisms. The *syllogism* is a systematic arrangement of arguments:

1. A *major premise*, which is a proposition stating a generalization ("All A's are B's")
2. A *minor premise*, which is a proposition stating a specific instance related to the generalization ("C is an A")
3. A *conclusion*, which necessarily must follow from these premises ("Therefore, C is a B")

When the major premise is fully stated—"All communists are *among those* who want the United States to cut defense spending"—it becomes readily apparent that the major term (B) is not used in a universal sense in the major premise and thus may not be distributed in the conclusion. Congressman Zilch might be a pacifist. The following is an example of an illicit minor—distributed in the conclusion but not in the minor premise.

Major Premise: All union presidents (A) favor the union shop (B).
Minor Premise: All union presidents (A) are members of unions (C).
   Conclusion: Therefore, all members of unions (C) favor the union shop (B).

In this example, the minor term (C) is not distributed in the minor premise, but is distributed in the conclusion. When the minor premise is fully stated—"All union presidents are *some* members of unions," it becomes readily apparent that the minor term (C) has not been distributed and that consequently the conclusion is invalid. The only conclusion that could be drawn from these premises is that *some* union members favor the union shop.

6. At least one of the premises must be affirmative. Obviously, no valid conclusion can be drawn from two negative premises. *Example:*

Major Premise: No Democratic senators (A) will vote for this bill (B).
Minor Premise: Senator Eliot (C) is not a Democratic senator (A).
   Conclusion: Therefore, Senator Eliot (C) will ____ ?

7. If one premise is negative, the conclusion must be negative.

Major Premise: No Republican senators (A) voted for this bill (B).
Minor Premise: Senator Eliot (C) is a Republican senator (A).
   Conclusion: Therefore, Senator Eliot (C) did not vote for this bill (B).

The following statement is an example of syllogistic reasoning:

All legally insane persons are incompetent to make binding agreements (*major premise*).
John Doe is legally insane (*minor premise*).
Therefore, John Doe is incompetent to make a binding agreement (*conclusion*).

In the various examples of syllogisms that follow, assume for the present that each premise is absolutely true. First, we will give consideration only to the structure of the argument. Later, we will consider the truth of the premises in Section I-C, "Formal Validity and Material Truth."

1. The Categorical Syllogism In the categorical syllogism, the major premise is an unqualified proposition. Such propositions are characterized by words like *all*, *every*, *each*, or *any*, either directly expressed or clearly implied.

Some thoughtful scholars object to this aspect of the categorical syllogism, maintaining that it is very difficult to make unqualified generalizations. It might be pointed out, for example, that all legally insane persons are not alike: the nature and degree of their illnesses, the types of treatment they require, and the possibilities for their recovery are quite different. They are identical, however, in that they are all incompetent to make binding agreements as long as they are legally insane. Thus, for the purpose of making binding agreements, we treat all legally insane persons in the same manner. As a practical consideration, we treat many matters as identical and make unqualified generalizations about them. The problem of the advocate is to determine when it is practical or necessary to make unqualified generalizations, within a specific context and when it is prudent or necessary to recognize the differences in apparently identical matters.

Certain tests may be applied to the categorical syllogism (*see inset, pages 126–127*).

2. The Disjunctive Syllogism The disjunctive syllogism is one with a major premise containing mutually exclusive alternatives. The separation of alternatives is usually indicated by such words as *either, or, neither, but,* and *although* either expressly stated or clearly implied.

Major Premise: Either Congress will amend this bill or the President will veto it.
Minor Premise: Congress will not amend this bill.
Conclusion: Therefore, the President will veto it.

Certain tests may be applied to the disjunctive syllogism (*see inset, page 129*).

3. The Conditional Syllogism The conditional syllogism, also known as the hypothetical syllogism, is a syllogism in which the major premise deals with uncertain or hypothetical events that may or may not exist or happen. The conditional event is usually indicated by *if, assuming, supposing,* or similar concepts, either expressly stated or clearly implied. For example, the following conditional syllogism was used in debates on the proposition "Resolved: That the federal government should adopt a program of compulsory wage and price controls":

Major Premise: If the present measures have checked inflation, then we will not need compulsory wage and price controls.
Minor Premise: Present measures have not checked inflation.
Conclusion: Therefore, we will need compulsory wage and price controls.

The major premise of the conditional syllogism contains an *antecedent* statement, which expresses the conditional or hypothetical event under consideration, and a *consequent* statement, which expresses the event that is maintained as necessarily following the antecedent. In the above example, the antecedent statement begins with the word *if* and the consequent statement begins with the word *then*. The *if–then* relationship is a convenient way of expressing the major premise in a conditional syllogism.

Certain tests may be applied to the conditional syllogism (*see inset, page 130*).

Tests: Disjunctive Syllogism

1. The major premise of the disjunctive syllogism must include all of the possible alternatives. In debates on the "energy" proposition some affirmative advocates cited the shortage of gasoline and maintained:

Major Premise: We must either have gas rationing or gas shortages.
Minor Premise: We don't want gas shortages.
   Conclusion: Therefore, we must have gas rationing.

Negative advocates meeting this syllogism recognized that the major premise did not include all possible alternatives. They were quick to point out other ways of dealing with gas shortages and they maintained that voluntary allocations, car pools and a 55-mile-an-hour speed limit would solve the problems of the gas shortage.

2. The alternatives presented in the disjunctive syllogism must be mutually exclusive. Some of the negative advocates meeting the above syllogism were quick to point out that gas rationing and gas shortages were not mutually exclusive. They argued that gas rationing merely exacerbates the gas shortage by adding the problems of bureaucracy and blackmarkets.

3. The minor premise must affirm or contradict one of the alternatives given in the major premise. If the minor premise neither affirms nor contradicts one of the alternatives in the major premise, no valid conclusion is possible. *Example:*

Major Premise: Congress must either raise taxes or reduce federal expenditures.
Minor Premise: Members of Congress will not cut their own salaries.
   Conclusion: Therefore, Congress must ____ ?

Since Congressional salaries are only a minor part of all federal expenditures, the premise that Members of Congress will not cut their own salaries might more accurately be phrased as "Members of Congress will not reduce *some* federal expenditures." Even though congresspersons will not cut their own salaries, it is possible for them to reduce *other* federal expenditures; therefore, this premise neither affirms nor contradicts one of the alternatives in the major premise.

B. The Enthymeme

There are two definitions of the *enthymeme*, both of which are important to the advocate (*see inset, page 131*).

1. Definitions of the Enthymeme The rigorous rules of the syllogism make it a valuable instument for testing arguments. At the same time they limit the situations in which it can be used. We rarely talk in syllogisms—we are more likely to express our arguments in less than complete syllogisms. Further, there are many situations in

Tests: Conditional Syllogism

1. The minor premise must affirm the antecedent or deny the consequent. If the minor premise affirms the antecedent, the conclusion must affirm the consequent; if the minor premise denies the consequent, the conclusion must deny the antecedent:

Major Premise: If the interest rate on treasury notes increases, then more of these notes will be purchased.

Minor Premise: The interest rate on treasury notes will increase.

Conclusion: Therefore, more of these notes will be purchased.

Note that, in this case, the minor premise affirms the antecedent and the conclusion affirms the consequent. The following example does just the opposite:

Major Premise: If compulsory wage and price controls are to be effective, then black-marketing must be prevented.

Minor Premise: Blackmarketing cannot be prevented.

Conclusion: Therefore, compulsory wage and price controls cannot be effective.

2. If the minor premise denies the antecedent or affirms the consequent, no valid conclusion can be drawn. *Example:*

Major Premise: If the interest rate on treasury notes increases, then more of these notes will be purchased.

Minor Premise: The interest rate on treasury notes will not increase.

Conclusion: Therefore, ____?

In this example, the absence of an increase in interest rates will not lead to more of these notes being purchased; but (since a change in any of a number of fiscal or monetary policies might lead to more of these notes being purchased), one cannot conclude that more notes will *not* be purchased. Thus, when the minor premise denies the antecedent, no valid conclusion can be drawn. Now consider this example:

Major Premise: If compulsory wage and price controls are to be effective, then black-marketing must be prevented.

Minor Premise: Blackmarketing can be prevented.

Conclusion: Therefore, ____?

Even if blackmarketing could be prevented, there are numerous other factors that might prevent the effective operation of a program of compulsory wage and price controls. Thus, when the minor premise affirms the consequent, no valid conclusion can be drawn.

Two Definitions of the Enthymeme

1. The enthymeme is a *truncated* syllogism in which one of the premises or the conclusion is not stated.

2. The enthymeme is a syllogism based on probabilities, signs, and examples, whose function is rhetorical persuasion. Its successful construction is accomplished through the joint efforts of speaker and audience, and this is its essential character.[1]

[1]Lloyd F. Bitzer, "Aristotle's Enthymeme Revisited," *Quarterly Journal of Speech*, Vol. 45, No. 4, p. 408.

which we must deal with probabilities rather than certainties. In these circumstances we make use of the *enthymeme*. As there are two discrete concepts involved, there are two definitions of the *enthymeme (see inset above)*.

This first definition of the enthymeme — as a *truncated syllogism* — is of great importance to the advocate. As we have noted earlier, people usually do not talk in syllogisms. Many of their arguments are expressed in the form of enthymemes. In a debate on federal aid for higher education, we might hear the following argument: "This plan would lead to federal control and is undesirable." Expressed in the form of an enthymeme, this argument would look like this:

Minor Premise: This plan leads to federal control.

Conclusion: Therefore, this plan is undesirable.

As advocates encountering this enthymeme, we would promptly seek out the unstated major premise. If the unstated major premise were "*Some* forms of federal control are undesirable," we would recognize that the middle term is not distributed and that therefore the conclusion is formally invalid. If the unstated major premise were "All forms of federal control are undesirable," the conclusion would be formally valid, but we might wish to raise a question about the material truth of the major premise.

Thus, when we encounter enthymemes in an argument — and we will encounter them frequently — we should seek out the unstated premise and determine whether the conclusion logically follows that premise or whether the unstated premise is materially true. In discovering the unstated premise, we may open up important avenues of analysis.

Sometimes advocates may find it psychologically advantageous to omit the conclusion. If the major and minor premises are clearly stated, the audience or judges will draw the conclusion and may hold it more firmly because they reached it "on their own"; or advocates may be able to make an unpleasant point without actually stating it. Thus a professor might say to a student, "Anyone who failed the midterm exam must get a B or better on the final to pass the course. You failed the midterm." The professor would, no doubt, "get the message across" without verbalizing it; and the student, drawing the inevitable conclusion, might be motivated to put extra effort into preparing for the final exam.

The enthymeme—as the term is used in the second definition (with the focus on probabilities and construction through the joint efforts of the speaker and audience)—may or may not omit one of the premises or the conclusion. This definition of the enthymeme is also of very real importance to the advocate, who is often concerned with probability rather than certainty and who often wishes to build on premises already established in the mind of the audience.

Many negative debaters use this objection to the cost of an affirmative plan:

Major Premise: All plans that cause inflation should be rejected.
Minor Premise: This plan *may* cause inflation.
  Conclusion: Therefore, this plan should be rejected.

In this case the debater hoped that the audience was predisposed to oppose inflation and would thus join with the debater in building the enthymeme by accepting the major premise. Syllogistically, this argument proves absolutely nothing. It has a formal validity of zero. The syllogism is a logical instrument for dealing with certainty; it is concerned with all of the factors in a certain classification and with matters that necessarily and inevitably follow from certain premises. However, many problems the advocate must consider are not subject to certainty or to absolute proof. If the negative can establish a reasonable degree of cogency for its argument—if it can establish a reasonable probability that the plan will cause inflation—it might well win the decision. Another enthymeme was used in some debates on the "tax sharing" proposition:

Major Premise: All tax programs which impede urban renewal are undesirable.
Minor Premise: The affirmative's plan of tax sharing *may* impede urban renewal.
  Conclusion: Therefore, the affirmative's plan of tax sharing is undesirable.

In this case the debater hoped that the audience was predisposed to favor urban renewal and would thus join with the debater in building the enthymeme by accepting the minor premise.

At the time of these debates the negative could cite some evidence to support the minor premise, and the affirmative could cite some evidence to refute it. As neither side could establish certainty, the decision on this clash would go to the side establishing a fair preponderance of evidence.

Enthymemes, like syllogisms, may be classified as categorical, disjunctive, and conditional. The same tests that would be used to determine the formal validity of a syllogism may be used to determine the formal *validity* of an enthymeme. Although the above-cited enthymemes are invalid as syllogisms, they are formally valid as enthymemes. Thus, if advocates can establish a preponderance of probability to support their arguments and can get the audience to join with them in the construction of the enthymeme, they may well persuade reasonable and prudent people to accept their conclusions.

The following enthymeme, however, is formally invalid; and thus, regardless of the degree of probability attached to the premises, the conclusion is worthless:

Major Premise: Some domestic industries are not harmed by Japanese imports.

Minor Premise: Textiles are a domestic industry.

    Conclusion: Therefore, textiles are probably not harmed by Japanese imports.

The fallacy of an undistributed middle term — *some* domestic industries — renders the conclusion of this enthymeme formally invalid.

2. Chain of Enthymemes. Frequently, arguments are stated in the form of a chain of enthymemes. A speaker may state only the conclusion of an enthymeme, use that as one premise of a second enthymeme, state the conclusion to the second enthymeme without indicating the other premise, and continue in this manner to build a chain of enthymemes. The omitted portion of the enthymeme sometimes will be readily evident and uncontestable; at other times, however, it may not be readily apparent or may be subject to refutation. Consequently, the advocate should recognize and analyze a chain of enthymemes, seek out the omitted portions of the argument, restructure the argument in syllogistic form, and apply the appropriate tests.

The advocate will frequently find it advantageous to begin to build a chain of enthymemes in the minds of the listeners. As Aristotle advised:

Our speaker, accordingly, must start out from . . . the [actual] opinions of the judges [audience], or else the opinions of persons whose authority they accept. And the speaker must make sure that his premises do appear in this light to most, if not all, of his audience. And he must argue not only from necessary truths, but from probable truths as well.[2]

Thus, if the advocate were speaking before a civil liberties group, analysis of the audience might lead him or her to conclude that the group would support the major premise "No law should abridge the freedom of the press." Building on this premise in the minds of the audience, the advocate might begin the argument by stating, in effect:

Minor Premise: The Decent Literature Act abridges the freedom of the press.

    Conclusion: Therefore, the Decent Literature Act must be repealed.

Or, if the speaker were addressing a gun club, analysis of the audience might lead him or her to conclude that the group would support the major premise "The right of the people to keep and bear arms shall not be infringed." Building on this premise in the minds of the audience, the speaker might begin the argument by stating, in effect:

Minor Premise: The Gun Registration Act infringes on our right to keep guns.

    Conclusion: The Gun Registration Act is unconstitutional.

---

[2]Aristotle, *Rhetoric*, II, 22.

Advocates should analyze their decision renderers carefully and seek out opportunities to build a chain of enthymemes on the premises already established in the minds of the audience or judge.[3]

C. Formal Validity and Material Truth

In the syllogisms and enthymemes considered thus far in this chapter, it has been assumed that each premise of each syllogism is absolutely true, and that each premise of each enthymeme is probably true. If they are true, the conclusions drawn from the formally valid syllogisms are matters of absolute certainty, and the conclusions drawn from the formally valid enthymemes must be accorded the degree of cogency appropriate to the probability found in the premises. If, however, any of these premises is false, then its conclusion is worthless regardless of the formal validity of the construction:

Major Premise: Any child can make a spaceship.
Minor Premise: John is a child.
   Conclusion: Therefore, John can make a spaceship.

This syllogism is formally valid; there is no question about that. Assume that John really is a child; the minor premise is then materially true. The major premise, however, has no foundation in fact. Obviously, the conclusion is worthless.

It must be noted that a materially true conclusion is not proof that the premises are materially true or that the syllogism is formally valid, as the following syllogism shows:

Major Premise: All nations that have received direct economic aid from the United States are
now military allies of the United States.
Minor Premise: Canada has not received direct economic aid from the United States.
   Conclusion: Therefore, Canada is a military ally of the United States.

The proof of this conclusion must come from a source other than this syllogism.

In order to establish the material truth of a premise, the advocate must apply the tests of reasoning and the tests of evidence, considered earlier. Since many premises are, in fact, conclusions from other syllogisms or enthymemes that may or may not have been stated in the argument, the appropriate tests of formal validity should be applied to them.

II. The Elements of Any Argument

The philosopher Stephen Toulmin maintains that six elements can be found in any wholly explicit argument. These elements are: (1) claims, (2) grounds, (3) warrants,

---

[3]See Chapter 15, Section I.

(4) backing, (5) modal qualifications, and (6) possible rebuttals.[4] Let us consider each of these in turn.

A. Claims

The claim(s) element of the argument is the conclusion we seek to establish by our argument. Our claim might be the proposition itself—for example, "Resolved: That the federal government should significantly strengthen the regulation of mass media communication in the United States," or "Resolved: That the federal government should significantly curtail the powers of labor unions in the United States." In practice, in order to establish those claims, we would first have to establish a series of other claims—for example, "Banning publicity will reduce terrorism," or "Work sharing will reduce unemployment in the United States."

B. Grounds

Once we have made a claim, we must advance good reasons that establish the foundation of our claim. We must provide evidence and reasoning to establish that our claim is solid and reliable.

C. Warrants

Once we have made a claim and indicated the grounds for that claim, we must then proceed to justify the move from the grounds to the claim. We must establish that the evidence and reasoning we have offered as grounds apply in this particular instance.

Let's pause here to consider how these three elements of argument were used by affirmative advocates on the "mass media" proposition:

Grounds	Warrant	Claim
Terrorists commit terrorism to gain publicity.	Sensational media gives terrorists publicity.	Banning publicity will reduce terrorism.

If the advocates have provided good evidence and reasoning to establish their grounds and to support their claim, they will have taken imporant steps toward establishing their claim.

Let's continue now with a consideration of the other elements of argument.

---

[4]Stephen Toulmin, Richard Rieke, and Allan Janik, *An Introduction to Reasoning* (New York: Macmillan, 1979), p. 25.

D. Backing

Our warrant will not be accepted merely on our say-so; we must provide additional evidence and reasoning to support our warrant. Applying this element to our mass media example, we expand our diagram:

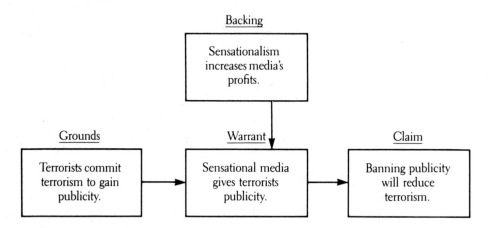

We see that the *warrants are not self-validating.*[5] Therefore we must provide additional evidence and reasoning to sustain our warrant in the form of backing.

E. Modal Qualifications

When we have considered the grounds, warrant, and backing offered in support of our claim, we are in a position to qualify that claim — that is, to express the degree of cogency (considered in detail at the beginning of Chapter 9) that we can attach to our claim. The degree of cogency, or modal qualification, we can attach to our claim may vary from certainty to possibility. Let us consider an example where the modality may be precisely verified:

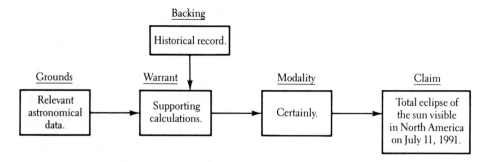

Students are invited to check with the astronomy department of their university: Do the professors there agree with the modality or degree of cogency assigned to this

[5]Ibid., p. 58.

claim? Students who consider this example after July 11, 1991, can verify this prediction from their memory of news stories of the event. Note that after July 11, 1991, this claim becomes a perfect example of judicial notice (see Chapter 6, Section I-A). If "everyone" knows there was a total eclipse of the sun on that date, one need only *mention* the fact in order to establish the claim. Since this is the last total eclipse of the sun that will be visible in North America in this century, or indeed in the lifetime of most readers of this book, it is likely to be a well-publicized event. Only after the lapse of some time will it be necessary to introduce evidence to support this claim.

Will the United States send a manned space expedition to Mars in 2005 or 2013? Will the United States and the Soviet Union send a joint manned space expedition to Mars in 2005 or 2013? In those years Mars will come relatively close to the earth. Scientists have made such proposals. However, an affirmative answer to these questions *cannot* be given with *certainty* until we are much closer to those dates. Eclipses and the orbits of planets can be predicted with certainty far in advance. The decisions of nations — and their ability to carry out these decisions — cannot be predicted with anything approaching the same precision.

Advocates rarely deal with certainty; most often they are concerned with establishing a lesser degree of cogency. As an example let us consider an argument that was made in the final round of an NDT tournament:

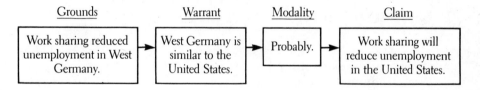

Grounds	Warrant	Modality	Claim
Work sharing reduced unemployment in West Germany.	West Germany is similar to the United States.	Probably.	Work sharing will reduce unemployment in the United States.

Did the advocates assign a reasonable degree of cogency (modal qualification) to their claim? Not surprisingly, the negative did not let this claim go unchallenged. In fact, the negative debaters did exactly what we would expect them to do — introduce rebuttal. This topic brings us to the last of Toulmin's elements of argument, which we will consider next.

F. Rebuttals

As discussed in Chapter 14, to rebut means to overcome opposing evidence and reasoning by introducing other evidence and reasoning that will destroy its effect. In the debate cited on the following page, the negative introduced rebuttal designed to destroy the degree of cogency that the affirmative assigned to its claim.

With the rebuttal and its backing now before us, we will either have to drop the claim or assign to it a considerably lower degree of cogency (modality). Depending on the evidence and reasoning the negative has used in its rebuttal, the chance that work sharing will reduce unemployment in the United States has now been lowered from a probability to at best a possibility.

Rebuttal, then, may be seen as an element of argument that may block or impede the movement of argument from grounds to claim and force us to reconsider and to define more precisely the degree of cogency we assign to our claim.

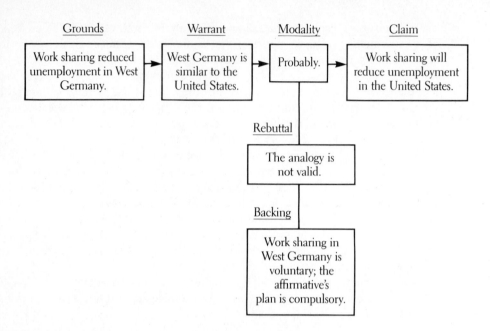

III. Extending the Elements of an Argument

The samples we have considered here are brief. In an actual argument or debate, the elements of argument are often extended and complex. In the example considered in Section F, the negative built on their backing, "Work sharing in West Germany is voluntary; the affirmative's plan is compulsory," to establish a disadvantage and advanced a revised version of that backing as grounds, "Unions despise compulsory work sharing," for their claim that "Unions will strike":

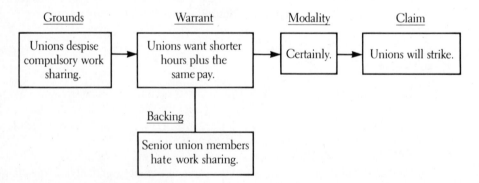

Naturally the affirmative responded with a rebuttal of its own, challenging the claim that the unions will certainly strike. Still more arguments were built on the strike argument as the opposing teams introduced evidence and reasoning to establish that the strikes would have a devastating impact on the economy or that the strikes wouldn't happen at all or that they would have only minimum impact on the economy.

Careful evaluation of the elements of argument will allow the advocate to detect flaws in an argument and thus launch an attack on an opponent's argument or replace or repair a flawed argument intended to support the advocate's own position.

Exercises

1. Find an argumentative editorial that has been published in a daily newspaper within the past month. Restate the arguments in the form of syllogisms or enthymemes. Analyze these arguments. Show why they are or are not formally valid.

2. Find an argumentative editorial as in Exercise 1. Lay out the major arguments in the form considered in Sections II and III of this chapter. Does the warrant justify the movement from grounds to claim? Has the editor established the modality of the claim accurately? Has sufficient backing been provided when needed? Have possible rebuttals been considered?

3. Select a major argument from one of the debates in the appendixes of this book. Lay out the argument in the form considered in Sections II and III of this chapter. Apply the questions listed in Exercise 2.

4. Select a major argument from one of the debates in the appendixes of this book. State the argument as a syllogism. Does it meet the appropriate tests of a syllogism?

5. Select a major argument from one of the debates in the appendixes of this book. State the argument as an enthymeme. Show why the enthymeme is or is not formally valid. If a premise is omitted, supply the omitted premise. Does the enthymeme establish a reasonable degree of probability?

9

Types of Reasoning

Reasoning is the process of inferring conclusions from premises; and the premises may be in the form of any of the various types of evidence. They may be stated as propositions, or they may be statements of conclusions reached through previous reasoning. Thus advocates use the premises they have previously established or asserted, and by a process of reasoning seek to establish something new—a conclusion they wish their audience to accept. If the audience perceives the premises as well grounded and the reasoning as rhetorically sound, it will be likely to accept the advocates' conclusion.

I. The Degree of Cogency

Rhetorical proof is the *degree of cogency* arising in the minds of the audience from the combination of premises with reasoning. (As we saw in Chapter 8, Toulmin used the term "modal qualifications" to express this concept.) Rhetorical proof may be said to establish certainty, probability, plausibility, or possibility. These degrees of cogency may be thought of as existing on a continuum, represented by the following diagram.

Cogency Continuun

Absolute
truth

A scintilla
of truth

Certainty

.... Probability

.... Plausibility

.... Possibility.............

These degrees of cogency are not discrete compartments. Rather they are terms used to suggest the relative compelling force of various logical proofs.

Certainty is associated with absolute truth. If a conclusion is a certainty, all competent observers are in agreement. Relatively little of the advocates' time is concerned with this degree of proof. Few matters of human affairs are subject to proof as certainty. Most of the advocates' efforts are in the realm of probability; they seek to demonstrate that their conclusions have a degree of credibility warranting acceptance. In criminal courts, which demand the highest standard of proof, all elements of the case must be proved beyond a reasonable doubt. This has been estimated to be over 90 percent certainty. Outside of the criminal courts we are often required to make decisions based on a lesser degree of certainty. For example, the Secretary of the Treasury, even with all of the resources of the federal government at his or her disposal, cannot establish as a certainty the proposition that a given tax bill will raise x number of dollars in revenue. Students who debated "tax sharing" and "higher education" found that estimates of state sales tax revenues and the yield from school tax levies were often inaccurate. Furthermore, matters that are a certainty are, by definition, not suitable subjects for debate. Matters that are a certainty, however, are often used as part of the evidence and with reasoning are used to establish new conclusions.

It must be noted that it is not only the evidence, but how the evidence is perceived, that will determine certainty and the other degrees of cogency. If our ego, politics, finances, or other interests are involved in the matter, our evaluation of the evidence will vary. While the judge or audience can consider some matters dispassionately and with great objectivity (fortunately, this is usually the case with the judge in academic debate), there are other times when the advocates must be very aware of audience attitudes and adapt their cases, reasoning, and evidence to their listeners' interests (see Chapter 15).

Probability is associated with a high degree of likelihood that a conclusion is true. As advocates, we will spend much of our time seeking to prove that our propositions have a high degree of probability, and that our propositions are more probably true than those of our opponents. For example, no method of contraception is 100 percent effective; even sterilization fails at times and other methods range from 76 percent to 97.6 percent in their effectiveness. Thus persons choosing to use contraceptives are basing their decisions on probabilities. In the physical sciences, the degree of probability of a proposition's being true can be established with great precision; often, thousands of cases can be examined under carefully controlled conditions. In other areas of human affairs, however, it is not always possible to measure so accurately and to control so precisely the variables affecting the proposition. In civil courts the standard of proof is the preponderance of evidence. This means a 51 percent chance of being true. Outside the civil courts we require the degree of cogency we deem appropriate to the situation. For example, the Secretary of the Treasury, in seeking to establish the proposition that a given tax bill will raise *x* number of dollars in revenue, will have to qualify his or her statement by saying that *if* the present level of employment is maintained, *if* spending is continued at the present level, *if* there isn't an international crisis, and *if* various other relevant factors don't change — then it is reasonable to assume that the tax bill will raise *x* number of dollars.

Plausibility is associated with a lesser degree of likelihood that a proposition is true. The advocate will use arguments having this degree of proof only when no better arguments are available. This type of proof was often used by the ancient Sophists and is often used today by modern propagandists. Arguments of this type are sometimes superficial or specious and have limited probative force for the thoughtful listener or reader. Sometimes, of course, we are forced to make decisions simply on the basis of plausibility, if this relatively low degree of cogency is the best available. Many life-or-death surgical decisions are made on this basis. When a new surgical procedure is first developed (heart transplants, for example), the surgeon tells the patient, in effect, "If you go on as you are, all our experience indicates that your condition will continue to deteriorate and you will die within a few months. We've developed a new surgical procedure that *could* help you. We've had some successes with this new procedure, but frankly it is still experimental and we do not have enough data to make firm estimates." Given this set of circumstances, would you take the gamble?

Possibility is associated with a very low degree of likelihood that a proposition is true. The advocate has only limited use for proofs with this degree of cogency and will always seek proofs having greater logical force. Until the closing weeks of the major league baseball season, a mathematical possibility usually exists that the last-place team could win the division pennant. If such a possibility requires, however, that the last-place team win all its remaining games and that the top three teams lose all their remaining games, this possibility would not warrant serious consideration. Sometimes, of course, we are forced to make decisions when proofs with this low degree of likelihood are the best available. In debating the proposition "Resolved: That the federal government should establish a national program of public work for the unemployed," some affirmative teams argued that the proposition should be adopted because a major recession might occur in the future and that such a program should be established and held in readiness to put into effect at the onset of the recession. At the time the proposition was debated, the country was enjoying a period of great prosperity and there was no evidence of a recession in the foreseeable future. Nonetheless, some affirmative teams were successful in arguing that on the basis of all our previous experience a recession was a possibility for which we should be prepared.

Recall the evidence considered in Chapter 6, Section II-H, "Evidence Aliunde": "the substance *could* be a one-shot cure for diabetes." As we saw, this evidence as presented is useless. But let's assume for a moment that the pharmaceutical company hoped to develop such a substance; after all, it's entirely *plausible*, indeed *probable*, that pharmaceutical companies would be interested in developing such a substance.

Let's assume that the company had conducted exhaustive studies that indicated that, by using certain techniques in the zero gravity of space, such a substance *could* be produced. Yet, prior to actual testing in space, one can only say "could." Until the experiment was actually performed in zero gravity and the results carefully evaluated, no one could say positively that the substance would in fact be a one-shot cure for diabetes. Yet, given the rewards that would come from such a discovery, it's entirely reasonable to believe that investors would risk large sums of money on the long odds.

Another example may be found in the effort to develop the next generation of computer chips. Although it is generally agreed that such a new-generation computer chip will come about, highly competent scientists have different ideas as to methods of design. At this time no one actually knows how or when it will be developed, but the cost–benefit ratio of being the first to develop such a new-generation computer chip is so great that billions of dollars are being poured into research on this project.

The balance of this chapter will consider the types and uses of the tests of reasoning. General tests applicable to all types of reasoning will be considered. Finally, specific tests will be indicated for (1) reasoning by example, (2) reasoning by analogy, (3) causal reasoning, and (4) sign reasoning.

II. Tests of Reasoning and Their Uses

Obviously, all reasoning does not have the same degree of cogency. Therefore, the thoughtful person will want to test reasoning to determine the degree of probability of the conclusions. Often more than one type of reasoning is involved in a given line of argument; therefore, the thoughtful person will apply all of the appropriate tests to each piece of reasoning that he or she considers. There are three uses for the tests of reasoning.

A. To Test the Validity of One's Own Reasoning

In the construction of a case, advocates will discover much reasoning advanced by others and will develop tentative lines of reasoning of their own. Before incorporating any of this reasoning into their case, they must apply the tests of reasoning so that they may reject invalid reasoning and include only what will stand up under scrutiny. By applying the tests of reasoning, they can anticipate the probable lines of refutation by their opponents and prepare their counterrefutation.

These tests of reasoning must also be applied outside the debate situation. As college students weigh the propositions that they should enter law school, or medical school, or a certain business, their future happiness and success require that they carefully apply the tests of reasoning to the arguments supporting these propositions.

B. To Test the Validity of the Reasoning Advanced by the Opposition

In preparing cases, advocates must try to discover the probable lines of reasoning their opponents will use, apply the appropriate tests to this reasoning, and plan refutation of it. In the course of the debate, they must be prepared to apply the appropriate tests as their opponent's actual lines of reasoning are presented and to develop their refutation accordingly.

C. To Test the Validity of Reasoning Advanced for a Decision

Often we may seek neither to advance our own arguments nor to refute arguments of others; rather, we function as decision renderers to whom various lines of reasoning are directed. As citizens, we are the target of arguments advanced by both political parties. To function as responsible citizens, we must apply the tests of reasoning to these arguments. If we plan to buy a car, purchase stock, buy a house, or undertake any significant purchase, our own self-interest compels us to apply the tests of reasoning to the arguments advanced by the salesperson. In fact, at any time when we are required to make a decision of any significance, prudence dictates that we must apply the tests of reasoning to the factors relating to that decision with a degree of rigor directly related to the importance of the decision.

In the course of the debate, we and our opponents are presenting reasoning to the audience or judges for their decision. The audience or judges will make a judgment as to what degree of cogency they assign to the conflicting arguments. We must be in a position to advance good reasons why they should accept our arguments and why they should reject the reasoning of our opponents.

III. General Tests of Reasoning

The general tests that must be applied to all types of reasoning are drawn from "The Elements of Any Argument" (Section II of Chapter 8). Once a claim is advanced we must apply these general tests to the supporting elements of the argument. The tests, of course, must be specific to the particular argument being considered. An affirmative answer to the following test questions implies that the reasoning is sound; a negative answer may imply the presence of a fallacy.

A. Are the Grounds Solid?

Have good reasons been given to establish the foundation of this claim? Has reliable evidence and reasoning been provided to establish solid grounds for the claim?

B. Does the Warrant Justify the Claim?

Has sufficient evidence and reasoning been given to provide good reasons justifying the movement from grounds to claim in this specific instance?

C. Is the Backing Adequate?

In many cases, the warrant or rebuttal is not sufficient to stand alone. Has additional evidence and reasoning been provided to establish adequate backing?

D. Has the Rebuttal Been Properly Evaluated?

Almost any argument is subject to rebuttal. Has sufficient evidence and reasoning been provided to offset or minimize the rebuttal? Has the rebuttal been properly evaluated?

E. Has the Degree of Cogency (Modal Qualification) Been Properly Determined?

As we have seen, the degree of cogency or modal qualification that may be attached to a claim may vary from certainty to possibility. Has the degree of cogency assigned to this particular claim been established accurately and precisely?

IV. Types of Reasoning and Tests for Each Type

Reasoning is often classified as deductive or inductive. *Deductive reasoning* claims to establish the *certainty* of a conclusion; *inductive reasoning* claims to establish a lesser degree of cogency for its conclusion. Copi points out:

> Although every argument involves the claim that its premises provide evidence for the truth of its conclusion, only *deductive* argument involves the claim that its premises provide *conclusive* evidence. . . . An inductive argument, on the other hand, involves the claim not that its premises give conclusive evidence for the truth of its conclusion, but only that they provide *some* evidence for it. . . . Inductive arguments may, of course, be evaluated as better or worse, according to the degree of likelihood or probability which their premises confer upon their conclusions.[1]

As a practical matter the advocate uses both deduction and induction, moving back and forth from one to the other many times while developing or analyzing an argument. The intermingling of deduction and induction will become apparent as we consider the principal types of reasoning and their related tests.

A. Reasoning by Example

The process of reasoning by example consists of inferring conclusions from specific cases. This process may be represented as follows:

$$\left.\begin{array}{l} \text{Case}_1 \\ \text{Case}_2 \\ \text{Case}_3 \\ \text{Case}_n \end{array}\right\} \text{Conclusion}$$

Sometimes a single case may be used to establish the conclusion or generalization. More frequently, however, a number of cases will be offered as the basis for the conclusion. Reasoning by example is a form of inductive reasoning and involves either cause or sign reasoning, since the advocate seeks to show that the examples or cases are a cause or a sign of the conclusion presented.

[1] Irving M. Copi, *Introduction to Logic*, 3rd ed. (London: Macmillan, 1968), pp. 20–21.

The advocate makes frequent use of reasoning by example. In debating the proposition "Resolved: That the United States should discontinue direct economic aid to foreign countries," some affirmative teams sought to establish the argument that recipient nations resented direct economic aid. They offered as examples a series of statements by various foreign leaders, maintained that these statements showed resentment toward direct economic aid, and from these cases drew the conclusion that resentment against such aid was widespread. Other affirmative teams debating this proposition maintained that direct economic aid was wasteful. They offered examples of expenditures of direct economic aid monies, maintained that these expenditures were unwise, and from these cases drew the conclusion that direct economic aid was wasteful.

The following questions serve as tests for reasoning by example:

1. *Is the example relevant?* The advocate must be careful to determine whether the cases offered are relevant to the matter under consideration. Some negative teams, refuting the argument that recipient nations resented direct economic aid, were quick to point out that some of the statements quoted by the affirmative were criticisms of American foreign policy generally and not of direct economic aid specifically; or that the statements quoted by the affirmative were criticisms of American military aid, not of direct economic aid. Thus, these negative teams demonstrated that the examples offered by the affirmative were not relevant examples of criticism of direct economic aid, however accurate they might be as examples of criticism of other aspects of American foreign policy. Consequently, they refuted the conclusion drawn from the examples.

2. *Are there a reasonable number of examples?* Although a single example may be used to establish a generalization or conclusion, the advocate's position is usually stronger with supporting examples. Even a very carefully controlled laboratory experiment is usually not accepted as establishing a conclusion until it has been repeated with the same results by other competent scientists — and, in medicine, not until thousands of cases have been studied.

   How many cases are enough? One method of obtaining enough cases is to make a complete enumeration. You could ask students in your argumentation class whether they own personal computers, and then, on the basis of complete enumeration, draw the conclusion that *x* percent of the students own personal computers. Complete enumeration, however, has obvious limitations, since it is often impracticable or impossible to consider every case; therefore, the advocate must seek to present enough cases to convince a reasonable and prudent person that there is a high degree of probability that a conclusion is correct.

   Some negative teams, answering the argument that direct economic aid was wasteful, did not attempt to refute the examples. Rather, they maintained that three or four examples of waste among thousands of projects were not sufficient to justify the conclusion that such aid, as a whole, was wasteful. Some negative teams carried this refutation a step further; they introduced reports of Congressional committees that had studied large numbers of projects and had concluded that such projects were, on balance, useful. Thus, although time limitations will often prevent our citing a large number of examples directly, we may give a few examples to illustrate our point and then, to substantiate our conclusion further, offer the testimony of persons who have studied large numbers of cases.

3. *Do the examples cover a critical period of time?* In many instances, the time at which the examples were studied, or the period of time covered by the examples, may be of critical importance. The advocate must seek to find examples representative of the period of time critical to the argument. If, in debating direct economic aid, the affirmative had chosen all of its examples of waste from the first year or two of the operation of the aid program, the negative might have maintained that some errors in administration could be expected at the start of a new program, and that the affirmative had offered no examples of waste in the recent or current operation of the program. Public opinion polls taken during election years often provide dramatic evidence of the importance of obtaining examples from the critical period of time. In 1988 Michael Dukakis had a substantial lead over George Bush in the polls taken just after the Democratic Convention. Although the polls may have accurately reported voter preference in August, they did not indicate how voter preference would change as the campaign developed. If the question was "who will win the election?" the critical period of time for the polls was early November. The early November polls correctly predicted Bush's victory — the August polls were history.

4. *Are the examples typical?* The advocate must be careful to determine whether the cases offered are really representative. In Senate debates on labor legislation, some senators have cited examples of corrupt labor practices and called for legislation to regulate labor unions. Other senators have opposed such legislation, maintaining that the few examples of corruption were not typical of labor unions generally.

5. *Are negative examples noncritical?* Advocates must discern whether the negative examples they discover are critical or noncritical. In matters of policy, it is unlikely that all of the examples will support one conclusion. Some examples may well be negative or contrary to the conclusion. In considering direct economic aid, advocates will find examples of waste and examples of excellent management; in considering employment practices, advocates will find examples of firms that practice discrimination and others that do not. They are well advised to remember that they are concerned more often with probability than certainty. They should not attempt to show that *all* direct economic aid projects are wasteful; rather, they should seek to show that the examples of wastefulness warrant the conclusion that waste is inherent in the program and that direct economic aid should be discontinued. On almost any proposition the opponents are likely to have negative examples; advocates must anticipate these examples and be prepared to offer adequate evidence that the examples are noncritical and do not invalidate their conclusion.

Reasoning by example may also be analyzed by laying out the argument in the manner considered in "The Elements of Any Argument" (Section II of the previous chapter).

Assume the advocate claims there are practical alternatives to nuclear power, as the diagram shows.

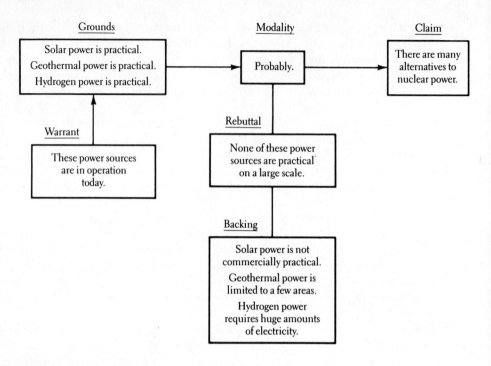

B. Reasoning by Analogy

The process of reasoning by analogy consists of making a comparison between two similar cases and inferring that what is true in one case is true in the other. Reasoning by analogy is a form of inductive reasoning, in which the advocate seeks to show that the factors in his or her analogy are either a cause or a sign of the conclusion presented. This process may be represented as follows:

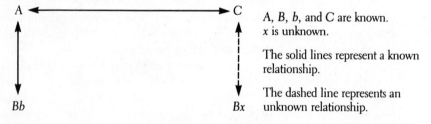

In the above diagram, A might represent Megalopolis, *Bb* might represent the type of city income tax in effect in Megalopolis, C might represent Gotham, and *Bx* might represent a type of city income tax proposed for Gotham. An advocate using reasoning by analogy might argue that, since a certain type of city income tax was desirable in Megalopolis, a similar city income tax would be desirable in Gotham. Similarly, in debating the proposition "Resolved: That the federal government should grant annually a specific percentage of its income tax revenue to the state governments," some negative teams sought to show that, as state income taxes were effective revenue producers for some states, such taxes could be used effectively by other states.

Analogies may be literal or figurative. The analogy is *literal* when the cases compared are in the same classification, as are Megalopolis and Gotham (if we will accept these as metropolitan cities for the purposes of our illustration) or the various state governments. The analogy is *figurative* when the cases compared are in different classifications. The statement "This car is a lemon!" is a figurative analogy. It has zero value as logical proof. It does, however, make the point rather effectively.

Carefully developed literal analogies may be used to establish a high degree of probability. Figurative analogies, on the other hand, have no value in establishing *logical* proof. If well chosen, however, they may have considerable value in establishing *ethical* or *emotional* proof, in illustrating a point, and in making a vivid impression on the audience.

The following questions serve as tests for reasoning by analogy:

1. *Are there significant points of similarity?* The advocate must be careful to determine whether significant points of similarity exist between the cases compared. In making an analogy between Megalopolis and Gotham, the advocate might be able to discover a number of significant points of similarity; both might have approximately the same population; both might have comparable inner city problems; both might have suburbs of about the same size and affluence; both might have about the same ratio of heavy industry to service businesses. Unless the advocate can demonstrate some significant points of similarity between the cases, no analogy can be made.

2. *Are the points of similarity critical to the comparison?* It is not sufficient that the cases merely have some significant similarities. The existence of significant points of similarity makes an analogy possible; but the analogy cannot have a reasonable degree of cogency unless it can be demonstrated that the cases are similar in *critical* points. We could easily demonstrate, for example, that there are some points of similarity between a water pump and the human heart. We would not conclude, however, that any skilled amateur mechanic is qualified to repair both of them. As indicated, we could find many significant similarities between Megalopolis and Gotham; however, in arguing that a certain type of city income tax is equally desirable in both cities, we would find these similarities noncritical. To support an analogy involving a city income tax, we would have to determine, for example, whether similar state income tax laws applied in both cities or whether there were similar state and city sales taxes in effect in both cities, similar reciprocity provisions for suburban city income taxes, similar taxes of other types, or similar financial policies. In other words, we would have to demonstrate that the two cities were similar in critical points.

3. *Are the points of difference noncritical?* The advocate will discover that no two cases are identical in every respect. Even when two cases are similar in critical points, there will still be certain points of difference. The task of the advocate, then, is to determine whether the points of difference are critical or noncritical. This very often depends on the context within which the comparison is made. For example, "identical" twins are usually similar in many respects, yet they have dif-

ferent fingerprints. This apparently minor difference might become critical and outweigh all similarities in a case where the identity of one of the twins was the issue and fingerprint evidence was available.

As another example, one might point to a very low level of malpractice suits against British physicians and the soaring rate of malpractice suits against American physicians and argue that British physicians must be providing far better medical care. In support of this, one could argue that an injured British patient would be just as willing to sue as an injured American patient, so the only possible reason for the difference in the ratio of malpractice suits must be the quality of medical care. However, there are critical differences in British and American law. In Britain, the lawyer's contingency fee is expressly forbidden; in America, it is almost the sole means of financing malpractice suits. Another critical difference is that in Britain all malpractice suits are held before a judge; in America almost all such suits are heard by juries. In order to defend an analogy, the advocate must be prepared to demonstrate that the similarities outweigh the differences in the cases compared and that the differences are not critical to the matter at issue.

4. *Is the reasoning cumulative?* An analogy is strengthened if it can be demonstrated that more than one comparison may be made in support of the conclusion. For instance, in defending the proposition that a city income tax would be advantageous in Gotham, the advocate would strengthen his case by making analogies not only between Gotham and Megalopolis, as mentioned, but also between Gotham and other comparable cities having city income taxes. If we were able to demonstrate that the similarities between the cities compared were critical and that the differences were noncritical, we would strengthen our case by using cumulative analogies.

5. *Are only literal analogies used as logical proof?* The advocate must remember that only literal analogies may be used to establish logical proof. Figurative analogies are useful as illustrations but have no probative force. When confronted with a figurative analogy, the advocate must be prepared to demonstrate its shortcomings as logical proof.

Reasoning by analogy may also be analyzed by using the elements of any argument. Assume the advocate claims that British medical care is better than American medical care (see the diagram).

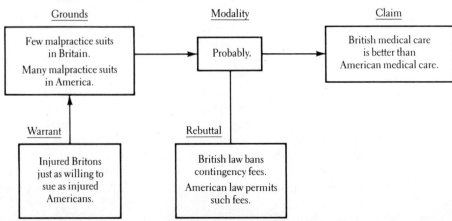

C. Causal Reasoning

In the process of reasoning by cause, one infers that a certain factor (a cause) is a force that produces something else (an effect). This process may be represented as follows:

$$C \text{ (known)} \xrightarrow{\hspace{4cm}} E \text{ (inferred)}$$

The same process may be used in reverse. If an effect is known to exist, it may be reasoned that it was produced by a cause. This process may be represented as follows:

$$C \text{ (inferred)} \xleftarrow{\hspace{4cm}} E \text{ (known)}$$

Causal reasoning may be cause-to-effect or effect-to-cause reasoning, and usually involves generalization. In using causal reasoning, the advocate seeks to show *why* the proposition is valid. The National Weather Service regularly reports the existence of low-pressure areas and other phenomena (causes) and predicts that we will have rain (an effect) tomorrow. The fact that the weather service is not always right emphasizes the point considered earlier. We often deal with matters in the realm of probability because we cannot establish certainty in many areas of concern to us. In debates on the discontinuance of direct economic aid, some affirmative teams tried to show that such aid was a cause of criticism among recipient countries. Continuing this argument, those advocates reasoned that if direct economic aid (the cause) were discontinued, then criticism (the effect) would also be eliminated. Conversely, the proponents of such aid argued that it was producing desirable effects.

Advocates must, of course, recognize that many causes are at work in any problem under consideration; at the same time, they must try to discern the practical, effective cause or causes in the matter at issue. Many debates on human affairs revolve around causal matters. The supporters of a "national program of public work for the unemployed," for example, saw such a program as a cause that would produce many desirable effects, whereas the opponents of this program saw it as a cause that would produce many undesirable effects. Causal reasoning influences our thinking on personal matters as well. Students may go to college because they see a college education as a cause that they hope will produce desirable effects in later life.

The problem, as we apply the tests of causal reasoning, is to discern the significant, practical, and effective causes in the matter at issue. The following tests of reasoning may be applied either to cause-to-effect or to effect-to-cause reasoning:

1. *Is the alleged cause relevant to the effect described?* Some observers have claimed that an increase in sunspot activity causes a rise in the stock market. Is there a relevant cause-and-effect relationship between these two phenomena? Most competent authorities have not been able to discern it. One college debater recently informed her professor that she expected to win because it was snowing the day the tournament began and she had previously won a tournament when snow had fallen at the start of the event. Her remark was facetious, of course, because she recognized that there was no causal relationship between snowfall and the winning of a tournament. Yet this very kind of reasoning has formed the basis of

many superstitions. The superstition that breaking a mirror will cause seven years of bad luck, for example, is based on the assumption that a cause-to-effect relationship exists where, in fact, there is no such relationship. Unless and until a causal link can be established between an alleged cause and an alleged effect, one cannot hope to develop causal reasoning.

2. *Is this the sole or distinguishing causal factor?* It is necessary to determine whether the alleged cause is the only causal factor in producing the effect under consideration or, if not, whether it is the distinguishing causal factor. In debates on the "mass media" proposition, some affirmative advocates used cause-to-effect reasoning to argue that television commercials for sugar-laden cereals caused children to eat these products, which, in turn, caused deleterious effects on their health. In countering this line of reasoning, some negatives argued that children naturally liked sweet foods and would eat sugar-laden cereals even if commercials for such products were banned from television.

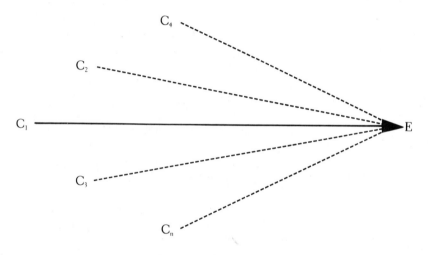

Is this the sole or distinguishing causal factor—or are there other causes that produce the effect under consideration?

Some negative advocates extended their argument by claiming that, if television commercials for such products were banned, the manufacturers would merely shift their advertising to newspapers, magazines, and billboards (that is, media not affected by the affirmative's plan) and that these media would produce the same effect as the television commercials had. Thus the negative advocates claimed that television commercials were neither the sole nor distinguishing causal factor in children's consumption of sugar-laden foods. The advocate must therefore be prepared to demonstrate that the alleged cause is the sole or distinguishing causal factor.

3. *Is there reasonable probability that no undesirable effect may result from this particular cause?* Usually a given cause will produce various effects in addition to the effect under consideration. Will these other effects be desirable, unimportant, or undesirable? If desirable, they will aid those advocating this particular cause; if

unimportant, they will have no adverse impact; if undesirable, they may provide good reason for rejecting the arguments in support of this cause. In debates on the "mass media" proposition, some negative teams developed a disadvantage argument by maintaining that, if the affirmative's plan of banning television commercials for sugar-laden cereals were put into effect, it would drastically reduce the demand for sugar, it would cause widespread unemployment among sugar producers, and the harms resulting from this unemployment would far outweigh any minor harms related to sugar consumption.

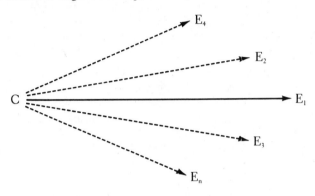

Are any of the other effects undesirable?

Some readers of this book can verify the following example from their own experience. Penicillin is a very effective cause for producing certain very desirable effects in some types of illness. Yet, in some persons, penicillin causes effects that are so undesirable that its use is contraindicated. The possible good effects are outweighed by the undesirable effects. Thus, advocates must determine what other effects will be produced by the cause they speak for and be prepared to demonstrate, at the least, that these other effects are not undesirable.

4. *Is there a counteracting cause?* When an effect that will take place in the future is the factor under consideration, it is necessary to determine that no counteracting cause, or causes, will offset the alleged effect. In debating the proposition on "mass media," some affirmative teams sought to ban the sale of pornographic material. Some negative teams meeting this case developed a series of plan-will-not-

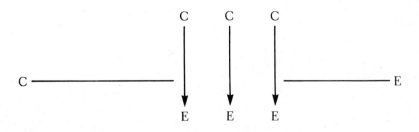

Do other counteracting causes prevent the operation of the cause under consideration?

achieve-claimed-advantage arguments by claiming that the sale of pornographic materials would continue virtually undiminished under the affirmative's plan because of these counteracting causes: (1) The courts would find it difficult or impossible to define pornography; (2) the affirmative's figures on the sales of pornographic material proved that a vast market exists for such materials—thus the criminal elements that produced it would have a strong incentive to circumvent the law; and (3) prosecutors would be reluctant to prosecute pornography cases, as prosecuting cases with little hope of obtaining convictions would be a waste of tax dollars. Thus advocates must be prepared to demonstrate that other causes at work in the situation will not counter the effect they claim a certain cause will produce.

5. *Is the cause capable of producing the effect?* Often various factors occur prior to a given event; yet these factors cannot be considered as causing the effect until it can be established that they are capable of producing it. For example, did the assassination of Archduke Ferdinand at Sarajevo cause World War I? Although this incident did immediately precede the outbreak of that war, the assassination of European royalty was not an altogether unusual occurrence and such occurrences did not cause wars. Most thoughtful historians do not regard this assassination as a cause capable of producing World War I, and thus they assign other causes to that war.

In debating the "guaranteed employment opportunities" proposition, many affirmative teams argued that their plan would cause the creation of jobs, thus guaranteeing the employment opportunities called for in the resolution. Of course, they had to prove that their plan was capable of generating several million new jobs.

When Geraldine Ferraro was given the Democratic Vice Presidential nomination, many of her supporters believed that her presence on the ticket would cause large numbers of women to vote Democratic. This causal reasoning turned out to be faulty; President Reagan won a majority of the women's votes.

In debating, as in politics and many other situations, a plan is often proposed as a cause that will produce a particular desired effect.

6. *Is the cause necessary and sufficient?* A necessary cause is a condition that is essential to producing the effect. Oxygen, for instance, is a necessary condition for fire. Oxygen alone will not cause fire, but we cannot have fire without it. Once we have identified the necessary condition for an event, we can *prevent* that event from occurring by removing one of the necessary conditions. In debating the "curtail executive control of foreign policy" proposition, some affirmatives argued that, when exposed *necessarily*, covert operations caused harm to American foreign policy and thus they advocated prohibiting the executive from carrying out covert operations.

A sufficient cause is a condition that automatically produces the effect. Decapitation, as the inventor of the guillotine well knew, is sufficient cause for death. The difference between a necessary and a sufficient cause is that, although a necessary condition must be present, it will not by itself produce the effect. The sufficient cause is by itself enough to produce the effect. Most often a sufficient cause is a collection of necessary causes all present at one time and place. For instance, oxygen, a combustible material, and the combustion point are all necessary conditions to fire. Together, all three constitute the sufficient cause for a fire. Once we have identified the sufficient conditions for an event, we can *produce* the event by bringing the sufficient conditions together. In debating the "comprehensive health care" proposition, some affirmatives argued that, if the government provided free medical care, trained more physicians and other medical personnel, and built more medical facilities, the *necessary* result would be better health for all citizens.

7. *How does a new cause affect the system?* In debates on the "comprehensive medical care" proposition, some affirmatives claimed as a need better medical care for slum residents and cited tragic cases of children bitten by rats as a need for providing medical care in slums. Some negatives countered this by arguing that there will be little point in treating the rat bite and then sending the child back to his slum home to be bitten again by another rat. Instead of spending the money on medical care, they argued, it would be better spent on providing better housing, better food, and other improved conditions for slum dwellers.

Causal reasoning may also be analyzed by using the elements of any argument.

Assume the advocate claims the Cost of Living Index will go up because of a recent increase in the cost of meat, as the diagram indicates.

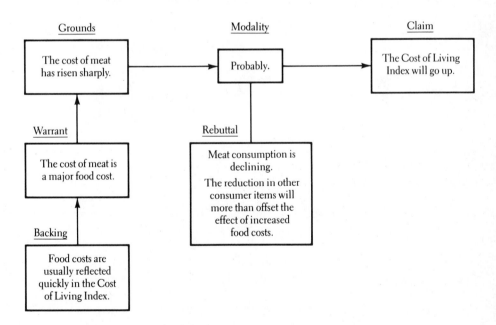

D. Sign Reasoning

The process of *reasoning by sign* consists of inferring relationships or correlations between two variables. One argues that two variables are so closely related that the presence or absence of one may be taken as an indication of the presence or absence of the other. This process may be represented as shown in the diagram.

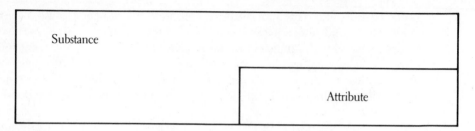

Reasoning by sign involves reasoning by analogy, by example, or from effect to effect as the advocate seeks to show that a proposition *is* valid. In causal reasoning, you will remember, the advocate seeks to show *why* a proposition is valid.

We use sign reasoning when we note that the leaves are falling from the trees and take this as a sign that winter is coming soon. The attribute is a part or a characteristic of the substance or totality with which we are concerned. In sign reasoning, the advocate may reason either from the attribute to the substance or from the substance to the attribute.

If one variable may be taken as a sign of another, the relationship between the variables is *reciprocal*. The relationship between the variables is *nonreciprocal* when one variable may be taken as a sign of the other, but the second variable is *not* a reliable sign of the first. For instance, if a person is President of the United States, we may take this as a sign that he or she is at least 35 years old. Obviously, we cannot take the fact that a person is 35 years old as a sign that he or she is President of the United States.

In debating the proposition "Resolved: That the United States should extend diplomatic recognition to Cuba," some negative advocates argued that we should not adopt the proposition because diplomatic recognition was a sign of approval of the government recognized.

The following questions serve as tests of sign reasoning:

1. *Is the alleged substance relevant to the attribute described?* It is necessary to determine whether there really is a sign relationship between the substance and the attribute under consideration. Some affirmative advocates, in meeting the argument that diplomatic recognition would be a sign of approval, maintained that diplomatic recognition is not a sign of approval. In support of this, they pointed out that the United States extended diplomatic recognition to the Soviet Union and to other regimes that followed policies we did not approve of; they maintained that no sign relationship exists between approval of a government and extending diplomatic recognition to that government. Unless and until advocates can demonstrate that a sign relationship exists between the substance and the attribute under consideration, they cannot develop sign reasoning.

2. *Is the relationship between substance and attribute inherent?* The advocate must determine whether the relationship between substance and attribute is inherent or merely incidental. A political commentator once noted that the Soviets had greatly increased the number of attachés at their embassy in a certain Eastern European country. He took this action as a sign that the Soviets were planning to invade that country. But was the relationship inherent? On some occasions, this type of action has been a sign of an invasion, as in Afghanistan; on other occasions, it has merely meant an increased propaganda or trade campaign.

3. *Is there a counterfactor that disrupts the relationship between substance and attribute?* It is necessary to determine that no counterfactor or factors disrupt the relationship. An increase in the number of attachés that one country assigns to another may, under some conditions, be a sign that the nation increasing its embassy plans to invade the other. When the United States expanded its embassy in the People's Republic of China, no one took this as a sign that the United States planned to invade the People's Republic; too many counterfactors disrupted that sign relationship.

4. *Is the sign reasoning cumulative?* Sign reasoning is strengthened by demonstrating that more than one sign relationship can be presented in support of the conclusion. An upturn in durable-goods orders might be a sign that an economic slump is ending. This sign is a relatively weak indicator when taken alone. If other signs can be found — such as increases in a number of indicators (productivity rate, orders for plants and equipment, orders for consumer goods, work week in industry, and new residential building permits) — the accumulation of a series of signs may add up to a conclusion with a high degree of cogency.

Sign reasoning may also be analyzed by using the elements of any argument. Assume the advocate claims the economy will improve in the next few months:

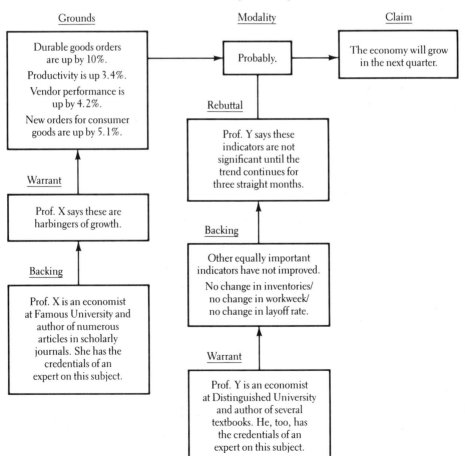

Exercises

1. Prepare a three-minute speech for presentation in class in which you develop one closely reasoned argument. Other members of the class will be invited to apply the tests of reasoning to your argument and see whether it is valid. Prepare an outline of your speech in which you indicate the types of reasoning, and hand this outline to your instructor.

2. Prepare a three-minute speech for presentation in class in which you develop one argument. In your speech, deliberately include some carefully concealed violations of sound reasoning. Other members of the class will be invited to apply the tests of reasoning and see whether they can discover the violations. Prepare an outline of your speech in which you indicate the types of reasoning used and the violations of good reasoning and hand this outline to your instructor.

3. Prepare a three-minute speech for presentation in class in which you develop a closely reasoned argument. After you have presented the speech, your instructor will designate another member of the class to present a three-minute refutation of your argument that will apply the tests of reasoning. Prepare an outline of your speech in which you indicate the types of reasoning used and hand this outline to your instructor.

4. Bring to class five examples of each of the four types of reasoning considered in this chapter. Draw your examples from newspapers or newsmagazines published within the past week. Apply the appropriate tests of reasoning to each example.

5. Attend an intercollegiate debate and prepare a brief paper in which you report four examples of reasoning used in the debate. Apply the appropriate tests of reasoning to each of these examples.

6. Attend an intercollegiate debate and prepare a brief paper in which you report four examples of reasoning used in the debate and the way in which the opposing team applied the tests of reasoning to refute them. Was the refutation effective or not? Justify your answer.

7. Bring to class one example of each of the four types of reasoning considered in this chapter. Draw your examples from recent public speeches by well-known national figures. Consult current publications for the full text of their speeches. Apply the appropriate tests of reasoning to each example.

10

Obstacles to Clear Thinking

Clear thinking is essential to all intelligent decision making. From the moment we begin to explore a problem until the end of the final debate on that problem, we must constantly be on guard against obstacles to clear thinking. The obvious obstacles are readily detected. One type of obstacle, however, which is more subtle and hence more deceptive, is called a *fallacy*. At first glance the error, unreasonableness, or falseness of the fallacy is not apparent, for the statement has the appearance of truth or reasonableness. Whately defined a fallacy as "any unsound mode of arguing, which appears to demand our conviction, and to be decisive of the question in hand, when in fairness it is not."[1]

Fallacies are usually recognized easily in isolation, but woven into the context of an argument they may pass unnoticed unless we are on guard against them. Debate affords those who render decisions one of the strongest protections against fallacies, since they not only have the opportunity to detect fallacies themselves but they also have the added safeguard that it is in the interest of the opposing advocates to point out fallacies in one another's cases.

Fallacies may be used accidentally or deliberately. Some advocates deliberately introduce fallacies into their arguments in order to exploit their listeners or readers and secure an unfair decision. A contemporary example of the apparently deliberate use of fallacies can be found in communist propaganda. Much of this propaganda is prepared by persons sufficiently intelligent to recognize the fallacies they are using, yet

[1] Richard Whately, *Elements of Logic* (Boston: James Munroe and Co., 1848), p. 143.

they deliberately introduce fallacies into their arguments. Some fallacies, on the other hand, may be introduced into argument unintentionally by honest people. Therefore, the advocate must be alert for obstacles to clear thinking at all times and from all sources.

For convenience, fallacies are classified here under various headings. In argument fallacies often are interwoven, and a fallacious argument may be a complex of several fallacies. In exposing fallacies in our opponent's case, we will do little good by declaiming "Aha, in his last statement my opponent has committed the fallacies of *circulus in probando* and *per negationem consequentiae!*" Although we may wish to identify and classify a fallacy for our own convenience, our task in the debate is not to name the fallacy but to be able to demonstrate to those who render the decision how or why the matter in question is fallacious. This task is complicated by the fact that fallacies are often field dependent; i.e., they must be considered in context. As Toulmin points out,

> Most disturbingly to some people, arguments that are fallacious in one context may prove to be quite solid in another context. So we shall not be able to identify any intrinsically fallacious forms of argument; instead we shall try to indicate why certain kinds of argument are, in practice, fallacious in this or that kind of context.[2]

One helpful way of exposing fallacies is to focus your attention on the warrants (considered in the previous chapter) and see whether the express or implied warrant actually justifies the claim made.

Some hold that there is no such thing as a fallacy; rather there is a failure to apply the appropriate tests of evidence or reasoning or language. In this chapter the conventional fallacies are discussed and the appropriate tests recommended. The use of the concept of fallacies provides us with a means of double checking our arguments and those of our opponents.

I.   Fallacies of Evidence

Theatre or film advertisements sometimes afford instances of fallacious use of evidence. For example, one critic wrote of a Broadway musical:

> *Interlude* represented an inept effort to make a dull story palatable by adding music. Unfortunately one brilliantly executed dance number in the first act was not enough to keep the show moving. Lavish costuming could not overcome the basic fact that the female lead simply does not have an adequate voice for the theater. The comedy routines showed brief flashes of inspiration, but they could not relieve the overall pedestrian pace of *Interlude*.

The newspaper advertisements quoted the reviewer as saying "*Interlude* . . . brilliantly executed . . . lavish costuming . . . flashes of inspiration." We can guard against this kind of fallacious use of evidence by asking, "Is any evidence omitted?"

One of the most common fallacies of evidence is the use of the unsupported assertion. Here, the speaker offers no evidence to support a statement; rather, he or she asks us to assume that something is so merely because he or she says it is so. The

[2]Toulmin, p. 157.

high-pressure used-car salesman may tell a customer, "This car is in perfect condition. You'd better buy it now before someone else gets it." The prudent buyer would not accept this unsupported assertion, but would look for evidence of the condition of the car. We can guard against this fallacy by asking, "Is the contention an unsupported assertion?"

The tests of evidence in Chapter 7 can help us guard against other fallacies of evidence.

II. Fallacies of Reasoning

Not only must we guard against fallacies of evidence; we must also be alert to fallacies that may occur in each of the types of reasoning we considered earlier.

A. Example

A speaker who maintained that the public schools are "failing to educate our children" offered as proof the following examples of their "failure":

> Last year 23% of the graduates of North High School who went to Omega State University were required to take remedial English; 37% of the North High graduates at Omega were required to take remedial math. I could cite dozens more examples of the failure of our schools, but this is enough to prove that we need a statewide system of competency testing before we grant high school diplomas.

Are you willing to accept this as an accurate picture of conditions statewide? Are the North High students typical of all the students in the state? Are the North High students who go to Omega State typical of North High students in general? We can quickly expose this fallacy by asking, "Are the examples given typical of the whole?"

Another common fallacy of reasoning by example is committed by the person who knows two or three motorcyclists who have criminal records and concludes that "they're all hoods." Here, one should ask, "Have sufficient examples been given?" A hasty generalization based on insufficient evidence often leads to unsound conclusions that will not be accepted by those who render the decision.

Additional questions that will aid us in guarding against other fallacies of reasoning by example may be found under "Reasoning by Example" in Chapter 9 (Section IV-A).

B. Analogy

A communist leader once told an American visitor to the Soviet Union, "With *glasnost* and *demokratizatsiya* we're completely democratic; we even have competing candidates running for some offices." The American exposed the fallacy in this analogy by replying, "In my country, however, we have at least two political parties." In this case the American applied the question "Are there critical differences in the factors compared?" and her reply pointed out one of the essential differences between American and Soviet elections.

See Chapter 9 (Section IV-B) for other questions that will help in detecting fallacies in reasoning by analogy.

C. Cause

There are many causal factors at work in most situations. Following the disastrous 1989 oil spill in Prince William Sound, Alaska, oil prices throughout the United States rose dramatically. Some consumer advocates were quick to charge that the price increase was excessive. Industry experts, however, pointed out that the price increase was only partially related to the costs of cleaning up the spill; OPEC had earlier decided to decrease oil production and new EPA regulations had just come into effect tightening summer grade fuel requirements. Was the price increase due solely to the costs of cleaning up the oil spill, or was it caused by a combination of factors? Fallacies of this type may be detected by asking, "Is a partial causal relationship treated as the sole or distinguishing causal factor?"

Additional questions we may ask to expose fallacies of causal reasoning may be found under "Causal Reasoning" in Chapter 9 (Section IV-C).

D. Sign

The ability to use sign reasoning effectively is an essential part of the work of all who seek rational decisions. The physician, for example, must constantly be on guard against fallacies in interpreting signs. In diagnosing a case, the neurologist may look for the Babinski sign, a certain type of movement of the toes after stimulus. This sign is apparently inherent in certain types of illness and, when found in adults, is taken as an indication of the presence of disease of the corticospinal pathway. The Rossolimo sign, a certain type of flexing of the toes after stimulus, indicates disease of the pyramidal tract. It is a much less reliable sign, however, because it is sometimes absent when the disease is present and it is sometimes found in normal patients. All who use sign reasoning should be on guard against fallacies that might lead to such false conclusions.

Questions that can help us to detect fallacies in sign reasoning in argumentative situations are considered in Chapter 9 (Section IV-D).

III. Fallacies of Language

The fallacies of language are often interwoven with other fallacies. Some of the more common fallacies of language that the advocate must guard against are cited here.

A. Ambiguity

Ambiguity arises when the meaning of a word, phrase, or passage may be reasonably interpreted in two or more ways. For example, what does a speaker mean when saying "I favor the American way of doing things"? A candidate for public office once campaigned on the slogan of "more teamwork in government." "Teamwork" may sound good, but what does it mean? A government official recently testified that he had not received any "improper" gifts from a constituent and that he had not made any "unreasonable" requests of governmental agencies on behalf of this constituent. His opponents viewed these same activities as "corruption" and "influence." Such terms as "New Deal," "New Frontier," "Great Society," and even "Democrat," "Republican," "conservative," and "middle of the road" have so many different meanings to so many different people that they are often ambiguous.

B. Verbalism

Verbalism arises when words are used so that they obscure meaning. *Time* magazine reported an example of this from one of Vice Presidential candidate Dan Quayle's campaign speeches:

> Making an argument for the Strategic Defense Initiative, Dan Quayle cited Indiana University's basketball coach. "Bobby Knight told me this: 'There is nothing that a good defense cannot beat a better offense.'" As listeners scratched their heads, Quayle explained, "In other words, a good offense wins." The candidate got it backward. Knight said—and SDI proponents contend—that good *defense* prevails.[3]

C. Loaded Language

Loaded language provides many possibilities for obstacles to clear thinking. Emotionally charged words are often used in an effort to establish a contention without proof. In a recent political campaign one candidate declared, "The time has come to throw this do-nothing, corruption-riddled Administration out of office." Obviously, such an administration should be thrown out of office, but the mere use of these labels did nothing to prove that the Administration was guilty of either of the charges. Consider the examples of loaded language in the following "conjugations":

I am economical.	I am a playboy.
You are a tightwad.	You are oversexed.
She is a miser.	He is a pervert.
I am revising my plans.	I am a freedom fighter.
You are impetuous.	You are a hijacker.
He is irresponsible.	She is a terrorist.

Are there extreme cases? Perhaps. Is a person who solicits memberships for a labor organization a "field representative," an "organizer," an "agitator," a member of a "goon squad," or a "hired thug"? It may depend on what paper we read. Is a successful businessperson a "robber baron," a "manipulator," an "exploiter," a "dynamic executive," or a "self-made person"? Once again, it may depend on what paper we read. Those who favor legal abortions call themselves "prochoice"; opponents of legal abortions promptly counter this label by calling themselves "prolife." The language is wonderfully loaded in both cases—who wants to be "antichoice" or "antilife"? When the Department of Health and Human Services proposed a regulation requiring those

[3]*Time*, September 19, 1988, p. 20.

who use tax dollars in supplying minors with contraceptive devices to notify the minors' parents, opponents promptly labeled it the "squeal rule." (If you want to denigrate an informer, use the label "squealer"; to hail an informer, use the label "whistleblower.")

Loaded language, or name calling, is all too often used in political campaigns. *Time* magazine reported this example from a Florida senatorial campaign:

> [George] Smathers used fancy language to convey sinister meanings to benighted rural listeners. "Are you aware that Claude Pepper is known all over Washington as a shameless extravert? Not only that, but this man is reliably reported to practice nepotism with his sister-in-law, and he has a sister who was once a thespian in wicked New York. Worst of all, it is an established fact that Mr. Pepper before his marriage habitually practiced celibacy."
>
> Pepper was defeated by 67,000 votes. "On election night people came up to our house in cars, shouting obscenities, cheering the fact that I had been defeated," Pepper recalls. "They wanted to destroy me and just about did."[4]

D. Grammatical Structure

Grammatical structure can, and often does, alter the meaning of a sentence. At a recent Republican Convention, the first draft of the party platform contained the sentence "[Republicans] oppose any attempts to increase taxes which would harm the recovery and reverse the trend to restoring control of the economy to individual Americans." A harmless bit of political rhetoric; of course everyone would oppose *harmful* tax increases; yet the door was left open to *unharmful* tax increases. The party's conservatives fought "The Battle of the Comma" and changed the sentence to read, "oppose any attempts to increase taxes, which would harm the recovery and reverse the trend to restoring control of the economy to individual Americans." The sentence, as punctuated with the comma, held *all* tax increases to be harmful. In reading the sentence aloud, the presence or absence of a pause would indicate the presence or absence of a comma.

Incomplete comparison is another grammatical fallacy — for example, "The present foreign aid program is unquestionably more effective." More effective than what? The advocate must guard against these and all of the other hazards of grammatical usage.

IV. Fallacies of Pseudoarguments

Pseudoarguments are fallacies created (by accident or design) by distortion, confusion, manipulation, or avoidance of the matters at issue or by substitution of matters not germane to the issue. Some of the more common fallacies are considered here.

A. Irrelevancy

The fallacy of irrelevancy carries an argument beyond its reasonable limits. For example, some opponents of "right-to-work" laws argued that these laws did not provide

[4]*Time*, April 25, 1983, p. 29.

jobs for the unemployed. These laws were not intended to provide jobs, but merely to eliminate the requirement of union membership as a condition of employment. It would be just as reasonable to criticize Salk vaccine, a serum designed to prevent polio, because it does not prevent pneumonia.

B. Arguing in a Circle

The fallacy of *arguing in a circle* occurs when one assumes as a premise for the argument the very conclusion one intends to prove. For example: "William Shakespeare is a greater writer than Danielle Steel because people with good taste in literature prefer Shakespeare." "How do you know who has good taste in literature?" "Why, that's simple; people with good taste in literature prefer Shakespeare to Steel." While Shakespeare is undoubtedly a greater writer than Steel, this circular argument does not prove the claim.

C. Ignoring the Issue

In a debate on the proposition, "Resolved: That the United States federal government should significantly increase exploration and/or development of space beyond the earth's mesophere," an affirmative team proposed a particularly weak and ineffective plan. In a thoughtful, closely reasoned refutation, the negative demonstrated that the affirmative's plan was completely unworkable. In their remaining speeches, the affirmative speakers completely ignored the issue of the workability of their plan; instead they spent their time claiming the great advantages that would come from their plan. By ignoring the issue, the affirmative lost this debate.

D. Baiting an Opponent

Sometimes advocates will *bait* their opponents by insulting them, attacking them personally, criticizing their friends, or doing anything that will cause them to lose their tempers. Once advocates lose their "cool," they are very likely to lose control of the argument and make reckless statements that will expose their case to defeat. Advocates can defend themselves against this kind of baiting only by holding their tempers during the argument; later, they may be able to "blow off steam" without damaging the case.

E. Repeated Assertion

The fallacy of *repeated assertion* occurs when an argument is repeated, with the repetition treated as proof. In a debate on guaranteed annual wages, members of the affirmative team stated repeatedly, without offering any proof, that American working persons need a guaranteed annual wage. A negative speaker, exposing this fallacy, pointed out that saying something three times did not make it true. This fallacy is not always so easily brushed off, however. Hitler developed to a fine art the technique of repeating a "big lie" so often that many came to believe it.

F. Structured Response

This fallacy is often found in cross-examinations or in any situation where the advocate has an opportunity to ask a series of questions. Using this fallacy, the advocate first asks a series of unimportant questions, which the respondent must answer in a predetermined way, until the pattern of a response has been established—then the critical question is asked. An old routine of insurance salespersons, for example, goes something like this: "You love your spouse, don't you?" "You love your children, don't you?" "You want your children to go to college, don't you?" "You want your family to continue to live in this lovely house, don't you?" "If something should happen to you, you want your family to be provided for?" "You would still want your children to go to college?" "You want to provide protection for them?" "To be safe, hadn't you better write your name on this routine form today?" Any prospects who have been lulled into a series of "yes" responses may find that they have signed an application for insurance without fully realizing the commitment they have undertaken.

The structured response was used effectively by Senator Edward Kennedy at the 1988 Democratic Convention, when after each recitation of a Republican shortcoming on Irangate he asked, "Where was George?" (The Republican candidate, Vice President George Bush, had stated that he was not present when certain controversial decisions were made.) The partisan audience quickly picked up the theme and chanted "Where was George?" along with Kennedy as he continued the list.

G. Special Pleading

The fallacy of *special pleading* occurs when advocates accept a line of reasoning and its conclusions but urge a special exception for their case. Examples of special pleading are sometimes found in Congress. In the early 1980s, there was tremendous pressure for Congress to produce a balanced budget. Virtually all members of Congress favored a balanced budget—except, of course, at the expense of cutting from the budget an item of interest to their constituents.

H. Substituting the Person for the Argument

This fallacy consists of the attempt to have an argument accepted or rejected, not because of any merit or defect intrinsic to the argument but because of the character of the person advancing the argument. For example, some people said that compulsory wage and price controls should be rejected because socialists favored them. Conversely, it may be argued that because someone is good in some respect, his or her arguments on some other matter must also be good. The defense attorney in a murder trial—as argument against the prosecution's claim that his or her client shot a business rival—sometimes tries to present the client as, for example, a kindly man who helps old ladies across busy streets, is good to his wife, kind to his children, generous to charities, and a member of the church choir. Traditionally the country rallies behind the President at the time of an international crisis, the theme being, "We must support the President during this crisis." Thus Roosevelt during World War II,

Kennedy at the time of the Bay of Pigs, and Carter at the time of the Iranian and Afghanistan crises enjoyed great initial support for policies that later came under criticism.

It should be noted that argument about a person is legitimate when the character of the person is intrinsic to the matter at issue. Evidence that John Doe is a convicted embezzler would be legitimate evidence if the issue were his employment as an accountant. Evidence that Jane Roe is a communist would be germane if she were urging that the United States adopt a certain foreign policy toward the Soviet Union. This example serves to emphasize the point, made at the beginning of this chapter, that "fallacies are often field dependent." Doe's criminal record and Roe's political beliefs are critical legitimate evidence in the context considered here; they would be irrelevant and thus fallacious in most other contexts.

I. Substituting Bombast for Argument

When no evidence or reasoning is available, advocates may sometimes attempt to support their argument by sheer noise and histrionics. In a debate on the "mass media" proposition, for example, a novice debater inserted in her affirmative case the impromptu claim that the federal government had a moral obligation to mandate a massive increase in the number of hours of closed-captioned programs that television stations provided for the hearing-impaired. The next negative speaker, in cross-examination, asked her to define moral obligation. Caught in her error, she replied with more hope than confidence, "My partner will define the term in the second affirmative." The second affirmative speaker, now on the spot, frantically searched his evidence files and was unable to find a single scrap of evidence defining moral obligation nor any notion of lines of argument that might be used to support his colleague's impromptu claim. There may have been some arguments to support this assertion, but they were not available to the advocate at that moment. In desperation he decided to bluff his way by *bombast*. He approached the lectern, wearing a well-simulated expression of deadly seriousness. In a voice seemingly choked with emotion he said, "The negative has asked us to define 'moral obligation.'" Eyes flashing with apparent righteous indignation he glared at his opponents: "We all know what 'moral obligation' is!" With a stern thump on the lectern, with ringing resolution, and an air of absolute finality, he cried, "A 'moral obligation' is a 'moral obligation'!" The negative, cowed by these histrionics, never dared mention the subject again. Had the next negative speaker assumed a calm and thoughtful air, providing a sharp contrast with the bombast of the affirmative, and quietly pointed out the absurdity of the affirmative's definition, he might well have punctured the balloon the affirmative speaker had used so effectively to conceal his lack of an adequate answer to a reasonable question.

J. Denying a Valid Conclusion

The fallacy of denying a valid conclusion occurs when an advocate admits or cannot refute the premises of an opponent, yet denies the conclusion that logically follows from these premises. For example, in a debate on federal aid for higher education, one negative team admitted that more money was needed for education and that the money must come either from federal aid or from increased aid by state and local governments; furthermore, the negative was unable to refute the affirmative's argument that many states and many local governments could not increase their aid to education. The logical conclusion from the admitted and unrefuted premises was that the federal government was the only source of the needed money; but the negative attempted to deny this valid conclusion.

The negative team's error was twofold. They admitted too much and failed to advance arguments they could have used. Other negative teams successfully argued that state and local governments could increase their aid to education and that the dangers of federal control outweighed the benefits of federal funds.

K. Popular Appeal

The fallacy of popular appeal occurs when an advocate seeks to gain support for a position by maintaining that he or she is just an "ordinary human" like everyone else. This device was particularly popular with rural politicians at the turn of the century and still has considerable currency today. During the 1988 Presidential campaign, Michael Dukakis liked to contrast his "son of immigrants" background with the "preppy" image of Vice President George Bush by proclaiming:

> My friends, there is only one country on the face of the earth where this son of immigrants could aspire to be the President of the United States, and that's the United States.

As the governor of Massachusetts, the son of a millionaire physician and a Harvard Law graduate himself, Dukakis was, of course, hardly a typical son of immigrants. And one might be pardoned for asking where else but the United States could one reasonably aspire to be President of the United States?

Another aspect of the same fallacy is the *"bandwagon" technique* — or arguing that something should be done because "everybody" is doing it. In many political campaigns, both candidates will announce their confidence that they will win by an overwhelming majority. They hope by this method to induce many undecided voters to vote for Doakes because Doakes is going to win anyway. Only one brand of cigarettes or soap or any other type of product can be the most popular; yet note the number of companies that claim their product is the "most popular." They hope their product will be bought because "everyone" is buying it.

L. "Straw Argument"

The fallacy of the *"straw argument"* occurs when advocates set up an issue just so they can knock it down. Sometimes they attack a minor argument of their opponents and claim that they have refuted the whole case, or else they refute an argument their opponents did not advance and claim that they have thus refuted their opponents' position.

An example of this fallacy occurred in a debate on the "guaranteed employment opportunities" proposition. Many affirmative plans were vulnerable to attack on the grounds that the plan to create more job opportunities was highly inflationary. One affirmative team carefully "spiked" its plan against this attack by including in the plan provisions to guard against inflation. A negative team, meeting this affirmative, failed to note the "spikes" in the affirmative plan and ran its own inflationary blocks attacking the plan. This was an attack on a "straw argument," which the affirmative quickly pointed out and the judge duly noted.

M. Appeal to Ignorance

The fallacy of the *appeal to ignorance* occurs when advocates maintain that something cannot be so because they, or the audience, have never heard of it. Uninformed persons, for example, at one time declared the telephone to be an impractical gadget because "Everyone knows you can't talk over wires." Another example of the appeal to ignorance occurred in a debate on guaranteed employment opportunities. The concept of "cyclical fluctuations" was important in many of these debates. One freshman debater, who had yet to take his first economics course, had never heard of the term when he met it in an early season debate. Faced with an unknown concept, he stoutly maintained, "Well, I never heard of — ah, uh — those — er — fluctuations, and I certainly don't think they influence our economy." The appeal to ignorance did not work in this instance — the judge *had* heard of cyclical fluctuations.

Unfortunately, the appeal to ignorance is sometimes successful with an uninformed audience. The defense against this fallacy is to provide the audience with the knowledge necessary to understand the argument. Unhappily, this is not always an easy task. Before the moon landings, it would have been almost impossible to refute the argument "Of course, you can't get to the moon, that's science fiction" before a popular audience without giving a lengthy technical explanation. In fact, the explanation might have had to be so lengthy and so technical as to be impossible to present within the available time.

N. Pseudoquestions

The fallacy of the *pseudoquestion* occurs when an advocate asks an unanswerable, "loaded," or ambiguous question; or a question based on a false assumption; or so many questions that an opponent cannot possibly answer them adequately within the available time. An example of this type of question is "Have you stopped cheating on examinations?"

Another example of this type of fallacy occurred when a second negative speaker posed a series of fifteen pseudoquestions about the plan. If the first affirmative rebuttalist had attempted to answer them, she would never have had time to get to the "case-side" arguments and would probably have lost the debate. Rather than attempting to answer the questions individually, she grouped them: "The first seven questions have to do with funding; please group them and note that our funding plank clearly provides. . . . The next four questions have to do with enforcement; please consider these together and note that our enforcement plank provides for. . . ." In this manner she was able to dispose of the fifteen questions quickly and effectively and thus meet her responsibilities of defending both the plan and the case.

O. Appeal to Tradition

The fallacy of the *appeal to tradition* occurs when the advocate maintains that we should follow a certain policy because we have "always" done things that way. Thus a negative speaker, in a debate on the "comprehensive medical care for all citizens" proposition, argued against the affirmative's plan, saying it was unnecessary since physicians and hospitals had always provided free medical care for the indigent. The fact that something has been a long-standing tradition does not prove its merit. As Senator Sam Ervin once pointed out, murder and larceny have been practiced in all nations in all ages, but this fact does not make either murder or larceny meritorious.

P. Non Sequitur

So far we have avoided the Latin names of fallacies, but this one — which simply is a conclusion that does not follow from the premises or evidence on which it is based — is best known by its Latin designation. In the "medical care" debates, some affirmatives cited evidence showing that numbers of people could not afford medical care and then argued that the government should provide free medical care for all citizens. In other debates, some negatives argued that the affirmative plan would be administered by a government bureau and would therefore be inefficient. Bureaucracy does have a bad reputation — but it does not follow that all government bureaus are inefficient.

Q. Post Hoc

This title is simply shorthand for the longer Latin phrase *post hoc ergo propter hoc* meaning "after the fact, therefore because of the fact." The fallacy lies in assuming a causal relationship where none is proven. American history provides one of the best-known illustrations of this fallacy. Every American President elected at twenty-year intervals since 1840 died in office (Harrison, Lincoln, Garfield, McKinley, Harding, Roosevelt, and Kennedy) until Reagan broke the morbid chain of coincidence. A remarkable coincidence, surely, but their election in a particular year was hardly the *cause* of their death.

Obviously there are many fallacies, and the possibility of their being introduced into arguments is almost unlimited. As advocates, we must be constantly on guard against these obstacles to clear thinking, not only in statements of others but in our own statements as well.

Exercises

1. Find the full text of a recent speech by a public figure. Compare this with excerpts of the speech printed in the newspapers or newsmagazines. Do you find a fallacy of omitted evidence? Remember, there is a great difference between an accurate condensation and the fallacy of omitted evidence.

2. Analyze some of the newspapers and newsmagazines published within the last month. Locate five fallacies in the editorial, opinion, or news sections of these publications; and locate five fallacies in the advertisements. Prepare a brief paper in which you state the fallacy as it appeared in its original form and explain why it is a fallacy.

3. Some of the following statements contain one or more fallacies. Prepare a list of the fallacies you discover in these statements:
  a. Now Wags Dog Food contains 50 percent more protein! Get Wags Dog Food for your dog today!
  b. Compulsory wage and price controls have worked successfully for years in Sweden; therefore, they will work in the United States.
  c. Gun control laws are bad; that's how Hitler came into power in Germany.
  d. Q: What will be the cost of this plan during its first five years of operation?
     A: Our country owes a debt of gratitude to the farmer. The farmer represents the American Way of Life. Farmers are good people. They live close to the soil. They have not come under the influence of socialist union bosses or Eastern intellectuals.
  e. Why is it that the Democratic Party always leads this country into war and the Republican Party always leads us into depression?

4. Prepare a five-minute speech in which you support or oppose a proposition of policy or value, as determined by your instructor. Although most of your speech will be developed in accordance with sound principles of argumentation and debate, include three carefully concealed fallacies. Present the speech before the class and invite your classmates to see if they can discover the fallacies. Prepare an outline for your speech, indicating the fallacies, and hand it to your instructor before you present the speech.

5. Prepare a five-minute speech in which you support or oppose a proposition of policy or value, as determined by your instructor. Make sure there are no fallacies in your speech. As soon as you have presented your speech to the class, your instructor will designate another member of the class to deliver a five-minute refutation of your arguments, exposing any fallacies he or she may discover.

11

Requirements of the Case

The *case* is defined as the specific arguments the affirmative advances as its reasons for adopting the resolution. It includes the affirmative's *definitive issues and designative issues on a value proposition and the affirmative's justification, plan, and advantages issues on a policy proposition*. From among the available options, the affirmative must select the one most likely to overcome the negative's opposition and to win favor with those who render the decision.

When several advocates on one side of a proposition seek to coordinate their efforts in securing a decision, the drafting of a case becomes a team function. Almost all debates conducted in parliamentary situations, almost all major courtroom debates, and almost all academic debates are team functions.

If the advocates on a given side of a proposition fail to coordinate their efforts and to agree on a case, they reduce their effectiveness and leave themselves open to attack by their opposition, who will be quick to point out inconsistencies in their position. Even in so vast an undertaking as a national political campaign, which involves literally thousands of advocates on each side, an effort is made to provide a highly specialized form of case in the statement of the party platform. The party leaders hope that members of the party will subscribe to this platform, or case, and use it as the basis for their campaign speeches. In practice, of course, there are numerous deviations by campaign speakers; and, if these deviations are serious enough, they may affect the final outcome of the campaign.

The two debaters in an intercollegiate debate — just as a block of senators in Congress or a battery of lawyers before the Supreme Court or the party spokespersons in a

Presidential campaign—will draft their case giving careful consideration to the various requirements of the case.

I. The First Requirement—To Present a Prima Facie Case—Value and Policy

The first requirement of any affirmative, whether debating a value or policy proposition, is that it must present a *prima facie* case—one that in and of itself provides good and sufficient reason for adopting the proposition. As a starting point, a prima facie case must provide effective issue statements to answer each of the stock issue questions. (See Chapter 4, Section III-A.) Moreover, it must be both structurally and qualitatively strong enough to be logically self-sufficient. It must convince a reasonable and prudent person and stand on its own merits until or unless it is refuted.

This requirement is unique to the affirmative. We will consider additional requirements of the case—first those that apply to value propositions, then those that apply to policy propositions, and finally those requirements common to both value and policy propositions.

The student is reminded that some value propositions are quasi-policy propositions and that while we may sometimes debate facts, values, or policies by themselves, we will find that on many occasions it is necessary to consider all of them together. (See Chapter 3, Section IV-B.) Thus it is in the student's interest to know the requirements that apply to both value and policy propositions.

II. Requirements of a Value Case

A. Requirement to Provide a Satisfactory Definition

As we saw earlier (Chapter 4, Section II-B), CEDA debate requires a reasonable definition of terms. In debating value propositions, definition is a stock issue essential to proving a prima facie case and is considered in that context here.

In debating the proposition "Resolved: That federal government censorship is justified to defend the national interest of the United States," it was essential to define "censorship." Did censor mean "keep correspondents out of the combat area" as the United States did in Grenada or "prohibit any mention of anything the government does not want mentioned and enforce this ban by harsh penalties" as the British did in the Falklands? Clearly there is a vast difference between these definitions.

In debating the proposition "Resolved: That individual rights of privacy are more important than any other Constitutional right," it was clearly necessary to define "rights of privacy." Actually there is no Constitutional right to privacy. Yet, in many cases, the courts act as if there were such a right. What is the best definition in these circumstances?

For many years the sex life of a political figure was considered to be a *private* matter. Times change, however. In 1988 Gary Hart's extramarital affair became a major news story and ended a once promising bid for a Presidential nomination.

Almost everyone is in favor of privacy. Yet we recognize that the public interest requires some exceptions. What exceptions can you justify as part of your definition?

B. Requirement to Provide a Satisfactory Criterion

Providing a reasonable criterion for each of the value terms in the proposition is critical for the affirmative in debates on value propositions. The negative must also consider carefully the criterion offered by the affirmative and be ready either to offer a better criterion or to exploit any error of the affirmative.

In debating the "commercial television" proposition, it was essential for the affirmative to provide carefully considered criteria for the value terms "detrimental" and "beneficial." If the criteria are well chosen, they establish a sound basis for the affirmative's case and greatly enhance the affirmative's chances of prevailing in the debate and winning the decision that it seeks. If the criteria were not well chosen, they would open up opportunities for the negative to defeat the affirmative by providing better criteria or to turn the criteria against the affirmative by providing value objections.

C. Requirement to Provide Application

Here the affirmative must address the question "What is the application of this value?" If the value set out in the proposition is accepted, what will happen? In debating the proposition "Resolved: That a unilateral freeze by the United States of the production and development of nuclear weapons would be desirable," the affirmative had to be prepared to demonstrate that such a unilateral freeze would indeed be desirable — that it would, for example, reduce the risk of World War III. Reducing the risk of World War III is indeed a highly desirable value, but would a unilateral freeze facilitate our achieving this goal? The negative would be certain to argue that the application of a freeze would actually increase the risk of World War III. The affirmative in value debates must be prepared to develop and defend its application issue in a way very similar to the development and defense of the advantages issue in policy debates.

D. Requirement to Prove Inherency

In value debates the advocates must sometimes prove that certain factors are inherent in various elements of the case they advance or in the relationship between certain of these elements. In debating the "privacy" proposition considered in Section A, debaters often had to establish just what was inherent in the right to privacy and why that was inherently more important than other constitutional rights. In debating the "censorship" proposition also considered in Section A, debaters sought to establish that certain factors inherent in censorship were inherently critical to the defense of the national interest of the United States. Inherency is sometimes a major issue in policy debate and will be considered in more detail in Section III-B.

E. Requirements of Significance

As in policy debate, the advocates in value debate must prove that the essentials of their case are significant. The values they advocate must be proved to be significant values, and the application of those values must be significant. In the example just considered about unilateral nuclear freeze, reducing the risk of World War III would seem to be a significant application. But *how much* would the risk be reduced? Enough to offset the negative's claim that adopting the affirmative's value would actually increase the risk of war? Thus, as in policy debate, significance is often established by weighing application *on balance* against the value objections. Significance, too, is often a major issue in policy debate and will be considered in more detail in Section III-C.

III. Requirements of a Policy Case

A. Requirement to Provide the Best Definition in the Debate

As we saw earlier (in Chapter 4, Section II-B), NDT debate requires the best definition in the debate. If, when challenged, the affirmative can prove that theirs is the best definition in the debate, they are then free to fight out the debate on their own grounds. If, however, the negative can prove that theirs is the best definition in the debate, they are now free to fight out the debate on their grounds. In debates on the "information gathering" proposition cited in Chapter 4, some affirmatives maintained that the best definition of "information" included citizens who used marijuana. Some negatives argued that the best definition of "information" was limited to computerized credit information. In such debates, the team proving theirs was the best definition won.

B. Requirement to Prove Inherency

The affirmative must prove that the essential elements of its case are inherent; the negative must prove that its attacks (that is, disadvantages) are inherent in the opponent's case. We will consider three types of inherency: structural, attitudinal, and existential.

1. Structural Inherency

There are two types of *structural inherency*: the presence of a structural barrier that prevents something from being done; or a structural gap, the absence of a structure necessary to permit or mandate a desired action.

a. Structural Barrier. This form of inherency may be important to both the affirmative and negative. For example, if an affirmative points to a certain need as a reason for adopting the proposition, it must prove that the need is inherent in the status quo; it must prove that the need could not be eliminated by repairs or that the need merely coexists with the status quo and could be eliminated without adopting the proposition.

    In debating the proposition "Resolved: That the federal government should guarantee a minimum annual cash income to all citizens," some affirmative teams argued that poor people needed cash to obtain food, medical care, and housing. They then proposed a "cash income" plan to meet this need. Some negative teams meeting this case were quick to point out that these problems did not constitute an inherent need for a "cash income." The need for food was being met by food stamps—and if more food stamps were needed, they could be supplied through repairs in the status quo; the need for medical care was being met through Medicare and other welfare programs — and if more medical care was needed, it could be provided through repairs in those programs; the need for housing was being met through various public housing programs — and if more housing was needed, those programs could be expanded.

A structurally inherent need is one that is intrinsic to the status quo. The affirmative must prove that the need cannot be resolved by modifications, adjustments, repairs, or any other means except by adopting the plan called for by the affirmative under the resolution. Some affirmative teams debating the "energy" proposition were able to establish that the status quo could not meet the nation's energy needs. As these debates took place during the Arab oil embargo, this need issue was usually easy to establish and the main clash of the debate focused on the plan arguments.

The affirmative will claim that certain advantages will flow from its plan. Here, too, it must establish inherency; the affirmative must prove that the advantages are inherent in its plan, that they are *caused* by the plan, and can be obtained *only* by the plan. If the advantages can be obtained without the plan, or by means other than the plan, the negative will argue that there is no reason to adopt the plan to obtain the advantages. Other advantages may come along with the plan without actually being inherent in the plan; the affirmative may claim these as "bonuses" or "plus factors" for their plan. The negative, however, will point out that these are incidental to, rather than inherent in, the plan and, if they are significant, may find ways to provide them without adopting the plan. Affirmative teams debating the "tax sharing" proposition were usually able to establish that the federal income tax was inherently more efficient than any other system of tax collection in the status quo or than any that the negative could propose as an alternative.

The negative must demonstrate inherency in its case. For example, the negative often argues that the affirmative's plan produces disadvantages. The negative must prove that a disadvantage it charges to the affirmative's plan is in fact inherent in that plan. In debating the "tax sharing" proposition, some negative teams offered the plan objection "The affirmative's plan will deprive the federal government of an important fiscal tool in combating economic fluctuations." In their analysis they pointed out that, by giving the states a specific share of the income tax revenues, the federal government would lose the ability to curtail expenditures in time of inflation or to increase them in time of recession as almost all that remained in the federal budget after tax sharing would be fixed expenditures (that is, Social Security, agricultural subsidies, veteran's benefits, and so on) that could not readily be changed to meet economic fluctuations. Some affirmatives, depending on the specific provisions of their plan, were able to demonstrate that this objection was not inherent in their plan. If their plan involved "only" $2 billion, they would argue that there were many other areas where the government could increase or decrease expenditures by many billions of dollars to meet a temporary economic problem without impinging on fixed expenditures.

In arguing inherency, the negative may sometimes use the phrase *not topical* and contend that the advantages claimed by the affirmative are not *unique* to the proposition, that they can be obtained without the proposition. In debating the "tax sharing" proposition, some affirmative teams pointed to the need for more funds for schools, proposed "tax sharing" with the requirement that the states spend the funds on schools, and then claimed the advantage of meeting the need of schools for more funds. A negative meeting this case argued that the advantage was "not topical," that the advantage came from giving the schools more money, and that the affirmative did not show any advantage in providing that money through tax sharing. The negative continued to demonstrate that there were other ways in which more funds could be provided for schools, thus the advantage could be obtained without adopting the proposition that called for tax sharing. Had the affirmative been able to establish that tax sharing was the most advantageous method of supplying the money, they then would have been able to establish the advantage of "more money through tax sharing" as inherent in adopting the proposition.

b. Structural Gap. Structural inherency can also take the form of the absence of a structure necessary to permit or mandate the policy desired by the affirmative. Opponents of abortion find that the structure of the status quo permits abortion. Therefore they call for a structural change — a constitutional amendment — to achieve their objective of banning abortions.

In debating the "mass media" proposition, some affirmatives called for regulations to require all television stations to greatly increase a standardized form of closed-captioned programming for the hearing-impaired and claimed as their advantage that this would benefit millions of hearing-impaired people. Obviously this *could* be done by the status quo. Closed captioning existed and two networks were broadcasting a few hours a week of such programs. Presumably the Federal Communications Commission *could* order the television stations to increase the number of hours devoted to closed-captioned programs anytime it wanted to. However, the affirmative's advantage, that *all* television stations *greatly increase a standardized* form of closed-captioned programming, could be achieved only through a structural change — by having the FCC actually issue a mandate requiring the action desired by the affirmative and thus closing the gap that existed in the status quo structure.

Structural gap inherency may also be argued by the negative to demonstrate that minor repairs or a counterplan may be instituted to solve the problem without the need of adopting the affirmative's plan and incurring the disadvantages that the negative will claim are inherent in the plan. In debating the closed-captioning case just considered, some negatives advanced as a counterplan the proposal that the National Association of Broadcasters (a voluntary organization) could institute a system of closed-captioned broadcasting that would achieve almost all of the advantages claimed by the affirmative. There was no structure to prevent this organization from doing so, and they would want to do so (see Section 2, "Attitudinal Inherency") in order to avoid the disadvantages of greater governmental control of their industry.

2. Attitudinal Inherency

This form of inherency may be important to both the affirmative and negative. Classic examples of *attitudinal inherency* as a need argument are found in the fields of civil rights and equal rights. Some believe that all citizens should be treated equally. A barrier to such treatment was perceived in the attitude of some whites who inherently refused to allow blacks to attend certain schools, eat at certain restaurants, and so on. This attitude was so strong that it could not be changed. Thus, equal rights advocates saw this attitude as a need for equal rights legislation. They recognized that they could not change the attitude, so they resorted to the coercion of law to change the behavior of persons with a certain attitude. In the same way, some women felt that many employers had an inherent attitude that always caused them to pay women less than men for the same work. They felt the attitude could not be changed and, therefore, constituted an inherent need for legislation, which would use the coercive power of law to change employers' behavior.

Another example of attitudinal inherency is found toward the use of automobile seat belts. It is a proven fact that using seat belts saves lives. One might have expected that once this fact was proved, the public, in the interest of saving lives, would rush to buy and use seat belts. As we know, this did not happen. Various safety councils mounted massive propaganda campaigns to persuade people to use seat belts. Yet few were persuaded. Finally, the federal government decided there was an inherent barrier in people's attitudes about using seat belts, and laws were enacted requiring manufacturers to install seat belts in all cars and to equip them in such a way that the car would not start or that buzzers would sound if the seat belts were not fastened. In this case, however, the attitude proved stronger than the structure. The public deluged Congress with complaints and threats of retribution in the next election. Congress promptly yielded — cars can now be started without using seat belts and the buzzer sounds for only a few seconds.

Attitudinal inherency may also be argued by the negative to demonstrate that a plan will not work. In debating the "energy" proposition, some affirmative teams proposed that an independent federal commission be appointed to control the oil industry and expected that this commission would significantly change the way the oil companies operated. Some negative teams meeting this case argued that it would not work because of attitudinal inherency. They argued that the only people with sufficient expertise to serve on the commission would be oil company executives. Although they might serve for a few years on the commission as a public service, they could not be expected to stay long at the lower-paying government jobs. After that, they would be rehired by the oil companies. Thus, the negative argued, such persons were inherently sympathetic to oil company policies and would be unlikely to make any rulings unfavorable to the oil companies.

The Eighteenth Amendment to the Constitution provided a classic example of attitudinal inherency blocking the workability of a plan. The amendment prohibited the manufacture, sale, or transportation of intoxicating liquors. In many jurisdictions, however, the attitude of the jurors was such that they did not believe there was anything wrong with manufacturing, selling, or transporting intoxicating liquors. Consequently, regardless of the evidence, they refused to bring in a guilty verdict.

3. Existential Inherency

Advocates will sometimes argue *existential inherency* when they are unable to find a cause in the form of a structure or gap that prevents the status quo from solving the problem. In 1989 President Reagan underwent surgery for Dupuytren's Contracture, a long-standing contraction of the ring finger of his left hand. The condition was inherent in the President's constitution, but as the attending physician admitted, "No one knows for certain what causes the problem" — an example of existential inherency. In using this type of argument, the affirmative maintains that the problem exists; therefore it must be inherent in the status quo, and it is necessary to adopt the affirmative plan to solve the problem. In debating the "employment opportunities" proposition, some affirmatives argued that unemployment had for many months been above the 7 percent level. They introduced evidence and argument to show that unemployment was undesirable. They then concluded that as unemployment was undesirable and as it had continued for many months at the 7 percent level, the status quo must be inherently incapable of solving the problem. (They pointed out that Congress, the President, the Federal Reserve Board, the Council of Economic Advisors, and other agencies all deplored the present unemployment rate. Since all recognized the problem and had been unable to solve it with status quo mechanisms, the status quo must be inherently incapable of solving it.)

In meeting this type of argument, the negative might argue minor repairs and maintain that the affirmative had given no reason why the status quo could not solve the problem. It might introduce evidence that the Comprehensive Employment and Training Act then in effect could be expanded to provide more jobs, that the interest rate could be changed to provide more jobs, and that a variety of other status quo mechanisms could be used, with only minor changes, to solve the problem cited by the affirmative.

Other negative teams meeting this existential inherency argument maintained that both structural and attitudinal barriers existed in the status quo. They maintained that there was an unemployment–inflation trade-off and that decreasing unemployment would increase inflation. They continued their argument by claiming that the President, the Congress, and various governmental agencies recognized this trade-off and that, because inflation was more harmful than unemployment, they were attitudinally opposed to the affirmative's plan. They then proceeded to develop the harms of inflation, which they argued were inherent in the affirmative's plan, as a major disadvantage that would justify rejecting the affirmative's plan.

C. Requirements of Significance

The advocates must prove that the essentials of their case are significant. If the affirmative claims there is a need to change the status quo, it must show the need to be significant; its plan must provide a significant change, and it must provide significant advantages. If only one or two advantages survive the negative's attack, they must be sufficiently significant in themselves to justify adopting the resolution. If the affirmative offers independent advantages and claims that any one of them is sufficient to justify adopting the resolution, then each advantage must in fact be of substantial significance. The negative will often argue that an insignificant need does not justify the cost (as measured in dollars or perhaps in just the inconvenience of change) of adopting the plan or that an insignificant advantage is outweighed by the serious disadvantages it finds inherent in the affirmative's plan. Thus significance is usually measured by comparison and contrast; that is, "This advantage is outweighed by this disadvantage." A well-conceived affirmative plan will produce some inherent advantages; and if the affirmative argues its case well, it may force the negative to admit this. Any plan, no matter how well conceived, may produce some disadvantages; and, again, if the negative argues its case well, it may force the affirmative to admit this. Thus the issue becomes "Do the advantages *on balance* outweigh the disadvantages?" If the advantages are not significant and the disadvantages are significant, the negative should win this issue. On the other hand, if the advantages are significant and the disadvantages are not significant, the affirmative should win the issue. If both the advantages and disadvantages are significant — a very real possibility in a good debate — then the decision on this issue should go to the side demonstrating that *on balance* the weight of advantage or disadvantage rests with the side that claims it. There are disadvantages in wearing eyeglasses, for example. Yet most people who wear them have decided that, on balance, these disadvantages are outweighed by the advantages gained.

One cigarette company urged people to buy its product on the ground that it was "a silly millimeter longer"; a breakfast food company touted its product as being "just a little bit better." Facetious or trivial advantages may serve as the basis for decision in minor matters. On major matters, however, the reasonable and prudent person requires that significance be established. Significance, of course, must be established *in context* — that is, within the framework of the problem being debated. In debating "wage and price controls," the affirmative's advantage was narrowed at the end of the debate to the claim that its "standby" controls could go into operation one month earlier than the negative's. Was that one-month advantage significant? The answer would turn on the ability of the teams to prove how much harm — or how little harm — to the economy would occur within the context of the situation they were describing. In early-season debates on the "mass media" proposition, some affirmatives sought to justify their plan for banning television commercials for sugar-laden products on the ground that such products caused an undetermined number of dental caries. Negatives quickly challenged the significance of a few tooth cavities as justification for massive government regulation. After losing a few rounds with this case, the affirmatives conducted further research and found more significant harms to justify their ban of television commercials for sugar-laden products.

Prudent advocates will seek to establish the greatest significance that the evidence and argument will permit, recognizing that their opponents will seek to minimize their claims. Significance may, as we will see in the next chapter, be developed as either quantitative or qualitative. Of course the advocate is in a stronger position if the significance is *both* quantitative and qualitative.

IV. Requirements Common to Both Value and Policy Propositions

A. Requirements Imposed by the Characteristics of Decision Renderers

Since the advocates naturally want to win the decision, they must consider carefully the person or persons who will render the decision and adapt their case accordingly.

Our objective is not to develop a case that is intellectually satisfying to us; rather it is to develop a case that will have sufficient cogency for those who render the decision to move them to vote for us. For instance, in debating the "mass media" proposition, the affirmative would do well to develop different cases for use before audiences consisting of PTA members, television station managers, and supermarket executives. If the decision is to be rendered by a critic judge or panel of judges, the debaters should adapt their case to these key individuals. In most intercollegiate debates, the decision is rendered by a single judge who scrupulously seeks to render the decision solely on the basis of which team did the better debating. However, as we will see in Chapter 17, such judges often do have a specific judging philosophy or a decision-making paradigm they prefer, and the experienced debater learns of these preferences and adapts to them. For example: "Judge A is an issues judge," "Judge B prefers the policymaker paradigm," "Judge C likes to be a hypothesis tester," "Judge D likes counterplans," and so on.

The debater should be aware that, in applied debates, the judge or judges are often influenced by the reactions of the nonvoting audience. In his messages to Congress, for example, the President may deliberately use the audience to influence those who render the decision. Supposedly such messages are addressed to the Congress, which will render a decision on the message by voting for or against the legislation the President proposes. In fact, however, the President frequently seeks to "go over the heads" of Congress and to present his case to the people in the hope that they will bring pressure to bear on Congress and influence the members to vote as the President wishes. President Franklin D. Roosevelt was particularly expert at this type of presentation; he revived the custom of delivering Presidential messages to Congress in person and broadcasting them to the nation at the same time. Roosevelt was usually far more concerned with the national audience listening to him on the radio than he was with the Congressional audience before him. This practice of "going over the heads" of the immediate audience that renders the formal decision and appealing to the nonvoting audience is by no means new, nor was it unique with Roosevelt. Reagan raised this technique to its zenith when he used joint sessions of Congress as a mere applause-line responder; his real target was preeminently the viewer at home. We know that legislators are not altogether uninfluenced by demonstrations in the gallery and that juries are not impervious to the reactions of the spectators in the courtroom.

Most frequently, as students or citizens, we will seek to influence a single individual or a small group of individuals. In such cases, we should seek to learn as much as possible about the key individual and adapt our case to this individual. Although the key individual will be the focal point of our presentation, the desirability of securing a favorable response from the nonvoting audience should not be overlooked, since this response may influence the person who renders the decision. In a certain large corporation, the purchasing manager had the sole authority to determine the make of automobile that would be purchased for the salespeople. After ordering a fleet of B cars, he confided to a friend, "A cars are really better, but the salespeople wanted B. There wasn't a great deal of difference between the two, so I let the salespeople have the one they wanted." Apparently, the advocates for B cars did the better job of influencing the nonvoting audience.

B. Requirements Imposed by the Occasion

Argument does not take place in a vacuum but in a specific context of time and place and with a certain relationship to events that precede and follow the argumentative speech or writing.

The college debater will find that the tournament situation calls for certain social amenities, graceful references to the opposing team, a courteous exchange with the judge, and a certain air of poised informality. The final round of a tournament requires a graceful reference to the host college and the opposing team and a judicious mixture of formality and wit. An international debate requires well-chosen references to international relationships and to the visitors' nation and customs.

The necessity of adapting to the occasion applies to all advocates. Speakers on the highest governmental level face this same requirement. A dramatic example of the occasion's influencing the debate may be seen in America's entry into World Wars I and II. On April 2, 1917, in a lengthy speech reviewing the events of the previous several months, President Wilson asked Congress for a declaration of war. The proposal was debated for several days and did not become law until April 6. On December 8, 1941, rejecting the advice of some of his Cabinet that he review the whole history of American-Japanese relations, President Roosevelt gave a brief speech dealing only with the events of the previous day and asked Congress for a declaration of war. His proposal became law within one hour after he had finished speaking. The difference in the approach used by the two Presidents showed an awareness of the different situations in 1917 and 1941. The advocate, whether a college debater or a President, must be aware of the occasion and make appropriate adjustment to it.

C. Requirements of Clarity and Relevancy

It is self-evident that the debate case must be clear, interesting, and relevant. The available time in a debate is always limited. In an intercollegiate debate, strict time limitations are imposed; and in other debates, such factors as limitations of radio or television time, an agreed-on time of adjournment, or simply practical considerations of sustained audience attention and interest place a limit on the time available to the advocates. Well-prepared debaters, therefore, always have at their disposal more material than they can possibly use in the time available. From the materials available to them, the advocates must select for use those items of evidence or illustration that will be most clear, most interesting, and most relevant to their purpose. Debaters speaking on the proposition "Resolved: That law enforcement agencies in the United States should be given greater freedom in the investigation and prosecution of crime" before a Massachusetts audience would certainly want to include references to the widespread criminal activity exposed by a Massachusetts crime commission at the very time this proposition was debated. Well-prepared debates will have several items of evidence available to support each issue of their case. Many of these items may have approximately equal value in fulfilling the logical requirements of the position; but debaters will select only those that will make their presentation most clear and interesting to the specific audience and that are clearly relevant to their overall purpose. A good rule for advocates is to make certain that everything included in their case is specifically relevant to their purpose and to exclude, ruthlessly, all materials that are not relevant. Here it should be noted that the social amenities of the debate and certain other factors of persuasion may not be relevant to the logical proof of the case; but they are relevant to the debater's purpose, which is to secure a decision.

The sequence in which the issues and materials of the case are presented is of great importance to the debater. Occasionally, the debater may find it advantageous to arrange materials in a fashion that will achieve maximum effect, even if this means a violation of logical organization.

D. Requirements Imposed by the Probable Case of the Opposition

The advocates' task is not to overcome all possible opposition to their case; rather, it is to overcome the specific case presented by their opponents within the context of a given debate. In order to do this, the debaters must, in advance of the debate, make the best possible estimate of the position that will be taken by their opponents. The advocates can gain a real understanding of the problem only when they have thoroughly analyzed both sides of the proposition.

Salespersons, lawyers, generals, diplomats, and others devote a considerable portion of their time to estimating the probable moves of their opponents and to planning their own actions so as to anticipate and defeat the opposition. Advocates are well advised to study carefully the probable moves of their opponents and to be prepared to meet them. Many teachers of argumentation, from classical times to the present, have encouraged students to debate on both sides of the proposition selected for academic debate. Most contemporary intercollegiate debate tournaments are structured to provide the student such an opportunity. This procedure gives the student an opportunity to acquire knowledge of both sides of the proposition and of the requirements of both affirmative and negative cases. Few teachers of argumentation are interested in training propagandists for or against a given proposition. They are interested, however, in using a proposition as an educational tool, by means of which they may teach the theory and practice of argumentation. A student would not, of course, be asked to advocate publicly a position contrary to his or her convictions, and such a problem rarely arises in academic debating. National academic debate propositions usually deal with matters on which the average student has an open mind. After a number of debates on both sides of the proposition, the student is better able to formulate a considered judgment based on an intelligent analysis of the problem.

E. Requirements of Consistency

If the two advocates in an academic debate allow themselves to present contradictory or inconsistent arguments, the effect is almost certain to be defeat. The same consideration applies outside academic debate. During the energy crisis when gasoline prices were soaring, oil company executives had to coordinate their position carefully when speaking in public. Before their stockholders there was a temptation to point with pride to the profits they had made. That is, after all, what corporate executives are supposed to do—and increased profits are an excellent justification for increased executive salaries and bonuses. At the same time, other executives were testifying before Congressional committees and various regulatory commissions. Before these groups there was a temptation to minimize their profits and to emphasize how poorly the oil companies had done in comparison to other industries. If their statements revealed inconsistencies, they could expect unfavorable action from at least one audience.

F. Requirements of Flexibility During the Debate

As advocates, although we make the best possible estimate of the case of our opposition, we should remember that we can only estimate what position our opponent *may* take; we can never be certain in advance. If we draw up our case on rigid lines, we may find ourselves unable to adapt to the case actually presented by our opponent, and we may be handicapped seriously by the inflexibility of our own position. We would do well to follow the example of Winston Churchill, one of the most skilled parliamentarians of the modern era, who carefully estimated the probable course of the debate in Parliament and often went into the House with seven or eight different, carefully prepared speeches. Once he learned the precise position his opponents took, he would select the most appropriate of his several prepared speeches. This tactic, of course, is exactly what today's skilled debaters do. Negative advocates, for example, develop a variety of "briefs" against possible affirmative positions. Once the affirmative has committed itself to a specific position, the negative then selects the appropriate preplanned briefs, adapts them to the affirmative arguments, and launches the attack.

The advocate's case should be sufficiently flexible to allow for adaptation during the debate itself. If several advocates join together to build a case, they should decide in advance what position they will take if the opposition presents a given course of argument, and they should be able to make a smooth transition to a different and previously prepared position. In academic debate, such adaptation typically occurs in the affirmative case at the start of the second affirmative speech. At this point, as at many others during the debate, there is a high premium on flexibility. Although the attacks must be anticipated, their exact form cannot be known until the first negative presents them. Then the second affirmative must move swiftly, smoothly, and consistently to refute the attacks made by the negative and must extend the issues introduced by his or her colleague. The prudent advocates are those who—in addition to making a careful estimate of the probable case of their opponents and preparing to meet that case—have also considered carefully every possible position that their opponents may take and have thoroughly prepared both their defense and attack for each of these positions. There is an answer for almost every argument that can be introduced into the typical debate dealing with probabilities. If we are taken by surprise by our opponent's argument, our answer must be impromptu and often it will be weak and ineffective. If, on the other hand, our opponent's argument has been anticipated, with the answer planned carefully in advance and held in reserve for just such an argument, we are much more likely to be effective.

In a debate, the clash seldom ends with our advancing a line of argument and our opponent's meeting that argument with an answer. We must assume that our opponent is well prepared and has counter argument ready for each of the major contentions of the debate. Therefore, we must prepare an answer not only for each of the probable arguments of our opponent but also for each counterargument that this opponent is likely to advance in support of his or her original contentions. In this way, we can prepare our arguments in depth and not only be ready to meet our opponent on the first level of argument — the initial clash of argument and counterargument — but also have additional evidence and argument at our disposal that we can use to reinforce our initial position through as many exchanges as may be necessary to sustain our position. This preparation is reflected in the debate card file, which should contain the evidence and argument we plan to use initially, as well as the supplementary materials we hold in reserve, should the occasion arise to draw on them.

Exercises

1. Consider the current CEDA proposition:
   a. What are the likely definitive issues?
   b. What are the likely criteria for the values?
   c. Do the facts correspond to the definition?
   d. What is the application of the values?

2. Consider the value applications of the current CEDA proposition:
   a. What value applications is the affirmative most likely to claim? Are they significant? Quantitatively? Qualitatively?
   b. What value objections is the negative most likely to advance? Are they significant? Quantitatively? Qualitatively?
   c. Are the value objections significant *on balance* when contrasted with the value applications?

3. If the current CEDA proposition is a quasi-policy proposition, what additional issues must be considered?

4. Consider the requirement to prove inherency in a debate on the current NDT intercollegiate proposition:
   a. Are there inherent needs in the status quo for adopting the proposition?
   b. Are there structural barriers that prevent the status quo from solving the problem?
   c. Are there structural gaps that prevent the status quo from solving the problem?
   d. Are there attitudes that prevent the status quo from solving the problem?
   e. Can the affirmative successfully argue existential inherency?
   f. Are the advantages claimed for the plan inherently caused by the plan?
   g. Can the advantages be obtained *only* by the plan?
   h. Are the disadvantages that the negative claims will be caused by the plan inherent in the plan?

5. Consider the requirement for proving significance in a debate on the current NDT intercollegiate proposition:
   a. If the affirmative claims there is a need to change the status quo, is this need significant? Quantitatively? Qualitatively?
   b. Is the plan a significant change in the status quo? Quantitatively? Qualitatively?
   c. Are the advantages significant? Quantitatively? Qualitatively?
   d. Are the advantages *on balance* significant when contrasted with the likely disadvantages that a negative will claim?
   e. Are the disadvantages significant? Quantitatively? Qualitatively?
   f. Are the disadvantages significant *on balance* when contrasted with the likely advantages that an affirmative will claim?

6. Consider a plan currently being debated in Congress, in your state legislature, or by the governing body of your college. Apply the questions on inherency listed in Exercise 4. Apply the questions on significance listed in Exercise 5.

7. What are the requirements that might be inherent in the attitudes, interests, and intellectual capabilities of each of the following if they were asked to judge a debate on the current CEDA proposition? on the current NDT proposition?
   a. A professor of argumentation
   b. A labor union official
   c. The president of a local chamber of commerce
   d. The members of a local parent-teacher association
   e. The members of a local Rotary Club
   f. The students at a high school assembly program
   g. A member of Congress

12

Building the Affirmative Case

In this chapter on the affirmative case and in the following chapter on the negative case, we will begin with a consideration of value propositions and conclude with a consideration of policy propositions. Outside of academic debate, of course, all of us will have occasion to debate both value and policy propositions as we apply the process of critical thinking to the problems of reasoned decision making.

I.   Objectives of the Affirmative Case

Both value and policy debate are usually in the area of probability, and time limitations — not only in academic debate, but in informal debate as well — do not permit the introduction of all possible evidence and argument. The affirmative, therefore, is not required to establish its case as a matter of certainty. Such a degree of cogency is seldom attainable in the realm of human affairs. Rather, the affirmative must establish a prima facie case that provides the highest possible degree of probability, giving those who render the decision good reasons to accept the resolution. For example, in debating the proposition "Resolved: That the American judicial system has overemphasized freedom of the press," the affirmative does not have to prove its position absolutely; rather it must establish sufficient good reasons to justify the judges accepting their position. In the same way, in debating the proposition "Resolved: That the United States should reduce substantially its military commitments to NATO member states," the affirmative is not required to establish its position as a certainty; rather they, too, are required to provide sufficient good reasons to justify the judges accepting their position.

II. Proposition of Value Affirmative Cases

As we saw in Chapter 3, in a debate on a proposition of value, the affirmative maintains that a certain belief, value, or fact is justified and that it conforms to the definition or criteria appropriate to evaluate the matter at hand.

In developing the affirmative case on a proposition of value, the advocate has the responsibility of presenting a prima facie case. As we saw in Chapter 4, Section III-A, the stock issues on a proposition of value are:

1. Definitive issues
   a. What are the *definitions* of the key terms?
   b. What are the *criteria* for the values?
2. Designative issues
   a. Do the facts *correspond* to the definitions?
   b. What are the *applications* of the values?

In addition to these issues, the debater will often find that it is necessary to establish other issues that will be discussed in detail in Section III, "Proposition of Policy Affirmative Cases."

A. A CEDA Debate Case

The CEDA debate case shown in the *inset*, p. 189, is a case that was used in the final round of a CEDA National Tournament. The proposition for which this case was built is, as many CEDA propositions are, a quasi-policy proposition. Note that in this case the debaters not only sought to establish the *definitive* and *designative* issues, but also sought to establish the issues of *significance, inherency,* and *solvency.* The use of these issues is critical to the affirmative's development of its case. These issues, as has been indicated, will be considered in detail in Section III.

The essential difference between debate on a proposition of value and debate on a proposition of policy is that plan is a stock issue in policy debate. In value debate a plan is often implicit in the proposition. In quasi-policy debate the plan is clearly implicit and it becomes necessary for the affirmative to demonstrate that the action (or plan) implicit in the resolution will provide solvency.

Typically the debate case is the product of several debaters working together. Once the outline of the case is in satisfactory form, the next step is to prepare a manuscript of the first affirmative speech.

The final draft of the manuscript should be the product of extensive rewriting and editing and should reflect the maximum skill of the advocate (or advocates, if the manuscript is a group effort) in speech composition. It must be so written that, when the speech is presented, the advocate can achieve maximum effectiveness in delivery. The student may find it helpful to review Chapter 15 (Presenting the Case: Composition) and Chapter 16 (Presenting the Case: Delivery) when building an affirmative or negative case.

A CEDA Debate Case*

"Resolved: That the American judicial system has overemphasized freedom of the press."

Our planet is on the brink of environmental disaster.   *Significance*

I. Freedom of the press is the right to publish facts,   *Definition*
   ideas, and opinions without government inter-
   ference and applies to both print and broadcast
   media.
   A. Print press denies claims of access.
   B. Broadcast press turning away from affirmative
      obligations.
II. Parameters and focus for debate.
   A. Ecological awareness of human extinction is   *Criteria*
      criteria.
   B. Preserve the ecology.
      1. Ecological systems are critical for continued   *Significance*
         human life.
      2. Status quo will destroy the present ecosystem.   *Inherency*
      3. Decision rule: 1988 is the pivotal year.

Two arguments in support of the resolution:

I. Freedom of the press entrenches the old paradigm.   *Inherency*
   A. Autonomous press supports the old worldview.
      1. Largely based on old Newtonian vision.
      2. Diverts us from the development of a new
         environmental ethic.
   B. New view requires access to the mass media.
II. Old paradigm must be deemphasized to save the   *Application*
   environment.
   A. Holistic awareness promotes environmental un-
      derstanding.
   B. Ecological understanding promotes environ-
      mental quality.

New environmental ethic of deep ecology is feasible.   *Solvency*

*See Appendix B for the full development of this case together with the supporting evidence and analysis.

Once the manuscript for the first affirmative speech is completed, the advocates must prepare "briefs"—short speech segments—that they will use to refute negative attacks and to extend affirmative arguments. Since these briefs must be adapted to the specific negative case met, they cannot simply be read from a manuscript but must serve as carefully planned outlines for an extemporaneous presentation. Well-executed *extensions* are the hallmark of the successful debater and are the initial responsibility of the second affirmative constructive speaker. Extensions consist of new evidence and analy-

Basic CEDA Speaker Responsibilities

First Affirmative Constructive

The basic responsibility is to present a prima facie case.

   I. The subject is Significant.
  II. Definitions
 III. Criteria
 IV. Inherency
  V. Application
 VI. Solvency

Second Affirmative Constructive

The basic responsibility is to refute the negative case attacks and to extend affirmative case arguments.

    I. Defend topicality if necessary.*
   II. Refute the first negative constructive's attacks on significance.
  III. Extend the first affirmative constructive's significance arguments with additional evidence and arguments.
   IV. Refute the first negative constructive's attacks on definition and criteria if necessary.
    V. Refute the first negative constructive's attacks on inherency.
   VI. Extend the first affirmative constructive's inherency arguments with additional evidence and argument.
  VII. Refute the first negative constructive's attacks on application.
 VIII. Refute the first negative constructive's attacks on solvency.
   IX. Extend the first affirmative constructive's solvency arguments with additional evidence and argument.

sis to carry forward arguments introduced earlier; they are not mere repetitions of previously introduced evidence and argument.

B. Basic CEDA Speaker Responsibilities

The outline in the *inset* on pages 190 and 191 demonstrates the basic speaker responsibilities for a quasi-policy proposition of value. With appropriate adjustments the outline may be adapted to propositions dealing with many different subjects. The beginning debater is advised to develop a clear and precise understanding of the speaker responsibilities. Once these responsibilities are firmly established, team members may, by prearrangement, develop any number of variations. Beginning debaters are advised to discuss proposed variations with their instructor before they undertake them so that they will know *why* they are structuring their case in a particular way and

(Note that the second affirmative constructive speaker deals with the issues in *exactly* the same order as they were presented by the first affirmative constructive speaker.)

First Affirmative Rebuttal

The basic responsibility is to refute off-case attacks and to extend the case arguments.

I. Refute the second negative constructive's off-case arguments.
II. Refute the first negative rebuttalist's attacks on the case and the case arguments in exactly the same order and same manner as the second affirmative constructive.

(Note that this speech requires very careful budgeting of time. The first affirmative rebuttalist must execute both responsibilities.)

Second Affirmative Rebuttal

The basic responsibility is to reestablish and clinch the affirmative's case arguments.

I. Refute the second negative constructive's off-case attacks.
II. Refute the second negative rebuttalist's attack on the case and extend case arguments.
III. Conclude by presenting the best reasons you have to justify a decision for the affirmative.

*See Chapter 13 for a discussion of this and other types of negative refutation.

---

know precisely *what* advantages they hope to gain. Experienced debaters in the final round of a major tournament, or lawyers arguing before a panel of learned judges, sometimes use exceedingly complex forms of case organization. This complexity is appropriate before audiences who are willing and able to follow such arguments. However, in the hands of a novice debater or before a lay audience, complex or unclear organization almost always leads to chaos. Thus the beginning debater is advised to develop and use a clear, clean, and simple organizational plan. All debaters are advised to use such an organizational plan before lay audiences.

III. Proposition of Policy Affirmative Cases

As we saw in Chapter 3, in a debate on a proposition of policy, the affirmative maintains that a certain policy or course of action should be adopted. In developing the affirmative case on a proposition of policy, the advocate has the responsibility of presenting a prima facie case. As we observed in Chapter 4, Section III-A, the stock issues on a proposition of policy are:

1. Justification
   a. Is the problem *inherent* in the status quo?
   b. Is the problem *significant*?

2. Plan
   a. Is the plan *workable?*
   b. Does the plan *solve* the problem?
3. Advantages
   a. Does the plan produce *advantages?*
   b. Do the advantages outweigh the *disadvantages?*

We will consider four types of affirmative policy cases in this section: (1) needs analysis affirmative, (2) comparative advantages analysis affirmative, (3) criteria affirmative, and (4) alternative justification affirmative. In addition, we will examine an NDT debate case and the basic NDT speaker responsibilities. The consideration of the needs analysis affirmative will discuss the issues of significance, inherency, and solvency, which, as we saw earlier, are important in the development of both value and policy propositions.

A. Needs Analysis Affirmative

The advocates select the *needs analysis* after study of the problem leads them to the conclusion that a significant inherent need in the status quo exists that can best be solved by adopting the plan advanced by the affirmative and that adopting this plan will solve the need and thus provide significant advantages.

The essential elements of the needs analysis affirmative are shown here:

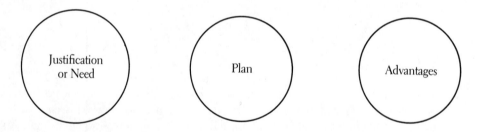

The *need* — or justification — portion of the case consists of arguments to establish the reasons for changing the status quo in the manner required or permitted by the proposition.

1. The Requirement to Prove Significance

As we saw in Chapter 11, significance may be quantitative, qualitative, or, best of all, both quantitative and qualitative. In debating the "guaranteed employment opportunities" proposition, first affirmative speakers often began by citing figures to prove that millions of U.S. citizens were unemployed. They continued to build significance by citing additional evidence to prove that millions of part-time workers were seeking full-time employment. Clearly if we are going to call for the federal government to adopt a new and costly program, we must provide justification in the form of a quantitatively significant need. In providing this type of justification, the affirmative seeks to show the greatest possible number of persons who are harmed by the status quo.

Usually it is also necessary to establish the qualitative significance of the need. If, in the example just cited, the first affirmative speaker provided only quantitative significance, the first negative speaker would quickly provide evidence showing that the numbers of people counted as unemployed were exaggerated and that the actual number of unemployed was much lower. The first negative would then produce evidence to demonstrate that there was no harm in unemployment—unemployed people receive unemployment compensation, food stamps, and many other welfare benefits. To anticipate this response and to firmly establish significance, the first affirmative must then complete the significance argument by establishing qualitative significance. The advocate must not only establish that large numbers of people are unemployed but must also prove that unemployment is harmful to these people. Thus, in the first affirmative speech, the advocate should not only prove that large numbers of people are unemployed but should go on to introduce evidence showing that unemployment causes poor health, suicides, crime, and other harmful conditions.

While advocates are usually in a stronger position if they can provide both quantitative and qualitative needs, it is not always possible to do so. In debating the "mass media" proposition, some affirmatives called for greater government control of the mass media's reporting of criminal trials on the ground that sometimes mass media coverage led to unfair trials. Debaters using this case found that they could document very few instances where media coverage had influenced juries. However, they argued that the Sixth Amendment right to an impartial jury was qualitatively so important that this right should be protected even if it was violated in only one out of thousands of trials.

2. The Requirement to Prove Inherency

As we saw in Chapter 11, inherency may be either structural (in the form of a barrier or a gap), attitudinal, or existential. The affirmative must demonstrate that there is some *cause* in the status quo that is either creating the need or preventing the status quo from solving the problem.

In the example just considered on mass media reporting of jury trials, affirmative advocates had an easy time establishing structural inherency. The First Amendment provides a formidable barrier to any governmental regulation of the press. The affirmative's plan could come into effect only by amending the Constitution and giving the federal government powers specifically denied it by the First Amendment.

In this same case the affirmative was often able to prove attitudinal inherency as well. It argued that sensationalism increased circulation of newspapers and increased ratings for television stations. Thus, they maintained, newspapers and television stations were predisposed to seek out and present lurid and often unproven or inadmissible (in court) news that might prejudice jurors.

If the affirmative fails to establish the inherency of its need, the negative will be quick to argue that there is no causal force preventing the status quo from meeting the need. It will also be quick to propose minor repairs, which, it will maintain, will be sufficient to solve all of the problems cited by the affirmative.

Depending on the nature of the proposition and the circumstances prevailing at the time of the debate, the objective of the affirmative may be to develop either a present or future need.

In developing a *present need*, the affirmative argues that conditions *right now* require us to adopt the proposition. The present-need argument was used by many who debated the "guaranteed employment opportunities" proposition. They argued, in effect, "Right now, *today*, significant numbers of people are suffering significant harms from unemployment. These harms are inherent in the status quo. We must act *now* to solve this problem by adopting the affirmative's plan."

In developing a *future need*, the affirmative argues that the status quo is inherently incapable of solving a problem that will or may come in the foreseeable future and that we must adopt the proposition to prepare to meet the future problem. The future-need argument was used by many who debated the "national program of public work for the unemployed" proposition. Debating at a time of relatively low unemployment, they argued, in effect, "Recessions are inherent in our economy. We *will* have a recession at some time in the foreseeable *future*. The status quo is inherently incapable of preventing a recession and the widespread and harmful unemployment that will come with it. Therefore, we must begin now to make plans for a national program of public work for the unemployed that we will put into effect when the recession strikes."

3. The Requirement to Provide a Plan

The plan is the connecting link between the needs and the advantages. It must solve the problems claimed in the justification as needs, and it must produce the advantages claimed by the affirmative. The affirmative's plan must be developed in sufficient detail to demonstrate that it can meet the alleged needs and that it can produce the claimed advantages.

The plan must be tailor-made to fit the resolution and the specific case of the affirmative. Although the variations in plans are limited only by the ingenuity and creativeness of plan builders, the beginning debater should master a *basic format*. After this basic format is thoroughly understood, the advanced advocate may make such variations as are desirable. The major parts of a plan are, in common usage, designated as "planks." The outline in the *inset* on p. 195 demonstrates the basic plan format. A plan may be seen in "An NDT Debate Case" on p. 209.

Advocates often find it desirable to provide plan *"spikes"* — that is, planks in their plan that will forestall possible negative attacks. In debating the "employment opportunities" proposition, most affirmative cases necessarily caused an increase in income for the people who gained employment. This argument opened the way for the negative to run a "grain-fed beef" disadvantage (arguing that, with increased income, people had a propensity to consume more grain-fed beef; and grain-fed beef, the negative argued, caused an increase in cardiovascular disease, thus killing off the very people whom the affirmative wanted to help). Some affirmatives, anticipating this attack, provided that their plan would be financed in part by a tax on grain-fed beef. This tactic either discouraged the negative from running the disadvantage or allowed the affirmative to answer it by claiming that the increased cost of the now-taxed grain-fed beef would hold consumption of it to present levels, thus incurring no new disadvantage. Note that the affirmative was careful not to decrease the consumption of grain-fed beef, which would have caused agricultural unemployment and exacerbated the need. "Spikes" must be nicely balanced.

Basic Plan Format

Plank 1 — Agency.   In this plank the affirmative specifies who will be responsible for administering its plan. Does the affirmative require an existing agency of the federal government to administer its plan? Does it create a new agency? Does the President appoint and the Senate confirm the new administrators? Or does the affirmative require the several states to join in a compact to implement their plan? In this plank the affirmative must provide the essential details of the agency that will put its plan into effect.

Plank 2 — Mandates.   In this plank the affirmative specifies the mandates given to the agency that administers the plan. The affirmative must specify exactly what it requires the agency to do. If new legislation is needed to carry out the affirmative's plan, this plank is the place to provide for it.

Plank 3 — Enforcement.   In this plank the affirmative specifies how the plan will be enforced. In the need and inherency issues, the affirmative has provided many reasons why people will resist its plan. Now it must provide a means of making people behave in the way it wants them to. The affirmative may find it necessary to provide fines, prison terms, or other forms of coercion or incentives to make people behave in the way necessary for its plan to work. In some circumstances the affirmative may be able to demonstrate that, under the new conditions created by its plan, people will act in the desired way because it is now in their self-interest to do so.

Plank 4 — Funding and staffing.   In this plank the affirmative specifies how it will get the funds and staff to permit the agency to carry out its mandates. Some cases on the "space development" proposition required billions of dollars in increased taxes; on the other hand, some cases on the "regulation of mass media communication" proposition required only a nominal increase in staff and funding to allow an existing agency to carry out the mandates.

Plank 5 — Addendum.   In this conclusionary plank the affirmative adds such further provisions as may be necessary to complete the implementation of its plan. For example, it might provide for the repeal of any conflicting legislation, indicate the intent of its plan, and provide such other details as might be necessary to make its plan comprehensive and readily understandable. *Spikes* (considered in the main text) might be provided here or inserted into earlier plan planks.

In debating the "consumer product safety" proposition, many affirmatives mandated that all new cars be equipped with air bags. Many negatives meeting this case diminished the affirmatives' claim that air bags would save 15,000 lives a year by arguing that this figure applied only if all cars were equipped with air bags — and many years would pass before all cars on the road had them. Anticipating this argument, some affirmatives "spiked" their plan by adding a provision for equipping all cars with air bags (mandating that new cars be equipped with air bags and that all other cars be equipped with them as a condition for being licensed, and also providing subsidies for low-income car owners).

The affirmative is not required to demonstrate that its plan will be adopted; but it does have the responsibility of demonstrating that its plan, if adopted, would be workable. As we saw earlier (Chapter 4, "The Meaning of 'Should' — Fiat Power"), the affirmative may fiat the *enactment* of its plan. It may not, however, fiat the *workability* of its plan if workability becomes an issue of the debate. If the plan calls for an increase in personal income taxes and a reduction of property taxes, it is pointless for the negative to raise the workability issue; the status quo has effective means of enforcing tax collections. In some cases, however, workability may become an all-important issue. In debates on "comprehensive medical care for all citizens," one affirmative plan called for annual physical examinations of all citizens. The affirmative sought to slough its responsibility by saying this provision of its plan would be "enforced by all necessary means." The negative established that millions of citizens — through fear, ignorance, or apathy — would not volunteer for such examinations and argued that the affirmative must provide an effective enforcement mechanism or lose its claimed advantage. The inexperienced affirmative debater, in a moment of excess, responded that this provision of the plan would be enforced by "drawing and quartering." The next negative speaker argued that the method of enforcement provided by the affirmative — drawing and quartering — was not only counterproductive to health, but was so repugnant to contemporary standards of law enforcement as to constitute grounds for rejecting the proposition. The judge agreed; drawing and quartering may have worked in the Middle Ages, but it was an unworkable plan provision for contemporary America.

Affirmatives may fiat reasonable provisions for their plan. For instance, they may stipulate that their administrative body be bipartisan or nonpartisan; they may stipulate geographic representation; they may provide that members of the body be lawyers, physicians, or accountants or meet various professional standards. Indeed, they may stipulate anything for which there is a reasonable warrant or relevant analogy.

Affirmatives may *not*, however, fiat unreasonable provisions for their plan. For instance, in a debate on consumer protection, the affirmatives may not fiat that their administrative body will be headed by Ralph Nader; in a debate on crime control, they may not fiat that the members of their administative body will be incorruptible;[1] if they designate a Congressional committee to investigate the CIA, they may not fiat that all of the members will be liberal Democrats. In short, the affirmative plan is subject to normal political processes and its members are subject to normal human frailties. The affirmative may not appoint "Jesus Christ Superstar" to its administrative body and stipulate that miracles will be passed to overcome attitudinal inherency and any other problems that block the status quo from functioning in a state of perfection.

In debating the proposition "Resolved: That the federal government should grant annually a specific percentage of its income tax revenue to the state governments,"

---

[1]Of course, one may attempt to provide for desirable qualities in appointees. The mayor of Cleveland once appointed a special committee of clergymen — promptly dubbed "The God Squad" by the media — to investigate crime. The mayor's supporters hailed the appointments on the ground that the clergymen would be incorruptible; his opponents scoffed that clergymen led sheltered lives and did not know enough about crime to investigate it.

the affirmative was not obliged to specify how much money would be given to each state, but it was obliged to present a policy by means of which such amounts could be determined.

Naturally, the importance of the plan in a debate on a proposition of policy will vary with the subject matter and with the attitude of those who render the decision. In many debates on the "energy" proposition, the plan was all-important. If the affirmative advocates could produce a satisfactory plan, they had a very good chance of winning. If the negative could demonstrate that the plan was unworkable or produced significant disadvantages, it had an excellent change of winning. In many debates on the proposition "Resolved: That the federal government should guarantee a minimum annual cash income to all citizens," the plan portion of the debate was of lesser importance. Since it is obviously *possible* for the federal government to make such a guarantee, most of the arguments on this proposition often centered on the *need* for the federal government to make such a guarantee and on the advantages (or disadvantages) that would result from the adoption of the proposition. In debates on "right-to-work" laws, some decision renderers were predisposed to agree with the affirmative if only it could produce a workable plan, whereas other decision renderers were interested not so much in the plan as in the need for such legislation.

4. The Requirement to Prove Solvency

Solvency is established by demonstrating that the plan can work to solve the claimed needs and that it can produce the claimed advantages. In building the plan the advocate must have solvency very much in mind. Care must be taken to provide the best agency to administer the plan. In debates on the "development of space" proposition, some affirmatives chose to have their plan administered by NASA, as NASA had the expertise to conduct work in space. These affirmatives were prepared to defend NASA as the best agency to solve the problem.

The mandates must be carefully drafted to achieve the desired objective. In debates on the "guaranteed employment opportunities" proposition, the affirmative could not say "The government will increase employment by 3 percent." Rather it was required to indicate very specifically what it would have the government do in order to achieve a 3 percent increase in employment. Some affirmatives mandated a reduction of the standard work week under the Fair Labor Standards Act and found that they had to spell out their mandate in considerable detail in order to demonstrate that the plan would solve the problem.

The enforcement plank must provide incentives or coercion to make people behave in the desired way. The recent enactment of legislation to increase the drinking age to 21 provides an interesting example of plan building to provide for enforcement. The minimum drinking age is clearly a matter of state legislation. The proponents of the age-21 minimum recognized that it would take years of endless lobbying to get all 50 states to enact the legislation they desired. Instead they chose to lobby the federal government and succeeded in getting the federal government to enact legislation requiring the states to raise the minimum drinking age to 21 or lose a substantial percentage of the highway construction funds they would otherwise get. This mixture of coercion and incentive provided the enforcement necessary to make the states pass the desired legislation. The proponents of the legislation felt that the states were doing a satisfactory job of enforcing drinking laws; what they wanted to change was the age at which the laws were enforced.

Funding and staffing must be nicely balanced; they must be sufficient to achieve the affirmative's objectives, yet not so great that they can easily be turned into disadvantages. In debates on the "space" proposition, many affirmatives found it necessary to provide for multi–billion dollar tax increases to fund their program, and multi–billion dollar tax incentives to encourage private corporations' participation in their program. In such cases it was necessary to indicate just how these vast sums would be raised. The "age-21 drinking law," of course, required no funding plank; to enforce compliance the government simply threatened *not* to spend monies already appropriated.

The addendum plank must supply any provisions needed to make the plan operate effectively. Sometimes an affirmative plan is against existing laws or constitutional provisions. Remember, as we saw in Chapter 4, "constitutionality is never an issue in academic debate." However, the plan must take appropriate action to make its provisions legal. People who wanted to lower the voting age to 18 were clearly proposing an unconstitutional action. The solution came in the form of the Twenty-Sixth Amendment. Thus, if the affirmative's plan is unconstitutional, illegal, or extralegal, the addendum plank should include the necessary provisions to legalize its proposal. If the negative can successfully argue that the plan is illegal or so unclear that lengthy court battles will ensue, the affirmative will lose solvency.

Solvency must be unique to the plan. In developing this portion of the case, the affirmative must be careful to demonstrate that *only* the plan can solve the problem in the most advantageous way. If the needs can be solved by some means other than the plan, there is little reason to adopt the plan. In debates on the "mass media" proposition, some affirmatives built cases claiming that violence on television was harmful and called for a plan that would have the federal government regulate television to ban violence. Some negatives meeting this case claimed that the National Association of Broadcasters (NAB)(a voluntary agency) could solve the problem without federal intervention. The affirmative responded by arguing that not all television stations belonged to the NAB and that not all NAB members followed all provisions of the NAB code. Thus the affirmative claimed that only its plan could guarantee full solvency of the needs by mandating that all television stations adhere to its regulations governing violence on television.

5. The Requirement to Prove Advantages

The advantages portion of the affirmative case must be developed in sufficient detail to demonstrate that the *plan meets the need* and corrects the deficiencies and weaknesses that the affirmative has found in the status quo. The affirmative must also take care to link the advantages to the plan and demonstrate that the advantages are *caused* by the plan, are *unique* to the plan, and cannot be obtained by other factors outside the scope of the plan.

In the first instance the advantages must be perfectly integrated with the needs. Thus, in a debate on the "guaranteed employment opportunities" proposition, if an affirmative argues that millions are unemployed and that these unemployed persons suffer from poor health, suicide, and crime, the affirmative must prove as its first advantage that it will provide employment opportunities for millions and that their health will improve and suicides and crime will be reduced as a result.

The affirmative's plan will almost invariably create some significant problems. Clearly it is in the negative's interest to discover and present the strongest possible set of disadvantages it can find and to prove that such disadvantages are inherent in the plan. The affirmative must, of course, be prepared to refute or minimize these disadvantages. Realistically, however, some disadvantages will be irrefutable. Thus the affirmative must be able to prove a net gain; that is, it must prove that the advantages *outweigh* the disadvantages.

An everyday example is found in contact lenses. If you or some of your friends wear them, you are aware of a disadvantage — there is the risk of losing them. Those who wear contact lenses, however, have decided that this disadvantage is outweighed by the advantages of convenience and appearance. They have chosen *on balance* to opt for contact lenses. The concept of balancing advantages against disadvantages is an important one to the debater. The affirmative seeks to show that on balance the advantages outweigh the disadvantages, whereas the negative seeks to show that the disadvantages outweigh the advantages.

In debating the "guaranteed employment opportunities" proposition, some negatives argued that employment causes more health problems than unemployment. They cited the number of injuries caused by industrial accidents and the number of illnesses caused by working with hazardous materials and claimed that, on balance, the affirmative's plan caused more ill health than did unemployment. Affirmatives meeting this disadvantage often responded that they were providing employment opportunities for the unemployed, not forcing them to take jobs. Thus, they argued, on balance it is better for a person to have the opportunity for a job and to have the freedom to choose whether to accept the potential hazards of the job.

Another method of demonstrating that the advantages outweigh the disadvantages is *risk analysis*. Here one must consider the *probability* (likelihood) of occurrence of some negatively evaluated state of affairs. One must also evaluate the *impact* of the negatively evaluated state of affairs.

We are all familiar with the evidence showing that wearing seat belts saves lives. Death is a high-impact disadvantage to not wearing a seat belt. However, the evidence is also clear that millions of drivers and passengers have decided that the likelihood of being involved in an accident where a seat belt might save their lives is remote, so they don't wear seat belts.

In debating the "guaranteed employment opportunities" proposition, some affirmatives presented a plan that mandated a cutback on imported oil and the conversion of all possible industries to fossil fuel (arguing that the high cost of imported oil caused unemployment and that the development of domestic fossil fuel would increase employment). In response, some negatives developed the disadvantage that the affirmative's plan would melt the polar ice caps by increasing emissions into the upper atmosphere and thus cause flooding of all the world's coastal cities — which, in turn, would cause trillions of dollars of damage.

Certainly the negative had high impact — trillions of dollars of damage is an awesome disadvantage. Some affirmatives meeting this disadvantage, however, were able to demonstrate that these events had a very low likelihood of occurring; melting of the polar ice caps would require a quantum increase of fossil fuel emissions on a world-wide scale, whereas the affirmative proposed that only the United States increase its use of fossil fuel. As the negative was usually unable to establish any threshold—the point at which burning 1 million more tons of coal would actually melt the polar ice caps—the affirmative was usually able to demonstrate that the likelihood of the disadvantage's occurring was remote, and thus the advantage outweighed the disadvantage.

In common usage a *turnaround* argument is any statement that one turns against the originator. David Brinkley provides a classic example:

> Nicholas Longworth, former speaker of the House, almost totally bald from an early age, [was] lounging in a leather chair when another member ran his hand over Longworth's shiny scalp and said, "Nice and smooth. Feels just like my wife's bottom." Longworth then ran his own hand over his head and said, "Yes, so it does."[2]

In debate usage the term is usually applied to the affirmative's *turning around* a negative's disadvantage and converting it into an advantage. The affirmative must be alert for such opportunities. In debates on the "employment" proposition, some affirmatives claimed as an advantage that their plan would "raise millions out of poverty." Some negatives meeting this case countered with the disadvantage that the affirmative plan would "increase cardiovascular disease" (arguing that, with increased income, people would drink more alcoholic beverages, which would cause more cardiovascular disease). Some affirmatives meeting this disadvantage were able to turn around the argument and claim the additional advantage of "improved health" (arguing that a moderate increase in consumption of alcoholic beverages actually reduced the risk of cardiovascular disease—the negative had merely shown that more people would drink alcoholic beverages, not that anyone would drink to excess).

The two disadvantages just cited were used frequently by second negative constructive speakers. Did they represent a hard-nosed assessment of the "real world" or were they merely "meatballs"—strategic ploys of little merit? Such arguments are made in real-world policy debates; all of the evidence came from reputable sources. The "real world" is a mixture of superb and "meatball" arguments, and the advocate must be prepared to respond to both. Only careful risk analysis will allow us to assess the merits of the argument and to demonstrate to those who render the decision whether the grounds, and the supporting arguments or intermediate conclusions, constitute good reasons for accepting the conclusion.

A familiar example of the turnaround was the prelaw student who considered taking an accounting course as an undergraduate because she felt she would need a knowledge of accounting in law school. A friend advised her, "Don't take accounting now—it will take too much time from your other courses." The prelaw student decided that this argument was a turnaround. She chose to take the accounting course as an undergraduate on the grounds that she could better afford the time it would take as an undergraduate than as a law student.

6. The Requirement to Integrate the Case

In order to build a prima facie case, the affirmative must carefully integrate its position. Justification, plan, and advantages must be so developed that they dovetail per-

---

[2]David Brinkley, *Washington Goes to War* (New York: Knopf, 1988), p. 195.

fectly. The justification — in this case, the need — must be sufficiently great to justify a change in the status quo; yet, at the same time, it must not be so great as to make it impossible for the plan to solve the need. The need and the plan must complement each other perfectly, and every point of need stated by the affirmative must be provided for in the plan advocated. Advantages, the third element of the affirmative case, are derived by demonstrating that the plan solves the claimed need and perhaps produces additional conditions not present in the status quo. Thus need, plan, and advantages must all be perfectly integrated into the whole structure of the affirmative case.

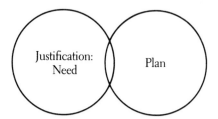

The plan is seen as the connecting link. It solves the problems raised by presentation of the need and produces the advantages that the affirmative maintains will follow the adoption of the resolution.

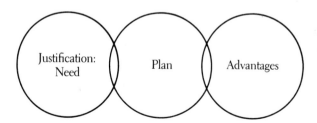

B. Comparative Advantages Analysis Affirmative

The advocates select the *comparative advantages analysis* after study of the problem leads them to the conclusion that there is a better way of attaining the goals of the status quo. They accept the goals of the status quo, present a plan of the type required or permitted by the proposition, and argue that their plan will produce comparative advantages.

Consider the example of the woman about to enter college. Her mother generously offers to allow her to take the family manual typewriter with her. The old Underwood served mother well in college. Since then it has been a family workhorse. It faithfully churned out countless letters, school themes, and book reports. Over the years it has required only *minor repairs* (see Chapter 13, Section II-E). In this case, the goal of both mother and daughter — the goal of the status quo — is to provide the daughter with an effective means of preparing the many term papers she will have to write in college. The daughter grants that the old Underwood would do the job but argues that a word processor would do the job *better*; that it has comparative advantages over the manual typewriter and that these advantages significantly outweigh the disadvantage of cost.

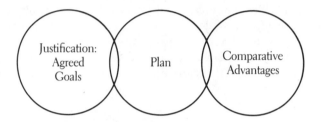

1. Essential Features

The four essential features of the comparative advantages case are (1) identify the goals of the status quo, (2) integrate the plan with the goals, (3) provide inherent, significant advantages, and (4) prove the advantages are comparative.

First, the affirmative must identify and accept the specific goals and assumptions of the status quo that are relevant to the proposition. The affirmative must isolate the "agreed goals" or "ends" that both the affirmative and negative wish to achieve.

Thus the need issue does not become an issue of the debate as it does when the need-plan-advantages analysis is used. If the affirmative has correctly analyzed the problem, and if it has correctly identified the goals and assumptions of the status quo, the negative will, in effect, concede the need issue. The negative cannot deny the need to reach the agreed goals in a way that will do more for us or enable us to reach our agreed goals more quickly, more efficiently, more fairly, or in some way that is more beneficial to us. Rather, the negative will argue that the proposal of the affirmative should be rejected because of inherent defects and disadvantages. If, however, the affirmative has not identified the goals of the status quo correctly, the negative may be able to develop arguments proving that the goals are incompletely identified or that other goals are equally or more important.

In debating the proposition "Resolved: That law enforcement agencies in the United States should be given greater freedom in the investigation and prosecution of crime," some affirmatives stated that one of the most urgent goals of society was to reduce crime. The negatives simply could not deny this statement; it would be pointless for them to attempt to debate it as a need issue. Some affirmatives, after stating this goal, then presented a plan to legalize wiretapping and argued that the advantage would be increased convictions and ultimately a reduction in crime. Negatives, meeting this type of case, often clashed with the plan and argued that wiretapping, when it was legal, had not been particularly effective in increasing convictions. They then sought — by setting out the disadvantage of invasion of privacy and all the abuses potentially existing in wiretapping — to counter the now-minimized advantage of a possible slight increase in convictions. These disadvantages, they argued, outweighed any possible advantage flowing from the affirmative's plan.

Note that the affirmative must identify and accept the *specific* goals and assumptions of the status quo that are relevant to the proposition. In the "law enforcement" example just cited, the affirmative was correct in stating that "reducing crime" is a goal of American society. In a debate on an international disarmament treaty, the affirmative would have to find certain agreed goals that were common to America, the Soviet Union, and other nations that might be parties to the treaty. In a debate in a business organization, "increased profits" would probably be the agreed goal of the board of directors. In a similar fashion, advocates must discover the agreed goals of the relevant group—their debate team, their business organization, American society, or the United Nations.

The goals just stated are phrased in general terms. For the purposes of debate, they must be specific. It is *not* the goal of American society to "reduce crime *by any means.*" No reputable business seeks "increased profits *by any means.*" Thus the plan to "reduce crime" must do so by socially acceptable methods. The plan to "increase profits" must be legal, ethical, and consistent with the other public and business responsibilities of the company.

While a general statement of the goal is often sufficient for the affirmative's opening statement of its rationale, the specific qualifications and limitations of the goal must be provided for in the plan. Many debates in which the "wiretap" case was used turned on the point of which was the more important goal of society—convicting some more criminals or assuring privacy for more citizens.

Second, the affirmative must present a plan that is perfectly integrated with the goals and assumptions it has specified. Note that this is an exact parallel of the need-plan-advantages analysis. In that case, the plan must solve the needs; in the comparative advantages case, the plan must satisfy the specified goals and assumptions. If the affirmative wishes to challenge the goals and assumptions of the status quo, it should move to a needs analysis and seek to establish a need for this change.

Third, the plan must produce advantages. Two considerations are involved here: (a) The advantages must be inherent in the plan. If the advantages can be achieved without the plan, or through some agency other than the plan, then there is no reason to adopt the plan. (b) The advantages must be significant. The reason for this consideration has been suggested in the "wiretapping" case already considered under the first essential.

Fourth, the affirmative must prove that these are comparative advantages. Two considerations are involved here: (a) The advantages must be better than any advantage that could be gained under the status quo. They must be better than any advantage produced by the status quo and better than any advantage that may *coexist* with status quo policies and agencies but that would be *excluded* by the affirmative's plan. (b) The advantages must outweigh the disadvantages. The negative is almost certain to stress the disadvantages of the plan, and the affirmative must be prepared to defend its plan.

The affirmative's proposal almost invariably will involve the loss of certain advantages gained under the status quo; and this loss is obviously a disadvantage of the affirmative's plan. The affirmative must be able to prove a net gain—that is, the advantage gained must be more valuable than the advantage lost.

The affirmative's proposal will almost invariably create some significant problems. Clearly, it is in the negative's interest to discover and present the strongest possible set of plan objections and to point out the inherent disadvantages of the plan. The affirmative will, of course, seek to refute or minimize these objections. Realistically, however, there will be some disadvantages that are irrefutable. Here again the affirmative must be able to prove a net gain; that is, even when handicapped and discounted by its inherent disadvantages, the advantages of the affirmative plan must outweigh, be more valuable than, be better than, or be comparatively advantageous to both the status quo and the status quo as it might be repaired by the negative.

Thus the affirmative is usually well advised to build its case to provide the most significant advantages it can reasonably claim. In debating the proposition "Resolved: That the federal government should grant annually a specific percentage of its income tax revenue to the state governments," an affirmative concluded the last rebuttal with the plaintive plea that its case was "just a little bit better" than the status quo and therefore merited the decision. As that debate drew to a close, it was apparent that the affirmative's plan did produce a taxing system that was "just a little bit" more progressive than the status quo and a method of tax collection that was "just a little bit" more efficient. Although the slogan "just a little bit better" may serve as the basis for choosing a breakfast food, it is a very slender—albeit in certain circumstances a reasonable—basis on which to claim victory in a hard-fought debate. In this case, the negative had established disadvantages and objections—loss of a fiscal tool to control the economy, the affirmative's inability to defend its distribution formula, the affirmative's failure to provide for "pass-through," and the affirmative's inability to guarantee that the funds would reach those areas specified as its goals—that outweighed the "little bit" claimed by the affirmative.

2. Integrating the Case

As with the needs analysis case, the comparative advantages case must be carefully integrated in order to establish a prima facie case. The agreed goals, the plan, and the comparative advantages must be so developed as to dovetail perfectly.

The agreed goals must be identified. As the advocate rarely accepts all of the goals of the status quo, we must identify the specific goals of the status quo that are relevant to the proposition. The plan must be perfectly tailored to the agreed goals and must be presented in sufficient detail to demonstrate how it differs from the status quo and how it will produce the comparative advantages. The comparative advantages must be inherent in the plan; they must be significant; they must be better than any advantage that exists because of the status quo or that could be obtained through any repairs proposed by the negative; and they must be better than any advantages that may coexist with the status quo policies under consideration.

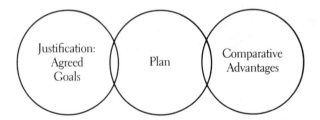

3. Some Examples

We have already considered some examples of comparative advantages cases. A few more examples may be helpful in gaining an understanding of how the comparative advantages case may be used.

To return to the business example: A business executive might attend a company board meeting and announce, "I have a plan that will increase our profits by 15 percent." In the typical business organization no one will ask, "But do we need more profits?" Profits are the agreed goal of most business organizations. It is also an agreed assumption that the board should constantly strive to improve the company's profit position—the company is committed to making more profits as quickly as possible within the limitations previously cited. Thus, the need issue is never debated. Probably the only issue debated at such a board meeting would be "Will the plan really work?" The opposition might develop such arguments as "it involves automation, and the union will strike" or "it will increase pollution and we're committed *not* to increase pollution from our plants" or "if we adopt this plan we'll have to close down the Widget Division and that's exchanging a proven profit maker for a risky speculation" and similar arguments designed to show that the plan will not actually produce profits or that it would in some way endanger the company's future profit position or create socially unacceptable problems.

As another example, an insurance salesperson recently called on a professor to try to sell her a tax-sheltered annuity. He did not waste time arguing that the professor needed to make investments to provide for future income; the professor had conceded the need issue when she gave the salesperson an appointment. The meeting actually turned out to be a debate in which the salesperson sought to establish that his proposal was comparatively advantageous to other investment opportunities available to the professor.

Or consider the case of the young couple who decide they want—or need—a new car. The problem they present to the salesperson is one that requires a comparative advantage analysis. There is no need issue to be argued—the couple has conceded it. The problem before the salesperson is to convince the couple that a product, or deal, is comparatively advantageous to competitive products or deals.

An actual example of the comparative advantages case in the field of politics may be found in the first campaign by Edward M. Kennedy for a seat in the U.S. Senate. He ran on the slogan "He can do *more* for Massachusetts." The effective use of the comparative advantage analysis—as expressed in this slogan—allowed Kennedy to focus much of the campaign on the issue of which candidate would have the greater success in securing federal grants and federal projects for Massachusetts and which candidate would have the greater success in bringing to Massachusetts the jobs that would result from these grants and projects. His opponent did not care to raise the issue of whether or not Massachusetts *needed* federal monies and the resultant jobs. No need issue was argued in the campaign—both contenders agreed that one of a senator's major goals was to obtain federal monies for his state. (We may wonder whether this *should* be one of the major goals of a senator. However, we must recognize facts—this is the way many senators campaign, and this is the basis on which many citizens decide their votes.)

The comparative advantages analysis is not appropriate for all of the issues of our times. The needs analysis is best suited to many situations. The advocate, after thorough study of the problem, must select the most effective type of analysis, taking into consideration the proposition, the status quo, the available evidence and argument, and the attitudes, interests, and intellectual capabilities of the audience and the occasion.

C. The Criteria Affirmative

The advocates select the criteria analysis after their study of the problem leads them to the conclusion that the status quo is inherently incapable of attaining an important goal of the status quo and that this failure causes significant harm. Care must be taken to establish that the goal cited by the affirmative is indeed a significant goal of the status quo, that the status quo is in fact inherently incapable of meeting this goal, and that significant harms result from the inability of the status quo to meet the goal in order to justify the case. The affirmative must also justify the criteria by which the attainment of the goal can be judged.

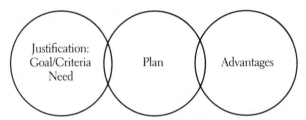

In debating the "tax sharing" proposition, one affirmative maintained that the goal of the status quo was to achieve the most effective utilization of public funds. The team stated, as criteria for judging plans to achieve this goal, that taxes should be collected by the most efficient agency and that tax revenues should be spent by the most responsive agency.

The affirmative pointed out that the status quo was inherently incapable of meeting this criteria, as tax raising and revenue spending were fragmented among federal, state, and local governments. The affirmative argued that this fragmentation resulted in significant harms as state and local governments were unable to meet urgent social needs because of the relatively high cost of collecting taxes. It them presented a plan to abolish all state and local taxes, raise the income tax rate to produce the corresponding amount of revenue, and have all taxes collected in the form of income taxes through the Internal Revenue Service—the agency it claimed was the most effective tax collector. An amount equal to the current state and local revenues would be turned over to state and local governments, the agencies it claimed were more responsive in spending tax revenues for state and local needs. The use of these agencies, it claimed, provided solvency for its plan. It claimed that, as advantages, these provisions met the criteria of using the most efficient agency to collect revenue and the most responsive agency to spend revenue; they met the goal of the status quo by achieving the most effective utilization of public funds; and they reduced the harms of unmet social needs.

D. Alternative Justification Affirmative

The advocates select the alternative justification analysis either because they believe there are multiple justifications for adopting the resolution or because it will increase their "maneuverability" during the debate.[3]

[3]Michael Pfau, "The Alternative Justification Affirmative," in *Advanced Debate*, ed. David A. Thomas (Skokie, Ill.: National Textbook Co., 1979), pp. 150–154.

In using this type of case, the affirmative advances multiple independent mini-cases as justification for adopting the resolution. Each of the minicases, of course, must carry all of the burdens of a prima facie case. The affirmative argues that any one of the minicases justifies the resolution.[4] By this argument the affirmative hopes to gain the strategic advantage of maneuverability. If the affirmative presents three minicases and the negative defeats one or two of them (or if the affirmative drops one or two of them to concentrate on carrying the second or third), the affirmative will claim it has still given sufficient justification for adoption of the resolution.

For example, in debating the "greater freedom in the investigation and/or prosecution of felony crime" proposition, one affirmative established the harms of crime as its

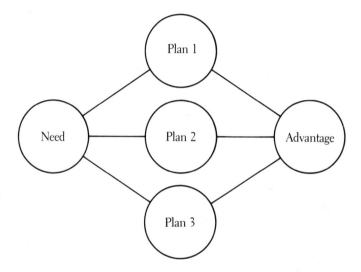

need and then offered three plans: legalize "no knock" searches to decrease drug traffic; and/or legalize "stop and frisk" searches to decrease street crime; and/or broaden "no bail" detention of previously convicted suspects to protect the public from recidivists.

The affirmative argued as its advantage that each plan would reduce crime.

The three minicases just considered are closely related and have essentially the same needs and advantages. Some debaters, however, use a different structure. In debating the proposition "Resolved: That greater controls should be imposed on the gathering and utilization of information about United States citizens by government agencies," one affirmative called for the licensing of auto mechanics (claiming that un-licensed auto mechanics made faulty repairs that caused harms) and the elimination of chiropractic care (claiming that chiropractic care caused harms). The affirmative claimed that both minicases were propositional as both cases gathered information to license or prohibit certain activities. The claimed advantages were the mitigation of the harms cited as needs.

[4]Allan Lichtman, Charles Garvin, and Jerry Corsi, "The Alternative Justification Affirmative: A New Case Form," *Journal of the American Forensic Association*, Vol. 10, No. 2 (Fall 1973), pp. 59–69.

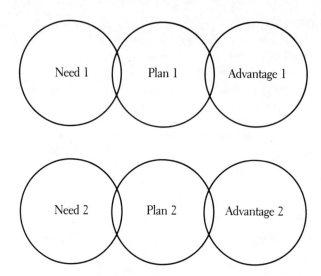

The student debater must consider three important constraints before selecting this approach: (1) The time limitations of academic debate may make it impossible for the debater to establish multiple prima facie minicases. This consideration is not overwhelming, however. Some "big" unitary cases tax debaters' ingenuity to meet the requirements of a prima facie case within the time limits. (2) Many judges hold that the integrity of the proposition constrains the affirmative to the advocacy of *one* policy change. They would thus view the minicases as parts of a whole and consider the disadvantages of any plan as applying to the entirety of the resolution. (3) Some judges feel that "the affirmative should not be permitted to capriciously abandon its own progeny without penalty."[5] These judges would then penalize a team that advances, say, three plans and then drops two of them to concentrate on the one for which the negative is least prepared.

E. An NDT Debate Case

The NDT debate case shown in the inset on p. 209 is a case used in the final round of an NDT National Tournament. As we saw with the CEDA case considered earlier, the case is often the product of several debaters working together. As with a CEDA case, once the NDT case outline is in satisfactory form the next step is to prepare the manuscript for the first affirmative speech. (See Section II-A.)

F. Basic NDT Speaker Responsibilities

The outline in the inset on pp. 210–211 demonstrates the basic speaker responsibilities for a needs analysis case. With appropriate adjustments the outline may be

[5]Tom Goodnight, Bill Balthrop, and Donn W. Parson, "The Problem of Inherency," *Journal of the American Forensic Association*, Vol. 10, No. 4 (Spring 1974), p. 235.

An NDT Debate Case*

Resolved: That the United States should reduce substantially its military commitments to NATO member states.

I. Nuclear proliferation is bad.	*Justification*
A. Proliferation increases risk of war.	*Significance*
1. Catalytic superpower war.	
2. Nuclear coups.	
3. Unauthorized use.	
4. Terrorism.	
5. Crazy leaders.	
6. Accidental nuclear war.	
7. Preemptive attacks.	
a. Preemption becomes inevitable.	*Inherency*
B. Impact: Regional wars would be devastating	
1. These wars will escalate.	*Qualitative*
2. Would cause nuclear winter.	*Significance*

Plan

Plank 1: Ban sale of nuclear powered submarines to Canada. — *Mandate*

Plank 2: Deny technology/technical safeguards/diplomatic measures/Defense Production Sharing Agreement. — *Agency*

Plank 3: Enforcement and funding through normal means. — *Enforcement and Funding*

Plank 4: Affirmative speeches will clarify what we mean. — *Addendum*

II. We reduce risks of proliferation.	*Advantage*
a. Canada wants nuclear powered subs.	*Inherency*
b. U.S. is committed to Canadian subs.	
c. Proliferation will be encouraged.	
d. Diplomatic actions will solve.	*Solvency*
1. Control of technology transfer.	
2. Canada had to seek U.S. permission.	
e. Importance of Canada's role.	*Significance*

*See Appendix C for the full development of this case together with the supporting evidence and analysis.

adapted to the other types of policy affirmative cases we have considered. As with the speaker responsibilities for a CEDA case, the student is advised to develop a clear and precise understanding of the obligations of each speaking position. Once these responsibilities are firmly established, team members may, by prearrangement, develop any number of variations. (See Section II-B.)

Basic NDT Speaker Responsibilities

First Affirmative Constructive

The basic responsibility is to present a prima facie case.

I. The need is significant.
  A. Quantitatively
  B. Qualitatively
II. The need is inherent.
III. Present the plan.
     Plank 1—Agency
     Plank 2—Mandates
     Plank 3—Enforcement
     Plank 4—Funding and Staffing
     Plank 5—Addendum
IV. The plan will solve the need, providing advantages.
  A. Prove solvency.
  B. Prove advantages.

Second Affirmative Constructive

The basic responsibility is to refute negative case attacks and to extend affirmative case arguments.

I. Defend topicality, if necessary.*
II. Refute the first negative constructive's attacks on significance.
III. Extend the first affirmative constructive's significance arguments with additional evidence and arguments.
IV. Refute the first negative constructive's attacks on inherency.

*See Chapter 13 for a discussion of this and other types of negative refutation.

IV. Building for Optimum Capability

Affirmative advocates of both value and policy propositions have the burden of proof; they must take the offensive and mount a strong attack and aggressively advance their case. Much of what we have considered thus far has to do with the affirmative's offensive position. It must be remembered, however, that debate does not take place in a vacuum and that an able negative will mount strong attacks against the affirmative. Therefore, the affirmative must build its case and deploy its evidence so as *to achieve the optimum balance of offensive and defensive capabilities.*

In building their case, the advocates must anticipate the probable areas of negative attack. In so doing, they frequently can adjust their case so as to avoid or blunt many

V. Extend the first affirmative constructive's inherency arguments with additional evidence and argument.

VI. Refute the first negative constructive's attacks on solvency.

VII. Refute the first negative constructive's attacks on advantages.

VIII. Extend the first affirmative constructive's advantage arguments with additional evidence and argument.

(Note that the second affirmative constructive speaker deals with the issues in *exactly* the same order as they were presented by the first affirmative constructive speaker. As the first negative constructive speaker usually does not make plan attacks, usually no need arises to defend the plan in this speech.)

First Affirmative Rebuttal

The basic responsibility is to refute plan attacks, to refute case attacks, and to extend case arguments.

I. Refute the second negative constructive's attacks on the plan.

II. Refute the first negative rebuttalist's attacks on the case, and extend the case arguments in exactly the same order and the same manner as the second affirmative constructive.

(Note that this speech requires very careful budgeting of time. The first affirmative rebuttalist must execute both responsibilities.)

Second Affirmative Rebuttal

The basic responsibility is to reestablish and clinch the affirmative's case, plan, and advantages.

I. Refute the second negative constructive's attack on the plan.

II. Refute the second negative rebuttalist's attack on the case and extend case arguments.

III. Conclude by presenting the best reasons you have to justify a decision for the affirmative.

---

negative attacks before they can be made. In developing cases on the "comprehensive medical care for all citizens" proposition, many affirmative advocates first considered adopting the widely publicized Kennedy proposal as their plan. As they studied possible negative attacks, they discovered that the $70-billion annual cost of the Kennedy proposal provided the negative with a myriad of plan attacks. After considering the difficulty of answering the potential attacks, many affirmative teams rejected the Kennedy proposal and opted for another plan. Some chose the Burleson Plan, favored by the Health Insurance Association of America, which cost "only" $4 billion annually. The same negative attacks still applied, but it was much easier to defend a $4-billion expenditure than a $70-billion expenditure.

On the same proposition, some affirmative advocates thought it would be a good idea to provide annual physical examinations for all citizens as a plank in their plan. At first they discovered a good deal of evidence recommending such examinations. Later they discovered evidence—which they were sure their opponents would also find—indicating that such examinations for the whole population were counterproductive when subjected to cost-benefit analysis. (The argument went that it would take so much time to give over 200 million physical examinations a year that physicians would not have time to do anything else.) Thus some affirmatives eliminated what had initially seemed to be a desirable plank for their plan and provided instead for multiphasic testing for the population. This method would check for many, but not all, diseases and, as the tests would be administered by physicians' aides and analyzed by computers, they were of low cost both in dollars and physicians' time.

Although it is defensively sound to tailor the plan to avoid the strongest negative attacks, advocates are *cautioned* that they still must provide a plan that will produce *significant* advantages. Obviously, it is easier to answer the cost attacks on a $1-billion plan than on a $70-billion plan. Given the context of the proposition, however, does the $1-billion plan produce significant advantages? The task of the affirmative advocates is to build a plan that achieves the optimum balance of offensive and defensive capabilities.

Prudent affirmatives will consider the most likely and effective attacks against their case and build in reasonable defensive provisions. An axiom of debate is that "a good case defends itself," and the well-planned case is built to provide for the maximally effective self-defense.

Exercises

1. Attend an intercollegiate debate and prepare an outline of the affirmative case. Attach to this outline a written critique (500 words) of the affirmative case, in which you evaluate the organization and development of the case.

2. Prepare an outline and a written critique (500 words) of an affirmative case on a contemporary problem as presented in a recent speech. For the texts of speeches, consult *Vital Speeches, Representative American Speeches,* the *New York Times,* or *U.S. News & World Report.*

3. Prepare the full manuscript (a ten-minute speech) for a first affirmative speech on a value proposition. Include all of the evidence and reasoning necessary to establish a prima facie case.

4. If time permits, your instructor may invite you to make an oral presentation of the manuscript prepared for Exercise 3 to the class (or you may arrange for duplicated copies of your manuscript to be distributed to the class). Conduct a class discussion:
   a. Is the definitive contention valid?
   b. Are the designative contentions valid?
   c. Is significance clearly established?
   d. Is inherency clearly established?
   e. Do the value applications advance the case?

5. Continue Exercise 4 by conducting a class discussion:
   a. What are the most likely negative attacks against your case?
   b. How can the case be improved to meet these attacks?

6. Prepare the full manuscript (a ten-minute speech) for a first affirmative speech on a policy proposition. Include all of the evidence and reasoning necessary to establish a prima facie case.

7. If time permits, your instructor may invite you to make an oral presentation of the manuscript prepared for Exercise 6 to the class (or you may arrange for duplicated copies of your manuscript to be distributed to the class). Conduct a class discussion:
   a. Is the case significant?
   b. Is inherency clearly established?
   c. Is solvency provided?
   d. Are the advantages inherent and significant?

8. Continue Exercise 7 by conducting a class discussion:
   a. What are the most likely negative attacks against your case?
   b. How can the case be improved to meet these attacks?

13

Building the Negative Case

The negative case requires flexibility in planning. A careful analysis of the proposition will probably enable the negative to determine the issues most likely to be advanced by the affirmative. Until the debate is actually underway, however, the negative team will not know what type of case the affirmative is using; it will not know what weight the affirmative will attach to each issue or what evidence and argument will be used by the affirmative in developing its issues. This uncertainty places a high premium on the negative's ability to adapt to the affirmative's case as it is presented.

I. Objectives of the Negative Case

As indicated earlier, the burden of proof rests on the affirmative. In theory, the negative need not even speak until the affirmative has presented a prima facie case. The prudent advocate will recognize, however, that popular audiences sometimes assume that "silence means consent" and may accept a proposition on the basis of less than a prima facie case. Therefore, the advocate must be prepared to reply to any affirmative case, even though it does not meet all the logical requirements of a prima facie case. In the courtroom, the defense may move that a case be dismissed on the ground that the prosecution or plaintiff has not presented a prima facie case. This procedure, however, is not generally available outside the courtroom.

While the burden of proof rests on the affirmative, the negative has the *burden of rebuttal*; that is, the negative must refute the issues of the affirmative, or the affirmative will prevail. The *burden of the negative*, then, is the burden of rebuttal, which the negative must seek to shift to the affirmative.

We will first consider the proposition of value negative case, then we will consider the proposition of policy negative case. The discussion of the policy negative case will include a consideration of many issues critical to both value and policy negative cases.

II. Proposition of Value Negative Cases

The negative has the burden of rebuttal and must attack the case that the affirmative presents. The negative knows that the affirmative will present definitive and designative issues. As we saw in the previous chapter, the affirmative may well find it necessary to introduce issues of significance, inherency, application, and solvency as well. The negative must refute at least one of the affirmative issues, or carry one of the issues the negative introduces, to win.

In developing the negative case the value debaters select the most appropriate combination of the various available options.

A. Attack Topicality

When advocates argue that a matter is not topical, they maintain that it is not related to, or does not directly stem from, the proposition being debated. In meeting the CEDA affirmative case outlined in Chapter 12, the negative maintained that the affirmative's case was not topical — it did not consider the whole resolution. The first negative constructive speaker argued, ". . . the affirmative is only talking about ecological impacts and only talking about ecological access. On that level not talking about the entirety of the resolution." The further development of this argument as it is continued through the various speeches of the debate may be seen in Appendix B. If the negative can convince the judges that the affirmative's case is not topical, they will win; if the affirmative can convince the judges that their case is topical, they will have safely won that issue.

B. Attack Definitions

Definitions have been considered in some detail earlier (in Chapter 4, Section II). As we saw, in CEDA debate the affirmative is required to present a reasonable definition. If the affirmative's definition is reasonable, the negative is well advised not to attempt to argue the matter, but to get on with attacks on issues it has a chance of winning. Note that in the first negative constructive speech in Appendix B the debater does just that, saying, "Definitions are fine, so we'll go specifically, go on to . . . " If, on the other hand, the affirmative's definition is perceived as unreasonable, then the negative may choose to attack the definition and if they prove their point will win.

C. Attack Criteria

In a debate on the proposition "Resolved: That significantly stronger third party participation in United States Presidential elections would benefit the political process," one
affirmative argued that "survival" was the ultimate value, that is, the most important
criterion. A negative meeting this case argued that "democracy" was the ultimate
value. As the debate developed, the negative was able to sustain their position that democracy was the most important criterion and thus won the decision of the judges. If
the negative can establish that other criteria are more important than those advanced
by the affirmative, and show that the affirmative does not meet these criteria, the
negative will usually prevail.

D. Attack Significance

The negative's objective in attacking significance is to prove that at least some of the
essential elements of the affirmative's case are not significant enough to justify adopting
the resolution. In the case considered in Chapter 12, the affirmative sought to establish the significance of the environment and the ecological systems. In this debate the
negative did not successfully attack significance. If the affirmative can establish the
significance of its case, it is in a strong position to counter other negative attacks. Thus
the negative must find ways and means to minimize the significance of at least some
of the essential elements of the affirmative's case.

E. Attack Inherency

The negative's objective in attacking inherency is to prove that at least some of the
essential elements of the affirmative's case are not inherent and thus do not warrant
adopting the resolution. In a debate on the "third party" proposition mentioned earlier,
one affirmative argued that significantly stronger third parties would inherently lead to
beneficial applications in the American political system. They cited the income tax,
direct election of senators, woman suffrage, labor legislation, and Social Security as
examples of desirable legislation originating with third parties. The negative meeting
this case pointed out that these laws were enacted under the status quo and that thus
they were not uniquely inherent in strengthened third parties. If the negative can
prove that some elements of the affirmative case are not inherent in the case or can be
obtained without adopting the resolution, they have successfully attacked the inherency claim of the affirmative.

F. Attack Application

In attacking application the negative seeks to prove that the value or quasi-policy advocated by the affirmative will not be applied to the problem. In a debate on the "third
party" proposition, one affirmative claimed that the application of the resolution
would result in strengthened third parties being able to enact important legislation
perceived as extreme by complacent majorities. A negative meeting this case attacked
the application by arguing it would not function as the affirmative claimed it would. The

negative maintained that a third party could not enact any legislation until it grew to major party size, and to do that it would have to drop its extreme position to attract enough voters.

G. Attack Solvency

In attacking solvency the negative argues that even if the application functions as the affirmative wants it to it will not solve the problem. In the debate in Appendix B the affirmative offered as its solvency issue in the first affirmative constructive, "a new environmental ethic of deep ecology is feasible." The negative's attack on solvency in the first negative constructive argued, "people must take action to solve . . . they don't show that there is any action taken whatsoever." The full development of this issue may be seen in Appendix B. If the negative is successful in winning the solvency argument there is no reason to adopt the resolution advanced by the affirmative.

H. Provide Value Objections

In providing value objections the negative argues that the affirmative's proposal will produce something so objectionable—in effect a disadvantage—that we should reject the affirmative's case. In the second negative constructive in the debate in Appendix B the speaker provided an extensive value objection, claiming the affirmative's proposal will, among other disadvantages, "kill the marketplace of ideas . . . chill the press . . . snowball to government control." This value objection was potentially the negative's strongest position. Its impact would have been greater had the headlining (labels) been clearer (see Chapter 15, Section V-C) and the substructure better organized (see Chapter 4, Section III-E). Note that value objections are introduced by the negative. When the negative introduces them, the affirmative must be prepared to demonstrate that they are not significant and that they are outweighed by other issues.

III. Proposition of Policy Negative Cases

As in value negative cases, the negative has the burden of rebuttal and must attack the case that the affirmative presents. The negative knows that the affirmative will present justification, plan, and advantage issues. The negative must refute at least one of the affirmative issues, or carry one of the issues the negative introduces to win. The specific development of the case and the particular issues the negative uses in any given situation will, of course, depend on the resolution under debate, the available evidence and arguments, the actual case of the opposition, the attitudes, interests, and intellectual capabilities of the audience, and the dynamics of the occasion.

It must be emphasized that each negative case is custom-built and adapted to the specific affirmative case it must oppose. The negative selects among its arsenal of potential issues and develops those best suited for use in a particular situation. Although carrying one issue—workability, for instance—could win for the negative, the prudent advocate recognizes that the able affirmative has anticipated and is prepared for all

Basic CEDA Speaker Responsibilities

First Negative Constructive

The basic responsibility is to attack the affirmative's case. This is done by attacking the affirmative's case in exactly the same order as the issues are presented by the first affirmative constructive. There is one exception: If the negative chooses to make a topicality argument, this is made first. The other off-case arguments are reserved for the second negative constructive. The following listing therefore *is suggestive only; the actual order must be adapted to the affirmative case.*

    I. Attack Topicality, if vulnerable.
   II. Attack Significance, if vulnerable.
  III. Attack Definitions, if vulnerable.
  IV. Attack Criteria, if vulnerable.
   V. Attack Inherency, if vulnerable.
  VI. Attack Application, if vulnerable.
 VII. Attack Solvency, if vulnerable.

Second Negative Constructive

The basic responsibility is to present the negative's off-case arguments. As with the first negative constructive, this speech must be tailor-made to attack a specific affirmative case.

    I. Prove Value Objections.
  II. Contrast Application and Solvency with Value Objections, and prove Value Objections outweigh them.

---

possible attacks. Thus, as the negative can rarely be sure of winning an issue until the debate is over, it usually finds that the wisest course is to attack all vulnerable areas of the affirmative case, concentrating its major attacks on the most vulnerable areas — for instance, not only attacking workability but also providing minor repairs and proving that disadvantages outweigh advantages.

A. Attack Topicality

When advocates argue that a matter is not topical, they maintain that it is not related to, or does not directly stem from, the proposition being debated. In the law courts, an attorney may object to evidence, a question, or an argument on the ground that it is not relevant to the case before the court. If the judge sustains the objection, the matter is excluded. In parliamentary debate, the chair should rule "out of order" any remarks or proposed amendments that are not germane to the business before the house. (The stringency with which this rule is enforced varies; for example, the U.S. Senate does not require that a senator's remarks be germane.) In academic debate, the topicality

First Negative Rebuttal

The basic responsibility is to refute the second affirmative's case arguments and to extend the first negative attacks on case.

   I. Reestablish and extend attack on Topicality, if necessary.
  II. Reestablish and extend attack on Significance, if necessary.
 III. Reestablish and extend attack on Definitions, if necessary.
 IV. Reestablish and extend attack on Criteria, if necessary.
  V. Reestablish and extend attack on Significance, if necessary.
 VI. Reestablish and extend attack on Inherency, if necessary.
VII. Reestablish and extend attack on Application, if necessary.
VIII. Reestablish and extend attack on Solvency, if necessary.

Second Negative Rebuttal

The basic responsibility is to reestablish and clinch the negative's off-case and case attacks.

  I. Reestablish and clinch the negative's Value Objections.
 II. Reestablish and clinch the negative's case attacks.
III. Conclude by presenting the best reasons you have to justify a decision for the negative.

---

issue — if the negative wins it against a major portion of the affirmative's case — usually becomes an "absolute voting issue," and the judge awards the decision to the negative. In less formal situations, reasonable persons tend to dismiss irrelevant arguments. Attacks on topicality are usually directed against the plan or one or more of the advantages.

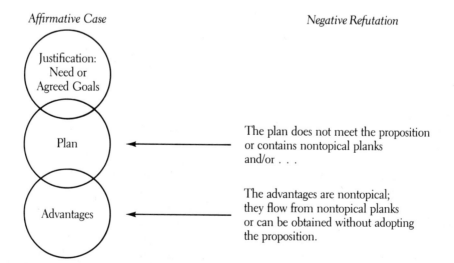

Affirmative Case　　　　　　　　　　　　　*Negative Refutation*

Justification: Need or Agreed Goals

Plan　←　The plan does not meet the proposition or contains nontopical planks and/or . . .

Advantages　←　The advantages are nontopical; they flow from nontopical planks or can be obtained without adopting the proposition.

1. Of the Plan. The proposition "Resolved: That the federal government should grant annually a specific percentage of its income tax revenue to the state governments" provides an interesting example. This proposition mandated four specific things for the affirmative's plan: (1) an annual grant, (2) a specific percentage of the revenue, (3) funds coming from federal income tax revenue, and (4) funds distributed by the federal government to the state governments. If any one of these items were missing, the negative would have grounds for arguing "not topical."

The affirmative may add some nontopical provisions to its plan to provide for a reasonable implementation of its proposal. For example, in debating the "revenue sharing" proposition, some teams provided that the funds could not be used for (1) matching federal funds for federal categorical grant programs or (2) highway construction.

In meeting the NDT affirmative case outlined in Chapter 12, the negative argued that the affirmative's case was "not topical: (1) The plan was not substantial, (2) it was not over 50 percent, (3) a comparison is required, and (4) a criterion for measurement is required." While these may seem to be very similar to definitional arguments (considered next) the negative chose to headline them as "topicality" arguments. The further development of this argument as it is continued through the various speeches may be seen in Appendix C.

2. Of the Advantages. The advantages must flow from the adopting of the resolution as operationally defined by a plan congruous with the resolution. If the negative can prove an advantage is nontopical, that advantage should be rejected as a reason for adopting the resolution.

If the advantages come from a nontopical provision of the plan, the affirmative is in trouble. On the "revenue sharing" proposition, some affirmative teams required the states to give the funds to the public schools and claimed the advantage of better education.

Negatives meeting this case were usually able to prove that the provision was nontopical and that the advantage of better education came from giving the money to the schools and not from any of the four items mandated in the resolution. They also demonstrated that the advantage was "not unique" to the resolution. The same advantage could be achieved by having the federal government give money (and not necessarily income tax revenue) directly to the schools.

As we have just seen, the advantage of "better education" was nontopical. As we have also seen, reasonable nontopical planks may be added to the plan to provide for its reasonable implementation. Any advantage that comes from a nontopical plank of the plan is in itself nontopical. For example, the provision that no revenue sharing funds be used for highway construction was a reasonable nontopical constraint. If, however, the affirmative claimed as an advantage that it would reduce waste in highway construction, such an advantage would be clearly nontopical; it stemmed from adopting a nontopical plank of the plan. Of course, it would also be "not unique" in that any waste in highway construction could be eliminated by legislation other than revenue sharing.

B. Attack Definitions

As we saw earlier (in Chapter 4, Section II), in NDT debate there is a preference for "the best definition in the debate." In many cases, as in the CEDA debate considered in Section II-B of this chapter, definitions do not become an issue. If the negative chooses to challenge the affirmative's definition, in NDT debate the clash comes on which team provides the best definition in the debate. In debates on the "information" proposition (see Chapter 4, Section II-B), the definition of information sometimes became critical in determining the outcome of the debate. Was the best definition of information one that was limited to credit data or one that included marijuana? The debaters sought to establish their position by applying the "Criteria to Prove a Satisfactory Definition" considered in that chapter.

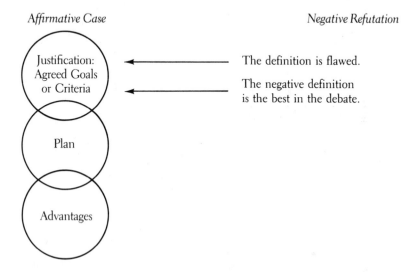

Affirmative Case   *Negative Refutation*

Justification: Agreed Goals or Criteria ← The definition is flawed.

← The negative definition is the best in the debate.

Plan

Advantages

C. Attack Goals or Criteria

In attacking the goals of a comparative advantage case, the negative may seek to demonstrate that (1) the goals are incompletely identified or (2) there are other, more important goals and these goals are incompatible with efforts to meet the affirmative goals. A similar analysis is made when attacking a criterion case.

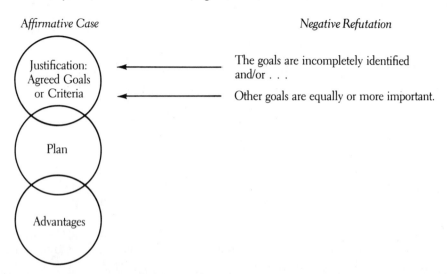

Affirmative Case   *Negative Refutation*

Justification: Agreed Goals or Criteria ← The goals are incompletely identified and/or . . .

← Other goals are equally or more important.

Plan

Advantages

1. Goals or Criteria Incompletely Identified. If the affirmative has incompletely identified the goals of the status quo or the criteria for the value advocated by the affirmative, the negative should point this out and identify the goals or criteria fully within the context of the appropriate reasoning. In a debate on the "crime" proposition, one affirmative speaker stated that the goal of society was "to reduce crime." A negative debater responded:

> Reducing crime is an incomplete statement of the goal of American society. We all want to reduce crime, but the negative today stands with the great legal scholar Blackstone who warned, "It is better that ten guilty persons escape than one innocent suffer." This is why we say the affirmative's goal is incompletely identified. The real goal of society is to reduce crime while preserving due process and other essential Constitutional rights.

2. Other Goals or Criteria More Important and Incompatible. If the affirmative's goals or criteria are valid, the negative may be able to prove that other goals or criteria are more important and that these goals are incompatible with efforts to meet the affirmative's goals. In a debate on the "tax sharing" proposition, an affirmative team maintained that the agreed goals of the status quo were to attain a more efficient system of tax collection and a more progressive system of taxation. A negative team meeting this case argued that a more important goal of the status quo was to maintain the American system of federalism. It was unable to refute the affirmative's claim that its plan would produce the advantages of "more efficient collection" and "more progressive taxes." However, the negative was able to minimize these advantages by demonstrating that repairs in the status quo could produce almost as much efficiency in tax collection and almost as progressive a system of taxation. It then developed its argument that the affirmative's plan destroyed the federal system by making the states dependent on the federal government for their revenues, thus reducing the states to *de facto* departments of a central government. It then cited the disadvantages it claimed were inherent in a system of central government. In weighing the now-minimized advantages against the disadvantages, the negative advocates claimed that, on balance, the affirmative's plan had a net disadvantage. As the goals of the affirmative and negative were incompatible, only one of the two competitive goals could be accepted.

D. Attack Need

The objective of the negative here is either to demonstrate that the affirmative has not proved the existence of a need or to prove that there is no need.

1. Need Not Proved. In debates on the "employment opportunities" proposition, some affirmative speakers advanced as a major need issue the argument that millions were unemployed and needed job opportunities. In support they cited the unemployment statistics and argued that the unemployed suffered from a loss of income. Negative advocates, using the attack on the need negative case, were quick to point out that the affirmative had not established any real need — it had not shown that any harm came to the people or to the economy because of unemployment — and that unemployed persons received unemployment compensation, food stamps, and many other welfare benefits. The negative speakers introduced further evidence to show that many

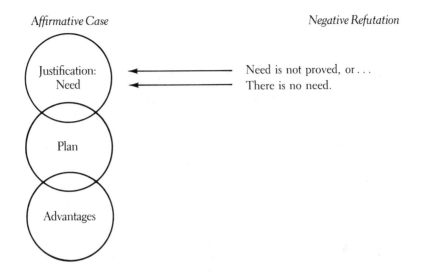

Affirmative Case

Justification: Need

Plan

Advantages

Negative Refutation

Need is not proved, or . . .
There is no need.

unemployed persons were members of families where others were employed. Thus, the negative maintained that even if the affirmative's unemployment statistics were true—and counterevidence produced by the negative cast doubt on the validity of the statistics—the affirmative had not proved a need for adopting the resolution.

2. No Existing Need. In debating the "energy" proposition, some affirmatives called for the federal government to ban any further construction of nuclear energy plants to generate electricity. They pointed out that the status quo was committed to the construction of such plants and argued, as their need issue, the claim that when we had 100 or more such plants there would be an intolerable risk of radiation leakage or explosion. Many negatives argued that no need existed or would exist. They maintained that nuclear power plants were perfectly safe and that any leakage or explosion was impossible. They cited evidence stating that no fatality had ever been caused by a civilian nuclear power plant and extended their argument by citing the elaborate safety precautions already in existence. The disaster at Chernobyl was irrelevant, the affirmative maintained, since the Soviet plant was built to a design inferior to American standards. Debates on this issue provided excellent examples of the clash of evidence. Excellent evidence was available to both sides, and the clash was inevitably won by the team that could provide the most recent evidence from the best qualified authorities, who could be quoted most directly to the point under dispute.

E. Provide Repairs or Modifications

Two types of repair or modification arguments may be used by the negative: (1) to solve needs and (2) to provide advantages. The repairs or modifications should be relatively few and relatively minor; they must be consistent with the status quo; there should be ample precedent for such actions; and they must be capable of being put into effect without making any structural change in the status quo.

1. To Solve Needs. This type of argument is used when the negative is forced to admit certain shortcomings in the status quo but believes they can be repaired by status quo mechanisms. Usually the negative first seeks to minimize the need issues (see Section F, "Attack Significance") and then presents its repairs. For example, in debates on the proposition "Resolved: That law enforcement agencies in the United States should be given greater freedom in the investigation and prosecution of crime," some negative teams argued that the laws already on the books were entirely adequate to deal with crime; all that was needed were more funds to provide for better enforcement. They maintained that more funds would provide more "hardware" — that is, more computers,

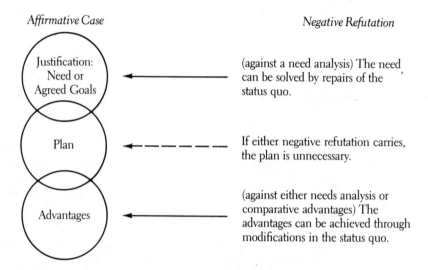

Affirmative Case	*Negative Refutation*
Justification: Need or Agreed Goals	(against a need analysis) The need can be solved by repairs of the status quo.
Plan	If either negative refutation carries, the plan is unnecessary.
Advantages	(against either needs analysis or comparative advantages) The advantages can be achieved through modifications in the status quo.

walkie-talkies, mobile communication centers; more funds would enable them to upgrade the police forces by paying higher salaries to attract and retain more able officers and to provide in-service training; more funds would provide more prosecutors and more judges, thus assuring prompt trials; more money would provide more effective rehabilitation programs in prisons; and more money would provide more parole officers to supervise the prisoners once they were released. This combination of repairs — while maintaining the status quo laws — would significantly reduce crime, they argued.

In debates on the "comprehensive medical care" proposition, many negative teams made effective use of repairs. If the affirmative limited its need analysis to the claim that "poor people can't afford medical care," the negative quickly offered repairs to extend Medicare, Medicaid, free clinics, the free care provisions of the Hill-Burton Act, and many other programs. The negative noted that all of these programs existed in the status quo, that they provided ample precedent for the government to provide free medical care for poor people, and that no structural change in any program was required.

In both of these examples, if the negative can show that the amount of money needed is relatively small and can be obtained without dislocating other government programs, they are true minor repairs. If the amount of money needed is massive and would require serious tax increases or the curtailment of other government spending, the negative would be arguing "major" repairs that might provide the affirmative with the opportunity to claim that the negative's proposal produced significant disadvantages.

The distinction between minor and major repairs is situational. Minor repairs utilize status quo mechanisms in a way that does not significantly alter the status quo or change its structure. Major repairs significantly alter the status quo and may well require a change in its structure. A plan that provided for the federal government to spend $1 billion more in grants to the nation's police forces would probably qualify as a minor repair. A senator commented on the scale of federal expenditures by observing wryly, "A billion here, a billion there, and pretty soon it adds up to real money." A $1-billion increase for police by even the largest of cities would, of course, require massive structural changes in the status quo.

2. To Achieve Advantages. This type of argument is used when the negative believes that the advantage claimed by the affirmative can be achieved without adopting the resolution — that the advantage is "not unique" to the proposition — but by merely making some modifications in the status quo. The debater might choose to make a conditional argument and show that the advantage *could* be provided by modifications without advocating that the advantage actually be achieved. If the advantage could be achieved without adopting the resolution, then it is not a justification for adopting the resolution.

In debating the "energy" proposition, some affirmatives introduced a plan to ban the use of coal in producing electricity and mandated the use of nuclear power plants. One of the advantages they claimed was "cleaner air." A negative team meeting this case argued that the status quo was already working to provide cleaner air and that, if we wanted still cleaner air, all we had to do was modify the standards of the Air Quality Act, since ample technology existed to make this cleanup practical. Thus, by merely making a minor modification in the status quo, we could achieve the advantage of cleaner air without adopting the affirmative's plan and suffering all the inherent disadvantages of nuclear power plants that the negative would seek to prove in the "disadvantages" portion of their case.

The negative, of course, must exercise discretion in making modifications or repairs. A multiplicity of repairs or modifications might open the way for the affirmative to argue that the negative has admitted the need or advantage of so many repairs or modifications that we should "go all the way" and adopt the resolution.

F. Attack Significance

The negative objective in attacking significance is to prove that the needs or advantages of the affirmative are not sufficiently significant to justify adopting the resolution.

1. Of Need. The negative will usually find it advisable to examine the affirmative's need for both quantitative and qualitative significance and attack the affirmative if either or both are not proved. In debates on the "mass media" proposition, some affirmatives argued that television commercials for sugar-laden food products caused dental cavities in children. Negatives meeting this case readily proved that an unknown number of

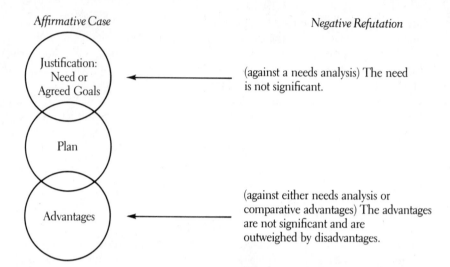

Affirmative Case

Justification:
Need or
Agreed Goals

Plan

Advantages

Negative Refutation

(against a needs analysis) The need
is not significant.

(against either needs analysis or
comparative advantages) The advantages
are not significant and are
outweighed by disadvantages.

dental cavities were not sufficient justification for government regulation of mass media communication. On the same proposition, some affirmatives argued that violence on television "affected children adversely." Here again negatives quickly refuted the significance of the harm—no significant numbers of children were proved to have been adversely affected, and no qualification was provided for the term "adversely affected."

In debates on the "guarantee employment opportunities" proposition, affirmatives could usually readily establish that millions were unemployed, thus establishing quantitative significance. Negative advocates often granted this argument readily enough and went on to argue that the affirmative had not proved any qualitative harm from unemployment. They continued this argument by introducing evidence to show that many unemployed persons received unemployment compensation, food stamps, and other welfare benefits. Thus, they maintained, the affirmative had not proved that the unemployed persons were harmed by their unemployment.

The negative may attack the affirmative for failing to prove quantitative significance, qualitative significance, or, in some circumstances, both quantitative and qualitative significance. Most often, of course, the affirmative will successfully establish some significance. The task of the negative then is to prove that the significance established by the affirmative is not sufficient "on balance" to outweigh the disadvantages the negative will seek to prove.

2. Of Advantage. In debates on the "energy" proposition, some affirmatives presented a plan providing for a ban of offshore drilling for oil and claimed the advantage of protecting the environment by (1) preventing unsightly oil rigs, (2) protecting fish life, and (3) preventing ecological damage from possible oil leakage. Some negative teams meeting this plan argued that the advantages were not significant as (1) the oil rigs would be miles offshore so no one could see them from the shore; (2) oil rigs provided a feeding ground for the fish, thus the fish population actually increased in this area (note this negative turnaround—the affirmative claimed that banning oil rigs protected fish life, and the negative turned this argument around, claiming that oil rigs increased the fish population); and (3) oil leakage was rare and, even in those few instances where it occurred, the wildlife population grew back to normal in two years. They concluded their argument by maintaining that the affirmative had provided neither quantitative nor qualitative significance for their advantage, since offshore wells did no harm to the environment and, in any event, the need for oil clearly outweighed the insignificant environmental considerations presented by the affirmative.

G. Attack Inherency

Since inherency has been considered earlier (Chapter 11, Section II-D, "Requirement to Prove Inherency"), we will treat it only briefly here. Three types of inherency arguments are often used by negative teams: (1) The status quo has no inherent barrier blocking the achievement of the advantage; (2) the status quo has no inherent gap preventing the attainment of the advantage; and (3) the advantages are not inherent in the plan.

1. Of the Status Quo Barrier. The negative seeks to prove that no justification exists for adopting the resolution, since the advantages claimed by the affirmative can be achieved without the plan. In debating the "energy" proposition, some affirmatives proposed a plan whereby the government would require all electric generating plants to use coal as their only fuel and to generate electricity by the magnetohydrodynamic (MHD) process. They argued that this method used cheap and plentiful coal and was far more efficient than the status quo methods of producing electricity. As an advantage they claimed that the oil now used by the electric plants — which was in critically short supply — would be made available to industries that could not substitute coal as a source of their energy. Some negatives meeting this type of case responded by pointing out that the affirmative had cited no reason why the electric industry would not adopt the MHD process of its own volition. Using a conditional argument, they maintained — since coal was both abundant and cheap — that, if the process really was more efficient, then it would obviously be more profitable for the electric companies to adopt MHD and that they would do so promptly, and hence there was no justification for the plan. Some affirmatives had difficulty in responding to this argument until they found evidence enabling them to argue that the very high initial cost of MHD equipment was an inherent barrier to its being adopted by electric companies. The cost was so high that many years would pass before the companies realized any profit from the changeover. Thus, they argued, the only way to obtain the advantages of MHD was to adopt the resolution and use federal control to require the electric companies to use this process.

2. Of the Status Quo Gap. In debating the "mass media" proposition, some affirmatives maintained that television violence was harmful and argued that a gap in existing laws permitted television to broadcast violent programs. Some negatives meeting this argument held that the legal gap was irrelevant and that other status quo means existed to control violence. Television networks and stations, they argued, were very responsive to public pressure, and they cited various examples of programs that had been taken off the air because of public opposition. If the affirmative's harms were valid, the negatives maintained, public pressure would be sufficient to cause the networks and stations to change their programming. Many negatives extended this argument by offering a minor repair—use voluntary means to keep violence off television—and claimed that this repair would achieve the affirmative's advantage of reducing television violence without the disadvantage of increased government control.

3. Of the Advantages. A good beginning point is to study carefully the affirmative's plan to discern whether any nontopical planks are present. Any advantages that flow from such provisions are clearly nontopical. In addition, the negative must be alert to the possibility of a noninherent advantage being claimed from a properly topical plan. In debating the "energy" proposition, some affirmatives called for the federal govern-

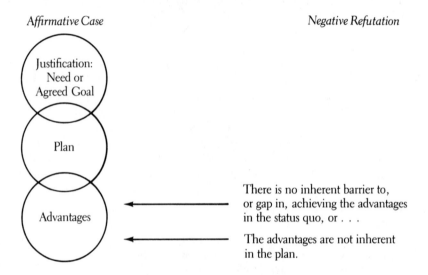

Affirmative Case   *Negative Refutation*

Justification: Need or Agreed Goal

Plan

Advantages

There is no inherent barrier to, or gap in, achieving the advantages in the status quo, or . . .

The advantages are not inherent in the plan.

ment to spend $10 billion on research on solar and geothermal sources and to mandate the use of these sources to supply the nation's electricity needs within ten years. The negative quickly pointed out that success is *not inherent* in research. Thus the affirmative could not guarantee that solar and geothermal sources could meet our electricity needs in ten years or indeed ever. After all, they noted, we have spent billions of dollars over many years on cancer research without finding a cure for cancer. And alchemists devoted centuries of research to the problem of the transmutation of the base metals into gold.

H. Attack Workability

The negative's objective here is to block adoption of the resolution by proving that the plan proposed by the affirmative is unworkable. To do so, the negative should present a series of concisely stated, closely reasoned arguments. In preparing for this, as with other negative issues, the advocates often develop a series of "briefs" against potential affirmative plans. When they hear the plan the affirmative is actually presenting, they pull the appropriate briefs from their file and adapt them to the specific plan presented by the affirmative.

Debating the "energy" proposition, one affirmative team cited the energy shortage as its need and proposed to solve the need by a plan that called for the federal government to require electric plants to phase out the use of oil and coal and to build solar, geothermal, and nuclear plants to produce electricity. Well-prepared negatives usually had briefs of arguments prepared for each of these energy sources. One negative argued against this plan by introducing evidence to establish:

1. Solar energy is unworkable because (1) it has never been proven in commercial use; (2) its potential is geographically limited by cloud cover; (3) the fuel cell method is prohibitively expensive — it would increase the cost of electricity one thousand times; and (4) the reflector method is prohibitive in land cost — it would require an area equal to the size of 21 states to solve the affirmative's needs.

2. Nuclear energy is unworkable because (1) there will be a long time lag before reactors can be built — all present nuclear plants are two to seven years behind schedule and future plants will be delayed even more because of lengthy lawsuits and hearings where the dangers to life and environment will be argued; and (2) there is now a shortage of uranium necessary to operate the present plants — there just will not be enough uranium to operate the number of plants proposed by the affirmative.

3. Geothermal is unworkable because (1) there are very few potential sources of commercially useful size; (2) these are located in earthquake prone areas, where drilling for the hot water might in itself cause earthquakes, or in areas remote from any population to use the electricity they might produce; and (3) there is a shortage of copper which makes it commercially impractical to transmit electric power over great distances.

The negative concluded its workability argument by demonstrating that all three of the energy sources proposed by the affirmative could not solve their need.

I. Prove Plan Will Not Accrue Claimed Advantages

In developing this argument, the advocate concentrates on attempting to prove that the plan — even if it works exactly as the affirmative wants it to — will not accrue the advantages claimed by the affirmative.

In debating the "comprehensive medical care" proposition, one affirmative, in its plan, provided free medical care for all citizens and claimed as one of its advantages "better medical care for the poor." The negative argued that the plan could not accrue this advantage because (1) few physicians practice in the rural and ghetto areas where most poor people live; (2) the poor lack the money to pay for transportation to travel to the areas where the physicians practice; (3) many of the poor are ignorant of the value of early medical care and will not seek it; (4) many of the poor are afraid of medical care and will not seek it until their condition is critical; and (5) many of the working poor cannot afford to take time off to seek medical care and do so only when their condition is critical.

In debating the "law enforcement" proposition, some affirmatives proposed as their plan that wiretapping be legalized for state and local police forces and claimed as their advantage that there would be more convictions of criminals as wiretaps would produce direct evidence of crimes. Negatives meeting this case argued that the plan would not accrue the advantage since criminals would assume their phones were tapped and

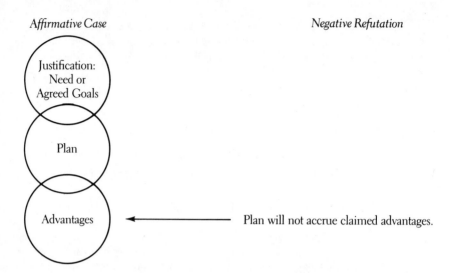

take countermeasures to circumvent the plan. They argued that the criminals would (1) reduce the use of the phone, (2) use scrambler phones, (3) use electronic devices to discover untapped phones and use those phones, (4) use randomly chosen public phones, (5) use frequently changed codes, (6) use frequently changed argot, and (7) use fragmentary references and identification.

J. Attack Solvency

Typically, the negative will seek to minimize the need (see Section F, "Attack Significance") and later prove that the plan will not work (see Section H, "Attack Workability").

In developing the "plan does not solve need" argument, the negative concentrates on attempting to prove that the plan — even if it works exactly as the affirmative wants it

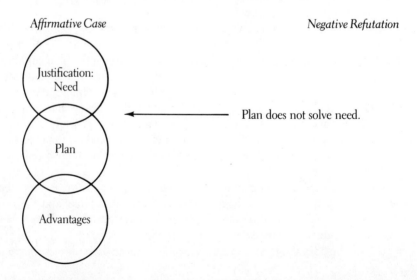

to — will not solve the need. For example, in debates on the "guaranteed annual wage for nonagricultural workers" proposition, some affirmatives argued, as their need issue, that the purchasing power of unemployed persons must be maintained; they cited evidence that millions of persons were unemployed annually and then presented a plan that would provide a guaranteed annual wage for employees with one year's seniority. Negatives meeting this case argued that it did not provide solvency because millions of the unemployed cited in the affirmative's need were agricultural workers, who were not covered in the plan (indeed they were excluded by the resolution), and then introduced evidence to show that most unemployed persons had less than one year's seniority prior to their discharge and hence would not receive the guaranteed annual wage provided for in the plan. The plan would work for the relatively few unemployed persons with one year's seniority, but not for the millions cited by the affirmative in their need issue.

In debates on the "guarantee employment opportunities for all U.S. citizens" proposition, some affirmatives proposed a plan to rebuild the inner cities and claimed as their advantage that this plan would provide jobs for all. Negatives meeting this case were quick to point out that the jobs created by this plan did not "guarantee employment opportunities" for those unskilled in the building trades or for those unsuited for the rigors of unskilled construction jobs.

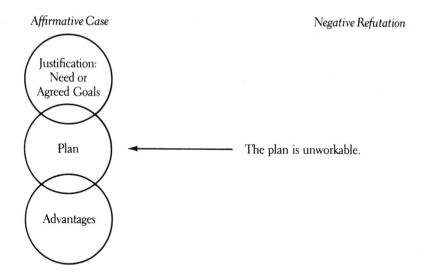

K. Prove Disadvantages

The negative's objective here is to block the adoption of the resolution by proving that the plan proposed by the affirmative will produce disadvantages and that these disadvantages outweigh any possible advantage the plan may achieve. To do so, the negative should present a series of concisely stated, closely reasoned arguments. In preparing for this argument, as with workability and other negative attacks, the advocate develops a series of "briefs" against potential affirmative plans and adapts them to the specific plan presented by the affirmative.

In debating the "energy" proposition, one affirmative, having established as its need that strip mining damaged the environment, provided a plan that banned all strip mining and claimed the advantage of a better environment. A negative meeting this case argued that banning strip mining (which it called surface mining) would produce the following disadvantages: (1) cause a shortage of copper (most copper came from surface mines and copper wire is essential for the transmission of electricity from generators to users); (2) cause a shortage of iron (most iron came from surface mines); (3) exacerbate the oil shortage (as oil would be used as a partial replacement for surface-mined coal); (4) increase the cost of electricity (as scarce oil and more expensive deep-mined coal would be used to replace surface-mined coal); (5) increase inflation (as a result of 1, 2, 3, and 4); (6) increase unemployment (as a result of 1, 2, 3, 4, and 5); (7) increase black-lung disease (as more people would work in deep mines under the affirmative's plan); (8) increase the number of mine accidents (working in deep mines is inherently more dangerous than working in surface mines); (9) cause dependence on unreliable foreign sources for coal (as present deep mines could not meet the demand for coal and, as it takes several years to get new mines into production, we would have to import coal; foreign sources might embargo coal, as the Arabs embargoed oil); (10) exacerbate the balance-of-payments problem (as dollars would flow out of the country to buy coal).

The negative then concluded this portion of its case by arguing that these disadvantages far outweighed whatever aesthetic advantages might be gained by viewing a landscape untouched by surface mining as contrasted with a landscape reclaimed after surface mining.

Of course, the negative must *prove* the disadvantage. As we saw earlier, on p. 41, "Whoever introduces an issue or contention into the debate has *a* burden of proof."

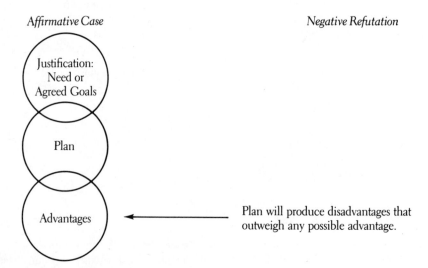

Affirmative Case

Justification:
Need or
Agreed Goals

Plan

Advantages

Negative Refutation

Plan will produce disadvantages that
outweigh any possible advantage.

1. Prove the Slippery Slope. When the affirmative's plan is not bad per se, the negative may seek to prove that the plan provides a precedent that will lead us down a *slippery slope* to the most deleterious consequences. In debates on the "mass media" proposition, an affirmative plan to ban advertising of sugar-laden food products would probably have the advantages of reducing children's dental cavities and probably improve their general health. Certainly these are desirable things in themselves. Negatives meeting such cases argued that this seemingly benign plan would lead us down the slippery slope of abridging the First Amendment. If we allowed advertising for sugar-laden foods to be banned, what would be next? It would set a dangerous precedent that could lead to the banning of advertising for books and for political candidates and would create intolerable barriers to free speech. Thus, the negative continued, we must avoid taking the first step down the slippery slope that could lead to clearly disadvantageous consequences.

The affirmative then had the burden of demonstrating that their proposal was a carefully measured and limited step and that their plan included safeguards (see "spikes," pp. 194–195) that will avoid the slippery slope.

2. Provide Generic Disadvantages. The disadvantages we have just considered were specific to the cases being attacked. Often, as we have noted, the negative will not know the affirmative's case until the debate is actually underway — and then it is too late to undertake specific research to refute the opponent's case. To provide for this situation, experienced negative advocates develop *generic disadvantages*. After careful analysis of the proposition, they discover certain provisions that an affirmative must *almost certainly* include in its plan. Although they cannot be certain in advance exactly what form these provisions will take, they can make realistic estimates. For example, in debating the "guarantee employment opportunities" proposition, some negative teams developed a series of generic disadvantages to any affirmative plan that would increase income. (By providing jobs for unemployed people, of course, the affirmative's plan usually did increase their income.) These negative teams argued: (1) When Americans' income went up, they ate more beef; (2) eating more beef would increase cardiovascular disease, thus causing millions of deaths; (3) as farmers would find it more profitable to feed cattle grain to produce more beef, there would be less grain for export to the less developed countries (LDCs); (4) millions of people in the LDCs would die, as they would be unable to get grain; (5) this would cause the LDCs to start World War III in order to obtain needed grain; and (6) World War III would cause the end of life on earth. Would an increase in employment in the United States *really* cause the end of life on earth? This issue was actually argued in many debates on this proposition. As we saw in Chapter 9, the advocate must be prepared to demonstrate that the cause is capable of producing the effect under consideration.

As we observed in the previous section ("Prove the Slippery Slope"), the negative debating the "mass media" proposition could develop effective arguments against banning advertising for sugar-laden foods. Negatives found that arguments used against this specific case could be adapted as generic disadvantages for use against a multiplicity of affirmative cases that imposed limitations on free speech. The negative could not know in advance if the affirmative would choose to ban saccharin ads, ban pornography, ban violence on television, or any of the other myriad variations available to the affirmative. Against many of these bans, however, the negative could run a slippery slope First Amendment disadvantage and claim that the affirmative's seemingly benign ban would result in the disadvantage of violating First Amendment rights, thus concluding that the disadvantage of violating free speech outweighed any advantage

Basic NDT Speaker Responsibilities

First Negative Constructive

The basic responsibility is to attack the affirmative's case. This is done by attacking the affirmative's case in exactly the same order as the issues are presented by the first affirmative constructive. There are two exceptions: If the negative chooses to make definitional or topicality arguments, these are made immediately after the rationale statement. The plan attacks are customarily reserved for the second negative constructive. The following listing therefore *is suggestive only; the actual order must be adapted to the affirmative case.*

I. State the negative's rationale, if desired.
II. Attack definitions, if vulnerable, and provide the best definitions in the debate.
III. Attack topicality, if vulnerable.
IV. Attack criteria, if vulnerable.
V. Attack need, if vulnerable.
    A. Need not proved.
    B. Need not quantitatively significant.
    C. Need not qualitatively significant.
    D. Need not inherent.
VI. Provide minor repairs, if desired.
VII. Attack advantages, if vulnerable.

Second Negative Constructive

The basic responsibility is to attack the affirmative's plan.
I. Attack workability, if vulnerable.
II. Attack solvency, if vulnerable.
III. Prove plan will not accrue advantages, if possible.

---

claimed by the affirmative. The ability to convert a specific disadvantage, with careful and appropriate adaptation, into a generic disadvantage is an important weapon in the negative's arsenal.

3. Avoid Turnarounds. As we saw in Chapter 12, the experienced affirmative will be alert for opportunities to "turnaround" disadvantages and convert them into advantages that will help it. Negative advocates, as they build disadvantages, must be aware of this affirmative strategy and carefully consider whether a disadvantage can be turned against them. If the negative advocates find that a disadvantage could be turned around against them, they *should not use it.* A successful turnaround means that the negative not only loses the disadvantage but that the affirmative gains an advantage.

In Chapter 8 we considered an argument made by a second negative constructive speaker that work sharing would cause strikes. These strikes, the negative argued, were a disadvantage of the affirmative plan. The first affirmative rebuttalist sought to turn-

IV. Prove plan will produce disadvantages, if possible.

V. Contrast now-minimized advantages with disadvantages and prove, if possible, that disadvantages outweigh advantages.

(Note that the second negative constructive must be tailor-made to attack the affirmative's plan. Thus the organization presented here is merely suggestive. It is possible, for example, that the second negative constructive might consist entirely of proving that the plan will produce disadvantages and that the disadvantages outweigh the advantages claimed by the affirmative.)

First Negative Rebuttal

The basic responsibility is to refute the second affirmative's case arguments and to extend the first negative attack on case.

I. Reestablish and extend negative's rationale, if necessary.

II. Reestablish and extend negative's definitions, if necessary.

III. Reestablish and extend the attack on topicality, if necessary.

IV. Reestablish and extend the attack on criteria, if necessary.

V. Reestablish and extend the attack on need, if necessary.

VI. Reestablish and extend minor repairs, if necessary.

VII. Reestablish and extend the attack on advantages, if necessary.

Second Negative Rebuttal

The basic responsibility is to reestablish and clinch the negative's plan and case attacks.

I. Reestablish and clinch the negative's attack on plan.

II. Reestablish and clinch the negative's attack on case.

III. Conclude by presenting the best reasons you have to justify a decision for the negative.

---

around the disadvantage by citing evidence that unions had gone on strike to obtain work sharing. This evidence proved, the rebuttalist argued, that the disadvantage of strikes would not occur. The rebuttalist went on to claim an additional advantage: labor relations would be more peaceful under the affirmative plan as unions would not have to go on strike to obtain work sharing.

Of course, new issues may not be introduced in rebuttal, but, since the second negative had introduced the issue of strikes, it was perfectly proper for the first affirmative rebuttalist to turnaround that issue.

L. Use Conditional Refutation

As we saw earlier (in Chapter 11, Section IV-E, "Requirements of Consistency"), the advocate must develop consistent arguments; and the arguments must be consistent with one another and with the arguments of his or her colleague. Clearly, debaters cannot say "There is no need, besides the need is insignificant, and furthermore minor repairs can solve this significant need." They may, however — *provided they make their position very clear* — offer conditional refutation. They must *not* present an argument in such a fashion that the audience "ought to be able to figure out" that it is conditional; rather, they *must* present it with such clarity that the audience *will inevitably* recognize it as conditional.

In debating the "guarantee employment opportunities" proposition, some negatives argued that (1) no harm from unemployment had been proved and (2) *if* unemployment did cause any harm, this harm was taken care of by status quo mechanisms. By using the type of argument considered in this chapter under "Provide Repairs or Modifications" (Section III-E), the negative would continue the conditional argument by maintaining that (3) *if* status quo mechanisms did not presently solve all of the harms, such harms could easily be solved by the minor repair of providing more unemployment compensation, more food stamps, and so on (note that these points are repairs to status quo mechanisms and do not require any structural change).

M. Counterplan Negative Case

The advocates select the *counterplan negative position* after their study of the problem and analysis of the affirmative case have led them to the conclusion that the affirmative has defined the needs or goals of the status quo incorrectly, or they may accept the affirmative's needs or goals and argue that the counterplan can attain them in a more advantageous way. The negative then proposes an entirely different plan, one inconsistent with the affirmative's plan and the resolution as the solution to the problem.

Note that this is exactly what the first negative constructive speaker did in the NDT debate in Appendix C when, after introducing the counterplan, he stated, "Observation one: It is not topical . . . Observation two: competition." The development of this counterplan and the clash of argument over it may be seen in Appendix C.

1. Developing the Counterplan

This case is difficult in that the negative, in redefining or accepting the needs or goals, may appear for a time to be conceding the debate. The negative also has the exacting tasks of presenting a plan that is inconsistent with the resolution and of demonstrating that this plan provides the best balance of risks and advantages.[1] In the event of a tie, the decision in an academic debate is awarded to the negative.

It should be emphasized that the negative's counterplan must be inconsistent with the proposition; otherwise the affirmative will be able to adapt the negative's proposals to its own plan and thus prevail. The principal clash in a debate in which the counterplan negative case is used comes in the efforts to demonstrate the superiority of a given plan in producing the optimum balance of risks and advantages. In using a case of this type, the negative does not necessarily accept the affirmative needs or goals (though it may). It may choose instead to redefine the needs or goals as presented by the affirmative; furthermore, the plan of the negative must not only be inconsistent with the plan of the affirmative — it must also be integrated perfectly with the needs or goals

[1]See Chapter 3 (Section III), "Presumption and Burden of Proof."

that the negative has accepted or redefined. If the negative accepts the needs or goals of the affirmative, the negative argues that its counterplan solves them with less risk (disadvantage) or at a higher level of solvency.

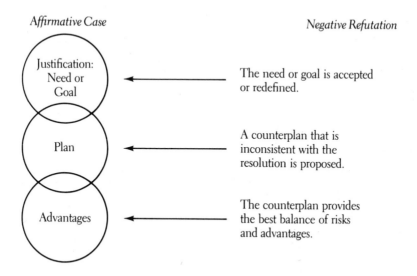

| *Affirmative Case* | *Negative Refutation* |

Justification: Need or Goal — The need or goal is accepted or redefined.

Plan — A counterplan that is inconsistent with the resolution is proposed.

Advantages — The counterplan provides the best balance of risks and advantages.

The negative may establish that its counterplan is nontopical in a number of ways. It may argue that the counterplan should be carried out by a different level of government than that called for in the resolution (for example, the states rather than the federal government should do it); or that a different agency should carry out the counterplan (for instance, it should be voluntary rather than mandated by law); or that finite funds should be used in a different way (for example, the funds available for space research should be used to send a probe to Mars rather than to Venus). In debates on the "mass media" proposition, negative counterplans often called for a voluntary agency such as the National Association of Broadcasters, rather than an agency of the federal government, to regulate television. In debates on the "consumer product safety" proposition, some negative counterplans called for action by the states rather than the federal government. A wide range of mechanisms are available to the negative for developing a counterplan that is nontopical. Indeed, once the affirmative has operationally defined the resolution, almost any inconsistent plan may constitute grounds for a counterplan. Careful study of the problem area of the proposition and its context will aid the negative in choosing the most effective one.

The negative must be careful to demonstrate that its counterplan provides the best balance of risks and advantages when compared to the plan and advantages of the affirmative. In debates on the "mass media" proposition, negatives calling for the NAB to regulate television violence often argued that the risk of loss of First Amendment freedoms was less if a voluntary agency regulated television violence than if the federal government did. In similar fashion on the "consumer product safety" proposition, negatives using a "states" counterplan argued that the states rather than the federal government should regulate a particular consumer product: If a plan turned out to be

Speaker Responsibilities in a Counterplan Debate — NDT

First Affirmative Constructive

Unchanged.

First Negative Constructive

I. Redefine the needs or goals, or accept them.
II. Present counterplan and advantages, as in the first affirmative constructive basic speaker responsibilities.
III. Demonstrate that the advantages of the counterplan outweigh the advantages of the plan and involve less risk.

Second Affirmative Constructive

I. Defend affirmative definition of needs or goals.
II. Prove the counterplan is topical and can coexist with the plan, if vulnerable; or
III. Attack the counterplan and advantages, as in the second negative constructive basic speaker responsibilities.
IV. Extend the affirmative case, as in the second affirmative constructive basic speaker responsibilities.
V. Demonstrate that the affirmative's advantages outweigh the advantages of the counterplan and involve less risk.

Second Negative Constructive

I. Attack the plan, as in the second negative constructive basic speaker responsibilities.
II. Extend the counterplan case arguments.
III. Demonstrate that the counterplan advantages outweigh the advantages of the plan and involve less risk.

undesirable, less harm would be done on a statewide basis than if the plan were nationwide. If the plan turned out to be desirable, then other states would adopt it.

The speaker responsibilities in a counterplan debate (*see inset on pp.* 238–239) demonstrate a method of organization the speakers may use. Note that this organization is more complex than the basic organization of speaker responsibilities. For that reason it is *not recommended* that negative debaters use a counterplan until they have acquired a backlog of sound experience in using the refutation negative analysis. Affirmative debaters should be familiar with the counterplan negative approach as — depending on the nature of the proposition and the experience of their opponents — they might meet it at any time.

First Negative Rebuttal

I. Refute the second affirmative constructive's case arguments, as in the first negative rebuttal basic speaker responsibilities.
II. Refute the second affirmative's attack on the counterplan.

First Affirmative Rebuttal

I. Refute the second negative constructive's attack on the plan, as in the first affirmative rebuttal basic speaker responsibilities.
II. Extend the affirmative's case arguments.

Second Negative Rebuttal

I. Reestablish and clinch the negative's attack on the plan.
II. Reestablish and clinch the negative's attack on the case.
III. Refute attacks on the counterplan.
IV. Refute attack on the negative's needs or goals.
V. Conclude by presenting the best reasons you have to justify a decision for the negative.

Second Affirmative Rebuttal

I. Refute the second negative rebuttalist's attack on the plan.
II. Refute the second negative rebuttalist's attack on the case, and extend case arguments.
III. Reestablish and clinch the attack on the counterplan.
IV. Reestablish and clinch the attack on the negative case.
V. Conclude by presenting the best reasons you have to justify a decision for the affirmative.

2. Integrating the Counterplan

The advocates using the counterplan negative case must take special care to integrate their positions. Although the counterplan case should be planned long in advance, the decision to use it in a given debate is usually best made only after the first affirmative presentation. Since the counterplan must be perfectly adapted to the specific affirmative case under attack, this adaptation frequently requires a good deal of during-the-debate coordination by the negative speakers. Not only must they integrate their counterplan with the needs or goals as they have redefined them; they must also carefully integrate their indictment of the affirmative plan to ensure that one speaker's plan attacks on the affirmative cannot be applied with equal force to the counterplan.

3. Conditional and Hypothetical Counterplans

The *conditional counterplan* is a variation of the conditional refutation considered earlier. In developing this type of case, the negative argues: (1) The status quo can solve the problem; and (2) *if* the status quo can't solve the problem, the negative counterplan can. Two important constraints the student debater must consider before selecting this approach are: First, the time constraints of academic debate may make it impossible to develop *both* the defense of the status quo and the counterplan adequately. Second, as we have seen earlier, conditional arguments must be presented with great clarity. This requirement for clarity, when combined with the difficult-in-itself counterplan, makes for a doubly complex problem for the debater.

The *hypothetical counterplan* was developed as a response to the alternative justification affirmative. One debater argued it this way:

> We would suggest a hypothetical counter plan. That is, at the end of the debate, if the affirmative doesn't carry all three advantages, adopt whatever ones they do carry and use the rest of the money to fund things like tax rebates, pollution control, et cetera. That, we suggest, would be a superior policy system unless they can carry all three advantages, which is the resolution.[2]

Student debaters are cautioned that many judges reject this approach, holding that the counterplan must be a fully developed policy and requiring the negative to argue its case in depth.

4. Studies Counterplan

The *studies counterplan* may be offered on its own merits or as a conditional counterplan. In developing the studies counterplan, the negative usually runs any combination of the refutation negative arguments that can be applied to the affirmative case and argues that: (1) The affirmative has not proved a need for a change in the status quo; (2) minor repairs can solve any minor problem in the status quo; (3) the plan will not solve the need; and (4) the plan will produce disadvantages. The negative then goes on to argue that, before a change can be justified, further study is needed. Its counterplan then proposes that specific studies be undertaken with a view to establishing conclusively whether there is a justification for adopting the affirmative's plan. Of course, it argues additionally that, since the studies will be conducted on a smaller scale than the plan, they involve less risk of the disadvantages that the negative claims are inherent in the plan.

For example, in the final round of the NDT tournament debate on the "guarantee employment opportunities" proposition, the first negative constructive speaker proposed that a variation of the affirmative's plan be adopted in two states, that the experience in the two states be studied for five years, and that after five years the results be submitted to Congress and the state legislatures for such action as they might wish to take.

Student debaters are *cautioned* that many judges view the studies counterplan as "an easy way out" for the negative and tend to reject it unless it is presented with great skill. It is true that almost any plan or proposal would benefit from further study. How-

[2]"Final Debate," *Journal of the American Forensic Association*, Vol. 10 (Summer 1973), p. 21.

ever, real-world decisions must be made on less than perfect knowledge, and proposals for further study must be justified by proving such study is clearly the superior policy.

5. Utopian Counterplan

In developing the *utopian counterplan* the negative typically mandates in a single plank that the nation or world will be arranged in a manner consistent with anarchy, world government, socialism, authoritarianism, or some other future strategy and claims that this strategy will better solve the problem than the federal government or whatever agency of change is provided in the proposition under debate.[3]

In debating the "federal government should . . . guarantee employment opportunities" proposition, some negative teams using a utopian counterplan argued that a socialist government rather than the federal government could better provide such a guarantee. In debating the "federal government should increase exploration and/or development of space" proposition, some negatives used a world government utopian counterplan.

The attraction of utopian counterplans for the negative is twofold: (1) Utopia is defined as "a place of ideal perfection, especially in laws, government, and social conditions" — certainly a most desirable locale for one's plan, and (2) the utopian counterplan may be the ultimate generic argument in that it may be applied to an almost limitless variety of affirmative cases.

The debater is *cautioned* that some judges object to utopian counterplans and are easily convinced to vote against them. They hold that such counterplans are topic limitless; that is, they may be used against any affirmative policy and thus are of doubtful educational value since debaters using them no longer have the incentive or need to research new topic-specific arguments.

Wise debaters, however, find it desirable to be familiar with these counterplans, because even if they do not choose to use them, they may encounter such counterplans.

Exercises

1. Attend an intercollegiate debate and prepare an outline of the negative case. Attach to this outline a written critique (500 words) of the negative case in which you evaluate the organization and development of the case.

2. From the Op Ed page of the *New York Times* or another major metropolitan paper find an article that is essentially a negative case against some contemporary proposal. Prepare a written critique (500 words) in which you evaluate the article as a negative case.

3. Select some contemporary proposal that you oppose. Write an essay suitable for publication as an Op Ed article in which you make the best possible negative case against this proposal.

---

[3]For a more detailed consideration of utopian counterplans, see the *Journal of the American Forensic Association*, Vol. 24 (Fall 1987), pp. 95–136, which presents four essays under the heading "Point–Counterpoint: Essays on Utopian Fiat."

4. Obtain an actual affirmative case (perhaps one prepared in your class for Exercise 3 in Chapter 12).

   a. Prepare a first negative constructive speech, attacking the case in the manner suggested in "Basic CEDA Speaker Responsibilities" in this chapter.

   b. Prepare a second negative constructive speech, attacking the case using the basic CEDA speaker responsibilities of this position.

5. Using the current national value debate proposition (or any other proposition approved by your instructor), prepare a series of generic value objections that you feel could be used against *many* specific affirmative cases under this proposition. Be prepared to justify your choice.

6. Using the current national policy debate proposition (or any other proposition approved by your instructor), prepare a series of generic disadvantages that you feel could be used against *many* specific affirmative cases under this proposition. Be prepared to justify your choice.

7. Select some contemporary policy proposal you oppose. Prepare a first negative constructive speech in which you present a counterplan.

8. Select a bill currently being debated in Congress. Study the arguments being used by the negative speakers against the bill. What type of negative case are they using? What issues are they developing?

14

Refutation

Debate takes place not in a vacuum — but in the presence of opposition. The debater is always confronted with the necessity of overcoming objections that are raised by the opponent. The process of overcoming these objections is known as *refutation*. Strictly interpreted, the term "refute" means to overcome opposing evidence and reasoning by proving that it is false or erroneous. The term "rebut," strictly interpreted, means to overcome opposing evidence and reasoning by introducing other evidence and reasoning that will destroy its effect. In practice, the terms "refutation" and "rebuttal" are used interchangeably, except that the second speech by each advocate in an academic debate is designated as the *rebuttal speech*.

In academic debate, advocates are required to refute only the specific arguments advanced by their opponents. In applied debate, advocates face the necessity of refuting any evidence and reasoning that may influence the decision renderers.

I.   Shifting Burden of Rebuttal

As the preceding chapters on cases indicated, the burden of proof always remains with the affirmative, whereas the burden of rebuttal is initially the negative's. This burden of rebuttal shifts back and forth between the opponents in the course of the debate and is finally placed on one side or the other. The side that bears the burden of rebuttal at the conclusion of the debate is the loser. In the typical academic debate, the first affirmative speaker usually establishes his or her case sufficiently well to place the burden of refutation on the negative. It is the task of the first negative speaker to shift that burden back to the affirmative. The second affirmative speaker, by rebuilding and extending the case, seeks to shift the burden to the negative again. At this point in the debate, the negative presents its second constructive speech and its first rebuttal. In these two speeches, the negative seeks to shift the burden of rebuttal back to the affirmative. Obviously, these consecutive presentations provide the negative with its maximum opportunity to shift the burden decisively. In each of the remaining rebuttal speeches, the advocates seek to carry their share of rebuttal and to shift the burden to their opponents. The affirmative's last opportunity comes in the final speech of the debate, wherein the second affirmative speaker has the opportunity to review the entire debate and to demonstrate that the negative has not carried its burden of rebuttal.[1]

II. Purpose and Place of Refutation

The process of refutation must be included in every speech of the debate. Obviously, the first affirmative speech, as it opens the debate, cannot include direct refutation since no opposition has preceded it. Even this speech, however, may well include a certain amount of anticipatory refutation, although care should be taken that such anticipatory refutation is directed to issues that the negative must inevitably support, and not against "straw men" that the affirmative hopes the negative will advance. (*See inset* for a list of processes of refutation.)

In general, advocates should refute an important issue early rather than allow it to stand unchallenged for any length of time. Possible exceptions to this practice might occur when advocates ignore an issue for the moment while waiting for the opposition to commit itself further on the issue. Sometimes advocates will attempt to foster this process deliberately by advancing a limited refutation, encouraging the opponents to pursue further a given line of argument that will fully commit them to a position the advocates will refute later. Thus the advocates are able to bring into the debate arguments their opponents might wish to avoid. For example, in debates on the proposition "Resolved: That the nonagricultural industries of the United States should guarantee their employees an annual wage," some affirmative advocates argued that significant numbers of persons were unemployed at the time this proposition was being debated. In using exploratory refutation, some negative advocates advanced a deliberately weak refutation — introducing evidence that some unemployed persons had built up substantial savings during the years they had worked — and drew the conclusion that some workers did not need a guarantee of annual wages. Some affirmative advocates responded to this refutation by answering that the vast majority of unemployed persons did not have substantial savings, since low-seniority workers were the first to be laid off and many of them had worked only a few months prior to their unemployment. Once the negative advocates had obtained such an admission from the affirmative as a result of their exploratory refutation, they were able, later in the debate, to focus on their main line of refutation. They then argued that, since the wage guarantees proposed by the affirmative required at least a year's seniority before becoming effective, the proposed

---

[1]See Chapter 18 for an outline of the speaking sequence and time allotments used in intercollegiate debating.

The Processes of Refutation

- Overthrowing the opposition's evidence by demonstrating that it is invalid, erroneous, or irrelevant.
- Overthrowing the opposition's evidence by introducing other evidence that contradicts it, casts doubt on it, minimizes its effect, or shows that it fails to meet the tests of evidence.
- Overthrowing the opposition's reasoning by demonstrating that it is faulty.
- Overthrowing the opposition's reasoning by introducing other reasoning that turns it to the opposition's disadvantage, contradicts it, casts doubt on it, minimizes its effect, or shows that it fails to meet the tests of reasoning.
- Rebuilding evidence by introducing new and additional evidence to further substantiate it.
- Rebuilding reasoning by introducing new and additional reasoning to further substantiate it.
- Presenting exploratory refutation—preliminary refutation offered for the purpose of probing the opponents' position and designed to clarify the opponents' position or to force them to take a more definite position.

plan did not meet the need of the low-seniority workers, who—according to the affirmative—made up the largest group of unemployed.

III. Preparation for Refutation

As advocates, we should prepare our refutation with the same care that we prepare other portions of our case. Effective refutation is seldom the result of improvisation but comes from careful analysis and preparation.

We must be thoroughly familiar with all evidence and reasoning related to the proposition under debate. Our knowledge of the subject should never be confined to our own case or to the case we expect the opponent to use; rather, it should include all possible aspects of the resolution. We should make certain that our research on the subject has been sufficiently detailed so that we will not be taken by surprise by new evidence or reasoning introduced by the opposition. We should recognize that on most propositions the evidence is seldom complete; new evidence, or new interpretations of evidence, may appear frequently. Thus, we should never assume that our research is complete but should continue it until the very moment of the debate.

One college debating team won a major tournament, in part because they used more recent evidence than the opposition. During the tournament, the President sent his budget message to Congress. This message contained some new information relating to the economic proposition debated in the tournament. One team redrafted its case overnight to include the new information. When this team met other teams that had not studied the President's message, it found that the opposing speakers were at a serious disadvantage when they attempted to refute new evidence with which they were not familiar.

The advocates should have a broad perspective in the preparation of their refutation. They should never limit themselves to one point of view or to one philosophy. They should seek to analyze carefully both sides and should consider fully all possible positions that may be taken on the proposition.

Student debaters will find that one of the best means of improving their refutation is to debate on both sides of the proposition. In this manner they will gain a wider perspective and avoid the danger of seeing only one side. The advocate in nonacademic debates drafts the strongest possible cases that the opponent might use and prepares refutation for each of these cases. The advocate should consider not only the evidence the opponent may use but also the lines of argument that may be introduced and the philosophical position that may form the basis of the opposition's case.

In planning answers to the possible cases advanced by an opponent, the advocate should give careful consideration to the phrasing of any refutation. If the advocate's thinking has proceeded merely to the stage "If the opposition quotes expert A, I will quote expert B," the refutation is likely to be verbose, uncertain, and lacking in specificity. Rather, the advocate should plan the phrasing of the refutation, making sure that the words are well chosen, sharp, and specific and that the reasoning is cogent.

IV. Arranging Material for Refutation

Until the debate is actually under way, the advocates cannot be certain what position their opponents will take; they must therefore have a broad and deep store of materials from which to draw refutation, and these materials must be so arranged that they are readily available.

One effective way of doing this is to prepare a refutation brief for each possible argument or piece of evidence the opposition may use and to record that reasoning or evidence in an easy-to-retrieve form. At the start of the season, one negative debater prepared a brief for use against possible funding provisions that affirmative teams might use on the "comprehensive medical care" proposition (see sample brief in the *inset*).

In his card file, this advocate *had evidence cards keyed to the retrieval numbers on his sheet.* As he heard the specific funding provisions of the affirmative plan, he would pull the appropriate disadvantage cards and adapt them to the specific plan before him. As the season went on and he learned of more possible funding provisions, he provided for them and increased the depth of his attacks on the provisions he was already familiar with.

The construction of detailed briefs and card files is the mark of conscientious student debaters. As advocates, we are well advised to prepare refutation with similar thoroughness, using any method of recording material that is convenient and readily accessible. As we gain in knowledge and experience, our dependence on mechanics will be reduced. At the start, however, specific, detailed preparation is essential.

V. Selection of Evidence and Reasoning

Just as our refutation file should contain more material than can be used in any one debate, our opponents' speeches will probably contain more evidence and reasoning than we can possibly refute in the allotted time. The problem before us, then, is one

Sample Refutation Brief

```
                        DISADVANTAGES

1000.1    FUNDING DISADVANTAGES

1000.11   MORE EXPENSIVE--Medicare and Medicaid cost 3 to
          4 times as much as government planners expected

1000.12   DEFICIT SPENDING--accelerate inflation

1000.13   INCOME TAX INCREASE--unstable collections

1000.14   RAISING TAXES--discourage both work and investment

1000.15   RAISING CORPORATE TAXES
          1000.151   worsen international competitive situation
          1000.152   burden on all income levels
          1000.153   cause employers to release marginal
                     employees

1000.16   CLOSE TAX LOOPHOLES--produce only $1-billion revenue

1000.17   END OIL DEPLETION ALLOWANCE--increase cost of gas,
          oil, and natural gas

1000.18   REDUCE CAPITAL DEPRECIATION--hinder long-term
          economic growth and employment opportunities

1000.19   TAX MUNICIPAL BONDS--harm economic growth

1000.20   CUT DEFENSE SPENDING--cause unemployment
```

of selection. The fundamental concept underlying refutation is that we must seek to refute the *case* of our opponent. To do so, we must have an accurate picture of that case as it is presented. Let us look first at a sample debate case (*see inset*). This is a simple, straightforward case that will be easy to follow. It is used here in preference to one of the debate cases found in Appendixes B and C because those affirmative cases and the negative cases used against them are, as one would expect to find in the final round of a national tournament, sophisticated, complex cases. After you have studied the sample debate case, turn next to the representation of the flow sheet (*see inset*).

This is a debate on a policy proposition; thus the arguments are recorded in two parts — case side and plan side. In a value or quasi-policy debate the division would be case side and off case side. In this debate the speakers followed the Basic NDT Speaker Responsibilities considered in Chapters 12 and 13. Typically the debaters and judges record the flow of argument on sheets of legal-sized paper or often on larger artist's pad sheets. The case arguments are usually recorded in seven columns on one

A Sample Debate Case*

Resolved: That the federal government should significantly strengthen the regulation of mass media communication in the United States.

I. Terrorism is a major threat to American society.   *Significance*
  A. Terrorism is significant.
    1. Many terrorist incidents occur.
      UN Report evidence
      NY Times evidence
    2. Terrorism is increasing.
      Wall Street Journal evidence
      U. of Mich. Law Rev. evidence
  B. Terrorism is harmful.
    1. Terrorism costs lives and money.   *Quantitative*
      a. Thousands of lives are lost.   *Significance*
        Amnesty Int'l Report evidence
        House Hearings evidence
      b. Billions of dollars worth of property damage occurs.
        Bus. Wk. evidence
        Senate Hearings evidence
      c. Billions are paid in ransoms.
        Fortune evidence
        Forbes evidence
    2. Terrorism threatens basic liberties.   *Qualitative*
      a. Liberties are lost.   *Significance*
        CLU Report evidence
        Wm. & Mary Law Rev. evidence
        U. of Penn. Law Rev. evidence
      b. Loss of liberties will snowball.
        Time evidence
        Senate Hearings evidence
        U.S. News evidence
  C. The harms of terrorism will increase.
    1. Terrorists can use nuclear devices.
      NY Times evidence
      Senate Hearings evidence
      Science evidence
    2. Terrorists can use chemical-biological agents.
      Wash. Post evidence
      Hudson Study evidence

*Adapted from a case prepared by Julia Davis, Lisa Garono, Timothy Ita, and Anthony Smith—John Carroll University debaters.

II. Present policies perpetuate terrorism.　　　　　　　*Inherency*
   A. Terrorists commit their crimes for publicity.
      FBI Report evidence
      Amnesty Int'l Study evidence
      Brookings Inst. Report evidence
   B. Sensationalism causes a lack of media restraint.
      NY Times evidence
      Editor & Publisher evidence
      Senate Hearings evidence

III. Plan
   Plank 1:　The plan will be administered by the Criminal　*Agency*
   Justice Division of the Department of Justice.
   Plank 2:　The federal government will enact legislation　*Mandates*
   limiting all media coverage of terrorist events to reporting the event. Names and causes of terrorists may not
   be reported.
   Plank 3:　Violations of this law will, upon conviction, result　*Enforcement*
   in fines of not less than 25% nor more than 50% of the
   gross annual income of the media company found quilty.
   Plank 4:　Any and all necessary funding will be derived　*Funding and*
   from an optimal mix of general revenues and a 10% sales　*Staffing*
   tax on all copies of *Argumentation and Debate.**
   Plank 5:　A. The Internal Revenue Service will be re-　*Addendum*
   quired to make available to the D.O.J. any and all
   records required for prosecutions under this law.
         B. Any laws or regulations in conflict with
   Plank 2 are hereby repealed.
         C. The Constitution will, if necessary, be
   amended to permit the effective enforcement of Plank 2.

IV. The affirmative significantly reduces terrorism.　　　*Advantage*
   A. Media coverage motivates terrorist actions.
      Bochin Study evidence
      NY Times Mag. evidence
      Hornung Report evidence
   B. Removal of media coverage will cause terrorism to　*Solvency*
   atrophy.
      Newsweek evidence
      Barron's evidence
      Senate Hearings evidence

*Debate is not all somber and serious. Debaters delight in slipping jokes into their presentation — such as this provision for a 10 percent sales tax on this textbook. If the joke can be made at near zero cost in time and does not open up any opportunity for the opponents to attack, the debater hopes to be rewarded by a chuckle from the judge or audience. Jokes, of course, must be adapted to the audience.

Case-Side Flow Sheet

IAC	INC	2AC	1NR	1AR	2NR	2AR
I. Terrorism major threat to Am. society	**I.** T– not a major threat	**I.** T– is sig major threat				
A. T– significant	→ A. Not sig.	→ A. T– sig				
1. many incidents	→ 1. most incidents abroad	→ 1. against U.S. nationals	→ 1. (drop)			
2. T– increasing	→ 2. only statistically	→ 2. sig Trend	→ 2. stat flawed	→ recent	→ not accurate	
B. T– harmful	→ B. Not sig harm	→ B. T– harmful	→ 1. no U.S. jurisdiction	(drop)		
1. T– costs lives and $	→ 1. most incidents abroad	→ 1. against U.S. nationals				
a. thousands of lives lost	a. not in U.S.	a. U.S. nationals				
b. billions in damage	→ b. not in U.S.	b. U.S.-owned property				
c. billions in ransoms	→ c. not in U.S.	c. ransom for U.S. citizens				
2. T– threatens basis liberties	→ 2. Not sig. threat	→ 2. T– threatens liberties				
a. liberties lost	→ a. not unique – wire taps etc. used for all crimes	→ a. massive increase in wire taps, etc. needed against T–	→ a. foreign gov'ts can wiretap	→ not all co-op w/ U.S.	→ (drop)	not all co-op w/ U.S.
b. loss will snowball	→ b. a prediction – not proof	→ b. 9 well-qualified experts. Best evidence	→ b. other experts disagree	→ best evidence	→ neg. source is better	→ aff. evidence more recent
C. Harms of T– will increase	→ C. Harms exaggerated	→ C.	1. not on			
1. nuclear	→ 1. T– can't get nuclear	→ 1. T– may already have needed	2. scale needed	→ can steal	→ need facilities	→ crude facilities enough
2. Chemical-biological	→ 2. chem-bio too sophisticated for T–	→ 2. any chem-bio grad student could make chem-bio agents				
II. SQ perpetuates T–	**II.** (grant)					
A. T– seek publicity						
B. Sensational media						
IV. Plan reduces T–	**IV.** Plan won't reduce T–	**IV.** Plan will reduce T–				
A. Publicity is motive	→ A. Publicity not only motive	→ A. Seek publicity vs. U.S. by actions against U.S. nationals abroad				
B. Remove media coverage – T– atrophy	1. T– want money for their cause	→ 1. media coverage increases T– helps T– get $	→ events reported	→ not cause		
	2. T– want to free imprisoned colleagues	2. few in U.S.				
	3. T– not rational	→ 3. Leaders are rational	→ fanatical	→ rational	→ eager to die for cause	→ leaders rational

Plan-Side Flow Sheet

III. Plan	2NC	1AR	2NR	2AR
1. Adm. by Criminal Justice Div. — DOJ	I. Plan won't work	I. Plan will work; media fears fines		
	A. Interney proves motive to circumvent			
2. Fed. legislation to limit media coverage of T— to event: no names or causes	B. Media has resources: will litigate for years	(Drop)	→B. Will litigate	
	C. Courts overloaded: will take years to reach S.C.	→C. Not unique. Courts overcrowded now	C. proves Plan not work	→C. not unique
3. Fines — 25% to 50% of gross annual income	D. SC sensitive to liberties: will dismantle aff plan	→D. SC conservative; will uphold plan	→D. SC pro free press	→D. SC more conservative now
4. Funding — gen. rev.	II. Disadvantage	II. Plan does not prevent public's knowing		
5. A. IRS give records to DOJ	1. If Plan works, it destroys public's right to know names and causes of T—	→1. Legitimate causes can get publicity w/o T—. Aff inherency proves media loves sensational		
B. conflicting laws repealed	A. Some causes may be legitimate			
C. Const. amend	B. Gov't is covering up illegal or unwise activities abroad			
	2. If Plan works, it destroys free media	→2. Evidence comes from Congressional committees, not T—		
	A. Becomes precedent	III. Not destroy media	III	
	B. Gov't wants to restrain media	→A. Plan strictly limited	→A. Precedent slippery slope	A. Plan strictly limited
	C. Destruction of the media greater threat to society than T—	B. Courts will check Gov't		
		→C. Not destroyed because of A & B	→C. Destroy free media	
	3. If Plan works, it escalates T—	IV. T— won't escalate	IV	
	A. T— escalate to force media coverage	→A. Plan blocks	→A. Incentive to escalate	→ Plan blocks
	B. Lack of news about T— means no public support for anti-T— measures	B. Full news of events only no names of causes		
		C. with full news of events public will support anti-T— measures		

side of the sheet—the case side. (The heading 1AC indicates the first affirmative constructive speech; 1AR, the first affirmative rebuttal; 1NC, the first negative constructive speech, and so on.) The plan and plan arguments are usually recorded on the back on this sheet—thus the name "plan side"—in five columns. If counterplans or topicality arguments are used, as was the case in Appendixes B and C, they are usually recorded on separate sheets. (Once the student has mastered the basic concept of a simple flow sheet, it will be an easy adjustment to provide additional sheets to record such arguments.) Typically the 2AC speaker does not flow the 1AC speech; rather the 2AC speaker will have prepared in advance an outline of the 1AC speech and will clip it to the flow sheet and then record the 1NC responses. Debaters and judges often use arrows and other symbols to record the flow of argument. Different colored pens may be used to record cross-examination data or to readily identify other items. Debaters and judges develop a system of abbreviations to save time. On the flow sheet in the inset, T- is used to represent terrorism or terrorists; SQ is used for the status quo or present policies; sig, of course, represents significance; and SC represents the Supreme Court. A granted argument (an opponent's argument that the speaker admits is valid; see II in 1NC) is noted and circled. In the same way, a dropped argument (an opponent's argument to which the speaker fails to respond; see IA1 in 1NR on Case Side and IB in 1AR on Plan Side) is also circled. With practice, debaters develop a system of abbreviations and symbols that enables them to record recurring words and phrases in a way that is both time saving and meaningful. Each column on the flow sheet should be the most accurate and detailed outline possible of that speech. Such an outline aids the debater in detecting dropped arguments or weak links in the structure. It takes time and practice to learn how to run an effective flow sheet, but debaters find it worthwhile to develop this essential skill. *With appropriate adjustments, the flow sheet can be adapted to any type of argumentative situation.* The college senior confronted with the happy problem of weighing two job offers might find it desirable to prepare a flow sheet weighing the relative merits of the two offers. A corporate purchasing agent charged with the responsibility of making a major purchase for the company might well prepare a flow sheet to help evaluate the advantages and disadvantages of competing products or services.

VI. Structure of Refutation

A. Basic Structure

The basic structure of refutation involves five clearly defined stages for the advocate:

1. Identify the argument you are attacking or defending clearly and concisely.
2. State your position succinctly.
3. Introduce evidence and argument to support your position.
4. Summarize your evidence and argument.
5. Demonstrate the impact of this refutation in weakening your opponent's case or in strengthening your own case.

This final stage is perhaps the most critical and is the one most frequently overlooked by the beginning advocate. Much of the effect of refutation is lost unless we relate it clearly to the case of the opposition or to our own case.

B. General Considerations

In addition to the basic structure of refutation, we should be aware of these general considerations of refutation:

1. Begin refutation early. It is usually to our advantage to begin refutation early — both early in our speech and early in the debate. The purpose of beginning refutation early in the speech is to offset immediately the effect of some of the opponents' arguments. This statement does not mean, however, that the first portion of the speech should be reserved for refutation and the balance of the speech devoted to a constructive presentation. Rather, the skilled debater will interweave refutation and constructive materials throughout the entire speech. It is usually not desirable to allow a major contention to go unrefuted for too long a time in the debate. Usually an argument should be refuted in the next available speech. Thus a plan attack made in the second negative speech must be answered in the first affirmative rebuttal. If the affirmative waits until the final rebuttal to answer this argument, the judge may weigh the answer lightly, saying "Well, yes, they did finally get around to it, but it was so late that the negative had no chance to reply."

2. Conclude with constructive material. Usually it is desirable for us to conclude a speech with constructive material designed to advance our own case. Thus, after giving the listeners reasons for rejecting the opponents' position, we give them positive reasons for concurring with our position.

3. Incorporate refutation into the case. Although we are usually well advised to open a speech with refutation, refutation is by no means confined to the first part of the speech. Since the well-planned case is prepared to meet many of the objections of the opposition, we will often find it advisable to incorporate refutation *into* our case. For example, in debating the proposition "Resolved: That the federal government should grant annually a specific percentage of its income tax revenue to the state governments," some negative teams objected to the adoption of the resolution on the ground that it would place an additional burden on the taxpayer. In refuting this objection, some affirmative teams made use of *built-in* refutation by pointing out that the gross national product was rising (as, indeed, it was at the time this proposition was debated); thus incomes would rise and revenue would be derived from the same tax rate.

4. Evaluate the amount of refutation. Advocates often ask, "How much refutation is necessary?" Unfortunately, no definitive answer is available, since the answer varies from one occasion to another and is found only in the mind of the judge or the audience. We should observe the judge or audience closely during the course of our speeches and should watch for both overt and inconspicuous signs of agreement or disagreement when presenting refutation, in order to adapt to our audience more effectively. As a minimum, we should develop our refutation through the five basic stages of refutation. Our goal is to introduce enough refutation to satisfy a reasonable and prudent person. We should avoid the too-brief statement of refutation, such as "The recent Brookings Institution study disproves this contention." Such a statement may suggest a line of refutation to the advocates; but until this line of refutation is actually developed within the context of the debate, it is of little value.

5. Use organized refutation. The advocate must use a carefully organized pattern of refutation that is clear and precise and allows those who render the decision to follow the refutation readily. The objective is to make it easy for the judge to "flow" your argument. Clearly identify the specific argument of your opponent that you are refuting, so that the judge will know exactly where you want your arguments to apply. The Basic Speaker Responsibilities considered in Chapters 12 and 13 indicate an organized pattern of refutation and a clear division of speaker responsibilities. The debater is advised to know and use this organization of refutation. Once this basic pattern has been mastered, then debaters, by prearrangement with their colleagues, may develop variations.

In informal situations where we may not have a colleague and there is no judge with a flow sheet, it is still important to have a clear and precise pattern of refutation. We want to make it easy for those who render the decision to follow our arguments.

6. Make use of contingency plans. Advocates will find it desirable to prepare *contingency plans* — that is, briefs of evidence and argument prepared in advance to raise against issues they believe will be fundamental in meeting the opposing case. Prudent advocates, in fact, will have a number of contingency plans available. In the course of the debate, they will determine which contingency plans are applicable to the case presented by the opponents; then, of course, they must adapt the contingency plan to the specific argument used by the opposition.

For example, in debates on a national program of public work for the unemployed, the negative could safely assume that the affirmative would have to argue that unemployment is harmful. A negative team prepared contingency plans to meet affirmative arguments on "frictional unemployment," "cyclical unemployment," "long-term unemployment," and so on. In their contingency plan on "long-term unemployment" (unemployment of fifteen weeks or more), they assembled evidence to establish that (a) a large percentage of the long-term unemployed had working spouses and were seeking a job to finance some luxuries rather than necessities, (b) a large percentage were elderly persons with retirement incomes, (c) a large percentage were teenagers seeking part-time jobs, and (d) only a very small percentage were heads of families. Recently, one good college team preparing to go to the National Debate Tournament learned that the 61 other teams participating in the tournament had a total of 117 different affirmative cases available — and had, of course, to assume that there were other cases they had not learned of. Before they arrived at the NDT, they prepared more than 117 contingency plans. This, of course, is the burden of the advocate who hopes to win. You must have available sufficient contingency plans to overcome the probable opposition.

VII. Methods of Refutation

A. Evidence

Evidence is refuted by applying the tests of evidence and demonstrating that the evidence advanced by the opposition fails to meet these tests. (See the tests of evidence considered in Chapter 7.) Counterrefutation against attacks on one's own evidence consists of demonstrating that the oposition has applied the tests of evidence incorrectly.

B. Reasoning

Reasoning is refuted by applying the tests of reasoning and demonstrating that the reasoning advanced by the opposition fails to meet these tests. (See the tests of reasoning considered in Chapters 8 and 9.) Counterrefutation against attacks on one's own reasoning consists of demonstrating that the opposition has applied the tests of reasoning incorrectly.

C. Fallacies

Fallacies are refuted by exposing the arguments of the opposition as fallacious. (Fallacies, and methods of refuting fallacies, are considered in Chapter 10.) Counterrefutation against attacks on one's own arguments as fallacies consists of demonstrating that the arguments are in fact valid.

Exercises

1. Prepare in written form your refutation of an editorial appearing in a recent issue of a daily newspaper. Hand the editorial and your refutation to the instructor.

2. Write a "letter to the editor" of your local newspaper in which you refute an editorial, an opinion expressed in a column, or another letter to the editor. If your letter is well written, brief, and signed with your name and address, there is a good possibility the paper may publish it.

3. Arrange to have a debate presented in class. Follow the debate carefully, making a detailed flow sheet. At the conclusion of the debate, conduct a class discussion in which you seek to determine at which points the burden of rebuttal shifted from one side to the other.

4. Attend an intercollegiate debate. Prepare a written report (500 words) in which you evaluate the effectiveness of the refutation of each team.

5. Study the debate in Appendix B or Appendix C. Which of the debaters did the most effective refutation? Cite some specific examples to support your conclusion.

15

Presenting the Case: Composition

The case, as indicated in earlier chapters, is the operational plan drafted by the advocates on one side of a proposition for the purpose of coordinating their reasoning and evidence and presenting their position with maximum effectiveness. The case outline incorporates some elements of speech composition and is an important starting point. It is not a speech, however, nor an editorial nor a book. It is the blueprint from which the advocates will develop their actual debate speeches. Although the case can serve with equal effectiveness as the basis for a written document, our concern here is with the *presentation* of the case. In presenting their case orally, the advocates are concerned with composing speeches that will gain the attention of the audience, hold interest, make it impossible for the listeners to fail to understand their arguments, and make it easy to agree with their case.

I. Analysis of the Audience

As we saw earlier (page 2), "argumentation is reason giving in communicative situations by people whose purpose is the justification of acts, beliefs, attitudes, and values." The first critical question in composing our arguments, then, becomes "Who are the people to whom our arguments are directed?" To answer this question the advocate must undertake an analysis of the audience. The questions in the *inset* (pp. 258–259) suggest information that the speakers need to know about an audience. Most of these questions are relevant for most advocates on most propositions. Special considerations may make some of them unnecessary or may make necessary the addition of other questions. Debaters know, or quickly learn, that the type of composition suited to the final round of an NDT tournament simply will not work before a campus audience in a debate with a visiting team from Japan or the Soviet Union. When the debater leaves campus to appear before community groups, each of these different audiences requires analysis, and the case must be adapted in the way best suited to the audience. If we are to speak before a familiar campus group where we already have a good idea of who will be in the audience, the answers to the questions in the inset will come quickly and easily. If, as is often the case, we are to speak before an unfamiliar audience, we must undertake specific research that will equip us to answer the questions effectively.

A dramatic example of the importance of audience analysis occurred during the second Bush-Dukakis debate. The first question was:

> Governor, if Kitty Dukakis were raped and murdered, would you favor an irrevocable death penalty for the killer?

Dukakis replied:

> No, I don't Bernard, and I think you know that I've opposed the death penalty during all my life. [The full text of Governor Dukakis's response may be seen in Appendix A.]

Any debater who opposes the death penalty knows, or certainly should know, that this is the very first question that would be asked in cross-examination. (Of course, the questioner would substitute girlfriend, sister, or mother for Kitty Dukakis.) The answer Governor Dukakis gave was well suited for a tournament debate. The judge would nod with approval and note that the respondent had kept his cool and calmly and dispassionately stayed with the issues.

But the debate did not take place in a tournament round; it took place before an audience of 62 million viewers. The general public is not cognizant of the requirements of tournament debate. An entirely different response was called for. *Time* magazine began the lead article in its postdebate issue with this critique:

> The question was in ghoulish taste, but it proved revealing. Moderator Bernard Shaw of CNN began the final presidential debate by demanding that Michael Dukakis reconcile his opposition to capital punishment with a macabre scenario in which his wife Kitty Dukakis was raped and killed. Such a hypothesis justified almost any conceivable answer. Dukakis could have vented his anger at the premise of the question or passionately explained his own feelings of outrage when his father was badly mugged. Such a response would have been a perfect way to introduce his view that the legal system is designed to temper human impulses for hang-him-high vengeance. But even as his political dreams hung in the balance, Dukakis mustered all the emotion of a time-and-temperature recording. He managed to turn a question about his wife being brutalized and murdered into a discourse on the need for a hemispheric summit on drugs.
>
> The debate — and perhaps even Dukakis' chance to inspire a late-inning rally to win the election — may have been lost in those opening two minutes.[1]

[1]*Time*, October 24, 1988, p. 18.

What the Advocate Needs to Know About the Audience

Audience Attitude Toward the Speaker

1. What is the probable audience attitude toward the speaker as a person?
2. What is the probable audience attitude toward the organization the speaker represents or is identified with?
3. What is the probable audience attitude toward the point of view the speaker represents?
4. What is the probable audience attitude toward the proposition the speaker is supporting (or opposing)?

The Occasion

1. Why have these people assembled as an audience?
2. What will precede the advocate's speech?
3. What will follow the advocate's speech?
4. Are there any customs, ceremonies, or traditions that relate to the occasion?
5. Who else will speak on this occasion?
6. What will the other speakers probably say?
7. What leaders of the group or distinguished guests will be present?
8. How will their presence influence the audience's decision?
9. How much time is available?
10. What is the physical condition of the room in which the advocate will speak?

Once again, we must emphasize the importance of audience analysis. The correct answer in a tournament round is not necessarily the correct answer for a public debate.

A. Analysis of the Audience During the Speech

In addition to audience analysis before a speech, we should also analyze our audience *during* the presentation, since the audience will react in various ways to the speech — and these reactions will give us useful clues. Such obvious demonstrations as applause, cheers, and cries of approval or disapproval are readily interpreted. The audience will also give the speaker important clues through the more subtle signs of body language. The truly effective advocate is highly skilled at picking up the "vibes" provided by the audience, interpreting them, and adapting the composition of the case to establish rapport with the audience.

The Audience

1. Is the audience homogeneous or heterogeneous?
2. Does one age group predominate in the audience?
3. What is the probable size of the audience?
4. Does the audience consist predominantly or exclusively of members of one sex?
5. What is the educational attainment level of the majority of the audience?
6. Are there significant numbers of any one occupational group in the audience?
7. Are there significant numbers of any one ethnic group in the audience?
8. What common interests do members of the audience share?
9. To what groups or organizations do significant numbers of the audience belong?

The Audience and the Advocate's Purpose

1. Will the audience know the speaker's purpose in advance?
2. What does the audience know about the subject area relating to the speaker's purpose?
3. What experience has the audience had with proposals similar to those of the advocate?
4. How would the audience be affected by the advocate's proposal?
5. What beliefs, prejudices, or predispositions does the audience have that relate to the speaker's purpose?

B. Analysis of the Key Individual

In many situations we do not have the problem of giving reasons to all the members of an audience; rather, we are concerned with winning a decision from a key individual or from a very small group of individuals who have the power of decision in a particular situation. The college student quickly learns that within various clubs, and even in the official business of the college, frequently key individuals have the power of decision on various matters. The intercollegiate debater may on occasion address very large audiences, but the decision is usually rendered by a single judge or by a panel of three or five judges. One of the great advantages of intercollegiate debating is that students usually have many opportunities to speak in the small audience situation and the opportunity to adapt arguments to a key individual. By analyzing the judge in an academic debate and adapting the case to him or her, students have an opportunity to gain experience in an argumentative situation closely paralleling many situations they will face in the future when directing arguments to a key individual. Although student speakers may hope that after graduation they will speak frequently in Madison Square Garden or over television networks, they will, in fact, address the majority of their arguments to small audiences or to key individuals. Even the President, who usually can command a larger national audience than any other individual, addresses vast audiences far less frequently than he argues with small groups of key congressional leaders who can decide the fate of legislation.

Many of the questions we must answer about the key individual are substantially the same as those we must answer about the audience. In preparing a list of questions about the key individual, the advocate may begin by reviewing "What the Advocate Needs to Know about the Audience" (pp. 258–259) and substituting the words "key individual" where applicable.

C. Analysis of the Key Individual During the Speech

The analysis of the key individual is both easier and more difficult than the analysis of the audience. It is more difficult in that it is usually inappropriate for the key individual to give such overt signs as applause or cheers. Often the key individual, such as the judge in the courtroom or the judge at an academic debate, will deliberately try to conceal any sign of approval or disapproval as the arguments are developed. At the same time, it is usually easier because we do not have to give our attention to many individuals, but only to one or to a very small group. When directing our whole presentation to the president of the bank, to the credit manager of the corporation, to the judge in the jury-waived trial, or to the judge in the academic debate, we have a better opportunity to study the subtle signs of agreement or disagreement, of attention or inattention, and thus have a better opportunity to adapt our argument than we do when we must consider the whole audience.

Evidence shows that debaters can "read" nonverbal stimuli and interpret it correctly. Sayer found, in one research study, that debaters in general evaluated the judges' nonverbal stimuli and predicted their decisions with 66.5 percent accuracy, whereas "better" debaters (defined as those with 5–3 or better records) were 80.7 percent accurate.[2] Although we do not know precisely what the nonverbal stimuli were—Sayer postulates they may have been eye contact, facial expression, and bodily movement and posture—or how the debaters interpreted them, it is apparent that debaters, operating on an intuitive basis, have considerable success in analyzing the key individual during the debate.[3]

The problem becomes more complex when an audience is present along with the key individual, such as the spectators at a court trial. In such a situation, we must give priority to those who render the decision—but must never neglect the nondeciding audience. Indeed, we must make specific efforts to secure responses from it, for it may exert a favorable influence upon those who render the decision.

---

[2]See James Edward Sayer, "Debaters' Perception of Nonverbal Stimuli," *Western Speech*, Vol. 38 (Winter 1974), pp. 2–6.

[3]See "Nonverbal Communication" (Section III) in Chapter 16.

II. **Written and Oral Styles**

Written and oral styles differ significantly. Wichelns pointed this out when he said:

> All the literary critics unite in the attempt to interpret the permanent value that they find in the work under consideration. That permanent value is not precisely indicated by the term beauty, but the two strands of aesthetic excellence and permanence are clearly found. . . .
>
> If now we turn to rhetorical criticism . . . we find that its point of view is patently single. It is not concerned with permanence, nor yet with beauty. It is concerned with effect. It regards the speech as a communication to a specific audience, and holds its business to be the analysis and appreciation of the orator's methods of imparting his ideas to his hearers.[4]

Writers can usually work at a more leisurely pace than speakers. They may often write and rewrite their arguments; they may polish and repolish style. They must consider enduring aesthetic standards and think of an "audience" that will read their arguments months or years afterward. A writer's "audience" may also proceed at leisure. Readers may stop to ponder a point, consult a reference work, or reread a passage.

Speakers, on the other hand, usually work under stricter time limitations. If they do not reply promptly to their opponents' argument, their opportunity to reply may be forever lost. While writers may hope that readers will reread their words, speakers have only one opportunity to reach their listeners. Their arguments must be instantly intelligible to the audience. If listeners miss an argument, its value is lost unless the speaker repeats it. Most important, the speaker is concerned with a very specific audience on a very specific occasion. Morely pointed out:

> The statesman who makes or dominates a crisis, who has to rouse and mold the mind of senate or nation, has something else to think about than the production of literary masterpieces. The great political speech, which for that matter is a sort of drama, is not made by passages for elegant extract or anthologies, but by personality, movement, climax, spectacle, and the action of the time.[5]

Although, as speakers, we are not concerned with the production of literary masterpieces, we are concerned with the production of masterful oral arguments. Our concern with style is neither more nor less than that of the writer; it is different. Activist Kunstler cites this example: "I've listened to Justice [William] Douglas speak — I've shared a platform with him several times — and he is a terrible speaker. And yet he can write the most beautiful opinions. So I guess it's a different thing."[6] The writer must strive for a style that will have permanence; the speaker must strive for a style that will be appropriate to the moment.

---

[4]Herbert A. Wichelns, "The Literary Criticism of Oratory," in *Studies in Rhetoric and Public Speaking in Honor of James Albert Winans*, by Pupils and Colleagues (New York: Century, 1925), pp. 208 ff.

[5]John Morely, *Life of William Ewart Gladstone* (New York: St. Martin's Press, 1903), Vol. II, pp. 589–590.

[6]Beatrice K. Reynolds, "An Interview with William M. Kunstler: Rebel Rhetor," *Today's Speech* (Fall 1974), p. 45.

III. A Philosophy of Style

No one style of speech is suitable to all speakers and to all time. The style of Webster was magnificent for his times, but today it would be considered too formal, too florid. Style also bears the stamp of the individual. Students will readily recognize the differences in the styles of George Bush, Ronald Reagan, Dan Quayle, Jessie Jackson, David Letterman, and Oprah Winfrey.

Debaters should study carefully and critically the styles of successful speakers on the contemporary scene. Rather than seeking to emulate the style of a favorite politician, television personality, or the winner of last week's big tournament, debaters should seek to develop the style best suited for them and develop that style to a high point modified by the occasion and the audience. An attorney, for instance, would use one style of speaking when addressing a rural jury and quite a different style when pleading before the Supreme Court; yet in both cases he or she would have the same purpose: to win an acquittal for the client. As another example, an advocate with a purpose of winning support for intercollegiate athletics would find it advisable to use one style of speaking in addressing a football rally and quite a different style in addressing a chapter of the American Association of University Professors. Even substantially similar audiences will expect important differences in style on different occasions. The style of speech appropriate for the stag banquet of the senior class would be quite different from the style appropriate to a commencement address.

IV. Factors of Style in Speech Composition

The factors of style considered here reflect the tastes of contemporary audiences. These general principles must be modified as special considerations enter the situation. A speech at a football rally, for example, would probably require very short sentences, informal (even flamboyant) vocabulary, violent partisanship, and overall brevity. A speech before a group of educators, on the other hand, would probably require somewhat longer sentences, more dignified vocabulary, more formal structure, more restrained partisanship, and a more lengthy overall development.

A. Conciseness

Short sentences and succinct phrases are preferred by contemporary audiences in contrast to the full, flowing prose popular in the last century. Today speakers should seek a concise expression of their ideas. Conciseness involves not only the succinct expression of ideas but also the overall length of the speech. One- or two-hour speeches were quite the usual thing in the day of Webster, Clay, or Calhoun. Perhaps the expense of radio and television time has helped to set the pattern of a half hour as the usual maximum for a speaker today, and the average speech if often briefer.

Time is precious to us as advocates. Those portions of our speeches that are under complete control (for example, the first affirmative, sometimes the plan attacks or value objections, and so on) should be the product of extensive rewriting and editing until each issue is stated with maximum conciseness and clarity and phrased for maximum impact on the judge or audience. Each piece of evidence should be presented with a cogent lead-in and edited to eliminate all extraneous words (while preserving with scrupulous honesty the author's intent.)

B. Clarity

Clarity is of overwhelming importance to us as advocates. A perfectly sound case, a case superior to the opposing case, may be defeated if the audience fails to see the connection between our arguments or if the listeners do not get the point of our evidence. Our objective is to present our case with such great clarity that it is impossible for the average member of the audience *not* to understand the case. Carefully planned organization, well-chosen examples, and precise language will help us achieve clarity.

C. Appropriateness of Vocabulary

Our vocabulary must be appropriate for the audience and the occasion. Experienced lecturer William Kunstler reports his method of adapting his vocabulary to his audience:

> For example, if I speak to an undergraduate audience I use a far different approach than when I am talking to the Junior Chamber of Commerce in Minnatonka, Minnesota, or a bar association, or a group of older people.
>
> The difference, I think, is that in talking to the young people I consciously try to use language, that while not being condescending, is at least in the genre to which they are accustomed. And I try to bring into the talk some relationship to the language of an undergraduate without sacrificing any content and without sacrificing any rhetorical artistry that you can utilize and without, I hope, condescension, because I think that condescension is probably the worst sin any speaker can commit.[7]

The task of the advocate is to present often complex messages in readily comprehensible language geared to the genre of the decision renderers and with rhetorical artistry that will have a favorable impact. Student debaters should note that their approach is often the exact opposite of Kunstler's. They should consciously try to use the language and genre to which their often older audiences are accustomed.

D. Simplicity of Structure

The overall structure of the speech must be simple. Our objective is to make it easy for those who render the decision to follow our case. We should seek simplicity, too, in the structure of our sentences and passages. The complex or compound sentence, replete with subordinate clauses and studded with commas and semicolons, may, on careful reading, serve to express an idea with considerable precision. Our listeners, however, cannot see the punctuation in our notes, nor do they have a chance to reread a difficult sentence. Simple sentences are more desirable for speakers.

[7]Ibid., p. 37.

E. Concreteness

Specific rather than vague or general words or phrases will increase the impact of our ideas. We should seek the word or phrase that will convey the exact shade of meaning we intend. The use of specific detail will often heighten interest and add an air of authenticity to the speaker's words. When a first affirmative constructive speaker sought to show the harms of unemployment, he avoided a pointless generalization such as "unemployment is deleterious" and provided specific, concrete examples:

> Unemployment causes massive human suffering. The grim toll of even marginal increases in unemployment was documented by the painstaking study of Dr. Harvey Brenner of Johns Hopkins University, undertaken for the Joint Economic Committee.... That controlled epidemiological study revealed that for each 1 percent increase in unemployment, the nation suffered a 4.1 percent increase in suicides; a 1.9 percent increase in cardiovascular, renal, and cirrhosis mortality; and a 1.9 percent increase in overall mortality—that is, each 1 percent of unemployment results in 36,000 needless deaths.

Of course, the negative argued about this evidence—but it was concrete.

Sometimes the speaker must use unfamiliar words or phrases. These can be made more specific by careful definition.[8]

F. Imagery

If we can paint a vivid picture in the minds of our audience, we enhance our opportunity of persuading them. A deftly phrased image will have an immediate impact on listeners and may linger in their memory to influence future as well as immediate decisions.

In a debate on the proposition "Resolved: That executive control of U.S. foreign policy should be significantly curtailed," a first affirmative speaker began by saying:

> "All the people who lined the streets began to cry, 'Just look at the Emperor's new clothes. How beautiful they are!' Then suddenly a little child piped up, 'But the Emperor has no clothes on. He has no clothes on at all.'" In 1947 the United States created the Central Intelligence Agency and donned the cloak of secrecy to pursue communism. Experience has proven the cloak we donned was nothing more than the Emperor's new clothes, hiding far less than we long pretended and exposing America to peril.

A new phrase—"iron curtain"—entered the world's vocabulary when Winston Churchill proclaimed, "From Stettin in the Baltic to Trieste in the Adriatic an iron curtain has descended across the Continent."[9]

---

[8]See Chapter 4 (Analyzing the Controversy) for methods of defining terms.

[9]A considerable literature has been built up around the phrase "iron curtain." In 1918 Vasiliy Rozanov wrote in his book *Apocalypse of Our Time*, "...an iron curtain is descending on Russian history." In *Through Bolshevik Russia* (1920), Ethel Snowden described that country as being behind an "iron curtain." In the last days of Hitler's Third Reich, Propaganda Minister Joseph Goebbels spoke of "an iron curtain." See Martin Gilbert, *Winston S. Churchill*, Vol. 8 (Boston: Houghton Mifflin, 1988), p. 7. Although he was not the originator of the phrase, it is Churchill's usage that the world remembers.

G. Connotation

Our concern with the selection of words and phrases is not limited to the choice of words within the vocabulary of our audience. We are also concerned with the problem of choosing words and phrases with a sensitive awareness of their emotional connotations. Consider the following examples of phrases that present a concept in a "good" and a "bad" light.

Unemployed persons over age 65 receive money from the federal government. Is this "Social Security" or a "dole for the indigent unemployables"? Billions of dollars are spent to provide medical care for the aged and poor. Are these programs "Medicare" and "Medicaid" or "bureaucratic bungling" and a "rip-off of the taxpayer by organized medicine and the drug industry"? United Fund organizations collect monies for various groups. Is this "voluntary giving" or an "organized shakedown"? Are people who are employed to secure favorable press notices about their clients "public relations counselors" or "hucksters"? Each of these designations involves an element of slanting. But decisions are often influenced by just such slanted phrases. The use of the words "Social Security," "Medicare," and "Medicaid" were important factors in securing the enactment of the programs now known by those names. Joseph Conrad said, "Give me the right word and the right accent and I will move the world."[10]

H. Climax

The development of climax is an important consideration in speech composition. The advocate's speech typically contains a series of issues. Each of these should be built up to a climax, and the speech as a whole should build toward a final major climax. We will often find it advantageous to place a strong climax very near the beginning of our speech to capture audience attention. Our final climax may frequently be in the form of an effective summary of our major arguments combined with a strong persuasive appeal. If we use an anticlimactic order, beginning with our strongest arguments and tapering off with our least effective arguments, we will diminish the force of our case and will leave a weak impression with those who render the decision. We have three problems relating to climax: (1) We must open with an attention-getting climax; (2) we must end at a high point, leaving a strong, lasting impression with our audience; and (3) we must offset the climax of a previous speech by our opponents.

V. Rhetorical Factors in Speech Composition

The rhetorical factors of *coherence, unity,* and *emphasis* aid the advocate in composing an effective, well-organized speech. Students may find it desirable to review the speaker responsibilities considered in Chapters 12 and 13 as they compose their speeches so that they will not only have a well-written speech or brief but one that also fulfills their speaker responsibilities.

[10]Joseph Conrad, *A Personal Record* (Garden City, N.Y.: Doubleday, 1923), p. xvi.

A. Coherence

The speech must be arranged so effectively that it will be instantly intelligible to those who render the decision. The intelligibility of a speech depends in large part on coherent organization. Often beginning advocates have a cluster of evidence and reasoning that seems convincing to them but has no effect on those who render the decision. The same evidence and reasoning rearranged by skilled advocates may win a decision. The difference here is that the skilled advocates have learned to arrange or order their materials carefully and to blend them together with effective transitions into a coherent whole.

1. Order. The materials of the speech must be presented in a carefully determined order designed to have maximum effect on those who render the decision. The issues of the proposition must be presented in an effective sequence. The supporting materials for each issue must be so arranged as to lend maximum support to the issues. Often, as advocates, we may first think of presenting our arguments in logical order. In many situations, logical order is the most effective arrangement. In other situations, however, we may find it desirable to arrange our arguments in a psychological order adapted to our audience.

Other arrangements that are effective in certain situations include the problem–solution order, the "this-or-nothing" order, the topical order, and the chronological order. Sometimes the use of one arrangement for the overall speech, and another for the development of certain supporting arguments, is effective. In debating the "energy" proposition, one debater used a combination of methods in his first affirmative speech. The organization of the debate case was *problem–solution*: the problem was identified and a solution proposed. Other types of organization were used in the development of the issues. Following is an excerpt from the outline of his speech:

I.   Today's energy crisis is not a matter of just a few years but of decades.
     (Under this heading the debater used *chronological* order to show how the crisis had come about and why it would project into the future.)
II. Alternative sources of energy are impractical.
     (Under this heading the debater used the *this-or-nothing* order, as he considered and dismissed various alternative sources, concluding that coal was not an alternative as both coal and uranium were needed.)
III. Nuclear power is safe.
     (Under this heading the debater used *chronological* order, reviewing the history of civilian nuclear power from its start to the present and claiming an unparalleled safety record.)
IV. There is no reasonable alternative to nuclear power.
     (Under this heading the debater again used the *this-or-nothing* order to argue that an energy famine would result unless the affirmative plan were adopted.)

Even though we may use a variety of methods, our objective is always to order and arrange our materials in such a way as to achieve coherence.

2. Transition. Transitions may be regarded as bridges between the various parts of the speech. A well-ordered series of arguments is not sufficient to provide coherence.

We must also connect the parts of our argument in a way that makes it easy to follow the development of the total case. In many cases, a transition may be only a word or a phrase. In a closely reasoned argument, however, an effective transition often includes three parts: (a) a terse summary of the preceding arguments, (b) a brief forecast of the next argument, and (c) a concise demonstration of the relationship between the two arguments.

The debater whose outline was cited above used the following transition in developing his fourth issue:

> Remember our analysis: One, the energy crisis will last for decades. Two, alternative sources are impractical and three, nuclear power is safe. With this in mind consider the statement signed by 31 scientists — including 10 Nobel Prize winners — appearing in the *New York Times* on the 16th of this month: "On any scale the benefits of a clean, inexpensive, and inexhaustible domestic fuel far outweigh the possible risks. We can see no reasonable alternative to an increased use of nuclear power to satisfy our energy needs." And that's our fourth issue: There is no reasonable alternative to nuclear power.

Well-planned transitions make it easier for the audience to see the relationship of various parts of the argument and to link the parts of the speech together into an effective whole.

B. Unity

We should have one clear, definite, and specific objective for a speech. Once we have established this objective clearly in our mind, we may proceed to compose a speech designed to attain that objective. The effective speech has unity of purpose and mood.

1. Unity of Purpose. Unity of purpose requires that the speaker have one and only one specific purpose for his speech. The rhetorical purpose of the advocate is to prove, or to disprove, the proposition of debate. Anything that does not contribute to the attainment of the purpose — no matter how interesting, amusing, or informative it may be — must be ruthlessly excluded from the speech.

An example from academic debating will serve to illustrate this point. One student, who had many of the qualifications of an excellent debater, consistently lost debates on the "energy" proposition. A senior physics major, he was particularly well informed on nuclear power reactors. His response to negative workability attacks were brilliantly informative speeches on nuclear reactors. In fact, one judge commented that the student had delivered one of the best informative speeches the judge had ever heard on the operation of nuclear reactors. The student's problem was that he presented so much information on workability that — although he clearly carried that issue — he failed to respond to the disadvantages attacks. When he restructured his response-to-workability briefs, deleted the fascinating, informative, but irrelevant material, and retained only the critical refutation, he then had time to get to other major arguments and enjoyed much more success in winning decisions.

2. Unity of Mood. Unity of mood requires that we sustain a certain mood, emotional feeling, or "tone" appropriate to our purpose, audience, and occasion. Our materials should be in perfect unity with the mood we have chosen for our speech.

Evidence and reasoning that may meet the logical requirements of the proposition but not the mood requirements should be replaced by materials that will meet both requirements.

A debater favoring a program of national compulsory health insurance decided she would seek to establish a mood of pity. To support her argument about the cost of medical care, she offered a series of examples of long-term illness. One ill-chosen example shattered the mood she sought to sustain:

> One young girl, just the age of many in this audience, spent seven long, lonely, tragically wasted years in the cold isolation of a TB hospital. One man in the prime of life, the age of many of your parents, spent five years in the living hell of bone cancer suffering the most terrible pain known to man. One dear old lady, the age of some of your grandparents, spent fifteen years in a mental institution knitting a 27-foot-long scarf.

The audience of high school youngsters was still chuckling about the old lady and her 27-foot-long scarf while the debater completed her arguments showing the high cost of long-term hospitalization.

C. Emphasis

Not all parts of a speech are of equal importance—some are indispensable to our case, others are of lesser importance. Our problem is to emphasize the more important parts of our speech. Emphasis makes it easier for the audience to grasp and retain the ideas we must get across if we are to prove our case. Emphasis may be achieved by *position*, by *time*, by *repetition*, by *headlining*, and by *perspective (Spin control)*.

1. Position. Emphasis may be achieved by the position given to an idea. The *beginning* and the *ending* provide greater emphasis than does the middle. This principle applies to the speech as a whole, to an argument within the speech, and even to a sentence.

Consider the following excerpts taken from speeches in debates on "right-to-work" laws. The speeches come from two different debates, but the same issue is involved. Note the difference in emphasis:

> They just don't work. That's the simple fundamental fact about "right-to-work" laws—they just don't work. Let's look at the record. Let's go right down the list of states with "right-to-work" laws. In every case we'll see they just don't work.

> Let us consider the feasibility of the proposal advanced by the affirmative. Let us examine the facts in those states where this plan has been tried. We will find that such legislation does not work effectively to produce any significant change in labor-management relationships. There are now seventeen states that have legislation of this type. As we review the evidence from these states, we find...

Both speakers maintained that "right-to-work" laws do not work. The first speaker emphasized this claim by giving it both first and last position; the second speaker buried it in the middle of his passage.

2. Time. Time is of the essence in argument—and we must spend our time wisely. The greater part of our time must be devoted to the important arguments. We never have sufficient time to cover all possible arguments or to refute fully all of the contentions of our opponent. Therefore, we must single out the important matters and emphasize them by the amount of time we give them.

3. Repetition. Repetition and redundancy are often viewed with disapproval in writing, and the author is given stern injunctions to avoid them. For the speaker, however, judicious repetition is essential. Repetition aids both clarity and emphasis. If listeners miss a critical word or phrase that is uttered only once, the speaker's case may never be clear to them. Listeners cannot turn back the page to reread something they missed the first time. We must compensate for the probable inattention among some members of our audience by reiterating critical material. The old slogan "Tell them what you're going to tell them, tell it to them, and tell them what you've told them" has considerable merit. We cannot use italics, capital letters, or boldface type, but we can use repetition. Repetition may be achieved by repeating the same idea in the same words or by restating an idea several times in slightly different ways.

The use of the *echo effect* is often an effective technique for the advocate. A key sentence — usually a headline (considered next) — is stated and then the speaker *immediately* echoes the sentence by repeating the critical words of the sentence. Such echoing in a written essay would undoubtedly be criticized as poor style, and justly so. However, it is a valuable stylistic device in oral presentations — just one more example of the differences in oral and written style.

A first affirmative speaker arguing the "employment" proposition repeated his major claims, saying:

> Our first issue: Unemployment will persist. Unemployment will persist. . . .
> Our second issue: Unemployment is a major social problem. Unemployment — a major social problem.

The repetition is intended to lodge the argument firmly in the minds of the judge and audience and to ensure that the judge will record the speaker's exact phrasing of this argument on a flow sheet. Such overt repetition is accepted by many judges, who recognize the pressures a speaker is under in a tournament. A more subtle method of repetition is required for general usage.

4. Headlining. Headlining, or signposting, is an essential technique in composing debate cases and, indeed, in composing a speech on any relatively complex matter.

The headlines, which are the first sentences of the major portions of the speech, should be short and succinct and should emphasize the major point you want to make. Recall the examples just cited:

> Unemployment will persist.
> Unemployment is a major social problem.

With these headlines the debater set out the need issues in short, succinct, and emphatic form.

All major portions of the case should be headlined in similar fashion. For example,

> Inherency: Present economic policies can't reduce unemployment.

In the plan, each of the planks should be clearly headlined. For example,

Plank 1 — Agency: NASA will administer the plan.
Plank 2 — Mandate: By 1994 NASA will . . .

The headlines must concisely and precisely express the key ideas the debaters wish to lodge in the minds of the decision makers. Imprecision or ambiguity in phrasing headlines are counterproductive for the debater. One newspaper headlined a story about President Reagan's illness with, "President Determined to Have Cancer." A small town Alabama newspaper startled its readers with, "Methodists Take Up Homosexuality." If the headline leaves the audience puzzled, angry, or amused by inept word choice, the headline is a failure. Experienced debaters find it worthwhile to write and rewrite their headlines until they are honed to perfection.

Both CEDA and NDT debaters find it desirable to continue the headlining down through the substructure of the case using numbers and letters to make their organization clear. Note that in the debates in both Appendixes B and C, the debaters not only headline their arguments but also use numbers and letters to label their own arguments and to identify the points in their opponents' arguments that they seek to refute. In nonformal debate, too, headlining is essential to add clarity and impact to the arguments. The phrasing will be more informal — "Now wait a minute, let's look at that second point Art made, about the fees for the MBA, you really can't compare . . ." — but it makes an important contribution to helping the listeners follow your argument. In any situation, carefully developed headlining will make it easy for those who render the decision to follow your arguments.

5. Perspective (Spin Control). As we saw earlier (in Chapter 7, Section II-J), data are often susceptible to more than one reasonable interpretation. This, of course, is not limited to statistical data. Advocates will find it advantageous to give the most favorable rhetorical perspective to their answers in cross-examination (see Chapter 18, Section I-B, "Considerations for the Respondent" 5) and, indeed, to all aspects of speech composition. This perspective or spin control should be applied to both the headline (see 4 above) and to the development of the statement.

Consider the story that appeared in the *Washington Post* under the headline "Neutron Killer Warhead Buried in ERDA Budget," which said that "The United States is about to begin production of its first nuclear battlefield weapon designed to kill people rather than destroy military installations. . . . "[11] The President's national security advisor later stated, "The *Post* article touched off a political explosion that reverberated throughout the United States and Europe." Was the story objective? Accurate? Fair? Many senior government officials didn't think so. The story presented the information from the reporter's *perspective.*

Later, with the luxury of hindsight, another writer suggested that the brouhaha might have been avoided had the government released the information *first*, putting its spin on the story by stating that

The US, as a part of its long standing modernization program of nuclear weapons in Europe, is about to begin production of a low-yield nuclear weapon designed to kill enemy

---

[11]Martin Linsky, *Impact: How the Press Affects Federal Policymaking* (New York: Norton, 1986), p. 21. ERDA refers to the U.S. Energy Research and Development Administration.

soldiers in Russian tanks through radiation, at the same time reducing collateral damage from blast in civilian areas.[12]

Both stories reported the same set of facts. The *perspective* or spin, however, is quite different.

The lesson for the advocate is clear: Present the material *from your perspective* — put your spin on it — and if at all possible get your perspective on record *before your opponent* plants a very different perspective (or spin) in the minds of the decision makers.

Spin control became a major priority during the 1988 Presidential campaign debates. Following the Vice Presidential debate in Omaha that year, the *New York Times* reported:

> They [the Quayle and Bentsen camps] had flown in from Washington, old pro pols, Senators, House members, campaign big wigs, and their sole aim was to put "spin" on the news and commentary about to flow forth from the pressroom. In journalistic jargon such partisans are referred to as "spin doctors" and tonight the carpet on which they held forth was candidly labeled "Spin Valley" by the debate's organizers.[13]

Exercises

1. Prepare a five-minute speech in which you support or oppose a proposition of value. Drawing on the factors of style considered in this chapter, compose a speech in the style best suited to an audience of one of the following:
   a. a panel of judges at the CEDA National Debate Tournament.
   b. the audience at a meeting of a local Kiwanis Club.
   c. the audience at an alumni club of your university.

2. From recent newspapers and newsmagazines, find the text of a speech that you feel represents effective speech composition.

3. What speaker, prominent on the public scene today, do you regard as being particularly effective in speech composition? Justify your choice by citing specific examples from that person's speeches.

4. Assume you are the affirmative (or negative — specify which) in a debate on the current CEDA proposition (or the current NDT or national off-topic proposition — specify which). Prepare a written set of answers to the questions listed in the inset "What the Advocate Needs to Know about the Audience" in terms of (a) your class, (b) a selected campus organization, (c) a community service organization (Kiwanis, Rotary, Lions), (d) a local consumer organization, and (e) a local political organization. Compare your answers with those of other members of your class.

5. Assume the same debate situation as in Exercise 4. Prepare a written set of answers to the questions suggested in the discussion of "the key individual" (Sections I-B and I-C) as applicable to (a) your college president, (b) the mayor of the city where your college is located, (c) one of the deans of your college, (d) your parents, and (e) the member of Congress from your district.

[12]Ibid., p. 220.
[13]*New York Times*, October 6, 1988, p. 13.

6. From the newspapers or news magazines of the past two weeks, find examples of a news story presented from different perspectives.

7. From the newspapers or news magazines of the past two weeks, find a news story on the current debate proposition written from a perspective that favors one side of the debate. Draw on your knowledge of the national proposition to show how the same information could be presented from a perspective that would favor the other side.

16

Presenting the Case: Delivery

Once we have composed our case, our next step is to deliver it. Although a well-composed case is essential, good composition is not sufficient to win a debate decision. In order for the speech to achieve its impact, we must add effective delivery. The importance of delivery in oral communication has been stressed since the days of Aristotle, who pointed out: "Success in delivery is of the utmost importance to the effect of the speech."[1] Modern students of communication theory confirm this classical dictum. McCroskey examined a number of experimental studies and concluded: "Good delivery allows the rhetorically strong message to have its normal effect. Poor delivery tends to inhibit the effect of a verbal message."[2] Once we have composed a rhetorically strong message, we must prepare to deliver that message in a way that will secure the desired decision from our audience.

I. Methods of Delivery

The four methods of delivery available to the speaker are: *impromptu, extemporaneous, manuscript,* and *memorization.*

[1]Aristotle, *Rhetoric,* III, p. 1.
[2]James C. McCroskey, *An Introduction to Rhetorical Communication* (Englewood Cliffs, N.J.: Prentice-Hall, 1968), p. 208.

A. Impromptu

We use the impromptu method of delivery when we make little or no preparation for the presentation of our thoughts. In fact, since the impromptu speech is made without specific preparation, we have no organized case and do not compose the speech in advance of delivery. If at this very moment we were asked to defend our views on U.S. foreign policy, our response would be impromptu. We could draw on our general knowledge of the subject, on such information as we happen to gather in our reading, and on such ideas as we may have formulated, but we would have to organize our ideas as we went along.

The one advantage of being familiar with the impromptu method is that in some circumstances it is the only method available to the advocate. When news of an important development is received in the Senate during the day's session, for example, a senator might find it desirable to speak on this matter at once. A sales representative might meet a prospective customer unexpectedly and find that this meeting is just the opportune moment to attempt to make a sale. The business executive, while attending a board of directors' meeting, might learn of a new problem for the first time and be called upon to participate in debate on the problem immediately. Each of them would probably have a good general background on the problem, but in these situations they would have had no opportunity to make specific preparations. Since the impromptu method is often the only available method, argumentation teachers sometimes require their students to present impromptu arguments, so they may have experience in organizing and presenting a case under impromptu conditions.

The best preparation for meeting the impromptu situation when it arises is experience in delivering prepared speeches. Actually, we may plan and organize the impromptu speech to a degree. We will have at least a few seconds in which to organize our thoughts, and, if we are experienced speakers, we can do much in a very short time. Some speakers have developed the faculty of thinking ahead and planning their future lines of argument while they are speaking on matters of lesser importance that do not require their full attention.

B. Extemporaneous

The extemporaneous speech is a prepared speech. In delivering the extemporaneous speech, we neither read from a manuscript nor memorize our entire speech. We may or may not make use of notes; we may or may not read short quotations as a part of our speech; and we may or may not memorize a few short passages of our speech.

The extemporaneous method provides almost all of the advantages found in other methods of delivery and very few disadvantages. Its greatest advantage lies in the fact that it is both prepared and flexible, allowing us to plan exactly what we wish to say and the way in which we wish to say it. Thus all of the advantages of building the case and speech composition may be brought to bear in the extemporaneous speech. In addition, because the speech is planned but not frozen, we can modify our presentation to adapt to the situation and to the statements of previous speakers. Since we can watch the audience closely during the speech, we can gauge the listeners' reaction and adapt the speech to their response.

The disadvantages of the extemporaneous method are few. The extemporaneous speech does admit a greater possibility of error than do the manuscript or memorized speeches, but careful planning and preparation can minimize this risk. When the time element is critical, as in a radio or television speech, the extemporaneous method may pose some problems for the beginning speaker. It is more difficult to control the time with this method than with the manuscript or memorized speech. Experienced speakers, however, develop an excellent sense of time, and the college debater has little difficulty in adjusting to the time limits prevailing in intercollegiate debate. The repeat guests on television talk shows are those who have learned to adapt to the strict time requirements while retaining the spontaneity of the extemporaneous method. Political candidates, who are faced with the necessity of making numerous speeches each day at the height of the campaign, usually develop "The Speech"—a block of material in which they can present their views extemporaneously in as little as five minutes or extend them to as much as twenty minutes as the occasion requires. Almost all debaters, be they students or senators, use the extemporaneous method of delivery. Only extemporaneous delivery provides for the carefully prepared on-the-spot adaptation and refutation so essential to effective debate.

The extemporaneous method most frequently makes use of note cards. Typically, they are 4 × 6 cards, which the speaker holds in hand or places on a lectern. For television much larger cards are used, and they usually are placed "off camera."

C. Manuscript

In using the manuscript method, we prepare our speech carefully, write it out in full, and read it to our audience. The advantage of the manuscript is that it provides us with the maximum opportunity to say exactly what we want to say in exactly the way we want to say it. The presence of the manuscript will give us assurance that, under the pressure of the debate, we will speak the words exactly as we have planned them. When minimizing the possibility of error is the prime consideration, the manuscript speech is generally used. In delivering a State of the Union message or other major state addresses, all Presidents of the United States, even those who were brilliant extemporaneous speakers, have used the manuscript method. A "slip of the tongue" in such a situation would be too dangerous; it might lead to a domestic or international crisis.

The disadvantages of the manuscript method include the lack of flexibility and the difficulty of reading the manuscript effectively. Since the manuscript is prepared in advance of the occasion, it does not provide for adjustments to the situation, to previous speeches, or to audience reaction. Furthermore, the manuscript often becomes a barrier between the speaker and the audience when the speaker's objective is to establish rapport with the audience. Audiences would rather have the speaker *talk with* them than *read at* them. Skilled speakers, when they find it necessary to use a manuscript, often plan their delivery in such a way as to create the impression that they frequently depart from the manuscript.

Experienced debaters have found it worthwhile to master the art of effective delivery from a manuscript. As we practice the delivery of our speech, we should give careful consideration to the "Steps to Good Delivery" considered later in this chapter.

Those portions of the speech that are under the advocate's complete control — that is, where there is little or no need or opportunity for adaptation — must reflect the maximum skill in speech composition. The first affirmative speech, for example, provides the greatest opportunity for advocates to say precisely what they want to say in precisely the way they want to say it and to deliver their carefully chosen words with maximum effectiveness. The well-planned first affirmative speech is a masterpiece of composition and delivery. The issues, the contentions, the transitions, the analysis, the evidence,[3] and the summaries should be polished to perfection so that they will be recorded on the judge's flow sheet — or lodged in the minds of the audience — precisely as the speaker wants them to be. The well-written and well-delivered first affirmative speech is a graceful, forceful, highly literate, lucid, cogent statement that should be a powerful factor in advancing the affirmative's case. A well-planned manuscript may be adapted to the situation at many points in a debate. Experienced debaters prepare briefs for these situations — that is, short manuscripts that may be blended into their total speech by use of extemporaneous methods. Negative debaters prepare briefs of plan attacks. The plan attacks, of course, must be adapted to the specific case of the affirmative. Frequently, however, it is possible to anticipate a considerable part of this portion of the negative's case. The negative speaker may select from a number of previously prepared briefs — choosing the one *directly* relating to the particular affirmative plan of the moment and carefully adapting it to the *specifics* of that plan. The debater is cautioned that judges and audiences do not like "canned arguments." The scripted plan attack will work effectively only if it is *adapted* to the exact plan used by the affirmative and only if it is presented so that it appears spontaneous.

The *reading copy* of the manuscript should be a carefully prepared document of professional quality. The manuscript in draft form will be covered with corrections, revisions, insertions, and deletions. Reading from such a paper presents challenges that are best avoided. (Of course, if you prepare your manuscript on a word processor, the problem is much simpler.) A professional-quality manuscript is easier to read and its appearance adds to the speaker's ethos.

A professional-quality manuscript is one that is typed on 8½ × 11-inch paper with 1½-inch margins on all sides. Double spacing makes it easier to read and allows space for last-minute changes.

Underlining, capitalization, highlighting, phonetic spelling of difficult words, and use of dashes or slash marks to indicate pauses help the speaker to achieve effective delivery. Leave extra space at the bottom of a page rather than break a key sentence between two pages. Begin a new argument at the top of a page rather than start it near the bottom of a page. Where possible, have one argument per page; the act of turning to a new page can help indicate to the audience that you are making a transition to a new argument.

Debaters often find it advisable to put manuscript pages into transparent jackets, thus keeping the pages fresh and easy to read even after repeated usage.

A well-prepared, professional-quality manuscript can help the speaker achieve more effective delivery and thus increase the impact of the arguments.

[3]Again the admonition: evidence may be edited to eliminate extraneous material, but the advocate must scrupulously preserve the author's intent.

Speaker's Brief Notes

```
OTHER BARRIERS TO RECEIVING COMPREHENSIVE MEDICAL CARE

A.   Ignorance rather than money is real barrier.
     1.  Advisory Board for Public Policy quote
     2.  Newsweek quote
     3.  Mueller quote
B.   Fear of physicians and hospitals is a barrier.
     1.  Sen. Hansen, Hearings quote
     2.  Health Care Story quote
C.   Shortage of physicians is a barrier.
     1.  Robbins quote
     2.  U.S. News and World Report quote
     3.  Cray quote
D.   Maldistribution of physicians is a barrier.
     1.  Nolan quote
     2.  N.Y. Times quote
     3.  Sen. Kennedy, Hearings quote
     4.  Time quote
     5.  Hayden quote
```

D. Memorization

Memorization of the entire speech is little used by advocates today. This method is still required in many college oratory contests, because it furnishes an educational opportunity to emphasize considerations of speech composition and delivery. Outside the contest situation, however, most advocates do not feel they can afford the time necessary to memorize a speech. The memorized speech is, in fact, a manuscript that has been memorized. It provides all of the advantages of the manuscript method, as well as the additional advantage that the manuscript is not present. Memorization also provides the maximum opportunity for polished presentation. With this advantage, however, a potential disadvantage exists. Inexperienced advocates who memorize their speeches often appear stilted and artificial and lacking in apparent spontaneity. Further disadvantages of the memorized speech include the time necessary for complete memorization, the lack of flexibility also found in the manuscript speech, and a special hazard in the possibility that the advocate may forget a portion of his or her speech. Many speakers, however, *do* find it advantageous to memorize speech segments.

The answer to an obvious plan attack may be rambling and ineffective the first time debaters respond to it. After they have met the attack in essentially the same form several times, they may hone their answers to perfection and present them concisely and incisively. Prudent advocates preplan answers to recurring problems—and to problems they anticipate may arise.

A consideration of the advantages and the disadvantages of the four possible methods makes it apparent that in most situations the best method for most advocates is the extemporaneous method. In using the extemporaneous method, we frequently find it necessary to have at hand evidence cards that contain quotations or statements we wish to use in a very specific form. Often we find it advantageous to memorize brief passages of our speech. For example, we might wish to conclude a speech with a very carefully phrased summary. If we felt that reading this summary from a card would lessen its effect and yet we wished to be very precise in that statement, we might memorize our concluding sentences. And when our opponent introduces important unexpected matters into the debate, we must meet them with impromptu refutation.

II. Steps to Good Delivery

A. The Speech Outline

The speech outline is different from the case outline. The case outline is an operational plan that coordinates the evidence and reasoning of the speakers on a given side of the proposition; the speech outline is a detailed plan of exactly what we intend to say, and it indicates the manner in which we intend to say it to a specific audience.

B. The Speaker's Notes

The speaker's notes in a debate typically take two forms. In the first instance the debater will record notes on the flow sheet (see pages 250–251) as an opponent is speaking. These notes are designed to guide the debater's response to an opponent's arguments. In the second instance the speaker's notes are prepared in advance in the form of briefs. The briefs are responses that will be *adapted* for use against the anticipated arguments of an opponent. (See the typical example of a speaker's brief on page 277—one of several "negative briefs" prepared by the second negative speaker for use in a debate on "comprehensive medical care.") In the course of the debate the speaker would make a note on the flow sheet to use this particular brief. On the brief itself the speaker would make additional notes adapting the brief to the specific arguments of the opponent. If, for example, the affirmative had anticipated the "shortage of physicians" argument by providing for more physicians in their plan, the debater would delete Section C (as seen in the inset).

C. Preparation

Just as we must prepare by building our case and composing our speech, we must also prepare the delivery of our speech. Experienced advocates do not deliver a speech for the first time to those who render the decision. Rather, they deliver it a number of times, preferably to colleagues who will be able to give useful suggestions on improving the delivery. If we consider the problems of delivery for the first time as we address those who render the decision, our statement will be far less effective than if we have delivered our speech or brief a number of times, anticipated the potential problems in delivery, and worked out the most effective way of presenting a position. The requirement of flexibility, of course, means that we will revise our speech up to the very moment of delivery. We should also anticipate probable arguments of our opponents and practice the way we will answer them should they be used.

At national political conventions, where a televised speech can make or break a career, knowledgeable politicians make elaborate efforts to assure that they are well prepared. In 1988 both major parties provided soundproof rooms containing life-sized replicas of the real podiums used in the convention halls where speakers could rehearse their speeches under the guidance of speech consultants. Michael Dukakis took the precaution of having three aides on hand to chant "Duke! Duke! Duke!" and simulate crowd interruptions during his rehearsals. The effort paid off. Previously Dukakis was considered to be an uninspiring speaker. His well-rehearsed acceptance speech was hailed as "an unexpected flight of oratory that electrified the convention."

III. Nonverbal Communication

We communicate with others not only through language — verbal behavior — but by means of nonverbal behavior as well. When we address an audience, we use not only verbal language but also *vocal expression* and *body language*. The meaning the audience perceives from our message comes not from our words alone, nor alone from vocal expression or body language. The message is perceived as an interrelation of all these factors. For example, such a simple verbal message as "Hi" can, with the addition of appropriate vocal expression and body language, be perceived to mean: "I love you," "Have I seen you somewhere before?", "Don't interrupt me now, I'm too busy to talk," or a wide variety of other meanings. Thus, it is our task, as advocates, to use the techniques of nonverbal communication to clarify and enhance our message. Nonverbal communications must be *consistent* with the verbal communications — the smile or frown, for example, reinforcing rather than contradicting the verbal message.

The importance of nonverbal communication is stressed by modern students of communication theory. Hance, Ralph, and Wiksell maintain "The ideas and feelings that we want to express to our audience are determined as much by nonverbal behavior and by vocal signals as they are by the words we use."[4] Harrison has estimated that "in face-to-face communication no more than 35 percent of the social meaning is carried in the verbal messages."[5] Much of the remaining 65 percent of social meaning comes from the delivery of nonverbal messages.

[4]Kenneth G. Hance, David C. Ralph, and Milton J. Wiksell, *Principles of Speaking*, 3rd ed. (Belmont, Calif.: Wadsworth, 1975), p. 250.

[5]Randall Harrison, "Nonverbal Communication: Explorations into Time, Space, Action and Object," in James H. Campbell and Hal W. Hepler, *Dimensions in Communication*, 2nd ed. (Belmont, Calif.: Wadsworth, 1970), p. 285.

A. Vocal Expression

We communicate with our audience partly by means of vocal expression. The words we pronounce are intended to be heard by our listeners and to have meaning to them. Some considerations of vocal expression important to the advocate include the following.

1. Rate. The rate at which we talk is important. We must speak slowly enough for the audience to follow us, but not so slowly that the audience will lose interest in our words. Beginning advocates sometimes try to pack too much evidence and reasoning into a short time; consequently, they are forced to deliver their speech at so rapid a rate that the audience cannot follow them without difficulty. Those who render the decision are not always willing to make the necessary effort to follow them, and the advocates may thus defeat their own purposes. The solution to this problem is often found in careful speech composition. Rather than using three pieces of evidence, and delivering them at too rapid a rate for easy comprehension, it would be better to use one well-chosen piece of evidence, integrating it carefully into the case and helping to drive it home by use of an effective rate. We may do well to listen to good speakers, both in audience situations and on radio and television, and note the rate they use; and we should adapt our own rate to suit the needs of our audience.

Experienced varsity NDT debaters operating in tournament situations on the national circuit are under great pressure to pack as much evidence and argument as possible into the time limits. Their delivery may often exceed 300 words per minute. Their opponents will strain to follow every word; the judge, usually an argumentation professor who may well have "been there," understands the situation and often is willing to concentrate on the speech and record the arguments accurately on a flow sheet. The human mind is easily capable of absorbing far more than 300 words a minute, *provided the listener is willing to concentrate and provided the delivery is intelligible.* We are warned, however, that audiences of the general public are not willing to provide the same degree of concentration that is available in the tournament situation. As selecting and using the appropriate rate for those who render the decision is often a difficult problem for the beginning debater, it is well to remember the question posed in Chapter 15 (Section I): "Who are the people to whom our arguments are directed?" The judges in an NDT national debate tournament will have one set of expectations about rate; the judges in a CEDA or off-topic debate will have another set of expectations; and an audience of the general public still a different set of expectations. In such circumstances a coach might well offer

> "The Coaches' Prayer
> God, give my debaters the speed and logos
>   to impress the NDT judge,
> The ethos and pathos to impress the CEDA
>   judge,
> And the audience analysis to distinguish
>   the one from the other."
>   (with apologies to
>   Reinhold Niebuhr)[6]

---

[6]Alan Cirlin, "Judging, Evaluation, and the Quality of CEDA Debate," *National Forensic Journal,* Vol. 4 (1986), pp. 81–151.

Successful advocates are able to adapt their rate to the requirements of the judge and audience. Observe the delivery of television network newscasters — their rate is usually ideally suited to general public audiences.

2. Pitch. Pitch refers to the tone level of the voice. Men generally have a deeper pitch than women and adults a deeper pitch than children. A pitch appropriate to the advocate's age and sex is an important consideration.

3. Intensity. Intensity refers to the loudness or softness of the speaker's voice. As a minimum, our voice must be loud enough to be heard easily by everyone we want to reach. In some circumstances, the use of a public address system may be necessary. In such cases, we should address the microphone with normal conversational intensity and allow the electronic system to provide the needed amplification rather than shout into the microphone. At the same time we must guard against too much intensity. Beginning debaters sometimes make the mistake of addressing a small audience in a classroom with an intensity that would be appropriate for a large gathering in an auditorium. Our intensity should be such as to make it easy and pleasant for those who render the decision to hear us.

4. Flexibility. We should be able to adapt our voice, as well as our arguments, to the situation. One type of delivery is appropriate at a football rally; quite another in a small committee meeting.

We may use variation of rate, intensity, and pitch to add effectiveness to our delivery. For example, when we come to a particularly important concept in a speech, we might use a much slower rate, greater intensity, and a deeper pitch than we had previously used. When we come to a minor transition, we might provide contrast by increasing rate, lowering intensity, and raising pitch. These variations must be accomplished with subtlety, however. If the variation is too obvious, it calls attention to itself rather than to the argument the speaker wishes to emphasize. Listen to good speakers in audience situations or on radio or television. Their use of variation to increase effectiveness will not be apparent on the surface, but if we look for the use of variation, we will see how good speakers vary their delivery to achieve a desired effect.

5. Quality. The quality of our voice is important; we want our voice to be such that people will find it easy and pleasant to listen to. Good quality results from the presence of good resonance and from the absence of undesirable noise elements in the voice. Undesirable qualities resulting from the improper production of tone are breathiness, nasality, huskiness, and throatiness. Other voice qualities, considered undesirable in most circumstances, include tones that are aspirate, guttural, falsetto, pectoral, metallic, or shrill. We should try to cultivate the presence of well-modulated, resonant tones. Under certain conditions (considered in "Expressional Patterns"), we will deliberately use unpleasant voice qualities to convey special meaning to our audience. With these special exceptions, which are confined to isolated words or brief passages, our overall quality should be such as to produce a pleasant reaction in the audience.

6. Fluency. We should cultivate verbal fluency. Because beginning speakers are sometimes at a loss for words, they may vocalize pauses while they grope for the next word and fill their speech with "er," "ah," and "uh." A good knowledge of the subject, a well-developed case outline, a well-composed speech plan, and advance delivery of the speech will help the advocate to overcome these problems and acquire the necessary verbal fluency. Practice in impromptu speaking also helps us to develop verbal fluency.

7. Expressional Patterns. Our concern with delivery is not limited to the production of clear, pleasant, readily intelligible speech. On many occasions we will use nuances of delivery to convey meaning. Skillful advocates use rate, pitch, intensity, quality, and inflection to create an expressional pattern giving special meaning and emphasis to certain words and phrases in their speeches. With a well-chosen expressional pattern, we can do much to clarify and communicate our meaning. Foreign demonstrators chanting for the television cameras can often convey their meaning across a language barrier. Expressional patterns can be used to express friendly as well as unfriendly attitudes. Ed McMahon on television's "Tonight Show" sets the stage with a warm and friendly "H-e-e-r-r-e's Johnny!"

B. Body Language

We communicate with our audience partly with verbal language, partly with vocal expression, and partly with body language. Just as audiences are influenced by the speaker they hear, so too are they influenced by the speaker they see. Radio speaking is, of course, an exception, but when the speaker appears before audiences—in person or on television—the audiences are influenced by what they see. Birdwhistell believes that we do most of our "talking" with our body movements. He maintains that we pour out information with our shrugs, our hand and body movements, our eyes, and our facial expressions and that these signals are often *more* reliable messages than the words we utter.[7] Some considerations of body language important to the advocate include the following.

1. Eye Contact. We should maintain direct eye contact with members of the audience throughout our speech. Of course, we will have to refer to our notes or manuscript, but this checking should be done as briefly as possible. The *vast majority* of our time should be spent in looking *at* and talking *to* our audience. If there is a key individual in the audience—such as a single judge for a debate—we may focus most of our attention on that key individual. We will, however, establish some eye contact with others in the audience. In a general audience situation, we should make sure that we establish eye contact with persons in all parts of the audience, thereby getting vital *feedback* from the audience.

---

[7]Ray L. Birdwhistell, *Introduction to Kinesics: An Annotation System for Analysis of Body Motion and Gesture* (Washington, D.C.: Foreign Service Institute, Department of State, 1952).

2. Movement. Our movement, when speaking, should be *purposeful*. Our movement should aid us in communicating with our audience. The way we approach the lectern, for example, is important. If we approach the lectern with a confident step and with quiet authority take possession of the rostrum, our ethos is enhanced. Our movements should be easy, economical, purposeful, yet apparently spontaneous. We should not remain in a fixed position behind the lectern, or rooted to one spot on the rostrum as if we were inanimate. For example, we might move away from the lectern and move closer to our audience to emphasize a major issue; we might move from one side of the rostrum to the other as we make a transition from one issue to another.

Our movement should never be such as to compete with our case for the attention of the audience. A story, which just might be true, is told of a young prosecuting attorney who lost his first case in a burglary trial, although he had ample evidence of the guilt of the accused. The novice lawyer was so nervous that in presenting his evidence he continually paced to and fro before the jury. This pacing so attracted the attention of the jury that they concentrated on estimating how many steps he took in each direction and how many miles he walked in the course of the trial, rather than following the case he was attempting to present.

3. Gestures. Our gestures should be purposeful, aiding our communication with the audience. A distinct preference is shown today for the restrained gesture in contrast to the flamboyant breast-beating of another century. As with movement, the gesture should be easy, economical, purposeful, yet apparently spontaneous. When we use a three-fingered gesture as we say, for example, "The three major issues are . . . ," it should appear natural and spontaneous rather than calculated.

4. Facial Expression. Our facial expression should be consistent with the attitude we are trying to express. One novice debater was so pleased to be participating in his first intercollegiate debate that he smiled happily as he said, "The energy crisis is going to produce the worst depression this country has ever seen." The incongruity of the speaker's pleasant smile did much to minimize the effect of his argument on this issue.

Experienced communicators such as Johnny Carson or William Buckley can convey a world of meaning by a tilt of an eyebrow, the toss of a head, the curl of a lip, or a slight change of expression. And, of course, others are constantly trying to "read" our facial expressions. After an important conference, reporters often tell us that the President or the Secretary of State looked "pleased" or "tense," "confident" or "worried."

Speech delivery and composition involve many considerations. As in many other arts, the great art is to conceal the art. As advocates, our purpose is to win a decision. We use the arts of speech communication to help attain this objective. When the debate is over, we are not interested in having the audience applaud our clever word choice, or comment on the quality of our voice, or note our graceful gestures; rather, we want it to make the decision we have argued. The arts of speech communication must never attract attention to themselves, but must be blended into the total communicative effort to secure the decision of the audience.

Exercises

1. Read a transcript of a Presidential press conference. Can you identify the questions the President expected and for which he had prepared an extemporaneous reply, and those questions that he did not expect and to which he gave impromptu replies? Report your findings to the class and support your conclusions with quotations from the press conference.

2. Use the following method to gain some experience in impromptu speaking. At one class meeting, the instructor will announce a proposition that will serve as the subject for impromptu speeches. At the next class meeting, the instructor will have a number of slips of paper, each containing a statement of an issue, line of argument, or piece of evidence important in this proposition. Draw one of these slips at random and support or refute the statement.

3. Use the following method to gain some experience in manuscript speaking. Prepare a three-minute speech in which you support or oppose a proposition. Plan this speech so that the greater part of your time will be spent in reading quotations or carefully phrased statements from 4×6 cards or from a manuscript. (Some speakers find it convenient to arrange their cards or script in acetate jackets.) Plan your delivery so that you will handle your materials smoothly and communicate effectively with the audience while reading. The instructor and your classmates will criticize your delivery and offer suggestions for improvement.

4. Use the following method to gain some experience in the use of vocal expression. Arrange with your instructor to prepare an audiotape recording outside of class. In the recording present a three-minute speech in which you support or oppose a proposition. Use the various considerations of vocal expression to make your delivery more effective. Play the recording in class. Your instructor and classmates will criticize your delivery and offer suggestions for improvement.

5. Use the following method to gain some experience in the use of body language. Arrange with your instructor to prepare a videotape recording outside of class. In the recording present a three-minute speech in which you support or oppose a proposition. Use the various considerations of body language to make your delivery more effective. Play the videotape recording in class. Your instructor and classmates will criticize your delivery and offer suggestions for improvement.

6. Prepare a three-minute speech in which you support or oppose a proposition. Use all the considerations of speech delivery to present your case with maximum effectiveness. Your instructor and classmates will criticize your delivery and offer suggestions for improvement.

17

Evaluating the Debate

We want to know "What was the vote?" "What was the verdict?" "Who won?" Members of Congress put their voting cards into the electronic slots, then the electronic scoreboards on the gallery walls light up, and we learn the fate of legislation. The judge in the courtroom asks the jury to state the verdict, and we learn the outcome of the trial. In academic debate the judge rises to announce the decision, or in a tournament situation the teams gather to await the announcement of results. Everything we have considered thus far builds to the climactic moment—the decision.

How do we evaluate the debate? What is the basis for the decision? The decision should be based either on the proposition of debate or on the debate itself. In applied debate, the decision should be rendered on the proposition itself; in academic debate, the decision should be based on the debate itself—that is, the comparative merits of the opposing teams, not the merits of the proposition. We shall consider here the role of the judge in academic debates.

I. Functions of the Judge

Judges in academic debates have two functions; they serve as decision makers and as critics. As decision makers, they must discern which team did the better debating; as critics, they must report their decisions in an educationally useful manner.

A. Discerning Which Team Did the Better Debating

Judges of academic debates must answer the question "Which team did the better debating?"[1] To answer this question, they are guided by certain principles:

1. Judges must apply their total knowledge of argumentation and debate.
In debates, an almost infinite range of possibilities may become factors in the decision-making process. Therefore, judges must be able to bring to bear a comprehensive knowledge of the principles of argumentation and debate in order to evaluate the arguments advanced for their decision. The First National Developmental Conference on Forensics stated:

> As decision maker the judge is called upon to make choices among alternatives emerging out of the proposition. The judge should value content above delivery and substance above technique. The stronger position on the issue should prevail, and the more credible evidence should prevail over a greater quantity of evidence having less probative force.[2]

2. Judges must set aside their special knowledge of the subject for the duration of the debate.
Although judges are usually expected to have only the knowledge of well-informed persons on the subject of the debate, often they have devoted much study to the subject and frequently acquire considerable special knowledge. This additional knowledge may produce certain attitudes, stereotypes, anticipations, or even occasional distortions in their thinking on the proposition. Their responsibility as judges requires that they set this knowledge aside for the duration of the debate and, in rendering the decision, consider only the evidence and reasoning that the students introduced into the debate. For example, one team may introduce some evidence found in an article by source A. The judge may know that source A's position is superficial and that it could easily be refuted by evidence found in a scholarly book written by source B. However, the judge must set aside this knowledge for the duration of the debate. Unless and until the opposing team refutes the weak evidence drawn from source A's article, that evidence must be accepted at its face value within the context of the debate. The subject-matter experts ordinarily do not make good judges for academic debates. Because of their very expertness in the field, they have usually formed considered judgments on the proposition, after long and careful study, and consequently find it exceedingly difficult to set aside these judgments for the duration of the debate.

Judges may properly draw on their special knowledge of the subject in critiques to suggest ways in which the debaters may improve their arguments. Here judges take cognizance of the strength or weakness of the subject-matter knowledge of the debaters and reflect their findings in the quality-rating points on the ballot. Should judges discover a deliberate misuse of evidence, they should impose an appropriate penalty. The National Debate Tournament has adopted a rule stipulating the following: "If a judge determines that distortion and/or falsification [of evidence] has oc-

---

[1]There are two penalty situations for which a team might be given an automatic loss. One, considered later in this section, involves the use of evidence of doubtful credibility. The second is a forfeit (usually for being late for the scheduled starting time of a debate) as stipulated in the rules of a tournament.

[2]James H. McBath, ed., *Forensics as Communication* (Skokie, Ill.: National Textbook Co., 1975), p. 30.

curred, the judge shall award the offending team a loss and award zero speaker points to the offending speaker(s)."

The judge's knowledge of the subject may also produce preferences for certain types of cases. These too must be set aside for the duration of the debate. The First National Development Conference on Forensics stated:

> In the area of case forms, students may evolve new paradigms that are consistent with the issues under consideration. The appropriateness of such paradigms should be determined primarily by the process of argumentation. In choosing between different interpretations of a proposition, the judge should encourage methods of analysis and reasoning about *meaning*. Only in those instances where the students themselves have failed to agree upon the basis for a reasonable interpretation of the proposition should the judge exercise his or her individual and carefully considered judgment.[3]

3. Judges must base their decisions on the debate as it is presented. Judges, since they are experts on argumentation and debate, could undoubtedly refute easily some of the arguments advanced in the debate. They might know that one team could have taken a much stronger position than it took. However, they must never require the students to debate *them* rather than the opposing team. They must never ask, "Could I refute a particular argument?" but rather "Did the opposing team refute that argument?" They do not ask whether a team's position was weak or strong in relation to the ideal position, but whether the team's position was weaker or stronger than that of their opponents. For example, in debating the proposition "Resolved: That executive control of U.S. foreign policy should be significantly curtailed," an affirmative team took the position that the United States should adopt a foreign policy of isolation. In the opinion of one educator who was asked to judge this debate, a foreign policy of isolation would be folly for the United States. His opinion, however, was irrelevant to his function as a judge. The question was not "Is isolation good or bad for the United States?" but rather "Did the affirmative team support its case for curtailing of executive control of U.S. foreign policy within the context of the debate?"

In fact, since the debate must be judged within its own framework, almost any statement made or any position taken by either team stands until refuted — with the exception of the last affirmative speech, when the judge may take judicial notice of the validity of evidence or of the introduction of a new concept. If a team fails to ask the judge to take judicial notice of an obvious error or contradiction in their opponents' case, the judge must assume they have failed to detect the error and it must stand against them.

Judges, of course, take cognizance of the strengths and weaknesses in a debate case and refer to them in their critiques and reflect their findings in the quality-rating points on the ballot.

4. Judges must take comprehensive notes during the debate. Experienced educators who have judged thousands of debates are known for the care with which they take notes during a debate. All judges would do well to de-

[3]Ibid.

velop a comprehensive notetaking system, so that they can record all of the significant developments during the debate in order to evaluate the debate effectively. Experienced educators judging academic debates find the flow sheet to be the most convenient method of taking comprehensive notes.

Judges using the flow-sheet method seek to record the development of each issue throughout the debate. This method is essentially similar to the debater's flow sheet considered in Chapter 14 but with one difference. The debater — on a flow sheet — may make notes to aid in planning future speeches; the judge, of course, will record the arguments only as they are actually presented by the debaters.

Although the methods suggested in Chapter 14 are designed specifically for use in judging the academic debate, they may be readily adapted for use in rendering a decision on an applied debate. Many trial judges and attorneys use a comparable method to follow a courtroom debate, and many business executives use a comparable "balance sheet" to aid them in weighing arguments in a debate on corporate policy. Whenever it is necessary to render a decision on an important debate, it is desirable to develop some system that will facilitate the process of analyzing and weighing the arguments.

B. Reporting the Decision in an Educationally Useful Manner

The decision, as part of the educational process of debate, must be reported in a manner that will contribute to the further educational attainment of the students. This reporting may be done either through the medium of an oral critique, by the use of a carefully prepared ballot, or by a combination of these methods.

1. The Oral Critique. If the oral critique is used, the judge is allowed a few minutes to review his or her notes before being called upon to present the critique. The effective critique should do the following:

1. Review the progress of the debate.
2. Cite examples of effective application of the principles of argumentation and debate.
3. Offer suggestions for improvement.
4. Cite the factors most significant in determining the decision.
5. Announce the decision.

When the oral critique is used, adequate time should be allocated for its presentation.

2. The Ballot. The ballot is the more common method of reporting decisions on academic debates today, because it is often desirable to secure a written or a lasting record of the decision. When a ballot is used, an oral critique may be presented as well; or the judge may be asked to prepare a written critique on those portions of the ballot that will be handed to the participating teams. The effective ballot should do the following:

1. Record the decision on the debate.
2. Record the rank and points of each debater in the debate.
3. Provide a place for a written critique.
4. Provide a record of the debate for each team.
5. Provide a record of the debate for the tournament director.

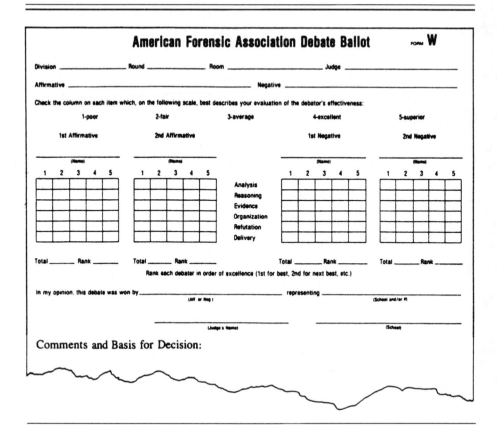

Three ballots that meet these requirements are shown in *insets*. The AFA Form W ballot, one of several ballots published by the American Forensic Association, is widely used for CEDA and NDT debates. The AFA Form H ballot is used for Lincoln-Douglas debates, and the cross-exam debate ballot may be used for cross-examination debates. These are prepared in convenient no-carbon form. The top sheet, recording the decision and points, can be sent to the tournament control room immediately upon the judge's reaching a decision. The judge may then complete the written critique at leisure and send the completed ballot to the control room in timely fashion. Completed copies of the ballot containing the critique are distributed to the participants after the preliminary rounds of the tournament are finished. A ballot for shift-of-opinion debating, which may be prepared locally and distributed to the audience, is also shown in an *inset*.

II. Judging Philosophies

All qualified judges for academic debate agree that the decision must be based on the answer to the question "Which team did the better debating?" However, judges may

CROSS EXAM DEBATE BALLOT ©1981

DIVISION _____ ROUND _____ ROOM _____ JUDGE _____

AFFIRMATIVE _____ NEGATIVE _____

CHECK EACH COLUMN ACCORDING TO YOUR EVALUATION – 1 = UNPREPARED 2 = FAIR 3 = GOOD 4 = EXCELLENT 5 = SUPERIOR

1st AFF.	VALUE 1 2 3 4 5	NAME	RANK IN ROUND		1st NEG.	VALUE 1 2 3 4 5	NAME	RANK IN ROUND
ANALYSIS/DEFINITION					ANALYSIS/DEFINITION			
EVIDENCE					EVIDENCE			
AUDIENCE ADAPTATION					AUDIENCE ADAPTATION			
REFUTATION/REBUTTAL					REFUTATION/REBUTTAL			
DELIVERY					DELIVERY			
ORGANIZATION					ORGANIZATION			
CROSS-EXAM.					CROSS-EXAM.			
COURTESY					COURTESY			
SUM TOTAL (40 Max.) →					SUM TOTAL (40 Max.) →			

2nd AFF.	VALUE 1 2 3 4 5	NAME	RANK IN ROUND		2nd NEG.	VALUE 1 2 3 4 5	NAME	RANK IN ROUND
ANALYSIS/DEFINITION					ANALYSIS/DEFINITION			
EVIDENCE					EVIDENCE			
AUDIENCE ADAPTATION					AUDIENCE ADAPTATION			
REFUTATION/REBUTTAL					REFUTATION/REBUTTAL			
DELIVERY					DELIVERY			
ORGANIZATION					ORGANIZATION			
CROSS-EXAM.					CROSS-EXAM.			
COURTESY					COURTESY			
SUM TOTAL (40 Max.) →					SUM TOTAL (40 Max.) →			

(X ONE)   **TEAM RATINGS**   (X ONE)

AFFIRMATIVE		NEGATIVE	
☐ UNPREPARED	☐ EXCELLENT	☐ UNPREPARED	☐ EXCELLENT
☐ FAIR	☐ SUPERIOR	☐ FAIR	☐ SUPERIOR
☐ GOOD		☐ GOOD	

BE SURE YOU HAVE CHECKED ALL AREAS

I am persuaded to vote for team: _____

of the _____ side.

_____   _____
JUDGE'S SIGNATURE   SCHOOL

NOTE TO JUDGES

(tear along here after reading)

Please fill out this ballot completely as the speaker points and team ratings are necessary to match following rounds. Each of the categories is described below:

1.) **Analysis/Definition:** Your evaluation of how clearly the teams present their definition of the terms of the resolution, and how significantly, fairly and completely that understanding of the topic is presented.

2.) **Evidence/Reasoning:** Do the debaters present sufficient, quality evidence to support their arguments? Is the evidence fully cited? Are inferences drawn from the evidence warranted?

3.) **Audience Adaptation:** Do the speakers make an effort to relate their arguments to you directly? Do they use audience analysis? Wit? Humor?

4.) **Refutation/Rebuttal:** Do the speakers clash with opponents' arguments? Are they able to synthesize and narrow the focus of clash during rebuttal time?

5.) **Delivery:** Do the speakers present their ideas at a tone and rate which the audience can follow and respond to?

6.) **Organization:** Are the speakers following a consistent pattern of organization and idea development? Do the debaters use adequate transitions and sign posting to make their ideas clear?

7.) **Cross Exam.:** Do the speakers utilize the cross examination time to clarify the opponents' case? Do they lead opponents through a series of questions designed to build examiners' ethos? Do they make subsequent use of matters raised under cross-examination?

8.) **Courtesy:** Do the speakers exhibit a respect for their opponents and the audience, and the worth of ideas?

SPECIAL NOTE: If this debate is on the "CEDA" resolution, it may be a "Value-oriented" proposition. If so, some specific aspects of "policy" debate, such as plans, traditional disadvantages and inherency arguments, may not be appropriate. Also, CEDA stresses debate adaptation to the audience, even if that audience is a single judge. They may use wit and humor to PERSUADE you, as well as all of the traditional techniques of sound argumentation covered by the 8 categories above. Remember, the debaters are **learners,** help them to become better advocates by rewarding them when they skillfully use tools of argumentation and persuasion to communicate their ideas to you in a clear, complete, logical, analytical, organized, evidenced, and pleasant manner. The debaters and their teachers depend on your comments for feedback in these areas in order to learn. Please assist them in learning by providing as specific and extensive commentary as appropriate. Thank you for your time in this effort. ©1981 by

use different philosophic approaches — or different decision-making paradigms — in answering this question.[4]

A. The Skills Judge

The *skills judge* focuses on the skills listed on the AFA ballot — analysis, reasoning, evidence, organization, refutation, and delivery — and carefully evaluates which team has argued better with regard to each of these skills. The judge in this case does *not* merely assign points and add up the score to "find out who won." The ballot is an instrument the judge uses to *report* decisions. Skills judges base their decision on their total knowledge of argumentation and debate and recognize that, although the skills are given equal weight in the ballot in an actual debate, one or two skills might outweigh all the others and constitute the reason for the decision. (For example, one team's use of evidence or its analytic skill in developing a particular critical issue might be decisive.)

B. The Issues Judge

The *issues judge* focuses on the stock issues (considered on pp. 55–59, Chapter 4). In order to win the decision from such a judge, the affirmative must win all of the stock issues, whereas the negative need win only one stock issue to win the debate. The affirmative is not required to win every argument and every contention in the debate, but it must win each stock issue. Note that issues are won or lost *in comparison* to the arguments of the opposing team. A negative team might establish that the affirmative's plan will cause substantial disadvantages. To win this issue, however, the negative must demonstrate that the disadvantage has greater impact than the significance of the need itself. If, in debating the "consumer safety" proposition, an affirmative argues that the lack of mandatory air bags in automobiles caused 14,000 deaths per year (thus establishing the significance of the need it claims that the plan would solve), and the negative argues as a disadvantage that the accidental deployment of air bags would cause 500 deaths a year, the affirmative clearly wins by saving 13,500 more lives than the negative. The advantage outweighs the disadvantage.

C. The Policymaker Judge

The *policymaker judge* takes the perspective of a legislator evaluating competing policy systems. The judge evaluates the affirmative's policy system (that is, its plan) representing a departure from the status quo, contrasts it with the negative's policy system (for example, a defense of the status quo, repairs, a counterplan, an attack on the affirmative's plan as unworkable, or any of the other options open to the negative) and then decides whether or not the affirmative has offered a viable plan. If the affirmative's plan is viable, the judge will also require that it be better than the negative's policy system. The policymaker judge would agree with the issues judge cited previously: Saving 13,500 more lives is clearly the better policy (unless, of course, the

---

[4]John D. Cross and Ronald J. Matlon, "An Analysis of Judging Philosophies in Academic Debate," *Journal of the American Forensic Association*, Vol. 15, No. 2 (Fall 1978), pp. 110–123.

negative introduced a new issue and argued that the 500 lives lost in the accidental deployment of air bags was an involuntary loss of life—whereas the 14,000 lives lost by the lack of air bags represented a voluntary assumed risk—and that consumers should be free to choose whether or not they want air bags in their cars). If this argument were introduced, the judge then would have to weigh it in the policy decision.

D. The Hypothesis-Testing Judge

The *hypothesis-testing judge* takes the perspective of a scientist seeking to determine the probable truth of a hypothesis. Unlike the policymaker judge, the hypothesis-testing judge does not seek to compare two policy systems. Rather, he or she is testing the hypothesis (that is, the affirmative case) alone. Thus the negative is free to defend anything or everything that is nontopical. If the negative demonstrates that no need exists for the proposition, the hypothesis-testing judge would conclude that the hypothesis is not true and should not be adopted. The hypothesis-testing judge tends to be receptive to conditional and hypothetical counterplans.

E. The Tabula Rasa Judge

The *tabula rasa judge* takes the position of having no judging philosophy and allows and expects the debaters to decide the theoretical framework for the decision as the debate evolves. Thus, if the affirmative is using a stock issue case and argues successfully that the debate should be decided on stock issues, this judge will vote for the affirmative if it carries the stock issues. If the negative offers a conditional counterplan and argues successfully that the judge should function as a hypothesis tester, the judge will vote for the negative if it carries the conditional counterplan. If neither team chooses to argue the judging philosophy, the judge may decide that a certain type of judging philosophy is implicit in the way the debate evolves and choose that philosophy as the basis for decision. If no judging philosophy emerges as clearly implicit in the debate, this judge may decide to select any one of the philosophies to use as the basis for decision.

F. Significance to the Debater

We have considered five different judging philosophies. As the debaters usually will not know the philosophy of the judge, the question arises: How can debaters adapt to the situation?[5] Two considerations are: First the debater should know argumentation theory and be prepared to argue that the judge should serve, for example, as an issues judge for "this" debate if the debater intends to argue the case on issues. Second, although judges have their preferences for specific judging philosophies, most judges are willing to consider arguments about judging philosophies from the debaters and

[5]Sometimes, of course, the judge will have judged one or both teams in a round previously, and from reading the judge's ballots from previous tournaments the debaters will know the judge's philosophy. At the National Debate Tournament and at district tournaments, judging philosophy booklets—in which the judges state their judging philosophy—are distributed to the debaters. As a practical matter, however, the debaters will know the judge's judging philosophy in only a very small minority of their debates.

apply the model most appropriate to a specific debate. Indeed, Cross and Matlon have found that "the majority of judges in the academic debate community view debates with extraordinary consensus regardless of their stated judging philosophies."[6]

We have considered the major decision-making paradigms used in academic debate. Students should be aware that in other forums the decision renderers often will have formulated decision-making paradigms they deem appropriate to the subject or occasion. Although these paradigms may not be as clearly stated or as precisely articulated as are the paradigms for academic debate, they are important and the advocate must discover them. (See Chapter 15, Section I, "Analysis of the Audience.") When necessary, the advocate must be prepared to debate the paradigm for decision as well as the issues and evidence relating to the resolution.

III. Functions of the Ballot

A. Reporting the Decision

The *ballot* is, in the first instance, an instrument for reporting the judge's decision. The debaters and the tournament director in a tournament situation want to know who won. The ballot furnishes this information.

B. Reporting the Quality of the Debaters' Work

For educational purposes, debaters should know not only the judges' decisions on debates, but also the judges' evaluation of the quality of their debating. Reference to the quality points tells how the judge evaluated their work, and it also indicates how the judge evaluated their work in comparison to that of the other participants in the debate. The quality points and rank may also be critical information to the tournament director as a means of determining speaker awards and as a device for breaking ties in a tournament. A tie in a debate is, of course, a logical impossibility.[7]

C. Serving as an Educational Tool

At the conclusion of the debate or tournament, the ballots are distributed to the participants. The ballots thus become available to the director of forensics as an important educational tool. After a tournament, debate directors often arrange conferences in which they review the judges' evaluations with each student. Although the quality of a student's work will vary from one debate to another and different judges may place a somewhat different emphasis on different aspects of argumentation, the reports of the student's work in a number of different debates as recorded by a number of different judges provide important insights into the student's ability and allow the director to plan a program of further study and training suited to the student's needs.

[6]Ibid., p. 123.
[7]See: Chapter 3 (Section III), "Presumption and Burden of Proof."

Although forensic directors ordinarily do not judge an intercollegiate debate involving a team from their own schools, they will judge many debates between their own students as they prepare for intercollegiate debates. The evaluations given at this time are often a most valuable part of the students' education. Usually time is available for a much more detailed critique than is possible in other circumstances. Since the directors have seen the students debate many times, often over a period of several years, they have considerable knowledge about their students' abilities and limitations and more insight into a student's problems than a judge who sees the student only once.

IV. Special Ballots for Special Purposes

The ballot presented on p. 289 may be used for most types of debate.[8] The exceptions are the Town Hall format of debate, which uses a division of the house, and Parliamentary debate, which may use any of the various methods of voting. In addition, audience-decision debating and Lincoln-Douglas debating require special ballots.

A. Ballot for Lincoln-Douglas Debating

Lincoln-Douglas debating requires a special ballot, since only two debaters participate in the debate. The AFA Form H ballot, shown on p. 295, is designed for use with these debates.

B. Ballot for Shift-of-Opinion Debating

Since lay audiences obviously lack the qualifications necessary to evaluate the debate as an educational process, their decision has value only when the merits of the proposition are being considered or when certain data are being collected for research purposes. An audience-decision ballot is sometimes used as a device to heighten audience interest. In such cases, a shift-of-opinion ballot may be used. The ballot shown on p. 296, a modification of the Woodward Ballot,[9] provides a means of compensating for the lack of understanding of the principles of argumentation and debate found among most audiences. Members of the audience are simply asked to state their beliefs about the proposition before and after hearing the debate, and the decision is based on the shift of audience opinion. At the conclusion of the debate, the ballots are collected and tabulated as those recording a shift to the affirmative, those reporting no change, and those reporting a shift to the negative. The team that has effected the greater shift of opinion is determined by an inspection of the tabulation. The results obtained by this method may be regarded as interesting but not necessarily significant. Carefully controlled tests of statistical reliability are necessary to guard against chance variables. These controls, or the use of other experimental methods,

[8]See: Chapter 18, Modern Procedures: Academic Debate Formats.
[9]See: Howard S. Woodward, "Measurement and Analysis of Audience Opinion," *Quarterly Journal of Speech*, Vol. 14 (February 1928), pp. 94–111.

AMERICAN FORENSIC ASSOCIATION

FORM **H**

LINCOLN-DOUGLAS DEBATE BALLOT

Round _____ Room _____ Date _____ Judge _____

	Name-Code	Points		Name-Code	Points
Aff.	_____	_____	Neg.	_____	_____

Scale: | 12-15 | 16-19 | 20-23 | 24-27 | 28-30 |
| Below Average | Average | Excellent | Outstanding | Exceptional |

COMMENT/RECOMMENDATION (REGARDING ANALYSIS, SUPPORT, REFUTATION, DELIVERY):

AFF.

NEG.

REASONS FOR DECISION (MIGHT INCLUDE ISSUES, REASONABLENESS OF POSITION, PERSUASION):

IN MY OPINION, THE BETTER DEBATING WAS DONE BY _____ REPRESENTING _____

CODE

AFF./NEG.

_____
SIGNATURE OF JUDGE

_____
AFFILIATION

UNIVERSITY DEBATING TEAMS

Audience Shift-of-Opinion Ballot

INSTRUCTIONS TO THE AUDIENCE:

The debaters will appreciate your interest and cooperation if you will, both before and after the debate, indicate on this ballot your personal opinion on the proposition of debate.
The proposition is: "Resolved: That (the proposition of debate is stated here)."

BEFORE THE DEBATE
FILL OUT THIS SIDE

(Check one)

_____ I believe in the
affirmative of the
resolution.

_____ I am undecided.

_____ I believe in the
negative of the
resolution.

AFTER THE DEBATE
FILL OUT THIS SIDE

(Check one)

_____ I believe more strongly in
the affirmative than I did.

_____ I believe in the
affirmative of the
resolution.

_____ I am undecided.

_____ I believe in the
negative of the
resolution.

_____ I believe more strongly in
the negative than I did.

---

require more elaborate statistical procedures than are practical for the average academic debate.

In presenting debates before popular audiences, the student gains valuable experience in addressing large groups and has an opportunity to analyze and adapt to the popular audience. Audience-judges challenge the student to win a popular response, whereas educator-judges challenge the student to win a critical response. It is educationally necessary that students have their work evaluated by persons who know more about argumentation and debate than the students do — the educators — rather than by persons who know less about argumentation and debate than they do — the popular audience. It is inherent in our tradition of liberal education that students should seek the highest rather than the lowest common denominator.

Exercises

1. Arrange for a debate to be presented in class. During the debate, members of the class will take comprehensive notes on the debate. Following the debate, they will complete the ballot chosen by your instructor. After the ballots are completed, hold a class discussion in which the decisions of the members of the class are considered and any differences in their decisions and quality ratings are analyzed.

2. Arrange for a debate to be presented in class. Have the class use the shift-of-opinion ballot presented on p. 296.

3. Attend an intercollegiate debate and prepare a ballot, chosen by your instructor, recording your decision on the debate. If possible, secure a copy of the ballot used by the judge for that debate. Write a brief paper in which you report your decision and that of the judge. What factors most influenced your decision? If your decision differs from that of the judge, what factors do you think account for the difference?

4. What judging philosophy would you prefer a judge to use when you are debating? Write a brief paper in which you state your preferences, and give good reasons to justify your preferences. If time permits, your instructor may arrange a class discussion on these papers.

18

Modern Procedures: Academic Debate Formats

Although debating is as old as civilization itself, the procedures of debating have evolved and changed considerably over the centuries. Academic debating today, while retaining the essential values of debating in ancient times, is an interesting example of rapid change as it adapts its form to contemporary interests. To gain the full benefit of academic debate, the student should be cognizant of its various formats.

I. Formats of Debate

The various formats of academic debate have certain common elements: (1) Both sides must have an equal number of speakers; (2) both sides must have an equal amount of time; and (3) the affirmative must speak first and last.

The First National Developmental Conference on Forensics has recommended that "More frequent use of alternative events and formats in forensics should be encouraged."

A. Standard Format

The standard format was *the* format of American collegiate debating from the 1940s to the mid-1970s when it was overtaken in popularity by the cross-examination format. We mention it first here because it is still used by many professors of argumentation as a starting point for their students, and a number of novice tournaments make use of this format. The organization of this format is as follows:

First affirmative	Ten minutes
First negative	Ten minutes
Second affirmative	Ten minutes
Second negative	Ten minutes
First negative rebuttal	Five minutes
First affirmative rebuttal	Five minutes
Second negative rebuttal	Five minutes
Second affirmative rebuttal	Five minutes

B. Cross-Examination Format

The most widely used format in college debating is cross-examination. Two popular organizations of this format are as follows:

	CEDA	NDT
First affirmative constructive	Eight minutes	Ten minutes
Cross-examination by second negative	Three minutes	Three minutes
First negative constructive	Eight minutes	Ten minutes
Cross-examination by first affirmative	Three minutes	Three minutes
Second affirmative constructive	Eight minutes	Ten minutes
Cross-examination by first negative	Three minutes	Three minutes
Second negative constructive	Eight minutes	Ten minutes
Cross-examination by second affirmative	Three minutes	Three minutes
First negative rebuttal	Four minutes	Five minutes
First affirmative rebuttal	Four minutes	Five minutes
Second negative rebuttal	Four minutes	Five minutes
Second affirmative rebuttal	Four minutes	Five minutes

Edward Bennett Williams, once called "the country's hottest criminal lawyer," gave this tough but practical advice on the most difficult of trial techniques, cross-examination:

> It is . . . the art of putting a bridle on a witness who has been called to do you harm, and of controlling him so well that he helps you. You must think of him as a man with a knife in his hand who is out to stab you, and you must feel your way with him as if you were in a dark room together. You must move with him, roll with him. You must never explore or experiment during cross examination. *You must never ask a question if you do not already know the answer.* If you do know it and the witness refuses to say what you know, you can slaughter him. Otherwise he may slaughter you. Never attack a point that is unassailable. And if you hit a telling point, try not to let the witness know it. Keep quiet and go on. The time to dramatize it to the jury is during your closing argument.[1]

[1]*Life* magazine, June 22, 1959, p. 116. Used by permission of Edward Bennett Williams and *Life*. (Italics added.)

All of the considerations of argumentation and debate apply to cross-examination debate. In addition, certain considerations arise from the form of this debate. Let us examine some of the considerations of cross-examination, beginning with the questioner:

1. Some portions of your opponent's speech may have been unclear — either by accident or design. Cross-examination affords an opportunity to clarify them.
   Q: *Your plan calls for placing a space station in orbit. What sort of an orbit will that be?*
   A: *Geosynchronous. That way we will be able to . . .*
   Q: *Thank you. That's what I wanted to know.*
   This brief exchange clarified the affirmative's plan. The negative now knows that the affirmative is going to use a high orbit that will be far more costly than a low orbit and will present many technical difficulties. With the now-clarified plan before them, the negative can begin to develop plan attacks specific to the type of orbit the affirmative is now committed to using in their plan.
2. If you know of a defect in your opponent's evidence, cross-examination gives you an excellent opportunity to expose it.
   Q: *You justify your plan for greater freedom for law-enforcement agencies by claiming that crime increased 16 percent last year?*
   A: *Yes, and not only last year; it has been a steady trend.*
   Q: *And the source of your evidence was?*
   A: *The Boston Globe.*
   Q: *And where did the Globe get its figures?*
   A: *[Consulting card] From, er, let me see. From the FBI. Yes, from an FBI report.*
   Q: *From the FBI report. Thank you, we'll come to that later. Now . . .*
   You will recall that this example was used in Chapter 6. The questioner has now established the source of the affirmative's evidence. In the next speech the negative will certainly emphasize the flaw in that evidence. You may recall that the FBI had warned against using these statistics to make year-to-year comparisons.
      Let's consider another example:
   Q: *You claim industry will move to escape environmental controls?*
   A: *Right. They certainly will.*
   Q: *Would you please read that card? I think it was the . . .*
   A: *State Street Report. "When faced with unreasonably high taxes and excessive regulation, industry will give serious consideration to their option to move to a location that offers a more favorable business climate."*
   Q: *That specifically says a combination of high taxes and unreasonable regulations, doesn't it?*
   A: *Well, er, yes, but I think the focus is . . .*
   Q: *Does the evidence say that any industry moved because of environmental regulations alone?*
   A: *Er, no, I don't think so. Not in this report, but environmental controls are a part of it.*
   Q: *Does the State Street Report specifically mention environmental controls?*
   A: *It cites "unreasonable regulations" and many of the . . .*

Q: No mention of environmental controls. Thank you. And it said industry would consider moving, didn't it?
A: Yes, and they have moved.
Q: Does your evidence say so?
A: Well, no, not this evidence. We have other evidence that my partner will read...
Q: We'll be looking for it in her speech. But so far there is no evidence of industry moving; no evidence about environmental controls. Thank you.

This cross-examination has given the questioner an opportunity to point out important flaws in the evidence. If the respondent's partner fails to provide the promised new evidence in her speech, the questioner's colleague should be prepared to point that out.

3. Cross-examination may be used to advance your position.
Q: You didn't respond to our argument that unemployment will persist, did you?
A: No. We give you that.

This brief exchange allowed the debater to emphasize that the other team had dropped an argument. The "development of space" resolution provides another example:

Q: Our evidence says that industry will make billions in the space station, doesn't it?
A: Yes, but industry is reluctant to go into space.
Q: You mean industry is reluctant to make billions in profits?
A: No. They're reluctant because they're not certain that the station will be built.
Q: Our plan mandates that the space station will be built, doesn't it?
A: Yes, but...
Q: And industry will certainly want those billions of dollars of profit, won't they?
A: Well, once it's built...
Q: Thank you.

4. Cross-examination may be used to respond to an attack made on your position.
Q: In your workability attack you said our plan wouldn't work because the people in the space station would get sick.
A: Right. The evidence shows they develop low blood pressure and lose bone marrow. Both Russians and Americans. And it takes three months...
Q: They get low blood pressure. So what?
A: Low blood pressure isn't good for you.
Q: Does the evidence say that?
A: Well, no, but everybody knows that low blood pressure...
Q: The evidence doesn't say it's low enough to do any harm, does it?
A: It says they develop low...
Q: The evidence doesn't say it gets low enough to stop them from working, does it?
A: Well, no, but everyone knows low blood pressure...
Q: No significance shown in low blood pressure. Now, about the bone marrow — so what?
A: They lose 5 percent of their bone marrow, and it takes three months to get it back to normal. Both Russians and Americans.

Q: Again no significance. The evidence doesn't say that they can't work, does it?
A: It does say that it takes them three months to . . .
Q: And they're back to normal. But the evidence doesn't attach any significance to a 5-percent loss, does it?
A: I certainly think it's significant.
Q: Do the physicians who made the report say it's significant?
A: Well, what they say is . . . they report . . . they report low blood pressure and loss of bone marrow.
Q: And in neither case do they say it's significant. Thank you.

Here the debater defended his case by establishing that the workability attack had no significance.

5. Questioners should avoid "open-ended" questions that allow the respondent freedom to roam at will.

Q: Do you think your "Star Wars" plan will work?
A: It certainly will. The Teller evidence makes it clear that it is entirely feasible. The Hearings prove that we have the technology. We can have everything in place and working by the early 1990s. We think that . . .

The "do you think" opening gives respondents license to say anything they want to. Of course, they think their position is favorable and will use this opportunity to advance it.

Lawyer and best-selling author Scott Turow admonishes, "A good trial lawyer never asks why, unless he knows the answer."[2] Turow echoes Williams' wise advice considered earlier (p. 299). Like the "do you think" opening, a "why" question invites respondents to give the best possible reasons for their position.

Further considerations of the questioner include:

6. Questioners should try to elicit brief responses (although questioners may not require a "yes" or "no" answer). They may not cut off a reasonable qualification, but they may cut off a verbose response with a statement such as "Thank you, that gives us enough information" or "That's fine, thank you. That makes your position clear."

7. Questioners should not develop arguments on the responses obtained during cross-examination. Cross-examination is a time for asking questions and getting responses. The significance of the responses should be argued in the constructive speeches or in rebuttal.

8. Questions should be brief and easily understandable. Rambling, ambiguous questions may confuse the opponent, but they may also confuse those who render the decision. Respondents would certainly ask for a clarification of such questions, and the resultant waste of time would reduce the number of questions that could be asked.

9. Questioners may set the stage for a question. For example, "You know, of course, that President Bush has announced his support for . . ."

10. Questioners should never ask a question unless they already know the answer. Remember the attorney Williams's advice given earlier.

[2]Scott Turow, *Presumed Innocent* (New York, Farrar, Straus & Giroux, 1987), p. 324.

11. Questioners should not attempt to attack unassailable points. Some of the arguments in the respondents' case will probably be so well established as to be irrefutable. An unsuccessful attack on them will merely make their strength more obvious to those who render the decision. Questioners should focus on the points they can carry.

12. Remember that the whole purpose of asking questions in cross-examination is to obtain information that you can *use* to your advantage in your *next speech*. Make notes of your questions and the responses you receive on your flow sheet—the judge will be doing this as well—so that you can refer to them directly. Don't assume that the significance of an opponent's response is self-evident. Drive your point home to your audience in your next speech.

> In cross-examination Gail admitted that their space station would be in geosynchronous orbit. Let's see what that really means in terms of cost...
>
> Roger admitted in cross-examination that their figures on increased crime came from the FBI. Now I'm going to tell you what the FBI itself said about using those figures for year-to-year comparisons...
>
> Remember when I asked Mark about the significance of his claim that people get sick in space stations? He couldn't give you any significance of low blood pressure. None. Again on bone marrow—Mark couldn't give you any significance there either. There's no significance shown in their workability attack...

Considerations for the respondent include:

1. Respondents must keep in mind that each question is designed to destroy their case or to advance the case of their opponents. Consequently, they must constantly be on guard.

2. Respondents must answer any reasonable question.

3. Respondents may refuse to answer ambiguous or "loaded" questions. Questions of the "Have you stopped cheating on examinations?" variety can be rejected by demonstrating that the question is ambiguous or "loaded" and by requesting a more reasonable rephrasing of the question.

4. Respondents may qualify their response. The "Yes, but..." qualification is weak. It is better to give the qualification first and then give a direct response.

   Q: *Do you believe that all branches of government should be responsive to the will of the people?*

   A: *I believe that the Supreme Court is responsive to the will of the people by protecting their Constitutional rights. With this important Constitutional safeguard, I would say that government should be responsive to the will of the people.*

5. Respondents must answer from their perspective. (See Chapter 15, Section V-C.) Real estate tycoon Donald Trump provides an excellent example of this: "When a reporter asks why I build only for the rich, I note that the rich aren't the only ones who benefit from my buildings. I explain that I put thousands of people to work who might otherwise be collecting unemployment, and that I add to the city's tax base every time I build a new project."[3]

---

[3]Donald J. Trump, *The Art of the Deal* (New York: Random House, 1987), p. 40.

6. Respondents should promptly admit not knowing the answer to a question.
   Q: *Do you know what methodology Kwarciany and Langer used in their study?*
   A: *They're reputable scholars. I'm sure they used an appropriate methodology. But, no, I don't know their exact methodology.*
7. Respondents should not attempt to defend an indefensible point. It is better to yield a point immediately than to allow questioners to wring admissions from the respondents in a series of questions that will only fix the point more firmly in the mind of those who render the decision.

Next we will examine some considerations that apply to both questioners and respondents:

1. The questions should focus primarily on arguments developed in the speech of the respondent. However, questions about arguments in a previous speech by the respondent's colleague, or any matter relevant to the proposition, are admissible.
2. The questioner and the respondent should treat each other with courtesy. Sarcasm, "browbeating," or obvious evasion will boomerang to the discredit of the one using them.
3. Both the questioner and the respondent should bear in mind that they are not conducting a private conversation but are asking questions and giving responses designed to have an effect upon the judge and audience. To facilitate communication with the audience, both speakers stand and face the audience during the question period.
4. Once the questioning has begun, neither the questioner nor the respondent may consult a colleague.
5. Finally, a special consideration for both questioners and respondents is: *practice.* Once you have prepared your affirmative case or your negative briefs, practice cross-examination. Give thoughtful consideration to the questions that a skilled opponent will ask. What are the points of your case that are most vulnerable to attack? What questions can hurt you most? What are the questions you will have the most difficulty answering? Ask yourself these questions *before* the debate, or have your partner ask them of you. Plan in advance how you will answer them. Work over your answers and rephrase them until you have concise, convincing, and effective responses. If you find some positions in your case or briefs that will not stand up under vigorous questioning, *now* — before the debate — is the time to redraft your position.

   In the same manner, plan in advance the questions you will ask of your opponent. What arguments is your opponent most likely to advance? What questions will you ask? How will your opponent most likely respond to those questions? How will you follow up on that response? Will a skilled opponent give a response that will help or hurt you? If it will help you, plan how you will follow up on it with further questions or with analysis and argument in your speech. If a question or line of questions does nothing for you or is likely to work against you, abandon that approach before the debate begins.

In summary, when cross-examination is used, it is an essential part of the debate and the advocate must prepare for it with the same care given to all other parts of the debate. This preparation should include planning and carefully phrasing the questions and answers you anticipate using. This practice must include an analysis of those who will render the decision. As we saw earlier (in Chapter 15, Section I), Governor Dukakis had apparently anticipated and planned for a question about capital punishment in his second debate with then Vice President Bush. His preparation, however, apparently did not include an analysis of how the audience would react to his calm and dispassionate response.

Advocates preparing for cross-examination might find it helpful to arrange with friends to emulate the "murder boards" used to prepare federal officials for Congressional cross-examination.

> It's called a "murder board" in the trade, and Dr. Louis W. Sullivan has been getting "murdered" regularly for the last week. "Murder board" is Washington jargon for a mock hearing, where officials who are about to face Congressional questioning train for the event.
>
> And Dr. Sullivan, President Bush's choice to head the Department of Health and Human Services, has gone through this grueling process three times with aides firing questions at him and picking apart his answers.
>
> After those sessions, Dr. Sullivan wearily told friends this week, "I find that I need to learn the language, the culture, and the etiquette of Washington so I'm not misunderstood."[4]

As the "murder boards" make clear, it is not sufficient to have *an* answer to a question in cross-examination. The answer must be phrased in a way to make a favorable impression on those who render the decision.

C. Lincoln-Douglas Format

The Lincoln-Douglas format is simply a two-person debate, named in honor of the two famous debaters who used this form. Interest in this format is growing in high schools and colleges and in politics, where the tendency is increasing for opposing candidates to meet in debate before the voters. The famous Kennedy-Nixon debates marked the first time in American history that Presidential candidates met in debate in the tradition of Lincoln and Douglas.

The organization of this format is as follows:

Affirmative constructive	Six minutes
Cross-examination by negative	Three minutes
Negative constructive	Seven minutes
Cross-examination by affirmative	Three minutes
Affirmative rebuttal	Four minutes
Negative rebuttal	Six minutes
Affirmative rebuttal	Three minutes

The time limits suggested here are often used in the classroom. In political debate, the time limits are usually tailored to radio or television requirements.

4*New York Times*, February 5, 1989, p. 20.

Customary Arrangements

Formats A through C are conducted in approximately the same manner. Formats D through F require certain special arrangements (see the discussion of each type).

- The physical arrangements customarily include a chair and a table placed at the rear center of the platform for the chairperson, a lectern placed at the front center of the platform for the speakers' use and a table and two chairs placed at each side of the platform for the debaters. Customarily, the affirmative is seated at the chairperson's right. The timekeeper is usually seated in the first row of the audience and is provided with a set of time cards (usually twelve 3 × 4 cards of light cardboard held together by a metal binding and bearing the markings: 10, 9, 8, 7, 6, 5, 4, 3, 2, 1, ½, STOP) and a stopwatch. The judge or judges are seated at convenient places in the audience and are provided with ballots on which to record their decisions and flow sheets on which to take notes during the debate. If the chairs in the room are not designed with a writing surface, clipboards should also be provided.

- The chair announces the proposition of debate and introduces the speakers to the audience. He or she may make other introductory remarks if appropriate, but the remarks should be brief and should not express any opinion on the proposition under debate.

- The timekeeper holds the cards so that they are constantly visible to the speaker, adjusting the cards each minute (each thirty seconds for the last two cards) to show the speaking time remaining. In tournament debates, the timekeeper also keeps track of "prep time." In many tournaments, although never in public debates, each team is allowed ten minutes of preparation time to use at its discretion. (For example, after the first affirmative speech, the first negative speaker may, in agreement with his or her partner, take several minutes to prepare before beginning the first negative speech, and so on for the interval between each of the remaining speeches.) The timekeeper announces the "time remaining" audibly at one-minute intervals (e.g., "The negative has seven minutes remaining"). It a team exceeds its prep time, any excess time is deducted from its speaking time.

- At the conclusion of the debate, the timekeeper collects the ballots from the judges and hands them to the chair, who announces the decision. If a critic judge is used rather than a panel of judges, the chair may by prearrangement invite the judge to give a critique and announce the decision. If an audience-decision ballot is used, the timekeeper and one or two assistants should collect the ballots at the conclusion of the debate. If a forum period is allotted, the ballots may be tabulated during this time and the result announced at the conclusion of the questions.

- In tournaments, since a number of debates are conducted simultaneously, no chair presides—only a timekeeper and a single judge in the preliminary rounds, or a panel of judges in the elimination rounds. In most tournaments, decisions are not announced at the conclusion of individual debates but are published at the conclusion of the tournament.

D. Mock Trial Format

The mock trial format emulates trial court debating. In mock trial debate the emphasis is on debate and argumentation skills and on cross-examination. This differs from moot court debate (see p. 15), widely used in law schools, which is very much concerned with the sometimes highly technical rules of procedure and which may emulate the appellate court rather than the trial court.

Instead of a proposition the debaters are provided with the facts of a legal case. The case may be a criminal one, in which case the affirmative becomes the prosecution and the negative becomes the defense; or a civil suit, in which case the affirmative is the plaintiff and the negative is the defendant.

This format is a popular exercise in argumentation and debate classes. Members of the class are assigned the various roles. Both sides are limited to the information about the case provided by the instructor. No additional information may be introduced into the mock trial. In the following format substitute plaintiff's attorney for prosecuting attorney if the case is a civil one.

Judge gives background information and outlines the procedure.	*Three minutes*
Prosecuting attorney outlines the case.	*Three minutes*
Defense attorney outlines the defense.	*Three minutes*
Prosecuting attorney calls three witnesses, and questions each one for four minutes.	*Twelve minutes*
Defense attorney may cross-examine each witness, asking each one a maximum of three questions.	*Six minutes*
Defense attorney calls three witnesses, and questions each one for four minutes.	*Twelve minutes*
Prosecuting attorney may cross-examine each witness, asking each one a maximum of three questions.	*Six minutes*
Defense attorney sums up and makes final plea.	*Three minutes*
Prosecuting attorney sums up and makes final plea.	*Three minutes*
The judge instructs the jury.	
The jury votes.	

E. Town Hall Format

The town hall format has been used at a number of Speech Communication Association conventions to debate issues of professional interest. This format may be used for any matter of interest to the participants and audience. A popular variation for campus debates provides for a student and a faculty member to serve as "kick-off" speakers for the motion and another student-faculty team to serve as "kick-off" speakers against the motion. (See points 3 through 6 below.)

Format

1. The Chair opens the debate by announcing the motion before the house and reviewing the rules of procedure.
2. The Chair introduces each of the four kick-off speakers in order.

3. A seven-minute speech moving the adoption of the motion.
4. A seven-minute speech opposing the motion.
5. A seven-minute speech moving the adoption of the motion.
6. A seven-minute speech opposing the motion.
7. The floor is then open to audience members, who may speak *not more than three minutes*. The Chair recognizes speakers alternately for and against the motion. Preference shall be given to those who have not previously spoken.
8. The debate proceeds in this manner usually for not more than 60 minutes. The Chair then recognizes each of the kick-off speakers to summarize the arguments, first *against* and then *for* the motion. The summary speeches last no more than three minutes each.
9. The Chair calls for a division of the house and announces the result.

Procedural Guides

1. All action on the floor is channeled through the Chair. It is the prerogative of the Chair to exercise best judgment in any action not explicitly covered in these regulations.
2. Any speaker except the maker of the motion may be interrupted at any time if a member wishes to call attention to a violation of the rules by "rising to a point of order" or if he or she wishes to question the speaker "on a point of information." The speaker may refuse to answer the question or even to give the member a chance to ask it. He or she cannot refuse to yield for points of order. The time involving in stating the point of information is not charged against the speaker; the time consumed in giving the information is.
3. Only these points of order will be considered: objections to the behavior of an audience member; objections that the speaker's remarks are irrelevant.
4. The timekeeper will give each speaker a one-minute warning and a termination signal. Members must conclude their remarks on receiving the second signal.
5. Unused time of a speaker may not be passed to a speaker on the same side.
6. The resolution before the house may not be amended.

Seating

Those favoring the motion at the beginning of the debate shall seat themselves to the Chair's right; those opposed to the Chair's left. A section is provided for the undecided. If, as a result of the debating, at any time the sentiment of a member should change, the member should then move from undecided to decided or across the aisle and sit with the side the member now favors.

F. Parliamentary Format

Parliamentary debate is a specialized format involving the use of special procedures. This format is considered separately in Chapter 19.

II. The Audience

The First National Development Conference on Forensics recommended:

> Audience debating should be promoted through public appearances on the national proposition and on issues of local concern, as well as through tournaments, or rounds within tournaments, based on the audience vote model.

Directors of forensics regularly provide opportunities for their students to speak before a variety of audiences. Since a number of debates are conducted simultaneously in a tournament, the audience for any one debate is usually small. The debaters thus have an opportunity to adjust to a limited audience and can gain experience in directing arguments to the key individual (in this case, the judge) in that audience. In the final round of a tournament, which is usually well attended, the debaters have an opportunity to address an audience well versed in argumentation; and they now seek to influence several key individuals, since three or more experts usually serve as the panel of judges for the final round of a tournament.

In addition to the audiences found in tournaments, general public audiences may be found on the campus and in the community. Sizable campus audiences are usually obtained for debates with traditional rival institutions. However, since audiences that may be obtained on any one campus are usually limited in size, debates are sometimes presented before various community audiences. Schools, church groups, and civic and social organizations are often interested in securing debates for their programs. Community audiences may be used for tournament as well as individual debates. Local commercial radio and television stations, as well as educational radio and television stations, may be interested in carrying well-planned debates adapted to their special needs, thus offering debaters further opportunities to obtain experience in various types of communication situations.

The tournament situation makes provision for both the novice and the experienced debater. In fairness to both the student and the audience, the director of forensics usually assigns only the more proficient debaters to appear before campus and community audiences. Debates conducted before such groups require that the debaters undertake a careful audience analysis and make specific preparation in terms of the audience. Factors of audience analysis and adaptation are considered in Chapter 15.

Although it is hoped that debates presented before public audiences will be both interesting and profitable for the audience, they should never be regarded as entertainment. Debates presented before public audiences should be regarded as an opportunity to educate the student about audience analysis and to educate the audience about debate. The listeners, of course, may attend a debate for a variety of reasons. Some may want to gain more information about the subject of the debate; some may hope to use the debate process to help them arrive at a decision on the proposition. These reasons, however, are subordinate to the educational reasons for presenting the debate.

When critic judges are used in the public-audience debate situation, they can make a significant contribution to the audience's knowledge about debate by explaining the factors leading to a decision in a manner that will be interesting and informative to the audience as well as profitable for the debaters.

Suggestions for Adapting to Media

Public Address System

- Avoid the use of a public address system unless it is clearly needed for the speakers to be heard in the auditorium.
- If possible, test the public address system before the audience arrives.
- Before beginning a speech, adjust the microphone to a convenient height and place it in a convenient location—so that it is sufficiently close to you but does not obstruct your access to the lectern or your view of the audience.
- Allow the public address system to amplify your voice; do not shout into the microphone.
- Remain close to the microphone during your talk, adjusting your movements and gestures to the microphone, and avoid moving "off mike."

Radio

- Adapt your style as though you were speaking to two, three, or four persons seated in their living room.
- Since you cannot ordinarily use visual aids in a radio speech, you must depend on vivid and precise words to paint the desired pictures in the minds of your audience.
- If you use a manuscript (for plan or negative briefs), remember that you must simplify complex arguments and present them in a conversational manner.
- The format of radio debates must be adjusted to the time available. Sometimes only half-hour or fifteen-minute time segments are allotted for the debate. In such situations, the speeches should be short, with a frequent change of speakers. Sometimes a program format may evolve wherein the moderator addresses questions, based on the principal issues of the debate, to members of each team alternately, and they respond with a one- or two-minute answer; in other cases a modification of cross-examination debate may be used. The best format for radio debate is usually worked out in consultation between a director of forensics who knows the problems of debate and a radio producer who knows the problems of radio.

Television

- Keep in mind the same considerations of style that apply to radio in your television debates.

III. Adapting the Debate to Communications Media

The use of public address systems, radio, or television enables debaters to reach larger audiences and poses the problem of adapting the debate to the special requirements of the media to be utilized. The public address system requires only a simple adjust-

- You may use visual aids in television, and their use is often effective. Visual aids must be prepared in consultation with the television program director, so that they meet the special requirements of television and so that necessary arrangements are made to get them "on camera" at the proper time.
- Movements, gestures, or facial expressions can be seen by the audience and have value in communicating to the television audience. Movement must be within previously defined limits — the speaker must not move "off camera." Gestures and facial expression as well as movement should be restrained, since the camera will frequently take a tight head "shot" of the speaker.
- Dress is important in the televised debate. Participants should avoid large, bright pieces of jewelry and noisy bracelets. Everyone should avoid clothing with sharply contrasting colors or "busy" patterns. Both men and women may need makeup for color television; this special makeup is usually applied by a studio makeup artist. If you wear eyeglasses only occasionally, remove them to simplify the problem of light reflection. If you wear eyeglasses constantly, however, you should wear them during the telecast, since you will probably feel more comfortable and you will avoid the tendency to squint.
- Keep the use of a manuscript to an absolute minimum. Most program directors strongly prefer that the speaker use the extemporaneous manner of speaking with a minimum of notes.
- The style of television debates must be adjusted to the time available and to the special problems of the medium. The sketches on p. 312 indicate floor plans used in various television debates. (*M* designates the program moderator; *L*, the lectern; *D*, a debater; *J*, a judge; and *A*, an audience member who appears on camera.)

Plan I: The moderator and debaters are seated at an L-shaped table.

Plan II: The moderator is seated apart from the debaters' table and the debaters speak from the lectern.

Plan III: The judges and a number of audience members are seated on raised chairs in "jury box" style. (Two lecterns are provided so that the debaters may stand facing each other during cross-examination.)

---

ment; radio and television require a more complex adjustment and afford the opportunity to develop a type of debate specifically designed for the medium and for the specific broadcast situation (*see inset on pp.* 310–311).

Speakers sometimes must use radio or television at the same time that they are addressing an audience assembled before them. Adapting a style of debate or a style of speaking to two such different audience situations is difficult. Although some superior speakers are able to reach both audiences effectively, it is usually preferable to concentrate on one audience. For debaters, the problem is simple. They must direct their principal attention to the audience that will render the decision. Most political speakers consider radio or television audiences more important, because the media audiences include a greater number of voters who will render the decision with their

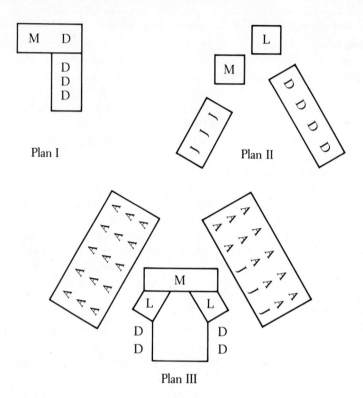

Plan I

Plan II

Plan III

ballots. Franklin Roosevelt was one of the first political speakers to make this decision. As early as 1928, he began to design some of his major political addresses primarily for the benefit of his radio audience and the press, rather than for the delegates and audience in the convention auditorium.

Present-day speakers sometimes have the problem of three audiences: the audience physically present before them, the radio audience, and the television audience. In such a situation, most speakers give priority to the television audience. Although speakers must decide which audience will receive principal attention, they should avoid any obvious neglect of the other audiences and should seek, insofar as possible, to include all audiences in the presentation. President Reagan—known to friends and opponents alike as "The Great Communicator"—was a master of this technique. His addresses to Congress often included specific references to representatives or senators present on the floor or to special guests present in the gallery, while he really concentrated on reaching the millions of television viewers.

In both radio and television debates, time is of great importance, and this factor places a premium on extemporaneous speeches, which allow speakers to condense or extend remarks as the situation may demand.

In television debates, two cameras are usually used; often one camera is turned on a participant other than the speaker to allow the audience to see various reactions to the speech. Speakers should direct their remarks to the "live" camera—the one with a small red light burning near the lens—unless the program format calls for addressing remarks to the moderator or to some other participant. If a monitor—a television set showing the program going out over the air — is in sight, the speakers should ignore it.

In general, television debates require more planning than radio debates, because the medium is more complex and the special problems of camera placement, sets, and lighting and the need for rehearsal time influence the format to be used. In planning the format of the television debate, debaters should remember that television is a *visual* medium; and the debate format should be selected and its presentation planned with this factor in mind.

Debaters should plan to arrive at the studio well ahead of broadcast or recording time to allow the producer or director to make the necessary arrangements: check for voice balance, adjust lighting, plan camera arrangements, and so on. For a radio debate, speakers should make a point of getting acquainted with the various signals that will be given from the control room as cues at different points during the program. For the television debate, speakers should make a point of acquainting themselves with the various signals the floor person will give from time to time during the debate, and they should prepare themselves to present their speeches in a conversational manner amid the apparent chaos of the movement of cameras and technicians during the broadcast.

Exercises

1. Plan and conduct a standard format debate in class. It may be necessary to modify the time limits to meet available class time.

2. Plan and conduct a cross-examination debate in class. It may be necessary to modify the time limits to meet available class time.

3. Plan and conduct in-class debates using some of the alternative formats considered in this chapter.

4. Listen to a radio debate. Prepare a written report (300 words) evaluating the effectiveness of the program format.

5. Watch a television debate. Prepare a written report (300 words) evaluating the effectiveness of the program format.

6. If audiotape-recording equipment is available, plan and record a debate using a format suitable for radio. Play the recording for the class. Conduct a discussion in which the class is invited to evaluate the effectiveness of the recording (a) as a debate and (b) as a format for radio debate.

7. If videotape-recording equipment is available, plan and record a debate using a format suitable for television. Play the recording for the class. Conduct a discussion in which the class is invited to evaluate the effectiveness of the recording (a) as a debate and (b) as a format for television debate.

8. As a class project, plan and conduct several debates before campus or community audiences.

19

Parliamentary Debate

Whenever a group finds it necessary or desirable to have formal debate, some rules for that debate must be provided to ensure order, efficiency, and impartiality. The law courts have special rules for debates conducted in the courtroom; the governing body of each city, town, or village conducts its debates under a special set of rules; civic, social, and business organizations have special sets of rules governing debate, as do the state legislatures and Congress. Parliamentary debate permits a large number of persons to participate and provides a means for a large group to reach a decision.

Parliamentary debate derives its name from the ancient parliaments of Britain. The details of parliamentary debate, however, vary from one group to another. The rules of debate for the British Parliament are different in many ways from the rules of debate in the American Congress. The rules of debate in the Senate, for example, are far too complicated and specialized for general use by other organizations. In fact, they are different in important aspects from the rules of debate in the House of Representatives. All well-conceived rules of parliamentary debate, however, have a common nature and certain common purposes.

Parliamentary debate provides for the orderly and efficient conduct of business. It does so by considering one matter at a time and by disposing of each matter before going on to another.

Parliamentary debate assures a decision. It does so by requiring that every motion must be acted upon in some way. Once a motion has been introduced, it must be passed, defeated, or postponed. A postponement, of course, is a decision *not* to pass a motion at the present time.

Parliamentary debate protects the rights of the majority. It does so by providing that the decisions of a sufficient number of members must prevail.

Parliamentary debate protects the rights of the minority. It does so by giving the minority many important privileges. For example, any member, without the necessity of securing a second, has the right to be heard on many important matters; only two members are required to introduce any motion; and one-third of the members plus one can exercise important restraints.

Parliamentary debate is impartial. Since the rules of procedure apply equally to all members, each member has an equal right to be heard and has equal voting power.

I. Sources of Parliamentary Debate Rules

Actually parliamentary debate has no one set of rules, although a body of commonly accepted practices and some legal requirements are recognized. As has been indicated, the two Houses of Congress do not debate under the same rules. The faculty and student governments of a university undoubtedly operate under different rules of parliamentary debate; and even two different clubs probably conduct their debates under somewhat different rules. Where, then, do the rules of parliamentary debate come from? Members of each group must adopt or create their own rules. If the decisions made by the group are of particular importance — for example, the decisions of a legislative body or a corporation — prudence dictates that those conducting the meeting have at hand expert parliamentarians familiar with general usage and attorneys familiar with the special laws applicable to the particular organization. For example, state laws, which differ considerably from one state to another, often dictate the methods of voting that must be used by corporations. For the average group, however, the problem is simpler. It is usually sufficient that its members follow one set of commonly accepted practices and make provision for their special needs. The rules of parliamentary debate for the average group come from five sources: (1) the constitution of the organization; (2) the bylaws of the organization; (3) the standing rules of the organization (which are recorded in the minutes of the organization); (4) the agenda of the meeting (although not necessary, an agenda is often convenient); (5) a stipulated source.

With the exception of national and state legislative bodies, very few organizations attempt to write their rules of parliamentary debate in full. Rather, most organizations provide a set of rules to take care of their most obvious needs and special requirements and then stipulate some source as the basis for rules not otherwise provided. Small groups, for instance, could stipulate the rules printed on pp. 320–321 as the source of their rules. Larger groups, or groups likely to be confronted with complicated problems, would select one of the various books devoted entirely to parliamentary procedure as the stipulated source of their rules.

Sometimes the special requirements of an organization make it desirable to set aside common usage in parliamentary practice. Groups that meet annually or infrequently often find it desirable to take from the motion to adjourn its customary privileged status and give it the lowest possible priority. This provision is usually unnecessary for groups that meet weekly, but it is often advisable for groups that meet only at infrequent intervals or in situations where a hastily passed motion to adjourn might seriously inconvenience the organization. Although deviations from common practice are sometimes desirable or necessary, they should be made infrequently and only after careful consideration of all of their implications.

II. Order of Business

The usual order of business for an organization using parliamentary procedure follows a clear, logical pattern.

The Call to Order: The call to order is usually a simple announcement by the chair: "The meeting will be in order" or "The National Convention of the Democratic [or Republican] Party is now in session."

The Roll Call: A roll call is taken only if one is required by the rules or customs of the organization. A roll call is a useful device in a larger organization; most smaller organizations find it unnecessary.

Reading of the Minutes of the Last Meeting: The minutes are usually read by the secretary in smaller organizations, although this reading may be omitted by unanimous consent. Larger organizations, and many smaller organizations as well, find it convenient to have the minutes printed or duplicated and distributed to the membership. Once the minutes have been presented, they may be corrected, amended, or accepted.

Reports of Standing Committees: Most organizations have various committees that are established by the constitution or whose duties continue for a long period of time, such as the executive committee or the finance committee. These committees report at this time.

Reports of Special Committees: Most organizations also have various committees that are appointed to serve for a shorter period of time or to deal with a special matter, such as a special fund-raising committee or the committee to recommend a site for next year's convention. These committees report at this time.

Unfinished Business: Unfinished business is that business not completed at the previous meeting. For example, if a motion was on the floor at the time the previous meeting adjourned, that motion now comes before the house as unfinished business. A motion that was postponed at a previous meeting, by a motion to postpone temporarily or "lay on the table," may be brought before the assembly at this time by a motion to resume consideration or "take from the table." The motion to postpone to a specified time often specifies that the motion shall come before the assembly as unfinished business at the next meeting.

New Business: Once the unfinished business has been disposed of, the floor is open to new business.

Miscellaneous: The last matter of business includes announcements and other miscellaneous items that may come before the group, such as "The executive committee will meet at eight o'clock" or "Members wishing to obtain tickets for the annual outing should see Bill Smith after this meeting."

Adjournment: Once the business of the meeting is completed, the chair may ask for a motion to adjourn. Such a motion may, however, be introduced earlier.

Larger organizations, or organizations that have many items of business to consider, find it convenient to prepare an *agenda*. An agenda is a special order of business, drawn up in advance of the meeting, which takes precedence over the usual order of business. The agenda may be changed by passing a motion setting a special order of business. The agenda often includes a detailed statement of the order in which reports will be presented and motions considered. When an organization's meetings extend over more than one day, it is particularly desirable to indicate in advance which matters will be considered on each day.

III. Presenting Motions

When motions are in order, a member who wishes to make a motion must first secure recognition from the chair. To gain recognition, the member rises and addresses the presiding officer: "Mr. Chairman" or "Madam Chairwoman." (If the constitution of the organization provides for a chairperson, the form of address is then "Mr. Chairperson" or "Ms. Chairperson.") The chair grants recognition by addressing the member: "Joe" would suffice in an informal group, "Mr. Smith" or "The delegate from Ohio" in a more formal group. If the member's name is not known, the chair may ask, "Will the member state his name?" The member replies, "Joe Smith, delegate from Ohio." In granting recognition, the chair replies, "The chair recognizes Mr. Smith from Ohio" (the chair always speaks in the third person; never, "I recognize...").

When several members seek recognition at the same time, the chair must decide which one to recognize. In granting recognition, the chair should consider the following factors:

1. Priority should first be given to the maker of the motion.
2. Priority should be given alternately to speakers favoring and opposing the motion if they are known to the chair. If the chair does not know which speakers favor or oppose the motion, he or she may state, "The chair will recognize a speaker favoring [or opposing] the motion."
3. Priority should be given to a member who has not spoken previously.
4. If none of the other considerations apply, the chair should, if possible, recognize the member who first sought recognition.

Once a member has gained recognition, he or she states the motion by saying "I move that..." In many organizations a member is required to give the secretary a written copy of the motion at the time it is introduced. The secretary has the privilege, should it be necessary, of interrupting a member to request a restatement of the motion so that it may be entered into the minutes accurately.

Before a main motion may be debated, it must be seconded by another member. Any other member, without the necessity of being recognized, may state, "I second the motion." If the motion is not seconded immediately, the chair may ask, "Is there a second?" If there is no second, the chair announces, "The motion is lost for lack of a second." The motion is then no longer before the house and a new motion is in order. If the motion is seconded, the chair announces, "It has been moved and seconded that . . ." and then recognizes the proposer of the motion to speak on that motion.

IV.   Precedence of Motions

In the interests of order and efficiency, a definite order of precedence of motions is followed. As shown in the table on pp. 320–321, the main motion has zero, or lowest, precedence, since it may be introduced only when no other business is before the house. Once a main motion is before the house, any of the other motions, when appropriate, may be applied to it. The highest precedence — 1 — is given to a motion to fix the time of the next meeting, and the other privileged motions follow this motion in precedence. The incidental motions rank after the privileged motions in precedence but have no precedence among themselves; they are considered in the order that they arise. The subsidiary motions follow the incidental motions in precedence and have a definite order of precedence among themselves. The table of precedence lists the motions most frequently used in parliamentary debate and the preferred rules applying to these motions. Some of the rules may be modified by special circumstances.

V.   Purposes of Motions

The four types of motions — *main, subsidiary, incidental,* and *privileged* — have different purposes, as outlined in detail below.

A.   Main Motions

Main motions bring substantive proposals before the house for consideration and decision. Main motions are the core of the conduct of business; they are the most important and most frequently used motions. Main motions are the *plan* by which the maker of the motion seeks to attain an objective. This may be very simple, such as a motion directing the treasurer to pay a small sum to the Scholarship Fund, or very complex. If the motion is other than very simple, the student will find it helpful to review the "Basic Plan Format" (see Chapter 12, Section III-A). The author of the plan illustrated in Exercise 6(g) at the end of this chapter had an easy task. This plan merely calls for an increase in an existing tax. The author had only to specify when the tax increases were to go into effect and to provide certain exemptions (the mandates). The agency to administer the excise tax and penalties to enforce it and the other elements of the plan are already in existence.

General Main Motion: To bring new business before the meeting.

Reconsider: To stop all action on a motion previously voted until the motion has been reconsidered. This motion may be made by any member (unless the rules of the organization specifically establish some limitation), but it may be made only the same day as the original motion was passed or on the next business day of a convention — *not* at the next weekly or monthly meeting or at the next convention. A motion to reconsider cannot be applied to a matter that has left the assembly. For example, if a motion has been passed directing the treasurer to pay five dollars to the Scholarship Fund and if the treasurer has already paid that money, the motion cannot be reconsidered. If carried, the motion to reconsider places the motion previously voted upon in the exact status it had before it was voted upon. If defeated, the motion to reconsider may not be renewed.

Rescind: To cancel an action taken at some previous meeting. This motion may be made at any time when other business is not before the meeting; it cannot be applied to a matter that has left the assembly.

Resume Consideration (take from the table): To bring a temporarily postponed motion (a motion that had been laid on the table) before the meeting in the same state that the motion held before it was postponed temporarily.

Set Special Order of Business: To set a date or time at which a certain matter will be considered.

B. Subsidiary Motions

Subsidiary motions are alternative aids for changing, considering, and disposing of the main motion. Consequently, they are subsidiary to the main motion.

Postpone Temporarily (lay on the table): To postpone consideration of a matter. This device may be used to allow more urgent business to come before the house or to allow time for some members to gather additional information before voting. It is also a way of "sidetracking" a matter in the hope that it will not be taken up again.

Vote Immediately (previous question): To close debate and bring the matter before the meeting to an immediate vote.

Limit or Extend Debate: To set, or extend, a limit on debate on a matter before the meeting.

Postpone to a Specified Time: To delay action on a matter before the meeting until a specified time.

Refer to Committee: To refer a matter before the meeting to a committee. If applied to an amendment, this motion also takes the main motion with it. It may be used to secure the advantage of having the matter studied more carefully by a small group, or to delay action on the matter.

Refer to the Committee of the Whole: To refer a matter to the committee of the whole, in order to debate the matter "off the record" and in the greater informality of the committee of the whole.

Amend on Amendment: To amend an amendment to a motion before the meeting. Most organizations find it advisable to prohibit an amendment to an amendment to an amendment.

Amend: To change a motion. A motion to amend may take any of four forms: (1) amend by striking out, (2) amend by substitution, (3) amend by addition, or (4) amend by dividing the motion into two or more parts.

Table of Precedence of Parliamentary Motions

Once a main motion is before the meeting, any of the following motions, when appropriate, may be made. In the following table the motions are arranged from the strongest—1—to the weakest—0. A stronger motion takes precedence over any weaker motion and becomes the business before the meeting.

Precedence Number	Interrupt Speaker?	Require a Second?	Debatable?	Vote Required?	Amendable?	Subject to Referral to Committee?	Subject to Postponement?	Subject to Reconsideration?
Privileged Motions								
1. Fix time of next meeting	No	Yes	No	Maj.	Yes¹	No	No	No
2. Adjourn	No	Yes	No	Maj.	No	No	No	No
3. Recess	No	Yes	No	Maj.	Yes	No	No	No
4. Question of privilege	Yes	No	No	Chr.	No	No	No	No
Incidental Motions								
Incidental motions are of equal rank among themselves; they are considered in the order they are moved.								
5. Appeal decision of the chair	Yes	Yes	Yes	Maj.	No	No	Yes	Yes
5. Close nominations	No	Yes	No	⅔	Yes¹	No	No	No
5. Division of the house	Yes	No	No	None	No	No	No	No
5. Object to consideration	Yes	No	No	⅔	No	No	No	No
5. Parliamentary inquiry	Yes	No	No	None	No	No	No	No
5. Point of order	Yes	No	No	Chr.	No	No	No	No
5. Suspension of rules	No	Yes	No	⅔	No	No	No	No
5. Request for information (Will the speaker yield for a question?)	Yes	No	No	Chr. or Speaker	No	No	No	No
5. Withdraw a motion	No	No	No	Maj.	No	No	No	No

Precedence Number	Interrupt Speaker?	Require a Second?	Debatable?	Vote Required?	Amend- able?	Subject to Referral to Committee?	Subject to Postpone- ment?	Subject to Recon- sidera- tion?
Subsidiary Motions								
6. Postpone temporarily (lay on the table)	No	Yes	No	Maj.	No	No	No	No
7. Vote immediately (previous question)	No	Yes	No	2/3	No	No	No	No
8. Limit or extend debate	No	Yes	No	2/3	Yes	No	No	No[4]
9. Postpone to a specified time	No	Yes	Yes	Maj.	Yes	No	No	No[4]
10. Refer to committee	No	Yes	Yes	Maj.	Yes	No	No	No[4]
11. Refer to the committee of the whole	No	Yes	Yes	Maj.	Yes	Yes	No	No
12. Amend an amendment	No	Yes	Yes	Maj.	No	Yes	Yes	Yes
13. Amend	No	Yes	Yes	Maj.	Yes	Yes	Yes	Yes
14. Postpone indefinitely	No	Yes	Yes	Maj.	No	No	No	No
Main Motions (Main motions are of equal rank among themselves. They have zero precedence since they may not be considered when any other motion is before the house.)								
0. General main motion	No	Yes	Yes	Maj.	Yes	Yes	Yes	Yes
0. Reconsider	Yes	Yes	Yes	Maj.	No	No	Yes[3]	No
0. Rescind	No	Yes	Yes	2/3[2]	Yes	Yes	Yes	Yes
0. Resume consideration (take from table)	No	Yes	No	Maj.	No	No	No	No[4]
0. Set special order of business	No	Yes	Yes	2/3	Yes	No	No	Yes

[1]Although the motion is not debatable, the amendment may be debated.
[2]Only a majority is required if previous notice has been given.
[3]May be postponed to a specified time only.
[4]Motion may be renewed after a change in the parliamentary situation.

Postpone Indefinitely: To suppress the main motion to which it is applied without the risk of adopting the main motion. This device is sometimes used to identify, without the risk of adopting the motion, who favors and who opposes it.

C. Incidental Motions

Incidental motions arise only incidentally out of the business before the house. They do not relate directly to the main motion but usually relate to matters that are incidental to the conduct of the meeting.

Appeal Decision of the Chair: To secure a reversal of a ruling by the chair.

Close Nominations: To prevent nomination of other candidates. Voting is *not* limited to those candidates who have been nominated.

Division of the House: To require a standing vote.

Object to Consideration: To prevent consideration of a matter.

Parliamentary Inquiry: To allow a member to ascertain the parliamentary status of a matter or to seek parliamentary information.

Point of Order: To demand that the chair rule on an alleged error, mistake, or violation of parliamentary procedure.

Suspension of Rules: To suspend rules to allow procedure contrary to certain rules of the organization.

Request for Information: To allow a member to ask the chair—or, through the chair, the speaker who has the floor—for information on a matter before the meeting.

Withdraw a Motion: To prevent action on a motion before the meeting.

D. Privileged Motions

Privileged motions have no direct connection with the main motion before the house. They relate to the members and to the organization rather than to substantive proposals. They deal with matters so urgent that they are entitled to immediate consideration. Privileged motions would be main motions except for their urgency. Because of their urgency, they are given the privilege of being considered ahead of other motions that are before the house.

Fix Time of Next Meeting: To fix a time at which the group shall meet next.

Adjourn: To close the meeting. This motion is also used to prevent further consideration of a matter before the meeting.

Recess: To suspend the meeting temporarily.

Question of Privilege: To request the chair to rule on a matter relating to the privileges of the assembly or the privileges of an individual member.

VI. Unanimous Consent

To expedite business on a routine or obviously desirable matter, any member may ask that approval for a certain course of action be given by unanimous consent. The chair will ask "Is there any objection?" and then, if no objection is made, will announce "Hearing none, it is so ordered." If any member objects, the required parliamentary procedure must be followed.

Exercises

1. Prepare a list of the organizations to which you belong that conduct their business through parliamentary debate. Evaluate the effectiveness of each group in parliamentary debate.

2. From your experiences in groups that conduct their business through parliamentary debate, can you recall an instance when the will of the majority was defeated by a minority better versed in parliamentary procedure? Prepare a brief report of this instance.

3. Select a proposition for parliamentary debate and hold a debate on this proposition in class.

4. Conduct a debate using the same arrangement suggested in Exercise 3. This time, by prearrangement with the instructor, select a small group of students who will seek to secure passage of the proposition; select a second small group of students who will seek to defeat the proposition. The majority of the class will be uncommitted on the proposition at the start of the debate.

5. Conduct a debate using the same arrangement suggested in Exercise 4. This time, the supporters of the proposition will be instructed to use every possible parliamentary motion in order to "railroad" the passage of the proposition. The opponents of the proposition will be instructed to use every possible parliamentary motion in order to obstruct or defeat passage of the proposition. The class will probably encounter some difficult problems in this exercise. In working their way out of these problems — with some help from the instructor, who will serve as parliamentarian when needed — the class will gain practical experience in parliamentary procedure.

6. Arrange to conduct a model congress in class. Elect a speaker and a clerk. Your instructor will serve as parliamentarian. Before the class meets, each student will prepare a bill on a subject that would be suitable for consideration by the Congress of the United States at the present time. Prepare enough copies of your bill for each member of the class and for your instructor. Distribute copies of your bill at the first meeting of the class as a model congress. Prepare bills in the following form:
   a. They must be typewritten, duplicated, and double-spaced on a single sheet of white, $8\frac{1}{2} \times 11$ inch paper.
   b. The first line shall consist of these words: "Congress Bill Number _____ ."

c. The second line shall consist of these words: "by [your name]."

d. Commencing with the third line, the title of the bill must be stated, beginning with the words "AN ACT" and containing a statement of the purpose of the bill.

e. The text of the bill proper must begin with the words: "BE IT ENACTED BY THE MODEL CONGRESS." The material following must begin with the word "That." Each line of the material that follows must be numbered on the left margin of the page, beginning with "1."

f. Every section shall be numbered commencing at "1." No figures shall be used in the bill except for the numbers of sections and lines. No abbreviations shall be used.

g. The following form is an illustration of the prescribed form for drafting bills:

```
Congress Bill Number_____

by John Doe


AN ACT to make the United States energy independent by the year 2000.

BE IT ENACTED BY THE MODEL CONGRESS


1.   Section 1.  That the federal excise tax on gasoline be

2.   increased by twenty-five cents a gallon effective thirty

3.   days after this bill becomes law.

4.   Section 2.  That the federal excise tax on gasoline be

5.   increased by an additional twenty-five cents a gallon

6.   effective one year from the date this bill becomes law.

7.   Section 3.  That gasoline purchased for agricultural and fishery

8.   purposes be exempt from this tax.

9.   Section 4.  That the . . .
```

A

A Presidential Debate

Presidential debates are the paramount example of applied debate. They become the focal point of Presidential campaigns and have sometimes been the decisive factor in determining the winner of the election. For days in advance of each Presidential debate, the media feature the coming event. The debates are carried on all major networks in the United States and are widely broadcast around the world; they are viewed by more people than any other debates in history. For days afterward the media continue to feature news about the debate, first seeking to determine who won and then assessing the impact of the debate on the campaign.

Presidential debates are a relatively new tradition in American history. On Election Day (November 3), 1959, a group of speech professors began to organize the Committee on Presidential Campaign Debates to call on the candidates for the Presidency to meet in debate

in the tradition of Lincoln and Douglas. Initially the committee consisted of all the past presidents of the American Forensic Association. The movement quickly gained momentum and was endorsed by the American Forensic Association, Delta Sigma Rho–Tau Kappa Alpha, and the Ohio Association of College Teachers of Speech. These organizations named additional members to the committee. Kennedy promptly endorsed the proposal as did all the potential candidates in 1960 except for Nixon. The idea of Presidential debates quickly captured the public's imagination. Soon editorials, columns, and articles appeared in support of the idea. Television networks indicated their willingness to cooperate.

September 26, 1960, brought the first Presidential debate between Senator John F. Kennedy and Vice President Richard M. Nixon. Four debates were held during the campaign; the first one, which was won by Kennedy, was judged to be the most important. *The New York Times* called the debates "the really decisive factor" in the election.

The Presidential debates have an interesting, tangled background of law and legal fiction. Under Federal Communication Commission rules, it was illegal for the networks to sponsor such debates. The "equal-time" rule required the networks to give equal time to all Presidential candidates. In 1960, for example, sixteen legally qualified Presidential candidates ran (including one who campaigned in an Uncle Sam suit on the platform "Drop the Bomb"). Naturally the networks would not consider giving equal time to sixteen candidates nor would the major candidates consider sharing a platform with near-unknown candidates who had no chance of winning. The problem was solved when Congress passed legislation suspending the equal-time requirement for 60 days in 1960.

The debates won widespread public approval, and great support was exhibited for more Presidential debates in 1964, 1968, and 1972. The candidates in those years (including Nixon, who once remarked that he had flunked debating in the Electoral College) didn't want to debate, and their allies in Congress found a convenient way to avoid the pressures for debate. Each House of Congress passed bills suspending the equal-time law during the campaign, which allowed the senators and representatives to report to their constituents that they had voted in favor of Presidential debates. However, as the House bill and the Senate bill differed in the number of days for which the law was suspended, the bills were referred to a Joint Conference Committee where they quietly died.

In 1976 the League of Women Voters found a way to have Presidential debates without the need to suspend the equal-time law. The League invited the major candidates to debate. The League, of course, is not subject to the equal-time law, and the networks maintained that the debates were a news event—not something sponsored by the networks—and thus not subject to the equal-time law. Ford and Carter accepted the invitation to debate. Although Carter credited his election to the wide exposure he gained in the debates, the debates themselves were marred by inept technical production and lackluster content. Ford's gaffe of stating that Poland was not under Soviet domination hurt his campaign. Members of the Committee on Presidential Debates generally regarded the debates as "eminently forgettable."

During the 1980 Presidential campaign President Carter declined to meet with Reagan and third party candidate John Anderson in a three-way debate. Reagan agreed to debate Anderson and won points for being a "good sport"; Carter, conversely, lost points for being a "bad sport." Later in the campaign Carter, apparently reluctantly, agreed to meet Reagan in one debate.

That debate was judged a draw by most qualified experts. However, the political context of debates appeared to have changed the usual rules of presumption and burden of proof. Public dissatisfaction with Carter's administration was widely reported in the media. By appearing to be the equal of a flawed President—and certainly not the incompetent and impulsive person the Carter camp had tried to paint him as being—Reagan was then perceived as an acceptable choice to many undecided voters and to many of those who were dissatisfied with Carter. After the election, both Reagan and Carter supporters and many independent commentators cited the debate as the "turning point" in the election and the major factor in Reagan's landslide victory.

After the 1984 conventions the League of Women Voters invited Reagan and Mondale for a series of debates. Mondale, sorely needing the visibility the debates would give him, eagerly accepted. Reagan, enjoying a twenty-point lead in the public opinion polls, was advised not to give Mondale the visibility and status the debates would bring. However, apparently remembering the "poor sport" charge that had hurt Carter in 1980, Reagan agreed to two Presidential debates and one Vice Presidential debate. (The first Vice Presidential debate was between Senator Dole and Mondale in 1976.) Mondale was generally credited with winning the first debate, in which Reagan was perceived as being tired and unsure of himself. In the second debate Mondale was credited with winning the issues, but Reagan, returning to his customary style that had won him the title of "The Great Communicator," clearly carried the *burden of communication* and won the decision of the voters.

The second Presidential debate of 1988 was held in Los Angeles on October 13 under the sponsorship of the Commission on Presidential Debates. (The Commission, organized in 1987 by the Democratic and Republican National Committees, had taken over the sponsorship of the debates.) The format might be described as a highly specialized type of joint press conference. However, the Presidential debates did have some important elements of real applied debates. Equal time was allotted for each debater, each had an opportunity for rebuttal, and closing statements were made by each candidate. Although the format fell short of a real debate, it did provide the American voters with their only opportunity to see and hear both candidates on the same platform at the same time as they responded to the journalists and each other.

The Second Bush-Dukakis Debate

Moderator On behalf of the Commission on Presidential Debates, I am pleased to welcome you to the second Presidential debate. I am Bernard Shaw of CNN, Cable News Network. My colleagues on the panel are Ann Compton of ABC News, Margaret Warner of Newsweek magazine and Andrea Mitchell of NBC News.

The candidates are Vice President George Bush, the Republican nominee, and Gov. Michael Dukakis, the Democratic nominee.

For the next 90 minutes we will be questioning the candidates following a format designed and agreed to by representatives of the two campaigns. However, there are no restrictions on the questions that my colleagues and I can ask this evening and the candidates have no prior knowledge of our questions.

By agreement between the candidates, the first question goes to Governor Dukakis; you have two minutes to respond.

Q. Governor, if Kitty Dukakis were raped and murdered, would you favor an irrevocable death penalty for the killer?

Dukakis No, I don't, Bernard, and I think you know that I've opposed the death penalty during all of my life. I don't see any evidence that it's a deterrent and I think there are better and more effective ways to deal with violent crime. We've done so in my own state and it's one of the reasons why we have had the biggest drop in crime of any industrial state in America, why we have the lowest murder rate of any industrial state in America.

But we have work to do in this nation. We have work to do to fight a real war, and not a phony war, against drugs and that's something that I want to lead, something we haven't had over the course of the past many years even though the Vice President has been at least allegedly in charge of that war. We have much to do to step up that war, to double the number of drug enforcement agents, to fight both here and abroad, to work with our neighbors in this hemisphere. And I want to call a hemispheric summit just as soon after the 20th of January as possible to fight that war.

But we also have to deal with drug education prevention here at home, and that's one of the things that I hope I can lead personally as the President of the United States. We've had great success in my own state, and we've reached out to young people and their families and been able to help them by beginning drug education and prevention in the early elementary grades.

So we can fight this war and we can win this war. And we can do so in a way that marshals our forces, that provides real support for state and local law enforcement officers, who have not been getting that kind of support; do it in a way which will bring down violence in this nation, will help our youngsters to stay away from drugs, will stop this avalanche of drugs that's pouring into the country and will make it possible for our kids and our families to grow up in safe and secure and decent neighborhoods.

Moderator Mr. Vice President, your one-minute rebuttal.

Bush Well, a lot of what this campaign is about, it seems to me, Bernie, gets to a question of values. And here I do have, on this particular question, a big difference with my opponent. You see, I do believe that some crimes are so heinous, so brutal, so outrageous—and I'd say particularly those that result in the death of a police officer—and for those real brutal crimes, I do believe in the death penalty. And I think it is a deterrent and I believe we need it. And I'm glad that the Congress moved on this drug bill and have finally called for that, related to these narcotics drug kingpins.

And so we just have an honest difference of opinion. I support it and he doesn't.

Moderator Now to you, Vice President Bush.

Q. I quote to you this from Article Three of the 20th Amendment of the Constitution: "If at the time fixed for the beginning of the term of the President, the President-elect shall have died, the Vice President-elect shall become President," meaning if you are elected and die before Inauguration Day, automatically—automatically Dan Quayle would become the 41st President of the United States. What have you to say about that possibility?

Bush I'd have confidence in him. And I made a good selection. And I've never seen such a pounding, an unfair pounding, on a young Senator in my entire life. And I've never seen a Presidential campaign where the Presidential nominee runs against my Vice-Presidential nominee. Never seen one before.

But, you know, Lloyd Bentsen jumped on, on Dan Quayle when Dan Quayle said he's had roughly the same amount of experience. He had two terms in the Congress. He had two terms in the Senate—serving his second term. He founded the—authored the Job Training Partnership Act that says to American working

men and women that are thrown out of work for no fault of their own that they're going to have jobs. We're moving into a new competitive age and we need that kind of thing.

He, unlike my opponent, is an expert in national defense—helped amend the I.N.F. treaty, so we got a good sound treaty when these people over here were talking about a freeze. If we'd listened to them, we would never have had a treaty.

And so I have great confidence in him. And he's—it's, it's turning around. You know, the American people are fair. They don't like it when there's an unfair pounding and kind of hooting about people. They want to judge it on the record itself. And so I'm proud of my choice.

And you know, I don't think age is the only criterion. But I'll tell you something: I'm proud that people that are 30 years old and 40 years old now have someone in their generation that is going to be Vice President of the United States of America.

I made a good selection. The American people are seeing it and I'm proud of it. That's what I'd say. And he could do the job.

Q. Governor Dukakis, your one-minute rebuttal.

Dukakis Bernard, this was the first Presidential decision that we as nominees were called upon to make. And that's why people are so concerned, because it was an opportunity for us to demonstrate what we were looking for in a running mate.

More than that, it was the first national security decision that we had to make. The Vice President talks about national security. Three times since World War II, the Vice President has had to suddenly become the President and Commander in Chief. I picked Lloyd Bentsen because I thought he was the best-qualified person for the job.

Mr. Bush picked Dan Quayle and before he did it he said: "Watch my choice for Vice President. It will tell a lot." And it sure did. It sure did.

Moderator Ann Compton for the Vice President.

Q. Thank you, Bernie. Mr. Vice President, yes, we read your lips. No new taxes. But despite that same pledge from President Reagan, after income tax rates were cut, in each of the last five years, some Federal taxes have gone up, on Social Security, cigarettes, liquor, even long-distance telephone calls. Now that's money straight out of people's wallets. Isn't the phrase "no new taxes" misleading the voters?

Bush No because that's—that—I'm pledged to that. And yes, some taxes have gone up. And the main point is taxes have been cut and yet income is up to the Federal Government by 25 percent in the last three years. And so what I want to do is keep this expansion going. I don't want to kill it off by a tax increase. More Americans at work today than at any time in the history of this country, and a greater percentage of the work force. And the way you kill expansions is to raise taxes. And I don't want to do that. And I won't do that.

And what I have proposed is something much better. And it's going to take discipline of the executive branch. It's going to take discipline of the Congressional branch. And that is what I call a flexible freeze that allows growth—about 4 percent of the rate of inflation—but does not permit the Congress just to add on spending.

I hear this talk about a blank check. The American people are pretty smart. They know who writes out the checks. And they know who appropriates the money. It is the United States Congress. And by 2 to 1 Congress is blamed for these deficits. And the answer is to discipline both the executive branch and the Congressional branch by holding the line on taxes. So I am pledged to do that. And those pessimists who say it can't be done—I'm sorry, I just have a fundamental disagreement with them.

Moderator Governor Dukakis, your one-minute response.

Dukakis The Vice President made that pledge. He's broken it three times in the past year, already, so it isn't worth the paper it's printed on. And what I'm concerned about is that if we continue with the policies that Mr. Bush is talking about here this evening, a flexible freeze. Somebody described it the other day as a kind of economic slurpee.

He wants to spend billions on virtually every weapon system around, says he's not going to raise taxes though he has broken that pledge repeatedly. He says he wants to give the wealthiest 1 percent of the people in this country a five-year, $40 billion tax break and we're going to pay for it. And he's been proposing all kinds of programs for new spending costing billions.

Now if we continue with these policies, this trillion and a half dollars worth of new debt that's already been added on the backs of the American taxpayers is going to increase even more, and if we continue with this for another four years, then, I'm worried about the next generation, whether we can ever turn this situation around. Now we need a chief executive who's prepared to lead; who won't blame the Congress but will lead, bring down that deficit, will make tough choices on spending—

Moderator Governor—

Dukakis —will go out and do the job that we expect of him and do it with the Congress of the United States.

Moderator And to Governor Dukakis.

Q. Governor, let me follow up on that by asking: you've said it many times that you have balanced 10 budgets in a row in Massachusetts. Are you promising the American people here tonight that within a four-year Presidential term you will balance the Federal budget?

Dukakis No, I'm not sure I can promise that. I don't think either one of us can, really. There's no way of anticipating what may happen. I will say this, that we'll set as our goal a steady, gradual reduction of the deficit which will require tough choices on spending. It will require a good strong rate of economic growth. It will require a plan that the President works out with the Congress—doesn't blame them—works it out with them, which brings that deficit down. It will require us to go out and collect billions and billions of dollars in taxes owed that aren't being paid in this country, and that's grossly unfair to the average American who's paying his taxes and paying them on time, and doesn't have any alternative. It's taken out of his pay check.

Mr. Bush says we're going to put the I.R.S.

on every taxpayer; that's not what we're going to do. I'm for the taxpayer bill of rights. And I think it's unconscionable that we should be talking, or thinking about, imposing new taxes on average Americans when there are billions out there, over $100 billion in taxes owed, that aren't being paid.

Now I think if we work together on this, and if you have a President that will work with the Congress and the American people, we can bring that deficit down steadily, 20, 25, 30 billion dollars a year. Build economic growth, build a good strong future for America, invest in those things which we must invest in. Economic development, good jobs, good schools for our kids, college opportunity for young people, decent health care and affordable housing and a clean and safe environment.

We can do all of those things and at the same time build a future in which we're standing on a good strong fiscal foundation. Senator Bentsen said as you recall at the debate with Senator Quayle, that if you give any of us $200 billion worth of hot checks a year we can create an illusion of prosperity. But sooner or later that credit card mentality isn't going to work, and I want to bring the White House a sense of strength and fiscal responsibility which will build a good strong foundation under which this country, or above which this country, can move, grow, invest, and build the best America for its people and for our kids and for our grandkids.

Moderator Mr. Vice President.

Bush The Governor has to balance the budget in his state: he's required to by law. He's raised taxes several times. I wish he would join me, as a matter of fact, in appealing to the American people for the balanced budget amendment to the Federal Government, and for the line-item veto. I'd like to have that line-item veto for the President because I think that would be extraordinarily helpful.

And I won't do one other thing that he's had to do: took $29 million out of his state pension fund. That's equivalent in the Federal level of taking out of the Social Security trust fund. I'm

not going to do that. I won't do that. So I'm still a little unclear as to whether he's for or against the tax increase. I have been all for the taxpayer's bill of rights all along. And this idea of unleashing a whole bunch, an army, a conventional force army of I.R.S. agents into everybody's kitchen. I mean he's against most defense matters and now he wants to get an army of I.R.S. auditors going out there. I'm against that. I oppose that.

Moderator I'm going to say this and I'm going to say it once to every person in this auditorium. What these candidates are about is of utmost seriousness to the American voters. They should be heard and you should be quiet. If you are not quiet, I'm going to implore the candidates to do something about crowding, or quieting their own partisans. But we cannot get through this program with these outbursts.

Margaret Warner for Governor Dukakis.

Q. Governor, you won the first debate on intellect and yet you lost it on heart.

Bush Just a minute.

Q. You'll get your turn.

Dukakis I don't know if the Vice President agrees with that.

Q. The American public admires your performance but didn't seem to like you much. Now, Ronald Reagan has found his personal warmth to be a tremendous political asset. Do you think that a President has to be likable to be an effective leader?

Dukakis Margaret, may I go back and just say to the Vice President that I didn't raid the pension fund of Massachusetts. You're dead wrong, George. We didn't do that. As a matter of fact, I'm the first Governor in the history of my state to fund that pension system, and I'm very proud of that. And you just have your—

Bush (Comment drowned out by applause.)

Dukakis No, we did not. No, we did not. I've been in politics for 25 years, Margaret. I've won a lot of elections and I've lost a few, as you know, and learned from those losses.

I won the Democratic nomination in 51 separate contests. I think I'm a reasonably likable guy.

I'm serious, though I think I'm a little more lovable these days than I used to be back in my youth when I began in my state legislature.

But I'm also a serious guy. I think the Presidency of the United States is a very serious office. And I think we have to address these issues in a very serious way.

So, I hope and expect that I'll be liked by the people of this country as President of the United States. I certainly hope I'll be liked by them on the eighth of November.

But I also think it's important to be somebody who's willing to make those tough choices. Now we've just heard two or three times from the Vice President that he's not going to raise taxes. I repeat, within days after you made that pledge you broke it.

You said, well, maybe as a last resort we'll do it. And you supported legislation this year that's involved in tax increases, not once but twice. So that pledge isn't realistic, and I think the Vice President knows it. I think the people of this country know it.

The fact of the matter is that the next President of the United States is going to have go to the White House seriously. He's going to have to work with the Congress seriously. He can't turn to the Congress and blame them for the fact that we don't have a balanced budget and that we have billions and billions of dollars in red ink.

And I'm going to be a President who is serious; I hope and expect will be liked by the American people, but more than that will do the kind of job that I'm elected to do; will do it with as much good humor as I can, but at the same time will do it in a way which will achieve the goals we want for ourselves and our people.

And I think we know what they are.

Moderator Governor.

Dukakis A good strong future, a future in which —

Moderator Your time has run out, sir.

Dukakis — there's opportunity for all of our citizens.

Moderator One minute from the Vice President.

Bush I don't think it's a question of whether people like you or not to make you an effective leader. I think it's whether you share the broad dreams of the American people; whether you have confidence in the people's ability to get things done.

Or whether you think it all should be turned over, as many of the liberals do, to Washington, D.C.

You see, I think it's a question of values, not likability or lovability. It's a question in foreign affairs of experience: knowing world leaders, knowing how to build on a superb record of this Administration in arms control, because you'd know exactly how to begin.

You have to learn from experience that making unilateral cuts in the defense system is not the way that you enhance the peace. You've got to understand that it is only the United States that can stand for freedom and democracy around the world, and we can't turn it over to the United Nations or other multilateral organizations.

It is, though, trying to understand the heartbeat of the country. And I know these campaigns get knocked, but I think I'd be a better President now for having had —

Moderator Mr. Vice President —

Bush — to travel to these communities and understand the family values and the importance of neighborhood.

Moderator Margaret Warner for the Vice President.

Bush Please.

Q. I'd like to follow up on that, Mr. Vice President. The tenor of the campaign you've been running in terms of both the issues and your rhetoric has surprised even some of your friends. Senator Mark Hatfield has known your family a long time and who knew your father, the late Senator Prescott Bush, said and I quote, "If his father were alive today, I'm sure his father would see it as a shocking transformation." Is Senator Hatfield right?

Bush What was he referring to?

Q. He was referring to your performance in the campaign.

Bush Well I think my dad would be pretty proud of me because I think we've come a long, long way. And I think, you know, three months ago I remember some of the great publications in this country had written me off. And what I've had to do is to define not just my position, but to define his. And I hope I've done it fairly. And the reason I've had to do that is that he ran on the left in the Democratic primary, ran firmly and ran with conviction and ran on his record.

And then at that Democratic convention they made a determination and they said there ideology doesn't matter, just competence. And in the process the negatives began. It wasn't me that was there at that convention, thank God, I was up in the—with Jimmy Baker camping out and I didn't have to hear all the personal attacks on me out of that Democratic convention. It was wonderful not to have to listen to it.

And I'm not the one that compared the President of the United States to rotting like a dead fish from the head down. I didn't do that. But I have defined the issues and I am not going to let Governor Dukakis go through this election without explaining some of these very liberal positions.

He's the one that said "I am a liberal—traditional liberal—progressive liberal Democrat." He's the one that brought up, to garner primary votes, the whole question of the A.C.L.U. And I have enormous difference with the A.C.L.U. on their political agenda, not on their defending some minority opinion on the right or left. I support that. But what I don't like is this left-wing political agenda. And therefore I have to help define that. And if he's unwilling to do it, if he says ideology doesn't matter, I don't agree with him.

Moderator One minute from Governor Dukakis.

Dukakis Well, Margaret, we've heard it again tonight and I'm not surprised—the labels. I guess the Vice President called me a liberal two or three times. Said I was coming from the left. In 1980 President Reagan called you a liberal for voting for Federal gun control. And this is some-

thing Republicans have used for a long time. They tried it with Franklin Roosevelt and Harry Truman and John Kennedy.

It's not labels. It's our vision of America and we have two fundamentally different visions of America. The Vice President is complacent, thinks we ought to stick with the status quo and doesn't think we ought to move ahead, thinks things are O.K. as they are. I don't. I think this is a great country because we've always wanted to do better, to make our country better, to make our lives better.

We've always been a nation which was ambitious for America and we move forward. And that's the kind of America I want. That's the kind of leadership I want to provide, but I don't think these labels mean a thing. And I would hope that tonight and in the course of the rest of this campaign we can have our good solid disagreements on issues. There's nothing the matter with that, but let's stop labeling each other and let's get to the heart of the matter, which is the future of this country.

Moderator Andrea Mitchell for the Vice President.

Q. Mr. Vice President, let me return for a moment to the issue of the budget because so much has already been put off limits in your campaign that most people do not believe that the flexible freeze alone will solve the problem of the deficit. So let's turn to defense for a moment.

Pentagon officials tell us that there is not enough money in the budget to handle military readiness, preparedness, as well as new weapons systems that have been proposed, as well as those already in the pipeline. You were asked at the first debate what new weapons systems you would cut. You mentioned three that had already been canceled. Can you tonight share with us three new weapons systems that you would cut?

Bush If I knew of three new weapons systems that I thought were purely waste and weren't protected by the Congress, they wouldn't be in the budget. They would not be in the budget. But you want one now? I'll give you one, that Hemtt, that heavy truck that's cost, what is it, $850 million, and the Pentagon didn't request it, and yet a member of Congress, a very powerful one, put it in the budget.

I think we can save money through this whole very sophisticated concept, Andrea, that I know you do understand, of competitive strategies. It is new and it is very, very different than what's happened. But it's not quite ready to be totally implemented, but it's very important.

I think we can save through the Packard commission report. And I'm very proud that David Packard, the originator of that report, is strongly supporting me.

So it's not a question of saying our budget is full of a lot of waste. I don't believe that.

I do think this: we're in the serious stages of negotiation with the Soviet Union now in the strategic arms control talks, and we are protecting a couple of options in terms of modernizing our strategic forces. My Secretary of Defense is going to have to make a very difficult decision in which system to go forward with. But we are protecting both of them, we're moving forward with the negotiations, and, you see, I just think it would be dumb negotiating policy with the Soviets to cut out one or the other of the two options right now.

The Soviets are modernizing. They continue to modernize. And we can't simply say we've got enough nuclear weapons, let's freeze. We can't do that. We have to have modernization, especially if we achieve the 50 percent reduction in strategic weapons that our President is taking the leadership to attain.

And so, that's the way I'd reply to it. And I believe we can have the strongest and best defense possible if we modernize, if we go forward with competitive strategies and if we do follow through on the Packard commission report.

Moderator Governor Dukakis, one minute.

Dukakis Well, Andrea, we've just had another example of why the Vice President's mathematics just doesn't add up. I think you know because you've covered these issues that there's no way that we can build all of the weapons systems the Vice President says he wants to build within

the existing defense budget. Everybody knows that, including the people at the Pentagon.

Now, my Defense Secretary is going to have to — a lot to do with some of those decisions, but it's going to be the President that's going to have to ultimately decide, before that budget goes to the Congress, what weapon systems are going to go and what are going to stay.

We are not going to spend the billions and trillions that Mr. Bush wants to spend on "Star Wars." We're not going to spend billions on MX's on railroad cars, which is a weapons system we don't need, can't afford and won't help our defense posture at all. We're not going to spend hundreds of millions on the space plane from Washington to Tokyo.

Those are decisions that the Chief Executive has to make. Yes, we're going to have a strong and credible and effective nuclear deterrent. We're going to go forward with the Stealth, the D-5 and the advanced cruise missile and good conventional forces. But the next President of the United States will have to make some tough and difficult decisions. I'm prepared to make them —

Moderator Governor.

Dukakis The Vice President is not.

Moderator Andrea has a question for you.

Q. Governor, continuing on that subject, then, you say that we have to do something about conventional forces. You have supported the submarine-launched missiles, the D-5 you just referred to. Yet from Jerry Ford to Jimmy Carter to Ronald Reagan, there has been a bipartisan consensus in favor of modernizing the land-based missiles. Now you have ruled out the MX and the Midgetman. More recently some of your aides have hinted at some flexibility that you might show about some other new form of missile. Can you tell us tonight why you have rejected the collective wisdom of people as diverse as Sam Nunn, Henry Kissinger, Al Gore — people in both parties — and what type of land-based missile would you consider?

Dukakis Well, Andrea, today we have 13,000 strategic nuclear warheads, on land, on air, in the sea. That's an incredibly powerful nuclear deterrent. I don't rule out modernization, and there are discussions going on now in the Congress and Pentagon about a less expensive, modernized, land-based leg of the triad.

But there are limits to what we can spend. There are limits to this nation's ability to finance these weapons systems. And one of the things the Vice President either ignores or won't address is the fact that you can't divorce our military security from our economic security. How can we build a strong America militarily that's teeter-tottering on a mountain of debt? And if we go forward with the kinds of policies the Vice President is suggesting tonight and has in the past, that debt's going to grow bigger and bigger and bigger. So military security and economic security go hand in hand.

And we will have a strong and effective and credible nuclear deterrent—we're going to have conventional forces that are well maintained, well equipped, well trained, well supported. And we have serious problems with our conventional forces at the present time, and they'll get worse unless we have a President who is willing to make some of these decisions. And we also have important domestic priorities—in education, in housing, in health care, in economic development, in job training, in the environment. Now all of these things are going to have to be addressed.

That's why I say again to all of you out there who have to deal with your household budgets and know how difficult it is, that the next President has to do the same. I want the men and women of our armed forces to have the support they need to defend us, the support they need when they risk our lives to keep us free and to keep this country free. But we cannot continue to live on a credit card. We cannot continue to tell the American people that we're going to build all of these systems, and at the same time invest in important things here at home, and be serious about building a strong and good America. And that's the kind of America I want to build.

Moderator One minute for the Vice President.

Bush I think the foremost—can we start the clock over? I held off for the applause—can I get—?

Moderator You can proceed, sir.

Bush I think the foremost responsibility of a President really gets down to the national security of this country. The Governor talks about limits—what we can't do—opposes these two modernization systems—talks now about, maybe we'll develop some new kind of a missile. It takes eight years, 10 years, to do that. He talked about a nuclear freeze back at the time when I was in Europe trying to convince European public opinion that we ought to go forward with the deployment of the I.N.F. weapons, and thank God the freeze people were not heard—they were wrong—and the result is we deployed, and the Soviets kept deploying, and then we negotiated from strength, and now we have the first arms control agreement in the nuclear age to ban weapons. You just don't make unilateral cuts in the naive hope that the Soviets are going to behave themselves. World peace is important, and we have enhanced the peace. And I'm proud to have been a part of an Administration that has done exactly that—peace through strength works.

Moderator Ann Compton for Governor Dukakis.

Q. Governor, today they may call them role models but they used to be called heroes; the kind of public figure who could inspire a whole generation, someone who was larger than life. My question is not who your heroes were. My question instead is who are the heroes who are there in American life today? Who are the ones that you would point out to young Americans as figures who should inspire this country?

Dukakis Well, I think when I think of heroes I think back, not presently, Ann. But there are many people who I admire in this country today. Some of them are in public life, the Senate and the Congress. Some of my fellow governors who are real heroes to me. I think of those young athletes who represented us at the Olympics, were tremendously impressive. We were proud of them, we felt strongly about them and they did so well by us. I can think of doctors and scientists—Jonas Salk who, for example, discovered a vaccine which cured one of the most dread diseases we ever had, and he's a hero.

I think the classroom teachers—classroom teachers that I have had, classroom teachers that youngsters have today who are real heroes to our young people because they inspire them. They teach them, but more than that, they are role models. Members of the clergy who have done the same; drug counselors out there in the street who are providing help to youngsters—who come up to me and others and ask for help and want help—and are doing the hard work, the heroic work which it takes to provide that kind of leadership, that kind of counseling, that kind of support.

I think of people in the law enforcement community who are taking their lives in their hands every day when they go up to one of those doors and kick it down and try to stop this flow of drugs into our communities and into our kids.

So there are many, many heroes in this country today. These are people that give of themselves every day and every week and every month. In many cases they're people in the community who are examples and are role models. And I would hope that one of the things that I do as President is to recognize them, to give them the kind of recognition that they need and deserve so that more and more young people can themselves become the heroes of tomorrow, can go into public service, can go into teaching, can go into drug counseling, can go into law enforcement and be heroes themselves to generations yet to come.

Moderator One minute for Vice President Bush.

Bush I think of a teacher right here. Largely Hispanic school. Jaime Escalante, teaching calculus to young kids, 80 percent of them going on to college. I think of a young man, now in this country, named Valladares, who was released from a Cuban jail, came out and told the truth in this brilliant book "Against All Hope" about what is actually happening in, in Cuba. I think of those people that took us back into space again, Rick Hauck, and that crew, as people that

are worthy of this. I agree with the Governor on, on athletics and there's nothing corny about having sports heroes. Young people that are clean and honorable and out there setting a—setting the pace. I think of Dr. Fauci. You've probably never heard of him. Oh, you did. Ann heard of him. He's a very fine research—top doctor at National Institute of Health—working hard doing something about research on this disease of AIDS. But, look, I also think we ought to give a little credit to the President of the United States. He is the one that has gotten that first arms control agreement and the cynics abounded.—

Moderator —Mr. Vice President—

Bush —And he is leaving office with a popularity at an all-time high—

Moderator —Mr. Vice President, your time has expired. —

Bush —as American people say he is our hero.

Moderator Ann has a question for you, Mr. Vice President.

Q. Let's change the pace a little bit, Mr. Vice President. In this campaign, some hard and very bitter things have been spoken by each side about each side. If you'd consider for a moment Governor Dukakis and his years of public service, is there anything nice you can say about him?—

Bush Yeah.

Q. —Anything you find admirable?

Bush Listen, you're stealing my close. I had something very nice to say.

Q. Somebody leak my question to you?

Bush No. Look, I'll tell you—Now let me tell you something about that. And Barbara and I were sitting there before that Democratic convention and we saw the Governor and his son on television the night before, and his family, and his mother who was there. And we're—I'm saying to Barbara, 'You know, we've always kept family as a bit of an oasis for us.' You all know me. And we've held it back a little. But we use that as a role model. The way he took understandable pride in his heritage. What his family means to him. And we've got a strong family and we watched that and we said, 'Hey, we've got to unleash the Bush kids.' And so you saw 10 grandchildren there jumping all over their grandfather at the, at the convention. You see our five kids all over this country, and their spouses. And so I would say that the concept of Dukakis family has my great respect. And I'd say that—I don't know if that's kind or not. It's just an objective statement.

And I think the man—anybody that gets into this political arena and has to face you guys every day deserves a word of praise because it's gotten a little ugly out there. It's gotten a little nasty. It's not much fun sometimes. And I would cite again Dan Quayle. I've been in politics a long time and I don't remember that kind of piling on, that kind of ugly rumor that never was true, printed. Now, come on. So some of it's unfair.

But he's in the arena. Teddy Roosevelt used to talk about the arena. You know, daring to fail greatly or succeed. Doesn't matter. He's in there. So I salute these things. I salute those who participate in the political process. Sam Rayburn had a great expression on this. He said, you know, here are all these intellectuals out there griping and complaining and saying there's negative coverage. Rayburn says, 'Yeah and that guy never ran for sheriff, either.' Michael Dukakis has run for sheriff and so has George Bush.

Moderator One-minute response, sir.

Dukakis I didn't hear the word 'liberal' or 'left' one time.

Bush That's not bad; that's the truth.

Dukakis And doesn't that prove the point, George. Which is that values like family and education, community,—

Bush If it's where you want to take the country.

Dukakis —decent homes for young people. That family on Long Island I visited on Monday where Lou and Betty Calamo bought a house for some $19,000 back in 1962. They've had seven children; they're all making good livings—they can't live in the community in which they grew up—which they grew up in.

Those are basic American values. I believe in them; I think you believe in them. They're not left or right; they're decent American values.

I guess the one thing that concerns me about this, Ann, is this attempt to label things which all of us believe in. We may have different approaches; we may think that you deal with them in different ways, but they're basically American.

I believe in them. George Bush believes in them. I think the vast majority of Americans believe in them. And I hope—

Moderator Governor.

Dukakis —the tone we've just heard might just be the tone we have the rest of the campaign. I think the American people would appreciate that.

Moderator Margaret Warner for the Vice President.

Q. Vice President Bush, abortion remains with us as a very troubling issue, and I'd like to explore that for a minute with you. You have said that you regard abortion as murder, yet you would make exceptions in the case of rape and incest.

My question is, why should a woman who discovers through amneocentesis that her baby will be born with Tay-Sachs disease, for instance; that the baby will live at most two years and those two years in incredible pain—be forced to carry the fetus to term. And yet a woman who becomes pregnant through incest would be allowed to abort her fetus.

Bush Because you left out one other exception—the health of the mother. Let me answer your question, and I hope it doesn't get too personal or maudlin.

Bar and I lost a child. You know that. We lost a daughter, Robin. I was over running records in west Texas, and I got a call from her to come home. Went to the doctor. The doctor said, beautiful child; your child has a few weeks to live. And I said, what can we do about it. He said, no, she has leukemia, acute leukemia, a few weeks to live.

We took the child to New York. Thanks to the miraculous sacrifice of doctors and nurses, the child stayed alive for six months and then died. If that child were here today and I was told the same thing, my granddaughter Noel, for example, that child could stay alive for 10 or 15 years or maybe for the rest of her life.

And so I don't think that you make an exception based on medical knowledge at the time. I think human life is very, very precious.

And, look, this hasn't been an easy decision for me to work—meet. I know others disagree with it. But when I was in that little church across the river from Washington and saw our grandchild christened in our faith, I was very pleased indeed that the mother had not aborted that child and put the child up for adoption.

And so I just feel this is where I'm coming from. And it is personal. And I don't assail him on that issue, or others on that issue. But that's the way I, George Bush, feel about it.

Moderator   One minute for Governor Dukakis.

Dukakis   Margaret, Kitty and I had very much the same kind of experience that the Bushes had. We lost a baby. It lived about 20 minutes after it was born.

But isn't the real question that we have to answer not how many exceptions we make, because the Vice President himself is prepared to make exceptions. It's who makes the decision. Who makes this very difficult, very wrenching decision?

And I think it has to be the woman, in the exercise of her own conscience and religious beliefs, that makes that decision.

Who are we to say, well, under certain circumstances it's all right but under other circumstances it isn't? That's a decision that only a woman can make, after consulting her conscience and consulting her religious principles.

And I would hope that we would give to women in this country the right to make that decision, and to make it in the exercise of their conscience and religious beliefs.

Moderator   Governor, Margaret has a question for you.

Q.   Governor, I'd like to return to the topic of the defense budget for a minute. You have said in this campaign that you would maintain a stable defense budget. Yet, you are on the board, on the advisory—

Dukakis   And incidentally, may I say that that's the decision of the Congress and the President has concurred.

Q.   —yet, you are on the board of a group called Jobs With Peace in Boston that advocates a 25 percent cut in the defense budget and the transfer of that money to the domestic economy. My question is do you share that goal perhaps as a long-range goal. And if not, are you aware of or why do you permit this group to continue to use your name on its letterhead for fund raising?

Dukakis   Well I think I was on the advisory committee, Margaret. No, I don't happen to share that goal. It's an example of how oftentimes we may be associated with organizations, all of whose particular positions we don't support, even though we support in general the hope that over time, particularly if we can get those reductions in strategic weapons, if we can get a comprehensive test ban treaty, if we can negotiate with the Soviet Union and bring down the level of conventional forces in Europe with deeper cuts in the Soviet side, yes, at some point, it may be possible to reduce defense outlays. And use those for important things here at home, like jobs and job training and college opportunity and health and housing and the environment and the things that all of us care about.

But I do think this, that the next President, even within a relatively stable budget, and that's what we're going to have for the foreseeable future, will have to make those tough choices that I was talking about and that Mr. Bush doesn't seem to want to make. And that really is going to be a challenge for the next President of the United States. I don't think there's any question about it.

But I also see a tremendous opportunity now to negotiate with the Soviet Union to build on the progress that we've made with the I.N.F. treaty, which I strongly supported and most Democrats did, to get those reductions in strategic weapons, to get a test ban treaty and to really make progress on the reduction of conventional forces in Europe. And if we can do that, and do it in a way that gets deeper cuts on the Soviet side, which is where they ought to come from, then I think we have an opportunity over the long haul to begin to move some of our resources from the military to important domestic priorities that can provide college opportunity for that young woman whose mother wrote me from Texas just the other day, from Longview, Tex. Two teachers, a mother and a father who have a child that's a freshman in college that's an electrical engineering major, a very bright student. And they can't afford to keep that child in college.

So I hope that we can begin to move those resources. It's not going to happen overnight. It certainly will have to happen on a step-by-step basis as we make progress in arms negotiation and arms control and arms reduction. But it certainly—

Moderator Governor.

Dukakis — ought to be a long-term goal of all Americans and I think it is.

Moderator One minute for the Vice President.

Bush The defense budget today takes far less percentage of the Gross National Product than it did in President Kennedy's time, for example — moved tremendously. And you see, I think we're facing a real opportunity for world peace. This is a big question, and it's a question as to whether the United States will continue to lead for peace. You see, I don't believe any other country can pick up the mantle. I served at the U.N. I don't think we can turn over these kinds of decisions of the collective defense to the United Nations or anything else.

So what I'm saying is we're going to have to make choices. I said I would have the Secretary of Defense sit down — but while the President is negotiating with the Soviet Union, I simply do not want to make these unilateral cuts. And I think those that advocated the freeze missed the point, that there was a better way, and that better way has resulted in a principle — asymmetrical cuts — Soviets take out more than we do and the

principle of intrusive verification, and those two principles can now be applied to conventional forces, to strategic forces, provided—

Moderator Mr. Vice President—

Bush —we don't give away our hand before we sit down at the table.

Moderator Andrea Mitchell for Governor Dukakis.

Q. Governor, you've said tonight that you set as a goal the steady reduction of the deficit, and you've talked about making tough choices, so perhaps I can get you to make one of those tough choices. No credible economist in either party accepts as realistic your plan to handle the deficit by tightening tax collection, investing in economic growth, bringing down interest rates and cutting weapons systems.

Dukakis And some domestic programs as well.

Q. And some domestic programs as well. So let's assume, now, for argument's purpose, that it is the spring of 1989, and you are President Dukakis, and you discover that all of those economists were right and you were wrong. You are now facing that dreaded last resort — increased taxes. Which tax do you decide is the least onerous?

Dukakis May I disagree with the premise of your question?

Q. For the sake of argument, no.

Dukakis As a matter of reality, I'm going to have to, because we have had not one but two detailed studies which indicate that there are billions and billions of dollars to be collected that are not being paid in. These are not taxes owed by average Americans. We don't have an alternative — we lose it when it's taken out of our paycheck before we even get it. But it's the Internal Revenue Service which estimates now that we aren't collecting a hundred billion dollars or more in taxes owed in this country, and that is just absolutely unfair to the vast majority of Americans, who pay their taxes and pay them on time.

The Dorgan task force, which included two former Internal Revenue Commissioners — one Republican, one a Democrat. It was a bipartisan commission — a study by two respected economists, which indicated that we could collect some $40, $45, $50 billion of those funds. The point is, you've got to have a President prepared to do this, and to begin right away, and preferably a President who as a Governor of a state has had very, very successful experience at doing this. In my own state we did it — in other states we've done it — Republican Governors as well as Democratic Governors, and we've had great success at revenue enforcement.

Now the Vice President will probably tell you that it's going to take an army of I.R.S. collectors again. Well, his campaign manager, who used to be the Secretary of the Treasury, was taking great credit about a year ago in asking and receiving from the Congress substantial additional funds to hire Internal Revenue agents to go out and collect these funds. I'm happy to join Jim Baker in saying that we agree on this. But the fact of the matter is that this is something that we must begin.

It's going to take at least the first year of the new Administration. But the Dorgan task force, the bipartisan task force, estimated that we could collect about $35 billion the fifth year, $105 billion over five years — the other study even more than that. And —

Moderator Governor —

Dukakis — that's where you begin.

Moderator One minute response, Mr. Vice President.

Bush Well, Andrea, you didn't predicate that lack of economist support for what I call a flexible freeze because some good, very good economists do support that concept. And I think where I differ with the Governor of Massachusetts is I am optimistic.

They jumped on me yesterday for being a little optimistic about the United States. I am optimistic and I believe we can keep this longest expansion going.

I was not out there when that stock market dropped, wringing my hands and saying this was the end of the world as some political leaders were. Because it isn't the end of the world. And what we have to do is restrain the growth of spending, and we are doing a better job of it. The

Congress is doing a better job of it. And the dynamics work.

They don't work if you go raise taxes and then the Congress spends it — continues to spend that. The American working man and woman are not taxed too little. The Federal Government continues to spend too much.

Moderator Mr. Vice President, Andrea has a question for you.

Q. Mr. Vice President, you have flatly ruled out any change in Social Security benefits even for the wealthy. Now can you stand here tonight and look a whole generation of 18-to-34-year-olds in the eye, the very people who are going to have to be financing that retirement, and tell them that they should be financing the retirement of people like yourself, like Governor Dukakis, or for that matter people such as ourselves here on this panel?

Bush More so you than me. But —

Q. We could argue about that.

Bush No, but you got to go back to what Social Security was when it was created. It wasn't created as a welfare program, wasn't created that — it was created as a whole retirement or help supplement to retirement program. It wasn't created as a welfare program. So here's what's happened.

We came into office and the Social Security trust fund was in great jeopardy. And the President took the leadership working with the Democrats and the Republicans in Congress. Some tough calls were made and the Social Security trust fund was put back into sound solvent condition.

So I don't want to fool around with it. And there's several, there's a good political reason, because it's just about this time of year that the Democrats start saying the Republicans are going to take away your Social Security. It always works that way. I've seen it in precinct politics in Texas and I've seen it at the national level.

We have made the Social Security trust fund sound and it is going to be operating at surpluses, and I don't want the liberal Democratic Congress to spend out of that Social Security trust fund or go and take the money out for some other purpose. I don't want that. And I will not go in there and suggest changes in Social Security.

I learned that the hard way. And the Governor and I both supported slipping the COLA's for one year. He supported it at the National Governors Conference and I supported it in breaking a tie in a major compromise package. And we got assailed by the Democrats in the election over that, and I am going to keep that Social Security trust fund sound and keep our commitment to the elderly.

And maybe down the line, maybe when you get two decades or one into the next century, you're going to have to take another look at it. But not now. We do not have to do it. Keep the trust with the older men and women of this country.

Moderator Governor, you have one minute, sir.

Dukakis Andrea, I don't know which George Bush I'm listening to. George Bush a few years ago said that Social Security was basically a welfare system. And in 1985 he flew back from the West Coast to cut that COLA. I voted against that at the National Governors Association. We won a majority, we didn't win the two-thirds that was necessary in order to pass that resolution, George, but everybody knew what we were doing, and I've opposed that.

The reason that we raise concerns—not just in election years but every year—is because Republicans, once they're elected go in there and start cutting. You did it in 1985. The Administration tried to do it repeatedly, repeatedly, in '81, '82. And I'm sure you'll try to do it again because there's no way that you can finance what you want to spend, there's no way you can pay for that five-year, $40 billion tax cut for the rich and still buy all those weapons systems you want to buy, unless you raid the Social Security Trust Fund.

Moderator Ann Compton for the Vice President.

Q. Mr. Vice President, there are three Justices of the Supreme Court who are in their 80's and it's very likely the next President will get a chance to put a lasting mark on the Supreme Court. For the record, would your nominees to the Supreme Court have to pass something that has been called a kind of conservative ideological litmus test? And would you give us an idea of perhaps who two or three people on your short list are for the Court?

Bush One, I don't have a list yet. I feel pretty confident tonight but not that confident! And secondly—secondly, I don't have any litmus test. But what I would do is appoint people to the Federal bench that will not legislate from the bench, who will interpret the Constitution. I do not want to see us go to again—and I'm using this word advisedly—a liberal majority that is going to legislate from the bench. They don't like the use of the word, but may I remind his strong supporters that only last year in the primary, to capture that Democratic nomination, he said, "I am a progressive liberal Democrat." I won't support judges like that.

There is no litmus test on any issue but I will go out there and find men and women to interpret. And I don't have a list but I think the appointments that the President has made to the bench have been outstanding, outstanding appointments.

Q. Including Bork?

Bush Yes.

Moderator Governor. You have a one-minute response time.

Dukakis If the Vice President of the United States thinks that Robert Bork was an outstanding appointment, that is a very good reason for voting for Mike Dukakis and Lloyd Bentsen on the 8th of November. And I think Mr. Bush supported the Bork nomination.

You know, Mr. Bush has never appointed a judge. I've appointed over 130, so I have a record. And I'm very proud of it. I don't ask people whether they're Republicans or Democrats. I've appointed prosecutors. I've appointed defenders. I don't appoint people I think are liberal or people who think I—who think—who I think are conservative. I appoint people of independence and integrity and intelligence, people who will be a credit to the bench. And those are the standards that I will use in nominating people to the Supreme Court of the United States.

These appointments are for life. These appointments are for life, and when the Vice President talks about liberals on the bench, I wonder who he's talking about. Is he talking about a former Governor of the State of California who was a former prosecutor—

Moderator Governor.

Dukakis —and a Republican, named Earl Warren? Because I think Chief Justice Warren was an outstanding Chief Justice. And I think most Americans do too.

Moderator Ann Compton has a question for you, Governor Dukakis.

Q. Governor, millions of Americans are entitled to some of the protections and benefits that the Federal Government provides, including Social Security, pensions, Medicare for the elderly, Medicaid for the poor. But in fact there are so many millions of Americans who are eligible, the Government just can't continue to pay for all of those programs as they're currently constituted.

A blue ribbon panel, shortly after the election, is likely to recommend that you go where the money is when you make budget cuts, and that means entitlements. Before the election would you commit yourself to any of those hard choices such as which one of those entitlements ought to be redrawn?

Dukakis Andrea, why do people who want to balance budgets, or bring the deficit down, always go to those programs which tend to benefit people of very modest means? Now, two-thirds of the people in this country who receive Social Security checks live entirely on that check. They have no other income. And yet, Mr. Bush tried to cut their cost-of-living increase in 1985.

Medicare is not getting less expensive. Medical care for the elderly is getting more expensive, with greater deductibles, with fewer benefits, the kinds of things that we've had under this Administration that have cut and chopped and reduced the kinds of benefits that one gets under Medicare.

Yes, we now have catastrophic health insurance, but it's going to cost, and that's going to be an additional burden on elderly citizens. It had bipartisan support, it should have had bipartisan support, but I suggest that we understand that those are going to be additional costs on senior citizens across this country.

So I'm not going to begin, and I'm not going to go to entitlements as a means for cutting that deficit when we're spending billions on something like "Star Wars," when we're spending billions on other weapons systems which apparently the Vice President wants to keep in his back pocket or someplace but which, if we continue to spend billions on them, will force us to cut Social Security, to cut Medicare, to cut these basic entitlements to people of very, very modest means.

Now, there are some things we can do to help people who currently do get entitlements to get off of public assistance. I talked at our first debate about the possibilities of helping millions and millions of welfare families to get off of welfare. And I'm proud to say that we finally have a welfare reform bill. And the Ruby Samsons and Don Lawsons, hundreds of thousands of welfare mothers in this country and in my state and across the country who today are working and earning, are examples of what can happen when you provide training for those welfare mothers, some day care for their children so that those mothers can go into a training program—

Moderator Governor.

Dukakis —and get a decent job. That's the way you bring a deficit down and help to improve the quality of life for people at the same time.

Moderator One minute for the Vice President.

Bush I think I've addressed it, but let me simply say for the record I did not vote to cut COLA's. And I voted the same way that he did three months before in a national governors' conference. And he said at that time, quote, and this is a paraphrase, a freeze, that's easy. So I don't believe that we need to do what you've suggested here. And I've said that I'm going to keep this Social Security entitlement, to keep that trust fund sound. But I do think there are flexible ways to solve some of the pressing problems, particularly that affect our children. And I have made some good sound proposals. But, again, we've got a big difference on child care, for example. You see, I want the families to have the choice. I want—I don't want to see the Federal Government licensing grandmothers. I don't want to see the, the Federal Government saying to communities, "Well you can't do this anymore; we're going to tell you how to do it all." I want flexibility. And I do—you know, these people laugh about the thousand points of life. You ought to go out and—light—you ought to go out and see, around this country, what's happening in the volunteer sector. Americans helping America. And I want to keep it alive in—

Moderator   Mr. Vice President—

Bush   —child care and in other entitlements.

Moderator   Margaret Warner for Governor Dukakis.

Q.   Governor, I'm going to pass on the question I originally planned to ask you to follow up on your rebuttal to a question Andrea asked. And that involved Social Security. Now it is true, as you said, that originally you sought an exemption for Social Security COLA's in this National Governors' Association vote. —

Dukakis   Right.

Q.   —But when you lost that vote, you then endorsed the overall freeze proposal and, what's more, you had great criticism of your fellow governors who wouldn't go along, as political cowards. You said—

Dukakis   That is absolutely not true—

Q.   —You said it takes guts—

Dukakis   No. That is absolutely—

Q.   —and it takes will.

Dukakis   It is absolutely not true. It had nothing to do with the debate on Social Security. It had to do with the discussion we had had the previous day on the overall question of reducing the budget—

Q.   My question is, aren't you demagoguing the Social Security issue?

Dukakis   No. And, and I have to—I have to—I just have to correct the record. That sim-

ply isn't true. Now, we're not a parliamentary body, the National Governors' Association. We vote on resolutions. If you don't get a two-thirds, then your resolution doesn't pass. But everybody knew that those of us who voted against the freezing of COLA's did so—we did so emphatically. And I never made that statement. Never would. The point is that as we look at this nation's future, and we have two very different visions of this future. I want to move ahead. The Vice President talks about a thousand points of light. I'm interested in 240 million points of light. I'm interested in 240 million citizens in this country who, who share in the American dream. All of them, in every part of this country.

But as we look at the decisions that the next President of the United States is going to have to make, I just don't believe the place you go first is those programs, those so-called entitlements which provide a basic floor of income and a modest amount of medical care for the elderly, for the disabled, for people who can't make their way on their own, and, in many cases, have given a great deal to this country. The Vice President did call Social Security a few years ago basically or largely a welfare program. It isn't. It's a contract between generations. It's something that we pay into now so that we will have a secure retirement, and our parents and grandparents will have a secure retirement. It's a very sacred contract and I believe in it.

So that's not where we ought to go. There are plenty of places to cut. There's lots we can do. In the Pentagon where dishonest contractors have been lining their pockets at the expense of the American taxpayer. There are—we certainly ought to be able to—

Moderator   Governor—

Dukakis   —give our farm families a decent income without spending 20 to 25 billion dollars a year in farm subsidies and I'm sure we can do that. That's where we ought to go and those are the programs that we ought to review first.

Moderator   One minute for the Vice President.

Bush   Well, let me, let me take him up on this question of farm subsidies.

We have a fundamental difference approach on agriculture. He favors this supply maintenance or production controls—he said that; he's been out in the states saying that, in these Midwestern states.

I don't. I think the farm bill that he criticizes was good legislation, outstanding legislation. And I believe the answer to the agricultural economy is not to get the Government further involved but to do what I'm suggesting.

First place, never go back to that Democratic grain embargo, that liberal Democrat grain embargo that knocked the markets right out from under us and made Mr. Gorbachev say to me when he was here: how do I know you're reliable suppliers? We never should go back to that.

And we ought to expand our markets abroad. We ought to have rural enterprise zones. We ought to move forward swiftly on my ideas of ethanol, which would use more corn and therefore make, create a bigger market for our agricultural product.

But let's not go back and keep assailing a farm bill that passed with overwhelming Democrat and Republican support—

Moderator Mr. Vice President.

Bush —The farm payments are going down, because the agricultural economy is coming back.

Moderator Margaret Warner has a question for you, Mr. Vice President.

Q. Mr. Vice President, I'd like to cover a subject that wasn't covered in the first debate. You have said in this campaign, I am an environmentalist—

Bush Uh-huh.

Q. —and described yourself as having zero tolerance for polluters. And yet your record does seem to suggest otherwise.

When you were head of the President's Task Force on Regulatory Relief, you did urge E.P.A. to relax regulations involving the elimination of lead from gasoline. I believe you urged suspension of rules requiring industries to treat toxic wastes before discharging them in sewers. And your group also urged OSHA to weaken the regulations requiring that workers be informed of dangerous chemicals at the works site.

Finally, I believe you did support the President's veto of the Clean Water Act. And my question is, aren't you—how do you square your campaign rhetoric with this record?

Bush Ninety percent reductions in lead since I chaired that regulatory task force—90 percent. It's almost—you remember that expression, get the lead out? It's almost out, almost gone. Clean water? I'm for clean water. But what I am not for—what I'm not for is measuring it the way the Democratic Congress does. We sent up a good bill on clean water, a sound bill on clean water, but the only way you can express your love for clean water is to double the appropriations for clean water, and then rant against the deficit. I am for clean water. I've been an outdoorsman and a sportsman all my life. I've been to these national parks. I led for the Earl Wallop Bill, or formerly Dingle Johnson. I headed the task force when I was a member of the Congress way back in the late-60's on these kinds of things on the Republican side. I led that. And so I refuse to measure one's commitment as to whether you're going to double the spending. That is the same old argument that's gotten us into the trouble on the deficit side. So I'll just keep saying I am one. I'm not going to go down there and try to dump the sludge from Massachusetts off the beaches off of New Jersey. I'm not going to do that.

That boo was excessively. Can you add five seconds, Bernie? Out of fairness—come on. Give me five. This guy, this is too much down there.

But I'm not going to do that. I am an environmentalist. I believe in our parks. I believe in the President's commission on outdoors. And I'll do a good job, because I am committed.

Moderator Governor Dukakis, you have one minute to respond.

Dukakis Margaret, I'm not sure I can get all of this in one minute. George, we have supply management today. Under the 1985 bill it's called set asides. Secondly, if you were so opposed to the grain embargo, why did you ask the Godfather of the grain embargo to be one of your top foreign policy advisers? I'm against the grain embargo. It was a mistake. I'm also against the pipeline embargo which you folks attempted to impose.

That was a mistake as well, and cost thousands of jobs for American workers in the Midwest and all over the United States of America.

Margaret, once again I don't know which George Bush I'm talking about here, or looking at. The George Bush who was a charter member of the environmental wrecking crew that went to Washington in the early 80's and did a job on the E.P.A. or the one we've been seeing and listening to the past two or three months. But let me say this, because he spent millions and millions of dollars in advertising on the subject of Boston Harbor. George, Boston Harbor was polluted for 100 years. I'm the first Governor to clean it up. No thanks to you. No thanks to you. And we've been cleaning it up for four years—

Moderator Governor.

Dukakis —and we've passed landmark legislation in '84. No thanks to you. You did everything you could to kill the Clean Water Act and those grants—

Moderator Governor.

Dukakis —to make it possible for states and local communities to clean up rivers and harbors and streams.

Moderator Andrea Mitchell has a question for you, Mr. Vice President.

Q. Mr. Vice President, Jimmy Carter has called this the worst campaign ever. Richard Nixon has called it trivial, superficial and inane. Whoever started down this road first, of negative campaigning, the American people from all reports coming to us are completely fed up. Now do you have any solutions to suggest? Is there time left to fix it? There are 26 days left. For instance, would you agree to another debate before it's all over so that the American people, so that the American people will have another chance before Election Day to compare you two?

Bush No, I will not agree to another debate. The American people are up to here with debates. They had 30 of them. We had seven of them. Now we've got three of them. I am going to carry this election debate all across this country in the last—whatever remains of the last three

and a half weeks or whatever we have—and the answer is no. I am not going to have any more debates. We don't need any more debates. I have spelled out my position.

In terms of negative campaigning, you know, I don't want to sound like a kid in a school yard—he started it—but take a look at the Democratic Convention. Take a look at it. Do you remember the Senator from Boston chanting out there, and the ridicule factor from that lady from Texas that was on there. I mean, come on. This is just outrageous. But I'll try harder to keep it on a high plane.

But if you could accept a little criticism—I went all across central Illinois and spoke about agricultural issues in about seven stops. We had some fun—Crystal Gayle, Loretta Lynn with us, and they got up and sang and went to little towns, and I talked agriculture. And not one thing did I see with respect on your network about my views on agriculture, and not one did I read in any newspaper. Why? Because you're so interested in a poll that might have been coming out. Or because somebody had said something nasty about somebody else.

And so I don't know what the answer is. I don't. Somebody hit me and said Barry Goldwater said you ought to talk on the issues more. How can Barry Goldwater, sitting in Arizona, know whether I'm talking on the issues or not when we put out position paper after position paper—he puts out position paper after position paper, and we see this much about it because everyone else is fascinated with polls and who's up or down today and who's going to be up or down tomorrow. So I think we can all share with respect in the fact that maybe the message is not getting out. But it's not getting out because there are too few debates. There will be no more debates.

Moderator Governor Dukakis, you have one minute to respond, sir.

Dukakis Well, I can understand after the Vice-Presidential debate why Mr. Bush would want no more debates.

Bush That's my five seconds.

Dukakis Andrea, I think we both have a responsibility to try to address the issues. Yes, we have fundamental differences. I think a great many of them have come out today. And I think if we get rid of the labels and, I'm not keeping count, but I think Mr. Bush has used the label "liberal" at least 10 times. If I had a dollar, George, for every time you used that label, I'd qualify for one of those tax breaks for the rich that you want to give away.

Isn't that the point? Most Americans believe in basic values. We have differences about how to achieve them. I want to move forward. I want this nation to move forward.

I'm concerned about the fact that 10 percent of our manufacturing and 20 percent of our banking and nearly half of the real estate in the city of Los Angeles are in the hands of foreign investors. I'm concerned about what that does to our future.

I'm concerned about the fact that so many of our securities are in the hands of foreign banks because of these massive deficits. But those are the issues on which we ought to be debating, and if we could just—

Moderator Governor.

Dukakis —put away the flag factories and the balloons and those kinds of things and get on to a real discussion of these issues, I think we'll—

Moderator Andrea Mitchell has a question for you, sir.

Q. Well we're talking about issues, so let's return to something you said earlier about the modernization of land-based missiles. You said that you didn't rule it out, but that there are limits to what we can spend. And then you went on to talk about a much more expensive part of our defense strategy, namely conventional forces.

Do you somehow see conventional forces as a substitute for our strategic forces? And in not talking about the land-based missiles and not committing to modernizing, do you somehow believe that we can have a survivable nuclear force based on the air and sea legs of our Triad?

Dukakis I think we ought to be looking at modernization. I think we ought to be exploring

less expensive ways to get it on land and we ought to make sure that we have an effective and strong and credible nuclear deterrent. But we also need well-equipped and well-trained and well-supported conventional forces.

And every defense expert I know, including people in the Pentagon itself, will tell you that given the level of dispense—defense spending and the level of defense appropriations, which the Congress has now approved and the President has signed, there's no way that you can do all of these things and do them well. That's why tough choices will be required, choices I'm prepared to make; Mr. Bush is not prepared to make.

But Andrea, I think we can go far beyond this as well because we have opportunities now, step by step, to bring down the level of strategic weapons and get a test ban treaty, negotiate those conventional force reductions.

I would challenge Mr. Gorbachev to join with us in limiting and eliminating regional conflict in the Middle East, in Central America. Let's get him working on Syria, their client state and see if we can't get them to join Israel and other Arab nations, if at all possible, and Arab leaders, in finally bringing peace to that troubled region. And I think that's one reason why we need fresh leadership in the White House that can make progress now in bringing peace to the Middle East.

Let's go to work and end this fiasco in Central America; a failed policy, which has actually increased Cuban and Soviet influence. The democratic leaders of Central and Latin America want to work with us. I've met with them. I know them. I've spent time in South America. I speak the language; so does Senator Bentsen. We want to work with them and build a new relationship and they with us.

But not a one of those key democratic leaders support our policy in Central America. And we've got to work with them if we're going to create an environment for human rights and democracy for the people of this hemisphere and go to work on our single most important problem, and that is the avalanche of drugs that is pouring into our country and virtually destroying those countries. Those are the kinds of priorities for national security and for foreign policy that I want to pursue. Mr. Bush and I have major differences on —

Moderator Governor.

Dukakis — and I hope very much to be President and pursue them.

Moderator Mr. Vice President, you have one minute.

Bush In terms of regional tensions, we have now gotten the attention of the Soviet Union. And the reason we've gotten it is because they see us now as unwilling to make the very kinds of unilateral cuts that have been called for and to go for the discredited freeze.

My opponent had trouble — criticized us on our policy in Angola. It now looks, because of steady negotiation, that we may have an agreement that will remove the Cubans from Angola.

We see the Russians coming out of Afghanistan. That wouldn't have stopped if we hadn't been willing — wouldn't have even started the Cubans — the Soviets coming out if we hadn't even been willing to support the freedom fighters there.

And the policy in Central America, regrettably, has failed, because the Congress has been unwilling to support those who have been fighting for freedom. Those Sandinistas came in and betrayed the trust of the revolution. They said it was about democracy, and they have done nothing other than solidify their Marxist domination over that country.

Moderator Ann Compton for Governor Dukakis.

Q. Governor, nuclear weapons need nuclear material replenished on a regular basis. And just this week yet another nuclear manufacturing plant was closed because of safety concerns. Some in the Pentagon fear that too much priority has been put on new weapons programs, not enough on current programs, and worry that the resulting shortage would be amounting to nothing less than unilateral nuclear disarmament.

Is that a priority that you feel has been ignored by this Administration, or are the Pentagon officials making too much of it?

Dukakis Well, it's a great concern of mine, and I think of all Americans, and perhaps the Vice President can tell us what's been going on. This is another example of misplaced priorities. An Administration which wants to spend billions on weapons systems that we don't need and can't afford, and now confronts us with a very serious problem in plants that are supposed to be producing tritium and plutonium and providing the necessary materials for existing weapons. Yes, if we don't do something about it, we may find ourselves unilaterally, if I may use that term, dismantling some of these weapons.

What's been going on? Who's been in charge? Who's been managing this system? Why have there been these safety violations? Why are these plants being closed down. I don't know what the latest cost estimates are, but it's going to be in the range of 25-50-75-100 billion dollars. Now, somebody has to bear the responsibility for this. Maybe the Vice President has an answer. But I'm somebody who believes very strongly in taking care of the fundamentals first, before you start new stuff. And that's something which will be a priority of ours in the new administration, because without it, we cannot have the effective and strong and credible nuclear deterrent we must have.

Moderator Mr. Vice President, you have one minute.

Bush That is the closest I've ever heard the Governor of Massachusetts come to support anything having to do with nuclear. That's about as close as I've ever heard him. Yes, this Savannah River plant need — needs to be more safe. Will he join me in suggesting that we may need another plant, maybe in Idaho, to take care of the requirements — nuclear material requirements — for our Defense Department? I hope he will. This sounds like real progress here because we've had a big difference on the safe use of nuclear power for our energy base.

I believe that we must use clean, safe nuclear power. I believe that we—the more dependent we become on foreign oil, the less our national security is enhanced. And therefore, I've made some proposals to strengthen the domestic oil industry by more incentive going in to look for and find and produce oil; made some incentives in terms of secondary and tertiary production. But we're going to have to use more gas, more coal and more safe nuclear power for our energy base.

So I am one who believes that we can—

Moderator Mr. Vice President.

Bush —and must do what he's talking about now.

Moderator Ann Compton has a question for you.

Q. Mr. Vice President, as many as a hundred officials in this Administration have left the Government under an ethical cloud. Some have been indicted, some convicted. Many of the cases have involved undue influence once they are outside of Government. If you become President will you lock that revolving door that has allowed some men and women in the Government to come back and lobby the very departments they once managed?

Bush Yeah, and I'll apply it to Congress too. I'll do both. I'll do both. Because I think, you see, I am one who—I get kidded by being a little old-fashioned on these things—but I do believe in public service. I believe that public service is honorable. And I don't think anybody has a, has a call on people in their Administrations going astray. His chief education adviser is in jail. He's in jail because he betrayed the public trust. The head of education. And yet this man, the Governor, equated the President to a rotting fish. He said that a fish rots from the head down as he was going after Ed Meese.

Look, we need the highest possible ethical standards. I will have an ethical office in the White House that will be under the President's personal concern. I will see that these standards apply to the United States Congress. I hope I will do a good job—as one who has had a relatively clean record with no conflicts of interest in his own public life, as has the Governor—to exhort young people to get into public service.

But there is no corner on, on this sleaze factor. Believe me. And it's a disgrace and I will do my level best to clean it up, recognizing that you can't legislate morality. But I do believe that with my record in Congress, having led the new Congressmen to a code of ethics through major, main emphasis on it in full disclosure, that I've got a good record. And there are more—if you want to talk about percentage appointments—more members of Congress who have been under investigation percentagewise, than people in the executive branch. And so it isn't—state governments have had a tough time. His—some of his college presidents aren't exactly holier than thou.

So let's, let's not be throwing stones about it. Let's say this isn't Democrat or Republican. And it isn't liberal or conservative. Let's vow to work together to do something about it.

Moderator Governor, you have one minute to respond.

Dukakis I would agree that integrity is not a Republican or a Democratic issue. It's an American issue.

But here again, I don't know which George Bush I'm listening to. Wasn't this the Mr. Bush that supported Mr. Meese? Called James Watt an excellent Secretary of the Interior? Provided support for some of these people—supported the nomination of Robert Bork to the Supreme Court of the United States?

Bush [drowned out by Dukakis].

Dukakis We've had dozens—we've and dozens and dozens of officials in this Administration who have left under a cloud or who have left with a special prosecutor on their arm; have been indicted, convicted.

This isn't the kind of Administration we need. And one of the reasons our selection of a running mate is so important and is such a test of the kinds of standards we'll set is because it tells the American people in advance of the election just what kind of people we're looking for.

I picked Lloyd Bentsen. Mr. Bush picked Dan Quayle.

I think that says a great deal to the American people about the standards we'll set and the quality of the people that we will pick to serve in our administration.

Moderator   To each of you candidates, regrettably, I have to inform you that we have come to the end of our questions. That's a pity. Before I ask the candidates to make their closing remarks on behalf of the Commission on Presidential Debates, I would like to thank all of you for joining us this evening.

Governor Dukakis, yours is the first closing statement, sir.

Dukakis   Twenty-eight years ago, as a young man just graduated from law school, I came to this city — came clear across the country to watch John Kennedy be nominated for the Presidency of the United States — right here in Los Angeles. I never dreamed that someday I would win that nomination and be my party's nominee for President. That's America. That's why I'm proud and grateful to be a citizen of this country.

Twenty-six days from today, you and millions of Americans will choose two people to lead us into the future as President and Vice President of the United States. Our opponents say things are O.K. — don't rock the boat — not to worry. They say we should be satisfied. But I don't think we can be satisfied when we're spending $150 billion a year on interest alone on the national debt — much of it going to foreign bankers. Or when 25 percent of our high school students are dropping out of school, or when we have 2½ million of our fellow citizens — a third of them veterans — who are homeless and living on streets and in doorways in this country, or when Mr. Bush's prescription for our economic future is another tax giveaway to the rich. We can do better than that — not working with government alone, but all of us working together. Lloyd Bentsen and I are optimists, and so are the American people. And we ask you for your hands and your hearts and your votes on the eighth of November so we can move forward into the future.

Kitty and I are very grateful to all of you for the warmth and the hospitality that you've given to us in your homes and communities all across this country. We love you and are grateful to you for everything that you've given to us. And we hope that we'll be serving you in the White House in January of nineteen hundred and eighty-nine. Thank you and God bless you.

Moderator   Vice President Bush, your closing statement, sir.

Bush   Sometimes it does seem that a campaign generates more heat than light. And so let me repeat, I do have respect for my opponent, for his family, for the justifiable pride he takes in his heritage.

But we have enormous differences. I want to hold the line on taxes and keep this the longest expansion in modern history going until everybody in America benefits. I want to invest in our children, because I mean it when I say I want a kinder and gentler nation. And by that I want to have to child care, where the families, the parents, have control. I want to keep our neighborhoods much, much better in terms of anti-crime. And that's why I would appoint judges that have a little more sympathy for the victims of crime and a little less for the criminals.

That's why I do feel if some police officer is gunned down that the death penalty is required. I want to help those with disabilities fit into the mainstream. There is much to be — be done. This election is about big things. And perhaps the biggest is world peace.

And I asked you to consider the experience I have had in working with a President who has revolutionized the situation around the world. America stands tall again, and as a result we are credible and we have now achieved a historic arms control agreement.

I want to build on that. I'd love to be able to say to my grandchildren four years after my first term, I'd like to say, "Your grandfather, working with the leaders of the Soviet Union, working with the leaders of Europe, was able to ban chemical and biological weapons from the face of the earth."

Lincoln called this country the last best hope of man on earth. And he was right then and we still are the last best hope of man on earth. And I ask for your support on Nov. 8 and I will be a good President. Working together, we can do wonderful things for the United States and for the free world. Thank you very, very much.

This debate, like many other Presidential debates, dramatically illustrates the importance of audience analysis and the ability of the candidate to adapt to the audience and to project an *image* that will win a favorable response from the audience. Reagan was the acknowledged master of this art form. In 1980 his response of, "There you go again!" defused a strong attack by Carter on Reagan's position on Social Security. In 1984 Reagan defused the potentially damaging issues of his age (he was the oldest person ever to serve as President) by smiling and saying, "I am not going to make age an issue of this campaign. I am not going to exploit for political purposes my opponent's youth and inexperience." The audience burst into laughter. Even Walter Mondale was seen laughing on camera.

Neither Bush nor Dukakis had Reagan's skill as a communicator. Dukakis was generally perceived as the winner of the first debate; yet Bush's standing rose in the public opinion polls immediately after that debate. Warner's question to Dukakis summed up this opinion, "Governor, you won the first debate on intellect and yet you lost it on heart.... Do you think a President has to be likable to be an effective leader?" It is perhaps worth noting that Eisenhower won two landslide elections on the slogan "I like Ike." The public perception of Dukakis as the "Ice Man" was not a campaign asset. Dukakis' response to the first question (see Chapter 15, Section I) certainly contributed to the Ice Man image.

Immediately after the debate the networks declared Bush the winner. The next day's newspapers tended to support the networks' analysis. In the days following the debate, Bush continued to hold his lead in the public opinion polls.

Academic debates are usually judged by critics using one of the judging philosophies considered earlier (see Chapter 17, Section II).

For Presidential debates the decision is made by the general public, and their decision is based on a different set of criteria. The "rules" for winning a Presidential debate appear to be:

1. Do better than expected. Kennedy achieved this in the first Presidential debate when the media pictured him as "youthful, immature, and inexperienced" while Nixon was perceived as "the man who stood up to Russian Premier Khrushchev in the famous 'kitchen debate.'" When Kennedy did much better than expected, he was declared the winner. Bush "lowered expectations" for his performance as a debater in 1988 by pointing out that Dukakis was a "professional debater" (Dukakis had served as moderator for a series of Public Broadcasting System television debates between his terms as governor of Massachusetts) and by claiming that Mrs. Bush fell asleep when he practiced for the debates.
2. Don't commit a gaffe. Gerald Ford provided one of the better-known gaffes in his Presidential debate with Carter when Ford said that Poland wasn't under Russian domination. When it became Carter's turn to debate Reagan, Carter committed a gaffe when he announced, "Just this morning I was discussing nuclear war with my daughter Amy." Dukakis' gaffe was his widely criticized answer to the first question of the debate about the hypothetical rape and murder of his wife.
3. Be the good guy. Neither Bush nor Dukakis won nor lost points on this. As noted above, Reagan won points for being a "good guy" by agreeing to debate Anderson and later Mondale.
4. Get the audience to laugh with you. Again neither Bush nor Dukakis won or lost points on this. Neither was noted for his public sense of humor. Once again we find that Reagan was the master of this art form. As noted above, Reagan's well-chosen and well-

delivered quips, "There you go again..." and, "I am not going to make age an issue of this campaign..." produced approving peals of laughter from the audience.

5. Be better prepared than your opponent. Kennedy spent far more time preparing for the first Presidential debate than did Nixon, and all subsequent Presidential debaters have followed and expanded on Kennedy's example by having extensive practice debates against a "stand-in" for their opponent. Dukakis' reply to the critical first question shows he was prepared for that question, but he was *not* prepared to give the answer the public expected. (See Chapter 15, Section I.)

6. Be the first to claim victory. Spin control (see Chapter 15, Section V-C) can be a critical factor in forming the public's perception of who won a debate. Typically the debaters each confidently claim victory. Bush's statement after his 1984 vice presidential debate against Geraldine Ferraro, "I kicked a little ass last night," was the least graceful of such claims, but it at least followed the rule that the candidate and the candidate's supporters must claim victory. Dukakis failed in this critical area.

> As soon as the debate was over, he marched offstage looking as if he were about to cry. He knew he had blown it.[1]

The claims of Dukakis' supporters that he had won carried little credibility after that nonverbal message.

As these rules for winning Presidential debates suggest, analyzing and adapting to the audience is of enormous importance. In applied debate one must not only win the arguments, but must also carry the burden of communication.

[1]*Time*, November 21, 1988, p. 56.

Exercises

1. Dukakis' reply to the first question was considered earlier (Chapter 15, Section I). Can you find other examples where the respondent's reply clearly helped or hindered his candidacy?

2. Who won the "choice of a vice president" issue? Justify your answer.

3. Who won the "no new taxes" issue? Justify your answer.

4. Who won the "balance the budget" issue? Justify your answer.

5. Who won the "likability" issue? Justify your answer.

6. Who won the "Bush's rhetoric" issue? Justify your answer.

7. Who won the "military budget" issue? Justify your answer.

8. Who won the "nuclear deterrent" issue? Justify your answer?

9. Who won the "abortion" issue? Justify your answer.

10. Who won the "defense budget" issue? Justify your answer.

11. Who won the "Social Security" issue? Justify your answer.

12. If you were Dukakis' debate coach, how would you have advised him to answer the "another debate" question? Explain the reasons for your advice.

13. Who won the "ethics" issue? Justify your answer.

14. Who gave the more effective closing statement? Justify your answer.

15. On the basis of your reading of this transcript of the debate, who did the better debating? Justify your answer.

16. Arrange to view a videotape of this debate. Is your decision the same as it was when you read the transcript? Explain why.

B

A CEDA Final Round

The debates presented here and in Appendix C are examples of contemporary intercollegiate debate. The debaters, at the time they participated in these debates, were about the age of the average college student.

The composition and delivery of the speeches in these debates and the exchanges in cross-examination are characteristic of intercollegiate tournament debate. Citations of evidence and authorities are, of course, subject to the usual omissions and errors of the extemporaneous method. Even Presidential candidates—as may be seen in Appendix A—make an occasional error under the pressure of debate. In studying these debates, it should be remembered that many of the classical models of the great argumentative "speeches" are not verbatim transcripts of the speech. The "text" of Patrick Henry's famous "Liberty or Death" speech, for example, was actually written by Henry's biographer, Wirt, some fifty years after Henry gave the speech.

As you read the texts of these debates you may well wonder whether the documentation of much of the evidence is so fleeting as to fall below the desideratum for the argumentative speech. The level of documentation is below the acceptable level for general argumentation. Yet, as we saw earlier in our consideration of judicial notice (in Chapter 6), this type of documentation is often acceptable in the final round of a tournament, as it was by the panel of judges for this debate.

The explanation is simple: The students were adapting to the highly specialized audience found in the final round of a national tournament. The four debaters, the panel of judges, and the debaters in the audience who had participated in the previous rounds of the tournament were all knowledgeable about the available evidence. All of them had researched the subject for months; a considerable body of evidence was common knowledge in the forensic community. Thus, a fleeting reference was sufficient to establish much of the evidence to this specialized audience.

Time is precious in a debate and, given the choice between citing four pieces of evidence incompletely or two pieces of evidence completely, the experienced debater in this situation would take the risk of incomplete citation. The "in-group," the experienced judges and debaters, would understand why the choice was made and, for better or worse, accept it in this situation.

This premium on time, as may be seen in this verbatim transcript, sometimes causes the debater to use fractured language or to fail to provide the audience with referents for the points being made. Note, however, that the debaters are aware of these problems and do provide headlining for both their main arguments and their substructure (see Chapter 15, Section V-C).

The following debate was presented in the final round at the Third National CEDA Debate Tournament. The decision was 5–2 for Southern Illinois University.

A CEDA Final Round*

Resolved: That the American judicial system has overemphasized freedom of the press.[†]

First Affirmative Constructive
John Lapham, Southern Illinois
University

I believe that our planet is now on the brink of environmental disaster. We agree with the con-

*John K. Boaz and James R. Brey, eds., 1988 Championship Debates and Speeches, Vol. 3, 1988. Sponsored by the Speech Communication Association and the American Forensic Association. Reprinted by permission of the American Forensic Association.

[†]The debate was transcribed from a cassette tape recording. Except for the correction of obvious unintended errors, this is as close to a verbatim transcript as was possible to obtain from the recording. Evidence used in the debate was supplied to the editor immediately following the round. Sources of the evidence have been verified as indicated in the Works Cited. Footnotes supply the exact quotation and other information when necessary. When the source was not available to the editor or was not located after a reasonable search, the term "source indicated" is used in the footnote together with any additional information provided by the debaters. Quotation marks surround statements from unverified sources only when the debater has provided the editor with a photocopy of the original. Descending time signals are included in brackets.

clusion of the 1980 International Conference on the Environmental Future. It is:

> There is now a high probability, almost a certainty, [if the world continues as at present] that within 50 years there will occur, exceeding past ecodisasters, the greatest catastrophe in the history of the world. This might be a world-wide famine or war, which could destroy civilization and nature, or it might be a combination of effects caused by unwise actions. But there is also the possibility that such a catastrophe can be averted if the right decisions about the environmental future are taken. Clearly decisions made now and during the next 30 years will determine the future of mankind and of the world. These decisions may be the most important of all time. (629)

Observation one is analysis of this semester's resolution. Initially we define the phrase freedom of the press as the right to publish facts, ideas, and opinions without interference from the government and note that this right applies both to the print and the broadcast media. The judicial system's historical understanding of this definition of the press was explained by Professor Benno C. Schmidt, former dean of the Columbia Law School, and now President of Yale, in 1976 when he wrote that the "First Amendment theory has long been the preserve of laissez-faire thinking" (29).

We delineate in two subpoints today. The (A) subpoint is the print press. For decades the American Judicial System has recognized [SEVEN] the concept of publisher autonomy at the expense of access claims. Professor Schmidt notes the historical protection from claims of access. "With one early exception, decisions concerning constitutional claims of access to private owned print media have denied claims of access for both ads and articles" (107).

Professor Steven Smith of the University of Idaho concurs in 1987:

> The Supreme Court has been largely unmoved by the argument for rights of access and indeed has ruled that the first amendment not only does not require rights of access, but in fact also precludes legislatures from granting rights in some contexts. (720)

The judicial system will apparently continue to emphasize publisher autonomy. Professor

Schmidt predicts in 1976 "The doctrines of freedom of the press may increasingly center on the concept of publisher autonomy" (239).

(B) subpoint is the broadcast press. Shortly after the Supreme Court's decision in Red Lion Broadcasting Co. v. FCC to uphold the constitutionality of the Fairness Doctrine, the Court adjudicated attempts to gain access to the broadcast press. Professor of Journalism at Drake University, William Francois noted in 1973 the effects of the Court's CBS v. DNC decision

> Instead of Red Lion being applied as an access case to the print media, as Professor Barron [SIX] believed might happen, it now is beginning to look as if the tradition of print journalism is going to be applied to broadcasting. . . . Access to the media appears to have been administered a severe setback. (188)

Professor Jerome Barron noted in '81: "The years since the CBS decision have, on the whole, seen a turning away from the interpretations of the 1st Amendment which would impose affirmative obligations upon the media" (3).

Observation two, rules for the road and paradigm. Parameters and focus for debate are noted initially in (A) subpoint, ecological awareness of human extinction is criteria. Mr. Rifkin argued in '80: "The only hope for the survival of the species is for the human race to abandon its aggression against the planet and seek to accommodate itself to the natural order" (256). We look to save the earth.

The (B) subpoint is preserve the ecology. The one subpoint is that ecological systems are critical for continued human life. Professor Paul Ehrlich of Stanford University explains in 1980 that the ecological systems maintain the quality of the atmosphere, dispose of our wastes, recycle essential nutrients, control the vast majority of potential pest and disease vectors, supply us with food from the sea, generate soils and run the hydrological cycle, among other vital services.[1]

The second subpoint is that the status quo will destroy the present eco-system. [FIVE] Ecology professor G. Tyler Miller of St. Andrew College notes the ominous implications in 1985 that:

[1]Source indicated.

> [I]f present trends continue, the world is headed for economic ruin, increased political instability, and threat of global nuclear war because (1) the maximum sustained yield of many of the world's renewable resources may be exceeded and (2) there will be shortage of affordable supplies of nonrenewable fossil fuels. . . . (8)

Subpoint three gives a decision rule. That is that 1988 is pivotal year. Sue Cross argued in March of this year. "1988 is the greatest biological crisis since evolution began three-and-a-half billion years ago" (A11).

We offer two contentions to support the resolution. Contention one, freedom of the press entrenches the old paradigm. Explanation in two subpoints. The (A) subpoint is the autonomous press supports the old world view. The mass media currently is based on the old paradigm. Environmentalist Hazel Henderson explains in 1978 that:

> Current mass journalism is still largely based on the old, fragmented Newtonian vision — where humans were the dispassionate, objective observer of the world. Even though few people still believe that humans can ever observe the world objectively because they are an interacting part of it, there is still a widespread lag on the part of our mass media in perception of this integral nature of reality. (274) [FOUR]

The mass media diverts us from the development of a new environmental ethic. Ecologists Devall and Sessions note in 1985:

> In technocratic-industrial societies there is overwhelming propaganda and advertising which encourages false needs and destructive desires designed to foster increased production and consumption of goods. Most of this actually diverts us from facing reality in an objective way and from beginning the "real work" of spiritual growth and maturity. (68)

Further, the mass media exacerbates environmental problems by overwhelming the voices of those who promote the new environmental ethic. The Science Action Coalition, an environmental group, concludes in 1980: "Those living simply are starting to speak out, but their power to publicize is minuscule compared to that of the mass media, which depend on complex living habitats for their livelihood" (Fritch, 6).

The (B) subpoint is the transition to the new view requires access to the mass media. The transition to this new consciousness will only be achieved through media dissemination of information about our environmental needs. Dr. Capra notes in his seminal 1983 work, *The Turning Point*:

> If the new ecological awareness is to become part of our collective consciousness, it will have to be transmitted, eventually, through the mass media. These are presently [THREE] dominated by business, especially in the United States, and their contents are censored accordingly. (409)

Access rights for key environmental groups will make the journalists ecologically aware, though, as Capra explains that:

> Once we succeed in reclaiming our mass media, we can then decide what needs to be communicated and how to use the media effectively to build our future. This means that journalists, too, will change their thinking from fragmentary to holistic modes and develop a new professional ethic based on social and ecological awareness. (409)

Further, the media can change attitudes about our environment today. Communication professors McLeod, Glynn, and Griffin explain in 1987 that "At least in regard to the energy issue, audience exposure to messages specifically dwelling on the topic seems to heighten agenda-setting effects" (34).

Absence of access rights will risk disaster for you. Henderson concludes in 1978 that to address adequately the need for more democratic access to public opinion, as well as to meet its huge responsibilities as our most powerful educational system, mass journalism, both electronic and print, must face up to a greatly enlarged function in a complex, mass society. If it fails, the environmental consequences will be disastrous.[2]

[2]"To address adequately the need for more democratic access to public opinion, as well as to meet its huge responsibilities as our most powerful educational system, mass journalism, both electronic and print, must face up to a greatly enlarged function in a complex, mass society. If it fails, the environmental consequences may be disasterous" (275).

Contention two, the old paradigm must be deemphasized to save the environment. [TWO] We must shift from the old Cartesian paradigm to a new holistic environmental ethic. Professor Miller argued in 1982 that:

> Our survival seems to depend on accepting this holistic world view. In other words, we must change from an agriculturalist society based on humans against nature to a sustainable earth society based on humans and nature. This means that we must cooperate with nature rather than blindly trying to control it. (27)

The (A) subpoint of contention two is holistic awareness promotes environmental understanding. Our position is summarized by philosophy professor Michael Fox in January, 1988 that:

> Truly understanding ecology demands that we see things whole, that we care for the entire biosphere, which can happen only when we abandon a human-centered value system and live in harmony with the world around us. (18)

We further note that holism is essential for solving for our environmental ills. The old Cartesian world view is terribly inadequate. Capra explained in 1983 that:

> We live in a globally interconnected world, in which biological, psychological, social, and environmental phenomena are all interdependent. To describe this world appropriately we need an ecological perspective that the Cartesian world view cannot offer. (19)

The (B) subpoint is that ecological understanding promotes environmental quality. Hope for solutions [ONE] to current environmental ills lies in the new environmental ethic. Devall and Sessions argue in 1985 that:

> If enough citizens cultivate their own ecological consciousness and act through the political process to inform managers and government agencies of the principles of deep ecology, some significant changes in the direction of wise long-range management policies can be achieved. (158)

The Ehrlichs concur in 1987 that "[h]uman beings already have the power to preserve the Earth that everyone wants — they simply have to be willing to exercise it" (252).

Fortunately we note that a transition to a new environmental ethic of deep ecology is feasible. After decades of abusing the environment, Americans are now prepared to [HALF] make a shift in consciousness. Ecology Professor Miller finally argued in 1982. Fortunately, the United States has never been in a better position to make such a transition as long as more of its citizens are willing to become environmentally aware and politically involved.[3]

Cross-Examination
David Israelite Questioning Lapham

Israelite: You indicate on the (A) subpoint the print analysis, right? The card from Benno Schmidt, correct? *Lapham:* Yep. *Israelite:* All right, what specific court case indicating no right of access to the print media? *Lapham:* You see, Schmidt goes so far beyond that. Through the entire American judicial system since 1919, which 1AC indicates as a holistic type of.... Now, let me answer the question so you'll have a better idea what's going on. Since 1919 there has only been one exception where they haven't granted access. That's what Schmidt argues.

Israelite: OK, what's been the latest case? *Lapham:* The latest case? I'm not concerned, because I argue the system and not the case. *Israelite:* Well, I'm concerned. Do you know the latest case? *Lapham:* I have no idea. *Israelite:* You have no idea what the latest case is? So, holistically they ruled against rights of access right? *Lapham:* Yeah.

Israelite: Now did the case ever come to the Supreme Court for environmental access specifically? *Lapham:* For environmental access specifically, no. *Israelite:* So the Supreme Court has never ruled specifically on allowing environmental access, right? *Lapham:* You see, you're missing the link to the resolution, I think which is the (A) subpoint. *Israelite:* I think I understand the link.

Israelite: (B) subpoint on broadcasting you indicate the Red Lion case, right? *Lapham:* Yes. *Israelite:* OK, what was the Red Lion case dealing with, what types of access? *Lapham:* The Red Lion case dealt with the fairness doctrine. It was more of a right to reply standard, but because that is mutated it also ended up denying access rights to broadcasting. *Israelite:* OK, but when the case came before the Supreme Court they dealt with the generic right to access, right? *Lapham:* No they dealt with the right to reply. Access ideas as mutated since then. *Israelite:* But the issues put before them had nothing to do with environmental issues, correct? *Lapham:* The issues before that case did not talk about deep ecology. You are correct.

Israelite: Has any case come to any court talking about specifically environmental rights to access? *Lapham:* Yes, I mean, that's why I argue observation one for you. *Israelite:* What cases? *Lapham:* Not just to kill time but to indicate that it is the autonomy of the press that has caused— *Israelite:* OK. I'd like to see case titles. *Lapham:* You see, I don't argue specific case titles. *Israelite:* I understand you don't argue, that. I'm asking if there ever in history has been a case that dealt specifically with this area. *Lapham:* Specifically, environmental ecology? *Israelite:* Yes. *Lapham:* I don't know if there's a Supreme Court case on the deep ecology. All I know is that in order to justify the resolution you look to whether or not the American judicial system has given too much autonomy.

Israelite: OK. Let's just make this real clear with one last question. Has the court ever ruled uniquely against environmental access? *Lapham:* Yes. *Israelite:* When? *Lapham:* When? I don't know the date. *Israelite:* What's the case? *Lapham:* The answer to your question— The court's say there is autonomous press. They don't have to grant rights of access. *Israelite:* Sir, that's not the question. I'm asking if there has ever been a case— *Lapham:* If you don't want an answer, why do you keep asking? *Israelite:* You said there's been a case, and you don't know the date. Do you know the title? *Lapham:*

[3]Source indicated.

Yes. [Laughter] *Israelite:* Could you tell us? *Lapham:* I mean I honestly, in 1AC, have no knowledge of the title. *Israelite:* No knowledge of the title? *Lapham:* I do not in first affirmative read you a single one case that talks about this. *Israelite:* Does Mark know? *Lapham:* I give the judicial system. You see, we are arguing the judicial system. I think William Jewell College needs to do the same thing.

Israelite: Now, solvency is dependent upon action taken after the access is used, right? *Lapham:* Solvency for the ethic? *Israelite:* Um hum. *Lapham:* Well, the (B) subpoint in contention two, if you want to— *Israelite:* Solvency, you have to prove one that the environmental groups will use the right and two that the public will respond, right? That's the burden? *Lapham:* The burden of solvency first of all does not impact on the resolution. *Israelite:* In order to prove no ecological harm you have to prove they will use the right and that the people will respond, right? *Lapham:* No, what you have to do is say that the overemphasis has occurred, because they have allowed the environmentalist not to have the access. When you don't have the access the Cartesian view is perpetuated.

First Negative Constructive
Raymond Roberts,
William Jewell College

Off case observation number one will be in terms of whole resolution. I'll tell you in terms of (A) subpoint standards. One subpoint intent of CEDA is whole resolution. Tomlison explains in 1983: "Another hallmark of CEDA has been to ask debaters to remember the intent of the resolution. These are qualities to be retained by any CEDA round. To ignore them is to reject the basic philosophy of the organization" (2).

Two subpoint under this is the focus of CEDA is on the resolution. *CEDA Yearbook* in 1987 explains. "The debate is limited to determining the truth of the resolution whether it is one value, a fact, or pseudo-policy" (21). In other words we're talking whole-res[olution] here.

(B) subpoint, violations. I will tell you first of all that the affirmative is only talking about ecological impacts and only talking about ecological access. On that level not talking about entirety of resolution. And I think that becomes very clear in cross-examination when David stands up here and tells you "OK, we're talking about access, right? Well, yes, no." What about cases, "Well, yes, no." Again, only a very narrow part of the resolution. On that level, I would say, (C) subpoint that this violation. It's a prima facia issue and should be a voting issue this round.

Observation, the one on top of case. Definitions are fine we'll go specifically go to the (A) [SEVEN] subpoint on printed press. The printed press is fine, but the only thing I want to go to is the Smith in '87 card. One response on this is going to be, Supreme Court says that it is unmoved on this specific situation. Two subpoint, on that level Supreme Court is not overemphasizing. Three subpoint, means Supreme Court is doing absolutely nothing, I mean affirmative evidence specifically tells you it is unmoved. Clearly would indicate to me no overemphasis.

On the (B) subpoint on broadcasting I will tell you in terms of one subpoint they give us no specific case to environmental rights of access. Two response on that, therefore, there is no condition of overemphasis by broadcasting or by any type of media because there is no specific case dealing with the right to access. I will extend, however, and make a distinction between press and broadcast.

I will tell you in terms of one response press is institutional and speech is individual. Lange explains in '75: "The role of the "autonomous" press is institutional in the sense that the press enjoys a separate constitutional status in the American society, a status quite apart from individual rights of free expression" (81).

Second response under this will be that framer's required and recognized the distinction. Stewart explained in '75:

> Between 1776 and the [SIX] drafting of our Constitution many of the state constitutions contained clauses protecting freedom of the press while at

the same time recognizing no general freedom of speech. By including both guarantees in the First Amendment, the Founders quite clearly recognized the distinction between the two. (633-4)

Next response on this is that legality infers different meanings. Nimmer explains in '75:

As nature abhors a vacuum, the law cannot abide a redundancy. The presumption is strong that language used in a legal instrument, be it a constitution, a statute, or a contract, has meaning, else it would not have been employed. (640)

Fourth response under this is speech is oral and press is written. Nimmer continues:

It may be surmised that this duality was deemed necessary because the reference to "speech" might be construed to protect only oral expression, so that the reference to in the press was added in order explicitly to protect written expression. (640)

Five subpoint under this broadcasting is not press. One extension on this is going to be from Lewis in '80: [FIVE] "I think whatever rights inure in those clause inure to everybody because I don't think the word 'press,' for the historical reasons I gave, meant the media. I think it meant the product of the printing press" (918). On that level broadcast does not apply. When we look on case broadcast is the major impact of all of the things that they talk about. On that level, not specific.

Observation two, (A) and (B) subpoints, group, please. This is talking about ecological awareness and our need to preserve the ecology. One response here is going to be this is all based on environmental ethic which I will get to later. Two response, the thesis of environmental ethic is that people will not act until there has been some kind of disaster. Three subpoint, on that level the environmental ethic will not change until there is some type of disaster and on that level access will not solve.

Specifically off of the little two card that they talk of destroying the ecology and renewed resources and a shortage. One response, this is talking about destroying the ecology. Two response renewed resources and a shortage. Three response

energy crisis in the early '70s when we were talking about running out of fuel and supposedly being the end of the world, — it didn't. On that level, I want to contend that this is the same thing here. Nothing is going to happen and there are going to be no impacts.

Specifically, on the third subpoint on decision rules. Simply an opinion here and I contend that it will not come about. [FOUR]

Contention one, on (A) subpoint talks about press being an old world view and it observes that view. One response to this is not due to the American judicial system, I mean the American judicial system is not telling the press how they should act on environmental issues. This is a press issue not a court issue.

Two subpoint. On that level the problem is not the fault of the system. Specifically, off the Sessions evidence on environmental ethics, apply the environmental ethics standard I give you above.

Specifically on the Scientific Action Group that they said was an environmental group. One, the evidence was from an environmental group. Two, on that level I would contend it is slightly biased towards saying that the environment needs to be protected.

Specifically, on the (B) subpoint. Group these answers. One response access supposedly equals more information. Two subpoint, we already have access. Three response, access says everyone has a right to get their views across or a right to express their views. Fourth response, however, does not say that they should all have equal amounts of time or equal impacts or equal [THREE] effects. On that level simply because people who support the environment don't get out and are not as involved and the press doesn't give them as much time is not the fault of rights of access and certainly not the fault of the American judicial system.

Contention two. First of all, on the Miller card he says we have to look at the whole world view. I would contend that's probably right, but I would contend in this debate round they should also look at the whole resolution.

On the (A) subpoint, on awareness equals understanding. Group all of these cards. One response says awareness equals understanding. Two response does not say that this understanding is going to do anything for protecting ecology. Third response specifically, off the Miller in '82 card says more critical awareness and political involvement is what is necessary. Fourth response this means people must take action to solve, specifically off of that card. Fifth response is that they don't show that there is any action taken whatsoever. They simply say that they will equal more awareness and more ability. And on that level I am going to contend that there is no solvency here.

I think this should be pretty clear, I mean when they are talking about the narrow example of ecology, [TWO] can't even give us one case that talks specifically about ecology where they have ruled in areas of rights of access I would contend that clearly shows it is not the fault of the American judicial system.

Also, when we're talking about rights of access equal rights of access is not guaranteed, it simply says that each person must be able to view their points. That is fine. Does not indicate that they must have equal amount of time to view those points.

Again on the contention two. They don't say that they are going to solve anything. Indicate some type of involvement and they must prove solvency.

Cross-Examination
John Lapham Questioning Roberts

Lapham: In order to make my partner happy I need to get the evidence you read on the (B) subpoint of observation one. *Roberts:* Sure. The cards marked and the top card on (C). *Lapham:* The whole resolution argument indicates that you should search the truth of the resolution, correct? *Roberts:* Indicates that you should search the truth of the whole resolution.

Lapham: All right. When people like Professor Bile write on whole resolution they're indicating that you must, in order to prove somebody is not whole resolution, set up some kind of standard for induction perhaps or indicate how the negative team is failing to induce their example, right? *Roberts:* Um hum. *Lapham:* What standards for inducement or for induction do you set up in the first negative speech? *Roberts:* We tell you that when you are only looking at environmental ethic its not looking at the entire area of rights of access is not— *Lapham:* In terms of the theoretical argument of whole resolution, what standards for induction do you set up that the affirmative team should meet? I realize that you say we are one example. What standards do you set up to indicate that say we should be six examples, we should be one big example, we should be one small example, or what? Which standards are we using? *Roberts:* The standards that I think should be used in this round is first of all you should at least be more than one example of the specific area you are talking about, i.e., access.

Lapham: Let me ask you this, which standard was argued in the first negative speech? *Roberts:* The standard is argued in the first negative speech is that the intent in this whole resolution is the focus should be on the resolution and not on the— *Lapham:* Which standards on induction were set up? *Roberts:* The standard of induction that was set up was that you only talk about an example you should be talking about the entire resolution.

Lapham: You say we talk about an example though, but you don't indicate how you prove that an example is whole-resolutional or how an example is not whole-resolutional, right? You simply indicate that an example can or cannot be. What standards do we use to indicate whether or not an example is whole-resolutional? *Roberts:* Whether or not an example is whole-resolutional or not is whether it encompasses the whole resolution. I mean when you're talking—

Lapham: I'm going in circles here. Let me try to change my question, all right? People at this tournament have to run cases that are whole-resolutional without standing up for eight minutes and reading eight different cases to give significance to the resolution, because there is a case that exists like ours that are the whole resolution. How would you determine through the standards you set up which cases are and which cases aren't? *Roberts:* Well, at the end of this round we'll find out whether or not your case is. *Lapham:* How in the first negative speech did we set this up? *Roberts:* We set it up in the first negative to say we should examine the entirety of the resolution. I contend that by only looking at environmental ethics you are not.

Lapham: OK. (B) subpoint of contention one, your second response is access now. I guess I missed the card or there wasn't one there because I don't seem to remember us having access now. That was why we read observation one on case, right? *Roberts:* Right. *Lapham:* There's not access now? *Roberts:* What I was getting at by that contention is the only thing that is granted under terms of access is that we are allowed to express our viewpoint. *Lapham:* What's — *Roberts:* That does not determine that we have to equal — *Lapham:* What's the substantiation to the second response for the (B) subpoint that says "access now"? *Roberts:* I didn't read any evidence on that. *Lapham:* Thank you.

Second Affirmative Constructive
Mark West, Southern Illinois University

I think that the environmental ethic is a very important thing that we should strive for, and I think that in a whole-resolutional analysis access prevention by the Supreme Court and by the entire American judicial system is bad and we should try to encourage access by certain groups.

I would like to begin with the off case observation on the whole resolution. I would begin with the (A) subpoint. My first response is that you should have a reasonable interpretation. If we are arguing that the entire autonomous press is bad that is certainly examining the entire resolution.

My second argument is that access is an extremely common case and when examining the topic and when examining general access cases that would be a common interpretation that the whole resolution and should be allowed.

On the (B) point where they argue violations. They only say we're only talking about ecological access and therefore we are not whole resolution. My first argument is that this is not true. We are talking about the entire system of preventing access by the autonomous press. So the violation in and of itself is incorrect.

My second argument is that we are also arguing that free press is bad. It is a very simple holistic interpretation of the topic and I don't understand the violation. I don't even think it's prima facially a violation because they only say we're talking about ecological access which is not correct.

My third argument is that the Schmidt evidence we [SEVEN] give you under observation one says that always the Supreme Court has held there is no right to access. If that is not a whole resolutional analysis throughout history I don't know what is.

My fourth argument is that additionally the Smith evidence that we provide under observation one says that they even go beyond not allowing access and that they prevent the legislature from allowing access. That is certainly an overactive American judicial system and a broad interpretation.

The fifth argument is that the Barron evidence, that is not discussed, either under observation one, says that there is a general trend to the future and how access will be denied.

The final argument is that if they demand a Supreme Court case that is specific to the environment I will provide one to determine that specifically that the environment is provided for as well. Goldstein argues in '86 the environment and how the Supreme Court has prevented environmental access:

> The court's present posture on Freedom of Speech and advertising was defined most clearly in 1980 in Central Hudson. . . . The court held the government interest in conserving energy, while important, could not overcome the utility's right to free speech. (26)

I certainly don't think this should be a voting issue if we have a reasonable interpretation of this topic under an access level. [SIX]

I would like to go to case now. Dealing with case, the definitions aren't really responded to. Under the (A) subpoint we discussed the print press. He first argues that the Supreme Court is unmoved and that the Supreme Court is not overemphasized.

My first argument is that the Smith evidence goes on to say, if they were to continue reading the evidence, that they've gone even beyond not allowing for access and stopped the legislature from providing access. That is quite an intrusion.

My second argument is that this guarantees autonomy of the press and that is free press being bad and that is our general position.

He argues under the (B) subpoint that it is not specific to case and it is not overemphasis. First argument, it is a systems analysis. We are saying that the system has generally prevented access. Secondly, we provide a specific example of how the environment is prevented as well when it comes to access. And finally, I would suggest that this violates the whole resolution, because they're asking us to discuss only one specific case rather than the whole resolution. Certainly they aren't consistent with their own position.

I would now like to argue the five arguments he says about how the press is special. I will argue this off case because there are a number of arguments. He first argues that press is a special case. [FIVE] My first argument is all his evidence says is that the press is being created as an autonomous press. This feeds our position. The press is autonomous, out of government control, and it can act on its own.

He next argues that the Framer's made a distinction. I don't think that Framers intent is what we should necessarily look to. The first argument is that there was no consensus in 1750 about the meaning of the first amendment. Don Pember argued as a professor at the University of Washington (my home) in 1977:

> There was probably little consensus on the exact meaning of the concept even among the Congressmen who drafted the First Amendment. There is little consensus today on the meaning of the First Amendment. Were it not for the Supreme Court,

which periodically defines the First Amendment, the law would be in a terrible state. (51)

The second subpoint is that the constitution does not even reveal how to interpret it. Richard Posner argues in '87:

> Even the decision to read the Constitution narrowly, thereby, "restrain" judicial interpretation, is not a decision that can be read directly from the text. The constitution does not say, "Read me broadly," or, "Read me narrowly." [4] We don't really know how to interpret it.

His third argument says that there is a different meaning. My first argument here is that this evidence only refers to one case and one case of interpretation. This is not necessarily whole resolutional [FOUR] as we discussed. My second argument again, this assumes framers' intent which above I argue we should not necessarily turn to.

His fourth argument says that speech is oral and press is written. My first argument, there is no free press distinction. They fall under the free speech principle. Schauer argued in '82:

> We may wish to say that some forms of communication represent a constraint on governmental power even greater than that established by a general Free Speech Principle, but this powerful constraint would properly be keyed as to political content, and not to the presence or absence of a printing press or transmitter. (109)

i.e., there is no distinction when you look at it generally.

The second argument is that the Supreme Court and the American Bar, for example, have always agreed with this. Don Gillmor and Jerome Barron argued in '74: "The Supreme Court like most of the American bar has engaged in a long standing practice of making interchangeable use of free speech cases in freedom of the press cases and vice versa" (8). Clearly this is not a distinction.

He next argues five subpoint that we're not dealing with broadcast. First argument, this is only dealing with framers' intent. My second argument, the difference is broken down. There is a trend

---

[4]Source indicated.

toward making these the same. Baron Carter, Professor of Communication and Lawyer, 81: [THREE] "Once subjected to scrutiny however the attempted differentiation of print and broadcast media breaks down in a number of ways" (49). There is not really this distinction.

Continuing on with case. Contention one, observation one we discussed criteria. They say that we are only dealing with the ethic and ethic only assumes we wait 'til a disaster happens. This is blatantly false. The first argument, you do not wait until a disaster happens when we are discussing the ethic. We are advocating that you move toward a holistic interpretation saying that man is as important as nature. This is a blatant assertion that is completely unsubstantiated in holistic thought.

He argues then under the (B) subpoint that under ecology that in 1970s this did not happen, and this is only dealing with ecology. My first argument is that this 1970s assertion does not take out our position, it only shows that we are building toward an ecological problem.

Second argument, please extend the evidence. The Rifkin in 1980 evidence under the (A) subpoint indicates that the earth is at risk. The (B) one subpoint from Ehrlich 1980 says that human survival is at stake. The very beginning of our case evidence from the International Task Force says in 1980 there is the greatest threat of danger we see. Extend as well that the status quo is destroying this and the decision rule is 1988. He says it's one opinion, I think [TWO] it's a good opinion.

Contention one. He says it's not the American judicial system. Our position is simply here is that it is the American judicial system because they have created an autonomous press.

Under the (A) subpoint the media is the old paradigm. He says not the system but please extend the media encourages the Cartesian paradigm they stop the ethic and that they prevent and encourage the environmental problems. He says that this evidence is biased, I think it's good it is biased, these people are shocking us into realizing that the environment is at risk.

The (B) subpoint says that you need access. I would argue first of all, we do not necessarily advocate there is equal time for everyone. We are saying that the environmentalists should get on the air and the autonomous press prevents it.

Second subpoint is that the media denies us access presently. Please extend. The Capra evidence says that only access will solve. Access, Capra in 1983 argues, that this is the most important thing to solve. And the McLeod evidence shows you studies indicating that it would indeed solve the problem.

Contention two argues that the old paradigm is bad. He says whole resolution must be examined. I think we are examining the whole resolution. He says that it's only one case [ONE] but it certainly is an examination of the whole resolution from an access level.

He says we don't show that they actually can solve. My first argument is that the studies indicate that they do solve. He ignores the McLeod evidence on case. Second argument is that studies prove that there is an actual attitude effect. Evidence comes from Fortner, and Lyon, 1985: "A comparison of test scores between the treatment group and the control group and within the treatment group indicates that people can learn from an environmental documentary on television" (18).

The next subpoint is that studies prove behavioral change occurs. Professor McLeod again in 1987: "Energy conserving role models from a local cable television programs produced some long-term [HALF] changes in energy conservation behavior among viewers participating in field experiments" (30).

The next subpoint is that the American public would adopt the ethic with this information. The Science Action Coalition again in '80:

> People want to get involved in environmental issues] but often don't know how. However, a hidden obstacle to the lack of urgency of procedures for going out to others, sharing with them, and joining forces with socially oriented citizens. (Fritch, 218)

He next argues that it is a political necessity. No the evidence says you need to adopt the ethic. Finally, he says you need action to solve. The evidence I give you says studies show people will act. Please extend the (A) to the (B) subpoints this is the best way to preserve the environment.

Cross-Examination
Ray Roberts Questioning West

Roberts: OK. First thing I need is Central Hudson card that you read me which is your environmental ethic case. *West:* It's not our environmental ethic case. *Roberts:* Well, I mean the case that talks about the environment.

Roberts: OK, now within the context of that card, it said that they ruled on speech and advertising in this case, right? *West:* Right. *Roberts:* What does that have to do with press? *West:* Speech and press are the same. *Roberts:* OK. Speech and press are the same thing. They ruled on advertising. What does that have to do with press. *West:* That's speech. *Roberts:* That's part of speech. So you're going to contend that commercial speech is press. It's all First Amendment. *West:* Right, you have to understand, I don't care about this piece of evidence that I read to you. I just did it to satisfy the need to have a Supreme Court case. *Roberts:* OK. *West:* That is not our position. Our position is that the media prevents environmental access and the Supreme Court and the American judicial system encourage an autonomous press. So I don't care about this piece of evidence.

Roberts: OK, all right. So the problem isn't actually the court system, the problem is that they've created an autonomous— *West:* The problem is certainly the court system. The court system has overemphasized a free press by creating an autonomous press that doesn't allow access.

Roberts: OK, so now then press is autonomous. Is it the fault of the Supreme Court that the editors in those papers will not print environmental ethic or will not run environmental PSAs or whatever the case may be? Is that the fault of the Court? *West:* Well, now we're getting into sort of a debate problem, and that is if you establish an initial link and then other teams require you to prove this link through out every single level until you get to your impact the result is

silly argumentation, because there are incredible burdens of proof that we cannot— *Roberts:* Could it also result in the fact that the link is simply not there? [Laughter] *West:* No, because the link— *Roberts:* Does that have anything to do with it? *West:* That has nothing to do with it. *Roberts:* OK. OK. *West:* Can I answer your question? *Roberts:* Yeah. I'd be glad to hear that.

West: I don't know why. We debated you guys on access cases before, and you didn't seem to have a problem with it. The argument is that the resolution must be proven true. Did the Supreme Court and the American judicial system overemphasize the free press? They did by creating an autonomous press. The result of that is that they don't allow access to environmentalists.

Roberts: OK. That's fine. Now then, let's just stop with autonomous press. What is the harm from autonomous press? Is there a harm from autonomous press? *West:* They don't let environmentalists on TV. *Roberts:* OK. So now then, the only reason there is an overemphasis is because there is a harm, i.e., that environmental ethic not being allowed, correct? *West:* That's kind of the way the debate has worked all this year.

OK, cool. Now who's fault is it that they're not allowing that environmental ethic? AJS? *West:* The judicial system. *Roberts:* Judicial system, why? *West:* Because they've created this autonomous press. [Laughter] *Roberts:* Now just a minute ago you told me there was no problem with autonomous press except that the fact that they wouldn't allow environmental ethics on there. Now is AJS telling them that they can't have an environmental ethic on there, or are they simply saying you're autonomous, you do whatever? *West:* I have no idea how this is relevant to this debate.

Roberts: OK, all right, that is fine. Third subpoint off of contention two (A) says behavior will change long term, right? Correct? *West:* I mean are you saying we can't argue an impact to a case? That's silly. *Roberts:* I have a question. '88 brink, right? *West:* The brink is subjective. A brink just means they have to start trying now.

Roberts: Oh, just start trying now, so there's really no threshold, here, right? *West:* No, the threshold is thirty years, and that's the evidence you drop on the top of case. *Roberts:* OK, cool.

Second Negative Constructive[5]
David Israelite, William Jewell College

Off case observation number one. Resolutional links. (A) subpoint is standards. First subpoint is, the word "has" in the resolution equals direct action. Second subpoint is, the Supreme Court will only rule on issues presented before it. Third subpoint, typicality. For the affirmative to be typical, they must deal with all cases and aspects of access. Final subpoint, therefore, you cannot deal with effects. For example, when the Supreme Court approved abortions, they did not approve all abortions.

(B) subpoint is links to my VO. If I can prove that when the Supreme Court or any court ruled on access they ruled correctly, or that the courts have never ruled on environmental access when they ruled on general access, then the affirmative is only left with effects and that's illegitimate.

(C) subpoint is impacts. Impacts in terms of solvency. Because the courts have not dealt with environmental access, it's not their fault. This now becomes a solvency press.

Second observation, and it is in terms of Central Hudson. The sole purpose of this observation is to demonstrate that the court has not ruled on environmental access. First, this was not an access case, therefore it's not the courts responsibility. Second response, it wasn't even an environmental case. Third subpoint is Posadas v Puerto Rico updates Hudson. This is from the *Hastings Constitutional Law Quarterly* 1987: "Indeed, the

[5]Due to technological problems, the first six minutes of the second negative constructive speech were not recorded. The information in brackets reflects the evidence, analysis and arguments offered by Mr. Israelite. The speech was reconstructed as accurately as possible based on the editors conversations with participants and judges. The evidence was verified based on the briefs given to the editor after the final round.

Court most recently applied the Hudson analysis in Posadas De Puerto Rico Associates vs. Tourism Company of Puerto Rico" (Nienow 878). Four subpoint, this equal protection.

Final subpoint is Posadas is a trend towards full protection. *Connecticut Law Review* in '87:. "The doctrine (in Posadas) has since matured into a rule affording nearly full first amendment protection to truthful commercial speech" (Almond, 125).

Please now go to off case value objection. Public access won't do any good. First subpoint is, access rights won't increase the flow of information. Baker in 1980: "Even if greater diversity is desirable, it is doubtful that access rights would significantly increase the flow of diverse information or viewpoints" (860). Second subpoint, wouldn't help society. Baker again in '80: "Assuming that the technical facilities necessary to handle public access requests existed and anyone who wished to print or broadcast a message could do so, society could gain little if few people listened" (860).

Next response is kills market place of ideas. Stanley Ingber, in 1984:

> In addition to being based on a naive belief of a "true" or "best" result, this reform approach also poses the danger of presenting the public with more information than it realistically can assimilate. Consequently, rather than guaranteeing all perspectives an opportunity for success, the equal access for viewpoints approach may only make the public perceive the marketplace as an arena full of nothing but "noise", and thereby decrease the public's willingness to reassess opinions it already holds. (53)

Four subpoint is too ambiguous. Ingber again in 84:

> Both forms of equal access, that which focuses on individuals as well as that which focuses on viewpoints, suffer additional infirmities. Both define ambiguously what must be equalized. For example, should a viewpoint indifferently held be a few receive access equal to that of a perspective passionately held by many? If so scarce resources may be wasted on trivial ideas, and the marketplace may reflect inaccurately the strength, and possibly the values of positions competing for adherents. (53-4)

Next subpoint and that is it actually increases marketplace of ideas bias. Ingber tells us:

> If the first amendment requires that unpopular ideas be given an opportunity to defeat established dogma, government officials should not be allowed to determine the adequacy of access. In short, adequate access proposals almost inevitably further the status quo market bias. (52-3)

Six subpoint is it's impossible to work. Ingber states:

> Regardless of equal access values in which the public have been indoctrinated or socialize will still prevail, and speakers with stature, influence, and skill will still be more persuasive than those without. Because equal access still allows variance in the opportunity to influence among differing individuals or viewpoints, equal opportunity to influence can be attained only through affirmative action such as giving that least popular or least able speaker the most access to the marketplace. (54)

My next subpoint will be seven, will not promote equal influence. Ingber in '84:

> Furthermore, guaranteeing such equal access is virtually impossible without an intricate and extensive leveling system of public subsidies and spending restrictions. Even if government officials could design and properly administer such a system, there is no guarantee that an opportunity for equal access would create an opportunity for equal influence. (54)

Next subpoint, causes government manipulation. Ingber in 84: "Second, such a process might invite manipulation by the very governmental bureaucrats appointed to insure access" (56). Next argument will be, cannot solve for bias. Ingber tells us in '84 that:

> Thus, overcoming the marked bias in favor of the statured communicator may create an even more unfortunate result: it may require us to be confronted most by those who may, in fact, have the least of significance to say. Equal access reform proposals, therefore, either prove insufficient to correct marketplace bias, or create problems equal to those they correct. Additionally, all market reform proposals pose the danger of unacceptable governmental interference with the market. (55)

My next extension is going to be that this will actually equal a chill to the press. If you will allow access you actually get a clouding of issues and you don't get anywhere. Ingber tells us in '84 that: "First if government requires media to bear the cost of providing access for those opposing a viewpoint that the media have presented, media managers may simply choose not to present controversial issues" (56). I.e., they just won't talk about it at all.

Next subpoint and that is that this will actually snowball to governmental control and again this will flip everything they give you on case. Ingber tells us in 1984:

> Finally, governmental interference may escalate from access regulation to more dubious types of governmental control. For example, giving government administrators discretion in access decisions risks the use of administrative machinery to force the media to conform to official positions. (56-57)

Exactly, if you have a generic right of access that's going to mean that the government actually expresses their views more than anyone else. And to that extent you just increase the bias.

Next subpoint, and that is going to be that this will actually violate newspaper individuality and that's why the court ruled against it. There are simply too many bad things to go with it. Lockhart tells us in 1987 that:

> I would also rely on that part of Tornillo . . . holding that a forced right of reply violates a newpaper's right to be free from forced [ONE] dissemination of view it would not voluntarily disseminate, just as we held that Maynard must be free from being forced by the State to disseminate views with which he disagreed. (PG&E vs CPUC 16)

Now I know what they're going to do, and I'm going to make a little preempt on the bottom of this. They're going to do one of two things. Claim one that the problem is the monopolies, or secondly, we have a link because they actually caused it. If they're going to claim a monopoly harm, I'm going to contend the courts didn't do that, because the problem is from the monopolies, not the courts. If they're going to claim that the courts are responsible for this, I'm going to contend that if you're going to hold the Court responsible for destroying the world then the nation that ruled on those issues.

At that point, if all they rule on is what comes before them and all that comes before them is political issues and then they never rule on environmental control then it is not their fault we don't have environmental access. That's why the Court has ruled in this favor.

If a case came to the Supreme Court and said we need environmental access it might have ruled differently, if they saw the great harm. But it is not their fault that the issue of environmental access never came to them. In light of that you have no resolutional link and you will vote negative.

Cross-Examination
Mark West Questioning Israelite

West: We can't look at the results of access, right? *Israelite:* Only direct results, not secondary results. *West:* What is the difference between a direct result and secondary result? *Israelite:* Direct result is if you want to talk about rights of access, you look directly at what they did; not secondary effects. *West:* You just repeated that. What is the difference? *Israelite:* The court never ruled against environmental access. What you're claiming is that they ruled against generic access if you don't have generic access then you don't have environmental access and therefore the Court is responsible.

West: The top level is American judicial system. *Israelite:* Yeah. *West:* I just want to get a little image here so we understand what we are talking about. First we have the American judicial system. It does something to access. It stops access, right? *Israelite:* O.K. *West:* So that's one to two. Three is the result of that stopping of access, right? *Israelite:* Not necessarily. *West:* Why not? Why doesn't the result— *Israelite:* Because when the Supreme Court when, the first step from one to two, when the Supreme Court stopped access, if you're going to hold them re-

sponsible for what they voted on or what they decided, you must look at the values and the ideas that were put before them to decide on. *West:* OK. You're jumping the gun. I'm not really talking about specifics, I'm just saying generally, like when humans think, you have the American judicial system which causes an absence of access which has results, right? I mean that's the way normal people think right? I mean is that— *Israelite:* Normal people? If you're going to look at the link of the rights of access—

West: Is there such a thing as a result of an absence of access? Is there a concept in the world like that? *Israelite:* Sure. *West:* OK. You discussed some of them. Your first one is there is no increase in information flow as a result of an absence of access. *Israelite:* Correct. *West:* You next argue there is not a help to society as a result of an absence of access, right? *Israelite:* Right. *West:* You next argue there is a killing of a marketplace of ideas as a result of an absence of access, right? *Israelite:* Yeah. You don't have to read each point. *West:* I would like to. Your next argument is that there is information overload as a result of an absence of access, right? *Israelite:* Yes. *West:* Your next argument is, well, too ambiguous is a different point. Well, I think I made my point. How come we can't talk about the results of an absence of access, i.e. the environmental ethic, but you can talk about the results? *Israelite:* Oh, you can talk about them all you want, but they're not going to vote for you, because there's no resolutional links. *West:* So, this is not. What you just make. The arguments, these twenty points you just made are not warrants against the resolution, is what you're saying? *Israelite:* They are warrants, all they're doing—I don't even want these weighed as VO's. That's not the purpose. *West:* Why do you read these? *Israelite:* The purpose. I read these to establish that when the Court ruled against access they did so correctly and they are not to be held responsible. *West:* So these are warrants then. *Israelite:* No. *West:* No? Then what are they? Just a way to make sound? [Laughter] *Israelite:*

I mean not in terms of impacts. *West:* I can't believe that we are not allowed to look at impacts. I guess that's what— *Israelite:* You are allowed to look at impacts that the American judicial system has caused. *West:* I only have thirty seconds. *Israelite:* Not impacts they didn't cause.

West: I only have thirty seconds. Final question. This is from Ingber right, I mean virtually the majority? *Israelite:* No. Um, first card and second card are not— *West:* All of that— *Israelite:* Um, fourteen, fifteen, sixteen card are not. *West:* And all of that refers to equal access, right? *Israelite:* Some of the cards do, some of them are theoretical access, although he talks about equal right a lot of his theories apply to all access, equal access.

First Negative Rebuttal
Raymond Roberts,
William Jewell College

Off of whole res[olution] on (A) subpoint, standards. He says we have to look to the intent of the resolution and he says his access case is looking at the entirety of access. I will say that is fine but when we show you that they do not look at all access, then you can vote on whole res[olution] and that should be clear.

Specifically, his next two responses off the (B) subpoint on violation, group those. I'll tell you in terms of one subpoint, system denied equals no access. Two response, then he says that the free press is bad. Three response, on that level American judicial system is not responsible because they don't control what the free press does, they allow a free press but they don't control what they do, i.e., they don't say that you have to allow someone to print environmental ethic ideas in your content.

Specifically, off the three and four cards where he talks about Schmidt card and the Smith card. One response, still says that they are unmoved specifically on environmental issues which feeds the whole resolution argument we give.

Fifth response and sixth response [FOUR] on trend and demand. One response, gives Central Hudson case ruling for here. Two response this was not an access case. Three response, not an environmental ethic case. Four response, long after the environmental problem ever came about. I mean they give us evidence that this is an environmental problem, we deny access and this is bad and then they give us the one case that they link to Central Hudson which is after all this has ever happened which again indicates that there's no American judicial system link. Fifth response, breeds no AJS link.

Case. (A) subpoint. Extends the Smith in '87 evidence that says it goes beyond and then says that this created an autonomous press. One response, did not deal with environmental ethic, and two response, the Supreme Court has been unmoved on the environmental issues. On that level, no AJS link.

Specifically, off the third response where he says systems prevent. One response, what has happened is not bad. Two response, no access is not bad unless it is specific to environmental access, and he grants me that in cross-examination. Three response, on that level what the Supreme Court did was not bad and had no impact. Fourth response, means that there is no overemphasis by American judicial system in this round and you vote negative.

(B) subpoint on broadcasting. Specifically, I want extended my first response that says that there is no specific environmental rights to access and that has not been denied.

Specifically off his first response, says autonomous [THREE] press has acted on its own. One response, that means autonomous press is bad and that is horrible if our resolution was that the autonomous press had overemphasized the freedom of the press, but it is not, it is American judicial system. Two response, on that level not American judicial system's fault.

Specifically next two responses. Says no consensus for framers and Supreme Court not interpret. One response, two conclusions and two separate clauses we have in the constitution not one. On that level I would contend they are separate and distinct.

Specifically off of my third response he says legislative differences. He says one, evidence is only talking about in one case and assumes framers intent. One response, all the evidence says is that its senseless for us to be redundant whether it be in a Constitution or in a contract or whatever. Two response, when we have two separate clauses, i.e., speech and press if they were meant to be the same they would have been included as one and the same and on that level there's no redundancy.

Specifically off his next response off my fourth, group those two. One response does not deny that there's a distinction between oral and written and that is all I need.

Fifth response, on broadcasting not press. He says it is only framers intent and the difference is broken down. One response, this is not talking about framers intent this is talking about [TWO] how another proceeds it. Two response, says the distinction is still there and three response, broadcasting is not part of the press on that level.

Observation two. Specifically, he says we don't wait until the environmental ethic has occurred or until a disaster has occurred we move on holistic. One, I will tell you in terms of first subpoint here that people simply don't believe something until they are convinced. Two, response, the oil spill on the Ohio river earlier this year was a prime example of that. I mean when that happened people became concerned, i.e., a disaster brought them to movement. It wasn't the added press coverage that brought them to movement but was the disaster itself.

Three response, on that level means that that brought attention. Fourth response, it allows environmental to have access. I mean this is a clear indication where there was an environmental problem and they got access, I mean for three days, four days, nothing on the news was there except for this environmental problem which would deny that there's no access to environmental information.

Two subpoint off of the environment. [ONE] One response says this assumes that this is not taking out and we're building toward. One response, if we are building toward. Two response, that means that this happened before the case which restricted access which is, three response, means this feeds that there is no American judicial system link. I mean he tells me perfectly this is building toward. We are moving forward on this level of having the problem with environmental ethic. But then he gives me a case that's after all this has already started, which would indicate that the American judicial system was not responsible. Again goes back to a time as press being responsible.

Contention one. Cross-examination. We find out that it's not bad auto autonomous press. Only thing is that autonomous press does is environmental ethic. On that level you have no American judicial system link.

Off of Contention two. The only thing I need here is that they have to show behavior is going to change. I mean they say thirty years down the road we're going to have a problem. Let's see that that behavior will change within that thirty year period. I think it's pretty clear that there's no link to American judicial system. Fault of problem here is autonomous press. On that level you vote negative.

First Affirmative Rebuttal
John Lapham,
Southern Illinois University

The (A) subpoint of observation one on case. He says it violates whole resolution. But first subpoint, we provided whole resolution by offering you a single case. The second subpoint is that we extend the (A) subpoint evidence. It gives you historical analysis, future preparation, and a guarantees of autonomy, all which is systems analysis we support the American judicial system for the resolutional requirements.

Please go to his last argument on observation one. He says doesn't mean Supreme Court is not bad and access equals environment not bad. The first subpoint is that both squads have certainly argued pejorative cases this year which require you to look to effects.

Second subpoint they have yet to justify you today why you do not look to effects. And certainly to evaluate the resolution properly in a value context you must do that as argued by Mark in the second affirmative speech. Please go to the (B) subpoint. He says that no specific cases. The first subpoint is that I'm glad we offer you no specific cases, I hate to violate whole resolution as I support the authors who write this. The second subpoint is the fault of the link on observation one which clearly guarantees autonomy for you.

He next says there are two classes of the Constitution and there are two clauses and they don't want to be redundant. The first subpoint is I'd ask you to extend the evidence in the second affirmative. It says the framers themselves had no consensus. [FOUR] Certainly clauses in a sentence don't prove this for you. The second response is that the Constitution then also does not reveal interpretation. And because they're both included under the First Amendment they are a single issue. You evaluate the single issue. Furthermore, please extend the evidence at the bottom of the (B) subpoint that says the distinction has to last, from Schauer in '84.

He combines the answers in observation one that there's no framers' intent. The first subpoint is, the evidence was specific to framer's intent. The second response is, because we are now presently evaluating the American judicial system you have to see that technology has advanced and therefore you need to look to broadcasting.

Observation two on criteria. He says people don't believe. The first subpoint is waiting is bad. That's the criteria, the decision rule in 2AC. The second response, you get the ethic from the (B) subpoint in contention one which indicates people will believe you when you go to the mass media. Third subpoint is, don't look for piecemeal solvency, instead look to the fact you can solve the right through the media.

Please go to (B) subpoint on observation two. He says build equals happened before. But, first

subpoint is the system requires whole resolution. Second, subpoint, whole resolution is proven in observation one (A) and (B) subpoint and I would argue by the negative team in terms of being [THREE] the whole resolution argument.

Contention one. He says autonomous equals environment. But, first, subpoint though is the affirmative — please extend the evidence media equals status quo. You divert solvency, you exacerbate the problem. The next subpoint then is overemphasis is proven by the (A) subpoint which clearly allows the American judicial system to do this.

Please also extend that you have guaranteed autonomy.

I would ask you to go to the (B) subpoint of contention one. He doesn't argue this. It indicates you do not allocate time. Media denies presently.

Contention two. He says show change. Well, I think Mark did an excellent job of doing this. He indicates studies will solve. Attitudes are effected. Behavior will change and we could adopt the ethical information. The only obstacle now is the media.

Please go to whole resolution. The first subpoint on whole resolution, he says that's fine but you need whole res[olution]. But, first subpoint is, we are all access. Second subpoint, we choose one case I mean we choose one impact in order to justify why the court is forcing the system of autonomy is bad. The third subpoint is our impact is justified as it is the largest one.

Please go to where he said AJS is not responsible. First subpoint, I've argued this before on case and above. He says the court is unmoved. The first subpoint, [TWO] the Schmidt evidence indicates they always rule this way. The final subpoint indicates they go beyond and preclude legislation.

Please go to the last answer. He say there's no environmental case. The first subpoint, that's because we justify the system. The second response is, communication is a speech and the autonomous press removes it. And the final response is it's not a voting issue, argued by the second affirmative speech, and not refuted by the first negative rebuttalist.

Please go to the first observation by the second negative. I will argue first subpoint and that is they preclude affirmative obligation with the AJS overemphasis. The second response is all cases since 1919 was the evidence in the first affirmative. Third subpoint is, the environment is the greatest threat and that is not argued in 1NC. The fourth subpoint then is that you look to the effect, because the system has continuously denied this. That's the evidence given in observation one.

Please go to solvency on the 2NC observation one. My first subpoint is that you need to preclude legislation in solvency. The second subpoint is this is direct from the court. Precludes affirmative obligation. Cross-[ONE]examination also shows direct results are legitimate and you must vote for these.

Observation two. My first subpoint is it indicates access does not because of the environment. The second response is the example is ruling on the environment to prove observation one is true and to prove why the American judicial system causes harm. The third subpoint is Posadas is one case. Certainly violates whole resolution. The final subpoint is commercial speech is not protected as it perpetuates Cartesian viewpoint.

Please go to value objection. The first subpoint is that they dejustify the resolution. The second subpoint is the court is justified and then they give the overemphasis because they have this definition which clearly decreases the marketplace of ideas.

Please go to the beginning of his argument. The first subpoint is that they ignore contention one which gives the only mass media solvency. The second response is when he applies the Glenn evidence here which indicates they can change. [HALF] (C) subpoint. One, Ingber says time is all equal ideas. Second response, affirmative doesn't advocate all equal ideas. I would argue next subpoint and that is government chill will be fine because right now the press is Cartesian viewpoint. There is no snowball because we indicate private censorship is far worse, and this

comes from Boyan in '74: "None of these rules requires any licensee to offer any time to anybody for any office, or to editorialize on any issue or to deal with any controversy. No one may use a licensee's facilities to reply to silence" (144).

Final subpoint is it is not a warrant against access. Jacklin in '81: "Given the preferences and power of the broadcast industry, the government has usually opted for no regulation. The fairness doctrine is rarely enforced" (279). And that is time and I would argue the value objection does not stand alone.

Second Negative Rebuttal
David Israelite, William Jewell College

1AR hands me the round when he mishandles the link off case. I'm on whole resolution. One response, he indicates that we are typical of access. At that point he grants the standard that they must be typical of access. At that point if they are typical of access throw the whole resolution out. They still have the burden of being typical access and that is exactly what off case is. That is all that I want from this. Especially down at Central Hudson. All I want to stay here is that was not abandoned that is not typical.

I am now off case. This is where William Jewell is going to win this round. He mishandles this. In terms of standards please group his four responses. One response, and that is, the system does not deny. Second response, you do not look at impacts at this point because I am talking about a resolutional link, I am not talking about weighing the impacts at this point.

I am on (A) one subpoint. Has equals direct action—granted. Two subpoint, the court will only rule on the issue before it—granted. Three subpoint, to be typical therefore you have to deal with all access—granted. Four subpoint, therefore you cannot deal with effects—granted. I don't care if you like it, I don't care if you believe it he should have dealt with it and he dropped it, at that point I want no new responses.

If I can prove to you that holistically access is a bad idea I absolutely win this round because

[FOUR] he does not deny that they have to be direct action. He does deny that they have to be typical, and he did not deny that the courts only rule on issues before it, if they do not have the issue of environmental ethic before them it is not their fault. He mishandles this so badly that it means we win the round.

I'm now on the off case or second observation on Hudson. My first response, is going to be this is not an access case, therefore it is not their responsibility. Second response, it's not an environmental case, it's talking about specifically just commercial speech again they're not being typical of the case. Third response indicates Posadas is a trend away and therefore we indicate trend is for full protection which turns everything. And fourth response, this is not whole res[olution] for us because we do not have to meet that burden.

I'm now on the VO. This round is won here. Because if I can prove that the court ruled correctly, they do not deal with environmental impact, or its a good idea not to have access then vote negative. In terms of the first two responses. I have one response, this does not deny theory above and that will take that out. On his second response, please group his two responses. My one response is contention one does not take this out either because it does not talk about impact in terms of environment.

On (C) subpoint please group the responses. You know, one response is *Miami Herald* and Red Lion the cases that the Court ruled on did talk about equal access and therefore the access cases talked about what [THREE] Ingber's theory talks about.

Now, I have a lot of responses that I give out telling you why I think access is bad. I think those are untouched. I would ask you to extend one, it does not increase information. Two it does not help. Third, it kills MOI. Four, it's bad. Fifth point, it increases bias. Six point, it won't work. Seven, eight, nine, extend it all because it is not touched. I want no cross applications, because 1AR doesn't do it. I want no 2AR answers on this, because it is not extended. And I will extend proving that access, generally is a bad idea.

First subpoint, public will not get information. Ingber tells us in '84:

> By equalizing access for all view points, these reformers seek to neutralize the advantages of "well-packaged" and frequently offered messages. In addition to being based on a naive belief in the existence of a "true" or "best" result, this reform approach also poses the danger of presenting the public with more information than it realistically can assimilate. (53)

Next subpoint and that is that it actually deters press freedom. Alpert tells us in '73:

> The newpaper's right to print what it wishes is protected by the First Amendment. If a newspaper is required, under the threat of the sanctions of the Florida Statute, to provide free space which it does not wish to provide and print words which it does not wish to print, it may very well be dotard from printing words it does wish to print. This chilling effect clearly destroys freedom of the press in its most basic sense. (25)

Next subpoint and that is, this will harm First Amendment. Alpert tells us in '73: "Since compulsory printing inhibits freedom of the press at least as much as civil damages, clearly, freedom of the press prohibits any legislatively required right to reply, particularly so when libel is not involved" (29).

Next subpoint and that is going to be, inconsistent with freedom of the press goals. [TWO] Paul and Bealey, '73:

> Though the issue in this case is not a technical one of state action. The issue is whether the government can tell newspapers what to print. Professor Emerson has pinpointed the reason that the Florida statute is unconstitutional, it means that the government can tell the newspapers that the newspapers can be force to print material they don't want to print. This is the very opposite of freedom of the press. (5)

You know, my extensions are not touched and I am going to contend that the Court ruled on this and they ruled correctly. He punts the above standards. That's the standard you have to use. They have to show a direct link, they have to show that they ruled on the issues, and they have to show that the resolution actually causes, and they can not do that, because I prove to you holistically access is a bad idea.

In terms of case side, you know they may be right. Environmental access may be a good idea, you might want to have it, so what. You may kill thousands of people if you don't have it, so what. It is not the fault of the American judicial system.

In terms of the (A) subpoint. [ONE] He indicates that we always talk about these kinds of harms, why change now? You know this is finals so lets just set the resolution straight here.

(B) subpoint on broadcasting. All I want to extend here is that there are no specific cases, therefore no link.

On the two subpoint on the framers' intent and that stuff. All I want to extend here is that they still continue and they don't change their position and most importantly even if it's not it should be. To that extent, even if you don't have a difference there should be a difference.

Observation two on rules. I want one response here that they do not meet the burden of balancing and down below I want to extend it here that it, that observation one (A) and (B) do not pose independent harms.

You know, contention one and contention two don't matter, you don't look to the impacts until you first look at prima facia burdens and if they can't prove a link to the resolution then you don't even go to looking at dead people on the flow. At that point what you will first go to when voting on this round is first go to my standards off case and what they have to prove. Look at the drops. Then you apply those standards on my VO and if you feel they don't show a direct link, if you feel the court has not ruled on this issue, or if you feel they are not typical of the whole resolution in terms of access, then you will vote negative and you will vote for William Jewell.

Second Affirmative Rebuttal

I think there's an important burden of rejoinder, and John makes some good arguments that I talk about in cross-examination. This enormous dump that he makes about this value objection is not relevant in this debate. Ingber is not talking about access, he's talking about equal access. And the position is that equal access requires a response and it requires an enforced diversity of ideas. We are not advocating an enforced diversity of ideas, we are saying that you should allow environmental people access and that is the impact of our case. One group, not people responding to each other, not diverse ideas, we think that's bad, because it crowds out environment.

I will discuss specifically this value objection now. All I want to respond— He says that we do not deal with the above stuff, but I will talk about the bad effects above. He says contention one is not beat. But I would suggest that impact. You know, look at the biggest impact in the round. He says that the reason. He reads extension evidence and the results in a danger to ideas. This assumes equal access, which is Ingber, which is not responded to. That is John's third argument in 1AR, he does not meet his burden of rejoinder, please extend it. All of this evidence assumes that.

He next argues that it destroys freedom of the press, [FOUR] harms the First Amendment, and it is inconsistent with freedom of the press goals. Grant. That is our position in this debate, that the freedom of the press is bad, the American judicial system has created an autonomous freedom of the press that does not allow access to environmental groups. You should be able to look at the effects of certain things. And I will now go to whole resolution in order to justify that argument.

He only extends on whole resolution that it must be typical of access. My argument first of all, is that, again, he doesn't meet his burden of rejoinder. Please extend the third argument from 1AR that says impacts are justified. You look at the largest impact when you are discussing access.

My second argument is that there is no warrant in this debate against access. The warrant that is presented against access is not relevant as he agrees in his second negative rebuttal. It is dealing with equal access, which is not access, that is right to respond, that is fairness doctrine, which is different, as John argues. Which means that the value objection is not relevant and

[FOUR] there is no warrant against our case. Our case now becomes the largest example of access and you look at our impacts, which he fluffs off in the 1NR and he fluffs off in the 2NR. You cannot do that when you are examining the third argument from 1AR on whole resolution that the impact is justified as far as the largest impact goes. I think this is very clear.

I'm now on the two resolutional arguments that he presents as far as resolutional standards. He wants to extend that the system is not justified and you do not look at effects, etc. First argument, effects are OK. Because as he's arguing, as I think I clearly indicate in cross-examination, this whole twenty point argument that he presents are all the effects of access. He justifies this contextually by arguing effects himself.

Secondly, you have to look at effects now, because the only argument presented by the negative is not relevant in this debate, because it is equal access, it is right to respond, which is not access, which is our case.

He next says that the system does not justify, I think you should look at the whole resolution, when I get back to case and discuss the top of [TWO] it.

He argues observation two, you don't look at specific cases, that's true, you shouldn't, you should look at the system and you should look at the top of case, that's where I am now.

He only wants to respond that there are no independent harms. Please extend the 1AC and the 1AR. He argues that they are violating whole resolution by requiring a look at each case. Extend the (A) subpoint that the Schmidt evidence, that they have always ruled against general access, the Smith evidence that they have stopped a legislature from ruling on general access, and the Schmidt evidence that this will increase in the future. The (B) subpoint also says that broadcast in 1AC the Barron evidence on the bottom says there is a trend toward a general movement against access. What you have is a general interpretation by the affirmative saying that general access is being ruled against by the American judicial system, and general access is good because this one group of people, the environmentalists want to get on, and they can't get on, and they should be able to get on without any kind of equal access, right to reply, fairness doctrine, [ONE] and stuff like that. They should be able to get on and have their say, and that is the first contention.

As far as these arguments on free speech and free press being the same, he basically collapses out of this and says that it should be the framer's intent. I think we read you better evidence saying framer's intent is not really true and not really, you know, relevant. This is not relevant to this debate anyway.

I am now on observation two, criteria. This is not responded to. Please extend. You argue a round, and you discuss criteria to evaluate that round. The criteria in this debate is the preservation of the ecosystem. [HALF] Who preserves the preservation of the ecosystem is the question that must be answered in order to determine who wins this debate. If any of this value objection dump impacts upon the ecosystem please vote against us. It doesn't. Please extend contention one and contention two, indicating (A) subpoint that the media is the old paradigm, it is supported by the autonomous press, and this is the greatest threat to man and the earth. That is the criteria.

William Jewell is a fine team, and I've enjoyed debating them throughout this year, but I certainly think that they have made an error in this debate. They don't make relevant arguments. Please support access. [Applause]

Exercises

1. Prepare a flow sheet of this debate.

2. What type of case did the affirmative use?

3. Was the affirmative's a prima facie case? Justify your answer.

4. Which team won the criteria issue? Justify your answer.

5. Which team won the significance issue? Justify your answer.

6. Which team won the solvency issue? Justify your answer.

7. Which team won the whole resolution issue? Justify your answer.

8. Which team won the value objections issue? Justify your answer.

9. Which team made the best use of cross-examination? Justify your answer.

C

An NDT Final Round

The debate presented here is another example of contemporary intercollegiate debate. Appendix B presented an example of CEDA debate; this appendix presents an NDT debate. In both debates the students were under the intense pressures that prevail in the final rounds of the great national tournaments. In this debate the students are skilled NDT debaters adapting to experienced NDT judges. The background of these debaters and the expectations of the judges are different from those that would be found in a CEDA round. A comparison of the two final rounds will help to develop insight and understanding of the differences between the two formats.

The composition and delivery of the speeches in this debate and the exchanges in cross-examination are characteristic of intercollegiate tournament debate. Citations of evidence and authorities are, as in Appendix B, subject to the usual omissions and errors of the extemporaneous method. The documentation of evidence is subject to the same shortcomings as in Appendix B and for the same reasons: The students were adapting to the highly specialized audience found in the final round of a national tournament.

In NDT and in CEDA debate (as we saw in Appendix B) there is a premium on time. This premium on time has made very rapid delivery a hallmark of NDT debating (see Chapter 16, Section III-A). Such speed is often a cause for criticism of NDT debate. Yet rapid delivery has a real-world parallel. Kennedy's aide Sorenson, commenting on the first Presidential debate, noted with evident approval that Kennedy's "rapid-style delivery crowded more facts and arguments into each severely limited time period than Nixon could answer."[1] This effect, of course, is precisely the motivating factor behind the rapid delivery of NDT debaters. NDT debaters appear to be trying to tie Kennedy's world record; the *Guinness Book of World Records* cites

[1] Theodore C. Sorenson, *Kennedy* (New York: Harper & Row, 1965), p. 200.

Kennedy as using the "highest speed by a speaker in public life" — 327 words per minute — in a speech in December 1961. If a President of the United States, especially one who was generally regarded as an excellent public speaker, used such a rate of delivery, we can at least understand, if not approve, NDT debaters using such delivery. Judges understand why this rapid pace happens in the pressure of an NDT national tournament, and some are willing to overlook it in these special circumstances. Note, however, that the debaters are aware of these problems and do try to provide headlining for both their main arguments and their substructure (see Chapter 15, Section V, C).

The following debate was presented in the final round at the Forty-Second NDT National Debate Tournament. The decision was 5 — 2 for Dartmouth College.

An NDT Final Round*

Resolved: That the United States should reduce substantially its military commitments to NATO member states.[†]

---

*John K. Boaz and James R. Brey, eds., *1988 Championship Debates and Speeches*, Vol. 3, 1988. Sponsored by the Speech Communication Association and the American Forensic Association. Reprinted by permission of the American Forensic Association.

[†]The debate was edited from a tape recording. Except for the correction of obviously unintended errors, this is as close to a verbatim transcript as was possible to obtain from the recording. Evidence and other materials used in the debate were supplied to the editor immediately following the debate by the participants. Sources of the evidence have been verified as indicated in the Works Cited. Footnotes supply the exact quotation and other information when necessary. When the source was not located after a reasonable search or was not available to the editor the term "source indicated" is used in the footnote together with any additional information provided by the debaters. Quotation marks surround quotations from unverified sources only when the debater has provided the editor with a photocopy of the original. For help in locating sources in this debate, the editor gratefully acknowledges the assistance of the library staff of Illinois State University.

First Affirmative Constructive
Shaun Martin, Dartmouth College

Contention (1): Nuclear proliferation is bad. We begin with (A), proliferation increases the risk of war. Representative Ed Markey argued in '82:

> As more and more nations crash the nuclear club, the risks inherent in nuclear proliferation rise geometrically; at any moment, a seemingly local crisis may suddenly escalate beyond any possibility of control. The entire earth could be in the grip, and at the mercy of, a "use it or lose it psychology" among nations with the bomb. (ix)

A number of specific scenarios follow: First of all, catalytic superpower war. Nye argued in '84: "[L]ooking further out into the future, if one imagined a rapid rate of proliferation of nuclear weapons, the number of candidates for attempts at catalytic action might increase (65)." Professor Beres concluded in '86:

> [I]n a region of many nuclear powers, it would become possible for a nuclear-armed aggressor to launch its weapons against another state without being identified. Unable to know for certain where the attack originated, the victim state might lash out blindly. In the resulting conflagration, a worldwide nuclear war enveloping even the superpowers might ensue. (9)

The second scenario is nuclear coups. Brian Jenkins of Rand argued in '80:

> [T]here are subnational actors other than terrorists who may come into the possession of nuclear weapons. One faction of a disintegrating government that already has nuclear weapons could seize the country's nuclear arsenal, or a political faction in a nuclear nation could seize and threaten to use nuclear weapons in a coup. (8)

Spector noted in February of '87: "Thus there are historical episodes that remind us that where you have internal turmoil and the presence of nuclear weapons, you can have a very, very dangerous combination (10)."

The third scenario is unauthorized use. Professor Beres argued in '86:

> [R]egional nuclear proliferation would also increase the probability of the unauthorized use of nuclear weapons. This is the case, again, not only because

of the expanded number of existing risks, but because the new nuclear powers would almost certainly lack the safeguards now in place in superpower arsenals. In response to the need for a quick-reaction nuclear force which can be fielded as soon as possible, new nuclear powers will inevitably turn to automatic or nearly automatic systems of nuclear retaliation which are not encumbered by complex and costly command and control checks. (6)

Stephen Meyer of MIT argued in 1984:

[N]uclear command and control could be so lax as to give lower level military command elements the prerogative to launch nuclear attacks. A particularly enthusiastic commander might decide that ever-lasting glory could be attained through the destruction of an American force. (163-4)

The fourth scenario is terrorism. Professor Friedlander argued in '86:

Demaris concludes his well-researched study of international terrorist organizations with a dire warning: "Nuclear terrorism is the wave of the future." With the proliferation of nuclear weaponry and the incremental growth of states capable of developing a nuclear military technology, the mathematical chances of a terrorist group stealing, adapting, or constructing a nuclear device is not beyond the realm of reasonable prediction. British security agencies reluctantly concede that a potential terrorist incident is undeniably credible. In their view, the issue is no longer *if* such an event is feasible, but rather *when* an episode of mass destruction will finally occur. (156)

Professor Beres argued in '86:

The expanded number of nuclear powers would create the conditions whereby microproliferation... might be accelerated. [A]n anonymous terrorist detonation could be mistakenly blamed upon another state by the attack victim. In this way, microproliferation could actually spark regional or systemwide nuclear war between states. (10)

The fifth scenario is crazy leaders. Professor Beres of Purdue argued in '76:

The greater the number of nuclear powers, the greater the probability of irrational national leaders with nuclear options. Such irrational leaders might initiate nuclear strikes against nuclear states even though enormously destructive or annihilating consequences were anticipated. (4-5).

Professor Beres continued:

What about *rationality?* The durability of any system of nuclear deterrence is always contingent upon this assumption.... Should a new nuclear weapons state fall under the leadership of a person or persons suffering from madness, severe emotional stress, or major physiologic impairment, this state might initiate nuclear first-strikes against other nuclear states even though enormously destructive retaliation could be anticipated. (3)

The choice of these leaders is often beyond our control. Lewis Dunn of the Hudson Institute argued in '82:

The significance [of these command-and-control deficiencies] is magnified by the domestic political instability of most of the countries that may acquire nuclear weapons by the early 1990s. Nearly all ... are developing countries, while many either have experienced a successful or aborted military coup d'etat within the past decade or could in the future. (75)

In the sixth scenario is accidental nuclear war. Prolif increases the risk. Leonard Spector with the Carnegie Foundation argued in '84:

The more nations that possess nuclear weapons, the greater the risk that such arms will be used accidentally or inadvertantly. No nuclear command and control system can be fool-proof. The greater the number of such systems, the higher the probility of failure. (4)

Proliferants won't have security systems. Nashif argued in '84:

Any mishap arising from technical or human failure, of course, would probably bring nuclear tragedy, and the guarantees against mishaps and errors are likely to be diminished as the proliferation of nuclear arms increases because small states cannot overcome the complex technical and administrative problems involved very easily. (70)

The seventh scenario is preemptive attack. Systems vulnerability would encourage preemption. Stephen Meyer argued in '84:

[T]he potential for crisis escalation is particularly strong. SNFs are likely to be small and vulnerable with fragile C^{3}I. Hence, there will be strong incentives for preemptive first use of nuclear weapons. (175)

Instability only adds to this risk. *Africa Today* argued in '85:

> The general instability affecting most regions of the world makes nuclear weapons in such areas a greater potential for pre-emptive conventional wars that could easily trigger nuclear exchange or pre-empt first-strike. The management and control of nuclear weapons in nations whose technological capacities are suspect can also create serious risks and dangers. (78)

Preemption, thus, becomes inevitable. Martin Goldstein argued in '80:

> For a proliferant to lose these weapons on the airstrip or the launching pad would be a catastrophe beyond the endurance of most political leaders. Hence, the compulsion to launch early would be enormous. . . . In such a situation, escalation is likely to be terrible and swift. (26)

The eighth scenario is first-strike. Bitter rivals will use nukes. The Carnegie Endowment for International Peace argued in March of '88: The presence of two nuclear-armed adversaries with a history of recent wars facing each other across a common border would present a far more volatile situation than can be found today between any pair of nuclear powers. (27)

Nashif argued in '84:

> To have a stable nuclear deterrence, it is not enough to have a nuclear technical balance. There should also exist a psychological balance. . . . [D]eep hatred and enmity. . . . increases the likelihood of a crisis developing into a nuclear war. (78)

An attack is, thus, inevitable. Professor Beres argued in '86:

> The expanded number of nuclear powers would ultimately create the conditions whereby first-strike attacks could be unleashed with impunity, whatever the condition of the intended victim's willingness to retaliate or the security of its retaliatory forces. (9)

(B) subpoint, impact. Regional wars alone would be devastating. Professor Beres argued in '86:

> Even the most limited nuclear exchange would signal unprecedented catastrophe. The immediate effects of the explosion — thermal radiation, nuclear radiation, and blast damage — would cause wide swaths of death and devastation. . . . Such a war could also have devastating climactic effects. (11-12)

There wouldn't be just one war. Professor Beres argued in '86: "If . . . the nuclear 'firebreak' were actually crossed . . . other pairs of antagonistic states would be more likely to think the unthinkable. A ripple effect would begin to be evident (9)." These wars would escalate. Senator Glenn in '87:

> What is the national security cost to the Administration's inconsistency. Fledgling nuclear weapons programs in volatile areas mean greater strategic uncertainty for the United States. They add to the risk that terrorists will gain access to nuclear materials, either through theft, capture, revolution, or coup; they threaten U.S. military forces deployed abroad; and they increase the chances that — through a premptive strike, an unauthorized or accidental use, or a premeditated nuclear attack — the United States could be drawn into a devastating nuclear exchange. (28)

Calogero of the University of Rome in '78: "[T]he spread of nuclear weapons . . . would also provide the most likely mechanism whereby the present nuclear-weapons states, especially the two superpowers, might be drawn into a nuclear conflict . . . (19-20)."

It would cause a nuclear winter, as Dr. Caldicott argued in '84: "[T]he explosion of 200 megatons on urban centers could induce a 'nuclear winter' which could destroy most biological systems on the planet (25)."

Guess you're wondering what the plan is. The sale of nuclear powered submarines to Canada will not be allowed. This will be done through denial of technology, use of technical safeguard agreements, and appropriate diplomatic measures with emphasis on incentives under the Defense Production Sharing Agreement of 1959 and other U.S.-Canadian defense procurement pacts. Enforcement and funding through normal means. Affirmative speeches will clarify what we mean.

Contention (II): We reduce the risks of proliferation. (A) Canada wants nuclear powered submarines. In June 1987, the Canadian government released a Defense White Paper which proposed, among other things, the acquisition of a fleet of nuclear subs. Since Canada lacks the technology to design and build nuclear subs, it will have to buy the boats. As the 1987-88 edition of *Jane's Fighting Ships* reported: "The Canadian government has . . . made a somewhat startling decision to purchase ten (or a dozen?) nuclear attack submarines (119).

(B) The U.S. is committed to Canadian subs. The U.S. is committed to assisting in the development of Canada's military capability. In general this commitment is embodied in the NATO treaty. As former Assistant Secretary of State Martin Hillenbrand testified in '70:

> Under Article 3, the parties agree to maintain and develop their *individual* and *collective* capacity to resist armed attack. The article provides that this is a *separate* and *joint* obligation, to be effectuated by means of "continuous and effective *self-help* and *mutual aid*. Under this article, therefore, the United States has undertaken . . . the obligation to assist the other parties to become and remain militarily strong. (2226-7)

The commitment to Canada was reported in *NATO's Sixteen Nations* in '85:

> Indicative of his Canadian Prime Minister [Mulroney's] approach is the joint declaration on international security which he made with President Reagan at the "Shamrock Summit". . . . In it the two countries *committed* themselves to "reinvigorate" their "defense and security partnership" through . . . [among other things] cooperation in defense production and procurement. . . . (33)

These commitments have been carried out with Canada's purchase of subs. According to the *New York Times* in 1988: "Mr. Shultz . . . said that . . . the United States would be prepared to sell certain [nuclear submarine] technology to the Canadian defense industry (A3)." The *Wall Street Journal* indicated in that year [1988]: "Mr. Schultz told reporters the U.S. would 'fully cooperate' with Canada's plan to expand its submarine fleet (19)."

(C) Proliferation will be encouraged. Nuclear subs must use highly enriched uranium. For Canada to obtain this weapons grade material would violate existing nuclear safeguards. *Canadian Dimension* editorialized in November of '87: "Should Canada proceed to purchase 12 nuclear powered submarines which use reactors fueled with weapons grade . . . uranium, we will also have violated the 1978 Canada-Euratom agreement as well as the Non-Proliferation Treaty (28).

Such a violation would undermine the existing non-proliferation regime. William Epstein of the UN Institute wrote in August 87:

> If Canada proceeds with the bizarre plan to acquire nuclear-powered subs . . . [i]t will create difficult problems for the International Atomic Energy Agency's non-proliferation regime ("New Defense" A7).

Canadian Centre on Arms Control and Disarmament Director, John Lamb, concurred in September of '87:

> If Canada does acquire nuclear powered submarines, it will . . . be easing the way for other countries, including some regarded as proliferation risks, to acquire unsafeguarded fissile material. As a result, the IAEA's work will be made more difficult, [and] the NPT regime will be weakened. . . . (11)

At this point, we should clarify what is meant by the Non-Proliferation regime. Structurally, the regime consists of the NPT, IAEA safeguards, and other agreements. While these arrangements include technical barriers to proliferation, their more important function is to maintain an international consensus against proliferation. Mitchell Reiss of the IISS explained in '88:

> [T]he international non-proliferation arrangements . . . attested to a view shared by most of the world community that nuclear proliferation should be prevented. . . . These arrangements in effect legitimized and universalized a consensus against nuclear proliferation. (263-4).

Reiss continued in '88:

> These arrangements . . . provided mechanisms with which countries could advertise their nonnuclear

intentions, both to those countries which were parties to these arrangements and those countries which were not. They specified and codified under international law a political commitment not to develop nuclear armaments, and projected this commitment into the future.... To the extent that the international nonproliferation arrangements achieved this objective, they had a restraining influence on the decisions to acquire nuclear weapons taken by Sweden, South Korea, Japan, Israel, South Africa, and India. (263)

Now is not the time to allow any actions which might threaten the NPT. Dr. Lamb wrote in October of '87:

If the NPT regime collapses (as nearly happened at the 1985 treaty review conference and as could yet happen at the 1990 review) and if countries like North and South Korea, India and Pakistan, Brazil and Argentina, and Israel and Iraq begin openly acquiring nuclear weapons, the world would be a lot more dangerous and the risk of Third World crises escalating into superpower confrontations would be much greater. This is hardly the time for Canada to take steps likely to weaken the Non-Proliferation Treaty regime. (18)

(D) Solvency. Diplomatic actions will solve. The efficacy of this approach was demonstrated by VMI professor Wayne Thompson in '88: "Ties with the United States restrain and complicate the making of Canadian defense policy. Canadians must always ask themselves what their partners want them to do . . . (106)."

Technical means involve control of technology transfer. The plan would not allow Canada the means to build the subs. The ability to control technology was reported by the *Financial Post* in '87: "U.S. Navy clearance is essential for these firms [General Dynamics and Newport News Shipbuilding to assist Canada in construction of submarines], because the navy owns some of the rights to all submarines it orders (2)."

Such control would be complete, since Canadian subs would inevitably require U.S. technology. For example, the *Alberta Report* reported in June ['87:] "[A]n American-designed pressurized water reactor . . . is the most likely

power source for the [Canadian submarine] fleet (15)."

Additionally, it should be noted that Canada had to seek U.S. permission to obtain nuclear technology, regardless of the source. The CSM [*Christian Science Monitor*] made this clear in [22] February of '88:

Canada is currently negotiating with both the British and French government a "memorandum of understanding" which will permit transfer of technology needed to build the subs in Canada.... Under a Canadian-American treaty of 1959, though, the U.S. congress must approve the sale to Canada of any "military nuclear reactors and/or parts." (11)

Thus, through diplomatic and technical means the plan avoids Canadian development and weakens the non-proliferation regime. The importance of Canada's role in the non-proliferation regime was noted by Weiss in '86:

[E]ffective persuasion is more likely to come from non-nuclear-weapons nations (such as Canada . . .) that had the obvious capability to become military nuclear powers but elected not to do so. It is in the context of active diplomacy that Europe and the United States must collaborate in engaging such third-party persuaders in this endeavor. (24)

The Council on Foreign Relations concluded in '86:

[I] is . . . essential to preserve and extend the international consensus against proliferation that now exists among most states capable of acquiring nuclear weapons or helping others to do so, and the international commitments reflecting and reinforcing that consensus. (7)

Cross Examination
Martin Loeber Questioning Martin

Loeber: It seems to me, why do the reactor sales, which is what gets sold, right? They're not armed with nuclear weapons. *Martin:* No, these forces are not armed with nuclear weapons. *Loeber:* Right, but they have nuclear reactors on them, right? *Martin:* That's nuclear subs. *Loeber:* Well, why wouldn't the sale or transfer of nuclear technology to Brazil, Argentina, West Germany, and a lot of countries in the world have the same effect of weakening the NPT as this did? *Martin:* Well, there are numerous answers to that question. *Loeber:* Why? *Martin:* The first of which being that Canada's the most important nation. The evidence we read— *Loeber:* Why? *Martin:* I believe on the last two cards it says, is because it would demonstrate most the— It would uphold most the NPT regime—if those nations which clearly had the technology to become military powers and used fissile material militarily—didn't exercise that option, and that would uphold the— *Loeber:* OK. *Martin:* —international consensus against proliferation. *Loeber:* So, why do people prolif? Out of security fears, or do they prolif just because they think it might be a good idea? *Martin:* I have no clue. *Loeber:* Can I see the whole link evidence you're reading to the proliferation rather? *Martin:* Yes, you may. *Loeber:* OK. *Loeber:* So when does the sale go through? *Martin:* When does the sale go through? *Loeber:* Um, hum. *Martin:* I believe they eventually acquire their subs, I don't know, about the year 2,000. Right? The sale is '88, but they don't— *Loeber:* OK. Let me ask you this. *Martin:* 1996, but the intention to buy makes proliferation— *Loeber:* Right. Right. Why is it that buying a nuclear sub creates the perception that people all of a sudden think nuclear weapons are a good thing? *Martin:* Well, it doesn't necessarily. *Loeber:* Well, why do people prolif? Just explain that. *Martin:* They have their own reasons. Maybe some envy— *Loeber:* They envy the nuclear subs. Why wouldn't they prolif with nuclear subs? *Martin:* Why wouldn't they prolif— *Loeber:* Why wouldn't they just build an SSN? *Martin:* Well, they might very well. Our argument is the non-proliferation regime constrains that by having an international consensus against proliferation. *Loeber:* Why is that? Why is Canadian proliferating by achieving these? *Martin:* Why is Canadian? That doesn't seem to be a sentence. *Loeber:* Why is Canadian—or Canada, rather,

proliferating? Or they're not proliferating, right? *Martin:* They're not proliferating. *Loeber:* Well, why is the atomic reactor part of the NPT that critical to the international consensus? *Martin:* Because it violates the Euratom-Canadian Agreement and the Non-Proliferation Treaty. It violates it. *Loeber:* So what if it violates it? Why is that important to the international— *Martin:* You are now using weapons grade material for military uses. *Loeber:* Oh, oh. I see. So, oh, OK. Which card says that they're weapons grade on the a— *Martin:* Oh. I talked to you about it. It is—the *Canadian Dimension* card. *Loeber:* OK. Thanks Cool. *Martin:* Is that it? *Loeber:* Yeah, that's all.

First Negative Constructive
J. Daniel Plants, Baylor University

Topicality. Overview. It's obviously an a priori voting issue. Each comparative interpretation of the topic decided [unintelligible]. Specific standards will be defended within each violation. The first violation is they're not substantial. The (A) subpoint interpretation of "substantially." Subpoint (1), substantial means "much" or "most." "Paving Plus vs. Professional Investments" says, "A building contract is 'substantially performed'... if all the essentials necessary to the full accomplishment of the purposes for which the thing contracted for has been constructed is performed except for some slight and unintentional defects... (271)." The second argument is they have to be over fifty percent. Where is this card? All right. *Words and Phrases* says in 1987: "'Substantially consummated,' for purpose of Bankruptcy Codes provision dealing with whether a Chapter 11 plan has been 'substantially consummated,' means more than half way and more than a mere preponderance (263)." Third, comparison is required. The only way to determine if a reduction is substantial is to evaluate it in the context of our overall military commitments to NATO. You have to look at the part as it relates to the whole. The fourth argument is criteria for measurement. We will embrace any objective criteria and permit the affirmative to defend that, whether it's monetary value, number of weapons systems, force levels, etc., but they have to defend an objective, quantifiable standard.

The (B) subpoint, they don't meet this. They won't be fifty percent of anything. They're just going to argue that they're important. (C) subpoint is our interpretation is better. We preserve meaning for the term "substantially." Each word serves a unique function in the topic. Ignoring one word distorts the meaning of the entire proposition. This is especially true for "substantially." CJS [Corpus Juris Secundum] says, "While it [substantially] must be employed with care and discrimination, it must, nevertheless, be given effect (765)."

Second violation, not a commitment. The (A) subpoint is definition of a commitment. It means a pledge to use force. This is from Paul in 1973: "The National Commitments Resolution . . . defines a national commitment as '. . . the use of the Armed Forces of the United States on foreign territory, or a promise to assist a foreign country . . . (6).'" The (B) subpoint is the violation. This has not anything to do with the pledge to use force. This is just a weapons system. The (C) subpoint is our interpretation is better. First, our definitions are contextual. It's from Paul who wrote a book called *Military Commitments*. The second is delimitation and [unintelligible] allow any single arms sales. We would indicate that it has to be something to do with the U.S. pledge which binds us to action in the future.

Counterplan. We offer the following conditional counterplan to be implemented through normal alliance decision-making processes: Consultation with all NATO allies regarding the reduction of the U.S. commitment to Canada will occur prior to any decision to reduce these commitments is made. Allied input and concerns will be given consideration in deciding whether commitments should be reduced. Funding and enforcement through normal means; negative speeches clarify what we mean.

Observation one: It is not topical. (A) It is not a reduction. There is no guarantee of topical ac-

tion. At best, an effects evaluation is required, which would mix burdens, reduce clash, and severely usurp negative ground. (B) It's not U.S. The counterplan involves NATO action, not United States.

Observation two: Competition. (A) Mutually exclusive. Counterplan postpones ultimate decision until consultation occurs, whereas the affirmative mandates immediate reduction. (B) Net beneficial. Effective consultation requires that no prior decision be made. Rose in '83:

> [N]o member should, without prior consultation, make a firm policy decision or pronouncement on a matter of major concern to an ally; members should take the views and interests of their Allies into account when developing their national policies. . . . (2)

Advantage: Consultation is good for NATO. Van Heuven says in '82:

> On balance, however, the argument favoring consultation within the Alliance is overwhelming. In defense, NATO manages common programs involving large sums of money. Even in those areas where members retain their national freedom of action, consultation is the essential element without which the Alliance defense effort would make little sense. (114-6)

First disad. West German prolif. The (A) subpoint here is that INF puts West Germany on the brink. The *Economist* says in 1987:

> In the present case, a sensible attempt to cull the world's oversupply of these weapons has produced . . . the danger . . . that emotions may now switch the other way, so that in the 1990s it finds itself facing a West European army with a German finger on its nuclear trigger. And all this because of an agreement to remove less than a 20th of the world's nuclear warheads. (18)

The (B) subpoint is the link. First, Canada is on the brink of neutralism now. Hasek says in 1987:

> This coincides with a time when Canadians who have personal memories of our nation as a vigorous, unafraid power, are fast retiring from positions of influence. War, and rumor of war, have taken on mythical qualities for the majority of the younger

generation. Canada is nearing a crisis of self confidence. (41)

Hasek says in 1987:

Therefore, any new defence policies must reaffirm our commitment to NATO, as the first part of a massive educational campaign designed to teach the media and the public the reasons for the maintenance of Western solidarity as well as for the existence of the Canadian military per se. The magnitude of the effort needed can only be comprehended when the methods and resources that are being used to neutralise Canada are examined. (38)

The third subpoint is this causes war. Hasek says in 1987:

If Canada were to withdraw from NATO and NORAD, the armed forces would be neutralised and Canadian sovereignty would be meaningless. While the political damage cannot be calculated, the balance between the Western democracies and the Soviet bloc would certainly become destabilised. This would immeasurably increase the risk of war. (38)

The fourth argument is decrease commitment equals West German prolif. Boston Study Group says in '82:

It is possible that . . . West Germany . . . will require nuclear weapons if the United States reduces or withdraws military force which, in their view, support their defense. In the cases of West Germany and Japan, we have gone to some lengths to avoid providing any incentive or excuse for increased armament or acquisition of nuclear weapons. (10)

The (C) subpoint is impact. World War. Calder in 1980:

[I]f West Germany makes the bomb it may be the end of the world, in the near-literal sense of nuclear war. As noted in the previous chapter such a move would enrage the Soviet Union and it is one of the very few imaginable events that could set the Soviet tanks rolling into Western Europe and into the nuclear war promised by NATO. (74)

Next disad, Southern discomfort. The (A) subpoint is on the brink now. Bush-Dukakis matchup will be real close. *Salt Lake Tribune* said two days ago, "In a Bush-Dukakis matchup, 46 percent of all registered voters polled said they favored Bush and 45 percent chose Dukakis (A3)." The (B) subpoint is they insure a Bush defeat. First, the plan equals Reagan soft line. Bush's fate will be tied to Reagan's. Broder says in 1988:

Even now, as he closes in on the GOP nomination, Bush can be faulted for his simplistic, sloganeering approach to the issues and for his nearly sycophantic dependence on the popularity of his silent patron, President Reagan. (30)

Second, soft line ensures defeat. Bush needs to be tough to persuade Southerners to vote for him. Nixon says in 1988:

It is fine to talk about being tough, but when your hand is called, you have to have something to be tough with. The lesson of every postwar U.S. election, except the anomalous victory of Jimmy Carter in 1976, is that no one can be elected president by advocating a policy of weakness abroad. (12A)

(C) subpoint, impact. Trade wars. Future protectionism will overwhelm any candidate except for Bush. *Wall Street Journal* in 1988: Signing this "acceptable" bill primarily will legitimize and keep alive the ghost of Richard Gephardt. The protectionists will return to present the next President with another assault on the world's economy. We now know that it is politically possible to stand up to this bunch. George Bush just proved that. (24)

It equals atomic war. Harrigan says in 1985: "Protectionism will breed stagnation, retaliation, and world-wide depression. Remember Smoot-Hawley. (30)" Cornish impacts in '80: "Even worse, an economic crisis could lead to a world war, as the bitter experience of the 1930s demonstrated so powerfully. (29)"

The next disad, Gorbachev. Glasnost at a critical stage now. *Washington Times* said in February of '88: "Mr. Gorbachev has set in motion a 'political earthquake' but still faces an uphill struggle within his own ruling dictatorship and a government bureaucracy hostile to his economic and political reforms. (3)"

The (B) subpoint is they save him. Coser says in 1987: "Gorbachev's reform measures will be followed up only if he feels that he is not forced to tighten the reins because of Reaganite threats and the beating of war drums by American rightist diehards (194)."

The link here is that these things would — if it would free U.S. SSNs for maritime strategy. (This one, or this one?) Sokolsky says in 1987:

> From the U.S. perspective, the Canadian decision to acquire SSNs offers some benefit yet also suggest future complications. The benefit would be that Canada would be able to assume more of the burden of North American defense, thus freeing U.S. Naval resources for duty elsewhere in the world. (15)

Our argument is that if these forces will be freed up then we can put pressure on the Soviets. That is what would stop Gorbachev, but if they act this way, it would keep him in power.

Also, maritime strategy link puts pressure on him. Leggett in 1987:

> Other objections to the Maritime Strategy leap to mind. Just when a Soviet leader seems genuinely intent on a military build-down, NATO has produced a plan involving attacks on the Soviet homeland, and has even begun to rehearse them in peacetime. Ammunition aplenty has been provided for Kremlin hawks to argue against the allure of disarmament. (12)

The first impact is equals Soviet adventurism. Glasnost strengthens Soviet aggressiveness. Metcalf in '87:

> [Glasnost] could be seen as the first stirrings of a potential economic giant, bent on aggression whose weight of natural resources and sheer industrial power, no longer hobbled by the Soviet system, could — in the long run and in the geo-political sense — prove irresistible in a bid for world dominance. (12)

Whelan says in 1986:

> So-called "wars of national liberation, Soviet supported and sometimes directed . . . has contributed immensely to the sense of interminable upheaval in the Third World. All of these varieties of regional conflicts have disrupted regional peace . . . and even endangered world peace by risking superpower confrontation (6-7).

The second impact is Yugoslav corridor. First, Romanian resistence to Glasnost causes the Soviets to invade. Urban in 1987:

> Ceausescu has been openly critical of Gorbachev's analysis of "real existing socialism" and said the Soviet way was not for him. . . .
>
> I can foresee a number of interesting developments. The spectacle of undernourished Communist Romania being "liberated" by Soviet tanks with popular Romanian approval is only one, if Gorbachev stays the course. (22)

Yugoslav-Romanian security ties equals nuclear war. Yugoslavia would have to come to Romania's assistance. That would draw the U.S. in. Winsor in 1981: "In general, then, the particular importance of Romania lies . . . in its association with Yugoslavia and in this potential for this association to detonate a major international conflict in the event of an East European crisis (207)."

The last impact is Soviet biological weapon breakout. Glasnost causes this. *Wall Street Journal* in 1987:

> We're beginning to get a fuller understanding of what a versatile concept *glasnost* is. In its constant efforts to steal Western technology, the Soviet Union has now come up with an aboveboard way to access secrets: use international organizations.
>
> . . . [T]he Soviet Union and its allies have shown an unusual interest in biotechnology, proposing resolutions to increase information and technology transfers between East and West. . . . (34)

The impact is a plague. Kucewicz in '84:

> Indeed, genetic engineering could carry mind-boggling military potential. An aggressor armed with such new biological weapons could, for example, vaccinate its own armed forces and population against this new disease, leaving them the only survivors of a world-wide plague. Another nation could be attacked surreptitiously. . . . (30)

Who would ever know who started the epidemic?

Case. We're starting on the third contention. On the (A) subpoint. They say that Canada wants these things. That's fine. On the (B) subpoint, the U.S. commitment. First, he says it's terrible. Doesn't say anything about how this is committed. It just says that we've agreed to give them to them. The second argument here doesn't even say that we're going to give them. It just says that we will assist them. The final argument, there's no indication that they have given these things — is a commitment. Our definition of a commitment is a pledge, not simply giving them a weapons system. Additionally, none of this — this — evidence just says that we're committed to their defense. Right? Which may be true, but that doesn't change our pledge to defend them, or anything like that. They would only change the means of doing this. Right? But that doesn't change the commitment. They're only changing a means for fulfilling that, but not an actual pledge.

On the (B) subpoint, equals prolif. The first thing here is they have to isolate all the scenarios. Right? Some of these cards talk about different countries, but they have to have specific impact scenarios for these countries. Right? They have to have evidence that says if Iran prolifs and this will happen in these other countries. Just reading the evidence up above, the generic evidence on prolifs, the plan doesn't apply.

Second argument is Canada won't have nuclear weapons on board. These things — Sokolsky in '87:

> Arms control groups, which have regarded Canada as an important actor in efforts to control the proliferation of nuclear weapons and as a country in a position to promote restraint on the growing strategic competition in the Artic, have also voiced misgivings. This, even though the SSNs will not be armed with nuclear weapons. (13)

Next argument here is plan to acquire is reasonable. Sokolsky in 1987:

> While some allied governments and groups abroad may regard the SSN announcement as a radical departure for Canada, the origins of the decision are rooted in Canadian defense . . . Western collective security system. Viewed in this context, Canada's plan to acquire SSNs appears to be reasonable, not only in terms of its own interests, but also in terms of allied interests. It is also a decision that need not stand in the way of new arms control efforts — to reduce the arms — (13)[2]

[2]"While some allied governments and groups abroad may regard the SSN announcement as a radical depar-

Down below on the (D) subpoint, solvency. The first argument here is not unique. They could get it in other ways. Britain and France and the U.S. already have these kinds of submarines. It's no indication that they couldn't get them that way. The next is nuclear power plants provide enriched plutonium. Thus, they could get it these ways. Donnally in 1987:

> Development of uranium enrichment capabilities continues in several countries, including some with less industrial standing. The development of laser isotope separation is also becoming more prominent. If this should succeed, and there seems little reason to expect otherwise, the ability to produce weapons-grade uranium could spread quickly. (176)

The next argument here is reactor-grade plutonium makes these weapons. Wilmshurst says in '84:

> Another source of concern was the acceptance by expert opinion in 1974 that the distinction hitherto made between "weapons-grade" and "reactor-grade" plutonium, though still a valid technical distinction in terms of isotopic content, was no longer a valid distinction in terms of proliferation risk. ("Development" 26)

The next argument here is that the NPT fails us. Marin[-Bosh] in 1985: "The present state of affairs regarding the NPT can be described as a distressing example of unfulfilled promise (45)."

The next argument here is that new proliferants threaten the treaty. Goldblat says in '86: Accession to the Non-Proliferation Treaty by the most critical threshold states is doubtful for the foreseeable future (38)," indicating that the NPT doesn't apply to the countries that are the greatest risk.

ture for Canada, the origins of the decision are rooted in Canadian defense policy and Canada's somewhat unique place within the Western Collective Security System. Viewed in this context, Canada's plan to acquire SSNs appears reasonable, not only in terms of its own interests, but also in terms of allied interests. It is also a decision that need not stand in the way of new arms control efforts relating to the Arctic."

The next argument here is threshold states are not members. This is from Wilmshurst in 1984:

> If no new gestures can be devised to bring the potential weapon states into the non-proliferation system, there is not only the risk of another weapon state appearing but an equal danger that the non-proliferation community may split. ("Reforming" 153)

The next argument here is that the superpowers will thwart it in other ways. McGrew in 1984:

> In 1980, the NPT Review Conference was unable to agree [on] a final communique partly as a result of assertions that the superpowers had abandoned any serious commitment to restraints on their own actions as implied in Article VI (5).

And that's the last argument there.

At the top. The first argument here is that prolif is inevitable. This is from Wilmshurst in 1984:

> The most essential component of a nuclear military programme is not the nuclear material nor the nuclear technology, but the political will, supported by a minimum of scientific and industrial capacity. If the political will is there, any country will, sooner or later, succeed in producing and creating the necessary nuclear material and technologies. ("Development" 46)

Also, they can't stop for this. Right? All their evidence says that they would be able to keep them in check, but this evidence indicates that there are other factors driving people to proliferate. They can get the weapons.

Next is nuclear power plants are a mechanism. I'm reading evidence on that below. The next argument here is no barrier. This is from Schwartz and Derber in 1986: "[T]his process has now advanced so far that it can only be a matter of time before the capacity to make or steal nuclear warheads becomes available to any nation or major organization that seeks it (43)."

Next argument here is nuclear states are increasing. This is uniqueness answer. Spector says in 1985:

> [V]irtually all the threshold countries appear to have taken steps, in some cases significant, toward

developing or expanding nuclear weapons capabilities. (11) This is also an empirical [unintelligible] to the impact, if all their preemption evidence is true about how people would strike before the people get the weapons.

The next argument here is prolif would be slow. Gummett in 1984: "Waltz, a leading exponent of the view that 'more may be better', objects to the term 'proliferation' on the ground that nuclear weapons have diffused too slowly to deserve that description (77)."

All this impact evidence assumes fast. The next argument here is doesn't equal use. Waltz in '83: "Fourth, the possibility remains of one side in a civil war firing a nuclear warhead at its opponent's stronghold. Such an act would produce a national tragedy, not an international one (121)." This also takes out escalation. "The question then arises: Once the weapon is fired, what happens next? The domestic use of nuclear weapons is, of all the uses imaginable, least likely to lead to escalation and to threaten the stability of the central balance (Waltz 121)." On the second channel, based on nuclear coups. Won't happen. Waltz in '83:

> Although one may prefer civil control, preventing a highly destructive war does not require it. What is required is that decisions be made that keep destruction within bounds, whether these decisions are made by civilians or soldiers. Soldiers may indeed be more cautious than civilians. *Uncertainty* about the course a nuclear war might follow, along with the *certainty* that destruction can be immense, strongly inhibits the first use of nuclear weapons. (123)

The second argument here is there is no indication that this will cause more [unintelligible] to be used. They will have to win crazy leaders to get this, that these people will be more militaristic.

On unauthorized use, the first argument here is the coup argument takes this out above. The second argument here is safety measures. This evidence that says they won't use them is bad. They could have safety measures. Authorities empirically denied by the superpowers have never been authorized use, and we'll say some more about the other scenarios later.

Cross-Examination
Shaun Martin Questioning Plants

Martin: All the links on disads are soft line, correct? *Plants:* Ah, no. *Martin:* Well, perhaps you'd like to explain which ones aren't? *Plants:* OK. The Canada argument isn't. *Martin:* The Canada argument, meaning the links to Gorbachev, or the SSNs? *Plants:* On the West German prolif argument it is linked directly off of Canada. The evidence says that we need to be able to reaffirm our commitment to them now. We don't do that. That causes Canadian neutralism. They take trips out of Europe. They decrease their European or Continental commitments, and that causes West Germany to prolif. *Martin:* Robert, did you listen to this? *Rob Wick:* No. *Martin:* The link to West German prolif is Canadian neutralism, and they pull their forces out of Europe. *Plants:* Right. *Martin:* Robert, did you hear that? *Wick:* Yes. Why should they go neutral? *Martin:* Why do they go neutral? *Plants:* Because we don't sell them the subs. *Martin:* Well, the evidence says that right now is a critical time to reaffirm NATO commitments. *Plants:* Right. *Martin:* For them, and the only — the motivation for them to do that is our commitments to them. *Plants:* Is any evidence specific to sub causing neutralism? *Martin:* Uhm, are any of the cards specific to subs? *Wick:* You could say, no. *Plants:* Or you could just say, yes. *Martin:* Gorbachev in here says they free up U.S. SSBNs. *Plants:* Right. *Martin:* Is that a good idea? *Plants:* We didn't take a position on that, but we did say that frees up U.S. SSBNs which means we could put more pressure on the Soviets. *Martin:* Is that good? *Plants:* Well, from the standpoint — *Martin:* Will you ever take — *Plants:* From the standpoint of Gorbachev — our position on Gorbachev, it's good. *Martin:* Will you every take the position that's bad? *Plants:* Maybe. *Martin:* How can you do that consistently, oh conditional counterplan master? [Laughter] *Plants:* Well, I mean, depending on the way the matrix oᶠ arguments in the debate come down, maybe we would end up taking that. *Martin:*

Well, my question is, once we straight flip this, can you then go the other way and say, huh huh, you've fallen into our trap. *Plants:* Well, we we haven't taken a position on whether or not maritime strategy is a deterrent. *Martin:* Does that mean, yes, you can do that. *Plants:* Yes. *Martin:* So what's the incentive for you not to just run links to all your disads and then kinda just sit back and see what we do? *Plants:* Well, but this is a link to another argument which has an impact to it. *Martin:* In that case, should you be allowed to go the other way on the impact? *Plants:* Not on West German prolif. We've already taken a position on — *Martin:* On Gorbachev, SSBNs? *Plants:* We couldn't go the other way on Gorbachev, either. I mean — *Martin:* Well, but could you go? *Plants:* The impacts — *Martin:* Once we flip this internally, can you say, that's bad? You're reserving the right to do that? *Plants:* We're reserving the right to go either way on whether maritime is good or bad. From the context of how it impacts Gorbachev, our position is consistent, and we won't — *Martin:* So, would it be consistent for us — uh. Thank you very much.

Second Affirmative Constructive
Rob Wick, Dartmouth College

"Substantial" topicality [unintelligible] argument. First, commitments is plural which proves that it doesn't have to be a commitment to all nations. Secondly, fifty percent is an arbitrary standard. Justify, three, fifty percent. It only has to be fifty percent to Canada. One NATO member state — one or more NATO member states, and this is clearly more than fifty percent to Canada. Next, has no exact meaning, because no rule can be laid down that fixes exact meaning. Next argument, it just means important words [unintelligible]. "Substantial" means a moment of being important. Next, "substantially" modifies "reduce." Thus, it is a relevant comparison to other reductions of commitments. This one is as large as any other that has occurred. Next, small reduction can be substantial. *Words and Phrases* in '87: "[D]efendant would be found to have transacted a 'substantial quantity of business' in Vermont . . . even where percentage of defendant's gross business done . . . was .036% . . . (282)," which takes out his objective quantification standard.

Next argument I guess is that reduction in these commitments is standard. The topic doesn't say reduce the commitment or all commitments, only that some commitments should be reduced. The next argument is reasonability is sufficient. *Words and Phrases* in '87: Defendant's conduct is a "substantial factor" where it is of sufficient significance in regard to reasonability.[3] The last argument is we give them plenty of ground. This has been run by Iowa. This has been run by lots of other teams. Oh, and the last argument is that it overlimits [unintelligible]. There would only be as few cases as fifty percent, and the other fifty percent, he says, use of armed forces. Number one, this overlimits. This means promise not to defend any NATO countries is the only case 'til we decrease the commitment to defend with those subs.

Next argument is that the arms sales are military commitments. We reduce them. *Congressional Quarterly* in '69: "In recent years, members have attempted to scale down U.S. commitments by reducing the annual military aid authorization request (70)." Next argument is we reduce the commitments to Article 3 of NATO. That's the Hillenbrand evidence from 1AC. Leonard Johnson in '85: "[T]he Treaty obligates members to maintain their individual and collective ability to resist armed attack . . . (51)." The next argument is that we reduce the commitments made at The Shamrock Summit. That's the 1AC *NATO's Sixteen Nation's* evidence that says we committed ourselves to the defense and security partnership through cooperation in defense production and procurement. Certainly stopping the sub reduces the cooperation on defense procurement. Next we reduce submarine pledges to Canada. 1AC

New York Times and Wall Street Journal evidence says Shultz pledged full cooperation on sub acquisition. Next we reduce our commitment to Britain and France. We eliminate the pledge to let them sell to Canada. *Financial Post* in '87: "These co-operative Canada-U.S. military procurement pacts, along with 17 similar memorandums of understanding between the U.S. Defence Department and other allies, are coming under the magnifying glass to see if they meet basic U.S. objectives (Gherson 46)." Finally, we decrease the commitment under NATO under Article 2 which says that you have to — you're pledging to help the entire alliance to protect each other and themselves.

The consultations counterplan he says is not topical. First of all, it's topical. It reduces from an unconditional commitment to a conditional commitment. For the counterplan, there's no doubt that after it there's a huge debt. Secondly, this is the U.S. acting in terms of reducing the commitment from conditional. Third, the impact is an affirmative ballot. It justifies the resolution. Only have to do it by one example. Next argument, traditional arguments are better. Rewards them. The more we clash with them, they should just throw them out. Also, you can't allow them to just kick you out in conditional argument because that's de facto conditionality.

(A) subpoint, mutual exclusivity. You can obviously go through most of the plan expressly [unintelligible]. Secondly, it adopts through normal means which includes consultation within member states. (B) subpoint, net benefits. First, it's not unique. The status quo does not consult. Secondly, do the plan, and then consult on whether or not you should reverse the plan. The third argument is, if adopting the policy without consultation precludes benefits, then the status quo is precluded benefits. Next, he can't take the submarines back, so you have to do the plan before you do the consultation. The next argument, there's no guarantee that they would actually do the plan, and any risk of the advantage would outweigh the nothing advantage of this counterplan. Next, two, the plan is a fall-

[3]"Defendant's conduct is a 'substantial factor' where it is of sufficient significance in predicting the harm as to lead reasonable persons to regard it as a cause and to attach responsibility (251)."

back in case the consultation doesn't come out the right way. Next argument, subtrafuge. Have the U.S. lead them to this conclusion in order to be sure of getting the advantage of the plan.

West German prolif. One, we saw the strong NPT regime would stop them from proliffing. They are among the specific countries mentioned in our solvency evidence. Two, this proves the case harms on a more general level. Three, it assumes that we decrease European commitments, and I will argue that the subs are directed against the U.S. Denied perceived as a hard line policy. *Washington Post* in '88: "External Affairs Minister Clark has acknowledged that the decision to spend several billion dollars for the submarines was driven more by concern over the United States than because of any fear of Soviet military activity in the Arctic (16)." Next, the subs free up lots of money for alternatives. *Electronic Times* in '87: In a recent paper he says the twelve nuclear powered submarines [unintelligible] twelve diesel-electric subs [unintelligible].[4] Next argument, there's no backlash. The solvency evidence says that Canada would acceed to us. Also, they avoid competition with the U.S. Lemco in 1987:

> It must be acknowledged at the outset, however, that it is never in Canada's interests publicly to embarrass the United States. For all the tensions that exist, Canadian officials will always try to put the best face on things for fear of irritating their giant neighbor. (91)

Next argument is subs are isolationist. These subs will trade off with the forces in Europe. Charles Doran in 1987: "[T]he realities of politics are such that the drive to establish a credible submarine force for continental defence may come at the expense of the commitment to Europe (9)." Next, subs trade off with surface ships which are more visible. *Jane's Fighting Ships* in '88:

> The effect on the destroyer frigate building programme could have an impact on NATO force levels of the "Halifax" class if not followed by sufficient new construction. The overall total of such ships

throughout NATO is now lamentably low and there is not a single fleet which is exempt from financial constraints on its building programme. (121)

Next visible systems are better. Visible systems are a better deterrent. Epstein in [Oct.] '87: "Nuclear-powered attack submarines would do little to . . . enhance deterrence in the Atlantic and Pacific. . . . Invisible submarines cannot do this nearly as well as can highly visible aircraft, icebreakers, and other surface ships (12)." The next argument, I guess, is that — nope, there is no more.

The Dukakis-Bush advantage. The first argument is it's not certain. It's far — wait. The first argument, there's no certain link. This is far from Europe which is what he talks about. His hard line link evidence talks about — ah, no. It's far from the election. That's what the "E" stood for. Secondly, we could just do the plan after the election. There's no reason you'd have to announce it now. The third argument is that it flips above; would take it out, and makes them look more [unintelligible]. Next, it's not unique. Troop decreases. Mann in '87: "U.S. troop withdrawals from Europe. This could become an issue by itself, apart from curtailments in conventional forces . . . (16)." Next, it's not unique, because of Carlucci [Frank C., Secretary of Defense]. Mann in '88: "The Reagan Administration's retreat from major increases in defense spending, began a year ago. This was accentuated by the appointment recently of Frank C. Carlucci . . . (18)." Next, the character does not fit the policies of the re-election. Mann in '88: "Thus far, the 1988 U.S. Presidential campaign has been dominated by controversies over the character and integrity of individual candidates. Issues and policy have been secondary, including national defense and the civilian space program (16)." Next, it's too early to impact. Mecham in '88:

> The lack of focus on defense does not surprise Stephen J. Wayne, a political scientist at George Washington University here, who specializes in the presidency. "It's too early in the campaign," he said. "It's not what the average person is looking forward to in the primaries (19)."

[4]Source indicated.

The next disadvantage is Gorbachev. First of all, the flips above would take it out. Secondly, there's no impact to Soviet adventurism if there's no prolif. Three, do the plan later on. Means Gorbachev has already consolidated his power. Four, the subs aren't going to be here until 1996, so there wouldn't be any shift in U.S. subs until then. Next argument is that the subs will just obstruct the U.S. maritime strategies. Sokolsky in '87:

> [I]t is difficult to see how Canada's abandonment of plans to acquire its own SSN fleet, capable of under-ice operations, will persuade the United States to abandon its plans. For those in Canada and elsewhere concerned about unilateral U.S. naval activity in the region, a greater Canadian presence can be seen as desirable since it would, at the very least, restrict U.S. freedom of action. (16)

Next, won't be built for years. *Christian Science Monitor* in [19 Feb.] '88: "The first sub is not scheduled to come out of a shipyard until 1996 (9)." Next, they trade off with AHW. No, I don't want that. The next argument is that they're too few subs to matter. Eayrs in 1987: "It is hard to see how a few additional boats—at most three in each ocean, three, in refit—would make much difference to the Soviet planners' calculation of the overall 'correlation of forces' (10)." Next, there's no big Soviet sub threat anyway. This is Donald Cox in '87: "With the development of... long-range ballistic missiles, there is no obvious reason for the Soviets to wish to deploy ballistic-missile-bearing submarines (SS-BNs) in the Canadian Arctic (100)." I guess that's— *Martin:* Not unique. *Wick:* The next argument is it's not unique. This is the *USA Today* today [28 March 1988]: "[T]he 3,200 troops deployed to Honduras... would be back by Wednesday. Another 1,100 troops, a Fort Bragg engineering unit in Honduras since January, also go home this week... (1A)." They argue at the bottom, CBW epidemic, but we're arguing—it says, we—unless you vote for us you'll break the taboo on using weapons of mass destruction which also includes biological weapons.

The (A) subpoint, he argues topicality. The evidence isn't bad. It distinctly says we have pledged to defend all of each other. The "Shamrock" sentiments, etc. He says, commitment is not a pledge, but we're pledging to—our pledge to help them—is to help them get the means to defend themselves.

(C) subpoint, prolif. He says, specific scenarios. We're getting them. He says, Canada doesn't have weapons on board, but the weapons grade uranium could be used to make a weapon. This is a source for other countries to make a weapon. He says, they have reasonable need, but this is answered on the flips also. It doesn't kick out prolif.

(D) subpoint, he says Britain and France, but they're under the NPT Treaty. They can have 'em. He says, you can, and France will give them, but they won't do so. We're preserving an international [unintelligible] against that. He says, reactor creates uranium, but which doesn't matter, because it's not concentrated enough to be weapons grade. There's the huge difference thats— The (C) subpoint evidence makes the distinction. He says, NPT falls first. First of all, prolif is not inevitable. This is from Lewis Dunn in '83:

> There is no inexorable dynamic leading to a world of many nuclear weapons states. On the contrary, such current estimates probably will prove as unfounded as those 1950s predictions that confidently warned of twenty-five or thirty nuclear weapons states of the mid-1970s—and for similar reasons. (205)

Next argument is that it has been successful. Fischer in '87: "[T]he NPT and its regime have been an effective break on further 'horizontal' proliferation. Far from unraveling, the treaty is more viable than in 1980 (228-9)." Next argument is it doesn't matter if the technical safeguards are broken. We're preserving the international consensus. Gets it. Which has empirically worked. That's the Council on Foreign Relations. Next, Canada is the key NPT state. That's the 1AC evidence. Next, the subs encourage prolif. Epstein in [Oct.] '87: "Canada's precedent would weaken the entire nonproliferation regime. It would create problems for the International Atomic Energy Agency's safeguards system and for Canadian compliance with it. It would encourage other states to do likewise (11)." They argue at the bottom that the superpowers would thwart the plan. Is an example of them not doing that. It preserves the ways that cannot do so. He argues at the top of the case that it's inevitable. He argues, we don't solve which is above. He says, nuclear power plants, but they're not good enough to give weapons grade uranium. That's in the (A) subpoint or (B) subpoint of case, forget which.

On contention (II). He says, no barriers to acquisition but the IEA safeguards and the international consensus deters people from doing it whether they've signed the treaty or not. He says, it's increasing, because of Pakistan. There's no proof of this. This is only speculation. Also, we would still preserve from other countries. He says, empirically no impact which is because there hasn't been prolif in the past. They've only been [unintelligible] with standing powers. He says, empirically been slow, and the impact evidence. It seems fast, but the impact evidence doesn't assume fast or slow, and if you get rid of these safeguards there will suddenly be a lot of increased prolif. On two, no. He says, eight, they wouldn't ever use them, but we're giving specific reasons why it would. Vulnerability, insanity, the fact that you could plant one, and nobody could tell who had planted it, and choose, etc. All confused. He says, it wouldn't happen, but the Jenkins says it would. Turmoil would make it dangerous. They would use in a coup or acquire it in a coup. It's empirically happened a lot of times. There's been lots of coups. He says, caution, but these people are fighting desperately for the lives. Also, all the unauthorized use and other stuff, and he says, no war without crazy leaders. But we're winning crazy leaders. He grants that. All the reasons why prolif is bad are granted. We're winning massively a link to proliferation. More evidence on the solvency of the

NPT Treaty if I get time. I seem to have time. That it's been successful. Flow this on the top. This is — right where he argues solvency. Louis Dunn in '87:

> [S]ince 1970 only one additional country is known to have detonated a nuclear explosive device. The treaty clearly is a success in helping check the further spread of nuclear weapons, serving the security of all its parties, indeed of all countries. (18)

Next argument is they don't show how you could get weapons grade uranium absent Canada's example in the plan. Also, the next argument — more evidence from *Non-Proliferation and Global Security* in '87: "The current non-proliferation regime, as enbodied in the Treaty on the Non-Proliferation of Nuclear Weapons (NPT) . . . , has been relatively successful despite growing criticism . . . (Ing 119).

Cross-Examination
J. Daniel Plants Questioning Wick

Plants: The first question I have for you is, your answer on one of the disads is these things won't be built 'til the late 90s, right? *Wick:* Yeh. *Plants:* Now, how is it that these other countries prolif once we give these to Canada? Is it that they get the weapons grade uranium from them? *Wick:* Two reasons. The first — well — the first is all this general weakening of all the laws, rules, and international consensus is like international pressure not to do it. *Plants:* But they don't have any access to the uranium that way. *Wick:* That's not true; they could get it also, that's the other thing, Canada presents the (C) and (D) subpoint, the (C) subpoint evidence says that. What they do is, they follow Canada's example. They buy themselves a nuclear power— *Plants:* Who's going to tell it to them? *Wick:* The same countries that'll sell it to Canada. *Plants:* The U.S.? *Wick:* —unless we prevent them. *Plants:* The U.S. *Wick:* Yes, or Britain or France. *Plants:* Do we have any commitment to do that now? To sell to these other countries? *Wick:* No, but that's because none of the other ones have the gumption to ask us to do this. Canada couldn't get away with it. We should shut 'em down. *Plants:* OK. Then, when would they do this? Like who wouldn't sell these subs to Canada 'til like 1996, and they wouldn't get them, and these other countries wouldn't get them 'til at least later, right? *Wick:* Than what? *Plants:* Than '97—I mean there's no way that we would be giving them subs— *Wick:* Well, you've assumed that they can't—that they don't have any access to uranium which obviously isn't true. *Plants:* Well, now, you made this distinction about how—what—a certain kind of uranium, there's only one kind that will do it. *Wick:* Well, what the distinction is is how enriched it is. *Plants:* OK. Well, how do they get that? *Wick:* I mean, they could steal it. They could buy it from China, the Soviet Union, France, or Britain, etc. *Plants:* Now, wait a second— *Wick:* While we're preserving a consensus that stops them from doing that. *Plants:* Wait. Rob, your answer to the first argument about how Britain and France would construct them, but the plan was, they were under the NPTs so that there was no way that they would give this weapons grade uranium to these other countries. Where are they going to get it from? *Wick:* Well, we solve this in two ways. We're preserving the international consensus which means the individual nation won't move to acquire the weapons grade uranium. And secondly the consensus stops other countries from selling it. If you violate that consensus, Britain would say, there's no reason we shouldn't do the same thing the U.S. does and make a few bucks by selling to, you know, to Y.

Plants: On West German prolif, does any of your evidence that says it frees up resources, any of it talk about the Canadian commitments and how they view their role in Europe or NATO? I mean, your card says that there is a monetary trade off. *Wick:* Yes, it's all from like the Canadian Defense Center and the Canadian Cabinet sources basically. *Plants:* Well, the cards say that like there would be less surface ships, but

there's no evidence about like continental defense, is there? Land troops? *Wicks:* This says, um, we the Canadian Parliament—I mean Cabinet have decided that this would trade off with our other purchase plans to increase our commitments.

Second Negative Constructive
Martin Loeber, Baylor University

You know, if you run a new case, you should at least listen to the link arguments that we make in the first negative. Our link answer, our link arguments that we're making in the first negative on defense consensus in Canada, there is no answer to this which means even if I grant all their evidence on how it trades off with conventional forces, big deal. If you have a defense cut, then it destroys the consensus. In addition, we'll read evidence below that says, the only way to get Canada to spend money on defense is to make them mad, and we make them mad by violating their straits, so they buy subs from us, so that's the only way to get a defense consensus. I think we'll clearly win the debate. In addition, if we win West German prolif, we'll link flip the case.

First argument, he says, we solve. NPT. First argument is that there's no evidence that says West Germany makes their decisions on this. They don't give a dang about the NPT. They only care about security considerations. Second argument is strong NATO stops. This is Kosminsky in '86:

Rather than resulting from a calculated decision to reinforce deterrence within an Alliance or European framework, a German move to acquire nuclear weapons would be more likely to occur under political and military conditions marked by a radical loss of confidence in its allies. (26-7).

Third argument is he concedes the brink evidence. More evidence on this from the *Economist* in January [1988]:

The first has emerged on West Germany's right wing, where mutterings can be heard that if West

Germany's allies will not defend it adequately (French and British nuclear weapons are seen as no substitute for American ones), then West Germany must have its own finger on a nuclear trigger. (11)

The last argument here is West German prolif equals world prolif. In addition I would point out that this is a faster time for him, because they're claiming on the case that they get 1996, right? But our argument here will be that as soon as you do the law Canada neutralizes. That causes West German prolif which out-flips and out-time-frames the case. Dunn says in '82:

> Should West Germany acquire nuclear weapons, at least some other European countries will be pressured to do the same. . . . And by acquiring nuclear weapons, those two countries would fundamentally undermine any remaining nonproliferation efforts. . . . [T]hose countries that had not "gone nuclear" before for fear of sanctions would have less reason to hold back and the position of opponents to the acquisition of nuclear weapons will be weakened. (67).

And I'd like to point out also that this evidence gives a much better rationale than the case, because it doesn't deal with reactor technology but more with the actual weapons themselves.

He says, second, case harms. We're flipping that. Third argument, assumes decrease European commitment. They're out of it. First argument, extend the evidence that says they're on the brink of neutralism. There's no answer to this which means Canada is on the brink which means they don't get any new answers. Also, Hasek says in '87:

> The campaign to disarm the West psychologically dates back more than half a century. Now, when the new Soviet leader has made it apparent that the Politburo is placing an unequalled emphasis on the whole programme of indirect attack the danger is greater than ever. (40-1).

Hasek says in '87:

> We are now witnessing the last phase of neutralisation. This is a concerted propaganda campaign which is designed to "Finlandise" Canada and to sever the links with NATO and NORAD. The psychological preparation for this campaign has been

evident for the past several years, but the overt mass appeal could be said to have started with the television showing. . . . Tina Viljoen cast doubt on the value of Canada's sacrifice in the past wars by arguing that the wars had nothing to do with Canada. In any case, from a long-term historical viewpoint, nothing was solved by them even in Europe. Therefore, according to the films, the only sensible option is for Canada to be concerned solely with its own sovereignty and to leave NATO and NORAD. (37)

And I'd also like to point out that this link evidence says that they don't have an inherent commitment which means the only way to secure that is to make them mad by violating their sovereignty and giving them subs.

Third argument is you have to reaffirm NATO commitment in order to keep them in NATO. The Hasek evidence says that new defense policies must reaffirm our commitment to NATO, i.e., something like a sub in order to educate the public and keep them involved in NATO. Hasek says in '87:

> The roots of the armed forces have to be firmly anchored in society at large by revitalizing the reserves and reforming the officer training corps and high school cadet units. The exposure of a greater proportion of young Canadians to military training will not only restore confidence in our ability to defence ourselves. . . . (41)

Fourth argument is he concedes the impact evidence that says if Canada neutralizes that that would destroy NATO, because our defenses would be weakened. Also, Hasek says in '87:

> Exploited by forces hostile to democracy, the continued crisis in Canadian defence can be fatal to Canadian sovereignty, cause irreparable damage to the Western Alliance and seriously destabilise the nuclear balance. It is time to enact policies which will permit a secure Canada to play a stronger part in maintaining peace. (36)

Next argument is C^3 [Command, control, communications] vulnerability equals West German fears. You'll note that all the link talks about NORAD and if we abandon NORAD that that would equal vulnerability of first strike. That scares the Germans. Williams in '86:

[I]f the Soviets know that they cannot decapitate the American command structure, U.S. retaliation being then imminent, the value of deterrence is increased. This knowledge must increase European confidence in the American extended deterrent system upon which their own security continues to rest. (8)

Next argument is perceptions of superiority equal West German prolif which would be likely if we lost NORAD. Drum says in '82:

> But there are certain possible shocks that might cause West Germany to rethink or question its reliance on the security framework provided by NATO. West German perceptions of increasing Soviet strategic superiority, for example, could lead to more vigorous questioning of the alliance's effectiveness and of the American guarantee. (66)

He says, number four, subs are directed versus the United States which is the reason they're asking for them in order to protect their sovereignty which proves the only way that you can get them to build their subs is to make them mad by violating their sovereignty. The second argument is that they wouldn't build anything else otherwise. The only reason they're doing this is to protect their sovereignty. Shallhorn in '87:

> At about the same time senior Department of National Defense officials began telling the parliamentary defense committee that nuclear-powered submarines were "affordable" and were being considered to replace Canada's three British-built Oberon diesel-electric submarines, Canada seemed prepared to spend billions on under-ice-capable nuclear-powered submarines just to keep tabs on the U.S. Navy. (16-7)

Aviation Week in '87: "A primary objective of the expanded maritime role is to deter, rather than simply monitor U.S. and Soviet intrusions into Arctic waters that the Canadian government considers to be violations of national sovereignty. (57)" Sokolsky in '87:

> It is these nuclear-powered submarines that will give the fleet a more balanced ASW capability. They will allow the navy to operate in all three oceans . . . . The passive fixed system will still be crucial for surveillance and sovereignty protection, since most of the time the SSNs will be in the At-

lantic and Pacific. But the government regards it as important to Canada's sovereignty, as well as to its ability to contribute to North American defense, that the navy have an active under-ice capability similar to the active air defense forces that back up ground-based radar. (14-5) Which proves that the reason they do it is in order to protect their sovereignty, but it is also useful in defending NATO.

He says, number five, sub prevents dollars for alternatives. First argument is they can build the subs. There's no cost problem. *Aviation Week* in '87: in 10 Canada's long-delayed defense white paper, scheduled for release in June, will decree a more active military role for the 21st century, with a three-ocean maritime strategy reliant on 10 new nuclear-powered attack submarines. . . . (56)

Next argument is that they enhance security. Sokolsky says in '87:

> Nor is the decision inconsistent with Canada's support for arms control measures. In the long run, Western collective security and the cause of arms control can be furthered by a greater Canadian maritime capability in all three of its oceans. (16)

Next argument is independently, they won't send any troops. Their troop level is low. Our link is no longer troops out rather NORAD and the collective defense of the Arctic. This is *McLean's* says in '87: "Canada could not live up to its 19-year-old NATO commitment to help defend Norway in wartime (14)." *McLean's* says in 87: ". . . Ottawa is preparing to surrender its commitments in Norway (14)." Also, Canada is second to the bottom in spending which means they don't spend money, and the only way to motivate them to spend money is to make them mad by violating their sovereignty. Simpson says in '87: "The raw numbers told it all: Canada was spending the second-lowest per capita amount on defense of all the NATO countries. Thank God, ran the joke, for Luxembourg (9).

Hamilton says in '87:

> Canada has been reluctant to do so, though it has recently reviewed its overall defense policy. Indications are that a greater emphasis on conventional defenses of Canada will result. In addition, Can-

ada, whose defense spending as a percentage of GNP is the second lowest among NATO allies, needs to do more for common western security. (E1758)

Sokolsky says in '87:

The total personnel level is about 85,000 and the defense budget is roughly $10 billion in Canadian dollars ($7.5 billion U.S.), which translates into just above two percent of gross domestic product, placing Canada next to last in NATO, just above Luxembourg. (13)

All this evidence proves that Canada doesn't spend that much which means that they have no inherent reason to do it. The only way you could do it is to force them to sovereignty, and the only thing they'll do when you violate their sovereignty is buy nuclear subs.

He says, six, there's no backlash, and they avoid embarrassment. That's not our link. Our argument is they have to reaffirm their commitment to NATO. Otherwise they'll become neutral which causes C^3 vulnerability. In addition it would also cause neutralism which could tip the balance to the West. Our Hasek evidence is better.

He says, seven, subs trade off with forces in Europe. All this evidence says is that if they spend more money on subs they might not be able to put forces in Europe. First argument is counterplan. We'll give Canada money. We will take the money from conventional forces in the United States that are not deployed anywhere. This will take out the flip, right? Which means they get money which gives them enough money to keep their forces in Europe. Second argument is there's no evidence that says that if you get the money — no, no — if they get more money by banning subs that they would build more conventional forces. Our above evidence says that they're unlikely to spend more money. They have an inherent reason not to.

He says, eight, trade off with surface ships and visibles are a better deterrent. First argument is even if it does we're still winning the NORAD and neutralization links. Second argument is

there's no evidence that says that abandoning subs would result in an increase in funding for surface ships. All it says is that if you spend money on subs you can't spend it on surface ships which means we're still winning on link. Third argument is the fact that it is visible and a better deterrent is not our link to West German prolif. We're still winning the Canadian neutralism debate.

Now we can concede all these arguments about trading off with surface ASW. There is no answer in the 2AC trading off with surface ASW. There is no answer in the 2AC to the Canadian defense consensus, and for them to reach an answer to this in the 1AR, I suggest, would be new which means we win the debate there.

Southern discomfort. He says, it's far from Europe — no, no — far from the election, but our evidence says the polls are close. In addition there's every reason to consider that this would be translating concern especially since the plan is done over the near term. He says, second, they could do the plan after election. First of all, this contradicts their conditionality bad arguments. They're changing the plan. If anything, it should be a reverse floating issue on them. I'm not going to claim that, but if they go for conditionality, make them eat this as well. Second argument is the plan doesn't do that, right? It does it immediately. In addition if you want to vote for them after the election, I suggest you do so. You should vote for us in this debate.

He says, third, the flips above. I'm sure the South perceives that. They're more likely to perceive as hosing over Canada. Perceptions of credibility are critical to Bush. This is *Wall Street Journal* in March [1988].

If a genuine liability was exposed Tuesday it is the belief that a candidate can build his agenda around polls or press clippings. . . .

The successful candidate for high office must have some credible, discernible core of beliefs. . . .

George Bush, after a long career, has achieved credibility with a large constituency. (24)

Next argument is the plan kills that, right? The plan ensures that Reagan looks bad. He reverses himself on this decision. That translates into Bush which means independently of whether or not — independently of whether or not they increase deterrence, they still make Reagan both bad by making them think that we're hosing over the Canadians.

He says, troop decrease and Carlucci. There's no evidence on why that's our link. In addition the Canadian link on how we're hosing them over would take this out.

He says, five — or six, that character doesn't affect the election. Our evidence says that they destroy Bush's character. In addition our evidence says that empirically that's the way to get himself elected.

He says, seven, it's too early to know whether defense has an impact. That's no longer our link. Our link is credibility of Bush being consistent with our allies.

And extend the impact. Trade users. There's no answer.

Gorbachev. He says, flipped above, but if I grant out the uniqueness answers, it'll take it out. He says, there's no impact to Red spread. That's true. He says, they do it later in 1996 which all takes this out. Oh, also the subs are not built 'til 1996 which takes out any kind of links in this, but it wouldn't play into West German prolif nor Southern discomfort, since they'd be perceived. He says, subs obstruct maritime strategy, but our evidence says — that — our evidence on the other side says, enhance security. He says, for years, that's fine.

Cross-Examination
Rob Wick Questioning Loeber

Wick: Marty, your argument is that rather than trading off with other naval forces — rather than trading off they would just put it into solve their deficit, right? *Loeber:* Who? *Wick:* Canada. *Loeber:* Ah, yeah. They might have a couple of AFDC programs, or something. I don't know. *Wick:* If that's true, then why wouldn't your counterplan to give Canada money just put money back into their deficit? *Loeber:* Oh, because

it's stipulated on them keeping the troops in Europe. *Wick:* Where do you — OK — Why doesn't this take out the link to your disadvantage? It proves that Canada is not going neutralist, because the U.S. is sitting there guaranteeing that — *Loeber:* That has nothing to do with Canadian — *Wick:* —Canada's forces stay in Europe. *Loeber:* No, no, no, no, no, no, no, no. That has nothing to do with Canadian neutralism. Our link to Canadian neutralism — *Wick:* Wait a minute, how can Canada be neutral if it's stationing forces in NATO European countries? *Loeber:* Our link to Canadian neutralism is that Canada no longer perceives a need to defend the West. All right? *Wick:* Yeah, so, Canada has forces in Europe. Why isn't that defending the West? Are they going to put them in Eastern Europe? *Loeber:* No, they're going to pull the troops out. *Wick:* Your counterplan makes sure that they cannot do that, so where's the link? *Loeber:* No, we don't. The counterplan just gives them money to do so. We don't, we don't like hold a gun to Canadian troops and make them stay in Europe. *Wick:* OK. So the counterplan gives them money and doesn't tie their hands at all? *Loeber:* No, the counterplan says, if you plan to put troops in Europe, we'll give you money for it. *Wick:* But otherwise, eh — *Loeber:* We won't. *Wick:* OK. Well, why wouldn't Canada just accept free money to to like pay for all their people to stay in Europe? *Loeber:* Well, because they might not like the risk. *Wick:* If they wouldn't like the risk, then the counterplan can't solve, correct? *Loeber:* Right. All this does is counterplan out your turns. *Wick:* Tell me word for word, what does the counterplan do? What are the stipulations? *Loeber:* The counterplan says, if Canada wants to maintain forces in Europe, we will help them do so.

Wick: If they want to maintain forces in Europe, we will help them. *Loeber:* Um, hum. *Wick:* OK. So we will make it like free for them to maintain forces in Europe. *Loeber:* No. We'll just help them pay the — keep the money. *Wick:* Pay them how much? *Loeber:* As much as they—as we think is necessary. *Wick:* Well, how the hell are Shaun and I supposed to figure how much that is? *Loeber:* Current levels. To maintain current levels, we will pay them. *Wick:* OK. So now where's the link to your disad, and how can they be neutral if they're keeping Western European troops in Europe? *Loeber:* See, you're making a wrong assumption. If they become neutralist by collapse of the Canadian consensus, then they no longer would desire to keep troops in Europe. *Wick:* OK. Now, em, why if Canada had troops in Europe would West Germany prolif? *Loeber:* What? *Wick:* Western—even if Canada was neutral, but they had troops in Europe defending Germany— *Leober:* For one thing, NORAD would collapse and they'd perceive C^3 vulnerability. They'd also perceive— *Wick:* What's the risk to NORAD vulnerability? *Loeber:* What? *Wick:* Isn't NORAD on land? How do you protect NORAD better? *Loeber:* What? NORAD is our defense command in the north, a part of the DEW line in Canada. *Wick:* On land, so how do subs defend it better? *Loeber:* We're not arguing that. That's the point. You missed the whole link in the first negative. *Wick:* You said NORAD vulnerability. *Loeber:* Right, because you erode the defense consensus.

First Negative Rebuttal
J. Daniel Plants, Baylor University

This bio weapons turn is silly. There's no way they get that. Extend the evidence. It says, Glasnost caused them to break up. They'll get our technology.

On the counterplan, non-topicality. He says, topical. Unconditional versus conditional. First, this does not explain. Second, they shouldn't get to explain it in 1AR. Second, it wouldn't be a substantial reduction. It would only be a small decrease in our pledge. Their argument, this is wrong. This commitment would remain until the reduction was actually implemented. There wouldn't be any reduction in commitment until we voted to do away with something. The fourth

argument here is it will be a political not a military commitment. Kennedy in '84: "Consequently, NATO consultation is a *political* rather than a legal imperative (12)."

[Unintelligible] he says will be the U.S. action, but it wouldn't be. We'd only be going into these things. Also, it would be a NATO decision. The [unintelligible]. He says impact. Affirmative justifies ballot. But, first, that's not true. The competition arguments are granted away. We can kick it out on that. Second, there wouldn't be any advantage to that. Even if they could seize it, even if they consist, there would not be an advantage to [unintelligible] for the topic. He's pimping the advantage on the counterplan when he's saying it doesn't mean anything. Wouldn't be a reason to vote.

Off conditionality, he argues, first, there's no impact to that. It's not a voting issue. Second, there's no impact as well. It's the counterplan advantage does not flip the [unintelligible] warning away from these things. Even if we were stuck with it, it wouldn't hurt us. The third argument here is no different from other things. We can grant out link arguments on these things. The fourth argument here is there is no impact to clash on any of these kinds of things as well.

I just want to go off the mutual exclusivity on the competition. He says the plan equals. That's fine. There's no value that they can give to the advantage. He says it's not worth anything. Also, the Rose evidence says you can do it at the same time. Then there isn't any value from this, from our claim of the counterplan any more. But, they're not getting any value off doing this.

Topicality. Voting issue. No [unintelligible] from the first violation. We're short enough on prep time as it is. The argument on commitment. He says, first, that would be overlimit. But it would not be over limitation. There would be lots of pledges. There would be U.S. troops, U.S. tacticals in there. Also, our first use pledge. We would indicate that our weapons would still be part of it. As long as our weapons are [unintelligible] a force to the future. But selling arms to someone else for them to have the arms independently, to be sovereign weapons, and that's not a pledge, because we're not bound to action. If those subs are sunk as whatever, then we're not necessarily bound to fill in.

Off the second argument, he says they meet that. But they don't or they don't decrease the pledge. All they do is change the means to fulfill that pledge. Right? This is the whole point of the argument. The pledge remains definitive. All they do is change the means to that. In order to be topical they have to do away with the pledge itself.

Off the third argument, he says that arms sales are military commitment. First, that's not true. [Unintelligible]. The (C1) subpoint is [unintelligible]. On limitation. Also the second argument here is this would legitimize all kinds of other cases. Anything dealing with arms also. The Paul definition supersedes this. He says, first, it won't decrease the commitment to NATO. Reading the Johnson evidence, or according to the Johnson evidence, defense pledge, they change the means to fulfill the pledge. It has not reduced itself. I explained that above. Second subpoint is their interpretation requires effects. That would require you to look at the effect of taking away with this and the effect it had on our overall capability to do the pledge. He says, at this point reduce the commitment to defense. Stop the subs. But the pledge to defend subs only proves we have a broader pledge to defense. It proves that they don't stop that pledge. They don't change the commitment.

Off six subpoint, he says decrease subs a commitment. The 1AC Schultz evidence. First this is not a commitment. We have only agreed to help them. Second, it is not a definition. He has casually discussing this in the literature. The Paul evidence is conjectural. He's trying to [unintelligible].

Off number seven, he says decrease [unintelligible]. First, no commitment to do this. Only a memorandum of understanding. Second, that's not a commitment. The Paul definition answers. He says the last thing is they decrease Article 3, the pledge to help them. That's only proving my

argument that the pledge is in effect. It changes the way we would do this.

Off the second contention, on the case, off the (B) subpoint, not U.S. commitment. He says, pledge to defend. Pledge to help. This evidence is terrible. You can read it at the end of the debate. None of these cards say that this is a military commitment. The cards talk about how we have an overall pledge to them. That just proves that they don't do away with this commitment. All they do is change the way that we would implement that.

Off the (B) subpoint, the prolif argument. He says, actually, first of all, they have to isolate scenarios. He says they do. That's not true. None of the evidence is country specific. Make them read evidence that says that Brazil prolifs or that Argentina will do this, or whatever, like that.

Off the second argument, Canada won't have the uranium. The uranium would be used. First they won't have the uranium. There won't be nuclear arms. He's conceding the evidence that says they won't put nuclear warheads on there. There will be no reason to have the uranium. Second it takes out the prolif link. There's no way that these other countries could get the uranium. So Canada wouldn't have it. Even if the subs are nuclear capable, it wouldn't be given to them. They wouldn't need it.

Off the third argument, the plan to acquire, to [unintelligible]. Oh, the last argument above, there's no evidence about future sales. Canada is a unique country. There's no way that we would sell these kinds of things to Chile or anyone like that. There's no reason that could do this. Down below, off the next group of arguments on solvency on the (D) subpoint, first of all, not unique. They can get it in other ways. He says these people are under the NPT. First, that takes out prolif. If that's true that these other countries are, then his argument about future sales to these people wouldn't happen. That proves that they wouldn't be giving it to them. Takes out all the prolif. Second, it's an absolute meaning to the case. International consensus will be eroded. They can say this through rebuttals all they want, because last word about international consensus, but if we're not selling things to these people and these people can't get access to this and the fact that barriers to prolif have gone down won't matter, because they can't get the stuff to prolif.

Off the second, nukes of the plan, he says France already has, but there is no indication that France would give these away.

Off the third argument, reactor. He says, not weapons grade proving that the countries couldn't get it.

Off number four, NPT fails. He says, inevitable. First, post dated. Second, the Fischer evidence concludes negative. It said that support is decreasing. The third subpoint, the international consensus argument is answered above. The fourth, subs don't lead to others. There's no indication why that's true. U.S., Great Britain, and France will already have these things which is unique. The fifth argument is not give to these other countries. There is no propensity for these sales to happen in the future. They're not indicating that these things should be done. The sixth argument that [unintelligible] states are not member states. That proves that support for the NPT is irrelevant. The countries that might prolif are on the fringe anyway. They're not within the NPT, so strengthening it doesn't help.

Off number seven, the superpower's [unintelligible]. He says, plan preserves, but he drops the Soviet Union. That's at least a part of what we need. Extend the evidence that says these things won't be armed with nuclear arms, et cetera. All that's granted away. He's not answering that.

Top of the case. All prolif is bad. The inevitability argument, he says, answered above. That's answered above. He says, can't solve. He says, above. That's fine. Our third subpoint, nuclear power plants. He says, not good enough. It's either meet need, or it proves that they won't be able to get these things in anyway. Off fourth subpoint, no barriers. He says, 1EA. An international consensus for our program up above that would [unintelligible] nuclear states is increasing. Extend that. Number six, prolif would be

slow. I don't have an answer to this. It takes out all the transitional stuff. Extend the evidence that they would do it slow. It solves for the impact as well. Off the stuff — now he reads more cards about how the NPT solve. It says the treaty helps, but he's dropping that these people want membership, so it doesn't matter. Off nuclear coups, extend my arguments there that says, assumes a past war. Also, there's no propensity for a coup to happen. He's not reading any evidence on general military instability. Off the [unintelligible] on unauthorized use, just extend that it's empirically denied by the superpowers, and he doesn't extend the other scenarios. Right? He doesn't even mention them. It's the same thing as putting time pressure on him, and any other way of forcing him to drop things. He doesn't even mention them in the 2AC. He shouldn't be able to claim them in the 1AR now.

First Affirmative Rebuttal
Shaun Martin, Dartmouth College

Topicality. We say went over limits. He says, it's like a first use pledge. But if first use is topical, then we're topical as well. We decrease this commitment [unintelligible]. On our second subpoint, decrease commitment, he says, you won't achieve your means. That's the same as their first use. You would overlimit. You would only make that — not responding — topical. Our third subpoint, emphasis on commitment, group his answers. First of all, doesn't legitimize all kinds of show. There's still little [unintelligible] for you debating. You can debate all the weapons systems. Second of all, you certainly get an [unintelligible] in this debate. Third of all, we reading contextual evidence. That's best. It's certainly in the literature. Fourth subpoint, decrease Article 3. Says, you only change the means. First of all, it's directly in the Treaty. That certainly a limitation enough. Second of all, it's not effects. It's under the specific arms control treaty. I see no answer to the fifth subpoint, reduces "Shamrock." Sixth subpoint we have a pledge to NATO. He says, not broader interpretation. However, release to decreasing that promise sets enough ground. Seventh subpoint, decrease commitment to Britain and France. He says, this is only political. We say, that's not true. It's contextual evidence. I think it's best. The eighth subpoint is show up above as well.

West German prolif, please. We say, first of all, we solve. Please group his answers. First of all, you can still constrain somewhat. At least we get somewhat of a flip. Second of all, NATO strong. It's flip to our tradeoff. That'll be argued below. Second of all, it's perceived as increase for NATO. He says, the link is ridiculous. Our argument is that it is perceived as isolationist, which is direct flip off the internal link. *Financial Post* in '87: "A nuclear fleet amounts to a declaration of independence from NATO doctrine (Bagnell 55)." Fourth of all, West German prolif doesn't necessarily equal war prolif. They could still be constrained by U.S. factors, etc.

Off our third subpoint, decrease— Oh, off the second subpoint, group all his extend the link answers. First of all, they don't do it against the United States. If anything, if they do do foreign ships against the United States, that means we specifically increase the U.S. directed commitment. The Canadian commitment to NATO isn't what's important. We're increasing U.S. commitment. Give that as a defended against us. Second of all, they're perceived isolationist. That's above. Third of all, allies oppose subs because of trade offs. They at least perceive this. Sokolsky in '87: "Canada's allies are understandably concerned that the SSN project will draw resources away from other Canadian contributions ... (15)." Fourth of all, Europe fears this. Sokolsky in '87: "NATO allies are concerned that expenditures on a fleet of SSNs will reduce resources available for Canada's land and air forces, as well as for other parts of its navy, especially surface ships (13)," which means the counterplan wouldn't solve. Fifth of all, Canadian forces are an important symbol. We uniquely increase them. Honderich in '87: "[T]here is a tremendous political utility in having a symbolic Canadian presence on the continent of Europe (19)."

Sixth of all the Canadian cuts sets precedents for U.S. cuts which takes out the counterplan as well. Sokolsky in '86: "There is pressure ... to reduce the size of the U.S. forces unless the Europeans spend more on defense, and some in Congress might seize upon a Canadian decision to pull out of Germany to support this call (102)." Next subpoint, the subs tradeoff with forces in Europe which is our specific flip. [Leyton-Brown][5] in '87: "[E]xpenditures on nuclear powered submarines will inevitably to distort priorities in Canada's defense budget (5)." They could decrease the Canadian troops in Europe. The next subpoint, his evidence isn't specific to Canada. Next of all, we don't stop [unintelligible]. That'll be on the fifth subpoint that there is no backlash. The last subpoint, we stop Soviet strategic superiority. Right? He's dropping all flips on FPMS. We're directly delivering that link.

Off the third subpoint, he says, wanting to do this is no reason to do it. First of all, it still flips the direct link. We're increasing the U.S. presence which increases U.S. superiority. Given these subs, they will [unintelligible] against us. Second of all, the evidence below will take out. This evidence says you can still use the subs. They would attack against the United States. And third of all, there's no link to the sovereignty link. He's just making up. Please read our cards.

Fourth subpoint says, free elsewhere. He says, there are no subs now. Group his answers. First of all, you might be able to build the subs, but they still turn off better things [unintelligible] disad. Second of all, we're flipping his troop evidence — his troop argument. His evidence contradicts the 1NC position, so it shouldn't be allowed. It only talks about Norway; it doesn't

[5]"A second group is less supportive, because of the fear that expenditures on nuclear-powered submarines will inevitably distort priorities in Canada's defence budget. There is concern that other needed modernizations could be delayed or eliminated, and some even fear that Canada will ultimately be faced with a choice between the submarine program and the continuation of Canada's troops in Europe, because it could not afford to do both."

talk about Canada. Third of all, we will make them mad, so they'd increase spending to defend their own straits which would flip this. Fourth of all, they're still modernizing forces. Blackburn in '87: "Nuclear submarines would require a huge expenditure that would use up scarce resources and force cancellation of other essential equipment purchases (17)."

He says, fifth subpoint, they backlash. He says, there's no link; you must reaffirm the commitment. Our argument is that there isn't a backlash. His argument requires them to get upset at us. Our fifth subpoint says, they won't get upset at us. Extend from Knelman in '87: "Canada is subservient to U.S. interests in all senses, including the geopolitical, economic, and geostrategic (32)." [Mahant and] Mount in '84: "Economic integration with the United States has reached a level where Canada simply cannot afford to confront the United States on just any issue where Canada's interests may be at stake (260)."

He says, sixth subpoint, subs increase commitment to Europe. He counterplans it out. First of all, that directly increases the commitment. Takes out the disad. Second of all, they shifted to deficit, and he doesn't have any evidence on this. Third of all, it would cause a deficit disad. *Boston Globe* in '87: "[T]he goal of deficit reduction through spending reduction must be paramount (1)." *Business Today* in '86 [1988]: If we don't resolve the budget deficit dilemma, the market told us that we would have a depression,[6] and he reads the [unintelligible] evidence.

He only counterplans out troops. We have an independent advantage, plus his counterplan is conditional.

Disad two, on Bush. We say, third subpoint flips above. Our evidence is specific. It says, they

perceive isolationist. Fourth subpoint said, now you achieve troop decrease. He says, why is this a link? It's at least topical on link. He drops the fifth subpoint, not unique. Carlucci. He says, character is irrelevant. Our argument is character is talking about Iran-contra, not this.

Gorbachev, please. We say, flips above. He says, takes out uniqueness. However, it still pulls the disad somewhat. He says, across (B) subpoint, it's structural, maritime [unintelligible] which flips the other disad. The seventh subpoint, too few [unintelligible] where also takes out the other disads. And the ninth subpoint, not unique. This evidence is from today. West German prolif would be happening now.

Contention (II). (B) subpoint is topicality. He says, our evidence is bad. Please read our evidence. It's only conjectural evidence. (C) subpoint is on the links. Please group his one, two, and three. First of all, there's no counter evidence on our scenarios. Second of all, it doesn't take out prolif. You won't grant out the fissionable material link, however, you still have the nonproliferation regime, and that stops their will to get this. (D) subpoint, solvency. He says, one, two, three. Britain and France. Group it. First of all, Britain and France are not unique. Canada is key. Second of all, his evidence up over the (A) subpoint says, they can't get this type of material which we uniquely solve. Four, five, and six. Group his big doubt. First of all, the NPT [unintelligible] empirical [unintelligible] taking out his argument. Second of all, this is relevant to will. We decrease their will. Third of all, Canada is key. Fourth of all, we're reading better evidence than his here.

Off the top of the case, please. He says—group all of the stuff on the top of the case. First of all, we have a lot of scenarios. We'll certainly get that. Second of all, his third subpoint evidence says, no barrier to doing it. We independently decrease their will. Third of all, this takes out his arguments on the U.S. The Soviet Union could stop them, because this evidence says they could have these materials in the future which we would deem to uniquely stop that. All

[6]"Richard Menschel, managing partner of Goldman Sachs, says that concern over the deficits will continue to worry investors. 'If we don't resolve the budget deficit dilemma, the market told us through the October 19th experience that they would resolve it for us . . . (37).'"

we're saying is, if you hold a nonproliferation regime, that individuals won't want to get nuclear weapons.

Second Negative Rebuttal
Martin Loeber, Baylor University

There are two considerations as to why we should win this debate on West German prolif. First of all, all these answers he makes in the 1NR are new. Rob didn't make any of these answers. For him to get up here and read isolationism evidence and perceives isolationism and allies perceive evidence, all this evidence is new. You shouldn't allow it. Secondly, is we out time-frame them. They're claiming on the case that they have 1996 time-frame, but if you West German prolifs equals world prolif that happens a lot faster than the case.

First argument, he says, off West German prolif that they're still constrained by the NPT. That's ridiculous. He doesn't answer my arguments that they don't care about it. All they care about is NATO commitments.

He says, second, NATO is strong. That's beside the point. If we win the Canadian demilitarization impact, then we would win the debate, because it says that it destroys Western Security independently. The C³ links are dropped as well.

He says, third it's perceived as isolationism. First of all, is the counterplan would solve for that. If we counterplan by giving Canada enough money to solve for their defense budget, then it would solve for that. Second is the counterplan wouldn't take out the link. If we win our argument as to why they have to have more and more defense programs in order to educate the public for the need for them. In addition we're reading evidence that says that they build SSNs for both sovereignty and NATO security reasons. Also, the subs would inevitably be coupled. This is *Aviation Week* says in '87:

> They believe surveillance of the Arctic could be conducted less provocatively with sonar technologies and that aggressive maritime operations with attack submarines might, in the event of war, em-

broil Canada in the U.S. maritime strategy of blockading the Soviet Northern fleet in the Barents sea, near Murmansk and the Kola Peninsula. (56)

He says, four. West German prolif doesn't equal world prolif reading us evidence.

Second argument, case harms. He says, first, they don't do it against— Oh, that they increase Canadian defense, etc. But, first argument, extend our argument that says if you do any defense cuts that it equals a perception of neutralism, and they begin to question their commitment to NATO. Second, this is especially true in this case, because they've promised to build these subs. People say that they're to defend themselves and NATO, and then all of a sudden they're reversing on that.

Third, it's counterplan takes out any turns. He says, second, isolation. That's above. He says, third. [unintelligible]. The counterplan solves. He says, four, Europe fears. First of all, is they fear C³ vulnerability works. Second argument is Canada wouldn't increase absent solve external motivation. I am making those link answers. He doesn't answer it. In other words, the only reason they're building the subs is because we're violating their sovereignty. They wouldn't build anything in return. They wouldn't build a stubby frigate. They wouldn't build anything, because the only way to get political capital is to violate their sovereignty.

He says, five Canadian forces are key, but there are not very many troops. The key thing is their commitments to NORAD, etc., which means even if they win this force trade off, it's irrelevant.

He says, six, Canadian cuts equals U.S. cuts. Counterplan solves. He says, seventh, it doesn't trade off, or it does trade off with Europe, but that's beside the point, because they don't have very many troops there. In addition, our evidence says that they're more concerned about NORAD. The Hasek evidence says, if Canada becomes neutral, it's more of an impact. He says, not Canada. Yes, it is. He says, nine, doesn't stop Canada with [unintelligible] which isn't true. Our link evidence says that if you have any decrease in commitments, it decreases the educational value to the public, and this is especially true, since they have committed themselves to building these subs.

Off the arguments on subs prevent alternatives. He says, they increase U.S. precedents. Well, we're flipping that, because we counterplan this out. He says below, use diesel subs, but my evidence is specific. It says they don't think diesel subs are sufficient. In addition, they're committed to nuclear subs which means any reversal at this point would destroy the defense consensus. He says, third, no link. That's above.

Off the arguments on no backlash. He says, they build the subs, and they flip troops. The counterplan will solve. He says, they don't make them mad, etc., or they do, but there's no reason for that. They only say that — to insure their sovereignty is to build subs. He says, modernizing forces equals a tradeoff which is answered above. He says that there's no backlash, no upset, no defense consensus, which isn't true. I'm extending the evidence that says that if you do something that cuts back on defenses that it makes them mad. In addition, our evidence says that the only way that you can motivate them to build up forces is to violate their sovereignty and the only thing that they'll build in response to that is nuclear subs.

He says, counterplan gets the disads, because it increases commitments which equals no disads, but the plan and the counterplan together gets the Canadian neutralism disad, because Canada withdraws on its subs which means the counterplan would solve for that. He says, no evidence. I don't need any. He says, four, deficits, and he counterplans out the troops. AC's not answering the argument that I make in the 2NC. That will just draw down U.S. forces that are based in the United States that are not committed to NATO in order to fund them. There's no answer to this. I don't have to answer this deficit stuff which means if you compare the plan and the counterplan, we get more of a link to West German prolif, because we avoid Canadian neutralization.

Southern discomfort. He can have the links. Gorbachev. There's no flip. It's long term. In addition, I granted out uniqueness answers. I don't have to answer this.

Top of the case. I'll concede all there scenarios, but I'd like to extend number three, the nuclear power plants are a meet need to the case. Also, extend the sixth, prolif is slow. Also, nuclear states are increasing now which takes out his arguments which means there's inevitability to this which means that you would want to vote negative in order to avoid this.

Contention (II). We say — oh, he can have the T[opicality] arguments. Off the (C) subpoint, he says, there's no counter evidence. Doesn't take out prolif. Talking about the international regime, but he's not answering our evidence that says, they don't have nukes. There's no reason why nuclear reactors would cause this. In addition, we won't sell 'em. All he's winning now is the regime link.

Off the (D) subpoint, solvency. Extend that Britain and France makes this not unique. He just makes some answer to this, but he doesn't answer this. Also extend that the NPT fails. He says, it's empirical, but it's not. Also, extend that threshold states are not members which means they're not winning any link, and the seventh argument is superpowers thwarts as well. We explain that West German prolif link flips the case and faster time-frame, because the subs don't cause prolif at least until 1997.

Second Affirmative Rebuttal
Rob Wick, Dartmouth College

I think we'll win a lot on case, but I also hope to persuade you that we're flipping only disadvantage in the round. The fourth argument, troop decreases makes the West German prolif disadvantage happen. Right? They want their allies to defend them. The United States, its strongest ally, is not defending them any more. The fifth subpoint, Carlucci has promised that he would pull United States forces out of Europe. He doesn't counterplan out that its only cause of

West German prolif. He said they care about the U.S. much more than Canada. Obviously the U.S. is the mainstay of the NATO alliance. The Gorbachev argument. We're arguing the fifth subpoint, obstructs the U.S. maritime strategy which means that isolationism is not new. We argued in the 2AC that this would be used to enforce Canadian sovereignty, that it would not be directed toward Europe, that it would be directed against the United States, so it — these isolationism arguments aren't new. Also, it decreases the maritime strategy, so it flips the link, it flips security, it flips protection of NORAD, etc. Also, the perception of Canadian neutralism would be flipped, because they're not isolationist any more. The seventh argument, there's too few to matter. He doesn't answer this. There's no perception by Germany that this is important, that this will cause Canadian neutralism or any decrease in security versus the Soviets. The ninth argument is an independent uniqueness argument. We decrease forces today which means it takes out the West German prolif disadvantage. At the top of the West German prolif disadvantage he says, it's the new one in our answers. I've already explained that we argued that it would be used against the U.S. It would be isolationist, that it would be used to protect sovereignty. More evidence that it will be used to [unintelligible] subs to U.S. David Cox in '87:

> Theoretically, Canadian nuclear submarines might take responsibility for patrol of the Canadian Arctic and denial of passage to the Soviets, but this will hardly please the U.S. Navy if their primary purpose is transit of the Arctic basin to achieve access to Soviet sanctuaries. (104)

The second argument is all these perceptions distinctions don't come out until the 2NC. Does the 1NC argue perception distinctions? No. So, we just argued that Europe does perceive the terms that we already argued. He says, secondly, the time frame is 1996. No. The incentive to acquire is immediate. Secondly, decreased security does not happen 'til West Germany 'til then. Right? So there would be no Canadian neutralism, or anything, 'til then. Also, there's no evi-

dence that West Germany would perceive that they would suddenly need these subs in 1996.

The third argument is that the surface forces are much more visible which means that it will reassure Germany more. Off of the first answer in the 1AR, contain somewhat, the West German prolif. He says, they don't care about it. They only care about the NATO commitment. They care about the international consensus. Right? The international consensus deters them. They don't want to alienate their security partners which are part of that international consensus. He says, two subpoint, Canadian demilitarization is bad, but the subs cut more visible programs which means it looks like they're demilitarizing even more. Off of the three subpoint in the 1AR, isolationist flip, he says, the counterplan solves this. The subs themselves are isolationist. Right? They're used to keep the United States away. *Aviation Week* in '87: "On a larger scale, the concentration on national maritime strategy will proceed hand in hand with a somewhat diminished international role (56)." The whole point of this is to protect the Soviets. The Calogero evidence in the 1AC. The second argument is the 2AC evidence or Gorbachev says that this constrains the United States and defends Canada alone. Next, his perception argument isn't in 'til 2NC. It's justified now in 1AR. Next, the counterplan only solves troops. That's what he says in the 2NC, so it doesn't solve the trade off for the surface frigates and all these other things. He says, doesn't take out the link on defense programs, but these are more visible defense programs. They're surface ships. We're reading evidence on this in the 2AC. This educates them, because these are more vulnerable. If they're more visible, he says, the subs are inevitably coupled, but they're more visible, he says, the subs are inevitably coupled, but they're used against the United States. We have the only on point evidence. He says, next the neutralism is perceived if cuts, but there's no backlash. The evidence is Russia. The United States can persuade them. They don't want to anger the U.S. That's all the evidence Shaun reads on the five subpoint. He says defend against. He says, defend selves, and NATO, etc. but the visible programs would do that better. Also, he says, the counterplan solves, but it's independently isolationist to have the subs at all. Off of the three and four subpoints, he says C^3 vulnerability, etc. is bad. The maritime strategy flips C^3 vulnerability. Also, Europe perceives and fears this trade off with European forces. The counterplan wouldn't solve the perceptions of that. He said next, NORAD is keeping — we increase the maritime strategy which defends NORAD. Also, it defends it more visibly. The rest of his arguments are repeats. The fourth argument, dollar trade off, he says, counterplan out, but he — this takes out the link to the disad. The U.S. is still maintaining the commitments to West Germany, and so is Canada. Also, he only counterplans out troops. We would cut other existing naval programs if we sold the subs. He says, up the five subpoint that the counterplan solves this which isn't true. The argument here — the argument on they need the subs to guarantee their sovereignty is a huge lie. We will continue to intrude on their sovereignty. Unless there is a tradeoff with other programs they would have to massively build up other programs if they didn't have the subs in order to try to get rid U.S. sovereignty programs. In terms of the sixth subpoint, counterplan, he says, no disadvantages which isn't true. We're still winning flips. Absent the counterplan, he says, the plan flips the counterplan. He says, neutralism. No, because we get tradeoffs with other more visible programs. [Unintelligible] can leave the counterplan directly, yet it insures that there will never be neutralism. Also, it doesn't solve the fact that the subs themselves are perceived as isolationism. Up the deficit disad, he says, decrease other forces. This is the link. It decreases U.S. forces somewhere. Secondly, it was new. It was not in the 2NC. Shifting in the 2NR is illegitimate. The third argument that it still links, this is from Owens in 1985: "[N]o shifting of resources among subcommittees under a single committee is permitted (E 4575)." Loeffler in '85: "Congress needs some good tough budget rules that can't be bent, broken, or simply ignored as they are now (H 8504)." Also, the impact of this is war. It doesn't solve the submarines themselves.

The case. Group all his solvency arguments together. First, we're getting something off of international consensus. Second argument is it is not inevitable. It's empirically worked. The third argument is nuclear power. It doesn't take out, because it's not high enough for weapons grade. Doesn't violate any sanctions. Next, France and Britain don't take out, because the prolif treaty explicitly allowed them to do this.

We're winning a hell of a lot of scenarios, at least some degree of solvency of them, and I think we're flipping West German prolif if anything.

Exercises

1. Prepare a flow sheet for this debate.

2. What type of case did the affirmative use?

3. Was the affirmative's a prima facie case? Justify your answer.

4. Which team won the advantage issue? Justify your answer.

5. Which team won the significance issue? Justify your answer.

6. Which team won the disadvantage issue? Justify your answer.

7. Which team won the counterplan issue? Justify your answer.

8. Which team's arguments were easier to follow? Justify your answer.

9. Which team made the best use of cross-examination? Justify your answer.

D

National Intercollegiate Debate Propositions (CEDA)

Following is a list of the national intercollegiate debate propositions (CEDA) for the academic years 1971–1972 to the present.[1]

1971–1972 Resolved: That the United States should withdraw all its ground combat forces from bases located outside the Western Hemisphere.

1972–1973 (1st Semester) Resolved: That the penal system in the United States should be significantly improved. (2nd Semester) Resolved: That the United States should seek to restore normal diplomatic and economic relations with the present government of Cuba.

[1]The list of CEDA propositions from 1971 through 1985 was furnished by Jack H. Howe, Executive Secretary of CEDA. Various issues of *Spectra*, as well as announcements by CEDA, publish the current CEDA propositions.

1973–1974 (1st Semester) Resolved: That "victimless crimes" should be legalized. (2nd Semester) Resolved: That the United States should reduce its commitment to Israel.

1974–1975 (1st Semester) Resolved: That the federal government should grant amnesty to all those who evaded the draft during the Viet Nam war. (2nd Semester) Resolved: That American television has sacrificed quality for entertainment.

1975–1976 Resolved: That education has failed its mission in the United States.

1976–1977 Resolved: That legal protection of accused persons in the United States unnecessarily hinders law enforcement agencies.

1977–1978 Resolved: That Affirmative Action promotes deleterious hiring practices.

1978–1979 Resolved: That a United States foreign policy significantly directed toward the furtherance of human rights is desirable.

1979–1980 Resolved: That compulsory national service for all qualified United States citizens is desirable.

1980–1981 (1st Topic) Resolved: That protection of the national environment is a more important goal than the satisfaction of American energy demands.
(2nd Topic) Resolved: That activism in politics by religious groups harms the American political process.

1981–1982 (1st Topic) Resolved: That unauthorized immigration into the United States is seriously detrimental to the United States.
(2nd Topic) Resolved: That the American judicial system has overemphasized the rights of the accused.

1982–1983 (1st Topic) Resolved: That a unilateral freeze by the United States on the production and development of nuclear weapons would be desirable.
(2nd Topic) Resolved: That individual rights of privacy are more important than any other Constitutional right.

1983–1984 (1st Topic) Resolved: That United States higher education has sacrificed quality for institutional survival.
(2nd Topic) Resolved: That federal government censorship is justified to defend the national security of the United States.

1984–1985 (1st Topic) Resolved: That the method of conducting Presidential elections in the United States is detrimental to democracy.
(2nd Topic) Resolved: That the United States is justified in aiding undemocratic governments.

1985–1986 (1st Topic) Resolved: That the United States is justified in providing military support to nondemocratic governments.
(2nd Topic) Resolved: That Membership in the United Nations is no longer beneficial to the United States.

1986–1987 (1st Topic) Resolved: That improved relations with the Soviet Union are a more important objective for the United States than increased military preparedness.
(2nd Topic) Resolved: That regulations in the United States requiring employees to be tested for controlled substances are an unwarranted invasion of privacy.

1987–1988 (1st Topic) Resolved: That continued United States covert involvement in Central America would be undesirable.
(2nd Topic) Resolved: That the American judicial system has overemphasized freedom of the press.

1988–1989 (1st Topic) Resolved: That significantly stronger third party participation in the United States Presidential elections would benefit the political process.
(2nd Topic) Resolved: That increased restrictions on the civilian possession of handguns in the United States would be justified.

E

National Intercollegiate Debate Propositions (NDT)

Following is a list of the national intercollegiate debate propositions from the academic year 1920–1921 to the present.[1] Initially these propositions were used by virtually all colleges and universities. With the emergence of CEDA debating these propositions were identified as NDT propositions. A list of CEDA propositions appears in Appendix D.

1920–1921   (Men) Resolved: That a progressive tax on land should be adopted in the United States.
(Men) Resolved: That the League of Nations should be adopted.
(Women) Resolved: That intercollegiate athletics should be abolished.

1921–1922   Resolved: That the principle of the "closed shop" is unjustifiable.

1922–1923   Resolved: That the United States should adopt the cabinet-parliamentary form of government.

1923–1924   Resolved: That the United States should enter the World Court of the League of Nations as proposed by President Harding.

1924–1925   Resolved: That Congress should be empowered to override, by a two-thirds vote, decisions of the Supreme Court which declare acts of Congress unconstitutional.

[1]See: George McCoy Musgrave, *Competitive Debate, Rules and Techniques,* 3rd ed. (New York: H. W. Wilson Co., 1957), pp. 143–145, for a list of intercollegiate debate propositions from 1920–1921 through 1956–1957; and E. R. Nichols, "The Annual College Question," *The Debater's Magazine,* Vol. 3 (December 1947), pp. 206–207, for a list of intercollegiate debate propositions from 1922–1923 through 1947–1948. Various issues of *Spectra,* as well as announcements issued by the Committee on Intercollegiate Debate and Discussion, publish the current NDT debate proposition.

1925–1926 (Men) Resolved: That the Constitution of the United States should be amended to give Congress power to regulate child labor.
(Women) Resolved: That the United States should adopt a uniform marriage and divorce law.

1926–1927 (Men) Resolved: That the essential features of the McNary-Haugen bill be enacted into law.[2]
(Women) Resolved: That trial by jury should be abolished.[3]
Resolved: That the Volstead Act should be modified to permit the manufacture and sale of light wines and beer.[4]

1927–1928 Resolved: That the United States should cease to protect, by force of arms, capital invested in foreign lands, except after formal declaration of war.

1928–1929 Resolved: That a substitute for trial by jury should be adopted.

1929–1930 Resolved: That the nations should adopt a plan of complete disarmament, excepting such forces as are needed for police purposes.

1930–1931 Resolved: That the nations should adopt a policy of free trade.

1931–1932 Resolved: That the Congress should enact legislation providing for the centralized control of industry.

1932–1933 Resolved: That the United States should agree to the cancellation of the interallied debts.

1933–1934 Resolved: That the powers of the President of the United States should be substantially increased as a settled policy.

1934–1935 Resolved: That the nations should agree to prevent the international shipment of arms and munitions.

1935–1936 Resolved: That the Congress should have the power to override, by a two-thirds majority vote, decisions of the Supreme Court declaring laws passed by Congress unconstitutional.

1936–1937 Resolved: That Congress should be empowered to fix minimum wages and maximum hours for industry.

1937–1938 Resolved: That the National Labor Relations Board should be empowered to enforce arbitration of all industrial disputes.

1938–1939 Resolved: That the United States should cease the use of public funds (including credits) for the purpose of stimulating business.

1939–1940 Resolved: That the United States should follow a policy of strict economic and military isolation toward all nations outside the Western Hemisphere engaged in armed international or civil conflict.

1940–1941 Resolved: That the nations of the Western Hemisphere should form a permanent union.

1941–1942 Resolved: That the federal government should regulate by law all labor unions in the United States.

1942–1943 Resolved: That the United States should take the initiative in establishing a permanent federal union with power to tax and regulate commerce, to settle international disputes and to enforce such settlements, to maintain a police force, and to provide for the admission of other nations which accept the principles of the union.

1943–1944 Resolved: That the United States should co-operate in establishing and maintaining an international

[2]Listed by Musgrave, op. cit.
[3]Ibid.
[4]Listed by Nichols, op. cit.

police force upon the defeat of the Axis.

1944–1945 Resolved: That the federal government should enact legislation requiring the settlement of all labor disputes by compulsory arbitration when voluntary means of settlement have failed.

1945–1946 Resolved: That the policy of the United States should be directed toward the establishment of free trade among the nations of the world.

1946–1947 Resolved: That labor should be given a direct share in the management of industry.

1947–1948 Resolved: That a federal world government should be established.

1948–1949 Resolved: That the federal government should adopt a policy of equalizing educational opportunity in tax-supported schools by means of annual grants.

1949–1950 Resolved: That the United States should nationalize the basic nonagricultural industries.

1950–1951 Resolved: That the noncommunist nations should form a new international organization.

1951–1952 Resolved: That the federal government should adopt a permanent program of wage and price control.

1952–1953 Resolved: That the Congress of the United States should enact a compulsory fair employment practices law.

1953–1954 Resolved: That the United States should adopt a policy of free trade.

1954–1955 Resolved: That the United States should extend diplomatic recognition to the communist government of China.

1955–1956 Resolved: That the nonagricultural industries should guarantee their employees an annual wage.

1956–1957 Resolved: That the United States should discontinue direct economic aid to foreign countries.

1957–1958 Resolved: That the requirement of membership in a labor organization as a condition of employment should be illegal.

1958–1959 Resolved: That the further development of nuclear weapons should be prohibited by international agreement.

1959–1960 Resolved: That Congress should be given the power to reverse decisions of the Supreme Court.

1960–1961 Resolved: That the United States should adopt a program of compulsory health insurance for all citizens.

1961–1962 Resolved: That labor organizations should be under the jurisdiction of anti-trust legislation.

1962–1963 Resolved: That the noncommunist nations of the world should establish an economic community.

1963–1964 Resolved: That the federal government should guarantee an opportunity for higher education to all qualified high school graduates.

1964–1965 Resolved: That the federal government should establish a national program of public work for the unemployed.

1965–1966 Resolved: That law enforcement agencies in the United States should be given greater freedom in the investigation and prosecution of crime.

1966–1967 Resolved: That the United States should substantially reduce its foreign policy commitments.

1967–1968 Resolved: That the federal government should guarantee a minimum annual cash income to all citizens.

1968–1969 Resolved: That executive control of

United States foreign policy should be significantly curtailed.

1969–1970 Resolved: That the federal government should grant annually a specific percentage of its income tax revenue to the state governments.

1970–1971 Resolved: That the federal government should adopt a program of compulsory wage and price controls.

1971–1972 Resolved: That greater controls should be imposed on the gathering and utilization of information about United States citizens by government agencies.

1972–1973 Resolved: That the federal government should provide a program of comprehensive medical care for all citizens.

1973–1974 Resolved: That the federal government should control the supply and utilization of energy in the United States.

1974–1975 Resolved: That the power of the Presidency should be significantly curtailed.

1975–1976 Resolved: That the federal government should adopt a comprehensive program to control land use in the United States.

1976–1977 Resolved: That the federal government should significantly strengthen the guarantee of consumer product safety required of manufacturers.

1977–1978 Resolved: That United States law enforcement agencies should be given significantly greater freedom in the investigation and/or prosecution of felony crime.

1978–1979 Resolved: That the federal government should implement a program which guarantees employment opportunities for all United States citizens in the labor force.

1979–1980 Resolved: That the federal govern-

ment should significantly strengthen the regulation of mass media communication in the United States.

1980–1981 Resolved: That the United States should significantly increase its foreign military commitments.

1981–1982 Resolved: That the federal government should significantly curtail the powers of labor unions in the United States.

1982–1983 Resolved: That all United States military intervention into the internal affairs of any foreign nation or nations in the Western Hemisphere should be prohibited.

1983–1984 Resolved: That any and all injury resulting from the disposal of hazardous waste in the United States should be the legal responsibility of the producer of that waste.

1984–1985 Resolved: That the United States federal government should significantly increase exploration and/or development of space beyond the earth's mesosphere.

1985–1986 Resolved: That more rigorous academic standards should be established for all public elementary and/or secondary schools in the United States in one or more of the following areas: language arts, mathematics, natural sciences.

Narrow: Resolved: That more rigorous academic standards should be established for all public elementary and/or secondary schools in the United States in the subject of mathematics.

1986–1987 Resolved: That one or more presently existing restrictions on First Amendment freedoms of press and/or speech established in one or more federal court decisions should be curtailed or prohibited.

Narrow: Resolved: That one or more presently existing national security restrictions on First Amendment freedoms of press and/or speech established in one or more federal court decisions should be curtailed or prohibited.

1987–1988   Resolved: That the United States should reduce substantially its military commitments to NATO member states.

Narrow: Resolved: That the United States should reduce substantially its nuclear military commitments to NATO member states.

1988–1989   Resolved: That United States foreign policy toward one or more African nations should be substantially changed.

Narrow: Resolved: That United States foreign policy toward South Africa should be substantially changed.

F

Glossary of Terms in Argumentation and Debate

Academic Debate: Debate conducted under the direction of an educational institution for the purpose of providing educational opportunities for its students. The same as *educational debate*.

ADA: American Debate Association.

Advantages: The benefits or gains that the affirmative claims will result from adopting its plan. These must be shown to outweigh the *disadvantages*.

Advocate: One who supports a position; to support a position.

AFA: American Forensic Association.

Affirmative: The side in a debate that argues for the adoption of the resolution.

Alternative Justification Case: The affirmative advances multiple independent minicases as justification for adopting the resolution.

Analogy, Figurative: A process of reasoning in which cases in different classifications are com-

pared and inferred to be alike. For example, used car dealers are like sharks.

Analogy, Literal: A process of reasoning in which cases in the same classification are compared and inferred to be alike. For example, New York is like Chicago.

Applied Debate: Debate presented before a judge or audience with power to render a binding decision on the proposition. (Compare with *Academic Debate*.)

Argumentation: Reason giving in communicative situations by people whose purpose is the justification of acts, beliefs, attitudes, and values.

Assertion: An argument offered without supporting evidence or reasoning.

Attitudinal Inherency: A widely held belief, bias, or attitude that blocks a change in the status quo and/or prevents a *plan* from working.

Audience Debate: A debate presented before and adapted to an audience. Usually the audience is not empowered to render a binding decision on the resolution.

Backing: Additional evidence and reasoning advanced to support our *warrant*.

Benefits: See *Advantages*.

Block: A prepared group of arguments designed to support or refute a single point.

Brief: Used interchangeably with *block*.

Burden of Proof, A: One must prove what one asserts. Applies to both the affirmative and the negative.

Burden of Proof, The: The affirmative must give good and sufficient reasons for adopting the resolution.

Burden of Refutation: One must refute those arguments that harm one's position. Applies to both the affirmative and the negative.

Case: The operational plan drafted by the advocates on one side of a proposition for the purpose of coordinating their reasoning and evidence and presenting their position with maximum effectiveness.

Categorical Syllogism: A syllogism in which the major premise is an unqualified proposition. Such propositions are characterized by words like *all, every, each,* or *any,* either directly expressed or clearly implied.

Causal Reasoning: The process whereby one infers that a certain factor (a cause) is a force that produces something else (an effect).

CEDA: Cross Examination Debate Association.

CEDA Debate: Value, non-policy debate; the style of debate associated with CEDA.

Circumvention Argument: The negative argues that the affirmative's *plan* won't work since many have the incentive and ability to check, evade, or otherwise defeat that plan. For example, gas rationing won't work because a widespread black-market will develop.

Claim: The conclusion we seek to establish by our argument.

Clash: The direct conflict over a specific argument between the two sides in a debate.

Coercion: The threat or use of force.

Comparative Advantages Case: The affirmative accepts the goals of the status quo and argues that their *plan* is a better way of attaining these goals and that their plan will produce greater advantages than the status quo.

Conditional Counterplan: The negative argues that *if* the status quo can't solve the problem, the negative counterplan can.

Conditional Syllogism: A syllogism in which the major premise deals with uncertain or hypothetical events. Usually identified by *if, assuming, supposing,* or similar concepts either expressly stated or clearly implied. Also known as the *hypothetical syllogism*.

Constructive Speech: The first and longer of the two speeches presented by a debater. New evidence and new arguments for or against the proposition are presented in this speech. (See *Rebuttal Speech.*)

Contention: Statements offered in support of an issue.

Counterplan: A plan proposed by the negative—one that is inconsistent with the affirmative's plan and with the resolution—as a solution to the problem.

Criteria: The standards on which a decision is to be made. A major issue in value debate.

Critical Thinking: The ability to analyze, criticize, and advocate ideas, to reason inductively and deductively, and to reach factual or judgmental conclusions based on sound inferences drawn from unambiguous statements of knowledge and belief.

Debate: The process of inquiry and advocacy, the seeking of a reasoned judgment on a proposition.

Degree of Cogency: The relative compelling force of an argument, expressed as certainty, probability, plausibility, or possibility. (See *Modal Qualification.*)

Definition, The Best in the Debate: Expected in NDT debate.

Definition, a Reasonable: Expected in CEDA debate.

Definition, A Satisfactory: One that meets the expectations of those who render the decision.

Disadvantages (DA's): The deleterious consequences that the negative claims will flow from the affirmative's *plan*. These must be shown to outweigh the *advantages*.

Disjunctive Syllogism: A syllogism in which the major premise contains mutually exclusive alternatives, usually indicated by such words as *either, or, neither, but,* and *although,* either expressly stated or clearly implied.

Educational Debate: Used interchangeably with *academic debate.*

Enthymeme: (1) A truncated *syllogism,* in which one of the premises or the conclusion is not stated. (2) A syllogism based on probabilities, signs, and examples, whose function is rhetorical persuasion. Its successful construction is accomplished through the joint efforts of speaker and audience.

Evidence: Facts, opinions, and objects that are used to generate proof.

Example, Reasoning by: The process of inferring conclusions from specific cases.

Extrajudicial Evidence: Evidence not admissible in court. Such evidence may be used outside the court.

Fiat Power: The power of the affirmative (in policy debate) to argue that a certain policy *should* be adopted and to dismiss as irrelevant arguments that the policy *would* not be adopted.

Flow Sheet: An outline of a debate with the arguments recorded in vertical columns and so arranged as to allow one to follow the flow of argument horizontally.

Generic Disadvantages: Disadvantages that may be applied to a number of possible affirmative *plans.*

Goals: In a value debate the goals are the values expressed in the resolution or argued by the debaters. In a comparative advantage case the affirmative argues that it can reach the agreed objectives of the status quo in a better way than the status quo can.

Good reasons: Reasons which are psychologically compelling for a given audience, which make further inquiry both unnecessary and redundant — hence justifying a decision to affirm or to reject a proposition.

Grounds: Evidence and reasoning advanced to establish the foundation of our *claim.*

Hypothesis-Testing Judge: The hypothesis-testing judge focuses on testing the affirmative case and requires that the affirmative overcome any negative attack to win the decision.

Hypothetical Syllogism: See *Conditional Syllogism.*

Inherency: The debater must prove that the essential elements of the case are inherent, essential, or intrinsic in things — for example, the affirmative must prove that the problem is inherent in the status quo; the negative must prove that the value objections or disadvantages are inherent in the affirmative's case.

Issues: Critical claims inherent in the proposition.

Issues Judge: The issues judge focuses on the *stock issues* and requires the affirmative to win all the stock issues to win the debate.

Judicial Debate: Debate conducted in the law courts or before quasi-judicial bodies.

Judicial Evidence: Evidence that is admissible in court.

Judicial Notice: Evidence introduced into an argument without substantiation; it is assumed to be so well known that it does not require substantiation.

Mock Court Debate: A form of academic debate that emulates trial court debating.

Modal Qualification: The *degree of cogency* we attach to our *claim*.

Moot Court Debate: An academic form of judicial debate used by law schools to prepare students for courtroom debate.

NDT: National Debate Tournament.

NDT Debate: Policy debate; the style of debate associated with the NDT.

Negative: The side in a debate that argues against the adoption of the resolution.

Negative Evidence: The absence of evidence that might reasonably be expected to be found if the issue in question were true.

Nonformal Debate: Debate conducted without formal rules.

Persuasion: Communication intended to influence the acts, beliefs, attitudes, and values of others.

Plan: A major element of the affirmative case in policy debate; the affirmative's method of solving the problems it claims exist and of producing the *advantages* it claims.

Planks: The major parts of the plan are called planks; they are agency, mandates, enforcement, funding and staffing, addendum.

Policy-Maker Judge: The policy-maker judge contrasts the affirmative's and negative's policy systems and requires that the affirmative's policy system be viable and better than the negative's policy system in order to win the decision.

Presumption: From the judicial perspective the presumption favors the *status quo*. From the policy perspective the presumption favors the position that provides the greatest advantages while incurring the least disadvantages. In value debate the presumption favors the greater over the lesser value.

Prima Facie Case: A case that in and of itself provides good and sufficient reason for adopting the *proposition*. It must provide effective issue statements to answer each of the *stock issue* questions.

Propaganda: The use of persuasion by a group (often a closely knit organization) in a sustained, organized campaign using multiple media for the purpose of influencing a mass audience.

Proposition: A statement of judgment that identifies the central issue in controversy.

Quasi-Policy Proposition: A proposition that expresses a value judgment about a policy.

Rebuttal: Evidence and reasoning introduced to weaken or destroy another's *claim*.

Rebuttal Speech: The second and shorter of two speeches presented by a debater. New evidence and new argument may *not* be presented in these speeches. (See *Constructive Speech.*)

Resolution: See *Proposition*.

Should: (As used in policy debate) means that intelligent self-interest, social welfare, or the national interest prompts an action that is both desirable and workable. (See *Fiat Power, Would.*)

Significance: The degree of importance attached to an issue. The advocate must prove that the essential elements of the case are quantitatively or qualitatively important.

Sign Reasoning: The process of inferring relationships or correlations between two variables.

Skills Judge: The skills judge focuses on the skills listed on the AFA ballot—analysis, reasoning, evidence, organization, refutation, and delivery—and awards the decision to the team that has done the better debating with regard to these skills.

Slippery Slope: The argument that a seemingly benign proposal in the affirmative's *plan* would be an irreversible first step leading inevitably to the most deleterious *disadvantages*.

Solvency: The ability of the plan to achieve what is claimed for it.

Special Debate: Debate conducted under special rules drafted for a specific occasion — for example, Presidential debates.

Spike: *Planks* in a *plan* designed to forestall possible negative attacks.

Spin Control: Presenting material from your perspective; putting a matter in the most favorable light. Should be done before your opponent plants a different spin in the minds of the decision makers.

Squirrel: A definition or the resultant case that the affirmative hopes in the first instance will find the negative unprepared and in the second instance that it can convince the judge to accept.

Status Quo: The existing state of things.

Stock Issues: In policy debate: justification, plan and advantages. In value debate: definitive and designative.

Structural Inherency: (1) A structural barrier that necessarily prevents something from being done. (2) A structural gap (the absence of a structure) necessary to permit something to be done.

Studies Counterplan: A counterplan (or conditional counterplan) that argues that further studies are needed before the affirmative's plan can be justified.

Syllogism: A systematic arrangement of arguments consisting of a major premise, a minor premise, and a conclusion. (See *Categorical Syllogism, Disjunctive Syllogism,* and *Conditional Syllogism.*)

Tabula Rasa Judge: The tabula rasa judge takes no position and allows and expects the debaters to decide the theoretical framework for the decision. If no judging philosophy emerges in the debate, the judge may select any of the various judging philosophies as seems appropriate as a basis for the decision.

Topicality Attack: An issue advanced by the negative that argues that the affirmative's case does not directly stem from the proposition being debated; it falls short of the resolution or, conversely, goes beyond it.

Turnaround: Turning around a negative's disadvantage and converting it into an advantage. In common usage, any statement that one turns against the originator.

Uniqueness: The negative argument that the advantages claimed by the affirmative are not unique to the resolution; they can be obtained without adopting the resolution.

Utopian counterplan: A counterplan proposed by the negative that mandates that the nation or the world will be arranged in a manner consistent with anarchy, world government, socialism, authoritarianism, or some other future strategy and claims that this strategy will better solve the problem than the federal government or whatever agency of change is provided in the proposition.

Value Objections (VO's): In value debate the negative argument that undesirable consequences will flow from adopting the affirmative's case. Similar to a *disadvantage* in policy debate.

Warrant: Evidence and reasoning advanced to justify the move from *grounds* to *claim.*

Workability: The issue, in policy debate, in which the negative argues that the affirmative plan is not feasible or practical, that it will not work. The affirmative argues the opposite.

Would: (In policy debate) the argument that a certain policy would not be adopted; made irrelevant by *fiat power.*

Index

AUSTIN J. FREELEY, Emeritus Professor of Communication at John Carroll University, is a nationally recognized authority in argumentation and debate. He is a founder and past president of the American Forensic Association and has also headed the Eastern Forensic Association, New England Forensic Association, and the Ohio Speech Communication Association. He has received the Distinguished Service Award from both the American Forensic Association (1980) and Delta Sigma Rho–Tau Kappa Alpha (1986). He has also served as Associate Editor of the *Journal of the American Forensic Association, Ohio Speech Journal, Speaker and Gavel*, and *Central States Speech Journal.*